Social Science

Based on Latest NCERT

Class 8

Social Science

Based on Latest NCERT

Class 8

Authors

Kriti Arora
Susmita Dhar

ARIHANT PRAKASHAN
(School Division Series)

卐 ADMINISTRATIVE & PRODUCTION OFFICES

Regd. Office

'Ramchhaya' 4577/15, Agarwal Road, Darya Ganj, New Delhi -110002
Tele: 011- 47630600, 43518550; Fax: 011- 23280316

卐 **Head Office**

Kalindi, TP Nagar, Meerut (UP) - 250002, Tel: 0121-7156203, 7156204

卐 SALES & SUPPORT OFFICES

Agra, Ahmedabad, Bengaluru, Bareilly, Chennai, Delhi, Guwahati, Hyderabad, Jaipur, Jhansi, Kolkata, Lucknow, Nagpur & Pune.

PO No. : TXT-59-T066246-07-25

Published By Arihant Publications (India) Ltd.

For further information about the books published by Arihant, log on to www.arihantbooks.com or e-mail at info@arihantbooks.com

Follow us on   

卐 PRICE ₹305.00

PRODUCTION TEAM

Publishing Managers
Mahendra Singh Rawat &
Keshav Mohan

Project Head
Ashwani

Cover Designer
Bilal Hashmi

Inner Designer
Ankit Tyagi

Page Layouting
Mayank Saini

Proof Readers
Mukul Kaushik
Manish Kumar

Inside the Book

Our Pasts-III (History)

Resources and Development (Geography)

Social and Political Life-III (Civics)

Disaster Management

Key Features

Social Science Class 8

Chapter Intro

A quick information about the coverage of the chapter to explain students about what they are going to study.

CHAPTER 1

Introduction : How, When and Where

History is about changes that occur over time. It is about finding out how things were in the past and how things have changed in the present. Sometimes people ask questions out of curiousness which are actually historical. For example, 'When did people begin to drink tea or coffee?', 'When were railways built?' and 'How did people travel long distances before the age of railways?'. All these questions encourage us to think about time.

Knowledge Plus

Additional but informational matter related to given concept. It helps & motivate students to explore more beyond their books.

KNOWLEDGE PLUS Plassey is an anglicised pronunciation of **Palashi** and the place derived its name from the palash tree. This tree is known for its beautiful red flowers that yield gulal, the powder used in Holi.

Boxed Matter

Information given in the boxes cover some important facts related to the concept given.

Movement for Entry in the Temple

Dr. BR Ambedkar was born in Mahar family. As a child, he experienced caste prejudice in everyday life. In school, he was forced to sit in the grounds outside the classroom, not allowed to drink water from the taps which were used by the **upper castes.**

In 1919, he wrote about 'upper caste power in contemporary society'.

Try These

A set of 3-5 Questions given in between the text, helps students to remain connected with the text while studying. They can instantly assess themselves for their understanding.

Try These

1. **Which European power established the first trading post in India?**
2. **When did the Mughal emperor appointed the Company as the Diwani of Bengal?**
3. **In which battle, Mir Jafar was defeated?**
4. **Who were called nabobs?**

NCERT Folder

To make students completely understand NCERT books, answers of all the NCERT Exercises have been given in each chapter in NCERT Folder. Accuracy, Detailing and Simplicity of Answers are the major features of this section.

NCERT FOLDER

Covering Intext Questions and Exercises of NCERT

NCERT ON PAGE 2 (ACTIVITY)

Q.1 Interview your mother or another member of your family to find out about their life. Now divide their life into different periods and list out the significant events in each period. Explain the basis of your periodisation.

Ans. Do it yourself.

NCERT ON PAGE 8 (LET'S IMAGINE)

Q.2 Imagine that you are a historian wanting to find out about how argriculture changed in a remote tribal area after independence. List the different ways in which you would find information on this.

Ans. The information about how agriculture changed in remote tribal area after independence, can be found in the following ways

- By studying administrative records related to the agriculture in tribal areas.
- By studying old records, notices and information about agriculture in tribal areas.

(iii) Mill, through his periodisation suggested that only British rule could civilise India. The British should conquer all the territories in India to ensure the enlightenment as if India was not capable of progress without British help.

Q.3 Why did the British preserve official documents?

Ans. The British preserve official documents due to the following reasons

- They believed the recorded documents would make it easier to research and debate afterwards.
- These documents recorded the thoughts and interests of the officials.
- They believed that believed that the act of writing was important, so every instruction, plan, policy decision, agreement, investigation had to be clearly written up.
- The notes and reports that district officials prepared, or the instructions and directives that were sent by officials at the top to provincial administrators can be studied in future.

---

1. **Historian** It refers to a person who studies and writes about history.
2. **Archives** A place where a collection of historical documents or records of government, a family, a place or an organisation are stored.
3. **Tahsildar** A revenue administrative officer incharge of obtaining taxation from a tehsil. A tehsil was an administrative division under British Raj.
4. **Calligraphist** A person who is specialised in the art of beautiful writing.
5. **Survey** The act of examining and recording the measurements, features, etc of an area of land in order to make a map or plan of it.

Terms in Footnote

Meaning or definition of important words/terms given on the pages.

Mind Map

A quick revision visual tool for the complete chapter.

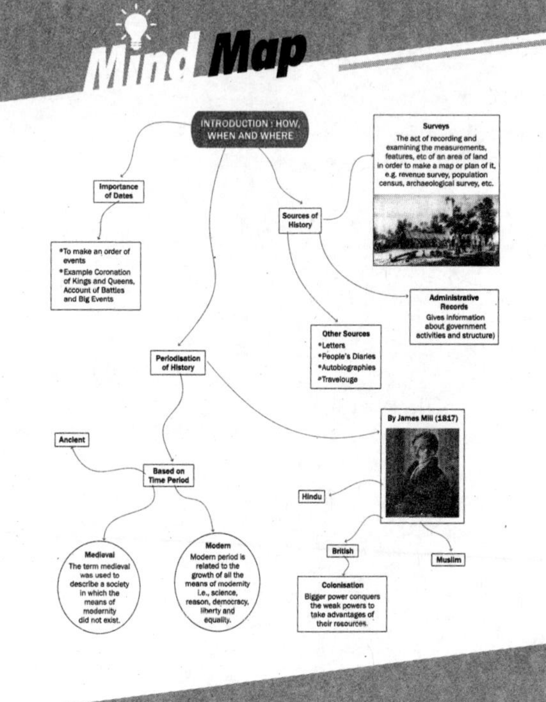

Introduction : How, When and Where

CHAPTER 1

History is about changes that occur over time. It is about finding out how things were in the past and how things have changed in the present. Sometimes people ask questions out of curiousness which are actually historical. For example, 'When did people begin to drink tea or coffee?', 'When were railways built?' and 'How did people travel long distances before the age of railways?'. All these questions encourage us to think about time.

1.1 Importance of Dates

Dates play a significant role in history. History is associated with dates as specific dates can be determined for the events in the past. History in the past was an account of battles and big events. It was about the rulers and their policies.

There can be specific dates for events such as when a king was crowned, when he fought a particular war, and when the next ruler succeeded to the throne. Thus, dates become important in history.

Sometimes, it is incorrect to fix specific dates to processes that happen over a period of time. For example, a single date cannot be fixed for the establishment of British rule or the beginning of the national movement. All these happened over a period of time.

Set of Dates which are Important

Dates are not important on their own. They become significant by focussing on a particular set of events as important. By changing the focus of study and looking at new issues, a new set of dates will become important.

For example, in the histories written by the British **historians**[1] in India, the rule of each Governor-General was important. These histories began with the rule of the **first Governor-General Warren Hastings** and ended with the **last Viceroy Lord Mountbatten**.

Periodisation of History

Periodisation of history means to divide history into different periods. This periodisation provide information about the significance of the change from one period to the next.

In 1817, **James Mill**, a Scottish economist and political philosopher, published a work **A History of British India** in three volumes.

In this work, he divided Indian history into three distinct periods which were **Hindu**, **Muslim**, and **British**. This periodisation became widely accepted.

Mill believed that all Asian societies were at a lower level of civilisation than Europe. According to Mill, before the British rule in India, Hindu and Muslim rulers ruled the country. At that time, societies were dominated by religious intolerance, caste restrictions and superstitious practices. This period before British rule was one of darkness.

According to Mill, only the British rule could civilise India as it represented all the means of progress and civilisation. He believed that it was necessary to introduce European manners, arts, institutions and laws in India.

Apart from Milli's classification, historians generally divided Indian history into **ancient**, **medieval** and **modern period**. This periodisation is borrowed from the West in which modern period is related to the growth of all the means of modernity i.e. science, reason, democracy, liberty and equality.

The term Medieval in this periodisation was used to describe a society in which these means of modernity did not exist.

Under the British rule, Indians did not have equality, freedom or liberty and there was no economic growth and progress. Thus, many historians refer to this period as **colonial**.

1 **Historian** It refers to a person who studies and writes about history.

Colonisation

A process in which one country conquers another and bring changes in its political, economic, social and cultural fields, is known as colonisation.

For example, the British came to conquer India and established their rule by defeating local nawabs and rajas. They established their control over the economy and society of the country. They also brought changes in values and tastes, as well as customs and practices.

1.2 Sources of History

Records of British Administration

The official records of the British administration are a significant source of history. These records include information about every instruction, plan, policy decision, agreement, and investigation.

During British, an administrative culture of memos, notings and reports was developed. Record rooms and specialised institutions like **archives**[2] and museums were established to preserve important documents and letters.

The record rooms were established for all administrative institutions like village **tahsildar's**[3] office, comissioner's office, etc.

In the early years of 19th century, the British administration records were copied and written by **calligraphists**[4]. With the spread of printing, by the middle of the 19th century, many copies of these records were printed as proceedings of each government department.

Surveys

The **practice of surveying** became common under colonial or British administration. By the early 19th century, detailed **surveys**[5] were carried out to know about the entire country.

Revenue surveys were conducted in villages to know about the **topography**[6], soil quality, flora, fauna, cropping pattern, local histories, etc. Apart from these, surveys like botanical surveys, zoological surveys, archaeological surveys, etc were also conducted.

From the end of the 19th century, **Census operations** were also started to be conducted every ten years. These included detailed records of the people in the provinces of India, like number of people, their castes, religions and occupation.

Other Sources

Other sources of history include diaries of people, accounts of pilgrims and travellers, autobiographies of important personalities, and popular booklets in local bazaars.

Limitations of Sources

- The official records only provide information about what the officials thought, what they were interested, and what they wished to preserve. They do not provide information about the feelings and reason behind the actions of other people in the country.
- All the sources were produced by literates. Thus, it is difficult to know about the lives of tribals, peasants, workers in the mines or the poor on the streets.

2 **Archives** A place where a collection of historical documents or records of government, a family, a place or an organisation are stored.
3 **Tahsildar** A revenue administrative officer incharge of obtaining taxation from a tehsil. A tehsil was an administrative division under British Raj.
4 **Calligraphist** A person who is specialised in the art of beautiful writing.
5 **Survey** The act of examining and recording the measurements, features, etc of an area of land in order to make a map or plan of it.
6 **Topography** It refers to the etc study and description (such as charts or maps) of the distribution, relative positions, elevations of natural and man-made features of a particular landscape, such as, mountains, rivers, valleys, etc.

INTRODUCTION : HOW, WHEN AND WHERE

Importance of Dates

- To make an order of events
- Example Coronation of Kings and Queens, Account of Battles and Big Events

Sources of History

Surveys

The act of recording and examining the measurements, features, etc of an area of land in order to make a map or plan of it, e.g. revenue survey, population census, archaeological survey, etc.

Administrative Records

Gives information about government activities and structure)

Other Sources

- Letters
- People's Diaries
- Autobiographies
- Travelouge

Periodisation of History

Based on Time Period

- Ancient
- **Medieval** The term medieval was used to describe a society in which the means of modernity did not exist.
- **Modern** Modern period is related to the growth of all the means of modernity i.e., science, reason, democracy, liberty and equality.

By James Mill (1817)

- Hindu
- Muslim
- British
  - **Colonisation** Bigger power conquers the weak powers to take advantages of their resources.

NCERT FOLDER

Covering Intext Questions and Exercises of NCERT

NCERT ON PAGE 2 (ACTIVITY)

Q.1 Interview your mother or another member of your family to find out about their life. Now divide their life into different periods and list out the significant events in each period. Explain the basis of your periodisation.

Ans. Do it yourself.

NCERT ON PAGE 8 (LET'S IMAGINE)

Q.2 Imagine that you are a historian wanting to find out about how argriculture changed in a remote tribal area after independence. List the different ways in which you would find information on this.

Ans. The information about how agriculture changed in remote tribal area after independence, can be found in the following ways

- By studying administrative records related to the agriculture in tribal areas.
- By studying old records, notices and information about agriculture in tribal areas.
- By collecting information from the documents produced by different researchers in country as well as outside the country.

EXERCISES

Q.1 State whether true or false.

(a) James Mill divided Indian history into three periods i.e. Hindu, Muslim, Christian.

Ans. False

(b) Official documents help us understand what the people of the country think.

Ans. False

(c) The British thought surveys were important for effective administration.

Ans. True

Q.2 What is the problem with the periodisation of Indian history that James Mill offers?

Ans. James Mill divided Indian history into three periods i.e. Hindu, Muslim and British. But this periodisation is not proper. There were some problems with this periodisation as follows

(i) It is improper to refer any period of history as 'Muslim' or 'Hindu' because a variety of faiths existed simultaneously.

(ii) It is also not justified to characterise an age through the religion of the rulers of the time. During ancient period, all the rulers did not share the same faith.

(iii) Mill, through his periodisation suggested that only British rule could civilise India. The British should conquer all the territories in India to ensure the enlightenment as if India was not capable of progress without British help.

Q.3 Why did the British preserve official documents?

Ans. The British preserve official documents due to the following reasons

- They believed the recorded documents would make it easier to research and debate afterwards.
- These documents recorded the thoughts and interests of the officials.
- They believed that the act of writing was important, so every instruction, plan, policy decision, agreement, investigation had to be clearly written up.
- The notes and reports that district officials prepared, or the instructions and directives that were sent by officials at the top to provincial administrators can be studied in future.

Q.4 How will the information historians get from old newspapers be different from that found in police reports?

Ans. The information from old newspapers tell us about the feelings and actions of common people of the country. This information may be affected by the personal views of the news editor, but from these, the historians can infer what common men thought about the incident.

On the other hand, the information in police reports tells us only about what officials thought, what they were interested in and what they wished to preserve for future generation. These records do not always help the historians understand what other people in the country felt and what lay behind their actions.

Q.5 Can you think of examples of surveys in your world today? Think about how toy companies get information about what young people enjoy playing with or how the government finds out about the number of young people in school. What can a historian derive from such surveys?

Ans. Today, different types of surveys are done by government and private companies.

These include geographical surveys, educational surveys, archaeological surveys, forest surveys, health surveys, etc.

The toy companies get information about what young people enjoy playing with by conducting a survey.

The government find out about the number of young people in school by conducting survey in school.

The historians can derive information like cultural practices, religion and occupation of the people in the past, from surveys.

REVIEW EXERCISE

Including Competency Based Questions

Part I

Multiple Choice Questions (MCQs)

1. Who was the first Governor-General of India?

(a) Lord Dalhousie (b) Warren Hastings
(c) Lord Canning (d) Lord William Bentinck

2. 'A History of British India' was written by

(a) Mahatma Gandhi (b) Lord Mountbatten
(c) James Mill (d) Dadabhai Naoroji

3. The National Archives of India came up in the

(a) 1920s (b) 1930s (c) 1940s (d) 1950s

4. Why the British preserve official documents ?

(a) The preserved documents reveal the progress made by country in the past.
(b) One can study the notes and reports which were prepared in the past.
(c) Their copies may be made and used in modern times.
(d) All of the above

5. Usually census operations in India are held

(a) every five years (b) every seven years
(c) every ten years (d) every twelve years

6. When did James Rennel produced the first map of India ?

(a) 1785 (b) 1782 (c) 1885 (d) 1830

7. The British thought surveys were important for

(a) effective administration (b) effective judgement
(c) writing history (d) None of the above

8. Who was the last Viceroy of India?

(a) Lord Ripon (b) Lord Mountbatten
(c) Lord William Bentinck (d) Lord Wellesley

9. When New Delhi was built, the National Museum and the National Archives were both located close to the

(a) Supreme Court (b) Parliament House
(c) Viceregal Palace (d) Red Fort

10. An advertisement for Lipton tea suggested that royalty all over the world was associated with this tea. When did this advertisement appear? Competency Based

(a) 1920 (b) 1925
(c) 1922 (d) 1932

11. Which of the following statements is/are correct?

I. James Mill divided the Indian history into three periods : Hindu, Muslim and British.
II. According to Mill, only British rules, culture and laws could make Indians civilised.

Codes

(a) Only I (b) Only II
(c) Both I and II (d) Neither I nor II

12. Which of the following statements is/are correct?

I. History is synonymous with dates.
II. British rule brought about changes in values and tastes, customs and practices.

Codes

(a) Only I (b) Only II
(c) Both I and II (d) Neither I nor II

Answers

1. (b) **2.** (c) **3.** (a) **4.** (d) **5.** (c)
6. (b) **7.** (a) **8.** (b) **9.** (c) **10.** (c)
11. (c) **12.** (c)

Match the Following

1.

List I	List II
A. James Mill	1. Scholar who write history
B. Warren Hastings	2. A History of British India
C. Historian	3. First Map of India
D. James Rennel	4. First Governor-General of India

Codes

	A	B	C	D
(a)	2	4	1	3
(b)	1	2	3	4
(c)	3	4	1	2
(d)	4	3	2	1

Ans (a)

Assertion-Reason

1. Assertion (A) The practice of surveying also became common under the Colonial administration.

Reason (R) The British believed that a country had to be properly known before it could be effectively administered.

Codes

(a) Both A and R are true and R is the correct explanation of A
(b) Both A and R are true, but R is not the correct explanation of A
(c) A is true, but R is false
(d) A is false, but R is true

2. **Assertion** (A) British came to India and established their rule by defeating local Nawabs and Rajas.

Reason (R) The British believed that the act of writing. i.e., preserving records of everything is very necessary.

Codes

(a) Both A and R are true and R is the correct explanation of A

(b) Both A and R are true, but R is not the correct explanation of A

(c) A is true, but R is false

(d) A is false, but R is true

Ans. 1. (a) Both A and R are true and R is the correct explanation of A

2. (b) Both A and R are true, but R is not the correct explanation of A

Fill in the Blanks

1. James Mill divided the Indian History into three periods that are ...., ... and ....
2. The Colonial Government gave much importance to the practice of ....
3. Census operations are held ....

Ans 1. Hindu, Muslim and British

2. surveying

3. every ten years

True/False

1. Botanical Gardens and natural museums established by the British collected plants specimens and information about their uses.
2. Old advertisement help us understand how markets for new products were created and new tastes were popularised.

Ans 1. True 2. False

Picture Based Question

1. **Identify the picture given below.**

(a) Parliament of India

(b) The National Archives of India

(c) President House

(d) None of the above

Ans. (b) The National Archives of India

Case Based Question

1. **Read the passage given below and answer the following questions.**

For that we need to look elsewhere. When we begin to search for these other sources, we find them in plenty, though they are more difficult to get than official records. We have diaries of people, accounts of pilgrims and travelers, autobiographies of important personalities, and popular booklets that were sold in the local bazaars. As printing spread, newspapers were published and issue were debated in public. Leaders and reformers wrote to spread their ideas, poets and novelists wrote to express their feelings.

(i) What types of sources are mentioned in the text apart from official records?

(a) Ancient manuscripts

(b) Fictional stories

(c) Diaries, accounts of pilgrims, autobiographies and popular booklets

(d) Scientific research papers

(ii) How did the spread of printing contribute to historical documentation?

(a) It led to the destruction of historical records.

(b) It allowed for the publication of fictional stories.

(c) It resulted in the availability of official records.

(d) It enabled the publication of newspapers and writings by various individuals.

(iii) Which of the following did leaders and reformers write for?

(a) To keep personal diaries.

(b) To express their feelings through poetry.

(c) To publish official records.

(d) To spread their ideas.

(iv) What sources were more difficult to obtain than official records?

(a) Ancient manuscripts

(b) Newspapers

(c) Autobiographies of important personalities

(d) Diaries, accounts of pilgrims and popular booklets

Ans (i) (c) Diaries, accounts of pilgrims, autobiographies and popular booklets

(ii) (d) It enabled the publication of newspapers and writings by various individuals.

(iii) (d) To spread their ideas.

(iv) (d) Diaries, accounts of pilgrims and popular booklets.

Part II

Very Short Answer Type Questions

1. How historians have divided Indian history?

Ans. Historians have divided Indian history into three periods i.e. ancient, medieval and modern.

2. What is history?

Ans. History is about findings out how things were in the past and how things have changed.

3. What is colonisation?

Ans. A process in which one country conquers another and bring changes in its political, economic, social and cultural fields, is known as colonisation.

4. Who was James Mill?

Ans. James Mill was a Scottish economist and philosopher who wrote the famous book 'A History of British India'.

5. What was James Mill's opinion about the Asian societies?

Ans. In James Mill's opinion, all Asian societies were at a lower level of civilisation than Europe.

6. Why did James Rennel produce the first map of India? **Competency Based**

Ans. James Rennel saw preparation of maps as essential to the process of British domination. Thus, he produced the first map of India in 1782.

7. Why do many historians refer to modern period as Colonial?

Ans. Under British rule, people did not have equality, freedom and liberty. Thus, many historians referred this period as 'Colonial' period.

8. Why do we try and divide history into different periods? **Competency Based**

Ans. We divide history into different periods in order to capture the characteristics of a time and its central features as they appear to us.

9. What evil practices according to James Mill dominated the Indian social life before the British came to India?

Ans. According to James Mill, the evil practices that dominated the Indian social life were religious intolerance, caste taboos and superstitious practices.

10. Suggest one of the most important sources used by historians in writing about the last 250 years of Indian history.

Ans. The official records of the British administration is one of the most important sources used by historians in writing about the last 250 years of Indian history.

11. How did paintings project the Governor-Generals of India? **Competency Based**

Ans. Paintings projected the Governor-Generals of India as powerful figures.

Short Answer Type Questions

1. Explain the importance of dates in history.

Ans. Dates play a significant role in history. History is associated with dates as specific dates can be determined for the events in the past. History in the past was an account of battles and big events. It was about the rulers and their policies.

There can be specific dates for events such as when a king was crowned, when he married, when he had a child, when he fought a particular war, when he died, and when the next ruler succeeded to the throne. Thus, dates become important in history.

2. Why and how do we periodise a time in history?

Ans. We periodise a time in order to characterise it into different periods on the basis of some significant events that have happened during those days.

These demarcations of time into different periods in the past is known as 'periodisation', which become important for history as they help to reflect our ideas quickly about the happenings and changes from one period to the next.

3. How did James Mill view India?

Ans. According to James Mill all Asian societies, including India had lower level of civilisation than Europe. According to him, before British came to India, Hindu and Muslim rulers controlled India. Society was then dominated by religious intolerance, caste taboos and superstitious practices.

Mill suggested that the British should conquer all the territories of India and it was necessary to introduce European manners, arts, institutions and laws for the enlightenment and happiness of the Indians.

4. What was the effect of colonisation on India?

Ans. The effects of colonisation on India are as follows

- The British established their rule in India, subjugating local nawabs and rajas.
- The British rule brought about the changes in values and tastes as well as customs and practices.
- The British rule brought about changes in political, economic, social and cultural sphere.

5. What is census? Explain about the surveys held during 19th century. **Competency Based**

Ans. Census operations included detailed records of the people in the provinces of India, like number of people, their castes, religions and occupation.

By the early 19th century, detailed surveys were carried out to know about the entire country.

Revenue surveys were conducted in villages to know about the topography, soil quality, flora, fauna, cropping pattern, local histories, etc. Apart from these, surveys like botanical surveys, zoological surveys, archaeological surveys, etc were also conducted.

Long Answer Type Questions

1. James Mill was a Scottish economist and political philosopher, who published a massive three volume work, 'A History of British India'.
He justified the British rule in India. Is it clear by his periodisation of history? Justify.

Ans. Yes, James Mill's periodisation of history justified the British rule in India. In his book, 'A History of British India', James Mill divided Indian history into three periods– i.e. Hindu, Muslim and British. He thought that all Asian societies were at a lower level of civilisation than Europe.

Mill pointed out that before the British came to India, Hindu and Muslim rulers ruled India. At that time, some factors like religious intolerance, caste taboos and superstitious practices dominated India's social life.

Mill felt that only British rule could save the Indians from the darkness. Thus, he advocated the theory of expanding colonisation, i.e. the British should conquer all the territories in India to ensure enlightenment and happiness for Indians. He strongly believed that India can be capable of progress only with the help of the British.

2. Historians divided Indian history into ancient, medieval and modern. But this division too has its problems. Explain about this periodisation and its problems. **Competency Based**

Ans. Many historians have divided Indian history into ancient, medieval and modern. This periodisation is borrowed from the West in which modern period is related to the growth of all the means of modernity i.e. science, reason, democracy, liberty and equality.

The term Medieval in this periodisation was used to describe a society in which these means of modernity did not exist.

If we accept this periodisation for our country, there must arise some problems. These are

- We can not justify the British Raj of India as the modern period.
- At that time, people did not have equality, freedom or liberty. There was no economic growth and progress in the society.

3. What are the sources that historians use in writing about Indian history? Explain.

Ans. The sources that historians use in writing about Indian history are

- **Records of British Administration** The official records of the British administration are a significant source of history. These records include information about every instruction, plan, policy decision, agreement, and investigation.
- **Surveys** The practice of surveying became common under colonial or British administration. By the early 19th century, detailed surveys were carried out to know about the entire country. Revenue surveys were conducted in villages to know about the topography, soil quality, flora, fauna, cropping pattern, local histories, etc. Apart from these, surveys like botanical surveys, zoological surveys, archaeological surveys, etc were also conducted.
- **Other Sources** Other sources of history include diaries of people, accounts of pilgrims and travellers, autobiographies of important personalities, and popular booklets in local bazaars.

Picture Based Questions

1. Look at the picture given below and answer the questions that follow.

(a) What does the advertisement of Lipton's Tea suggest?

(b) In which year this advertisement was published?

(c) Who is seen in the picture?

(d) What title was he given? **NCERT**

Ans. (a) The advertisement for Lipton Tea suggests that Royal people all over the world prefer this tea.

(b) This advertisement was published in 1922.

(c) Prince Arthur, the third son of Queen Victoria is seen in the picture. In the background of an Indian Palace, he is seen on a horse back.

(d) He was given the title Duke of Connaught.

2. Look at the picture given below and answer the questions that follow.

(a) Name the artist of this painting.

(b) What activity is going on in this painting?

(c) How does the painting depict the scientific nature of the project? **NCERT**

Ans. (a) The painting was drawn by James Prinsep in 1832.

(b) In this painting, mapping and survey operations are going on in Bengal.

(c) In this painting, we find that different types of instruments that were used in surveys are placed in the foreground. This emphasises the scientific nature of the project.

3. Look at the picture given below carefully and write a paragraph explaining how this image projects an imperial perception. **NCERT**

• Brahmans offering

Ans. Shastras to Britannia, frontispiece to the first map produced by James Rennel, 1782 Rennel was asked by Robert Clive to produce maps of Hindustan.
An enthusiastic supporter of British conquest of India, Rennel saw preparation of maps as essential to the process of domination. The picture here tries to suggest that Indians willingly gave over their ancient texts to Britannia – the symbol of British power – as if asking her to become the protector of Indian culture.

4. Look at the picture given below and answer the following questions.

(a) Name the personality in the above picture.

(b) What do you know about him? **NCERT**

Ans. (a) Warren Hastings, the first Governor-General of India is seen in the above picture.

(b) Warren Hastings was the first Governor-General of Bengal from 1773 to 1785. He is credit with laying the foundation of the British Empire in India. In 1779-1784 he led process of the East India company against a coalition of native states and the French. He was all used of corruption and impeached in 1787, but after a long trial, he was acquitted in 1795.

5. Look at the picture given below and answer the following questions.

(a) What event is shown in the picture?

(b) Where are such images found?

(c) What is the caption of the painting? How did the British painters illustrate them? **NCERT**

Ans. (a) The event shown in the picture is the Revolt of 1857.

(b) Such images are found in several illustrated books produced by the British after the 1857 rebellion.

(c) The caption of the painting is 'Mutinous sepoys share the loot'.
According to the British, the rebels were greedy, vicious and brutal. So, the British painters illustrate them as mere looter. The British historians tended to overlook the civil and national aspects of the revolt and called it merely a sepoy mutiny.

Case Based Questions

1. Read the passage given below and answer the following questions.

Source 1

Reports to the Home Department

In 1946, the Colonial Government in India was trying to put down a mutiny that broke out on the ships of the Royal Indian Navy. Here is a sample of the kind of reports the Home Department got from the different dockyards:

Bombay Arrangements have been made for the Army to take over ships and establishment. Royal Navy ships are remaining outside the harbour.

Karachi 301 mutineers are under arrest and a few, more strongly suspected are to be arrested. All establishments are under military guard.

Vizagapatnam The position is completely under control and no violence has occurred. Military guards have been placed on ships and establishments.

No further trouble is expected except that a few men may refuse to work.

Director of Intelligence. HQ.
India Command, Situation
Report No. 7 File No. 5/21/46
Home (Political), Government of India

Source 2

"Not fit for human consumption"

Newspapers provide accounts of the movements in different parts of the country. Here is a report of a police strike in 1946.

More than 2000 policemen in Delhi refused to take their food on Thursday morning as a protest against their low salaries and the bad quality of food supplied to them from the Police Lines kitchen.

As the news spread to the other police stations, the men there also refused to take food ... One of the strikers said: "The food supplied to us from the Police Lines kitchen is not fit for human consumption. Even cattle would not eat the *chappattis* and *dal* which we have to eat."

Hindustan Times,
22nd March, 1946

Look at Sources 1 and 2. Do you find any differences in the nature of reporting? Explain what you observe. **NCERT**

Ans. **Source 1** is an official record. This report is given by the Director of Intelligence. It is a report of an eye-witness. It is non-biased and true report.
Source 2 is a newspaper report. This report is given from the stand point of the news editor. It may be personal, facts may be distorted. But from this report, we can know the feelings of common men.

ASSESSMENT EXERCISE

Multiple Choice Questions (MCQs)

1. A Scottish economist and political philosopher, who wrote a three volume book 'A History of British India' was ....
(a) James Rennel (b) James Mill
(c) Johny Walker (d) Lord Mountbatten

2. In the book 'A History of British India', writer was divided Indian history into three periods, i.e. Hindu, Muslim and
(a) Buddhist (b) Jainism
(c) British (d) Sikhism

3. Colonisation means ....
(a) changes in political, economical aspects of the society.
(b) changes in political, economical, social and cultural field of the society.
(c) changes in economic and culture only of the society.
(d) changes in accounts of the indigeneous.

Subjective Questions (VSA, SA & LA)

1. What do you understand by the historical dates?
2. In how many period, history is divided?
3. How do surveys are important?
4. What is said by James Mill about the Asian societies?
5. How dates are important in history? Give examples and elaborate.
6. Historians use different sources in writing about the Indian history. Mention any two of the sources.
7. Write a short note on James Mill.
8. How do we know about our past? Explain.
9. How do we capture the characteristics of a time? Explain.

From Trade to Territory
(The Company Establishes Power)

CHAPTER 2

Aurangzeb was a powerful Mughal ruler who controlled a large part of India. After his death in 1707, many Mughal governors (subedars) and big landowners (zamindars) started to assert their authority and establish their own regional kingdoms. Thus, Delhi could no longer function as an effective centre.

From the second half of 18th century, the British began to emerge as a new power in India. They originally came as a small trading company and did not want to acquire territories.

2.1 Arrival of East India Company

In 1600, the East India Company acquired a **charter**[1] from **Queen Elizabeth** ruler of England. According to this charter, the East India Company got the sole right to trade with the East and no other trading group in England could compete with it.

With this charter, the Company could travel across the oceans, looking for new land from where they could buy goods at a cheap price and carry them back to Europe to sell them at higher prices.

During this time, **Mercantile**[2] trading companies made profit primarily by excluding competition, so that they could buy cheap and sell at higher prices.

The royal charter could not prevent other European powers like the Portuguese, Dutch, and French from entering the Eastern markets.

By the time, the first English ships reached the West Coast of Africa, round the **Cape of Good Hope** and crossed the Indian ocean, the Portuguese had already established their base in Goa.

By the early 17th century, the Dutch also started arriving and soon the French traders arrived.

All these companies were interested to buy the same things. These include the fine qualities of cotton and silk, pepper, cloves, cardamom and cinnamon in India which had a great demand in Europe.

Competition amongst these European companies led to increase in the prices at which the goods could be purchased, and reduced the profits that could be earned.

This competition also led to battles between these companies for securing their markets. Trade was carried on with arms and trading posts were protected through fortification.

KNOWLEDGE PLUS Vasco da Gama, a Portuguese explorer discovered the sea route to India in 1498.

East India Company Begins Trade in Bengal

In 1651, the **first English factory** was set up on the bank of Hugli River which served as a base for the Company's traders, called **factors**. The factory had a warehouse to store goods for export and offices for Company officials.

When the trade expanded, the Company encouraged merchants and traders to settle near the factory and by 1696, they began building a fort around the settlement.

They also bribed Mughal officials and acquired control over three villages which include **Kalikata**, that later became Calcutta, and now known as Kolkata. They also persuaded Aurangzeb to issue a **farman**[3] granting the Company the right to trade without paying duties.

However, after getting the farman, the officials of the Company also carried on private trade without paying the duties. This led to a huge loss of revenue for Bengal due to which Murshid Quli Khan, the Nawab of Bengal protested.

1 **Charter** It is a formal written document outlining the rights, privileges, or purpose of an organisation.
2 **Mercantile** It refers to a business enterprise that makes profit primarily through trade, buying goods cheap and selling them at higher prices
3 **Farman** It is a royal edict or a royal order.

Trade Led to Battles

In the early 18th century, the conflict between British East India Company and Nawabs of Bengal increased. The Nawabs, like Murshid Quli Khan, Alivardi Khan and Sirajuddaulah, were strong rulers who refused to give special privileges to the Company.

They demanded high tributes for the Company's right to trade, and prevented them from extending fortifications and minting coins.

On the other hand, the Company declared that the unfair demands of the local officials were ruining their trade and they demanded duty free trade. They needed to expand their settlements and rebuild forts to grow trade.

This conflict between the Company and the Nawab of Bengal finally led to the famous **Battle of Plassey**.

The Battle of Plassey

In 1756 Alivardi Khan died and Sirajuddaulah became the Nawab of Bengal.

The Company wanted a **puppet**[4] ruler instead of Sirajuddaulah, who would willingly give trade privileges. So they tried to help a **rival**[5] of Sirajuddaulah to become the Nawab.

Sirajuddaulah asked the Company to stop interfering in political affairs, stop building forts and pay the revenues. However, these **negotiations**[6] failed. Thus, Sirajuddaulah captured the English factory at Kassimbazar and the Company's fort at Calcutta.

In response to this, the Company officials in Madras sent forces under the command of Robert Clive. After the negotiations with the nawab failed, Robert Clive led the company's army against Sirajuddaulah at Plassey.

In this batle, Clive gained the support of Mir Jafar, one of the commanders of Sirajuddaulah. The Company promised to make him Nawab after defeating Sirajuddaulah.

The company defeated Sirajuddaulah and this battle became famous as it was the Company's **first major victory** in a battle in India.

Incidents after the Battle of Plassey

Incidents that happened after the Battle of Plassey were as follows

- After the defeat at Plassey, Sirajuddaulah was killed and Mir Jafar was made the nawab.
- When Mir Jafar protested, he was removed and Mir Qasim was made the Nawab.
- In 1764, when Mir Qasim protested against the Company, he was defeated in the **Battle of Buxar** and Mir Jafar was again made the Nawab of Bengal.
- In 1765, Mir Jafar died and the Company decided to become the Nawabs themselves.
- In 1765, the Mughal Emperor appointed the Company as the **Diwan of Bengal**. The diwani allowed the Company to use the vast revenue resources of Bengal.
- The Company used these revenues from India to finance its expenses. These revenues could be used to purchase cotton and silk textiles in India, maintain Company troops and meet the cost of building the Company fort and offices at Calcutta.
- The outflow of gold from Britain slowed after the Battle of Plassey entirely stopped after the acquiring Diwani.

KNOWLEDGE PLUS Plassey is an anglicised pronunciation of **Palashi** and the place derived its name from the palash tree. This tree is known for its beautiful red flowers that yield gulal, the powder used in Holi.

Company Officials become Nabobs

After the Battle of Plassey, the British East India Company officials forced the actual Nawabs of Bengal to give land and large amount of money as gifts.

Robert Clive, a Company official who had come to Madras (now Chennai) from England in 1743, acquired a lot of wealth when he left India in 1767. He was appointed as Governor of Bengal in 1764. In 1772, he was examined by the British Parliament due to his immense wealth and the ultimately committed suicide in 1774.

All the Company officials were not succeeded in acquiring wealth like Robert Clive. Many died an early death due to disease and war. Many of them desired to earn enough money to return to Britain for a comfortable life.

The officials who succeeded in accumulating wealth and return to Britain were called **Nabobs** which is an anglicised version of Indian word Nawab. They were often seen as **social climbers**[7] in British society.

4 **Puppet** This term is used disapprovingly to refer to a person who is controlled by someone else.
5 **Rival** It refers to a competitor or opponent in a contest, competition, or struggle for superiority or success.
6 **Negotiations** These refer to discussions at which people try to decide or agree something.
7 **Social Climber** It refers to a person who wants to gain higher social status.

Try These

1. Which European power established the first trading post in India?
2. When did the Mughal emperor appointed the Company as the Diwani of Bengal?
3. In which battle, Mir Jafar was defeated?
4. Who were called nabobs?

2.2 Company Rule Expands

From 1757 to 1857, the East India Company annexed various Indian states. Instead of a direct military attack, it used political, economic and diplomatic methods to extend its influence before **annexing**[8] an Indian kingdom.

After the Battle of Buxar in 1764, the Company appointed **Residents** in Indian states who were their political or commercial agents.

The Company officials began to interfere in the internal affairs of Indian states through these Residents. They tried to decide that who would be the successor and who would be appointed in administrative posts.

They sometimes forced Indian states into a **subsidiary alliances.** According to the terms of this alliance, Indian rulers were not allowed to have their independent armed forces. They had to pay for the 'subsidiary forces' that the Company was supposed to maintain, for providing them protection.

If the Indian rulers failed to make the payment, then a part of their territory was taken away as penalty. For example, the territories of Awadh and Hyderabad were taken away by the Company as they had failed to pay for the subsidiary forces.

Tipu Sultan–The Tiger of Mysore

The British East India Company used direct military attack when it saw a threat to its political or economic interests. This was the case in Mysore.

Mysore became powerful under the rulers like **Haidar Ali** (ruled from 1761-1782) and his son **Tipu Sultan** (ruled from 1782-1799). Mysore controlled the profitable trade of the Malabar coast where the Company purchased pepper and cardamom.

In 1785, Tipu Sultan stopped the export of sandalwood, pepper and cardamom through the ports of his kingdom. He also disallowed local merchants from trading with the Company.

He established a close relationship with the French traders and modernised his army with the help of the French.

The British saw Haidar and Tipu as a threat, and fought four wars with Mysore (1767-69, 1780-84, 1790-92 and 1799).

In the last battle, the **Battle of Seringapatam**, the Company ultimately won the war and Tipu Sultan was killed. Mysore was placed under Wodeyars dynasty and a subsidiary alliance was imposed on it.

KNOWLEDGE PLUS In 1782, Tipu Sultan earned the nickname 'Tiger of Mysore' after he fought unarmed with a tiger and killed it. He also had the image of tiger on his flag.

War with Marathas

From the late 18th century, the British East India Company wanted to weaken and defeat the Marathas. In 1761, the Marathas were defeated in the **Third Battle of Panipat**.

The Marathas were divided into different states ruled by chiefs (sardars) belonging to dynasties such as **Sindhia, Holkar, Gaikwad** and **Bhonsle**. They were led under a Peshwa (Principal Minister) in a **confederacy**[9] based in Pune.

The Marathas were defeated in a series of wars against the British. These were

- In the **First Angl-Maratha War**, there was no clear victory and it ended in 1782 with the Treaty of Salbai.
- In the **Second Anglo-Maratha War** (1803–05), the British defeated Marathas and gained control over Orissa and the territories North of the Yamuna river including Agra and Delhi.
- In the **Third Anglo-Maratha War** (1817–19), the British again defeated the Maratha and suppressed their power. They removed Peshwa and sent away to Bithur near Kanpur with a pension. They gained complete control over the territories South of the Vindhyas.

The Claim of Paramountcy

From the early nineteenth century, the Company adopted the policy of territorial expansion. Under **Lord Hastings** (Governor General from 1813 to 1823), a new policy of **paramountcy** was initiated.

According to this policy, the company claimed that its authority was paramount or supreme, thus its power was greater than that of Indian states.

---

8 **Annex** It means to take control of or incorporate a territory, region, or land into an existing entity.

9 **Confederacy** It is a union of sovereign states or entities, often for mutual cooperation or governance.

This policy was opposed by some Indians like **Rani Channamma** of Kitoor (Karnataka) and **Rayanna**, (a poor chowkidar of Sangoli in Kitoor), who led anti-British movements but were arrested and executed.

In the late 1830s, the British worried about Russian expansion into India from the North-West. To secure control over the region, they fought wars with Afghanistan between 1838 and 1842, took over Sind in 1843, and annexed Punjab in 1849.

The Doctrine of Lapse

This policy was devised by Lord Dalhousie who was the Governor-General from 1848 to 1856.

According to this doctrine, if an Indian ruler died without a male **heir**[10], his kingdom would 'lapse' and become the part of the Company territory.

Kingdoms that were annexed under this doctrine were Satara (1848), Sambalpur (1850), Udaipur (1852), Nagpur (1853) and Jhansi (1854). In 1856, the Company also took over Awadh and argued that they had to take over Awadh in order to free the people from the **misgovernment** of the Nawab.

The people of Awadh were angered by the humiliating way in which the Nawab was removed, so they joined the great revolt that broke out in 1857.

2.3 Setting up New Administration

Warren Hastings (first Governor-General from 1773 to 1785) played a significant role in the expansion of Company power. By his time, the British East India Company had control over Bengal, Bombay and Madras.

The British territories were divided into administrative units called **Presidencies**. There were three presidencies–Bengal, Madras and Bombay. Each of these was ruled by a Governor. The Governor- General was the suprence head of the administration.

Warren Hastings introduced several administrative reforms, especially in the area of justice. A new justice system was established in 1772, with two courts in each district, which were

- **Civil Court (*diwani adalat*)** European district collectors presided over civil courts with the assistance of Indian Maulvis and Hindu pandits who interpreted Indian laws.

  There was a major problem in this justice system that the Brahman pandits gave different interpretations of local laws on the basis of different schools of the **Dharmashastra**. Thus, in 1775, eleven pandits were asked to make a compilation of Hindu laws which was translated by **NB Halhed** into English.

- **Criminal Court (*faujdari adalat*)** It was under the control of a **qazi**[11] and a **mufti**[12], but they work under the supervision of the collectors. In 1778, a code of Muslim laws was also compiled for European judges.

Under the Regulating Act of 1773, a new Supreme Court was established, and the **Sadar Nizamat Adalat**, a court of appeal, was also set up in Calcutta.

The most important person in an Indian district was the **Collector** who was responsible for collecting revenue and taxes and maintaining law and order. His office, the **Collectorate**, become the new centre of power and authority.

The Company Army

The power of the Colonial rule in India was based on its military strength. The Company adopted the same method of recruitment for its army, like the Mughals.

The Mughal Army was mainly composed of cavalry (***sawars*** trained soldiers on horseback) and infantry, that is, foot paidal soldiers. Soldiers were trained in archery (*teer-andazi*) and the use of the sword.

The cavalry dominated the army and the Mughal state did not feel the need to have a large professionally trained infantry. The rural areas had a large number of armed peasants and the local zamindars often supplied foot soldiers to the Mughals.

In the 18th century, a change occurred when Mughal successor states like Awadh and Benaras started recruiting peasants into their armies and training them as professional soldiers.

Sepoy Army

The army of the East India Company was known as the sepoy army. The word 'sepoy' was derived from the Indian word '*sipahi*', meaning soldier.

When the warfare technology changed from the 1820s, the cavalry requirements of the Company's army declined.

10 **Heir** It refers to a person who inherits property, titles, or rights from a deceased family member.

11 **Qazi** It refers to a judge in Islamic law who is responsible for interpreting and applying Sharia principles in legal matters.

12 **Mufti** It refers to a jurist of the Muslim community responsible for proposing the law that the qazi would administer.

This was because the British were fighting wars in Burma, Afghanistan and Egypt where soldiers were armed with **muskets**[13] and **matchlocks**[14].

In the early 19th century, the British developed a uniform military culture. Soldiers were increasingly subjected to European style training, drill and discipline that their life became more regulated.

However, this created problems as caste and community feelings were ignored in building an army of professional soldiers.

Conclusion

The East India Company started as a trading company but transformed gradually into a colonial power.

This transformation process was aided by the introduction of steam technology in the 19th century.

Steamships reduced the journey time making it easier for Britishers and their families to come to a far-off country like India.

The Company also had significant indirect influence over the rest of India, which means that virtually it had control over the whole of India.

Try These

1. **When did the Battle of Seringapatam take place?**
2. **What was the British policy of territorial expansion called in the early 19th century?**
3. **What is the Indian term for a soldier in the Company's army?**
4. **Name the doctrine that allowed the British to annex Indian kingdoms without male heirs.**

13 **Musket** It refes to a heavy gun used by infantry soldiers.
14 **Matchlock** It was an early type of gun in which the powder was ignited by a match.

Mind Map

FROM TRADE TO TERRITORY (The Company Establishes Power)

Setting Up New Administration

Warren Hastings

Civil Court (Diwani Adalat)

Criminal Court (Faujdari Adalat)

The Company Army
18th century, Awadh and Benaras recruited peasants into their armies and trained them as professional soldiers.

The Sepoy Army
Army of East India Company.

Arrival of East India Company

East India Company Begins Trade in Bengal
First English factory was set up on the bank of Hugli river in 1651.

Trade Led to Battles
Conflict between the Company and the Nawab of Bengal.

The Battle of Plassey
- First major victory in a battle in India. The Company defeated Nawab of Bengal Sirajuddaulah.
- After Battle of Plassey, Robert Clive was appointed as the Governor of Bengal in 1764.

Company Rule Expands

The Claim of Paramountcy
Initiated under Lord Hastings.

Tipu Sultan-The Tiger of Mysore
The Company won the last battle with Mysore, the battle of Seringapatam and Tipu Sultan was killed.

The Doctrine of Lapse
Devised by Lord Dalhousie.

War with Marathas

First Anglo-Maratha War (1775-1782)
Ended with Treaty of Salbai

Second Anglo-Maratha War (1803-05)
British gained control over Orissa and the territories North of the Yamuna river including Agra and Delhi.

Third Anglo–Maratha War (1817-19)
British removed Peshwa and sent him to Bithur near Kanpur with a pension.

NCERT FOLDER

Covering Intext Questions and Exercises of NCERT

NCERT ON PAGE 18

Q.1 Imagine that you have come across two old newspapers reporting on the Battle of Seringapatam and the death of Tipu Sultan. One is a British paper and the other is from Mysore. Write the headline for each of the two newspapers.

Ans. Headline for the British paper would be 'The East India Company crushes Tipu Sultan.'

Headline for the local paper would be 'Mysore Tiger sacrifies life for the people of Mysore'.

NCERT ON PAGE 19

Q.2 Imagine that you are a nawab's nephew and have been brought up thinking that you will one day be king. Now, you find that this will not be allowed by the British because of the new Doctrine of Lapse. What will be your feelings? What will you plan to do so that you can inherit the crown?

Ans. I would be disappointed and angry to know that British are not giving my rights due to Doctrine of Lapse.

To inherit and secure the crown, I will form an alliance with other kingdom who had suffered due to this policy and negotiate with British.

EXERCISES

Q.1 Match the following.

A. Diwani	1. Tipu Sultan
B. 'Tiger of Mysore'	2. Right to collect land revenue
C. Faujdari adalat	3. Sepoy
D. Rani Channamma	4. Criminal court
E. Sipahi	5. Led an anti-British movement in Kitoor

Codes

	A	B	C	D	E		A	B	C	D	E
(a)	2	1	4	5	3	(b)	1	2	3	4	5
(c)	3	1	2	5	4	(d)	4	5	3	1	2

Ans. (a)

Q.2 Fill in the blanks

(i) The British conquest of Bengal began with the Battle of ....

(ii) Haidar Ali and Tipu Sultan were the rulers of ....

(iii) Dalhousie implemented the Doctrine of ....

(iv) Maratha kingdoms were located mainly in the .... part of India.

Ans. (i) Plassey (ii) Mysore (iii) Lapse (iv) Southern

Q.3 State whether true or false.

(i) The Mughal empire became stronger in the 18th century.

(ii) The English East India Company was the only European company that traded with India.

(iii) Maharaja Ranjit Singh was the ruler of Punjab.

(iv) The British did not introduce administrative changes in the territories they conquered.

Ans. (i) False (ii) False (iii) True (iv) False

Q.4 What attracted European trading companies to India?

Ans. European trading companies were attracted to India for its valuable resources. There was a great demand of Indian fine quality silk and cotton in European countries. Indian spices like pepper, cloves, cardamom and cinnamon too were in great demand.

These things were easily available in India at low prices. European trader could sell it at higher prices in Europe. Thus, the European traders came to India to gain profit.

Q.5 What were the areas of conflict between the Bengal nawabs and the East India Company?

Ans. The areas of conflict between the Bengal Nawabs and the East India Company were

- The nawabs of Bengal (Murshid Quli Khan, Alivardi Khan and Sirajuddaulah) were strong rulers. Sirajuddaulah refused to grant the Company concessions and demanded large tributes to the Company's right to trade.
- The nawabs denied the Company any right to mint coins and stopped the Company from extending its fortifications.
- They accused the Company of cheating. They claimed that the Company was depriving the Bengal Government of huge amounts of revenue and undermining the authority of the nawabs.
- The Company declared that the unjust demands of the local officials were ruining their trade.
- The Company refused to pay taxes and tried to humitate the nawabs and their officials by writing disrespectful letters.

Q.6 How did the assumption of Diwani benefit the East India Company?

Ans. In 1765, the Mughal emperor appointed the East India Company as the Diwan of Bengal. The assumption of Diwani benefitted the East India Company in the following ways

- The diwani allowed the Company to use the vast revenue resources of Bengal.
- The outflow of gold from Britain blowed after the Battle of Plassey entirely stopped after the acquiring Diwani.
- The Company used revenues from India to finance its expenses. These revenues could be used to purchase cotton and silk textiles in India, maintain Company troops and meet the cost of building the Company fort and offices at Calcutta.

Q.7 Explain the system of 'subsidiary alliance'.

Ans. Subsidiary alliance was introduced by Lord Wellesley under which Indian rulers were not allowed to have their independent armed forces. They were to be protected by the Company. They had to pay for the subsidiary forces that the Company was supposed to maintain for the purpose of protection.

If the Indian rulers failed to make the payment, then part of their territory was taken away as penalty. Some territories of Awadh and Hyderabad were taken as they failed to pay for the 'subsidiary forces'.

Q.8 In what way was the administration of the Company different from that of Indian rulers?

Ans. The administration of the Company was different from that of the Indian rulers in the following ways

- Indian rulers divided its administrative units as district, paraganas and tehsils whereas the Company divided its administrative units as presidencies. There were three presidencies-Bengal, Madras and Bombay. Each Presidency was ruled by a Governor of administrative units whereas districts were ruled by the Collectors.
- The Governor-General was the Supreme head of the Company's administration. On the other hand, in India, the head of the administration was king.
- The Company established a new system of justice in 1772. In each district, two courts i.e, a Criminal Court (Faujdari Adalat) and a Civil Court (Diwani Adalat).

Q.9 Describe the changes that occurred in the composition of the Company's army.

Ans. The changes that occurred in the composition of the company's army are as follows

- Company stopped recruiting cavalry.
- They started recruiting peasants into their armies and trained them as professional soldiers.
- They started recruiting soldiers armed with muskets and matchlocks.
- They began to develop a uniform military culture in the early 19th century.
- They started giving European-style training, drill and discipline to the soldiers which regulated their life. However, this ignored caste and community feelings.

Q.10 After the British conquest of Bengal, Calcutta grew from a small village to a big city. Find out about the culture, architecture and the life of Europeans and Indians of the city during the colonial period.

Ans. During the colonial period, after the British conquest of Bengal, Calcutta witnessed significant changes in its culture, architecture, and the lives of both Europeans and Indians. Here are some key points about the city during that time

- **Culture** Calcutta became a fusion of diverse cultures as British colonisers, along with other European communities, settled in the city.

  This led to the emergence of a hybrid culture influenced by British, Indian and other European traditions.
- **Architecture** The British established their administrative and commercial centers in Calcutta, leading to the construction of impressive colonial buildings, such as the Writers' Building and St. John's Church. These structures showcased a blend of British architectural styles with local influences.
- **European Lifestyle** The Europeans in Calcutta lived a luxurious and privileged lifestyle. They built elegant mansions, known as 'bungalows,' and enjoyed recreational activities like horse racing, polo and social gatherings.
- **Indian Life** The Indian population in Calcutta experienced a mixture of opportunities and challenges. The city became a center for trade, attracting merchants and artisans. However, many Indians also faced poverty and social inequalities under colonial rule.

REVIEW EXERCISE

Including Competency Based Questions

Part I

Multiple Choice Questions (MCQ)

1. Who discovered the sea route to India in 1498?

(a) Robert Clive (b) Vasco da Gama
(c) Columbus (d) None of these

2. Nawab Sirajuddaulah was the ruler of

(a) Bihar (b) Bengal
(c) Awadh (d) Mysore

3. Name the ruler who gave permission to the East India Company to establish trade relations with the East. Diksha

(a) Henry V (b) Henry VI
(c) Queen Elizabeth II (d) Queen Elizabeth I

4. Which of the following was not the Presidency? Competency Based

(a) Bengal (b) Madras
(c) Pune (d) Bombay

5. When was the Third Battle of Panipat fought?

(a) 1743 (b) 1752 (c) 1767 (d) 1761

6. Rani Channamma was the ruler of

(a) Bengal (b) Kitoor
(c) Agra (d) Delhi

7. When did the first English factory set-up ? Competency Based

(a) 1651 (b) 1600
(c) 1630 (d) 1665

8. Who was the powerful ruler who stopped trade with the East India Company in 1785?

(a) Haidar Ali (b) Tipu Sultan
(c) Bahadur Shah Zafar (d) Rani Laxmi Bai

9. Haidar Ali was the ruler of

(a) Bhopal (b) Hyderabad
(c) Mysore (d) Karnataka

10. Identify the Governor-General who introduced the policy of 'paramountcy' ?

(a) Warren Hastings (b) Lord Hastings
(c) William Bentinck (d) Lord Dalhousie

11. Which one of these was annexed on the basis of Dalhousie's 'Doctrine of Lapse'?

(a) Punjab (b) Satara
(c) Calcutta (d) Saurashtra

12. After Alivardi Khan, ... became the Nawab of Bengal.

(a) Murshid Quli Khan (b) Sirajuddaulah
(c) Haidar Ali (d) Mir Qasim

13. The Governor-General who was impeached by the British Parliament was .... Competency Based

(a) Lord Mountbatten
(b) Warren Hastings
(c) William Bentinck
(d) Lord Dalhousie

14. Consider the following statements and choose the correct option.

I. The British East India Company gained control over Bengal, Bihar and Orissa in 1765.
II. The British East India Company received the Diwani rights for these regions.

Codes

(a) Both I and II (b) Only I
(c) Only II (d) None of these

15. Consider the following statements and choose the correct option.

I. The Battle of Plassey took place in 1757.
II. The British East India Company defeated the French in the Battle of Plassey.

Codes

(a) Both I and II (b) Only I
(c) Only II (d) None of these

16. Arrange the following European powers' arrival in India in chronological order.

(i) French (ii) Portuguese
(iii) Dutch (iv) British

Codes

(a) (ii), (iii), (i), (iv) (b) (iii), (ii), (i), (iv)
(c) (ii), (i), (iii), (iv) (d) (iii), (ii), (iv), (i)

17. Arrange the following events related to the British East India Company's expansion in India in chronological order Competency Based

(i) Battle of Plassey
(ii) Arrival of the Portuguese in India
(iii) Treaty of Allahabad
(iv) Granting of Diwani rights to the British East India Company

Codes

(a) (ii), (i), (iii), (iv) (b) (i), (ii), (iv), (iii)
(c) (ii), (i), (iv), (iii) (d) (ii), (i), (iii), (iv)

Answers

1. (b)	2. (b)	3. (d)	4. (c)	5. (d)
6. (b)	7. (a)	8. (b)	9. (c)	10. (b)
11. (b)	12. (b)	13. (b)	14. (a)	15. (b)
16. (c)	17. (c)			

Match the Following

1.

List I	List II
A. Diwani	1. Landlords who collected revenue on behalf of the British East India Company
B. Zamindars	2. System introduced by Lord Cornwallis for fixed land revenue in Bengal
C. Permanent Settlement	3. Rights granted to the British East India Company to collect revenue and administer territories

Codes

	A	B	C		A	B	C
(a)	1	2	3	(b)	2	3	1
(c)	3	1	2	(d)	3	2	1

2.

List I (European Trading Company)	List II (Location)
A. Portuguese	1. Surat
B. Dutch	2. Hugli
C. English	3. Pulicat

Codes

	A	B	C		A	B	C
(a)	1	3	2	(b)	2	3	1
(c)	1	2	3	(d)	3	1	2

3.

List I	List II
A. Lord Dalhousie	1. Tipu Sultan
B. Sawars	2. A heavy gun used by infantry soldiers
C. Seringapatam	3. Trained soldiers on horseback
D. Musket	4. The Doctrine of Lapse

Codes

	A	B	C	D		A	B	C	D
(a)	2	1	3	4	(b)	4	3	1	2
(c)	1	3	4	2	(d)	3	2	1	4

Ans. 1. (c) 2. (a) 3. (b)

Assertion-Reason

1. Assertion (A) The British East India Company was initially interested in trading and had no intention of establishing political control in India.

Reason (R) The British East India Company signed several treaties with local rulers to secure trade privileges.

Codes

(a) Both A and R are true and R is the correct explanation of A

(b) Both A and R are true, but R is not the correct explanation of A

(c) A is true, but R is false

(d) A is false, but R is true

2. Assertion (A) The British East India Company's control over Indian trade led to the decline of Indian merchants and artisans.

Reason (R) The British East India Company imposed high tariffs and destroyed the local textile industry in India.

Codes

(a) Both A and R are true and R is the correct explanation of A

(b) Both A and R are true, but R is not the correct explanation of A

(c) A is true, but R is false

(d) A is false, but R is true

Ans 1. (b) Both A and R are true, but R is not the correct explanation of A

2. (a) Both A and R are true and R is the correct explanation of A

Fill in the Blanks

1. After the death of ...., the Bengal nawabs asserted their power and autonomy.

2. When Alivardi Khan died in ...., Sirajuddaulah became the Nawab of Bengal.

3. In ...., the East India Company acquired a charter from Queen Elizabeth I.

4. The Battle of Buxar was fought in .... between Mir Qasim and the British.

Ans 1. Aurangzeb 2. 1756 3. 1600 4. 1764

True/False

1. Warren Hastings was appointed as the Governor of Bengal in 1772.

2. Murshid Quli Khan was followed by Sirajuddaulah.

3. Tipu Sultan disallowed the local merchants from trading with the Company.

4. The Company took away parts of territories from Punjab and Satara on the basis of 'subsidiary alliance'.

5. From 1775, a new system of justice was established.

Ans 1. True 2. False 3. True 4. False 5. False

Picture Based Questions

1. Who is the famous personality in the below picture?

(a) Mir Jafar (b) Haidar Ali
(c) Tipu Sultan (d) Mahadji Sindhia

2. What was the purpose of the British painters in depicting scenes such as Cornwalis receiving the sons of Tipu Sultan as hostages?

(a) To showcase the defeat of the British Company against Haidar Ali and Tipu Sultan.
(b) To depict the signing of a treaty between Tipu Sultan and British Company
(c) To portray the triumph and dominance of British Power in India.
(d) To illustrate the role of the Marathas and the Nizam of Hyderabad in British Indian relations.

Ans. 1. (c) Tipu Sultan
2. (c) To portray the triumph and dominance of British Power in India.

Case Based Questions

1. Read the passage given below and answer the following questions.

If we analyse the process of annexation of Indian states by the East India Company from 1757 to 1857, certain key aspects emerge. The Company rarely launched a direct military attack on an unknown territory. Instead it used a variety of political, economic and diplomatic methods to extend its influence before annexing an Indian kingdom.

After the Battle of Buxar (1764), the Company appointed Residents in Indian states. They were political or commercial agents and their job was to serve and further the interests of the Company. Through the Residents, the Company officials began interfering in the internal affairs of Indian states. They tried to decide who was to be the successor to the throne, and who was to be appointed in administrative posts. Sometimes, the Company forced the states into a 'subsidiary alliance'.

(i) Which method did the East India Company primarily employ to extend its influence before annexing an Indian kingdom?
(a) Direct military attack
(b) Political interference
(c) Economic sanctions
(d) Diplomatic negotiations

(ii) What role did the Residents play in Indian states after the Battle of Buxar (1764)?
(a) Commanders
(b) Advisors
(c) Political and commercial agents
(d) Leaders

(iii) What authority did the Company officials exercise through the Residents in Indian states?
(a) Policy making
(b) Military force
(c) Interfering in internal affairs and succession matters
(d) Interfering in trade

(iv) What term was used to describe the alliance imposed by the Company on some Indian states?
(a) Agreement
(b) Contract
(c) Subsidiary alliance
(d) Treaty

Ans (i) (b) Political interference
(ii) (c) Political and commercial agents
(iii) (c) Interfering in internal affairs and succession matters
(iv) (c) Subsidiary alliance

2. Read the given passage and answer the following questions.

Warren Hastings (Governor-General from 1773 to 1785) was one of the many important figures who played a significant role in the expansion of Company power. By his time the Company had acquired power not only in Bengal, but also in Bombay and Madras. British territories were broadly divided into administrative units called Presidencies. There were three Presidencies: Bengal, Madras and Bombay. Each was ruled by a Governor. The supreme head of the administration was the Governor- General. Warren Hastings, the first Governor-General, introduced several administrative reforms, notably in the sphere of justice.

From 1772 a new system of justice was established. Each district have two courts—a criminal court (faujdari adalat) and a civil court (diwani adalat). Maulvis and Hindu pandits interpreted Indian laws for the European district collectors who presided over civil courts. The criminal courts were still under a Qazi and a Mufti but under the supervision of the collectors.

(i) Which Governor-General gained control over the regions Bengal, Madras and Bombay?

(a) Richard Wellesley (b) Robert Clive
(c) Warren Hastings (d) None of these

(ii) How were British territories in India divided administratively during Warren Hastings' time?

(a) Provinces (b) States
(c) Districts (d) Kingdoms

(iii) What was the role of the criminal court established under the new justice system introduced by Warren Hastings?

(a) Interpreting Indian laws for district collectors
(b) Presiding over civil court cases
(c) Enforcing British laws in Indian territories
(d) Adjudicating criminal cases under the supervision of Qazi and Mufti

(iv) Who helped European district collectors in understanding Indian laws in Civil Courts?

(a) British judges (b) European scholars
(c) Maulvis and Hindu pandits (d) Indian lawyers

Ans (i) (c) Warren Hastings
(ii) (c) Districts
(iii) (d) Adjudicating criminal cases under the supervision of qazi and mufti
(iv) (c) Maulvis and Hindu pandits

Part II

Very Short Answer Type Questions

1. Who was the ruler of England in 1600?

Ans. Queen Elizabeth I was the ruler of England in 1600.

2. What was the main reason of defeat of Sirajuddaulah at Plassey? Competency Based

Ans. The main reason of defeat of Sirajuddaulah was Mir Jafar, one of Sirajuddaulah's commanders, who supported the British in the Battle of Plassey.

3. Whom did the Company install as nawab of Bengal in place of Mir Jafar?

Ans. The Company installed Mir Qasim as Nawab of Bengal in place of Mir Jafar.

4. Name the village which the Company got from the Mughal officials

Ans. The Company got the village Kalikata from the Mughal empire, which later known as Calcutta.

6. When was the Second Maratha War fought?

Ans. The Second Maratha War was fought from 1803 to 1805.

7. When did the Company appoint the Residents of states?

Ans. The Company appointed the Residents of states after the Battle of Buxar (1764).

8. State the period of Lord Hasting's Governor Generalship.

Ans. The Period of Lord Hasting's Governor-Generalship was 1813 to 1823.

9. Name the kingdoms which were annexed on the basis of 'Doctrine of Lapse'.

Ans. The kingdoms like Satara, Sambalpur, Udaipur, Nagpur and Jhansi were annexed on the basis of 'Doctrine of Lapse'.

10. Which new power began emerging on the political scene after the fall of Mughals?

Ans. The British began emerging on the political scene as a new power after the fall of Mughals.

11. Why could Delhi no longer function as an effective centre? Competency Based

Ans. Delhi could no longer function as an effective centre because powerful regional kingdoms emerged in various parts of India.

The powerful technology changed from the 1820s, and the British empire used muskets and Makhlocks in the wars.

12. 'The warfare technology changed from the 1820s, and the British empire used muskets and matchlocks in the wars'. What was musket?

Ans. Musket was a heavy gun used by infantry soldiers.

13. What was the result of the Second Anglo-Maratha War?

Ans. After the Second Anglo-Maratha War, the British gained Orissa (now Odisha) and the territories North of the Jamuna river including Agra and Delhi.

Short Answer Type Questions

1. What was written in the charter from the Queen Elizabeth I to the East India Company in 1600?

Ans. In 1600, the East India Company acquired a charter from Queen Elizabeth ruler of England. According to this charter, the East India Company got the sole right to trade with the East.

It means that no other trading group in England could complete with East India company. They got the right to establish trading posts and forts in the East.

This charter gives the company rights to reach new lands for trade to buy goods at cheap price and sell in Europe at higher prices.

2. Through the early 18th century, the conflict between the Company and the Nawabs of Bengal intensified. Justify. Competency Based

Ans. Through the early 18th century, the conflict between the company and the Nawabs of Bengal intensified.

The Nawabs, like Murshid Quli Khan, Alivardi Khan and Sirajuddaulah, were strong rulers who refused to give special privileges to the Company demanded high tributes for the Company's right to trade, and prevented them from extending fortifications and minting coins.

On the other hand, the Company declared that the unfair demands of the local officials were ruining their trade and they demanded duty free trade.They needed to expand their settlements and rebuild forts to grow trade. This conflict between the Company and the Nawab of Bengal finally led to the famous Battle of Plassey.

3. What was the job of the Residents appointed by the Company? Diksha

Ans. Residents were appointed by the Company in the Indian states after the Battle of Buxar (1764). They were political or commercial agents and their job was to serve for the Company. Through the Residents, the company officials began to interfere in the internal affairs of the Indian states. They tried to decide who was to be the successor to the throne and who would be appointed in administrative posts.

4. How did East India Company begin trade in Bengal? What caused huge loss of revenue in Bengal? Diksha

Ans. East India Company began its trade in Bengal by establishing first English factory on the banks of river Hugli in 1651.

The huge loss of revenue in Bengal was caused as a result of Aurangzeb's farman. This farman had granted the Company only the right to trade duty free. But the officials of the Company misused this facility. They were carrying on private trade and stopped paying duty for their personal profit. This caused a huge loss of revenue in Bengal.

5. What were the condition of Nawabs after the Battle of Plassey?

Ans. After the defeat at Plassey, Sirajuddaulah was killed and Mir Jafar was made the nawab. When Mir Jafar protested, he was removed and Mir Qasim was made the Nawab.

In 1764, when Mir Qasim protested against the Company, he was defeated in the Battle of Buxar and Mir Jafar was again made the Nawab of Bengal. In 1765, Mir Jafar died and the Company decided to become the Nawabs themselves. In 1765, the Mughal Emperor appointed the Company as the Diwan of Bengal.

6. Why were the British furious with Tipu Sultan? Competency Based

Ans. The British got furious with Tipu Sultan because

- Mysore under Tipu Sultan controlled the profitable trade of the Malabar coast from where the Company purchased pepper and cardamom. In 1785, Tipu Sultan stopped the export of sandalwood, pepper, cardamom through the ports of his kingdom.
- Tipu Sultan established a close relationship with the French in India and modernised his army with their help.

7. Explain about the wars between the Marathas and the British.

Ans. The Marathas were defeated in a series of wars against the British. These were

- In the First Angl-Maratha War, there was no clear victory and it ended in 1782 with the Treaty of Salbai.
- In the Second Anglo-Maratha War (1803–05), the British defeated Marathas and gained control over Orissa and the territories North of the Yamuna river including Agra and Delhi.
- In the Third Anglo-Maratha War (1817–19), the British again defeated the Maratha and suppressed their power. They removed Peshwa and sent away to Bithur near Kanpur with a pension. They gained complete control over the territories South of the Vindhyas.

8. What was the 'Doctrine of Lapse'? Diksha

Ans. The Doctrine of Lapse was a policy of annexation followed by the British East India Company. It was introduced by Lord Dalhousie (Governor-General from 1848-1856).

The doctrine state that if an Indian ruler died without a male heir, his kingdom would lapse and automatically become part of the East India company's territories.

9. 'From 1772, a new system of justice was established by the British'? Discuss this sytem.

Ans. 'From 1772, a new system of justice was established by the British. In this system, two courts were established in each district, which were

- **Civil Court (*diwani adalat*)** European district collectors presided over civil courts with the assistance of Indian Maulvis and Hindu pandits who interpreted Indian laws.
- **Criminal Court (*faujdari adalat*)** It was under the control of a qazi and a mufti, but they work under the supervision of the collectors. In 1778, a code of Muslim laws was also compiled for European judges.

Long Answer Type Questions

1. Why is the Battle of Plassey famous in the history of India?

Ans. The Battle of Plassey holds significant historical importance in India due to following reasons

- **British East India Company's Victory** The battle was fought on 23rd June, 1757, resulted in the victory of the British East India Company led by Robert Clive over the Nawab of Bengal, Siraj ud-daulah.
- **British Control over Bengal** The British victory established the Company's political control over Bengal, marking the beginning of British territorial expansion in India.
- **Economic Consequences** The battle allowed the British East India Company to gain access to the rich resources and revenue of Bengal, leading to the economic exploitation of the region.
- **Consolidation of Power** The battle set the stage for the Company's later acquisition of the Diwani rights, which granted them the power to collect revenue and administer territories.

2. How was Mysore captured by the British? Explain.

Ans. Mysore was captured by the British after its four wars with Mysore (1767-69, 1780-84, 1790-92 and 1799). Mysore became powerful under the rulers like Haidar Ali (1761-1782) and his son Tipu Sultan (1782-1799). Mysore controlled the profitable trade of the Malabar coast where the Company purchased pepper and cardamom.

In 1785, Tipu Sultan stopped the export of sandalwood, pepper and cardamom through the ports of his kingdom. He also disallowed local merchants from trading with the Company. He established a close relationship with the French traders and modernised his army with the help of the French.

These conditions led to the wars between the East India Company and Mysore kingdom. In the last battle, the Battle of Seringapatam, the Company ultimately won the war and Tipu Sultan was killed. As a result, Mysore was placed under Wodeyars dynasty and a subsidiary alliance was imposed.

3. Who introduced the policy of paramountcy? What did it mean? What sort of resistance did the Company face? **Competency Based**

Ans. Governor-General Lord Hastings (1813-1823) introduced a new policy of 'paramountcy' in India.

It meant that the power of the Company was paramount or supreme, i.e. the power of the Company was greater than that of Indian states. In order to protect its business interest, the Company could annex or threaten to annex any Indian kingdom.

This policy of the British was followed by the later rulers. But this policy of the British was resisted by revolts. For example, when the British tried to capture the small state of Kitoor, Rani Channamma revolted against this annexation. As a result, she was arrested and later died in the prison in 1829. This resistance movement did not stop. It was carried on by Rayanna, a poor chowkidar of Sangoli in Kitoor. He got support from the common people and destroyed many British camps and records. In 1830, he was caught and hanged by the British.

4. A historian is writing an article about the process of expansion of Indian states by the British East India company from 1757 to 1857. Mention the points that historian needed to discuss in his article about the process of expansion.

Ans. Different types of political, economic and diplomatic methods were used by the British East India company to expand in India.

Initially, the company focused on expanding its control over Bengal and Bihar. The company defeated the nawab of Bengal and began to collect taxes on behalf of Mughal Emperor.

The Company also defeated Marathas to gain control in central and Western India. The Company imposed subsidiary alliance to gain territories. If Indian rulers failed to make the payment of subsidiary force, then part of their territory was annexed. Awadh and Hyderabad was annexed on this basis.

The Company used military action when it was threatened to its political or economic interests. It fought Anglo-Mysore war and killed Tipu Sultan.

The Company also used the policy of paramountcy to establish their supremacy over different territories. The company secure North-West front by fighting Afghan war and impose indirect rule in Afghanistan. Lord Dalhausie annexed many kingdom using Doctrine of Laspse like Satara, Udaipur, Jhansi, etc.

Picture Based Questions

1. Look at the picture given below and answer the questions that follow.

Ans. Bahadur Shah Zafar and his sons were being arrested by Captain Hodson.

(ii) **Why was the person being arrested and forced to leave the kingdom?**

Ans. In the First War of Independence of 1857, Bahadur Shah Zafar was seen as the natural leader. So, he was forced to leave the kingdom when the revolt was put down by the British Company.

2. Look at the picture given below and answer the questions that follow.

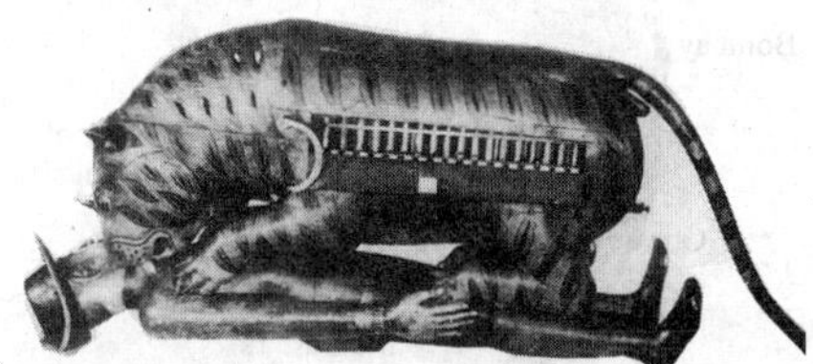

(i) **Who possessed the mechanical toy in the picture?**

Ans. Tipu Sultan, the ruler of Mysore, possessed the mechanical toy in the above picture.

(ii) **What happened when the handle of the toy was turned?**

Ans. When the handle of the toy was turned, the toy tiger roared and the soldier shrieked.

(iii) **Where is the toy tiger now kept?**

Ans. This toy tiger was taken by the British when Tipu Sultan died in 1799. The toy was then kept in the Victoria and Albert Museum in London.

Case Based Questions

1. Read the passage given below and answer the following questions.

The promise of riches

The territorial ambitions of the mercantile East India Company were viewed with distrust and doubt in England. After the Battle of Plassey, Robert Clive wrote to William Pitt, one of the Principal Secretaries of State to the English monarch, on 7th January, 1759 from Calcutta: But so large a sovereignty may possibly be an object too extensive for a mercantile Company ... I flatter myself ... that there will be little or no difficulty in obtaining the absolute possession of these rich kingdoms: ... Now I leave you to judge, whether an income yearly of two million sterling with the possession of three provinces ... be an object deserving the public attention ...

(i) **Who was William Pitt?**

Ans. William Pitt was one of the Principal Secretaries of state to the English monarch.

(ii) **What did Robert Clive write to William Pitt after the Battle of Plassey?**

Ans. After the Battle of Plassey, Robert Clive wrote to William Pitt on 7th January, 1759 about the advantage of expanding British colony in India. He stated that there was no difficulty in obtaining the absolute power of the rich kingdoms of India. The Company earned yearly two million sterling by possessing only three provinces at that time.

2. Read the passage given below and answer the following questions.

The Nawab complains

In 1733, the Nawab of Bengal said this about the English traders: When they first came into the country they petitioned the then government in a humble manner for liberty to purchase a spot of ground to build a factory house upon, which was no sooner granted but they built a strong fort, surrounded it with a ditch which has communication with the river and mounted a great number of guns upon the walls. They have enticed several merchants and others to go and take protection under them and they collect a revenue which amounts to ₹ 100,000 ... they rob and plunder and carry great number of the king's subjects of both sexes into slavery into their own country ...

(i) **What was the initial intention of the English traders?**

Ans. Initially, when the English traders first came to India, they were very polite. They petitioned the then government in a humble manner for permission to purchase land to build a factory house there.

(ii) **How did the activities of the British traders change later on?**

Ans. The activities of the British traders later on changed from trade to conquest. They began to built forts, accuiqre military power and expand its territorial holdings. They also started asking concessions and try to interfere in internal politics of local rulers.

3. Read the source given below and answer the following questions.

What power did the Residents have?

This is what James Mill, the famous economist and political philosopher from Scotland, wrote about the Residents appointed by the Company. We place a Resident, who really is king of the country, whatever injunctions of non-interference he may act under. As long as the prince acts in perfect subservience, and does what is agreeable to the residents, that is, to the British Government, things go on quietly; they are managed without the resident appearing much in the administration of affairs ... but when anything of a different nature happens, the moment the prince takes a course which the British Government think wrong, then comes clashing and disturbance.

(i) Who was James Mill?

Ans. James Mill was a famous economist and political philosopher from Scotland.

(ii) Who enjoyed the real power in an Indian state? Discuss.

Ans. According to James Mill, Residents enjoyed the real power in an Indian state. After the Battle of Buxar, the East India Company appointed Residents in Indian state. They were political and commercial agents of the Company. Their job was to serve and further the interests of the Company.

Through them, the Company officials began interfering in the internal affairs of Indian States. They decided who was to be the succession of throne and who was to be appointed in administrative post.

Map Based Questions

1. Look at the Maps a, b and c along with a present day political map, of India. In each of these maps try and identify the different parts of India that were under the British rule.

Map (a)

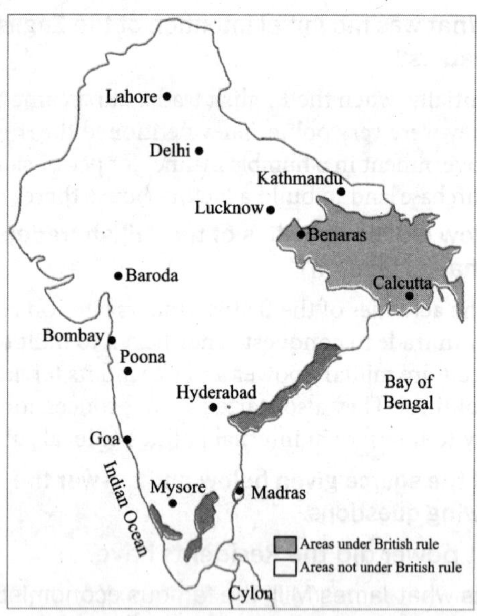

Ans. In the above map, the areas which were under the British rule were some parts of East UP, Bihar, Bengal, Coastal Andhra Pradesh, Madras city, some parts of Tamil Nadu and Kerala.

Map (b)

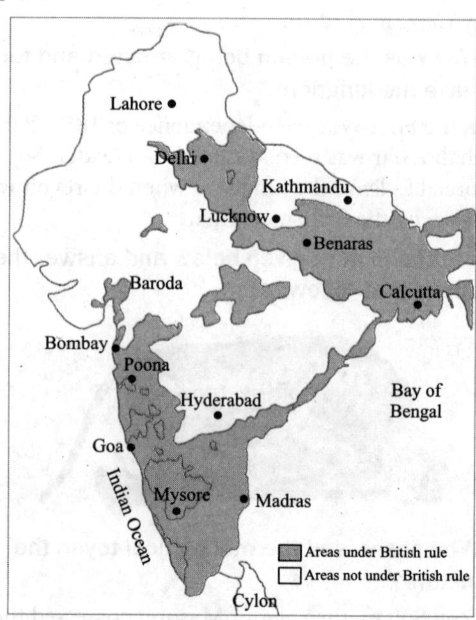

Ans. In the above map, the areas which were under the British rule were some parts of Himachal Pradesh, Punjab, Rajasthan, Gujarat, Madhya Pradesh, Orissa, etc.

Map (c)

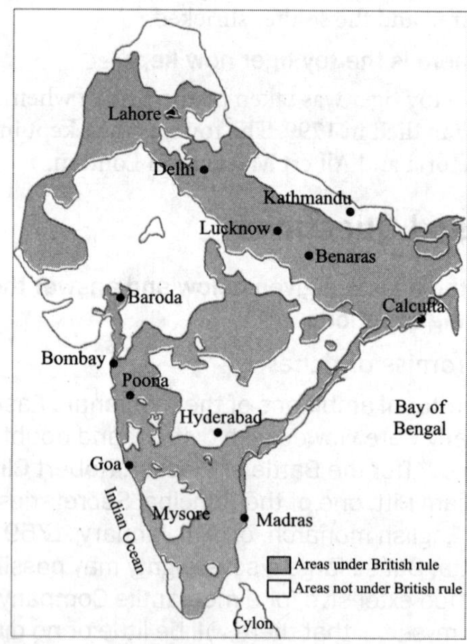

Ans. In the above map, the areas which were under the British rule were some parts of Jammu and Kashmir, Himachal Pradesh, Rajasthan, Gujarat, Madhya Pradesh, etc.

ASSESSMENT EXERCISE

Multiple Choice Questions (MCQs)

1. In 1600 AD, who was the ruler of the England?
(a) Queen Elizabeth-II
(b) Queen Elizabeth-I
(c) King Ronald James
(d) King Charles-V

2. Which of the following Europeans got their base in Goa?
(a) Britisher (b) Portuguese
(c) French (d) Dutch

3. Who was the puppet of the British after Battle of Plassey?
(a) Sirajuddaulah (b) Mir Jafar
(c) Mir Kasim (d) None of these

4. Who did devise a policy that came to be known as the Doctrine of Lapse?
(a) Lord Wellesley
(b) Dadabhai Naoroji
(c) Lord Dalhousie
(d) Lord Hastings

Subjective Questions (VSA, SA & LA)

1. Mention the names of the things which had a big market in Europe.

2. What do you mean by Nabobs?

3. What is the meaning of Subsidiary Alliance?

4. What are the Presidencies? Name any three.

5. Which matters raised the anger of the Nawab of Bengal, Murshid Khan?

6. How did the company rule influence the states?

7. What is the policy of paramountcy?

8. Mention any two changes in the Britisher's Army.

9. What were the effects of the 'Battle of Plassey'?

10. What were the contributions of Tipu Sultan?

11. Mention the differences between the Mughal Army and Sepoy Army.

Ruling the Countryside

CHAPTER 3

After acquiring the Diwani of Bengal in 1765, the East India Company gradually started to introduce new methods or system to increase produce in order to earn more revenue. This led to several rebellions by the people of countryside.

In this chapter, we will discuss how the company came to colonise the countryside, organise revenue resources, redefine the rights of people and produce the crops it wanted.

3.1 The Company becomes the Diwan

On 12th August, 1765, the Mughal emperor appointed the East India Company as the **Diwan**[1] of Bengal.

The Company as Diwan became chief financial administrator of the territory it controlled. The Company now had to think of administering the land and organising its revenue resources in a way that enough revenue could be earned to meet the growing expenses of the company.

Over the years, the Company also learnt about the need to pacify those who had ruled the countryside in the past and enjoyed authority and prestige. Those who had held local power had to be controlled but they could not be entirely eliminated.

Revenue for the Company

Initially, the British East India Company was only interested in collecting revenue. It became the Diwan but it still regarded itself as a trader. It did not want to establish a regular system to assessment and collection but aimed to increase its revenue, and buying fine cotton and silk cloth as cheaply as possible.

The value of goods bought by the Company doubled in five years. Before 1765, the Company had purchased goods in India by importing gold and silver from Britain, but now it could purchase the goods for export from the revenue collected in Bengal.

However, this led to a crisis in Bengal as

- Artisans were being forced to sell their goods to the Company at low prices and so they were leaving their villages.
- Peasants were not able to pay their dues that were being demanded.
- There was a decline in artisanal production and agricultural cultivation.
- In 1770, a famine killed about one-third population in Bengal.

The Need to Improve Agriculture

Most Company officials began to feel that investment in land had to be encouraged and agriculture had to be improved.

Finally, the Company introduced the **Permanent Settlement** in 1793. **Charles Cornwallis** was the Governor-General of India during this period.

The Permanent Settlement

According to the Permanent Settlement, rajas and taluqdars were recognised as zamindars. They were responsible for collecting rent from peasants and paying a fixed amount of revenue to the Company.

The Company officials felt that it would ensure a regular flow of revenue into the Company's treasury. The Company also encouraged the zamindars to invest in improving the land.

1 **Diwan** A "diwan" is a term for a high-ranking administrative officer or a public office in certain historical and contemporary contexts.

As the revenue demand of the state was fixed and could not be increased, the zamindar would benefit through increased production from the land.

Problems with the Permanent Settlement

The Permanent Settlement created several problems. These were

- The zamindars were not investing in improvement of the land.
- The revenue that had been fixed was so high that the zamindars found it difficult to pay. A zamindar who failed to pay revenue lost his zamindari.
- By the early 19th century, the prices in the market rose and cultivation slowly expanded. This meant an increase in the income of the zamindars but no gain for the Company as it could not increase a revenue demand that had been fixed permanently.
- The Permanent Settlement was extremely oppressive for the cultivators. The rent they paid to the zamindars was high and they often had to take loan from the moneylenders. Failure of payment of the rent meant removal of cultivators from the land.

Development of a New System

By the early 19th century, the Company officials realised to change system of revenue because the Company needed more money to meet its expenses of administration and change. Thus, the Company introduced **Mahalwari Settlement** and **Ryotwari** System.

These are discussed below.

- **Mahalwari Settlement** This system was developed by **Holt Mackenzie**, an Englishman in the North-Western Provinces of the Bengal Presidency. It came into effect in 1822.
- Under this system, the revenue collectors were asked to visit villages, inspect the land, measure the fields and record the customs and rights of different groups.

  The estimated revenue of each plot within a village was added up to calculate the revenue that each village (**mahal**[2]) had to pay. This rate of revenue was not fixed and to be revised periodically.

  The charge of collecting the revenue was given to village headman rather than the zamindar.
- **Ryotwari or the Munro System** This system was introduced by **Captain Alexander Read** and further developed by **Thomas Munro**. This system was gradually extended all over South India.

  Under this system, as there were no traditional zamindars in the South, these settlement had to be made directly with the cultivators (*ryots*[3]). Their fields had to be carefully and separately surveyed before the revenue assessment was made.

Both these systems of the Company were a failure as they were introduced to increase the income from land, but the revenue demand was very high. Peasants were unable to pay the revenue, ryots moved to the countryside, and people left villages in many regions.

Try These

1. **When was the East India Company appointed as the Diwan of Bengal?**
2. **Who introduced the Ryotwari system?**
3. **Mention the aim of the Permanent Settlement introduced in 1793.**
4. **What was the new revenue system in British-controlled South India called?**

3.2 Crops for Europe

The British realised that the countryside could grow the crops that Europe required.

By the late 18th century, the Company wanted to expand the cultivation of opium and indigo. However, after 18th century, the British forced the cultivators in different parts of India to produce other crops like

- jute in Bengal
- tea in Assam
- sugarcane in the United Provinces (now Uttar Pradesh)
- wheat in Punjab
- cotton in Maharashtra and Punjab
- rice in Madras

2 **Mahal** In British revenue records, mahal is a revenue estate which may be a village or a group of villages.

3 **Ryot** A "ryot" was a term used in India during the British colonial era to refer to peasant farmers who worked the land.

Indigo

India was the **biggest supplier** of indigo in the world in the 19th century. Indigo was used to dye the clothes in Europe as it provide rich blue colour. In India, indigo was also used in **Kalamkari print** created by the weavers of Andhra Pradesh.

KNOWLEDGE PLUS The blue dye used in the Morris prints in 19th century, Britain was manufactured from indigo plants cultivated in India.

Demand for Indian Indigo

The indigo plant grows primarily in the tropics. By the 13th century, Indian indigo was being used by cloth manufacturers in Italy, France and Britain to dye cloth. However, only small amounts of Indian indigo reached the European market and its price was very high.

Thus, European cloth manufacturers had to depend on another plant called **woad** for making blue and violet dyes. Cloth dyers preferred indigo as a dye in place of woad because indigo produced a rich blue colour, whereas the dye from woad was pale and dull.

By the 17th century, the French began cultivating indigo in **St Domingue** in the Caribbean islands, the Portuguese in Brazil, the English in Jamaica and the Spanish in Venezuela. Indigo **plantations**[4] also started in many parts of North America.

By the end of the 18th century, the demand for Indian indigo grew due to **industrialisation** in Britain. Cotton production expanded dramatically which created a large demand for indigo.

Britain Turns to India for Indigo Cultivation

With the rising demand for indigo in Europe, the Company in India looked for ways to expand the area under indigo cultivation.

From the late 18th century, indigo cultivation in Bengal expanded rapidly. In 1788, only about 30 per cent of the indigo was imported into Britain from India which increased to 95 per cent by 1810.

The demand for indigo increased but its supplies from the West Indies and America decrease between 1783 and 1789. Thus, the cloth dyers in Britain started looking for new sources of indigo supply.

Systems of Indigo Cultivation

There were two main systems of indigo cultivation i.e. **nij** and **ryoti**.

The Nij System

In this system, the planter produced indigo in lands that he directly controlled. He either bought the land or rented it from other zamindars and produced indigo by directly employing hired labourers.

The problems with nij cultivation were as follows

- The planters found it difficult to expand the area under nij cultivation. Indigo could be cultivated only on fertile lands and all these were already densely populated.
- The planters attempted to rent the land around the indigo factory and evict the peasants from the area which always led to conflicts.
- A large number of labour was required for large plantation of indigo. However, it was not available at a time when peasants were usually busy with rice cultivation.
- Nij cultivation on a large scale required many ploughs and bullocks. Investing on purchase and maintenance of ploughs was a big problem.
- Till the late 19th century, planters did not want to expand area under nij cultivation due to which less than 25 per cent of the land producing indigo was under this system.

The Ryoti System

Under the ryoti system, the planters forced the ryots to sign an agreement (*satta*). Sometimes, they forced the village headmen to sign the contract on behalf of the ryots.

The ryots who signed the agreement got cash advances from the planters at low rates of interest to produce Indigo. However, they had to cultivate Indigo on at least 25 per cent of the area of their land.

The problems with Ryoti system were as follows

- When the crop was delivered to the planter after the harvest, a new loan was given to the ryot and the cycle started all over again.
- The price they got for indigo production was very low.

4 **Plantation** A large farm operated by a planter employing various forms of forced labour. Plantations are associated with the production of coffee, sugarcane, tobacco, tea and cotton.

- The planters usually demanded to cultivate indigo on the best soils in which peasants preferred to cultivate rice.
- Indigo, moreover, had deep roots and it exhausted the soil rapidly.
- After an indigo harvest, the land could not be sown with rice.

3.3 The 'Blue Rebellion'

This rebellion started in March 1859, when thousands of ryots in Bengal refused to grow indigo. The ryots also refused to pay rents to the planters and attacked indigo factories. Women also joined the rebellion.

Gomasthas who were the agents of planters, were beaten up in this rebellion.

The local zamindars, and village headmen who had been forced to sign indigo contracts, also joined the rebellion.

When the rebellion spread, the government sent military for the protection of the planters and set-up the **Indigo Commission** to enquire into the system of indigo production.

The commission declared the following

- It held the planters guilty and criticised them for using coercive methods to control the ryots.
- It declared that indigo production was not profitable for ryots.
- It asked the ryots could fulfil their existing contracts, but they could refuse to produce indigo in future.

After the Blue Rebellion

After the Blue Rebellion, indigo production declined in Bengal. The planters shifted their operation to Bihar. Their business was severly affected with the discovery of synthetic dyes in the late 19th century, but they managed to expand production.

When Mahatma Gandhi returned from South Africa, a peasant from Bihar persuaded him to visit Champaran and see the condition of indigo cultivators.

Mahatma Gandhi visit Champaran in 1917 and marked the beginning of the **Champaran Movement** against the indigo planters.

Try These

1. **What was the primary source of indigo in the 19th century?**
2. **Which region of India dominated the global indigo market in the 18th century?**
3. **Name the systems adopted for indigo cultivation in India in 18th century.**
4. **Who initiated the Champaran Movement against indigo planters in 1917?**

RULING THE COUNTRYSIDE

Indigo

- In the 19th century, India was the biggest supplier of Indigo in the world.
- It was used in Kalamkari print created by the weavers of Andhra Pradesh.

The Nij System of Cultivation

Indigo was planted in lands that the planter directly controlled

Crops for Europe

British forced the cultivators in different parts of India to produce other Groups like

- Jute in Bengal
- Tea in Assam
- Sugarcane in United Provinces (UP)
- Wheat in Punjab
- Cotton in Maharashtra and Punjab

The Ryoti System of Cultivation

The planters forced the Ryots to sign an agreement (Satta)

The Company becomes the Diwan

Mughal emperor appointed the East India Company on 12th August, 1765

The Blue Rebellion

- Started in March 1859.
- Gomasthas were beaten.
- Indigo Commission was set up to enquire into the system of Indigo production.
- Indigo production declined after the Blue Rebellion.

The Need to Improve Agriculture

Revenue for the Company

Before 1765, the Company had purchased goods in India by importing gold and silver from Britain, but now it could purchase the goods for export from the revenue collected in Bengal

The Permanent Settlement

Rajas and Taluqdars were recognised as Zamindars

The Mahalwari Settlement

Developed by Holt Mackenzie

The Ryotwari System

Introduced by Captain Alexander Read and further developed by Thomas Munro.

NCERT FOLDER

Covering Intext Questions and Exercises of NCERT

NCERT ON PAGE 28 (ACTIVITY)

Q.1 Why do you think Colebrook is concerned with the conditions of the under-ryots in Bengal? Read the preceding pages and suggest possible reasons.

Ans. Colebrook is concerned with the conditions of the under-ryots or under-tenants in Bengal. These depressing conditions are due to some social economic reasons which are as follow

- In 1765, the British East India Company got the Diwani of Bengal.
- The Company was only interested to collect a large amount of revenue with which it could purchase fine cotton and silk from India.
- Artisans were paid very low prices, so they fled from villages.
- Agricultural production collapsed, the under-ryots could not pay the high rate of revenues.
- About one-third population of Bengal was wiped out in famine of 1770.
- The Permanent Settlement (1793) fixed a high rate of revenue which was not changeable in any condition.
- Zamindars had no interest in improving the conditions of land.

NCERT ON PAGE 30 (ACTIVITY)

Q.2 Imagine that you are a Company representative sending a report back to England about the conditions in rural areas under Company rule. What would you write?

Ans. As a Company representative, I would write the following conditions in rural areas of India under the Company rule

- The Company has made a policy of permanent settlement with the zamindars. This would provide a definite and regular supply of revenue to the Company.
- The zamindars are asked to take care of their tenants. They have been directed to do enough for the improvement of land.
- Farmers have been provided with the required irrigation facilities. They have been asked to focus on some crops which the Company needs for its trade.
- The farmers are being given payment in advance for the crops they grow for the Company.
- Small scale industries have been supported by the Company. The weavers are being provided loans, both for machines and tools and for raw materials.
- The overall situation in the Company ruled areas is satisfactory. The conditions seem satisfactory and promising to me both for the common people and the Company.

NCERT ON PAGE 36 (ACTIVITY)

Q.3 Imagine you are a witness giving evidence before the Indigo Commission. WS Seton Karr asks you "On what condition will *ryots* grow indigo?" What will your answer be?

Ans. The ryots will grow indigo on the following conditions

- They will pay revenue which is reasonable.
- They will cultivate indigo as per their will and convenience.
- They will not be forced in any manner.
- They will sell their produce in open market which will bring profit to them.

NCERT ON PAGE 38 (LET'S IMAGINE)

Q.4 Imagine a conversation between a planter and a peasant who is being forced to grow indigo. What reasons would the planter give to persuade the peasant? What problems would the peasant point out? Enact their conversation.

Ans. Do it yourself.

EXERCISES

Q.1 Match the following.

List I	List II
Ryot	Village
Mahal	Peasant
Nij	Cultivation on ryot's lands
Ryoti	Cultivation on planter's own land

Ans.

Ryot	Peasant
Mahal	Village
Nij	Cultivation on planter's own land
Ryoti	Cultivation on ryot's land

Q.2 Fill in the blanks.

(a) Growers of woad in Europe saw .... as a crop which would provide competition to their earnings.

(b) The demand for indigo increased in late 18th century Britain because of ....

(c) The international demand for indigo was affected by the discovery of ....

(d) The Champaran Movement was against ....

Ans. (a) indigo (b) expansion of cotton production (c) synthetic dyes (d) indigo planters

Q.3 Describe the main features of the Permanent Settlement.

Ans. The main features of the Permanent Settlement were

- By the terms of the settlement, the rajas and taluqdars were recognised as zamindars.
- Zamindars were asked to collect rent from the peasants and pay revenue to the Company.
- The amount to be paid by the zamindars was fixed permanently, i.e. it was not to be increased ever in future.
- It would ensure a regular flow of revenue into the Company's treasury and at the same time encourage the zamindars to invest in improving the land.
- As the rate of revenue was fixed, the zamindar would benefit from the increased production of land.

Q.4 How was the Mahalwari system different from the Permanent Settlement?

Ans. Following are the differences between Mahalwari system and Permanent Settlement

Mahalwari System	Permanent Settlement
The Mahalwari system came into effect in 1822.	The Permanent Settlement was introduced by the Company in 1793.
In Mahalwari system, it was decided that the rate of revenue was to be revised periodically, not permanently fixed.	Under the Permanent Settlement, the rate of revenue was fixed permanently, i.e. it was not to be increased ever in future.
In the Mahalwari system, the charge of collecting the revenue and paying it to the Company was given to the village headman.	In the Permanent Settlement, the zamindars were given the charge of collecting revenue from the peasants and paying it to the Company.

Q.5 Give two problems which arose with the new Munro system of fixing revenue.

Ans. The two problems with the new Munro system of fixing revenue were as follows

(i) The revenue officials wanted to increase the income from land and make more money, so they fixed a very high revenue demand which peasants were unable to pay.

(ii) It was believed that the new system would transform the peasants into rich farmers, but it failed to happen.

Q.6 Why were the ryots reluctant to grow indigo?

Ans. The ryots became reluctant to grow indigo for a number of reasons such as

- Indigo could be cultivated only on fertile lands, but the peasants preferred to cultivate rice there. Indigo plant had deep roots and exhausted the soil rapidly and after an indigo harvest, the land could not be useful for rice cultivation.
- Peasants who were initially tempted by the loans given by the planters, soon realised that the system was very harsh. The price they got for the indigo they produced was very low and cycles of loans never ended. They were trapped in a cycle of loan.

Q.7 What were the circumstances which led to the eventual collapse of indigo production in Bengal?

Ans. The collapse of indigo production in Bengal was primarily due to the exploitative indigo cultivation system imposed by British planters. Peasants were forced to cultivate indigo on a large scale, neglecting food crops, leading to famine. Additionally, British indigo planters subjected farmers to harsh terms, low wages, and excessive indigo production.

The discontent among peasants fuelled the Indigo Revolt of 1859-60, leading to widespread protests and boycotts. The British government, acknowledging the unjust practices, enacted the Indigo Commission recommendations, abolishing coercive indigo cultivation and contributing to the eventual collapse of the industry.

Q.8 Find out more about the Champaran Movement and Mahatma Gandhi's role in it.

Ans. Mahatma Gandhi started the Champaran movement in 1917 against the indigo planters.

The role of Mahatma Gandhi in this movement was

- He organised meetings with the peasants, listened to their grievances, and helped them organize a nonviolent resistance campaign against the British authorities and plantation owners.
- He encouraged them to organize themselves and stand up for their rights and as a result a law was passed to protect the farmers from the indigo planters.

Q.9 Look into the history of either tea or coffee plantation in India. See how the life of workers in these plantations was similar to or different from that of workers in indigo plantations.

Ans. The life of workers in tea or coffee plantations was similar to the life of workers in indigo plantations in the way they were exploited. They were given low wages. Their housing was poor and they lacked social mobility.

REVIEW EXERCISE

Including Competency Based Questions

Part I

Multiple Choice Questions (MCQs)

1. The East India Company was appointed as the Diwan of Bengal in

(a) 1760 (b) 1762
(c) 1764 (d) 1765

2. In which of the following states about ten million people were killed in the terrible famine of 1770?

(a) Bengal (b) Punjab
(c) Bihar (d) Orissa

3. What do you mean by Mahal in British revenue records?

(a) Farmer and fields
(b) A village or a group of villages
(c) Seeds and crops
(d) Local name of land revenue

4. In which state, the weavers created Kalamkari print in cotton clothes?

(a) Orissa (b) Madhya Pradesh
(c) Andhra Pradesh (d) Bengal

5. Who was William Morris?

(a) A famous actor (b) A famous cricketer
(c) A famous poet and artist (d) A famous scientist

6. What changes occured in the production of indigo between 1783 and 1789 in the world? Competency Based

(a) It fell by half
(b) It became larger
(c) It was not encourage
(d) It became a profitable business

7. Who was the Governor of Madras in 1819 to 1826?

(a) Thomas Munro (b) William Bentinck
(c) Thomas Disilva (d) Warren Hastings

8. In 1788, only about 30 per cent of the indigo was exported to Britain from India which rose to which per cent by 1810?

(a) 70 per cent (b) 80 per cent
(c) 95 per cent (d) 85 per cent

9. H.T. Colebrook described the conditions of the under-tenant farmers in

(a) 1806 (b) 1810
(c) 1815 (d) 1820

10. What affected the International demand of indigo?

(a) Synthetic dyes (b) Woad
(c) Blue colour (d) None of the above

11. The Permanent Settlement was introduced at the time of

(a) Charles Cornwallis (b) Thomas Munro
(c) Lord Dalhousie (d) Warren Hastings

12. The Indigo Commission was set-up to enquire into the system of indigo production. Whom did the Commission hold guilty? Competency Based

(a) The ryots (b) The government
(c) The planters (d) Both (a) and (b)

13. After the indigo production collapsed in Bengal, the planters shifted their operation to

(a) Gujarat (b) Bihar (c) Orissa (d) Maharashtra

14. Imagine you are one of the zamidars of Bengal. What role did you play in the indigo rebellion at 1859? Competency Based

(a) I supported the planters against the indigo peasants.
(b) I stayed neutral and did not intervene in the conflict.
(c) I encouraged the indigo peasants to resist the planters.
(d) I sought to maintain the power of the planters over the peasants.

15. Which of the following statements is/are correct? Competency Based

I. On 12th August, 1765, the Mughal emperor appointed the East India Company as the Diwan of Bengal.

II. As Diwan, the Company became the chief financial administrator of the territory under its control.

Codes

(a) Only I (b) Only II
(c) Both I and II (d) Neither I nor II

16. Consider the following statements and choose the correct option. Competency Based

I. In the British territories in the South, there was a similar move away from the idea of Permanent Settlement.

II. The new system that was devised came to be known as the ryotwar (or ryotwari).

III. The settlement, they argued, had to be made directly with the cultivator (ryots) who has tilled the land for generations.

Codes

(a) Only I (b) Both I and II
(c) Both II and III (d) All of these

17. Which one of the following is arranged in chronological sequence?
(i) Blue Rebellion
(ii) Mahalwari System
(iii) Permanent Settlement
Codes
(a) (iii), (i), (ii) (b) (iii), (ii), (i)
(c) (i), (ii), (iii) (d) (ii), (iii), (i)

Answers

1. (d)	2. (a)	3. (b)	4. (c)	5. (c)
6. (a)	7. (a)	8. (c)	9. (a)	10. (a)
11. (a)	12. (c)	13. (b)	14. (a)	15. (c)
16. (d)	17. (b)			

Match the Following

1.

List I	List II
A. 1793	1. Period of Thomas Munro
B. 1770	2. Permanent Settlement
C. 1819-26	3. The Company got Diwani of Bengal
D. March 1859	4. A terrible famine in Bengal
E. 12th August, 1765	5. Blue Rebellion

Codes

	A	B	C	D	E		A	B	C	D	E
(a)	2	4	1	5	3	(b)	5	4	3	2	1
(c)	2	1	4	5	3	(d)	4	2	5	1	3

2.

List I	List II
A. Kalamkari	1. Printing style of Andhra Pradesh
B. Mahalwari	2. Mackenzi
C. Satta	3. Contract
D. Gomastha	4. The agent of planters

Codes

	A	B	C	D		A	B	C	D
(a)	1	2	3	4	(b)	4	3	2	1
(c)	3	1	4	2	(d)	2	4	1	3

Ans 1. (a) 2. (a)

Assertion-Reason

1. **Assertion** (A) In the North-Western Provinces of the Bengal Presidency (most of this area is now in Uttar Pradesh), an Englishman called Holt Mackenzie devised the new system which came into effect in 1822.

Reason (R) He felt that the village was an important social institution in North Indian society and needed to be preserved. **Competency Based**

Codes
(a) Both A and R are true and R is the correct explanation of A
(b) Both A and R are true, but R is not the correct explanation of A
(c) A is true, but R is false
(d) A is false, but R is true

2. **Assertion** (A) The British realised that the countryside could not only yield revenue, it could also grow the crops that Europe required.

Reason (R) By the late 18th century, the Company was trying its best to expand the cultivation of opium and indigo.

Codes
(a) Both A and R are true and R is the correct explanation of A
(b) Both A and R are true, but R is not the correct explanation of A
(c) A is true, but R is false
(d) A is false, but R is true

Ans 1. (a) Both A and R are true and R is the correct explanation of A
2. (a) Both A and R are true and R is the correct explanation of A

Fill in the Blanks

1. Cornwallis was the Governor-General of Bengal when the .... was introduced.
2. Ryotwari system was also known as ....
3. 'Rural Life in Bengal, 1860' is written by ....
4. Indigo was cultivated by the .... in Brazil, the .... in Jamaica and the .... in Venezuela.
5. Between .... and ...., the production of indigo in the world fell by half.

Ans 1. Permanent Settlement 2. munro system
3. Grant Colesworthy 4. Portuguese, English, Spanish
5. 1783, 1789

True or False

1. By the first decade of the 19th century, cultivation system developed and the prices in market rose.
2. Permanent Settlement recognised the rajas and taluqdars as zamindars.
3. The conditions of under-tenants in Bengal was described by HT Colebrook in 1806.
4. The indigo villages were usually around East India Company's headquarters.
5. Mahatma Gandhi visited Champaran for Quit India Movement.

Ans 1. False 2. False 3. False 4. Flase 5. False

Picture Based Questions

1. Identify the revolt associated with the given picture.

(a) Kol revolt (b) The slave revolt
(c) Santhal revolt (d) Revolt of 1857

2. Identify the person depicted in the given image.

(a) Thomas Munro (b) Charles Cornwallis
(c) Warren Hastings (d) Lord Clive

Ans 1. (b) The slave revolt 2. (a) Thomas Munro

Case Based Question

1. Read the passage given below and answer the following questions.

By the end of the 18th century, the demand for Indian indigo grew further. Britain began to industrialise and its cotton production expanded dramatically, creating an enormous new demand for cloth dyes. While the demand for indigo increased, its existing supplies from the West-Indies and America collapsed for a variety of reasons. Between 1783 and 1789, the production of indigo in the world fell by half. Cloth dyers in Britain now desperately looked for new sources of indigo supply.

(i) What led to the increased demand for Indian indigo by the end of the eighteenth century?

(a) Decrease in cotton production in India.
(b) Expansion of the spice trade.
(c) Industrialisation in Britain and a rise in cotton production
(d) Increased availability of indigo from the West- Indies

(ii) Why did the demand for indigo grow as Britain industrialised?

(a) Indigo was used as a fuel
(b) Indigo was used as a primary material
(c) Both (a) and (b)
(d) Indigo was used for dyeing cloth

(iii) What caused the collapse of existing indigo supplies from the West Indies and America?

(a) Successful negotiation of trade agreements with India
(b) Decreased demand for cloth dyes in Britain
(c) Increase in local production of indigo in the West Indies and America
(d) None of the above

(iv) During the 1783 and 1789, the production of .... in the world fell by half.

(a) sugarcane (b) indigo
(c) black pepper (d) None of these

Ans (i) (c) Industrilisation in Britain and a rise in cotton production.
(ii) (d) Indigo was used for dyeing cloth
(iii) (d) Various reason that are not specified.
(iv) (b) Indigo

Part II

Very Short Answer Type Questions

1. When did the Company was appointed as the Diwan of Bengal?

Ans. On 12th August, 1765, the Mughal emperor appointed the East India Company as the Diwan of Bengal.

2. Why were Bengal artisans deserting villages?

Ans. Bengal artisans were deserting villages because they were being pressurised to sell their goods to the Company at low prices.

3. What were the consequences of 1770 famine in Bengal?

Ans. In the terrible famine of 1770, ten million people were killed in Bengal. About one-third of the population was wiped out.

4. When did the Mahalwari system come into existence?

Ans. In 1822, the Mahalwari system came into existence.

5. What was used to produce the rich indigo colour?

Ans. The rich blue colour or indigo which was used to dye clothes, was produced from a plant called indigo.

6. Why did European cloth manufacturers have to depend on woad?

Ans. European cloth manufacturers had to depend on woad for violet and blue dyes because only small amounts of Indian indigo reached the European market and its price was very high.

7. Why did cloth dyers prefer indigo instead of woad as dye? **Competency Based**

Ans. Cloth dyers preferred indigo as a dye, as it produced a rich blue colour, whereas the dye from woad was pale and dull.

8. How did Company purchase goods in India before 1865? **Competency Based**

Ans. Before 1865, the East India Company had purchased goods in India by importing gold and silver from Britain.

Short Answer Type Questions

1. Why were the planters reluctant to expand the area under nij cultivation?

Ans. The planters were reluctant to expand the area under nij cultivation because of the following reasons

- Indigo could be cultivated only on fertile lands, but these lands were already densely populated. The planters hardly got large areas in compact blocks.
- The planters needed a large number of labour at a time when peasants were busy with rice cultivation.
- Nij cultivation on a large scale also required many ploughs and bullocks. They could not get the supplies from peasants as their ploughs and bullocks were busy on rice fields.

2. Why did the cultivator find the system of Permanent Settlement oppressive?

Ans. The cultivator found the Permanent Settlement extremely oppressive because of the following reasons

(i) The rent that the cultivator paid to the zamindar was high and his right on the land was insecure.

(ii) To pay the rent, the cultivator had to often take a loan from the moneylender.
When he failed to pay the rent, he was evicted from the land which he had cultivated for generations.

3. What crisis was faced by the Bengal economy?

Ans. In the 18th century, the Bengal economy was facing a deep crisis because

- Artisans were forced to sell their goods to the Company at low prices. Thus, artisans were leaving their villages and artisanal production was in decline.
- The rajas and taluqdars were not interested in the improvement of lands, thus agricultural cultivation was declining. Peasants were unable to pay the taxes that were demanded from them.
- In 1770, a terrible famine killed almost one-third of the population of Bengal.

4. After becoming the Diwan of Bengal in 1765, the Company realised that it had to move with some cautions. What caution the Company had to take after it became the Diwan? **Competency Based**

Ans. After becoming the Diwan of Bengal in 1765, the Company realised that it had to move with some cautions. These cautions were

The Company now had to think of administering the land and organising its revenue resources in a way that enough revenue could be earned to meet the growing expenses of the company.

The Company had also learnt about the need to pacify those who had ruled the countryside in the past and enjoyed authority and prestige. Those who had held local power had to be controlled but they could not be entirely eliminated.

5. Who was Holt Mackenzie? Explain the system devised by him.

Ans. Holt Mackenzie was an Englishman in the North-Western Provinces of the Bengal Presidency. He devised the Mahalwari system which came into effect in 1822.

Under this system, the revenue collectors were asked to visit villages, inspect the land, measure the fields and record the customs and rights of different groups.

The estimated revenue of each plot within a village was added up to calculate the revenue that each village (mahal) had to pay. This rate of revenue was not fixed and to be revised periodically. The charge of collecting the revenue was given to village headman rather than the zamindar.

Long Answer Type Questions

1. The indigo villages were usually around indigo factories owned by planters. After harvest, the Indigo plants was taken to the vats in the indigo factory. Describe different stages of the production of indigo. **Competency Based**

Ans. The production of indigo dye involves several stages, from cultivating the indigo plant to extracting and processing the dye. These stages are

- The indigo plant were harvested and taken to the vats in the indigo factory. Three or four vats were needed to manufacture the dye. Each vat had a separate function.
- Leaves of the indigo plant were first soaked in warm water in the fermenting vat for several hours.
- When the plants fermented, the liquid began to boil and bubble. Now, the rotten leaves were taken out and the liquid was drained into the second vat, known as the beater vat.

- The solution was continuously stirred and beaten with paddles. When the liquid gradually turned green and then blue, lime water was added to the vat.
- Gradually, the indigo was separated out in flakes. A muddy sediment settled at the bottom of the vat and a clear liquid rose to the surface.
- The liquid was drained off and the sediment, i.e. the indigo pulp was transferred to another vat, known as the settling vat. Then the pulp was pressed and dried for sale.

2. Write a short note on Blue Rebellion.

Ans. The Blue Rebellion started in March 1859, when thousands of ryots in Bengal refused to grow indigo. The ryots also refused to pay rents to the planters and attacked indigo factories. Women also joined the rebellion. Gomasthas who were the agents of planters, were beaten up in this rebellion.

The local zamindars, and village headmen who had been forced to sign indigo contracts, also joined the rebellion. When the rebellion spread, the government sent military for the protection of the planters and set-up the Indigo Commission to enquire into the system of indigo production.

The commission declared the following

- It held the planters guilty and criticised them for using coercive methods to control the ryots.
- It declared that indigo production was not profitable for ryots.
- It asked the ryots could fulfil their existing contracts, but they could refuse to produce indigo in future.

3. Under the ryoti system, the planters forced the ryots to sign a contract, an agreement (satta). Explain this system and its problems.

Ans. Under the ryoti system, the planters forced the ryots to sign an agreement (satta). Sometimes, they forced the village headmen to sign the contract on behalf of the ryots.

The ryots who signed the agreement got cash advances from the planters at low rates of interest to produce Indigo. However, they had to cultivate Indigo on at least 25 per cent of the area of their land.

The problems with ryoti system were as follows

- When the crop was delivered to the planter after the harvest, a new loan was given to the ryot and the cycle started all over again.
- The price they got for indigo production was very low.
- The planters usually demanded to cultivate indigo on the best soils in which peasants preferred to cultivate rice.
- Indigo, moreover, had deep roots and it exhausted the soil rapidly.
- After an indigo harvest, the land could not be sown with rice.

Picture Based Questions

1. Look at the picture given below and answer the questions that follow.

Fig (a) Fig (b)

(i) Who designed and produced the floral cotton design in the pictures of Fig (a) and Fig (b)?

(ii) How was the blue in these prints produced?

(iii) What do you know about Kalamkari art?

Ans. (i) The picture in Fig (a) is Kalamkari print. It was created by weavers of Andhra Pradesh in India.

The picture in Fig (b) is a floral cotton print. It was designed and produced by William Morris, a famous poet and artist of 19th century Britain.

(ii) The blue colour was produced by indigo. This indigo gave rich blue colour and was produced in India.

(iii) Kalamkari is a type of hand-painted or block-printed cotton textile, produced in parts of India. It is also produced in Iran. There are two distinctive styles of Kalamkari art in India i.e. Srikalahasti style and Machilipatnam style. 'Kalam' or pen is used for drawing the subject in this art form.

2. Look at the picture given below and answer the questions that follow.

(i) What is shown in the above picture?

(ii) Where did French planters produce indigo?

(iii) What did the African slaves do when they rose in rebellion in 1791?

(iv) What is the other name of this rebellion?

(v) When did France abolish slavery? What was its consequences?

Ans. (i) The Slave Revolt in St Domingue in August, 1791 is shown in the above picture.

(ii) In the 18th century, French planters produced indigo and sugar in the French colony of St Domingue in the Caribbean islands.

(iii) The African slaves who worked on the plantations rose in rebellion in 1791. They killed 4000 Whites and burned, and destroyed 180 sugar plantations and hundreds of coffee and indigo plantations.

(iv) The other name of the Slave Revolt is Haitian Revolt.

(v) In 1792, France abolished slavery in the French colonies. It led to the collapse of the indigo plantations on the Caribbean islands. By 1792, slave rebels controlled one-third of the island. The success of this slave rebellion caused the newly elected Legislative Assembly in France to grant civil and political rights to free men in the colonies.

3. Look at the picture given below and answer the questions that follow.

(i) Who is shown in the above picture?
(ii) Which post did he hold?
(iii) Which system was introduced when he held that post?

Ans. (i) Charles Cornwallis is shown in the above picture.

(ii) He was the Governor-General of India.

(iii) Permanent Settlement was introduced by him. He was appointed as the Governor-General of India in 1786.

His greatest achievement in India was the reorganisation of the land taxation, known as the Permanent Settlement of 1793. He granted legal ownership of their land to the zamindars. In return, they had to pay the government 90 per cent of the rent which they collected from the farmers.

As per Permanent Settlement, rajas and taluqdars were recognised as zamindars. The zamindars were supposed to collect the land revenue from the peasants.

4. Look at the picture given below and answer the questions that follow.

(i) What is shown in the picture?
(ii) Why did peasants and artisans from rural area regularly come to these markets?
(iii) When were these markets badly affected?

Ans. (i) A weekly market (which is known as haat) in Murshidabad in Bengal is shown in the picture.

(ii) Peasants and artisans from rural areas regularly came to these weekly markets to sell the goods that they produced and to buy the goods that they required.

(iii) These markets were badly affected during the economic crisis. At the time of economic crisis, artisanal production and agricultural cultivation declined.

Case Based Questions

1. Read the passage given below and answer the following questions.

"I would rather beg than sow indigo".

Hadji Mulla, an indigo cultivator of Chandpore, Thana Hardi, was interviewed by the members of the Indigo Commission on Tuesday, 5th June, 1860. This is what he said in answer to some of the questions

WS Seton Karr, President of the Indigo Commission Are you now willing to sow indigo; and if not on what fresh terms would you be willing to do it?

Hadji Mulla I am not willing to sow, and I do not know that any fresh terms would satisfy me.

Mr Sale Would you not be willing to sow at a rupee a bundle?

Hadji Mulla No, I would not; rather than sow indigo I will go to another country; I would rather beg than sow indigo.

(i) Why was Hadji Mulla reluctant to cultivate indigo?

Ans. Hadji Mulla was reluctant to cultivate indigo due to exploitative practices, bad working conditions and the thought that indigo cultivation offered limited economic possibility.

(ii) **How did the Hadji Mulla's statement reflect the challenges faced by indigo cultivators during that period?**

Ans. Hadji Mulla's statement tells that the indigo farmers were not happy during the time when the British ruled India. They were not treated well.

They thought it was bad job to grow indigo as there was too much exploitation and unfair treatment of indigo farmers.

2. Read the passage given below and answer the following questions.

Colebrook on Bengal ryots.

In many villages of Bengal, some of the powerful *ryots* did not cultivate, but instead gave out their lands to others (the under-tenants), taking from them very high rents.

In 1806, HT Colebrook described the conditions of these under-tenants in Bengal

The under-tenants, depressed by an excessive rent in kind, and by usurious returns for the cattle, seed, and subsistence, advanced to them, can never extricate themselves from debt.

In so abject a state, they cannot labour in spirit, while they earn a scanty subsistence without hope of bettering their situation.

(i) **What did some powerful ryots in Bengal do instead of cultivating their lands?**

Ans. Some powerful ryots in Bengal did not cultivate their lands instead they leased them to under-tenants and impose very high rents.

(ii) **Why were the under-tenants unable to escape from debt?**

Ans. The under-tenents were unable to escape from debt because of the excessive rent they had to pay, as well as the high interest rates on loans for cattle, seed and subsistence.

ASSESSMENT EXERCISE

Multiple Choice Questions (MCQs)

1. In which of the following Emperor regime Diwani of Bengal was gone in the hand of the British?
   (a) Farukh Siyar (b) Shah Alam-II
   (c) Akbar- II (d) Murshid Khan
2. Which of the following Governor-General of India introduced the Permanent Settlement in 1793?
   (a) Lord Ripon (b) Lord Cornwallis
   (c) Lord Hastings (d) Lord Wellesley
3. Ryotwari system is introduced by
   (a) Holt Mackenzie (b) Cornwallis
   (c) Alexander Read (d) Thomas Munro
4. How many per cent of the land producing Indigo was under the Nij system?
   (a) 75 per cent (b) 25 per cent (c) 29 per cent (d) 50 per cent

Subjective Questions (VSA, SA & LA)

1. Mention any one crop, which is forced to cultivate by Britishers.
2. Mention any one problem of nij system.
3. Why there was demand for Indian Indigo in the Europe?
4. What do you mean by ryoti system?
5. What were the changes occurred when the East India Company established?
6. What were the effects of Blue Rebellion?
7. What were the problems faced by Ryoti system?
8. What were the suggestions of the Indigo Commission?
9. By the early 19th century, Company needed more money to meet its expenses. Thus, company introduced new systems. What were the new system? Discuss.
10. Indigo was used to dye the clothes in Europe, therefore the Britisher forced to the Indian farmer to do Indigo cultivation. Explain the systems of the Indigo cultivation.
11. The company was just interested in collecting its revenue? Explain.

Tribals, Dikus and the Vision of a Golden Age

CHAPTER 4

The British rule led to many changes due to which tribal groups like **Mundas**, **Santhals** and **Oraons** were unhappy and had to face many problems. The British rule had an influence on their traditional ways of living, their livelihood and their religion.

The tribal customs and rituals were different from those laid down by the Brahmans. Unlike the caste societies, the societies of tribal did not have the sharp social divisions. Those who belonged to the same tribe shared common ties of **kinship**[1]. However, social and economic differences were present within tribes.

4.1 Lifestyle of Tribal Groups

By the 19th century, tribal groups in different parts of India were involved in a variety of activities like

- Jhum Cultivation
- Hunting and Gathering
- Herding
- Settled Cultivation

Jhum Cultivation

Some of the tribal people in 19th century practiced jhum cultivation or shifting cultivation. This was done on small patches of land, mostly in forests. The cultivators burnt the vegetation to clear for cultivation. Then, they spread the ash which contained potash to fertilise the soil.

They used equipments like axe and the hoe for this cultivation. Instead of ploughing the land and sowing the seeds, they scattered the seeds on the field.

Once the crop was ready and harvested, they moved to another field. A field that had been cultivated once was left **fallow**[2] for several years.

Shifting cultivators were found in the hilly and forested areas of **North-East** and **Central India**.

Hunting and Gathering

In many regions, tribal groups lived by hunting animals and gathering forest produce. These included tribal groups like the **Khonds** living in forests of Odisha.

They ate fruits and roots collected from the forest, and cooked food with the oil they extracted from **sal**[3] and **mahua**[4] seeds.

They sold the forest produce in the local markets. The local weavers buy *kusum* and *palash* flowers from Khonds to colour their clothes and leather.

Sometimes, Khonds exchanged forest produce for rice and other goods. At other times, they bought goods with their small earning. They earned this from doing odd jobs in villages or labouring in the fields of farmers, when supplies of forest produce reduced.

However, many tribes like **Baigas** of the Central India opposed to work for other. They depend only on the produce of the forest and it was below the dignity of a Baiga to become a labourer.

Tribal groups were often depended on traders and moneylenders for buying and selling the goods that were not produced within the locality.

The traders sold the goods at high prices. Moneylenders provided loans to the tribals to met their cash needs, but they usually charge a very high rate of interest.

Thus, market and commerce often meant debt and poverty for the tribals. They regarded the moneylender and trader as evil outsiders and the cause of their misery.

Herding Animals

Many tribal groups in the 19th century herded and reared animals for their livelihood. They were pastoralists who moved with their herds of cattle or sheep according to the seasons. When the grass in one place was exhausted, they moved to another area.

1 **Kinship** It refers to the relationship between the members of the same family.
2 **Fallow**It is a field left uncultivated for a while so that the soil recovers fertility.
3 **Sal**It is a tree known for its hardwood and resin.
4 **Mahua**It is a flower that is eaten or used to make alcohol.

Some examples of these pastoralists include the **Van Gujjars** in Punjab and **Labadis** in Andhra Pradesh, who were cattle harders, Gaddis in Kulu who were **shepherds** and **Bakarwals** in Kashmir who reared goats.

Settled Cultivation

Before the 19th century, many tribal groups started settled cultivation in which they settled down and cultivated their fields instead of moving from place to place. They began to use the plough and gradually got rights over the land on which they lived.

In tribal groups, like the **Mundas** of **Chottanagpur**, all the members had right on the land. Most of the times, some people within the group acquired more power and they often rented out their land instead of cultivating it themselves.

According to the British officials, settled tribal groups like the Gonds and Santhals were more civilised than hunter-gatherers or shifting cultivators.

Try These

1. **Name some activities in which tribal groups were involved in 19th century.**
2. **On whom tribal groups were dependent for buying and selling their goods?**
3. **Give some examples of Pastoralists in the 19th century.**
4. **What do you mean by settled cultivation?**

4.1 Effect of Colonial Rule on Tribal Lives

The British or Colonial rule affect and changed the lives of the tribal groups. These effects are discussed below

Effect on Tribal Chiefs

Before the arrival of British, tribal chiefs enjoy certain economic and administrative powers for controlling their territories. They have their own police in some places and decided local rules of land and forest management.

Under the British rule, the tribal chiefs lost their administrative power and had to follow the laws made by British officials in India.

They still had the right over their land but they had to pay tribute to the British. They lost their authority and had to control the tribal groups on behalf of the British.

Effect on Shifting Cultivation

The British wanted the tribal groups who were shifting cultivators to settle down and become peasant cultivators because settled peasants were easier to control and administer.

The British wanted a regular revenue source for the state. So they introduced land settlements in which they measured the land, defined land rights, and fixed the revenue demand for the state.

However, their efforts to settle shifting cultivators were not successful because settled plough cultivation is not suitable in areas where water is not sufficiently available and the soil is dry.

Thus, the shifting cultivators in North-East India insisted on continuing their traditional practices and as a result of their protests, the British allowed them to carry on shifting cultivation in some parts of the forest.

Forest Laws and their Impact

The British brought several changes in forest laws which affected the tribal lives. These were

- The British extended their control over all forests and declared that forests were state property.
- Some forests were classified as **reserved** forests as they produced timber which the British wanted. In reserve forests, people were not allowed to move freely, practise jhum cultivation, collect fruits or hunt animals.

  As a result of this, many jhum cultivators moved to other areas in search of work and livelihood and British faced the problem of shortage of labour.
- In many regions, the Forest Department established forest villages in which jhum cultivators were given small patches of land to cultivate but they had to provide labour to the Forest Department.

Many tribal groups reacted against these laws. They disobeyed the new rules, continued practices that were declared illegal and sometimes involved in open rebellion. For example, the **Revolt of Songram Sangma** in 1906 in Assam and the **Forest Satyagraha** of the 1930s in the Central Provinces.

The Problem with Trade

During the 19th century, tribal groups in India faced problems with traders and moneylenders who came into the forests to buy forest produce, offer cash loans, and ask them to work for wages.

In the 18th century, Indian silk was in great demand in European markets due to its fine quality. Hence, the East India Company officials tried to encourage silk production to meet the growing demand.

The **Santhals** reared cocoons in Hazaribagh (in present day Jharkhand). The silk traders sent their agents who gave loans to the tribal people and collected the cocoons.

The tribes were paid 3 to 4 rupees for a thousand cocoons. These were then exported to Burdwan or Gaya where they were sold at five times the price.

Thus, the silk growers earned very little but traders or middlemen made huge profits. Many tribal groups, due to this, saw market and the traders as their main enemies.

The Search for Work

As the tribals were not able to carry on their traditional practices, they had to go far away from their homes in search of work.

From the late 19th century, tea plantations started to be established and mining became an important industry. Tribals were recruited in large numbers to work at the tea plantations of Assam and the coal mines of Jharkhand.

However, they were recruited through contractors who paid them very low wages, and did not allow them to return to their homes.

A Closer Look at the Rebellion

In the 19th and 20th centuries, various tribal groups in India rebelled against the changes in laws, the taxes they had to pay the restrictions on their practices and exploitation by traders and moneylenders.

The rebellions of the tribal groups included

- The rebellion of Kols in 1831–32
- The revolt of Santhals in 1855
- The Bastar Rebellion in Central India in 1910
- The Warli Revolt in Maharashtra in 1940
- The Birsa Movement of 19th century

Birsa Munda

Birsa was born in the mid-1870s in a poor family in Chottanagpur, Jharkhand. He belonged to Munda tribal group.

Birsa was deeply influenced by many of the ideas during his growing-up years.

In 1895, Birsa became popular because people believed that he had miraculous power. He declared that God had chosen him to save his people from troubles and free them from the control of **dikus**[5] (outsiders).

Birsa started the movement of reforming tribal society. He encouraged the Mundas to give up drinking liquor, clean their village, and stop believing in witchcraft (black magic). He regarged the missionaries and Hindu landlords as outside forces that were destroying the lifestyle of Mundas. He also wanted people to once again work on their land, settle down and cultivate their fields.

As the Birsa movement spread, the British arrested Birsa in 1895. When he was released in 1897, he started a revolt with support of villagers. They attacked police stations and churches, and raided the property of zamindars and moneylenders. They raised the white flag symbolising **Birsa Raj**.

In 1900, Birsa died and the movement ended. However, the movement was significant in two ways

(i) It forced the colonial government to introduce laws so that the land of the tribals could not be easily taken over by dikus.

(ii) It showed that the tribal people had the capacity to protest against injustice and express their anger against colonial rule.

Try These

1. **What were the different livelihoods of tribal groups in the 19th century?**
2. **Mention any one effect of shifting cultivation.**
3. **Who were *dikus*?**
4. **Mention any one impact of Birsa Munda's movement?**

5 **Dikus** It referred to non-tribal people, often the Britishers.

TRIBALS, DIKUS AND THE VISION OF A GOLDEN AGE

Lifestyle of Tribal Groups

Hunting and Gathering

It was practiced by tribal groups like the Khonds living in forests of Odisha.

Herding of Animals

It was practiced by pastoralists in Punjab, Kullu, Andhra Pradesh and Kashmir.

Jhum Cultivation

It was practiced in North-East and Central India.

Settled Cultivation

It was practiced by tribal groups like Mundas of Chhottanagpur.

Effect of Colonial Rule on Tribal Lives

Effect on Shifting Cultivation

The British efforts to settle shifting cultivation by introducing land settlements failed.

Effect on Tribal Chiefs

They lost their administrative power and had to control the tribal groups on behalf of the British.

A Closer Look at the Rebellion

- The rebellion of Kols in 1831-32.
- The revolt of Santhals in 1855.
- The Bastar Rebellion in Central India in 1910.
- The Warli Revolt in Maharashtra in 1940.
- The Birsa Movement of 19th century.

Forest Laws

- Forests were declared as state property.
- Forests producing timber were classified as reserved forests.
- Revolt of Songram Sangma (1906) and Forest Satyagraha (1930s).

The Problem with Trade

- The Santhals reared cocoons in Hazaribagh and earned very little profits.
- From late 19th Century, tea plantations started to be established and mining became an important industry.

NCERT FOLDER

Covering Intext Questions and Exercises of NCERT

NCERT ON PAGE 47 (ACTIVITY)

Q.1 Find out whether the conditions of work in the mines have changed now. Check how many people die in mines every year and what are the reasons for their death.

Ans. Yes, the conditions of work in the mines have changed now as the number of accidents and death have relatively reduced in number as compared to past.

Many miners die in mines every year. The main reasons for this are

- Flooding of the coal mines. Number of accidents and death have
- Falling of the mine walls.
- Breaking out of fire in the mines.

NCERT ON PAGE 50 (LET'S IMAGINE)

Q.2 Imagine you are a Jhum cultivator living in a forest village in the 19th century. You have just been told that the land you were born on no longer belongs to you. In a meeting with British officials, you try to explain the kinds of problems you face. What would you say?

Ans. There are some of the following problems we would try to explain in a meeting with British officials.

- We shall not be able to produce to our requirements.
- We shall not have any cash to buy food.
- We shall be unemployed.
- No one would help us.

EXERCISES

Q.1 Fill in the blanks.

(i) The British described the tribal people as ....

Ans. wild and savage

(ii) The method of sowing seeds in Jhum cultivation is known as ....

Ans. broadcasting

(iii) The tribal chiefs got .... titles in Central India under the British Land Settlements.

Ans. land

(iv) Tribals went to work in the .... of Assam and the .... in Bihar.

Ans. tea plantations, coal mines

Q.2 State whether true or false.

(i) Jhum cultivators plough the land and sow seeds.

Ans. False

(ii) Cocoons were bought from the Santhals and sold by the traders at five times the purchase price.

Ans. True

(iii) Birsa urged his followers to purify themselves, give up drinking liquor and stop believing in witchcraft and sorcery.

Ans. True

(iv) The British wanted to preserve the tribal way of life.

Ans. False

Q.3 What problems did shifting cultivators face under British rule?

Ans. The problems faced by shifting cultivators under British rule were

- The life of shifting cultivators was directly connected to the forest. So, when the British brought changes in forest law, their life was badly affected.
- The British extended their control over all forests and declared that forests were state's property.
- Some forests were classified as Reserved forests due to valuable timber which the British wanted to acquire. In these forests, people were not allowed to move freely and the jhum cultivators. Thus, many cultivators had to move to other areas in search of work.

Q.4 How did the powers of tribal chiefs change under colonial rule?

Ans. The power of tribal chiefs were significantly diminished and changed under colonial rule in the following ways

- Under the British rule, the tribal chiefs lost their administrative power and had to follow the laws made by British officials in India.
- They still had the right over their land but they had to pay tribute to the British. They lost their authority and had to control the tribal groups on behalf of the British.

Q.5 What accounts for the anger of the tribals against the dikus?

Ans. The reasons for the anger of the tribals against the dikus (outsiders) were

- The tribals practised shifting cultivation, but the British forced them to follow settled agriculture and also forcefully introduced land settlements.
- Under British rule, the tribal chiefs lost the authorities that they had enjoyed earlier. Further, they had to pay tribute to the British.
- By introducing forest laws, the British evicted the tribals from their own lands. As a result, they became homeless and were forced to find other work to earn their livelihood.

Q. 6 What was Birsa's vision of a golden age? Why do you think such a vision appealed to the people of the region?

Ans. Birsa talked about a golden age, (a satyug), an age of truth in which, like in the past, the tribal people would live a good life, construct embankments, tap natural springs, work on their lands, plant trees and orchards, and practise cultivation to earn their living.

He visualised an age when the Mundas would again be free of the oppression of dikus and their ancestral rights would be restored. He talked of an age in which the tribals would not kill one another and would live an honest life.

His golden age consisted of a reformed tribal society in which there was no place for vices like liquor consumption, unclean living, witchcraft or the influence of evil outsiders like Christian missionaries, landlords, moneylenders, traders and Europeans. They would all be driven out and the government would set-up a Munda Raj with Birsa as its head.

This vision appealed to the tribal people as all the vices and outside forces that Birsa talked about were believed by all of them as the root causes of their misery and suffering.

Q.7 Find out from your parents, friends or teachers, the names of some heroes of other tribal revolts in the twentieth century. Write their story in your own words.

Ans. Do it yourself.

Q.8 Choose any tribal group living in India today. Find out about their customs and way of life, and how their lives have changed in the last 50 years.

Ans. Do it yourself.

REVIEW EXERCISE

Including Competency Based Questions

Part I

Multiple Choice Questions (MCQs)

1. In jhum cultivation, why is a field left fallow for many years after being cultivated once? **Competency Based**

(a) To enable forest to grow on it again.
(b) To allow the groundwater to seep in again.
(c) To enable the soil to recover its fertility.
(d) All of the above

2. The mahua is a flower ....

(a) used to flavour food cooked by the tribals.
(b) used for dyeing the clothes by the tribals.
(c) used to make alcohol.
(d) blooms in summer.

3. ...... were flowers used to dye clothes and colour leather.

(a) Mahua and sal
(b) Kusum and sleeper
(c) Palash and kusum
(d) Palash and mahua

4. How the hunter-gatherer tribes got their supplies of rice and other grains? **Competency Based**

(a) By buying these grains with their meagre earnings from selling forest produce.
(b) By exchanging them for forest produce.
(c) By doing odd jobs.
(d) All of the above

5. The .... lived by herding and rearing animals.

(a) Labadis (b) Santhals
(c) Oraons (d) Bhils

6. When did the Bastar Rebellion take place?

(a) 1895 (b) 1910 (c) 1930 (d) 1940

7. The movement started by Birsa Munda identified the .... as the main cause of the misery of the tribals.

(a) Hindu landlords
(b) British Government
(c) missionaries and moneylenders
(d) All of the above

8. The usual work done by the Baigas during the month of Baisakh was

(a) harvesting of the crop
(b) sowing of seeds
(c) holding dances and marriages
(d) setting forests on fire to clear land for cultivation

9. Where does the term 'Bewar' mean shifting cultivation?

(a) Jharkhand (b) Madhya Pradesh
(c) North-East India (d) Andhra Pradesh

10. Which of the following statement is correct?

I. Jhum cultivation is also known as shifting cultivation.
II. Shifting cultivation were found in the hilly and forest tracts of North-East and Central India.

Codes

(a) Only I (b) Only II
(c) Both I and II (d) None of these

11. Arrange the following in the correct sequence.

I. Kol rebelled in Chottanagpur
II. Warli revolt in Maharashtra
III. Forest Satyagraha in Assam
IV. Birsa Munda arrested

Codes

(a) I, III, II, IV (b) III, IV, II, I
(c) IV, II, I, III (d) I, IV, III, II

12. Arrange the following in the correct sequence.

I. Criminal Tribals Act II. Birsa was died
III. Revolt of Songram Sangma IV. Santhals revolts

Codes

(a) I, II, III, IV (b) IV, II, III, I
(c) II, III, IV, I (d) IV, I, II, III

Answers

1. (c) **2.** (c) **3.** (c) **4.** (d) **5.** (a)
6. (b) **7.** (d) **8.** (d) **9.** (b) **10.** (c)
11. (d) **12.** (d)

Match the Following

1.

List I	List II
A. Hunting and clearing land of trees	1. Kuar, Kartik and Aghan
B. Worked in the fields	2. Baisakh
C. Hunting and burning forest	3. Chait
D. Hunting continued and sowing seeds	4. Asadh to Bhadon
E. Crops and fruits ripen and are harvested	5. Jeth

Codes

	A	B	C	D	E		A	B	C	D	E
(a)	3	4	2	5	1	(b)	5	4	3	2	1
(c)	1	2	3	4	5	(d)	3	2	5	4	1

2.

List I	List II
A. Warli revolt	1. Central India
B. A flower used to make alcohol	2. Assam
C. Gaddis	3. Kulu
D. Songram Sangma	4. Mahua
E. Baigas	5. Maharashtra

Codes

	A	B	C	D	E		A	B	C	D	E
(a)	2	1	3	4	4	(b)	5	4	3	2	1
(c)	1	2	3	4	5	(d)	5	4	1	3	2

Ans. 1. (a) 2. (b)

Assertion-Reason

1. Assertion (A) Birsa was born in a family of Mundas, a tribal group that lived in Chottanagpur.

Reason (R) Shifting cultivation were found in the hilly and forested tracts of North-East and Central India.

Codes

(a) Both A and R are true and R is the correct explanations of A
(b) Both A and R are true, but R is not the correct explanations of A
(c) A is true, but R is False
(d) A is False, but R is true

2. Assertion (A) The Kols rebelled in 1831-32, Santhals rose in revolts in 1855, the Bastar Rebellion in Central India broke out in 1916.

Reason (R) Birsa was born in Assam.

Codes

(a) Both A and R are true and R is the correct explanations of A
(b) Both A and R are true, but R is not the correct explanations of A
(c) A is true, but R is False
(d) A is False, but R is true

Ans. 1. (b) Both A and R are true, but R is not the correct explanations of A
2. (c) A is true, but R is False

Fill in the Blanks

1. The Santhals reared .... in Hazaribagh.

2. In shifting cultivation, a field that had been cultivated once was left .... for several years.

3. The Labadis pastoralists were cattle herders of ....

4. Birsa spent some time in the company of a prominent .... preachers.

Ans. 1. cocoons 2. fallow
3. Andhra Pradesh 4. Vaishnav

True/False

1. Birsa himself declared that God had appointed him to save his people from the slavery of outsiders.
2. It was below the dignity of a Baiga to become a labourer.
3. In the 1930s, Verrier Elwin visited the land of the Baigas - a tribal group in Central India.
4. The Warli revolt took place in Chottanagpur.

Ans. 1. True 2. True 3. True 4. False

Picture Based Questions

1. **Look at the picture below and answer the question that follow.**

Who recruited tribals for coal mine and tea plantations ?

(a) Britishers (b) Zamindars
(c) Pujani's (d) Contractors

2. **Look at the picture below and answer the question that follow.**

Khonds had collected the fruits and roots from forest and cooked food with the oil they extracted from the seeds of the .... and mahua.

(a) sunflower (b) tulsi
(c) fruit (d) sal

Ans. 1. (d) Contractors 2. (d) sal

Case Based Question

1. **Read the passage given below and answer the following questions.**

Some of them practised jhum cultivation, that is, shifting cultivation. This was done on small patches of land, mostly in forests. The cultivators cut the treetops to allow sunlight to reach the ground, and burnt the vegetation on the land to clear it for cultivation. They spread the ash from the firing, which contained postash, to fertilise the soil. They used the axe is cut trees and the hoe to scratch the soil in order to prepare it for cultivation. They broadcast the seeds, that is, scattered the seeds on the field instead of ploughing the land and swing the seeds.

Once the crop was ready and harvested, they moved to another field. A field that had been cultivated once was left fallow for several years. Shifting cultivators were found in the hilly and forested tracts of North-East and Central India. The lives of these tribal people depended on free movement within forests and on being able to use the land and forests for growing their crops. That is the only way they could practise shifting cultivation.

(i) A field that had been cultivated once was left fallow for

(a) several years (b) one year
(c) life time (d) five years

(ii) Shifting cultivators were found in which areas?

(a) Plain areas (b) Coastal areas
(c) Hilly and forested (d) None of the above

(iii) Jhum cultivation is also known as

(a) Forest cultivation (b) Shifting cultivation
(c) Beach cultivation (d) Land cultivation

(iv) Why the burnt ash is spread on the soil

(a) To clear the trees
(b) To make it dry
(c) To increase its fertility
(d) To spread the seeds

Ans. (i) (a) several years
(ii) (c) Hilly and forested
(iii) (b) Shifting cultivation
(iv) (c) To increase its fertility

Part II

Very Short Answer Type Questions

1. **How will you define tribals?**

Ans. Tribals are a group of people within a traditional society sharing customs and beliefs and led by a chief.

2. **List two different occupations of tribal groups before the British enacted the tribal laws.**

Ans. The two different occupations of tribal groups before the British enacted the tribal laws are shifting cultivation and settled cultivation.

3. Where did khonds live?

Ans. Khonds lived in the forests of Odisha.

4. What privileges did the tribal chiefs lose with the arrival of the British?

Ans. The tribal chiefs lost the authority that they had earlier over their people and also they were unable to fulfil their traditional functions.

5. Why did the British want tribal groups to settle down and become peasant cultivators? **Competency Based**

Ans. The British wanted the tribal groups to settle down and become peasant cultivators because settled peasants were easier to control and administer.

6. Why did the British introduced land settlements?

Ans. The British introduced land settlements in order to get a regular revenue source of the state.

7. Why were some forests classified as reserved forests?

Ans. Some forests were classified as reserved forests because these forests produced timber which the British wanted.

8. Whom did the Santhal tribals rearing silk cocoons view as their main enemies?

Ans. The Santhal tribals rearing silk cocoons viewed the market and the traders as their main enemies.

9. On what charges was Birsa convicted by the British and for how long was he jailed?

Ans. Birsa was convicted by the British on charges of rioting and jailed for 2 years.

10. Which groups of people were referred to as dikus by the tribals?

Ans. The groups of people referred to as dikus by the tribals were the British, traders and moneylenders.

Short Answer Type Questions

1. Describe the land settlement introduced by the British.

Ans. The British introduced land settlements to ensure a regular revenue source for the state. Under these settlements

- The British measured the land, defined the rights of each individual to that land and fixed the revenue demand for the state.
- Some peasants were declared landowners and other tenants. The tenants were to pay rent to the landowner who in turn paid revenue to the state.

2. Why did the British favour settled cultivators over jhum cultivators?

Ans. The British favoured settled cultivators over the jhum cultivator because the British were uncomfortable with groups which moved about (like jhum cultivators) and did not have a fixed home they wanted tribal groups to settle down and become peasant cultivators, who were easier to control and administer than people who were always on the move.

3. Write a short note on silk growers.

Ans. In the 18th century, Indian silk was in great demand in European markets due to its fine quality. The silk growers were the Santhals who reared cocoons in Hazaribagh in (present day Jharkhand). The silk traders sent their agents who gave loans to the tribal people and collected the cocoons. The tribes were paid 3 to 4 rupees for a thousand cocoons.

These were then exported to Burdwan or Gaya where they were sold at five times the price. Thus, the silk growers earned very little but traders or middlemen made huge profits. Many tribal groups due to this, saw market and the traders as their main enemies.

4. How was the silk industry more profitable for the silk traders than the tribal growing silk cocoons?

Ans. The silk industry was more profitable for the silk traders than the tribal growing silk cocoons as traders had control over key aspects of the industry.

Traders purchase cocoons at very low price from tribals and sell at very good price. Traders exports the silk to other countries and made huge profits.

5. What were the results of tribal dependence on traders and moneylenders?

Ans. Tribals dependence on traders and moneylenders were resulted in

(i) Traders came around with things for sale and sold the goods at high prices. Moneylenders gave loans with which the tribals met their cash needs, in addition to what they earned.

(ii) The interest charged on the loans was usually very high. So, for the tribals, market and commerce often meant debt and poverty.

(iii) The tribals came to see the moneylenders and traders as outsiders and the cause of their misery.

6. What was the impact of the achievements of Birsa Munda after his death?

Ans. The impacts of the achievements of Birsa Munda after his death in 1900 were

- The Birsa movment forced the colonial government to introduce laws so that the land of the tribals could not be easily taken over by dikus.
- It showed that the tribal people had the capacity to protest against injustice and express their anger against colonial rule.

Long Answer Type Questions

1. How was the cultivation traditionally practiced by tribal groups carried out? **Competency Based**

Ans. Traditional cultivation practices among tribal groups varied depending on their specific cultural and environmental conditions, but they also shared some common features such as shifting cultivation.
The tribals traditionally practiced jhum cultivation, i.e. shifting cultivation. This was done on small patches of land, mostly in forests.

The cultivators cut the trees to allow sunlight to reach the ground and burnt the vegetation on the land to clear it for cultivation. Then, they spread the ash of the vegetation to fertilise the soil, as it contained potash. Then, they scratched the soil to prepare it for cultivation. They used the axe to cut trees and the hoe to scratch soil in order to prepare the land for cultivation.

Then, the seeds were scattered on the field instead of ploughing the land and sowing the seeds. Once the crop was ready and harvested, they moved to another area. A field that had been cultivated once was left fallow for several years to recover its fertility.

2. Why did the tribals agitate under British rule? **Competency Based**

Ans. The tribals agitated under British rule because

- The powers and functions of tribal chiefs were reduced to keeping their land titles and renting out their lands only.
- They lost much of their economic and administrative power over their tribes and had to pay tribute to the British.
- Their method of shifting cultivation was stopped and they had to settle down at fixed places to become peasant cultivators. Besides, they had to give fixed revenue to the state.
- Their gathering of forest products for use or sale was stopped, as the British declared forests as 'reserved', meaning that the tribals could not either live in the forests or enter them at will or take out forest produce.

3. Why did the British introduce land settlement in the tribes? What was the net result of this?

Ans. When the British could not get a regular fixed revenue for the state from shifting cultivators, they introduced land settlement in the tribes. Under this, they measured the land, defined the rights of each individual to that land and fixed the revenue demand for the state.

Tribal chiefs were declared landowners, to enable them to collect revenue for the state from the others, who were declared tenants. Such peasant cultivators were also easier to control and administer than people who were always on the move.

The net result of this land settlement was negative on tribal communities. They lost their traditional lands and many were forced to leave their homes. The British also took resources from them and made them pay taxes, which made their lives harder. Some tribes also rebelled against these changes which lead to a lot of conflict during British rule.

4. How were the traders and moneylenders the major cause of the tribals' misery? **Competency Based**

Ans. The traders and moneylenders were the major cause of the tribals' misery as the tribals needed to buy some goods for their daily necessities which were not produced by traders and moneylenders. The traders exploited them by selling these goods at very high prices in exchange for forest produce or other goods produced by tribals. These goods were bought at very low prices by the traders for sale in other places at very high rates.

In case the tribals did not have goods worth enough to exchange with traders, they borrowed cash from moneylenders at very high interest rates, adding to the debt burden of the tribals. Both the traders and moneylenders exploited the tribal people.

Thus, the tribal people believed the moneylenders and traders as evil outsiders and the cause of their misery.

5. Why was the Birsa movement significant? How did Birsa Munda resume the Birsa movement?

Ans. The Birsa movement was significant because it marked one of the earliest and most influential tribal uprisings against British colonial rule in India.
Birsa was deeply influenced by many of the ideas during his growing-up years. In 1895, Birsa became popular because people believed that he had miraculous power. He declared that God had chosen him to save his people from troubles and free them from the control of dikus (outsiders).
Birsa started the movement of reforming tribal society. He encouraged the Mundas to give up drinking liquor, clean their village, and stop believing in witchcraft (black magic).

He regarged the missionaries and Hindu landlords as outside forces that were destroying the lifestyle of Mundas.

He also wanted people to once again work on their land, settle down and cultivate their fields. As the Birsa movement spread, the British arrested Birsa in 1895.When he was released in 1897, he started a revolt with support of villagers. They attacking police stations and churches, and raided the property of zamindars and moneylenders. They raised the white flag symbolising Birsa Raj.

Picture Based Question

1. **The picture given below is of a Santhal girl carrying firewood is shown.**

(i) **What was the occupation of the Santhals?**

(ii) **Why were the Santhals unhappy under the British Raj?**

Ans. (i) The Santhals traditionally undertook jhum cultivation and also hunting-gathering.

(ii) The occupations were affected by the forest laws made by the British, as the Santhals were not allowed to enter the forests at will to carry out these activities. Thus, they had to seek alternative occupations, which made them unhappy.

Case Based Questions

1. **Read the passage given below and answer the following questions.**

A time to hunt, a time to sow, a time to move to a new field

Have you ever noticed that people living in different types of societies do not share the same notion of work and time? The lives of the shifting cultivators and hunters in different regions were regulated by a calendar and division of tasks for men and women. Verrier Elwin, a British anthropologist who lived among the Baigas and Khonds of Central India for many years in the 1930s and 1940s, gives us a picture of what this calendar and division of tasks was like. He writes: In Chait women went to clearings to cut stalks that were already reaped; men cut large trees and go for their ritual hunt. The hunt began at full moon from the East. Traps of bamboo were used for hunting. The women gathered fruits like sago, tamarind and mushroom. Baiga women can only gather roots or kanda and mahua seeds. Of all the adivasis in Central India, the Baigas were known as the best hunters. In Baisakh the firing of the forest took place, the women gathered unburnt wood to burn. Men continued to hunt, but nearer their villages. In Jeth sowing took place and hunting still went on. From Asadh to Bhadon the men worked in the fields. In Kuar the first fruits of beans were ripened and in Kartik kutki became ripe. In Aghan every crop was ready and in Pus winnowing took place. Pus was also the time for dances and marriages.

In Magh shifts were made to new bewars and hunting-gathering was the main subsistence activity. The cycle described above took place in the first year. In the second year there was more time for hunting as only a few crops had to be sown and harvested. But since there was enough food the men lived in the bewars. It was only in the third year that the diet had to be supplemented with the forest products. Adapted from Verrier Elwin, Baiga (1939) and Elwin's unpublished 'Notes on the Khonds'

(Verrier Elwin Papers, Nehru Memorial Museum and Library)

Read carefully the tasks that Baiga men and women did. Do you see any pattern? What were the differences in the types of work that they were expected to perform?

Ans. There is a pattern in the tasks that Baiga men and women did. We notice that the men did the physically harder work and work which required them to go far from home, like working in the fields and going for hunting animals. Meanwhile the Baiga women did the physically less demanding work and which kept them near their homes probably to look after their children and the home, gathering fruits for consumption and unburnt woods for fuel etc.

The types of work that they were expected to perform was different on the basis of traditional gender roles of men and women. Men generally did hunting, farming and construction and women did the work near the house like gathering forest produce, household chores, weaving and took care to children.

2. **Read the passage given below and answer the following questions.**

"In this land of the English how hard it is to live"

In the1930s Verrier Elwin visited the land of the Baigas – a tribal group in Central India. He wanted to know about them – their customs and practices, their art and folklore. He recorded many songs that lamented the hard time the Baigas were having under British rule.

In this land of the English how hard it is to live. How hard it is to live. In the village sits the landlord. In the gate sits the Kotwar. In the garden sits the Patwari. In the field sits the government. In this land of the English how hard it is to live. To pay cattle tax we have to sell cow. To pay forest tax we have to sell buffalo. To pay land tax we have to sell bullock. How are we to get our food?

(i) Who are the Baigas and what was their main occupation? Why did they find it difficult to live under the British?

Ans. (i) The Baigas were a tribal group inhabiting the forested areas of Central India.

Their main occupation had been shifting agriculture.

(ii) They found it difficult to live under the British because of the taxes they had to pay for working on settled cultivation introduced by the British (land tax, forest tax, cattle tax etc as expressed in the poem). They had not been paying any such tax earlier.

3. Read the passage given below and answer the following questions.

'Blood trickles from my shoulders'

The songs the Mundas sang bemoaned their misery. Alas! under [the drudgery of] forced labour Blood trickles from my shoulders Day and night the emissary from the zamindars, Annoys and irritates me, day and night I groan Alas! This is my condition I do not have a home, where shall I get happiness Alas!

The song depicts the grievances of the Mundas. Who were the Mundas and what was the aim of their movement?

Ans. The Mundas were a tribal group inhabiting in the Chottanagpur region. They had started working on settled agriculture, with the land belonging to the clan as a whole. The Munda movement led by Birsa Munda had the following aims

- **Social and Religious Reform** Birsa aimed to revive and strengthen the traditional Munda way of life by promoting practices like cleanliness, giving up harmful practices like drinking, and resisting the influence of external forces like missionaries and Hindu landlords.
- **Land Rights** The movement also sought to reclaim the ancestral lands of the Munda people that were being encroached upon by the colonial government, moneylenders, and landlords.
- **Political Autonomy** Ultimately the movement aspired to establish a Munda Raj, a self-governing kingdom led by Birsa himself, which would be free from the control and oppression of outsiders.

ASSESSMENT EXERCISE

Multiple Choice Questions (MCQs)

1. What is the other name of Jhum cultivation?
   (a) Settled cultivation
   (b) Shifting cultivation
   (c) Gathering
   (d) Herding
2. Khonds tribes are mainly reside in which of the following state ....
   (a) Odisha (b) Chhattisgarh
   (c) Jharkhand (d) Madhya Pradesh
3. Who was talk about the golden age before dikus?
   (a) Birsa Munda
   (b) Tana Bhagat
   (c) Mahatma Gandhi
   (d) Cornwallis
4. Which of the following tribals started revolt in 1855?
   (a) Mundas (b) Kols
   (c) Santhals (d) Gondas

Subjective Questions (VSA, SA & LA)

1. Who were more civilised tribe according to the British officials?
2. Why did tribal people think Britishers as evil outsiders?
3. When did Birsa's movement fade out?
4. Mention any one impact of Forest law.
5. By the 19th century, many tribal people engaged in jhum cultivation. What do you mean by jhum cultivation?
6. What were the main occupations of the tribal people? Mention any one with broad view.
7. What were the effect of colonial rule on tribal chiefs?
8. By 19th century, tribal groups in different parts of India were involved in a variety of activities. Explain any three.
9. The lives of tribal groups are changed during the colonial era. Explain the effects on cultivation and silk growers.

When People Rebel : 1857 and After

CHAPTER 5

In 1857, a revolt started in India due to the policies introduced by the British. This chapter highlights the significance of the Revolt of 1857 as a major turning point in the history of British rule in India. It highlights the widespread nature of the rebellion, involving soldiers, peasants, artisans, and other sections of society. It also explores the brutal suppression of the rebellion by the British and its long-lasting consequences, including the end of Mughal rule and the strengthening of British control over India.

5.1 Policies and the People

The policies of the East India Company affected the life of kings, queens, peasants, landlords, tribals and soliders in many ways.

People had resisted policies and actions that harm their interests or go against their sentiments.

Nawabs Lose their Power

Since the mid-18th century, **nawabs** and **rajas** had gradually lost their authority and honour, their freedom was reduced, their armies were disbanded, and their revenues and territories were taken away.

Many ruling families like the **Peshwa Nana Saheb** and **Rani Lakshmibai** tried to negotiate with the Company to protect their interests, but they were unsuccessful.

In 1801, a subsidiary alliance was imposed on Awadh, and in 1856 it was taken over by the British.

In order to end the Mughal dynasty, the Company removed the name of the Mughal king from the coins minted by it.

In 1849, **Governor-General[1] Dalhousie** announced that after the death of Mughal king Bahadur Shah Zafar, his family would be shifted out of the Red Fort.

In 1856, **Governor-General Lord Canning** decided that Bahadur Shah Zafar would be the last Mughal king and after his death, his descendants would not be recognised as kings and just called princes.

The Peasants and the Sepoys

In the countryside, many peasants and zamindars were unable to pay back loans that they took from the moneylenders to pay the high taxes levied by the Company. Thus they gradually lost their lands.

The Indian sepoys under the Company's army were unhappy about their pay, allowances, conditions of service, and new rules that violated their religious beliefs.

During this period, many people believed that if they crossed the sea, they would lose their religion and caste. Thus, the sepoys in 1824 refused to follow the order of the Company to travel to Burma by the sea route, to fight on behalf of the Company.

In 1856, the Company passed a new law according to which every person who was employed in the Company's army had to serve overseas, if required.

Responses to the Reforms of the British

The British passed many laws to reform the Indian society. These included

- Laws were passed to stop the practice of sati and to encourage the remarriage of widows.
- English-language education was actively promoted.
- After 1830, the British allowed Christian missionaries to function freely under their empire, and even own land and property.
- In 1850, a new law was passed which allowed an Indians who had converted to Christianity to inherit the property of their ancestors.

As a result of these laws, many Indians started feeling that the British were destroying their religion, social customs and traditional way of life.

---

1 **Governor-General** It refers to the person that head the East India Company in India.

5.2 A Mutiny becomes a Popular Rebellion

In May 1857, a massive rebellion started in India against the English East India Company. This **mutiny**[2] or rebellion started by Sepoys in Meerut and a large number of people from different sections of society joined this rebellion.

From Meerut to Delhi

On 8th April 1857, **Mangal Pandey** (a young soldier) was executed for attacking his officers in Barrackpore.

Some sepoys of the regiment in Meerut refuse to use new **cartridges**[3] which were suspected of being coated with fat of cows and pigs. As a result of this, 85 sepoys were dismissed from service and sentenced to 10 years in jail on 9th May, 1857.

On 10th May, other sepoys released the imprisoned sepoys and declared war on the British by attacking and killing British officers. They captured guns and ammunition, and set fire to buildings and properties of the **firangis**[4].

After this, the sepoys of Meerut reached the Red fort in Delhi, in the palace of Bahadur Shah Zafar and declared him as the leader of rebellion.

He encouraged all the chiefs and rulers of the country through letters, to organise a **confederacy**[5] of Indian states to fight against the British.

Spread of the Rebellion

The mutiny of the sepoys was successful to took out the British from Delhi. After this, mutinies or rebellions also spread to other states. The major events of the rebellion were

- Many troop regiments mutinied and joined the other troops at Delhi, Kanpur and Lucknow.
- People from towns and villages rallied around local leaders, zamindars and other leaders who wanted to establish their authority and fight the British.
- **Nana Saheb** in Kanpur who was the adopted son of the late Peshwa Baji Rao, gathered an army to displace the British forces from the city. He declared himself Peshwa and a Governor under the Mughal king Bahadur Shah Zafar.
- In Lucknow, **Birjis Qadr** who was the son of the deposed Nawab Wajid Ali Shah, was proclaimed the new Nawab. His mother, **Begum Hazrat Mahal**, took active part in organising the uprising against the British.
- In Jhansi, **Rani Lakshmibai** joined the rebel sepoys and fought the British along with **Tantia Tope**, the General of Nana Saheb.
- In the Mandla region of Madhya Pradesh, **Rani Avantibai Lodhi** of Ramgarh raised and led an army against the British.
- In Awadh, a situation of widespread rebellion developed.
- **Ahmadullah Shah**, a **maulvi**[6] from Faizabad, gathered a large force of supporters and came to Lucknow to fight the British.
- In Delhi, a large number of **ghazis** (religious warriors) came together to took out the British.
- **Bakht Khan**, a soldier from Bareilly, led a large number of fighters who came to Delhi.
- In Bihar, an old zamindar **Kunwar Singh**, joined the rebel sepoys and battled with the British for many months.

5.3 The Company Fights Back

The Company started suppressing the revolt by bringing additional troops from England.

It recaptured Delhi from the rebels in September 1857. Bahadur Shah Zafar was tried in court and sentenced to life imprisonment in Rangoon jail, where he died in November 1862.

In March 1858, the British recaptured Lucknow from the rebels and Rani Lakshmibai was defeated and killed in June 1858. Rani Avantibai was also defeated.

Tantia Tope continued to fight with the support of many tribal and peasant leaders. However, he was captured, tried and killed in April 1859.

Many people lost faith in the rebels after they were defeated by the British. The British tried to win back the loyalty of the people. They announced rewards for loyal landholders and to have their traditional rights over their lands.

The British also told that the rebels who had not killed any white people, would remain safe and have the rights over their lands. However, despite this, many sepoys, rebels, nawabs and rajas were tried and hanged.

2 **Mutiny** When soldiers as a group disobey their officers in the army, it is called mutiny.
3 **Cartridges** It refers to a casing fitted with a bullet.
4 **Firangis** Forangi is aterm used to refer to Foreigners. especilly the British duning colonial times in India.
5 **Confederacy** A body or league formed by persons or states for an unlawful purpose
6 **Maulvi** It refers to a Muslim religious scholar.

5.4 Aftermath of the Rebellion

After the suppression of the rebellion and regaining the control of the country by the end of 1859, the British introduced some important changes. These were

- The British Parliament passed a new act in 1858 and transferred the powers of the East India Company to the **British Crown**[7] for ensuring a more responsible management of Indian affairs.
- A member of the British Cabinet was appointed Secretary of State for India. He was made responsible for all matters related to the governance of India. He was given a council to advise him, called the **India Council**.
- The Governor-General of India was given the title of **Viceroy** i.e. a personal representative of the Crown.
- All ruling chiefs were assured that their territory would never be annexed in future. They were allowed to pass on their kingdoms to their heirs, including adopted sons. However, they had to control their kingdoms as **subordinates**[8] of the British Crown.
- The number of Indian soldiers in the army were reduced and the number of European soldiers were increased.
- It was decided to recruit more soldiers from the Gurkhas, Sikhs and Pathans, instead of recruiting soldiers from Awadh, Bihar, Central India and South India.
- The land and property of the Muslims were taken over as the British believed that they were significantly responsible for the rebellion.
- The British decided to respect the customary religious and social practices of the people in India.
- Policies were made to protect landlords and zamindars and give them security of rights over their lands.
- All these changes began a new phase of history after 1857.

7 **British Crown** If refers to the British ruler (here it was Queen Victoria).
8 **Subordinates** These are individuals or entities having less power or authority than somebody else.

The Peasants and the Sepoys

- In 1824, the sepoys denied to travel to Burma by sea-route to fight for the Company.
- In 1856, the East India Company made a rule : Army recruits had to serve overseas.

Responses to the Reforms of the British

- Laws were passed to stop the practice of Sati and to encourage the remarriage of widows.
- English language education was actively promoted.

Nawabs Lose their Power

- In 1801, a Subsidiary Alliance was imposed on Awadh.
- In 1856, Awadh was taken over by the British.

Policies and the People

WHEN PEOPLE REBEL : 1857 AND AFTER

The Company Fights Back

- The Company recaptured Delhi in September, 1857.
- Bahadur Shah Zafar died in the Rangoon jail 1862.

Aftermath of the Rebellion

- In 1858, British Parliament transferred the East India Company's powers to the British crown.
- The Governor-General of India was given the title of Viceroy.

A Mutiny becomes a Popular Rebellion

From Meerut to Delhi

- On 8th April, 1857, Mangal Pandey was executed.
- On 10th May sepoys at Meerut declared war on the British.
- Bahadur Shah Zafar was declared as the leader of Rebellion.

Spread of the Rebellion

- Many troop regiments mutinied and joined troops at Delhi, Kanpur and Lucknow.
- Major Leaders-Nana Saheb of Kanpur, Birjis Qadar and his mother Begum Hazrat Mahal, Rani Laxmibai and Rani Avantibai.

NCERT FOLDER

Covering Intext Questions and Exercises of NCERT

NCERT ON PAGE 52 (ACTIVITY)

Q. 1 Imagine you are a sepoy in the Company army, advising your nephew not to take employment in the army. What reasons would you give?

Ans. As a sepoy in Company, I would give the following reasons for not taking employment in the army

- The pay and other allowances in the army are very low. There is also a discrimination between the British soldiers and the Indian soldiers regarding pay scale.
- The British do not have any respect for Indian religious sentiments and beliefs.
- The service conditions in the army are very harsh. Thus, it is not easy for Indians to cope with them.
- There is a chance that Indians may be posted outside India in overseas but this is against Hindu religious belief to cross the sea.

NCERT ON PAGE 55 (ACTIVITY)

Q. 2 What were the important concerns in the minds of the people according to Sitaram and according to Vishnubhatt?

Ans. The important concerns in the minds of the people according to Sitaram Pande were

- The seizing of Awadh was the main reason of sepoy's resentment.
- The cartridges used for the new rifles were greased with the fat of cows and pigs and both Muslims and Hindus would be defiled by using it.

The important concerns in the minds of the people according to Vishnubhatt were

- The British were determined to destroy the religions of the Hindus and the Muslims.
- According to Vishnubhatt Godse's book, 'Majha Pravaas', the British presented a list of eighty-four rules in a gathering of kings and princes in Calcutta. The kings rejected the rules and warned of severe consequences and upheaval if implemented.

Q. 3 What role did they think the rulers were playing? What role did the sepoys seem to play?

Ans. Vishnubhatt and Sitaram Pande thought that the British ruler did not care for the religious sentiment and beliefs of both the Muslims and the Hindus.

The colonial ruler wanted to convert all Indians into Christians and exploit them to fulfil their own interest.

The role of the sepoys was

- The date and plan for the war of religion was circulated among the sepoys and they were ready to start the mission.
- In May 1857, the sepoys mutinied in several places of India.

NCERT ON PAGE 58 (ACTIVITY)

Q. 4 Why did the Mughal emperor agree to support the rebels?

Ans. The Mughal Emperor Bahadur Shah Zafar agreed to supports the rebels because he felt that if the rebellion was successful, he would be able to rule again. Many people in India were not happy with the British rulers and Emperor felt the same way. He also wanted India to be free from British control.

Q. 5 Write a paragraph on the assessment he may have made before accepting the offer of the sepoys.

Ans. Bahadur Shah might have made several assessments before accepting the offer of the sepoys. He knew that he was old enough to lead the rebels. He was aware of the might and strength of the British. At the same time, he knew the value of the name of his dynasty.

He was aware of the initial victory of the rebels. He might have presumed that most of the sepoys would revolt and this way the British would become weakened itself. He also knew that the rulers who had lost their regions to the British would definitely come ahead to support them.

NCERT ON PAGE 59 (ACTIVITY)

Q. 6 Make a list of places where the uprising took place in May, June and July 1857.

Ans. The uprising took place in Meerut, Delhi, Kanpur, Lucknow, Jhansi and Awadh in May, June and July 1857.

NCERT ON PAGE 62 (LET'S ACTIVITY)

Q. 7 Imagine you are a British officer in Awadh during the rebellion. What would you do to keep your plans of fighting the rebels a top secret?

Ans. I would take the following steps to keep my plans of fighting a top secret

- I would discuss my plans with the British officers personally.

- I would have personal meetings with the British officers at a very secret place, so that no one would be able to know about the meeting.
- All the decisions that had been taken in the meetings would be conveyed through Britishers only to the concerned officers.

EXERCISES

Q.1 What was the demand of Rani Lakshmibai of Jhansi that was refused by the British? Diksha

Ans. Rani Lakshmibai of Jhansi wanted the East India Company to recognise her adopted son as the heir to her kingdom after her husband's death. This demand was refused by the Company.

Q.2 What did the British do to protect the interests of those who converted to Christianity?

Ans. In 1850, the British passed a law to allow Indians who converted to Christianity to continue to inherit the property of their ancestors.

In this way, this law protected the interests of those who converted to Christianity.

Q.3 What objections did the sepoys have to the new cartridges that they were asked to use?

Ans. The sepoys raised the objection that the new cartridges they had been asked to use were coated with the fat of cows and pigs.

Q.4 How did the last Mughal emperor live the last five years of his life? Diksha

Ans. In the last five years of his life, the last Mughal emperor, Bahadur Shah Zafar was tried in court for supporting the revolt against the British and sentenced to life imprisonment.

He and his wife Begum Zinat Mahal were sent to prison in Rangoon in October 1858. Bahadur Shah died in the Rangoon jail in November 1862.

Q.5 What could be the reasons for the confidence of the British rulers about their position in India before May 1857?

Ans. The reasons for the confidence of the British rulers about their position in India before May 1857 were

- Since the mid-18th century, Nawabs and Rajas had gradually lost their authority and honour. Residents had been stationed in many courts, the freedom of the rulers was reduced, their armed forces disbanded and their revenues and territories were taken away by the stages.
- The Company decided to end the Mughal dynasty. In 1849, Governor-General Dalhousie announced that after the death of Bahadur Shah Zafar, the family of the king would be shifted out of the Red Fort.

  In 1856, Governor-General Lord Canning decided that Bahadur Shah Zafar would be the last Mughal King and after his death his descendants would not be recognised as kings and just called princes.

Q.6 What impact did Bahadur Shah Zafar's support to the rebellion have on the people and the ruling families?

Ans. Bahadur Shah Zafar's support to the rebellion had a significant impact. Threatened by the expansion of British rule, many of the ruling families felt that if the Mughal emperor could rule again, they would be able to rule their own territories once again, under Mughal authority. When people saw an alternative possibility which appealed to them, they felt inspired and enthused. It gave them the courage, hope and confidence to act.

Some examples of this impact were

- Many troop regiments mutinied to join other troops at nodal points like Delhi, Kanpur and Lucknow.
- Nana Saheb proclaimed himself Peshwa and a Governor under the Mughal king.
- Birjis Qadr, son of the deposed Nawab Wajid Ali Shah in Lucknow, acknowledged that he ruled under the Mughal king.
- In Jhansi, Rani Lakshmibai joined the rebel sepoys and fought the British along with Tantia Tope, the general of Nana Saheb.

Q.7 How did the British succeed in securing the submission of the rebel landowners of Awadh?

Ans. The British secured the submission of the rebel landowners by a Carrot and Stick policy in the following ways

- They tried and hanged a number of rebel leaders who had challenged their authority and could do so again in the future.
- They tried their best to win back the loyalty of the people by announcing rewards for loyal landowners. They were assured that they would be allowed to continue to enjoy traditional rights over their lands.

Q.8 In what ways did the British change their policies as a result of the rebellion of 1857?

Ans. The changes in the policies of the British as a result of the rebellion of 1857 were

- The British Crown took over the control of administration with the British Parliament passing an act in 1858 under which the powers of the East India Company were transferred to the British Crown.
- They provided a sense of security to the local rulers by assuring them that their territories would never be annexed by the British in future.

- They abolished the Doctrine of Lapse, so that rulers could pass on their kingdoms to adopted sons also.
- They provided a sense of security to landowners by making policies to protect landlords and zamindars, as well as the security of rights over their lands.
- They reorganised the Army by reducing the proportion of Indian soldiers and increasing the proportion of European soldiers.

Q.9 Find out stories and songs remembered by people in your area or your family about San Sattavan ki Ladaai. What memories do people cherish about the great uprising?

Ans. Do it yourself.

Q.10 Find out more about Rani Lakshmibai of Jhansi. In what ways would she have been an unusual women for her times?

Ans. Do it yourself.

REVIEW EXERCISE

Including Competency Based Questions

Part I

Multiple Choice Questions (MCQs)

1. What was the objective of the new law passed by the Company in 1850?

(a) Converting all Muslims and Hindus to Christianity.
(b) To divide the Indians on religious lines.
(c) Making religious conversion to Christianity easier.
(d) Not allowing Christians to inherit the land of their ancestors.

2. What was the reason for the hanging of sepoy Mangal Pandey?

(a) For refusing to use the greased cartridges
(b) For killing British women
(c) For attacking his officers
(d) For disobeying orders

3. The mutiny started from ....

(a) Meerut (b) Delhi
(c) Barrackpore (d) Lucknow

4. Where was Nana Saheb living when the mutiny started?

(a) At Gwalior (b) On his farm near Delhi
(c) At Jhansi (d) Near Kanpur

5. Who was the son of the deposed Nawab Wajid Ali Shah of Awadh?

(a) Begum Hazrat Mahal (b) Birjis Qadr
(c) Ahmadullah Shah (d) Bakht Khan

6. Where did Bahadur Shah Zafar die?

(a) In Rangoon (b) In Delhi
(c) On the battlefield (d) In Lucknow

7. When was Lucknow recaptured by British forces?

(a) 21st March, 1858 (b) 1st November, 1858
(c) 20th September, 1857 (d) None of these

8. The British regained control of the country in the year

(a) 1860 (b) 1859 (c) 1858 (d) 1880

9. When was the act transferring the power to rule India from the East India Company to the British Crown passed?

(a) 11th February, 1856 (b) 29th March, 1857
(c) 21st March, 1858 (d) 1st November, 1858

10. Which of the following changes was not made by the British after the revolt was quelled? **Competency Based**

(a) The powers of the East India Company were transferred to the British Crown.
(b) The Hindus were treated with suspicion and hostility, being responsible for the mutiny.
(c) Landlords' and zamindars' rights on their land were protected in the new policies made.
(d) None of the above

11. Identify the correct option that describe about the given statements.

I. He was sent to prison in Rangoon.
II. He was the leader of 1857 revolt.
III. He died in November 1862.

Codes

(a) Nana Saheb (b) Vir Kunwar Singh
(c) Bahadur Shah Zafar (d) Wajid Ali Shah

12. Consider the following statements and choose the correct option. **Competency Based**

I. The sepoys captured Delhi on 10th May, 1857.
II. Rani Laxmibai Bai was the Queen of Delhi.

Codes

(a) Only I (b) Only II
(c) Both I and II (d) None of these

13. **Arrange the following in the correct sequence.**

I. Lord Wellesley introduced Policy of Subsidiary Alliance. **Competency Based**

II. Governor-General Dalhousie announced that after the death of Bahadur Shah Zafar, the family of the king would be shifted out of the Red Fort.

III. The Company allowed Christian missionaries to function freely in its domain

IV. Sepoy mutiny was started from Meerut.

Codes

(a) I, II, III, IV (b) II, III, IV, I

(c) II, I, IV, II (d) I, III, II, IV

Answers

1. (c) **2.** (c) **3.** (a) **4.** (d) **5.** (b)
6. (a) **7.** (a) **8.** (b) **9.** (d) **10.** (b)
11. (c) **12.** (a) **13.** (d)

Match the Following

1.

List I	List II
A. Ahmadullah Shah	1. Calcutta
B. Bakht Khan	2. Lucknow
C. Begum Hazrat Mahal	3. Faizabad
D. Governor-General Dalhousie	4. Bareilly

Codes

	A	B	C	D		A	B	C	D
(a)	3	4	2	1	(b)	4	3	2	1
(c)	1	2	3	4	(d)	1	4	3	2

2.

List I	List II
A. Henry Lowrence	1. Bihar
B. Kunwar Singh	2. Barrackpore
C. Mangal Pandey	3. Delhi
D. Nana Saheb	4. Kanpur

Codes

	A	B	C	D		A	B	C	D
(a)	4	1	2	3	(b)	1	2	3	4
(c)	2	3	4	1	(d)	1	4	3	2

Ans. 1. (a) 2. (a)

Assertion-Reason

1. **Assertion** (A) The recapture of Delhi did not lead to end of the rebellion; people continued to resist the British.

Reason (R) The British had to fight for two years to suppress the massive forces of popular rebellion, and many rebel leaders like Rani Lakshmibai, Rani Avantibai and Tantia Tope continued their resistance even after Delhi was recaptured.

Codes

(a) Both A and R are true and R is the correct explanation of A

(b) Both A and R are true, but R is not the correct explanation of A

(c) A is true, but R is false

(d) A is false, but R is true

2. **Assertion** (A) Leaders like Ahmadullah Shah, Bakht Khan and Kunwar Singh rallied people and organised forces to fight against the British colonial rule.

Reason (R) Several new leaders emerged during the rebellion, and they played significant roles in the resistance against the British.

Codes

(a) Both A and R are true and R is the correct explanation of A

(b) Both A and R are true, but R is not the correct explanation of A

(c) A is true, but R is false

(d) A is false, but R is true

Ans. 1. (a) Both A and R are true and R is the correct explanation of A

2. (a) Both A and R are true and R is the correct explanation of A

Fill in the Blanks

1. On 10th May, 1857, the soldiers marched to the jail in .... and released the imprisoned sepoys.

2. Nana Saheb, the adopted son of ...... pleaded to the British for pension.

3. In 1856, Governor-General .... decided that Bahadur Shah Zafar would be the last Mughal king and his descendants would just be called princes.

4. On 29th, March, 1857, a young soldier .... was hanged to death for attacking his officers in Barrackpore.

Ans. 1. Meerut 2. Peshwa Baji Rao II
3. Lord Canning 4. Mangal Pandey

True/False

1. Meerut was one of last areas to be recaptured by the British.

2. The British were very happy after the 1857 revolt.

3. After the revolt was quelled, the powers of the East India Company to govern India were transferred to Queen Victoria.

4. Rani Laxmibai was defeated and killed in April 1857.

5. Nawab Wajid Ali Shah had been deposed by the British before the mutiny started.

Ans. 1. False 2. False 3. True
4. False 5. True

Picture Based Questions

1. Look at the picture given below and answer the question that follow.

Identify the personality in above picture who lead the revolt 1857 in Bihar.

(a) Nana Saheb
(b) Tantia Tope
(c) Mangal Pandey
(d) Kunwar Singh

2. Look at the picture given below and answer the question that follow.

Who is depicted in the picture ?

(a) Nan Fadanvis
(b) Nana Saheb
(c) Tantia Tope
(d) None of these

Ans. 1. (d) Kunwar Singh 2. (b) Nana Saheb

Case Based Question

1. Read the passage given below and answer the following questions.

85 sepoys were dismissed from service and sentenced to 10 years in jail for disobeying their officers. This happened on 9th May, 1857. the response of the other Indian soliders in Meerut was quite extraordinary. On 10th May, the soldiers marched to the jail in Meerut and released the imprisoned sepoys. They attacked and killed British officers. They captured guns and ammunition and set fire to the buildings and properties of the British and declared war on the firangis.

The soldiers were determined to bring an end to their rule in the country. But who would rule the land instead? The soldiers had an answer to this question – to Mughal emperor Bahadur Shah Zafar. The sepoys of Meerut rode all night of 10th May to reach Delhi in the early hours next morning. As news of their arrival spread, the regiments stationed in Delhi also rose up in rebellion. Again British officers were killed, arms and ammunition seized, buildings set on fire. Triumphant soldiers gathered around the walls of the Red Fort where the Badshah lived, demanding to meet him. The emperor was not quite willing to challenge the mighty British power but the soliders persisted. They forced their way into the placed and proclaimed Bahadur Shah Zafar as their leader.

(i) What was the initial reason for the outbreak of the 1857 Indian Rebellion?

(a) Economic exploitation
(b) Religious discrimination
(c) Sepoys were dismissed from service
(d) Land reforms

(ii) Why did the soldiers gather around the Red Fort in Delhi during the rebellion?

(a) To seek protection from the British
(b) To demand reforms in the military
(c) To proclaim Bahadur Shah Zafar as their leader
(d) To organise a peaceful protest

(iii) What were some of the long-term consequences of the Indian Rebellion of 1857?

(a) The fall of the Mughal Empire and direct British rule over India.
(b) Increasing religious tensions between Hindus and Muslims.
(c) Strengthening of the British army
(d) All of the above

(iv) What were some of the key factors that contributed to the outbreak of the Revolt of 1857?

(a) The greased cartridge issue alone.
(b) Growing dissatisfaction with British rule, economic hardships and social grievances.
(c) A sudden and spontaneous rebellion without any underlying causes.
(d) The influence of foreign powers seeking to destabilise British rule.

Ans. (i) (c) Sepoys were dismissed from service
(ii) (c) To proclaim Bahadur Shah Zafar as their leader
(iii) (d) All of the above
(iv) (a) The greased cartridge issue alone

Part II

Very Short Answer Type Questions

1. What reason was given by the British for taking over the rule of the territory of Awadh? **Competency Based**

Ans. The British declared that Awadh was being misgoverned and British rule was needed to ensure proper administration.

2. What was the first step taken by the Company to end the Mughal dynasty?

Ans. The first step taken by the Company to end the Mughal dynasty was that the Company removed the name of the Mughal king from the coins minted.

3. What measure of the British was resented by the zamindars and peasants in rural areas?

Ans. The high taxes levied by the Company and their inflexible methods of revenue collection were resented by the zamindars and peasants in rural areas.

4. What laws regarding women were passed by the British?

Ans. Laws prohibiting the custom of sati and encouraging the remarriage of widows were passed by the British.

5. Name the major centres of the revolt of 1857.

Ans. The major centres of the revolt of 1857 were Meerut, Delhi, Lucknow, Jhansi, Kanpur, Faizabad and Bareilly.

6. What was the Maulvi Ahmadullah Shah's prophecy?

Ans. The prophecy of Ahmadullah Shah, a maulvi from Faizabad, was that the rule of the British would soon come to an end.

7. Who was Tantia Tope?

Ans. Tantia Tope was the general of Nana Saheb who fought the British along with Rani Lakshmibai.

8. After the revolt was quelled, why were the powers of the East India Company transferred to the British Crown?

Ans. The powers of the East India Company were transferred to the British Crown to ensure a more responsible management of matters related to India.

9. What was thought by the kings and princes called to Calcutta as the reason for the British formulating the eighty-four rules?

Ans. The kings and princes called to Calcutta thought that the eighty-four rules were formulated so as to destroy the religions of the Hindus and the Muslims.

Short Answer Type Questions

1. What reforms did the British introduce in Indian society and what did the people of India feel about them?

Ans. The reforms introduced by the British were

- They passed laws to stop the practice of sati and encourage the remarriage of widows, as well as a law allowing an Indian convert to Christianity to continue to inherit the property of his ancestors.
- English-language education was actively promoted.
- They allowed Christian missionaries to function freely in their domain.

The people of India had mixed feelings about these reforms. Some people were happy with the new things, like school and railways. But some people did not trust the British and thought they were only doing these things to control India and take its resources.

2. "The British had regained control of the country by the end of 1859, but they could not carry on ruling the land with same policies". **Competency Based**

(i) How did the British regain control of India by the end of 1859?

Ans. The British managed to regain control of India by the end of 1859 through a combination of military suppression and reinforcement of their rule, which included using additional troops and re-establishing their authority over various regions.

(ii) Why the British changed their policies after the 1857 rebellion?

Ans. The British changed their policies after the 1857 rebellion due to widespread opposition. To appease Indian sentiments and prevent further uprisings, they adopted more cautions, implementing reforms in education, administration and religious practices.

3. List the steps taken by the British to reform their army after the rebellion was suppressed.

Ans. The steps taken by the British to reform their army after the rebellion was suppressed were

- The number of Indian sepoys was reduced and the number of European soldiers increased.
- It was decided to recruit more soldiers from the Gurkhas, Sikhs and Pathans, instead of recruiting soldiers from Awadh, Bihar, Central India and South India.
- Troops were no longer in the service of the East India Company. They would serve directly under the British Crown.

4. What do you think was the main or immediate cause of the uprising against British rule in India?

Ans. The main or immediate cause of the uprising against the British rule in India was that some sepoys of the regiment in Meerut refuse to use new cartridges which were suspected of being coated with fat of cows and pigs. As a result of this, 85 sepoys were dismissed from service and sentenced to 10 years in jail on 9th May, 1857. This angered the other sepoys and the uprising was started.

5. The atrocities committed by both sides during the uprising were horrifying. What were the reasons for such atrocities? Competency Based

Ans. The atrocities committed by both sides during the uprising, such as the Indian Rebellion of 1857, were driven by a combination of factors. Tensions had been building up due to various social, economic and political issues as follows

- **Cultural and Religious Divide** There was a perceived cultural and religious threat among both Indian and British forces. The use of greased cartridges rumoured to be coated with animal fat, which offended both Hindu and Muslim sepoys, triggered widespread discontent.
- **Economic Grievances** Economic exploitation by the British East India Company, high taxes, and land annexations contributed to the resentment among the Indian population.
- **Political Discontent** The annexation of various Princely States and the imposition of direct British rule eroded the authority and power of local rulers, leading to political dissatisfaction.
- **Social Injustice** The British implementation of social reforms, often perceived as interference in local customs and traditions, angered many Indians.

6. Did the Revolt of 1857 have a popular character? Give arguments to support your answer.

Ans. Yes, the Revolt of 1857 had a popular character due to two reasons. These were

- The revolt was started by the Indian sepoys employed by the East India Company and continued by them all over North India.

  These sepoys were mostly ordinary people from peasant families in rural areas and so it was a popular uprising.
- The leaders of the revolt were the local rulers and chieftains, most of whom were well-liked by the populace due to their treatment of the people under their control. Thus most of them, with a few exceptions, were popular rulers.

Long Answer Type Questions

1. How did the uprising that started in Meerut in 1857 manage to spread across different parts of the country, finally became a widespread rebellion against British rule?

Ans. The uprising that started in Meerut in 1857 manage to spread across different parts of the country, finally became a widespread rebellion against British rule in the following ways

- On 10th May, other sepoys released the imprisoned sepoys and declared war on the British by attacking and killing British officers. They captured guns and ammunition, and set fire to buildings and properties of the firangis.
- After this, the sepoys of Meerut reached the Red Fort in Delhi, in the palace of Bahadur Shah Zafar and declared him as their leader the rebellion. He encouraged all the chiefs and rulers of the country through letters, to organise a confederacy of Indian states to fight against the British.
- As the mutiny of the sepoys was successful to took out the British from Delhi. After this, mutinies or rebellions spread to other states also.
- Many troop regiments mutinied and join the other troops at Delhi, Kanpur and Lucknow. People from towns and villages rallied around local leaders, zamindars and other leaders who wanted to establish their authority and fight the British. These leaders included Nana Saheb (Kanpur), Rani Lakshmibai (Jhansi), Birjis Qadr (Lucknow), etc.

2. The British gradually took over India. How do you think the British justified this takeover? Do you think it was justified? Why or why not?

Ans. The British took over India gradually and tried to justify their rule using economic, political and moral reasons.

The British said they were helping India become more civilised, claiming that the local traditions were backward. However, many people think these justifications were just excuses to cover up their real goal, which was often seen as exploiting India.

Economically, the British took valuable products from India at very low prices or as taxes to fund their rule. This made India poorer and more dependent on the British.

This policy was not justified because India lost much of its resources to the British, resulting in the poverty which we see and feel even today. Further, there were many loopholes in the policy which could be used by individuals for their personal gain and enjoyment at the cost of the country.

3. What steps did the British take to suppress the revolt, which were successful?

Ans. The British took several steps to suppress the revolt, and some of these measures were successful

- **Reinforcement** The Company brought additional troops from England to bloster their military presence in India, increasing their manpower.
- **New Laws** The British passed new laws to expedite the conviction of rebels, making it easier to bring them to justice.
- **Recapture of Delhi** They successfully recaptured Delhi from the rebel forces in September 1857, which was a significant centre of the revolt.
- **Trial of Bahadur Shah Zafar** The British tried and sentenced the last Mughal emperor, Bahadur Shah Zafar, to life imprisonment which effectively end his symbolic leadership of the rebellion.

- **Rewards for Loyalty** The British offered rewards for loyal landholders and assured them that they could retain their traditional right over the lands. This strategy aimed to win back the suport of those who had not rebelled.
- **Assurances for Surrendered Rebels** Rebels who had not killed any British individuals were promised safety and protection of their rights and claims to land, if they submitted to British authority.

4. Why were the Indian sepoys employed by the Company discontented?

Ans. Indian sepoys employed by the British East India Company were discontented for several reasons

- **Pay and Allowances** They were dissatisfied with their pay, allowances and overall compensation, as they believed it to be inadequate and unfair in comparison to British soldiers.
- **Conditions of Service** The working conditions and treatment of Indian sepoys were often unsatisfactory. They faced discrimination and unequal treatment in the army.
- **Religious Sensibilities** Some of the new rules and practices introduced by the British violated the religious sensibilities and beliefs of the sepoys. For example, the use of cartridges rumored to be coated with cow and pig fat was deeply offensive to both Hindu and Muslim sepoys.
- **Overseas Service** The sepoys were apprehensive about serving overseas, especially via sea routes, as it was believed by many in the country that crossing the sea could result in the loss of one's religion and caste. When they were ordered to go to Burma by sea in 1824, they refused, leading to severe punishments. The 1856 law that required all new recruits to agree to serve overseas further increased their discontent.

5. "After a hundred years of conquest and administration, the East India Company faced a massive rebellion that started in May 1857 and threatened the company's very presence in India". Why did the English East India Company face a major rebellion in May 1857 and how did it endanger the Company rule in India after a century o **Competency Based**

Ans. The English East India company confronted a major rebellion in May 1857 because of combination of political, economic, and social grievances that had been growing for years.

The primary cause of rebellion was the use of new Enfield rifle, whose cartridges were rumored to be coated with animal fat. This sparked the initial mutiny in Meerut, which rapidly spread.

Moreover, the British had increasingly centralised power and undermined the authority of India rulers. They also imposed heavy taxes and implement land revenue policies which created economic hardships for Indian population.

The social and cultural insensitivity of British policies, such as the suppression of local customs further fueled dissatisfaction.

All these factors causes rebellion, which became a significant threat to the East India Company's rule in India. This finally led to the end of the Company's control and beginning of direct British rule over the subcontinent.

Picture Based Question

1. Look at the picture given below carefully and answer the questions .

(i) Why did the revolt broke out on 10th May, 1857 ?

Ans. The Revolt broke out on 10th May, 1857 because some sepoys of the regiment in Meerut refused to do the army drill using the new cartridges which were suspected of being coated with fat of cows and pigs.

(ii) Describe the role of Mangal Pandey in the Revolt of 1857.

Ans. Mangal Pandey was a sepoy of the British East India Company. He played a key role in the Sepoy Mutiny of 1857. He attacked British officers at Barrackpore, inspiring other sepoys to rebel, which quickly led the mutiny spreading to other parts of India.

On 29th March, 1857 Mangal Pandey was hanged to death. Mangal Pandey's Martydom turned him into a hero among the Indian people and he is remembered as one of the first freedom fighters of India.

Case Based Questions

1. Read the passage given below and answer the following questions.

The list of eighty-four rules

Given here are excerpts from the book Majha Pravaas, written by Vishnubhatt Godse, a Brahman from a village in Maharashtra. He and his uncle had set out to attend a yajna being organised in Mathura. Vishnubhatt writes that they met some sepoys on the way who told them that they should not proceed on the journey because a massive upheaval was going to break out in three days.

The sepoys said:

The English were determined to wipe out the religions of the Hindus and the Muslims they had made a list of eighty-four rules and announced these in a gathering of all big kings and princes in Calcutta. They said that the kings refused to accept these rules and warned the English of dire consequences and massive upheaval if these are implemented ... that the kings all returned to their capitals in great anger ... all the big people began making plans. A date was fixed for the war of religion and the secret plan had been circulated from the cantonment in Meerut by letters sent to different cantonments.

Vishnubhatt Godse, Majha Pravaas, pp. 23-24.

(i) Who was Vishnubhatt Godse ? Where was he going and for what purpose ?

Ans. Vishnubhatt Godse was a Brahman from a village in Maharashtra. He was going to Mathura to attend a yajna.

(ii) Whom did he meet on the way ? What did they tell him?

Ans. He meet some sepoys on the way.

The sepoys told him that he should not proceed on the journey because a massive unheaval was going to break out in three days.

(iii) What further information did they give to Vishnubhatt ?

Ans. The sepoys further informed Vishnubhatt about the ways the British were destroying the religions of the Hindus and that spread due to it among the rulers and the comon mass. All the big people had fixed a date for the war of religion and that date would be coming in three days .

2. Read the passage given below and answer the following questions.

"There was soon excitement in every regiment"

It is my humble opinion that this seizing of Oudh filled the minds of the Sepoys with distrust and led them to plot against the Government. Agents of the Nawab of Oudh and also of the King of Delhi were sent all over India to discover the temper of the army. They worked upon the feelings of sepoys, telling them how treacherously the foreigners had behaved towards their king. They invented ten thousand lies and promises to persuade the soldiers to mutiny and turn against their masters, the English, with the object of restoring the Emperor of Delhi to the throne. They maintained that this was wholly within the army's powers if the soldiers would only act together and do as they were advised.

It chanced that about this time the Sarkar sent parties of men from each regiment to different garrisons for instructions in the use of the new rifle. These men performed the new drill for some time until a report got about by some means or the other, that the cartridges used for these new rifles were greased with the fat of cows and pigs. The men from our regiment wrote to others in the regiment telling them about this and there was soon excitement in every regiment.

Some men pointed out that in forty years' service nothing had ever been done by the Sarkar to insult their religion, but as I have already mentioned the sepoys' minds had been inflamed by the seizure of Oudh.

(i) What atrocity did the British commit on Subedar Sitaram Pandey although he was a loyal British soldier and why?

Ans. The British killed the Subedar's son in front of his eyes because the son was a rebel, although he was a loyal British solider.

(ii) In Subedar Sitaram Pandey's opinion, what was the major event which led the sepoys to plot against the government?

Ans. The major event, according to Subedar Sitaram Pandey, was the seizure of the state of Awadh by the British.

Map Based Question

1. The outline map of India mark the important centers of the revolt. Identify the centers.

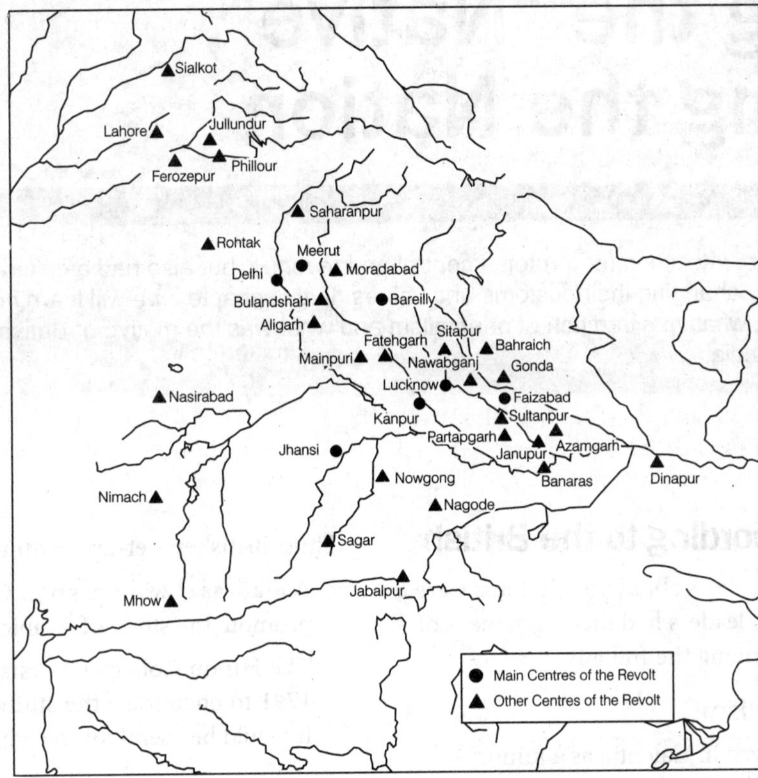

Ans. In the above map, the areas which are important centers of revolt are Meerut, Kanpur, Bareilly, Delhi, Lucknow, Faizabad and Jhansi.

ASSESSMENT EXERCISE

Multiple Choice Questions (MCQs)

1. Which of the following decided that Bahadur Shah Zafar would be the last Mugal King?
(a) Lord Canning
(b) Lord Dalhousie
(c) Lord Wellesley
(d) Captain Rose

2. Peshwa, Baji Rao of Kanpur adopted son was
(a) Birjis Qadr
(b) Nana Saheb
(c) Tantia Tope
(d) Wajid Ali Shah

3. Which event triggered the widespread rebellion of 1857?
(a) Sepoy Mangal Pandey's revolt
(b) Introduction of cartridge greased with animal fat
(c) Annexation of Awadh by the British
(d) All of the above

4. Who was the leader of the rebellion of 1857 in Delhi?
(a) Bahadur Shah Zafar (b) Rani Lakshmibai
(c) Nana Saheb (d) Tantia Tope

Subjective Questions (VSA, SA & LA)

1. How did company plan to end the Mughal dynasty?

2. Why did many Indian sepoys refuse to use new cartridges?

3. How did the British government check the power of East India Company?

4. How did company fight back to Suppress the Revolt?

5. How did the Mutiny become a popular rebellion?

6. How did the Nawabs and kings lose their powers in the company rule?

7. What were the important changes in the governance of British in India? Explain.

Civilising the "Native", Educating the Nation

CHAPTER 6

British rule in India not only aimed for territorial control and revenue, but also had a cultural mission to "civilise the natives" by changing their customs and values. In this chapter, we will learn how British saw Indian Education, what was tradition of orientalism and what was the motive of British to introduce English Education in India.

6.1 Education According to the British

The Britishers had their own views about how Indians were to be educated but some Indian leaders had their own ideas of how to improve education among the Indians.

The Tradition of Orientalism

In 1783, **William Jones** arrived in Calcutta as a junior judge at the Supreme Court established by the East India Company. Apart from being expert in law, Jones was a **linguist**[1] with knowledge of Greek, Latin, French, English, Arabic and Persian.

Jones learnt Sanskrit language, grammar and poetry from pandits in Calcutta. He also studied ancient Indian texts covering various subjects like law, philosophy, religion, politics, morality, arithmetic and medicine.

Other Englishmen living in Calcutta like **Henry Thomas Colebrooke** and **Nathaniel Halhed** also had similar interests as Jones'. They were known as **Orientalists**[2]. Jones along with them established the **Asiatic Society of Bengal** and initiated a journal named **Asiatick Researches**.

Jones and Colebrooke had a deep respect for both Indian and Western ancient cultures. For promoting Indian heritage, they started discovering ancient texts and translating them.

Many Company official were influenced by Jones and Colebrooke. They felt that institution should be set-up to encourage the study of ancient Indian texts and teach Sanskrit and Persian literature and poetry.

Thus, Britishers set-up institutions like

- A **madrasa**[3] was set-up in Calcutta in 1781 to promote the study of Arabic, Persian and Islamic law.
- The Hindu College was established in Benaras in 1791 to encourage the study of ancient Sanskrit texts. It would be useful for the administration of the country.

Great Mistakes of the East

In the early 19th century, many British officials criticised the orientalist view of learning. They believed that Eastern knowledge was full of errors (mistakes) and unscientific thoughts, and it focused more on non-serious literature.

James Mill criticised Orientalists and argued for emphasising practical and useful education, like scientific and technical advances of the West.

By the 1830s, **Thomas Babington Macaulay** strongly criticised Orientalists. He viewed India as uncivilised and advocated for teaching English language to civilise the people.

The criticisation of Macaulay led to the introduction of **English Education Act** of 1835. It aimed to make English as the medium of instruction for higher education and end support for Oriental institutions like Calcutta Madrasa and Benaras Sanskrit College. English textbooks started to be produced for schools after this act.

---

1 **Linguist** It refers to someone who knows and studies several languages.

2 **Orientalists** It refers to a person Those with a scholarly knowledge of the language and culture of Asia.

3 **Madrasa** It is an Arabic word for a place of learning; any type of school or college.

Education for Commerce

In 1854, the Court of Directors of the East India Company in London sent an educational **despatch**[4] to the Governor-General in India. It was issued by **Charles Wood**, the President of the Board of Control of the Company, and known as **Wood's Despatch.**

Wood's Despatch emphasised the practical benefits of European learning over Oriental knowledge for Indians.

It highlighted the economic advantages as follows

- European education would help Indians understand the benefits of expansion of trade and commerce.
- European learning would change Indian tastes, create a demand for British goods, and increase trade.
- European education would improve the moral character of Indians, making them trustworthy civil servants.

As a result of this Despatch, the British implemented several measures like extending control over educational matters, establishing a system of university education and making changes within the system of school education. In 1857, universities were established in Calcutta, Madras and Bombay.

6.2 The Local Schools

In the 1830s, a Scottish missionary, **William Adam**, toured the districts of Bengal and Bihar to make report on the progress of education in **vernacular**[5] schools.

The Report of William Adam

The report of William Adam mentioned the following

- There were over 1 lakh small **pathshalas**[6] in Bengal and Bihar with around 20 students each. These pathshalas were set up by wealthy individuals or the local community and sometimes by a teacher (*guru*).
- The education system in the pathshalas was flexible with no fixed fees, no printed books, no separate school building, no benches or chairs, no blackboards, no system of separate classes, no annual examinations, no regular time-table, etc. In some places classes were held in open space, in the corner of a village shop or temple or at the guru's home.
- Fees was based on parents' income. Teaching in these schools was oral and the *guru* decided what to teach.
- The school system was suited to local needs. For example, classes were not held during harvest time when the rural children worked in the field.

New Routines and New Rules

Until the mid-19th century, the Company focused on higher education and allowed local pathshalas to function freely.

After 1854, the Company decided to improve vernacular education by introducing order, routines and rules.

The company appointed Government pandits to visit the pathshalas and improve the standards of teaching.

Teaching was now based textbooks and learning was to be tested through annual examination. Apart from this, students were asked to pay a regular fee, attend regular classes sit on fixed seats and obey new rules.

Pathshalas which accepted the new rules were supported through government grants.

However, these new rules and routines had consequences as follows

- The *gurus* found it difficult to compete with the government aided and regulated pathshalas.
- As the discipline of the new system demanded regular attendance, the children of poor families who had to work in the fields during harvest, came to be regarded as indiscipline and having the lack of desire to learn.

KNOWLEDGE PLUS By the mid-19th century, both Christian missionaries and Indian reform organisations were involved in establishing schools for girls.

6.3 The Agenda for a National Education

From the early 19th century, many thinkers from India felt the need for widespread education. They were influenced by developments in Europe and believed that Western education would help modernise India.

They encouraged the British to open more schools and spend more funds for education.

However, some Indians like **Mahatma Gandhi** and **Rabindranath Tagore** reacted against Western education.

4 **Despatch** It is an official report, for example, wood's Despatch.

5 **Vernacular** It is a term generally used to refer to a local language or dialect as distinct from what is seen as the standard language.

6 **Pathshalas** These refer to local small schools which were set-up by wealthy people or the local community.

Mahatma Gandhi's Views about English Education

Mahatma Gandhi argued that colonial education created a sense of inferiority in the minds of Indians.

According to him, colonial education had made the Indians to see Western education superior that their own culture. He believed that it had enslaved Indians, as Indians began admiring British rule. During the national movement, he encouraged students to leave educational institutions.

Gandhi advocated for teaching in Indian languages . He criticised Western education for focusing on reading and writing rather than oral knowledge, and valuing textbooks rather than practical knowledge.

These nationalist sentiments led to the exploration of a new system of national education that would be different from the British system.

Tagore's 'Abode of Peace'

Rabindranath Tagore's ideas of education were influenced by the experience of his school days. He wanted to set-up a school where children could be happy, free, and creative, exploring their thoughts and desires.

He believed that childhood should be a time of self-learning. He wanted teachers to be imaginative and understanding. He thought existing schools restricts a child's natural creativity.

He established **Santiniketan** in 1901 in Calcutta. He saw Santiniketan as an 'abode of peace,' promoting creative learning in harmony with nature.

Santiniketan aimed to teach science, technology, art, music and dance.

Differences between the Ideas of Mahatma Gandhi and Rabindranath Tagore

Many ideas of education of Mahatma Gandhi and Rabindranath were similar, however there were differences also.

Mahatma Gandhi criticised the Western civilisation and its admiration of machines and technology.

On the other hand, Rabindranath Tagore wanted to combine elements of modern Western civilisation with some elements within Indian tradition.

CIVILISING THE "NATIVE", EDUCATING THE NATION

Education According to the British

The Tradition of Orientalism

- William Jones along with Henry Thomas Colebrooke and Nathaniel Halhed established the Asiatic Society of Bengal and initiated a journal named Asiatic Researches.
- A madrasa was set up in Calcutta in 1781 to promote the study of Arabic, Persian and Islamic law.

Great Mistakes of the East

- James Mill and Thomas Babington Macaulay criticised Orientalists.
- Introduction of English Education Act of 1835.

Education for Commerce

- In 1854, Wood's Despatch was issued by Charles Wood, the President of the Board of Control of the Company.
- In 1857, universities were established in Calcutta, Madras and Bombay.

The Agenda for a National Education

- Mahatma Gandhi criticised the Western civilisation and its admiration of machines and technology.
- Rabindranath Tagore wanted to combine elements of modern Western civilisation with some elements within Indian tradition.

The Local Schools

The Report of William Adam

- There were over 1 lakh small Pathshalas in Bengal with around 20 students each.
- Flexible education system with no fixed fees.
- Fees was based on parent's income.

New Routines and New Rules

- Government Pandits were appointed to visit the Pathshalas.
- Teaching was then textbook based and learning was to be tested through annual examination.

NCERT FOLDER

Covering Intext Questions and Exercises of NCERT

NCERT ON PAGE 69 (ACTIVITY)

Q.1. Imagine you are living in the 1850s. You hear of Wood's Despatch. Write about your reactions.

Ans. Living in the 1850s and hearing about Wood's Despatch, my reaction would likely be a mix of curiosity and expectation. The despatch, led by Sir Charles Wood, aimed to reform education in British India, emphasising the need for a more systematic and widespread approach.

I might feel hopeful about the potential positive impact on education accessibility and standards. At the same time, there could be some doubt and concern about how these reforms would be implemented and whether they would genuinely address the diverse educational needs of the population. Overall, the news of Wood's Despatch would likely spark interest and discussions about the future of education in the context of British India during that time.

NCERT ON PAGE 72 (ACTIVITY)

Q.2 Imagine you were born in a poor family in the 1850s. How would you have responded to the coming of the new system of government regulated pathshalas?

Ans. If I were born into a poor family in the 1850s and the new system of government-regulated pathshalas (schools) were introduced, my response would likely have been a mix of hope, curiosity and cautious optimism. In this new system, the students are asked to pay a regular fee, attend regular classes, sit on fixed seats and obey the new rules of discipline.

Being a child of a poor family, it is not possible for me to give fees. Not only that, regular attendence is also impossible for me as I have to go to the fields with my parents during harvest time. Flexible timings of our pathshala is suitable for us. New rules or policies of government are not beneficial for us, they only hampers our right to education.

Q.3 Did you know that about 50 per cent of the children going to primary school drop out of school by the time they are 13 or 14? Can you think of the various possible reasons for this fact?

Ans. Yes, about 50 per cent of the children going to primary school drop out of school by the time they are 13 or 14. Possible reasons for drop out of the children from schools are as follows

- Uneducated and unemployed parents discourage their child to continue education.
- Overall poverty forces the child to do any type of job. they depend on their parents who makes decisions for them.
- The parents do not give much importance to the education of girls in comparison to their sons which leads to more drop outs in case of girl child.
- Old traditional methods of learning can not attract the students.
- Lack of basic facilities in schools is one of the important causes of school drop outs.

NCERT ON PAGE 76 (LET'S IMAGINE)

Q.4 Imagine you were witness to a debate between Mahatma Gandhi and Macaulay on English education. Write a page on the dialogue you heard.

Ans. Do it yourself.

EXERCISES

Q.1 Match the following

A. William Jones	1. Promotion of English education
B. Rabindranath Tagore	2. Respect for ancient cultures
C. Thomas Macaulay	3. Gurus
D. Mahatma Gandhi	4. Learning in a natural environment
E. Pathshalas	5. Critical of English education

Ans. A-2, B-4, C-1, D-5, E-3

Q.2 State whether true or false.

(i) James Mill was a severe critic of the Orientalists.

Ans. True

(ii) The 1854 Despatch on education was in favour of English being introduced as a medium of higher education in India.

Ans. True

(iii) Mahatma Gandhi thought that promotion of literacy was the most important aim of education.

Ans. False

(iv) **Rabindranath Tagore felt that children ought to be subjected to strict discipline.**

Ans. False

Q.3 Why did William Jones feel the need to study Indian history, philosophy and law? Diksha

Ans. William Jones felt the need to study Indian history, philosophy and law due to the following reasons

- He had a deep respect for ancient cultures, both of India and the West.
- He thought that Indian civilisation had attained its glory in the ancient past, but had later declined.
- He believed that in order to understand India, it was necessary to discover the sacred and legal texts of ancient periods.

Q.4 Why did James Mill and Thomas Macaulay think that European education was essential in India? Diksha

Ans. James Mill thought that European education was essential in India because

- The knowledge of the East was full of errors and unscientific thoughts.
- The aim of education ought to be to teach what was useful and practical.

Thomas Macaulay thought that European education was essential in India because

- India was an uncivilised country that needed to be civilised.
- No branch of Eastern knowledge could be compared to Western knowledge. Oriental learning was of no practical use.

Q.5 Why did Mahatma Gandhi want to teach children handicrafts? Diksha

Ans. Mahatma Gandhi wanted to teach children handicrafts for the following reasons

- Education ought to develop a person's mind and soul. Simple learning to read and write by itself did not count as education.
- If children are allowed to work with hands, learn a craft and know how different things are operated, this would help their mind and their capacity to understand.

Q.6 Why did Mahatma Gandhi think that English education had enslaved Indians? Diksha

Ans. Mahatma Gandhi thought that English education had enslaved Indians because

- English education created a sense of inferiority in the minds of Indians.
- Indians educated in these institutions, started appreciating everything that came from the West and began admiring British rule. It made them see Western civilisation as superior.
- This education destroyed the pride that Indians had in their own culture and country.

Q.7 Find out from your grandparents about what they studied in school.

Ans. Do it yourself.

Q.8 Find out about the history of your school or any other school in the area you live.

Ans. Do it yourself.

REVIEW EXERCISE

Including Competency Based Questions

Part I

Multiple Choice Questions (MCQs)

1. In which year did William Jones arrive in Calcutta?

(a) 1783 (b) 1743 (c) 1793 (d) 1885

2. Who have scholarly knowledge of Asiatic language and culture ? Diksha

(a) Linguistic (b) Orientalists
(c) Vernacularists (d) Munshis

3. A madrasa was set-up in Calcutta in 1781 to promote the study of

(a) Arabic (b) Muslim religion
(c) Urdu (d) Ancient scriptures

4. Among the following who was the first British officials to attack the view of Orientalists. Diksha

(a) Thomas Macaulay (b) James Mill
(c) William Adam (d) Both (a) and (b)

5. The English Education Act was introduced in the year

(a) 1825 (b) 1835 (c) 1845 (d) 1855

6. William Adam toured the districts of .... in the 1830's to prepare a report on Education in Vernacular schools. Diksha

(a) Bihar and Orissa (b) Bihar and Bengal
(c) Bengal and Rajasthan (d) Orissa and Madhya Pradesh

7. **Who were appointed by the company in 1854 to took after four to five schools?**

(a) Government pandits (b) Government officials
(c) Government teachers (d) Government servants

8. **'English education had enslaved Indians'. Identify the person who had given this statement.**

(a) Mahatma Gandhi (b) Rabindranath Tagore
(c) Raja Rammohan Roy (d) Subhash Chandra Bose

9. **Identify the correct option that describe about the given statements.** **Competency Based**

(i) He started a journal called Asiatick Researches.
(ii) He setup Asiatic society of Bengal.
(iii) He arrived in Calcutta in 1783.

Codes

(a) William Jones (b) HT Colebrooke
(c) Warren Hastings (d) James Mill

10. **Consider the following statements and choose the correct option.** **Competency Based**

I. Thomas Babington Macaulay saw India as a civilised country.
II. William Jones was a minister of education.

Codes

(a) Both I and II (b) Only II
(c) Only I (d) None of these

11. **Consider the following statements and choose the correct option.** **Competency Based**

I. William Jones set up the Asiatic society of Bengal.
II. Vernacular education system was established by Britishers.

Codes

(a) Only II (b) Only I
(c) Both I and II (d) None of these

12. **Which of the following is the correct sequence?** **Competency Based**

(i) Madrasa was set up in Calcutta.
(ii) The English Education Act was implemented.
(iii) William Jones arrived in Calcutta.
(iv) Hindu college was established in Benaras.

Codes

(a) (i), (ii), (iii), (iv) (b) (iv), (i), (iii), (iv)
(c) (i), (iii), (iv), (ii) (d) (i), (iiii), (ii), (iv)

13. **Which of the following is the correct sequence?** **Competency Based**

(i) Wood's Despatch was issued.
(ii) System of Annual examination was started.
(iii) Rabindranath Tagore established Santiniketan.

Codes

(a) (i), (ii), (iii) (b) (iii), (ii), (i)
(c) (i), (iii), (ii) (d) (ii), (iii), (i)

Answers

1. (a)	2. (b)	3. (a)	4. (d)	5. (b)
6. (b)	7. (a)	8. (a)	9. (a)	10. (d)
11. (b)	12. (c)	13. (c)		

Match the Following

1.

	List I	List II
A.	A person who can read, write and teach Persian	1. Pathshala
B.	A local language or dialect, distinct from standard language	2. Madrasa
C.	An Arabic word for a place of learning	3. Munshi
D.	In this type of institution, teaching was oral and Guru decided what to teach	4. Vernacular

Codes

	A	B	C	D		A	B	C	D
(a)	3	4	2	1	(b)	1	2	3	4
(c)	1	4	3	2	(d)	4	1	2	3

2.

List I	List II
A. Hindu College	1. 1854
B. William Jones	2. 1791
C. William Adam	3. Linguist
D. Charles Wood Despatch	4. Scottish missionary

Codes

	A	B	C	D		A	B	C	D
(a)	1	2	3	4	(b)	3	1	4	2
(c)	2	3	4	1	(d)	2	4	3	1

Ans. 1. (a) 2. (c)

Assertion-Reason

1. **Assertion** (A) Mahatma Gandhi said that Western education focused on reading and writing rather than oral language.

Reason (R) European education value textbook rather than lived experience and practical knowledge.

Codes

(a) Both A and R are true and R is the correct explanation of A
(b) Both A and R are true, but R is not the correct explanation of A
(c) A is true, but R is false
(d) A is false, but R is true

2. **Assertion** (A) In many senses, Tagore and Mahatma Gandhi thought about education similar ways.

Reason (R) From the early 19th century, many American officials began to criticise the orientalist vision of learning.

Codes

(a) Both A and R are true and R is the correct explanation of A

(b) Both A and R are true, but R is not the correct explanation of A

(c) A is true, but R is false

(d) A is false, but R is true

Ans. 1. (a) Both A and R are true and R is the correct explanation of A

2. (c) A is true, but R is false

Fill in the Blanks

1. In 1857, universities were being established in Calcutta, Madras and ....
2. The Journal Asiatick Researches was started by ....
3. Charles Wood emphasised the practical benefits of a system of............ learning.
4. Mahatma Gandhi favoured .... languages as a medium of instruction.
5. There was no system of annual examinations in ....

Ans. 1. Bombay 2. Jones 3. European 4. Indian 5. pathshalas

True/False

1. In pathshalas, classes were not held during harvest time.
2. A madrasa was set-up in Agra in 1781 to promote the study of Arabic.
3. Until 1813, the East India Company was opposed to missionary activities in India.
4. The University of Calcutta was established in 1859.

Ans. 1. True 2. False 3. True 4. False

Picture Based Questions

1. **The image given below is of the statue of Warren Hastings. Where is this statue situated ?**

(a) Agra (b) Delhi (c) Calcutta (d) Mumbai

2. **Observe the picture carefully and identify the famous personality.**

(a) Mahatma Gandhi (b) Rabindranath Tagore

(c) Sir Aurobindo Ghose (d) None of these

Ans. 1. (b) Delhi 2. (c) Sir Aurobindo Ghose

Case Based Question

1. **Read the passage given below and answer the following questions.**

In 1783, a person named William Jones arrived in Calcutta. he had an appointment as a junior judge at the Supreme Court that the Company had set up. In addition to being an expert in law, Jones was a linguist. He had studied Greek and Latin at Oxford, knew French and English, had picked up Arabic from a friend, and had also learnt Persian. At Calcutta, he began spending many hours a day with pandits who taught him the subtleties of Sanskrit language, grammar and poetry. Soon he was studying ancient Indian texts on law, philosophy, religion, politics, morality, arithmetic, medicine and the other sciences.

(i) Which society was setup by William Jones?

(a) Bengal British India Society

(b) Asiatic Society of Bengal

(c) East India Association

(d) Royal Society of India

(ii) What was William Jones known for in addition to being a judge?

(a) Hix expertise in law

(b) His knowledge of Green and Latin

(c) His proficiency in French and English

(d) His linguistic abilities

(iii) Why did the British Government appoint William Jones as a Judge?

(a) He was expert in law.

(b) He was expert in Sanskrit.

(c) He was expert in policy making.

(d) All of the above

(iv) Why did William Jones study ancient Texts?

(a) Understanding Indian culture

(b) For linguistic discovery

(c) For philological research

(d) All of the above

Ans. (i) (b) Asiatic Society of Bengal

(ii) (d) His linguistic abilities (iii) (a) He was expert in law

(iv) (d) All of the above

Part II

Very Short Answer Type Questions

1. Who was William Carey?

Ans. William Carey was a Scottish missionary who helped to establish the Serampore Mission.

2. What did William Jones have as an appointment?

Ans. Willam Jones had an appointment as a Supreme Court Judge.

3. How many languages were known by William Jones?

Ans. William Jones knew French, English, Greek, Latin, Arabic, Persian and Sanskrit.

4. Who was Henry Thomas Colebrook?

Ans. Henry Thomas Colebrook was a scholar of Sanskrit and ancient sacred writings of Hinduism.

5. For what purpose was madrasa set-up in Calcutta in 1781?

Ans. A madrasa was set-up in Calcutta in 1781 to promote the study of Arabic, Persian and Islamic law.

6. When was Santiniketan set-up and by whom?

Ans. Santiniketan was set-up by Rabindranath Tagore in 1901.

7. Name some important Oriental institutions.

Ans. Some important Oriental institutions were
(i) Madrasa in Calcutta
(ii) The Hindu College in Benaras

8. Why was the Hindu College established in Benaras?
***Or* When did Hindu colleges started to promote study of Hindi religious Texts?** **Diksha**

Ans. In 1791, the Hindu College was established in Benaras to encourage the study of ancient Sanskrit texts that would be useful for administration of the country.

9. Name two individuals who sharply attacked the Orientalists.

Ans. James Mill and Thomas Babington Macaulay are two individuals who sharply attacked the Orientalist.

10. Which institutions were seen as 'temples of darkness that were falling of themselves into decay'?

Ans. Oriental institutions like the Calcutta Madrasa and Benaras Sanskrit College were seen as 'temples of darkness that were falling of themselves into decay.'

11. Name the places where the British established universities.

Ans. Calcutta, Madras and Bombay were the places where British established universities.

12. What type of education was given to the children in pathshalas?

Ans. In pathshalas, teaching was oral and the guru (teacher) decided what to teach.

13. Name two Indians who reacted against Western education.

Ans. Mahatma Gandhi and Rabindranath Tagore reacted against Western education.

Short Answer Type Questions

1. What did William Jones discover in Calcutta? What did he set-up?

Ans. When William Jones was learning Sanskrit language, grammar and poetry from pandits in Calcutta, he discovered that other Englishmen living in Calcutta like Henry Thomas Colebrooke and Nathaniel Halhed also had similar interests as Jones'.

Along with them, Jones established the Asiatic Society of Bengal and initiated a journal named Asiatick Researches.

2. Write a short note on 'Grave errors of the East'.

Ans. 'Grave errors of the East' refers to the criticisation of Orientalists by other English officials.

In the early 19th century, many British officials criticised the orientalist view of learning. They believed Eastern knowledge was full of errors (mistakes) and unscientific thoughts, and it focused more on non-serious literature.

James Mill criticised Orientalists and argued for emphasising practical and useful education, like scientific and technical advances of the West.

By the 1830s, Thomas Babington Macaulay strongly criticised Orientalists. He viewed India as uncivilised and advocated for teaching English language to civilise the people.

3. Issued by Charles Wood, the President of the Board of Control of the Company, the education despatch came to be known as Woods Despatch. What were the recommendations of the Woods Despatch? **Competency Based**

Ans. The recommendations of the Wood's Despatch were

- An education department was to be set in every province.
- Universitites on the model of the London University to be established in big cities such as Bombay, Calcutta and Madras.
- At least one government school be opened in every district.
- Affiliated private schools should be given grant in aid.
- The Indian natives should be given training in their mother tongue also.

4. What was done to promote Indian learning in India?

Ans. Some measures that were taken to promote Indian learning were

- A madrasa was set-up in Calcutta in 1781 to promote the study of Arabic, Persian and Islamic Law.

- The Hindu College was established in Benaras in 1791 to encourage the study of ancient Sanskrit texts that would be useful for the administration of the country.

5. Define the term 'Vernacular'. Why did the British use this term in colonial countries like India?

Ans. The term 'Vernacular' is generally used to refer to a local language or dialect as distinct from what is seen as the standard language of a country.

In colonial countries like India, the British used this term to mark the difference between the local languages of everyday use and English, the language of the colonial masters (Britishers).

6. Write the main features of educational method followed in pathshalas.

***Or* What were the special features of a pathshalas?** Diksha

Ans. The main features of educational method followed in pathshalas were

- The system of education in pathshalas was flexible.
- There were no formal schools.
- There were no fixed school fee, no books, no regular time-table, no roll-call registers and no annual examinations.
- In some places, classes were held in open space, sometimes in the corner of a village shop or temple or at guru's home.
- Teaching was oral and the guru (teacher) decided what to teach.
- Students were not separated out into different classes.

7. What were differences between Tagore's idea of education with Mahatma Gandhi's idea?

Ans. Rabindranath Tagore and Mahatma Gandhi had different educational philosophies.

Tagore believed in a well-rounded education that included art, music and nature. He wanted students to be creative. He started a school called Santiniketan, where students learned in open-air classrooms and through the arts.

On the other hand, Gandhi's idea was more practical. He wanted students to learn skills like spinning and weaving. Gandhi advocated for teaching in Indian languages. He criticised Western education for focusing on reading and writing rather than oral knowledge, and valuing textbooks rather than practical knowledge.

8. What were Tagore's experiences as a student?

Ans. As a student, Rabindranath Tagore had a negative experience with formal education. He disliked school, considering it oppressive and prison-like, as it stifled his freedom and creativity. His mind often wandered during lessons, and this disillusionment, shaped his views on education.

Tagore envisioned a school where children could be happy, free and creative, exploring their thoughts and desires. He believed in self-learning and opposed the rigid discipline of British-influenced schooling. Tagore emphasised the importance of imaginative teachers who understood and nurtured a child's curiosity.

9. "Mahatma Gandhi argued that colonial education created a sense of inferiority in the minds of Indians." Competency Based

(i) How did the Mahatma Gandhi argue that colonial education was harmful to Indians?

Ans. Mahatma Gandhi argued that colonial education made Indians feel inferior to Europeans. It also caused Indians to neglect their own culture and to admire British rule.

(ii) What did Mahatma Gandhi want education to achieve for Indians?

Ans. Mahatma Gandhi wanted education to help Indians recover their dignify and self-respect. He believed that education should be accessible to all Indians, regardless of their caste or social class.

10. Explain Tagore's motive behind setting up Santiniketan.

Ans. Rabindranath Tagore's motive behind setting up Santiniketan was

- He wanted to set-up a school where the child was happy, free, creative and could be able to explore his own thoughts and desires.
- Tagore felt that childhood should not be restricted in the strict schooling system set-up by the Britishers.
- He believed that creative learning could be encouraged only within a natural environment.

Long Answer Type Questions

1. What were the differences between the Orientalists and the Anglicists? Competency Based

Ans. The differences between the Orientalists and the Anglicists were

Orientalists	Anglicists
The Orientalists had a deep knowledge about the languages and culture of Asia. They favoured the development of Sanskrit and Persian language in India.	Anglicists preferred English language and urged that English should be the medium of instruction in the educational institutions.
The Orientalists tried to set-up such institutions that encouraged the study of ancient Indian texts.	Anglicists like TB Macaulay urged that the British Government in India stop promoting Oriental institutions.

Orientalists	Anglicists
The Orientalists translated many Sanskrit and Persian texts into English, set-up the Asiatic Society and started a journal called Asiatick Researches.	Anglicists like Macaulay emphasised that teaching of English could be a way of civilising people, changing their tastes, values and culture.
Orientalists argued that the study of Eastern languages and cultures will also help British administrators to understand India better and govern it more effectively.	Anglicisis argued that the teaching at English will help to spread British values and culture in India.

2. What measures were undertaken by the Company to improve the system of vernacular education?

Ans. The measures undertaken by the Company to improve the system of Vernacular education were

- It appointed a number of government pandits, each in charge of looking after four to five schools. The task of the pandit was to visit the pathshalas and try to improve the standard of teaching.
- Each pandit or teacher was asked to submit periodic reports and take classes according to a regular time-table.
- Teaching was based on textbooks and learning was to be tested through a system of annual examination.
- Students were asked to pay a regular fee, attend regular classes, sit on fixed seats and obey the new rules of discipline.
- The Company established a number of vernacular schools in major towns throughout India.
- The Company developed new vernacular textbooks which cover subjects like science, mathematics, history and literature.

3. A historian was asked to analyse the report of William Adam. Write about the points that should be included in the analysis. **Competency Based**

Ans. Some of the points that should be included in the analysis of the 'report of William Adam' are

- Adam's report highlights the existence of over 1 lakh pathshalas in Bengal and Bihar. There were small institutions with a limited number of students.
- Many pathshalas were established by wealthy individuals, local communities, or individual teachers.
- Adam point out that there was absence of fixed fees, printed materials, benches, etc.
- The report highlights that teaching was mainly oral with gurus deciding what to teach, based on the needs of their students.
- It was very flexible system which accommodate the local needs of rural students like classes were not continued during the harvest season, allowing children to assist in agricultural work.
- There was good socio-economic aspect of this educational system like fees were determined on the basis of parent's income.

4. Why did many Company officials in India want to promote Indian rather than Western learning?

Ans. Many Company officials in India argued that the British ought to promote Indian rather than Western learning because

- They felt that institutions should be set-up to encourage the study of ancient Indian texts and teach Sanskrit and Persian literature and poetry.
- The officials thought that Hindus and Muslims ought to be taught what they were already familiar with and what they valued, not subjects that were unknown to them.
- The officials believed that by introducing these measures, the British could hope to win a place in the hearts of the 'natives' and only then they could expect to be respected by their subjects.
- The officials realised that they needed to understand Indian society and culture in order to govern India effectively.
- The Company officials believed that by promoting Indian learning, they could create a class of Indians who were proud of their culture and were loyal to the British.

Picture Based Questions

1. Look at the picture given below and answer the following questions.

(i) Identify the personality.

Ans. The given picture is of Henry Thomas Colebrooke.

(ii) What do you know about him?

Ans. Henry Thomas Colebrooke was an English Orientalist. He was a scholar of Sanskrit and ancient sacred writings of Hinduism. He had a deep respect for ancient cultures both of India and the West.

2. Look at the picture given below and answer the following questions.

(i) Identify the famous personalities in the above picture.

Ans. (i) In the above picture , Mahatma Gandhi along with Kasturba Gandhi was sitting with Rabindranath Tagore.

(ii) What was the occasion and when it happened?

Ans. In 1940, Mahatma Gandhi and Kasturba Gandhi visited Santiniketan. It was Gandhiji's last meeting with Rabindranath. They had ideological differences, but they had mutual respect for each other.

Case Based Question

1. Read the passage given below and answer the following questions.

In 1854, the Court of Directors of the East India Company in London sent an educational dispat79ch to the Governor-General in India. Issued by Charles Wood, the President of the Board of Control of the Company, it has come to be known as Wood's Despatch. Outlining the educational policy that was to be followed in India, it emphasised once again the practical benefits of system of European learning, as opposed to Oriental knowledge. One of the practical uses the dispatch pointed to was economic. European learning, it said, would enable Indians to recognised the advantages that flow from the expansion of trade and commerce, and make them see the importance of developing the resources of the country. Introducing them to European ways of life, would change their tastes and desires, and create a demand for British goods, for Indian would begin to appreciate and buy things that were produced in Europe.

(i) Who was Charles Wood?

Ans. Charles Wood was the President of the Board of Control of the Company. He is famous for sending a despatch to Lord Dalhousie, which suggested that primary schools must adopt Vernacular languages.

(ii) What was the primary emphasis of Wood's Despatch regarding education in India?

Ans. Wood's Despatch emphasised the practical benefits of European learning over Oriental knowledge for the education system in India.

(iii) According to Wood's Despatch, what was one of the practical uses of European learning in India?

Ans. One of the practical uses of European learning, as pointed out in Wood's Despatch, was its potential economic impact. It was believed that European learning would enable Indians to recognise the benefits of expanding trade and commerce and create a demand for British goods, as Indians would develop a taste for European products.

ASSESSMENT EXERCISE

Multiple Choice Questions (MCQs)

1. A madrasa was set-up in Calcutta in year

(a) 1751 (b) 1781
(c) 1761 (d) 1771

2. The Hindu College was established in

(a) 1781 (b) 1791 (c) 1771 (d) 1751

3. Who among the following Indians strongly reacted against Western education?

(a) Jawaharlal Nehru (b) Rabindranath Tagore
(c) B R Ambedkar (d) None of these

4. Rabindranath Tagore started a school named Shantiniketan in

(a) 1905 (b) 1901 (c) 1911 (d) 1921

Subjective Questions (VSA, SA & LA)

1. Who set-up the Asiatic society of Bengal?

2. Who was Henry Thomas Colebrooke?

3. Madrasas was set-up to promote which langauge?

4. What do you mean by term 'vernacular'?

5. Which types of education system Gandhiji want?

6. Write short note on New Routines of Company after 1854?

7. What are the features of English Education Act of 1835?

8. Explain Wood Despatch and its advantages.

9. Discuss, 'Tagore's Abode of Peace'.

CHAPTER 7

Women, Caste and Reform

In today's world women are respected, they can work, study and even get married when they want. However, this was different 200 years ago as the lives of women were comparatively difficult from what it is now. There were various limitations or restrictions imposed on women. The caste system was also one of the biggest issues during those times. In this chapter, we will learn about various social reforms for the upliftment of women, caste and social reforms and other non-brahman movements.

Two hundred years ago, our society was very different. Most children got married at an early age. Both Hindu and Muslim men could marry more than one wife.

In some parts of the country, **Sati**[1] practice was prevalent in which widow women burnt themselves on the funeral pyre of their husbands.

Women's rights to property were restricted. Most of the women had no access to education.

In most regions, people were divided on the basis of castes. These included **Brahmans** and **Kshatriyas** who considered themselves as upper castes, **Vaishyas** (traders and moneylenders) and **Shudras** (weavers and potters).

The people who were involved in keeping cities and villages clean, were considered at the lowest level. The upper castes considered their work or jobs as 'polluting' and treated them as **untouchable**.

They were not allowed to enter temples, draw water from the wells used by the upper castes, or bathe in ponds where upper castes bathed.

Over the 19th and 20th centuries, these norms and perceptions slowly changed, leading to greater equality and opportunities for women and lower caste individuals.

7.1 Working Towards Change

From the early 19th century, there was development in new forms of communication. Books, newspapers, magazines, leaflets and pamphlets were printed.

Ordinary people could read these, and many of them could write and express their ideas about social, political, economical and religious issues in their own languages.

These led to various reforms or changes in society that were initiated by Indian reformers and reform groups.

Reforms for Changing the Lives of Widows

Raja Rammohun Roy (1772–1833) was an Indian reformer who initiated reforms for changing the lives of widows. He had a good knowledge of Sanskrit, Persian and several other Indian and European languages.

He founded a reform association known as the **Brahmo Sabha** (later known as the **Brahmo Samaj**) in Calcutta.

He wanted to spread the knowledge of Western education in India and bring about greater freedom and equality for women.

He started a campaign against Sati practice. He argued that the practice of widow burning had no sanction in ancient texts. British officials also supported Raja Rammohun and in 1829, Sati was banned.

Ishwarchandra Vidyasagar was another reformer belonging to 19th century who used the ancient texts to suggest that widows could remarry.

By the second half of 19th century, the movement in favour of widow remarriage spread to other parts of the country.

In the Madras Presidency, **Veerasalingam Pantulu** formed an association for widow remarriage and in the North, **Swami Dayanand Saraswati** founded the reform association called **Arya Samaj** which supported widow remarriage. In 1856, a law was passed by the British officials, permitting widow remarriage.

1 **Sati** It literally means virtuous women.

Reforms for Girls Education

Many reformers felt that education for girls was necessary in order to improve the condition of women. Vidyasagar in Calcutta and many other reformers in Bombay set up schools for girls.

Throughout the 19th century, most educated women were taught at home by liberal fathers or husbands. Sometimes women taught themselves.

For example, **Rashsundari Debi** secretly learned to read and write in the light of candles at night. It is because, many people feared that schools would prevent women from doing their domestic duties and girls had to travel through public places in order to reach school.

In aristocratic Muslim households in North India, women learnt to read the Koran in Arabic. Reformers like **Mumtaz Ali** reinterpreted verses from the Koran to support women's education.

The **first Urdu novels** were began to be written from the late 19th century, to encourage women to read about religion and domestic management in a language they understand.

Women Reformers

From the early 20th century, Muslim women like the **Begums of Bhopal** played an important role in promoting education among women. They founded a primary school for girls at Aligarh.

Another women, **Begum Rokeya Sakhawat Hossain** started schools for Muslim girls in Patna and Calcutta.

By the 1880s, Indian women began to enter universities. Many women began to write about the position of women in society.

For example, **Tarabai Shinde** wrote **Stripurushtulna**[2], criticising the social differences between men and women, and **Pandita Ramabai** wrote a book about the miserable lives of upper caste Hindu women.

Pandita Ramabai founded a widows' home at Poona to provide shelter and training to women so that they could be economically independent.

By the end of the 19th century, women wrote books, edited magazines, founded schools and training centres, and set-up women's associations.

From the early 20th century, women formed political **pressure groups** and some of them took part in nationalist and socialist movements.

In 20th century, leaders like Jawaharlal Nehru and Subhas Chandra Bose supported the demand for women's equality and promised **suffrage**[3] for all men and women after India gained independence.

Law against Child Marriage

In 1929, the **Child Marriage Restraint Act** was passed. According to the act, no man below the age of 18 and woman below the age of 16 could marry. Later, these limits were raised to 21 for men and 18 for women.

Try These

1. **How did the caste system not only divide people but also influence their occupations?**
2. **Which organisation was founded by Raja Rammohun Roy?**
3. **Which controversial practice was challenged and abolished by the reformers that was associated with widows?**
4. **Which movement was supported by Swami Dayanand Saraswati?**

7.2 Caste and Social Reform

Some of the social reformers also criticised caste inequalities. To remove these, different steps were taken that were

- Raja Rammohun Roy translated an old Buddhist text that criticised caste.
- The **Prarthana Samaj** followed the tradition of Bhakti that believed in equality of all castes.
- In Bombay, the **Paramhans Mandali** was founded in 1840 to work for the abolition of caste and organise secret meetings where they violated caste restrictions on food and touch.
- Christian missionaries began setting up schools for tribal groups and 'lower' caste children.
- Many poor people from villages, including people from lower castes moved to cities for work, to escape from the oppressive control of upper-caste landlords. Many of them like **Mahar people** who were regarded as untouchable, joined Mahar Regiment in the army.

---

2 **Stripurushtulna** It was a book published by Tarabai Shinde. It means a comparison between women and men.

3 **Suffrage** It refers to the right of citizens to participate in the political process by casting votes in elections.

Demands for Equality and Justice

In the second half of 19th century, Non-Brahman castes in India started organising movements to fight against caste discrimination, and demanded social equality and justice. These included the following

- **Guru Ghasidas** He founded the **Satnami Movement** in Central India. He worked among the leather workers and organised a movement to improve their social status.
- **Haridas Thakur** He belong to **Matua sect** who worked among the low caste Chandala cultivators in Eastern Bengal. He criticised Brahmanical texts that supported the caste system.
- **Shri Narayan Guru** He was a guru from the **Ezhava caste** in Kerala. He proclaimed the ideals of unity of all people. According to him, all human kind belonged to same caste i.e. their is one caste, one religion and one god for humankind.
- **Jyotirao Phule** He was born in 1827. He protested against the Brahman's claim that they were superior to others as they were the Aryans.

  Phule argued that the Aryans were foreigners, who came from outside the subcontinent, and defeated and conquered the original inhabitants of the country.

  According to him, the upper castes had no right to their land and power, and the land belonged to indigenous people i.e. the low castes.

  Phule founded **Satyashodhak Samaj** which promoted caste equality. In 1873, Phule wrote **Gulamgiri** (slavery) and dedicated it to Americans who fought to free black slaves and established a link between the conditions of low-caste people in India and black slaves in America. Phule was also concerned about the condition of upper caste women, the miseries of the labourer, and the humiliation of the low castes.
- **Others** Some other non-caste Brahmans who continued caste reform movement in the 20th century were **Dr. BR Ambedkar** in Western India and **EV Ramaswamy Naicker** in the South.

Movement for Entry in the Temple

Dr. BR Ambedkar was born in Mahar family. As a child, he experienced caste prejudice in everyday life. In school, he was forced to sit in the grounds outside the classroom, not allowed to drink water from the taps which were used by the **upper castes.**

In 1919, he wrote about 'upper caste power in contemporary society'. In 1927, he started a temple entry movement opposing Brahman priests who became angry when the Dalits used water from the temple tank. He led three such movements for temple entry between 1927 and 1935.

The Non-Brahman Movement

The Non-Brahman Movement started in the early 20th century. It was initiated by educated, wealthy and influential non-Brahman castes.

For example, EV Ramaswamy Naicker (Periyar) founded the **Self-Respect Movement**. He believed that all religious authorities considered that the social divisions and inequality are given by God.

He inspired untouchables to achieve social equality. He criticised Hindu scriptures like the Codes of Manu, the *Bhagavad Gita* and the *Ramayana* for establishing the authority of Brahmans over lower castes and the domination of men over women.

However, the movements of lower caste leaders were challenged by orthodox Hindu society. They founded **Sanatan Dharma Sabhas** and the **Bharat Dharma Mahamandal** in the north, and associations like the **Brahman Sabha** in Bengal to support caste distinctions as a basis of Hinduism.

Important Reform Movements

Some important reform movements organised in the 19th century are discussed below

The Brahmo Samaj

It was founded by Raja Rammohun Roy in 1828. It prohibited all forms of **idolatry** and sacrifice. It believed in upanishads, and restrict its members from criticising other religious practices.

It was based upon the ideals of religions, especially of Hinduism and Christianity.

Young Bengal Movement

It was initiated by **Henry Louis Vivian Derozio**, a teacher at Hindu College in the 1820s to promote radical ideas and encouraged his students to question all authority.

His students criticised tradition and custom, demanded education for women and campaigned for the freedom of thought and expression.

The Ramakrishna Mission

Swami Vivekananda established the Ramakrishna Mission to emphasise on the ideal of **salvation** through social service and selfless action. It was named after his Guru Ramakrishna Paramhansa.

He was formerly known as Narendra Nath Dutta, combined the teaching of Sri Ramakrishna with a modern perspective and shared them worldwide.

Swami Vivekananda was the first Indian in modern time, who re-established the importance of the Vedanta philosophy on a global scale.

The Prarthana Samaj

It was established in 1867 at Bombay. It worked to remove caste restrictions, abolish child marriage, remove the ban on widow remarriage and encourage women education.

Its religious meetings were based upon Hindu, Buddhist and Christian texts.

The Veda Samaj

It was established in Madras (Chennai) in 1864. It worked to abolish caste distinctions and promote widow remarriage, women's education, etc.

The Aligarh Movement

It was initiated by **Sayyaid Ahmed Khan** who founded the Mohammedan Anglo-Oriental College, in 1875 at Aligarh, which later became the **Aligarh Muslim University**. The institution offered modern education, including Western science to Muslims.

The Singh Sabha Movement

The first Singh Sabhas were formed at Amritsar in 1873 and at Lahore in 1879. They were reform organisations of the Sikhs.

They promoted education among the Sikhs, often combining modern teachings with Sikh teachings.

Try These

1. **Who set up a school for girls in Maharashtra?**
2. **Who wrote the book Stripurushtulana?**
3. **In which year Paramhans Mandali was founded?**
4. **Which movement was founded for promoting education among the Sikhs?**

WOMEN, CASTE AND REFORM

Working Towards Change

Women Reformers

- Begums of Bhopal founded a primary school for girls at Aligarh.
- Begum Rokeya Sakhawat Hossain started schools for Muslim girls in Patna and Calcutta.
- Pandita Ramabai wrote a book about miserable lives of upper caste Hindu women.

Reforms for Changing the Lives of Widows

- Raja Ram Mohan Roy founded the Brahmo Samaj and supported banning of Sati.
- Ishwarchandra Vidyasagar suggested widow remarriage.
- In Madras Presidency, Veerasalingam Pantulu formed an association for widow remarriage.
- Swami Dayanand Saraswati founded Arya Samaj.

Reforms for Girls Education

- Vidyasagar in Calcutta and many other reformers in Bombay setup schools for girls.
- Reformers like Mumtaz Ali reinterpreted verses from the Quran to support women's education.

Caste and Social Reforms

Demands for Equality and Justice

- Guru Ghasidas founded the Satnami Movement.
- Shri Narayan Guru proclaimed the ideals of unity of all people.
- Jyotirao Phule founded Satyashodhak Samaj.
- BR Ambedkar and EV Ramaswamy Naicker continued caste reform movements in 20th century.

Important Reform Movements

- The Brahmo Samaj (1890)
- Young Bengal Movement (Henry Louis Vivian Derozio)
- The Ramakrishna Mission (Named after Ramakrishna Paramhansa, Swami Vivekananda's Guru)
- The Prarthana Samaj (1867 at Bombay)
- The Veda Samaj (1864 in Madras)
- The Aligarh Movement (Mohammedan Anglo-Oriental College founded by Sayyid Ahmed Khan in 1875)
- The Singh Sabha Movement (leaders established Khalsa College in 1892)

NCERT FOLDER

Covering Intext Questions and Exercises of NCERT

NCERT ON PAGE 79 (ACTIVITY)

Q.1 Can you think of the ways in which social customs and practices were discussed in the pre-printing age when books, newspapers and pamphlets were not readily available?

Ans. In the pre-printing age when books, newspapers and pamphlets were not readily available, people could adopt some methods in which social customs and practices would be discussed.

Some of these methods were

(i) General meetings
(ii) Face to face discussions
(iii) Cultural programmes

NCERT ON PAGE 91 (LET'S IMAGINE)

Q.2 Imagine you are a teacher in the school set-up by Rokeya Hossain. There are 20 girls in your class Write an account of the discussions that might have taken place on any one day in the school.

Ans. An account of the discussion that might have taken place was

I am fortunate enough to impart education to my 20 girls. It is one of the first schools that has been started for all of you. We live in a world where men have more power and sometimes they seem more important, we are brave enough to speak out against unfair traditions and beliefs that hold girls back.

We deserve equal status, we should not be told that we must stay inside or that education will harm us by learning and studying, we become stronger, wiser and able to stand on our own feet. We can face the difficulties of society not by bowing down, but by standing up and fighting for what is right.

EXERCISES

Q.1 What social ideas did the following people support.

(i) Raja Rammohun Roy (ii) Dayanand Saraswati
(iii) Veerasalingam Pantulu (iv) Jyotirao Phule
(v) Pandita Ramabai (vi) Periyar
(vii) Mumtaz Ali
(viii) Ishwarchandra Vidyasagar

Ans. (i) Raja Rammohun Roy spread the awareness about the education of women.

(ii) Dayanand Saraswati was a strong critic of the caste system. He promoted vedic education.

(iii) Veerasalingam Pantulu campaigned against child marriage and encouraged the women's right like widow remarriage and women education.

(iv) Jyotirao Phule was a strong advocate for the rights of the lower castes and Dalits.

(v) Pandita Ramabai was a social reformer who worked for upliftment of women status in India. She established a shelter for widows in Pune.

(vi) Periyar founded Self Respect Movement to fight untouchability. He criticised the Hindu scriptures for establishing the authority of Brahmans over lower castes and the domination of men over women.

(vii) Mumtaz Ali was the first to argue for Muslim women rights. She was associated with the Aligarh Movement which aimed to modernise and reform Islam.

(viii) Ishwarchandra Vidyasagar was a promoter of women's rights and played an important role in passage of Widow Remarriage Act which allowed widows to remarry.

Q.2 State whether True of False.

(i) When the British captured Bengal, they framed many new laws to regulate the rules regarding marriage, adoption, inheritance of property, etc.

Ans. True

(ii) Social reformers had to discard the ancient texts in order to argue for reform in social practices.

Ans. True

(iii) Reformers got full support from all sections of the people of the country.

Ans. False

(iv) The Child Marriage Restraint Act was passed in 1829.

Ans. False

Q.3 How did the knowledge of ancient texts help the reformers promote new laws?

Ans. The reformers tried to improve the status of women in the society using the knowledge of ancient texts in the following ways

- Raja Rammohun Roy pointed out that the practice of widow burning had no sanction in ancient texts.
- Ishwarchandra Vidyasagar used the ancient texts to suggest that widows could remarry.
- Swami Dayanand showed that many social evils of today had no religious sanctions in the Vedas.

Q.4 What were the different reasons people had for not sending girls to school? Diksha

Ans. There have been various reasons for not sending girls to school and reasons varies across cultures, time periods, etc. Some common reasons are

- They feared that schools would take girls away from home and prevent them from doing their domestic duties.
- They felt that girls should stay away from public places. Girls had to travel through public place in order to reach school and this would have a corrupting influence on them.

Q.5 Why were Christian missionaries attacked by many people in the country? Would some people have supported them too? If so, for what reasons?

Ans. Christian missionaries were attacked by many people in our country because people did not support their activities. Further many Hindu nationalists felt that Hindu women were adopting Western ways and this would corrupt Hindu culture and destroy our family values.

Some people had supported the activities of Christian missionaries because

- During the 19th century, Christian missionaries, began setting up schools for tribal groups and 'lower caste children'. This education made them capable to adjust with the changing world.
- Christian missionaries condemned Sati system and child marriage. They set-up many schools for women, where women were trained so that they could support themselves economically.

Q.6 In the British period, what new opportunities opened up for people who came from castes that were regarded as 'low'?

Ans. There were several new opportunities opened up for people who were considered 'low caste' such as

- The poor began leaving their villages to look for jobs that were opening up in the cities. There was work in the factories and jobs in municipalities.
- Drains had to be dug, roads had to be laid, buildings had to be constructed and cities had to be cleaned. Coolies, diggers, carriers, bricklayers, sewage cleaners, sweepers, palanquin bearers, rickshaw pullers were required.
- Some of them also went to work on plantations in Assam, Mauritius, Trinidad and Indonesia.
- Many of them like Mahar people who were regarded as untouchable, joined Mahar Regiment in the army.

Q.7 How did Jyotirao, the reformer, justify his criticism of caste inequality in society?

Ans. The founder of Satyashodhak Samaj, Jyotirao Phule was low-caste leader. He criticised the caste inequality in our society in the following ways

- He opposed the idea that Brahmans were superior just because they were Aryans. He argued that Aryans were foreigners, who came from outside the sub-continent and defeated and subjugated the original inhabitants of our country. These native people had lived here before the coming of Aryans.
- He claimed that the upper castes had no right to their land and power, in reality the land belonged to the natives of the country.
- He proposed that Shudras (labouring castes) and Ati Shudras (untouchables) should unite to challenge caste discrimination.

Q.8 Why did Phule dedicate his book *Gulamgiri* to the American Movement to free slaves?

Ans. In 1873, Jyotirao Phule wrote a book 'Gulamgiri', meaning slavery. Phule dedicated his book to all those Americans who had fought to free slaves. By dedicating his books to the American Movement, he tried to establish a link between the conditions of the lower castes of India and the black slaves in America.

Q.9 What did Ambedkar want to achieve through the Temple Entry Movement?

Ans. Ambedkar led three movements for temple entry between 1927 and 1935. Through these movements, he wanted to make everyone see the power of caste prejudice within society as Brahman priests were outraged when the Dalits used water from the temple tank.

Q.10 Why were Jyotirao Phule and Ramaswamy Naicker critical of the National Movement? Did their criticism help the national struggle in any way?

Ans. Jyotirao Phule was critical of the anti-colonial nationalism that was preached by upper-castes leaders. He urged that the unity between high and low castes in our society could only make progress.

Ramaswamy Naicker criticised the National Movement when as a member of the Congress, he attended a feast organised by the nationalists. He found that the seating arrangement there followed caste distinctions, i.e. the lower castes were made to sit at a distance from the upper castes.

Yes, their ideas were respected and helped to strengthen the national struggle. The forceful speeches, writings and movements of lower caste leaders led to rethinking and some self-criticism among upper caste nationalist leaders.

REVIEW EXERCISE

Including Competency Based Questions

Part I

Multiple Choice Questions (MCQs)

1. Widow Remarriage Act was passed in the year

(a) 1826 (b) 1846
(c) 1856 (d) 1876

2. Satyashodhak Samaj was founded by which among the following reformers? Diksha

(a) Periyar (b) Mumtaz Ali
(c) Jyotirao Phule (d) Dr BR Ambedkar

3. What were peasants and artisans were referred to in the early 19th century?

(a) Vaishyas (b) Shudras
(c) Untouchables (d) Kshatriyas

4. Ishwarchandra Vidyasagar supported which of the following social causes? Diksha

(a) Girl education (b) Caste system
(c) Widow remarriage (d) Sati custom

5. The first Urdu novels began to be written from

(a) the late 19th century
(b) the late 18th century
(c) the late 16th century
(d) the late 17th century

6. Name the educationist who started schools for Muslim girls in Patna and Calcutta.

Or **Which woman reformer started girls schools in Patna and Calcutta?** Diksha

(a) Jyotirao Phule
(b) Rabindranath Tagore
(c) Begum Rokeya Sakhawat Hossain
(d) Mumtaz Ali

7. A widow's home was established at Poona by

(a) Tarabai Shinde
(b) Pandita Ramabai
(c) Bal Gangadhar Tilak
(d) Begum Rokeya Sakhawat Hossain

8. Name the national leader(s) who lent support to demand for greater equality and freedom for women.

(a) Jawaharlal Nehru
(b) Shri Narayan Guru
(c) Subhash Chandra Bose
(d) Both (a) and (c)

9. EV Ramaswamy was also known by the name

(a) Phule (b) Periyar
(c) Vidyasagar (d) Babasaheb

10. Which of the following was not a goal of the Prarthana Samaj?

(a) Abolishing caste restrictions
(b) Promoting education for women
(c) Both (a) and (b)
(d) Enacting land reforms

11. Identify the movement with the help of given information. Competency Based

I. The Mohammedan Anglo-Oriented College, founded by Sayyid Ahmed Khan 1875.
II. Mohammedan Anglo-Oriented College offered Modern education, including Western science to Muslims.

Options

(a) Khilafat Movement (b) Temple Entry Movement
(c) Self-Respect Movement (d) The Aligarh Movement

12. Identify the correct option that describes about the given statements. Competency Based

I. He founded a reform association known as the Brahmo Sabha.
II. He began a campaign against the practice of Sati.
III. He was given the title of Raja by Akbar II.

Options

(a) Raja Rammohun Roy (b) Ishwar Chandra Vidyasagar
(c) Dayanand Saraswati (d) Narayana Guru

13. Which of the following statements is/are correct?

I. Most of the women had access to education, two hundred years ago.
II. Brahmo Sabha was established by Mahatma Gandhi.

Codes

(a) Only I (b) Only II (c) I and II (d) None of these

14. Which of the following statements is/are correct?

I. Begum Rukeya Sakhawat Hossain started school for Muslim girls in Patna and Calcutta.
II. Jyotirao Phule started schools for girls in Assam.

Codes

(a) Only I (b) Only II (c) I and II (d) None of these

15. Arrange the following according to their year of happening.

I. Temple Entry Movement
II. Sati was banned

III. Veda Samaj

IV. Mohammaden Anglo-Oriental College

Codes

(a) I, IV, III, II (b) II, III, IV, I

(c) I, II, III, IV (d) III, IV, I, II

16. Arrange the following in the correct sequence in chronological order.

I. The Arya Samaj

II. Child Marriage Restraint Act

III. Widow Remarriage Act

IV. Prarthana Samaj

Codes

(a) III, I, IV, II (b) I, II, IV, III (c) III, IV, I, II (d) III, IV, II, I

Answers

1. (c)	**2.** (c)	**3.** (b)	**4.** (c)	**5.** (a)
6. (c)	**7.** (b)	**8.** (d)	**9.** (b)	**10.** (d)
11. (d)	**12.** (a)	**13.** (d)	**14.** (a)	**15.** (b)
16. (c)				

Match the Following

1.

List I	List II
A. The Brahmo Samaj	1. Madras
B. The Singh Sabha Movement	2. Calcutta
C. Veda Samaj	3. Bombay
D. The Prarthana Samaj	4. Amritsar

Codes

	A	B	C	D		A	B	C	D
(a)	2	4	1	3	(b)	1	2	3	4
(c)	3	2	4	1	(d)	4	3	2	1

2.

List I	List II
A. Periyar	1. Singha Sabha Movement
B. Pandit Ramabai	2. Widow's Home
C. Swami Vivekananda	3. Self Respect Movement
D. Khalsa College	4. World Parliament of Religion

Codes

	A	B	C	D		A	B	C	D
(a)	1	2	3	4	(b)	3	2	4	1
(c)	2	4	3	1	(d)	3	1	4	2

Ans. 1. (a) 2. (b)

Assertion-Reason

1. Assertion (A) In 1873, Jyotirao Phule wrote a book named Gulamgiri.

Reason (R) In 1927, Ambedkar started a Temple Entry Movement, in which his Mahar caste followers participated.

Codes

(a) Both A and R are true and R is the correct explanation of A

(b) Both A and R are the true, but R is not the correct explanation of A

(c) A is true, but R is false

(d) A is false, but R is true

2. Assertion (A) Ishwarchandra Vidyasagar used ancient text to suggest that widows could remarry.

Reason (R) His suggestions were adopted by the British officials and a law was passed, permitting widows remarriage in 1856.

Codes

(a) Both A and R are true and R is the correct explanation of A

(b) Both A and R are the true, but R is not the correct explanation of A

(c) A is true, but R is false

(d) A is false, but R is true

Ans. 1. (b) Both A and R are the true, but R is not the correct explanation of A

2. (a) Both A and R are true and R is the correct explanation of A

Fill in the Blanks

1. Tarabai Shinde wrote a book named ....
2. The Satnami Movement was founded by .... who belonged to a low caste family.
3. The Prarthana Samaj adhered to the tradition of ....
4. Ambedkar was born into a .... family.
5. Brahmo Sabha was later known as ....
6. In aristocratic Muslim household in North India, women learnt to read the .... in Arabic.

Ans. 1. Stripurushtulna 2. Ghasidas 3. bhakti 4. Mahar 5. Brahmo Samaj 6. Koran

True/False

1. Raja Ram Mohan Roy founded the Arya Samaj in 1875.
2. The Begums of Bhopal started schools for Muslim girls in Patna.
3. Pandita Ramabai was a great scholar of Sanskrit and she founded a widow's home at Poona.
4. Rashsundari Devi secretly learned to read and write in the flickering light of candles at night.
5. The Arya Samaj was an organisation that attempted to reform Hinduism.

Ans. 1. False 2. False 3. True 4. True 5. True

Picture Based Questions

1. Who was the reformer in the given picture?

(a) Periyar (b) Jyotirao Phule
(c) Swami Vivekananda (d) Raja Rammohun Roy

2. Who was the famous personality in the given picture?

(a) Swami Vivekananda (b) Swami Dayanand Saraswati
(c) Raja Rammohun Roy (d) Jyotirao Phule

Ans. 1. (d) Raja Rammohun Roy
2. (b) Swami Dayanand Saraswati

Case Based Question

1. Read the passage given below and answer the following questions.

The new demands in the towns increased the requirement of the labourers. Drains had to be dug, roads laid, buildings constructed and cities cleaned. This required coolies, diggers, carriers, bricklayers, sewage cleaners, sweepers, palanquin bearers, rickshaw pullers. Where did this labour come from? The poor from the villages and small towns, many of them from low castes, began moving to the cities where there was a new demand for labour. Some also went to work in plantations in Assam, Mauritius, Trinidad and Indonesia. Work in the new locations was often very hard. But the poor people from low castes, saw this as an opportunity to get away from the oppressive hold that upper-caste land owners exercised over their lives and the daily humiliation they suffered.

(i) Why did people from the low caste moved to the cities?
(a) There was a demand for labour
(b) To get rid of humiliation
(c) To get away from oppressive upper caste landowners.
(d) All of the above

(ii) Where did the people come from for the jobs like coolies, diggers, carriers, bricklayers, sewage cleaners, sweepers, palanquin bearers, rickshaw pullers?
(a) People from cities
(b) People who were reformers
(c) People from villages and small towns
(d) Women who were widows

(iii) Name the plantations and places where people went to work.
(a) Assam, Mauritius, Trinidad and Indonesia.
(b) Assam, Awadh and Nagpur
(c) Mauritius, Nagpur and Awadh
(d) Indonesia, Awadh and Nagpur

(iv) Why were the labours needed in the city?
I. To dig the drains
II. To laid the roads
III. To construct the buildings.
IV. For plantation

Codes
(a) I, III, IV (b) I, III, IV
(c) II, III, IV (d) I, II, III

Ans. (i) (d) All of the above
(ii) (c) People from villages and small towns
(iii) (a) Assam, Mauritius, Trinidad and Indonesia.
(iv) (d) I, II, III

Part II

Very Short Answer Type Questions

1. Who are considered as upper castes in our society?

Ans. Brahmans and Kshatriyas are considered as upper castes in our society.

2. Name the founder of Arya Samaj.

Ans. Swami Dayanand Saraswati founded the reform association of Arya Samaj.

3. Who was Mumtaz Ali?

Ans. Mumtaz Ali was a social reformer who reinterpreted verses from the Koran to argue for the education of women.

4. Name the founder of Satnami Movement in Central India.

Ans. The Satnami Movement in Central India was founded by Ghasidas, who came from a low caste.

5. Who were Aryans according to Jyotirao Phule?

Ans. According to Jyotirao Phule, the Aryans were foreigners, who came from outside the sub-continent, and defeated and subjugated the original inhabitants of the country.

6. What was the Satyashodhak Samaj? Who founded it?

Ans. The Satyashodhak Samaj was an association that propagated class equality. It was founded by Jyotirao Phule.

7. When did Dr BR Ambedkar start temple entry movement?

Ans. Dr BR Ambedkar started temple entry movement in 1927 and led three such movements between 1927 and 1935.

8. Name the Hindu scriptures which were criticised by Periyar.

Ans. Periyar was an outspoken critic of Hindu scriptures, especially the Codes of Manu, the ancient lawgiver, and the Bhagavad Gita and the Ramayana.

9. Name some orthodox Hindu associations.

Ans. Some orthodox Hindu associations were Sanatan Dharma Sabhas, Bharat Dharma Mahamandal and Brahman Sabha.

10. How did social reformers bring changes in society?

Ans. Social reformers brought changes in society by persuading people to give up old practices and adopt a new way of life.

11. What langauges did Raja Rammohun Roy well versed in?

Ans. Raja Rammohun Roy was well versed in Sanskrit, Persian and several other Indian and European languages.

12. When did Khalsa College of Amritsar established?

Ans. Khalsa College of Amritsar was established in 1892 by the leaders of the Singh Sabha Movement.

13. Why people like Raja Rammohun Roy were called reformers ? Diksha

Ans. People like Raja Rammohun Roy were called reformers because they dedicated their lives to fight against harmful social practices and advocating for positive change in Indian society during the 18th and 19th centuries.

14. Name one of the lower castes of Gujarat who work for the upper caste.

Ans. Dublas was one of the lower castes of the Gujarat who work for the upper castes. They cultivated the fields of upper caste landowners and also worked at landlord's house.

15. Name the girl's school which provided girls with the kind of learning that was usual for boys in the 19th century.

Ans. The Hindu Mahila Vidyalaya was one of the first institutions to provide girls with the kind of learning that was usual for boys in the 19th century.

16. When was Brahmo Samaj formed and who was its main leader? Diksha

Ans. Brahmo Samaj was formed in 1830 and Keshab Chandra Sen was one of its main leaders.

Short Answer Type Questions

1. Write about the contribution of Raja Rammohun Roy to end the practice of Sati.

Ans. Raja Rammohun Roy was deeply moved by the conditions of widows in our society. He began a campaign against the practice of Sati.

He tried to prove that the practice of widow burning had no mention in ancient texts. Many Britishers supported Raja Rammohun. As a result of his contribution, in 1829, the practice of Sati was banned by the Governor of Bengal William Bentinck.

2. Describe the role played by Muslim women in promoting education among women.

Ans. From the early 20th century, some Muslim women played a significant role in promoting education among women. Begums of Bhopal founded a primary school for girls at Aligarh.

A leading feminist writer and social worker Begum Rokeya Sakhawat Hossain started schools for Muslim girls in Patna and Calcutta. Begum Rokeya criticised the conservative ideas of the religious leaders which were responsible for the inferior place of women in society.

4. Write the short note on the work of women reformer Pandita Ramabai.

Ans. Pandita Ramabai was a great scholar of Sanskrit and a pioneer or women's education in India. She was a strong critic of the Hindu caste system and the oppression of women within it.

Ramabai was determined to improve the lives of Hindu women. In 1889, she founded the Sharada Sadan, a widow's home in Poona. The Sharada Sadan provided shelter and education to widows who had been treated badly by their husband's relatives. Women at the Sharada Sadan were trained in a variety of skills, including swing, typing and teaching. This enabled them to support themselves economically and live independent lives.

5. Write a short note on Ramakrishna Mission.

Ans. Ramakrishna Mission was founded by Ramakrishna's chief disciple Swami Vivekananda in 1897. It is an organisation which forms the core of worldwide spiritual movement known as the Ramakrishna Movement or Vedanta Movement.

The mission conducts extensive work in healthcare, disaster relief, rural management, tribal welfare, elementary and higher education and culture.

6. Write a short note on Singh Sabha Movement.

Ans. The Singh Sabha Movement was a Sikh movement, aimed at the revival of the Sikh Guru's teachings, the production of religious literature in the Punjabi language using the Gurumukhi script and a campaign to increase literacy.

The first Singh Sabhas were formed at Amritsar in 1873 and at Lahore in 1879. The Sabhas promoted education among the Sikhs by combining modern instruction with Sikh teachings. It tried to abolish superstitions, caste distinctions and practices seen as non-Sikh from the Sikh religion and its practices.

7. Who was known as Periyar? Why was he famous?

Ans. EV Ramaswamy was known as Periyar. He was a prominent social reformer and politician of South India. He was famous for fight against caste discrimination and untouchability. He started Self Respect Movement or Dravidian Movement for demanding equal rights for the untouchables and women. He propagated the principles of nationalism, self-respect, women's rights and eradication of caste. He also opposed the dominance of the Brahmin caste and North Indian influence in South Indian society and politics.

8. Who was Keshub Chandra Sen? What was done by the Brahmo Samaj after 1830?

Ans. Keshub Chandra Sen was a social reformer who attempted to incorporate Christian theology within the framework of Hindu thought. He became a member of Brahmo Samaj in 1856, but founded his own breakaway 'Brahmo Samaj of India' in 1866.

Brahmo Samaj was founded by Keshub Chandra Sen in 1830. The Brahmo Samaj literally denotes community (Samaj) of men who worship Brahman, the highest reality. Brahmo Samaj reflected the ideas of Bengal Renaissance in all fields of social reforms, including abolition of caste system, dowry system, emancipation of women and improving the educational system especially for women, etc.

9. In some parts of the country, widows were praised if they choose death by burning themselves on the funeral pyre of their husbands. Competency Based

(i) What were the women called who choose death by burning themselves on the funeral pyre of their husbands? What were the thoughts of advocate of sati on women?

Ans. Women who choose death by burning themselves on the funeral pyre of their husbands were called Sati. Advocates of Sati often held traditional and patriarchal views on women's roles in society. Some proponents believed that Sati was a virtuous act and a demonstration of the widow's dedication, love and loyalty to her deceased husband. They saw it as a woman's duty to follow her husband into the afterlife and the act was sometimes glorified as a symbol of ultimate sacrifice.

(ii) What were the thoughts of opponent of sati on women?

Ans. Opponents of Sati believed it was a cruel and oppressive practice, denying women their right to life and freedom. They argued that women should not be forced into self-immolation, emphasising the importance of women's rights, dignity, and the need to protect them from societal pressure and coercion. Abolishing Sati was seen as a crucial step towards promoting gender equality and ensuring the well-being of women.

Long Answer Type Questions

1. What was the condition of women in 19th century?

Ans. The condition of women in the 19th century varied significantly depending on their location, social class and cultural context.

The condition of women was as follows

- Women were married at an early age.
- Women were forced to burn themselves on the funeral pyre of their husbands. Women who died in this manner were called Sati which meant virtuous women.
- Women's rights to property were also restricted.
- Women had virtually no access to education. In many parts of the country, people believed that if a woman was educated, she would become a widow.

2. Discuss the work and contribution of Ishwarchandra Vidyasagar for the upliftment of women.

Ans. Ishwarchandra Vidyasagar was a social reformer, philosopher, academician, philanthropist and a key figure of the Bengal Renaissance.

His works and contribution for the upliftment of women were as follows

- He advocated for the education of women, because he believed that it was our primary duty to educate a woman as she was the real teacher of her child. He opened and ran many schools for girls at his own expense.
- He strongly protested against polygamy and child marriage.
- It was due to his effort, the Hindu Widow Remarriage Act, 1856 was passed which allowed the widows to remarriage. He had also opposed the sati system.
- He worked endlessly to provide equal education to all men and women irrespective of their caste, religion and gender. He believed that the status of women and all kinds of injustice and inequalities that they face could be changed only through education.

3. Reformers in the 19th century felt the changes or reforms were necessary in society, and unjust practices needed to be done away with. Explain these reforms. Competency Based

Ans. Some of the reforms in the 19th century were

Reforms for Changing the Lives of Widows

Raja Rammohun Roy (1772–1833) was an Indian reformer who initiated reforms for changing the lives of widows. He founded a reform association known as the Brahmo Sabha (later known as the Brahmo Samaj) in Calcutta.

He started a campaign against Sati practice. He argued that the practice of widow burning had no sanction in ancient texts. British officials supported also Raja Rammohun's and in 1829, Sati was banned.

Ishwarchandra Vidyasagar was another reformer belonging to 19th century who used the ancient texts to suggest that widows could remarry.

By the second half of 19th century, the movement in favour of widow remarriage spread to other parts of the country. In the Madras Presidency, Veerasalingam Pantulu formed an association for widow remarriage and in the North, Swami Dayanand Saraswati founded the reform association called Arya Samaj which supported widow remarriage. In 1856, a law was passed by the British officials, permitting widow remarriage.

Reforms for Girls Education

Vidyasagar in Calcutta and many other reformers in Bombay set up schools for girls. Reformers like Mumtaz Ali reinterpreted verses from the Koran to support women's education.

The first Urdu novels were began to be written from the late 19th century, to encourage women to read about religion and domestic management in a language they understand.

4. Mention the important factors which contributed to the rise of the social reforms movements in India.

Ans. The two important factors which contributed to the rise of the social reforms movements in India were as follows

- The conditions of women in our society was miserable. Social evils like Sati system, purdah system, child marriage, illiteracy, strict rules for widows were present at that time.
- Caste prejudice and injustice due to casteism were prevalent among people in the society. The people of high castes exploited the people of low castes.
- The upper castes treated many of the lower castes as untouchables.

5. In the early twentieth-century the non-Brahman Movement started. The initiative came from those non-Brahman castes that had acquired access to education, wealth and influence.

Can you explain the origin and objectives of the non-Brahman Movement? How did access to education wealth and influence contribute to the initiation and goals of this movement? Competency Based

Ans. The Non-Brahman Movement was originated as the response to the deeply rooted caste-based hierarchies and discrimination spreaded in Indian society.

The aims or objectives of non-Brahman Movement were

- It aimed to challenge the Brahman caste's monopoly on power, education and resources.
- The movement aimed to promote social justice and equality by challenging the rigidity of the caste system.
- It sought to address economic indifferences by advocating for a more equitable distribution of resource and opportunities in Indian society.
- It played a significant role in reshaping the social and political landscape of India.
- Access to education empowered non-Brahman leaders to raise awareness about their injustice and mobilise support for their cause. Accumulation of wealth and influence allowed these leaders to actively participate in social and political reforms.

Case Based Questions

1. Read the passage given below and answer the following questions.

'We First Tie Them Down to the Pile'

Raja Rammohun Roy published many pamphlets to spread his ideas. Some of these were written as a dialogue between the advocate and critic of a traditional practice. Here is one such dialogue on sati

Advocate of Sati

Women are by nature of inferior understanding, without resolution, unworthy of trust. Many of them, on the death of their husbands, become desirous of accompanying them; but to remove every chance of their trying to escape from the blazing fire, in burning them we first tie them down to the pile.

Opponent of Sati

When did you ever afford them a fair opportunity of exhibiting their natural capacity? How then can you accuse them of want of understanding? If, after instruction in knowledge and wisdom, a person cannot comprehend or retain what has been taught him, we may consider him as deficient; but if you do not educate women how can you see them as inferior.

This argument was taking place more than 175 years ago.

Write down the different arguments you may have heard around you on the worth of women. In what ways have the views changed?

Ans. Some arguments I may have heard on the worth of women are

- Spending time on education can prevent women from doing their domestic duties.
- Travelling through public places to reach educational institution would corrupt the women.
- If a woman was educated, she would become a widow.
- Widow's sight regarded as a bad omen, thus no permission was given to widows to attend auspicious functions.

These views have been changed in the following ways

- Equal educational opportunities are given to women with men.
- Right to vote and right to property are given to women.
- Law has been made which prescribes equal wages for equal work.
- Women can participate in politics and administration and are entitled to do any type of job in every sphere of life.

2. Read the passage given below and answer the following questions.

No Place Inside the Classroom

In the Bombay Presidency, as late as 1829, untouchables were not allowed into even government schools. When some of them pressed hard for that right, they were allowed to sit on the veranda outside the classroom and listen to the lessons, without "polluting" the room where upper caste boys were taught.

(i) Imagine that you are one of the students sitting in the school veranda and listening to the lessons. What kind of questions would be rising in your mind?

Ans. Following are some questions that arise in my mind when I was allowed to sit on the veranda outside the classroom.

- How can we pollute the classroom with our humble presence?
- Why are we considered inferiors to others?
- How do the upper castes deprive us of our Right to Education?

(ii) Some people thought this situation was better than the total lack of education for untouchable people. Would you agree with this view?

Ans. I do not agree with this view. The Right to Education is reflected in international law in Article 26 of the Universal Declaration of Human Rights.

The fulfilment of the Right to Education can be assessed using the 4 'As' frame work which are Availability, Accessibility, Acceptability and Adaptibility.

According to Accessibility, all children should have equal access to school services regardless of gender, race, religion, ethnicity or socio-economic status.

Thus, it is not right to allow the untouchable to sit on the veranda outside the classroom. They must fight for their own right.

3. Read the passage given below and answer the following questions.

Me Here and You Over There

Phule was also critical of the anti-colonial nationalism that was preached by upper-caste leaders. He wrote:

The Brahmans have hidden away the sword of their religion which has cut the throat of the peoples' prosperity and now go about posing as great patriots of their country. They give this advice to our Shudra, Muslim and Parsi youth that unless we put away all quarrelling amongst ourselves about the divisions between high and low in our country and come together, our country will never make any progress. It will be unity to serve their purposes and then it will be me here and you over there again.

What do you think Jyotirao Phule meant by 'me here and you over there again'?

Ans. Jyotirao Phule believed that though the upper caste leaders were then asking people all over the country (Shudra, Muslim, Parsi, etc) for fighting the British, once the British had left, they would continue with their oppressive caste politics, thereby causing divisions amongst the very people they were trying to unite.

He believed that the upper castes only wishes for unity to serve their purposes, and once the purposes had been served, the divisions would creep in again. Thus, Phule said, 'then it will be me here and you over there again'.

4. Read the passage given below and answer the following questions.

Periyar on Women Periyar Wrote

Only with the arrival of words such as Thara Mukurtham, our women had become puppets in the hands of their husbands we ended up with such fathers who advise their daughters ... that they had been gifted away to their husbands and they belong to their husband's place. This is the result of our association with Sanskrit.

Why does caste remain such a controversial issue today? What do you think was the most important movement against caste in colonial times?

Ans. Political leaders and social reformers like Jyotirao Phule, Gandhiji, BR Ambedkar and EV Ramaswamy Naicker advocated and worked to establish a society in which caste inequalities are absent. Partly due to their efforts and partly due to other socio-economic changes, caste and caste system in modern India have undergone great changes.

But these assertions did not go unchallenged. Orthodox Hindu society also reacted by founding Sanatan Dharma Sabhas, Bharat Dharma Mahamandal, Brahman Sabha, etc. The objective of these associations was to uphold caste distinctions as a cornerstone of Hinduism and show how this was supported by the scriptures.

Thus, debates and struggles over caste continued beyond the British period and still remain a controversial issue today.

I think 'The Temple Entry Movement' started by BR Ambedkar was the most important movement against caste in colonial times. Ambedkar led three such movements for temple entry between 1927 and 1935.

Picture Based Question

1. Look at the given picture and answer the following questions.

Painting 1

Painting 2

(i) Name the artist of painting 1 and 2.

Ans. Balthazar Solvyn is the artist of painting 1 and Rembrandt Peale is the **artist** of painting 2.

(ii) With the efforts of several reformers in which year Sati practice was abolished?

Ans. Sati practiced was abolished in 1829.

(iii) As seen in Painting 1 is practice of Sati. Who campaigned against the practice of Sati?

Ans. Raja Rammohun Roy campaigned against the practice of Sati.

ASSESSMENT EXERCISE

Multiple Choice Questions (MCQs)

1. Brahmo Samaj was founded in the year
(a) 1830 (b) 1828
(c) 1826 (d) 1929

2. A law relating to Widow Remarriage Act passed in a year
(a) 1855 (b) 1856 (c) 1854 (d) 1857

3. Begum Rokeya Sakhawat Hossain started school for Muslims girls in
(a) Patna and Calcutta (b) Patna and UP
(c) Patna and Gujarat (d) Patna and Kashmir

Subjective Questions (VSA, SA & LA)

1. Name the Guru of Swami Vivekananda.

2. Name the Begum of Bhopal who played a significant role in promoting education among women.

3. Who founded the Widow's Home at Poona?

4. How Raja Rammohun Roy worked for widows?

5. What do you mean by Gulamgiri? Explain.

6. Why education for girls is necessary? Discuss.

7. Give a brief description of the Non-Brahman Movement.

The Making of the National Movement : 1870s-1947

CHAPTER 8

The national movement of India played a significant role in the independence of the country. The commencement of the national movement started in the late 19th and early 20th century, and it was a process that took several years to become successful. In this chapter, we will learn about the emergence of nationalism, birth of INC (Indian National Congress), the growth of mass nationalism, partition and independence.

8.1 The Emergence of Nationalism

The British exercised control over the resources of India and the lives of its people for many years. With the formation of political associations after 1850, an awareness emerged among Indians that the British control had to end to make India the country for Indians.

After 1850, many political associations were formed, especially the associations formed in the 1870s and 1880s. Most of these were led by English educated professionals.

Some of the important associations were

- Poona Sarvajanik Sabha
- The Indian Association
- The Madras Mahajan Sabha
- The Bombay Presidency Association
- The Indian National Congress

Many of these associations functioned in specific parts of the country, but their goals were similar to the goals of the people of India. They worked with the idea that people of India should be **sovereign**[1], i.e. people should be empowered to take decisions regarding their affairs.

In 1870s and 1880s, the dissatisfaction with British rule among India intensified. In 1878 two acts were passed by the British. These were

(i) **Arms Act** This act disallowed Indians from possessing arms.

(iii) **Vernacular Press Act** This act empowered the government to take over the assets of newspapers including their printing presses, if the newspaper published anything **objectionable**.

In 1883, the government tried to introduce Ilbert Bill. This made provisions for trial of British or European persons by Indians, and tried to bring equality between British and Indian judges in the country.

However, the **Britishers** opposed the bill and forced the government to withdraw it. Thus, a need for an all India organisation of educated Indians arose.

The Indian National Congress

The Indian National Congress was established in 1885 at Bombay when 72 delegates from all over the country met at Bombay in December 1885.

The early leaders of the Indian National Congress mainly belonged to Bombay and Calcutta. Some of the important leaders were

- Dadabhai Naoroji
- Badruddin Tyabji
- Surendra Nath Banerji
- S Subramania Iyer
- Pherozeshah Mehta
- WC Bonnerji
- Romesh Chandra Dutt

AO Hume, a retired British official, played a significant role in bringing Indians from the various regions together.

A Nation in the Making

In the early years, the Congress was **moderate** in its objectives and methods as follows

- It demanded a greater role for Indians in the government and administration. It wanted better representation of Indians in the **Legislative Councils**[2].
- It made a demand for civil service examinations to be held in India, so that Indians could be place in high positions in the government.

1 **Sovereign** It refers to the capacity to act independently without outside interference.
2 **Legislative Council** It is an appointed or elected body of people with an administrative, advisory or representative function.

- It demanded for the separation of Judiciary and Executive, the **repeal**[3] of the Arms Act, and the freedom of speech and expression.

The early Congress also raised a number of economic issues like increase in the land revenue which had affected peasants and zamindars, and exports of grains to Europe which had created food shortages. So, the early Congress made the following economic demands

- It demanded reduction in revenue and military expenditure, and alloting more funds for irrigation.
- It passed various resolutions on the salt tax, treatment of Indian labourers abroad and the suffering of forest dwellers.

The moderate leaders wanted to develop public awareness about the unjust nature of British rule, through writing articles and delivering speeches.

They believed that the British had respect for the ideals of freedom and justice, so they would accept the just demands of Indians.

Freedom is Our Birthright

By the 1890s, many leaders in Bengal, Maharashtra and Punjab, like Bepin Chandra Pal, Bal Gangadhar Tilak and Lala Lajpat Rai began to criticise the political style of Congress and moderate leaders.

They emphasised on more radical objectives and methods. They emphasised that people must rely on their own strength, not on the 'good' intentions of the government and people must fight for **Swaraj**.

Tilak raised the slogan, that 'Freedom is my birthright and I shall have it'.

Partition of Bengal

In 1905, **Viceroy Lord Curzon** partitioned Bengal, which was the biggest province of British India at that time and included Bihar and parts of Orissa.

The British separated East Bengal and merged it with Assam.

For partition of Bengal, the British argued that it was divided for administrative convenience. However, the main motives of the British were to reduce the influence of Bengal politicians and to split the Bengali people.

The partition of Bengal enraged people all over India. Both the sections of the Congress, the Moderates and the Radicals, opposed the partition. Large public meetings and demonstrations were organised and new methods of mass protest developed.

The struggle against the partition of Bengal came to be known as the **Swadeshi Movement**. It was strongest in Bengal and known as **Vandemataram Movement** in deltaic Andhra.

The main aims of Swadeshi Movement were

- Oppose the British rule.
- Encourage the ideas of self-help.
- Encourage Swadeshi enterprise, national education and use of Indian languages.

During Swadeshi movement, the radicals advocated mass mobilisation and boycott of British institutions and goods, in order to fight for swaraj. Some individuals suggested **revolutionary violence**[4] to overthrow British rule.

Developments in Early 20th century

In the early 20th century, several developments were made which were

- A group of Muslim landlords and nawabs formed the **All India Muslim League** at Dacca in 1906. It supported the partition of Bengal and demanded for a separate electorate which was accepted by the government in 1909.
- The **Congress split in 1907** into two groups and was dominated by the moderates. The two groups reunited in December 1915.
- In 1916, the Congress and the Muslim league signed the historical **Lucknow Pact** and decided together to work for representive government in the country.

Try These

1. **Write the name of two importance political associations that were formed after 1850.**
2. **Which groups supported the partition of Bengal?**
3. **What was conceded by the government in response to the All India Muslim League's demand in 1909?**
4. **Why was the Lucknow Pact signed?**

3 **Repeal** It means to officially end the validity of something such as a law.

4 **Revolutionary Violence** It refers to the use of violence to make a radical change within society.

8.2 The Growth of Mass Nationalism

After 1919, the struggle against British rule gradually became a mass movement involving peasants, tribals, students, women, factory workers and certain business groups.

The First World War changed the economic and political situation in India. There was a huge rise in defence expenditure of government of India and in return, the government increase taxes.

However, business groups earned large profits from the war because it increased the demand for industrial goods and decline of imports from other countries into India. Thus, Indian industries expanded during the war, and the business groups began to demand more opportunities for development.

During the war, many people from the villages were forced to serve in the British army. A large number of soldiers were sent to serve abroad. They were exploited by the colonial powers and many of them returned after the war with a desire to oppose colonial rule in India.

In 1917, a revolution took place in Russia. The news about peasants' and workers' struggles in this revolution and ideas of **socialism**[5] spread widely, and inspired the Indian nationalists.

The Advent of Mahatma Gandhi

Mahatma Gandhi came to India in 1915 from South Africa. He was already a respected leader because of his movements against racial restrictions in South Africa,

Mahatma Gandhi spent his first year in India by travelling throughout the country and understanding the people, their needs and the overall situation.

He participated in local movements in **Champaran, Kheda** and **Ahmedabad** where he came into contact with Rajendra Prasad and Vallabhbhai Patel. In 1918, he led a successful mill workers strike.

The Rowlatt Satyagraha

The Rowlatt Act was passed in 1919. The act restricted the fundamental rights like the freedom of expression and strengthened the powers of police.

Gandhiji gave a call for Satyagraha against the Rowlatt Act. He asked the Indian people to observe 6th April, 1919 as a day of non-violent opposition to the Rowlatt Act, as a day of 'humiliation and prayer', and organise hartal (strike). **Satyagraha Sabhas** were set up to launch the Satyagraha. This Satyagraha became the **first all-India struggle** against the British Government.

During the Rowlatt Satyagraha, Gandhiji appealed both the Hindus and Muslims to fight unitedly against the British rule.

In April 1919, a number of demonstrations and hartals were organised in the country and the British Government used brutal measures to suppress them. **The Jallianwala Bagh Massacre** (13th April, 1919) in Amritsar by General Dyer, was an example of such brutal measures.

Rabindranath Tagore renounced his **Knighthood**[6] in protest of Jallianwala Bagh incident.

The Khilafat Agitation and the Non-Cooperation Movement

After the First World War, a harsh treaty was imposed on the Turkish Sultan or Khalifa. Thus, the Khilafat agitation was started under **Mohammad Ali** and **Shaukat Ali.**

Muslims wanted that the Khalifa should be allowed to retain control over Muslim sacred places in the erstwhile Ottoman Empire. The leaders of the Khilafat agitation associated with Gandhiji and Non-Cooperation Movement was started.

During the year 1921-22, the Non-Cooperation Movement gained momentum. Many students left government controlled schools and colleges, and joined the movement.

Many lawyers such as Motilal Nehru, CR Das, C Rajagopalachari and Asaf Ali gave up their practices. Professionals gave up their jobs, British titles were surrendered, legislatures were boycotted and foreign clothes were destroyed.

People's Initiatives

The Non-Cooperation Movement remained non-violent at most of the places. However, some people interpreted the message of Gandhiji in their own manner and link their movements to local grievances. Some examples of this were

- In Kheda (Gujarat), Patidar peasants organised non-violent campaigns against the high land revenue demand.

5 **Socialism** It refers to principle that emphasises on the control of masses or public over a property or natural resource.

6 **Knighthood** It was an honour granted by the British Crown for exceptional personal achievement or public service.

- Liquor shops were **picketed**[7] in Andhra Pradesh and Tamil Nadu.
- Tribals and poor peasants in Guntur district (Andhra Pradesh) organised a number of **forest Satyagrahas** against the restrictions on the use of their forest resources.
- Muslim traders and peasants in Sind (now in Pakistan), and people in Bengal enormously supported the Khilafat-Non-Cooperation Movement.
- In Punjab, the Akali agitation of the Sikh demanded to remove the corrupt **Mahants**[8] from Gurudwaras.
- In Assam, the tea garden labourers demanded a big increase in their wages. In Assamese Vaishnava songs, Gandhiji was referred to as 'Gandhi Raja'.

The People's Mahatma

Sometimes people thought about Gandhiji as a Messiah who could help them to overcome their misery and poverty.

Sometimes people gave the credit of their own achievements to Gandhiji. At some other times, tribals and peasants undertook actions using Mahatma's name that did not follow his idealism.

The Events of 1922-1929

- In February, 1922 a police station in Chauri Chaura was set on fire by a crowd because the police had fired on their peaceful demonstration. Twenty two policemen were, killed in this incident. Due to this incident, Gandhiji called off the Non-Cooperation Movement.
- After the Non-Cooperation movement was over, some leaders such as Chitta Ranjan Das and Motilal Nehru argued for contesting elections to the councils to influence government policies.
- Two important parties, **Rashtriya Swayamsevak Sangha** (RSS) and the **Communist Party of India** (CPI), were formed in the mid-1920s.
- The revolutionary leader **Bhagat Singh** was also active in this period.
- In 1927, the British Government in England decided to send a commission headed by **Lord Simon** to decide India's political future. However, this commission was opposed as it had no Indian representative.
- In 1929, the Congress under the presidentship of Jawaharlal Nehru adopted the resolution to fight for **Purna Swaraj** (complete independence).

Consequently, **Independence Day** was observed on 26th January, 1930 all over the country.

Hindustan Socialist Republican Association (HSRA)

It was founded by **Bhagat Singh, Chandra Shekhar Azad** and **Sukhdev** in 1928 at Ferozeshah Kotla in Delhi.

Its aim was to fight the colonial rule and the rich exploiting classes through a revolution of workers and peasants.

On 17th December, 1928 Bhagat Singh, Azad and Rajguru assassinated **Saunders**, a police officer who was responsible for the death of Lala Lajpat Rai.

On 8th April, 1929, Bhagat Singh along with BK Dutta threw a bomb in the Central Legislative Assembly.

On 23rd March, 1931, Bhagat Singh, Sukhdev and Rajguru were executed.

8.3 The March to Dandi

In 1930, Gandhiji declared that he would lead a March to break the Salt Law. According to this law, the state had monopoly over manufacture and sale of salt.

Gandhiji and his followers marched for over 240 miles from Sabarmati to the coastal town of **Dandi** where they broke the government law by making salt from sea water.

The **Government of India Act of 1935** prescribed **provincial autonomy**[9] and the government announced elections to the provincial legislatures in 1937. The Congress formed governments in 7 out of 11 provinces.

In 1939, Second World War broke out. Congress leaders were ready to support the British but in return they demanded independence after the war.

This demand was refused by the British and the Congress ministries resigned in protest.

Women in the Freedom Struggle

Women from different backgrounds participated in the National Movement. Their involvement was significant for the freedom struggle, women's movement as well as for themselves personally.

Ambabai was a widow from Karnataka who participated in freedom struggle and picketed foreign cloth and liquor shops. She was arrested and sent to jail.

During Salt Satyagraha, Gandhiji was initially opposed to women's participation, but **Sarojini Naidu** persuaded him to allow women to join the movement.

7 **Picket** It refers to people protesting outside a building or shop to prevent others for entering.

8 **Mahants** These refer to religious functionaries of Sikh Gurudwaras.

9 **Provincial Autonomy** It refers to the capacity of the provinces to make relatively independent decisions while remaining within a federation.

8.4 Quit India and Later

In August 1942, **Quit India Movement** was initiated under the leadership of Mahatma Gandhi.

Gandhiji urged the people to **Do or Die**. Gandhiji and other leaders were jailed, but the movement spread. Communications and symbols of state authority were attacked. In many areas the people set up their own government.

By the end of 1943, many people were arrested and many were killed in police firing. This movement ultimately brought the British Raj to its knees.

Towards Independence and Partition

In 1940, the Muslim League moved a resolution demanding 'Independent States' for Muslims in the North-Western and Eastern areas of the country. The resolution did not mention partition or Pakistan. This was demanded due to the following reasons

- From the late 1930s, the League began to visualise the Muslims as a separate nation from the Hindus. This belief was responsible to develop the tension between Hindu and Muslim groups in 1920s and 1930s.
- The results of the provincial election of 1937 convinced the League that Muslims were a minority.
- The Congress' rejected the League's desire to form a Joint Congress-League Government in the United Provinces in 1937.
- The Congress failed in mobilising the Muslims in the 1930s. This allowed the league to widen its support base.

In the provincial elections of 1946, the Congress gain majority in the **General constituencies**[10] but the League had a remarkable success in the seats reserved for Muslims.

The League continued its demand for 'Pakistan'. In March 1946, the British cabinet sent a three member mission to Delhi to examine the demand and suggest suitable framework for independent India. However, the purpose of the mission failed.

Direct Action Day

After the failure of the Cabinet Mission, the Muslim League announced 16th August, 1946 as 'Direct Action Day'. On this day, riots broke out in Calcutta which resulted in the death of many people.

By March 1947, violence spread to different parts of Northern India. Many people were forced to flee from their homes, tortured and killed. Women had to face cruelty during the partition.

Many cities of India were changed due to the partition. On 14th August, 1947, a new country 'Pakistan' was born.

KNOWLEDGE PLUS C. Rajagopalachari, popularly known as **Rajaiji** served as free **India's first Governor-General.**

Try These

1. **Who were the leaders of the Khilafat Movement?**
2. **In which year did the Chauri-Chaura incident happen?**
3. **When did the British Government send the Simon Commission to India?**
4. **In which year government announce election to the Provincial Legislature?**

10 **General Constituencies** These refer to election districts with no reservations for any religious or other community.

THE MAKING OF THE NATIONAL MOVEMENT : 1870S - 1947

The Emergence of Nationalism

Indian National Congress
- Established in 1885 at Bombay.
- AO Hume played a significant role.

Political Associations Formed after 1850
- Poona Sarvajanik Sabha
- The Indian Association
- The Madras Mahajan Sabha
- The Bombay Presidency Association

Partition of Bengal
- In 1905, Viceroy Lord Curzon partitioned Bengal.
- During Swadeshi Movement, people struggled against it.

The March to Dandi
- Started in March 1930.
- March from Sabarmati Ashram to Dandi-240 miles and broke salt law.
- Government of India Act 1935 provided provincial autonomy.

Quit India and Later
- Initiated by Mahatma Gandhi in 1942.
- Muslim League demanded separate Muslim state in 1940.
- Provincial elections were held in 1946. INC won majority in General constituencies.
- 14th August, 1947-Independence of Pakistan.
- 15th August, 1947-Independence of India.

The Growth of Mass Nationalism

The Rowlatt Satyagraha
- Rowlatt Act passed in 1919.
- Rowlatt Satyagraha was first all India non-violent struggle against British rule.
- On 13th April, 1919-the Jallianwala Bagh massacre by General Dyer.
- Rabindranath Tagore gave up Knighthood.

The Events of 1922-1929
- A police station in Chauri-Chaura was set on fire in February 1922.
- **Rashtriya Swayamsevak Sangha** (RSS) and the **Communist Party of India** (CPI) were formed.

The Advent of Mahatma Gandhi
- Mahatma Gandhi came to India in 1915 from South Africa initiated.
- He participated in local movements at Champaran, Kheda and Ahmedabad.

People's Initiatives
- Patidar peasants organised non-violent campaigns in Kheda (Gujarat).
- Tribals and poor peasants organised Forest Satyagrahas in Guntur (Andhra Pradesh).

NCERT FOLDER

Covering Intext Questions and Exercises of NCERT

NCERT ON PAGE 95 (ACTIVITY)

Q.1 From the beginning the Congress sought to speak for and in the name of, all the Indian people. Why did it choose to do so?

Ans. From the beginning the Congress sought to speak for and in the name of, all the Indians people because India is a country of various religions and cultures.

The Congress always wanted the contribution of all the people in achieving independence from the British.

NCERT ON PAGE 98 (ACTIVITY)

Q.2 Find out which countries fought the First World War.

Ans. The countries which fought First World War were United Kingdom, France, Russia, Japan, Germany, Austria-Hungary, Ottoman Empire, etc. The war began in 1914 and lasted until 1918.

NCERT ON PAGE 100 (ACTIVITY)

Q.3 Find out about the Jallianwala Bagh Massacre.

(i) What is Jallianwala Bagh?

Ans. Jallianwala Bagh is a garden near the Harmandir Sahib in Amritsar.

(ii) What atrocities were committed there? How were they committed?

Ans. The Jallianwala Bagh massacre occurred on 13th April, 1919, when British troops, led by Brigadier General Reginald Dyer, opened fire on a peaceful gathering of thousands of Indians.

This atrocity resulted in the death of hundreds, possibly over a thousand, and left many more injured.

NCERT ON PAGE 100 (LET'S IMAGINE)

Q. 4 Imagine that you are involved in the Indian National Movement. Based on your reading of this chapter, briefly discuss your preferred methods of struggle and your vision of a free India.

Ans. If I were involved in Indian National Movement during the struggle for independence, I would emphasise the power of peaceful protest, moral strength and unity to challenge British rule.

My methods of freedom struggle will include Non-Cooperation and Civil-Disobedence Movement as this approach is inspired by Mahatma Gandhi.

My vision of a free India would be one that supported the principles of democracy, equality, unity, and social justice. Independent would have unity in divesity, equality for all and also have aim to promote sustainable development and economic self-reliance.

EXERCISES

Q.1 Why were people dissatisfied with British rule in the 1870s and 1880s? **Diksha**

Ans. People were dissatisfied with the British rule in the 1870s and 1880s as in 1878, two acts were passed by the British. These were

(i) **Arms Act** This act disallowed Indians from possessing arms.

(iii) **Vernacular Press Act** This act empowered the government to take over the assets of newspapers including their printing presses, if the newspaper published anything objectionable.

Q.2 Who did the Indian National Congress wish to speak for?

Ans. The Indian National Congress wished to speak for all the people of India, irrespective of class, colour, caste, creed, language or gender.

It stated that India, its resources and systems were not for any one class or community of India, but for all the different communities of India.

Q.3 What economic impact did the First World War have on India? **Diksha**

Ans. The First World War have the following economic impacts on India

- There was a huge rise in the defence expenditure of the Government of India.
- The government increased tax on individual incomes and business profits.
- There was a great demand for industrial goods due to the war and this resulted in the decline of European goods being imported into India. This in turn gave the Indian Industrialists a chance to expand their production.

Q.4 What did the Muslim League Resolution of 1940 ask for? Diksha

Ans. In 1940, the Muslim League passed a resolution demanding independent States for Muslims in the North-Western and Eastern areas of the country. The resolution did not mention partition of India or Pakistan.

Q.5 Who were the moderates? How did they propose to struggle against British rule? Diksha

Ans. Moderates were the leaders of the Congress who presented their demands to the British in a moderate way and they wanted gradual reforms. They aimed at better and friendly association with the British.

The moderates included leaders like Surendra Nath Banerjee, Pherozeshah Mehta and Gopal Krishna Gokhale. They proposed methods to struggle against the British government in the following ways

- The demands were presented to the British through petitions, meetings, speeches and resolutions.
- Their whole attitude was of reconciliation and not confrontation.
- They would do nothing which would offend the British rulers.

Q.6 How was the politics of the radicals within the Congress different from that of the moderates? Diksha

Ans. The politics of the radicals within the Congress different from that of the Moderates during the freedom movement. Moderates suggested slow constitutional change. They depend on negotiations and petitions to seek self-governance.

On the other hand, radicals favoured direct action and civil disobedience to get independence.

Moderates aimed for reforms and representation with in existing colonial system while radicals sought complete self rule. These differences also led to division within the Congress.

Q.7 Discuss the various forms that the Non-Cooperation Movement took in different parts of India. Diksha

Ans. The Non-Cooperation Movement was launched by Mahatma Gandhi in 1920. It took the following forms in different parts of India.

- Indian boycotted British goods encourging the use of Swadeshi products.
- Students and teachers refused to participate in British-controlled educational institution.
- Lawyers refused to practice in British courts.
- Large-scale peaceful protests were held across the country.
- General strikes were organised.
- Muslims joined the Non-Cooperation Movement under the leadership of the Khilafat leaders.
- Tribal communities organised revolt against exploitative colonial policies.
- Indians renounced their British granted titles and honours.

Q.8 Why did Gandhiji choose to break the Salt Law? Diksha

Ans. Mahatma Gandhi choose to break the Salt Law as the strategic and symbolic act of civil disobedience against British colonial rule. The British introduced a law stating that the state had a monopoly on the manufacture and sale of salt. It also imposed a tax on the sale of salt. Mahatma Gandhi and other national leaders felt that it was wrong to impose tax on salt which was an essential commodity for food. Thus, leaders decided to oppose this tax.

In 1930, Gandhiji declared that he would lead a march to break the Salt Law. The Salt March was related to the desire for freedom felt by all the rich and the poor. Gandhiji and his followers marched for over 240 miles from Sabarmati to the coastal town of Dandi where they broke the government law by gathering natural salt found on the sea shore and boiled sea water to produce salt.

Q.9 Discuss those developments of the 1937-47 period that led to the creation of Pakistan. Diksha

Ans. The developments of the 1937-47 period that led to the creation of Pakistan were as follows

- In 1937, the government announced elections to the Provincial Legislatures. The Congress was victorious in 7 out of 11 provinces and formed governments in the 7 provinces. This result convinced the Muslim League that Muslims were a minority.
- In 1940, the Muslim League passed a resolution demanding 'Independent States' for Muslims in the North-Western and Eastern areas of the country.
- In 1946, elections to the provinces were held. The Congress did well in the 'general constituencies' but the League had a remarkable success in the seats reserved for Muslims.

Q.10 Find out how the National Movement was organised in your city, district, area or state. Who participated in it and who led it? What did the movement in your area achieve?

Ans. Delhi was crucial hub of the National Movement. Various local committees were led by leaders like Mahatma Gandhi and Jawaharlal Nehru. They organised public meetings, protests and acts of civil disobedience. It was participated by many local activities including Mahatma Gandhi and Jawaharlal Nehru.

It plays an important role in National Movement which influenced British policies leading to important reforms. The movement also played a key role in unifying the local population and encouraging sense of nationalism across the country.

Q.11 Find out more about the life and work of any two participants or leaders of the National Movement and write a short essay about them. You may choose a person not mentioned in this chapter.

Ans. **Chakravarti Rajagopalachari** He was a veteran nationalist and leader of the Salt Satyagraha in the South. He is popularly known as Rajaji. He served as member of the Interim Government of 1946 and as free India's first Governor-General.

Sardar Vallabhbhai Patel He was a foremost organiser of the freedom movement from 1918 onwards. He served as President of the Congress in 1931. He played an important role in the negotiations for independence during 1945-47. Patel hailed from an impoverished peasant-proprietor family of Nadiad, Gujarat.

REVIEW EXERCISE

Including Competency Based Questions

Part I

Multiple Choice Questions (MCQs)

1. The Vernacular Press Act was enacted in
(a) 1878 (b) 1894
(c) 1905 (d) 1920

2. Which bill allowed for trial of Europeans by Indians ?
(a) Vernacular Press Act (b) Ilbert Bill
(c) Judiciary Bill (d) Arms Bill

3. Who established National Congress?
Or Who was the founder of Indian National Congress?
(a) Mahatma Gandhi (b) Jawaharlal Nehru
(c) Netaji Subhas Chandra Bose (d) None of these

4. Who raised the slogan 'Freedom is my Birthright'?
(a) Lala Lajpat Rai (b) Bal Gangadhar Tilak
(c) Laxmibai (d) Mahatma Gandhi

5. When and where was All India Muslim League formed?
(a) 1850, Calcutta (b) 1906, Dhaka
(c) 1920, Bombay (d) 1910, Delhi

6. Which among the following parties signed a historic Pact of Lucknow in 1916 with Muslim League ?
(a) Communist Party (b) Socialist Party
(c) Congress Party (d) Hindu Mahasabha

7. When did Jallianwala Bagh massacre occurred ?
(a) 1918 (b) 1919 (c) 1920 (d) 1921

8. When did Gandhiji arrive in India from South Africa?
(a) 1910 (b) 1915 (c) 1920 (d) 1925

9. Which movement among the following was the first successful movement led by Gandhiji in India?
(a) Kheda Movement
(b) Champaran Movement
(c) Quit India Movement
(d) Civil Disobedience Movement

10. Which incident became reason for calling off Non-Cooperation Movement by Mahatma Gandhi?
(a) Chauri Chaura (b) Kanpur **Competency Based**
(c) Bithoor (d) Ahmedabad

11. Who was the first Indian Governor-General of free India?
(a) Jawaharlal Nehru (b) Dr Rajendra Prasad
(c) C Rajagopalachari (d) Sardar Vallabhbhai Patel

12. Congress fought for Purna Swaraj under the leadership of .... in 1930.
(a) Subhas Chandra Bose (b) Lala Lajpat Rai
(c) Jawaharlal Nehru (d) Bal Gangadhar Tikal

13. Hindustan Socialist Republican Association was founded by ....
(a) Chitta Ranjan Das (b) Bhagat Singh
(c) MK Gandhi (d) Annie Besant

14. Who led the Dandi March in 1930?
(a) Mahatma Gandhi (b) Sarojini Naidu
(c) Indira Gandhi (d) SC Bose

15. Which among the following movements was launched in 1930?
(a) Civil Disobedience Movement
(b) Swaraj Movement
(c) Khilafat Movement
(d) Workers Movement

16. Name the movement associated with the arrest of 90,000 people and killing of 1000 people by police firing.
(a) Civil Disobedience Movement
(b) Swaraj Movement
(c) Khilafat Movement
(d) Quit India Movement

17. **Lala Lajpat Rai was a nationalist from**
(a) Bengal (b) Punjab (c) Bihar (d) Uttar Pradesh

18. **When did Second World War end?**
(a) 1910 (b) 1941 (c) 1942 (d) 1945

19. **The book 'Poverty and Un-British Rule in India' is authored by**
(a) Dadabhai Naoroji (b) Mahatma Gandhi
(c) Jawaharlal Nehru (d) Sarojini Naidu

20. **Kesari, a Marathi newspaper was edited by**
(a) Bepin Chandra Pal (b) Dadabhai Naoroji
(c) Bal Gangadhar Tilak (d) Sardar Vallabhbhai Patel

21. **Who was the founder of Khudai Khidmatgars ?**
(a) Mohammad Ali (b) Khan Abdul Ghaffar Khan
(c) Shaukat Ali (d) Abul Kalam Azad

22. **Among the following which was formed by Subhas Chandra Bose ?**
(a) Indian National Army (b) Army Regiment
(c) Judicial Movement (d) Swarajya Party

23. **Identify the correct option that describes the movement given int he statements.** Competency Based
(i) It started in the year 1921-22.
(ii) Students left government controlled schools and colleges in this movement.
(iii) Many nationalist leaders also gave up their law practices in this movement.

Options
(a) Non-Cooperation Movement
(b) Civil Disobedience Movement
(c) Rowlatt Satyagraha
(d) Quit India Movement

24. **Identify the correct option that describes the movement given in the statements.** Competency Based
(i) It was turned out to be the first all India struggle against British rule.
(ii) Jallianwala Bagh incident was the part of expression of this movement.
(iii) It was against the act passed to curb fundamental rights.
(iv) Gandhiji gave a call for a satyagraha in 1919.

Options
(a) Rowlatt Satyagraha (b) Salt Satyagraha
(c) Khilafat Movement (d) Civil Disobedience

25. **Which of the following statement is/are correct?** Competency Based
I. The Indian National Congress was established by Mahatma Gandhi.
II. AO Hume was the first President of the Indian National Congress.

Codes
(a) Both I and II (b) Only II
(c) Only I (d) None of these

26. **Which of the following statements is/are correct? The main aim(s) of the Swadeshi Movement was/were** Competency Based
I. to oppose the British rule.
II. to encourage the ideas of self-help.
III. to encourage national education and use of Indian languages.

Codes
(a) Both I and II (b) Only II
(c) Only I (d) All of these

27. **Arrange the following events according to their happening and choose the correct option.** Competency Based
I. The Arms Act was passed
II. Ilbert Bill controversy.
III. Viceroy Curzon partitioned Bengal.
IV. The Indian National Congress was established.

Codes
(a) I, II, III, IV (b) I, IV, II, III (c) I, III, IV, II (d) I, II, IV, III

28. **Which of the following is/are the correct sequence?** Competency Based
I. Mahatma Gandhi called off the Non-Cooperation Movement.
II. The Vernacular Press Act was passed.
III. The Quit India Movement started.
IV. Gandhiji launched the Dandi March.

Codes
(a) I, II, III, IV (b) II, I, IV, III
(c) I, III, IV, II (d) II, I, III, IV

Answers

1. (a)	2. (b)	3. (d)	4. (b)	5. (b)
6. (c)	7. (b)	8. (b)	9. (b)	10. (a)
11. (c)	12. (c)	13. (b)	14. (a)	15. (a)
16. (d)	17. (b)	18. (d)	19. (a)	20. (c)
21. (b)	22. (a)	23. (a)	24. (a)	25. (d)
26. (d)	27. (d)	28. (b)		

Match the Following

1.

List I	List II
A. Picket	1. The capacity to act independently without outside interference
B. Quit India Movement	2. To undo law
C. Sovereign	3. People protesting outside a building or shop to prevent others from entering.
D. Repeal	4. Do or die

Codes

	A	B	C	D		A	B	C	D
(a)	3	4	1	2	(b)	1	2	3	4
(c)	4	3	2	1	(d)	2	3	4	1

2.

List I	List II
A. Forest Satyagraha	1. Jallianwala Bagh Massacre
B. General Dyer	2. Government of India Act 1935
C. Lal, Bal, Pal	3. Tribal of Andhra Pradesh
D. Provincial Autonomy	4. Radical Group of Congress

Codes

	A	B	C	D		A	B	C	D
(a)	3	1	4	2	(b)	1	4	2	3
(c)	1	2	3	4	(d)	4	3	2	1

Ans. 1. (a) 2. (a)

Assertion-Reason

1. **Assertion** (A) In 1905, Lord Curzon announced the division of Bengal into Bengal, Eastern Bengal and Assam.

   Reason (R) The main British motives were to curtail Bengali politicians' influence and split the Bengali people.

   Codes

   (a) Both A and R are the true and R is the correct explanation of A
   (b) Both A and R are the true, but R is not the correct explanation of A
   (c) A is true, but R is false
   (d) A is false, but R is true

2. **Assertion** (A) The Arms Act was passed in 1878, disallowing Indians from possessing arms.

   Reason (R) The Vernacular Press Act was passed in 1878. This act allowed the government to confiscate the assets of newspapers including their printing presses.

   Codes

   (a) Both A and R are the true and R is the correct explanation of A
   (b) Both A and R are the true, but R is not the correct explanation of A
   (c) A is true, but R is false
   (d) A is false, but R is true

Ans. 1. (a) Both A and R are the true and R is the correct explanation of A

2. (b) Both A and R are the true, but R is not the correct explanation of A

Fill in the Blanks

1. .... is the word which literally means of or for all the people.
2. .... addressed the Congress as President in 1887.
3. The Jallianwala Bagh atrocities, inflicted by .... in Amritsar on Baisakhi Day, 1919.
4. Mahatma Gandhi abruptly called off the .... Movement when it took violent turn.
5. In 1905, the Viceroy Lord Curzon partitioned ....

Ans. 1. Sarvajanik 2. Badruddin Tyabji 3. General Dyer 4. Non-Cooperation 5. Bengal

True/False

1. People were satisfied with the British rule in the 1870s and 1880s.
2. In 1885, Ilbert Bill was introduced.
3. WC Bonnerji was a moderate Congress leader.
4. Moderate leaders demanded that the civil service examinations would be held in India also, not just in London.
5. Subhas Chandra Bose was a moderate nationalist.

Ans. 1. False 2. False 3. True 4. True 5. False

Picture Based Questions

1. **In the picture given below Gandhiji is breaking the Salt Law. In which year did this incident take place?**

(a) 1931 (b) 1930
(c) 1932 (d) 1929

2. **Identify the personality in the picture given below who had thrown a bomb in the Central Legislative Assembly along with BK Dutta.**

(a) Chandra Shekhar Azad (b) Bal Gangadhar Tilak
(c) Bhagat Singh (d) Lala Lajpat Rai

Ans. 1. (b) 1930 2. (c) Bhagat Singh

Case Based Question

1. Read the following context and answer the question that follows.

In 1919, Gandhi gave a call for a Satyagraha against the Rowlatt Act that the British had just passed. The act curbed fundamental rights such as freedom of expression and strengthened police powers.

Mahatma Gandhi, Mohammad Ali Jinnah, and others felt that the government had no right to restrict people's basic freedoms. They criticised the act as devilish and tyrannical. Gandhi asked the Indian people to observe 6th April, 1919 as a day of non-violet opposition of this act, as a day of "humiliation and prayer" and hartal (strike). Satyagraha Sabhas were set up to launch the movement. The Rowlatt Satyagraha turned out to be the first all-India struggle against the British government although it was largely restricted to cities.

In April 1919, there were a number of demonstrations and hartals in the country and the government used brutal measures to suppress them. The Jallianwala Bagh atrocities, inflicted by General Dyer in Amritsar on Baisakhi day (13 April), were a part of this repression. On learning about the massacre, Rabindranath Tagore expressed the pain and anger of the country by renouncing his knighthood.

(i) Why did Mahatma Gandhi started Satyagraha in 1919?

(a) To protest against Rowlatt Act.
(b) To oppose the partition of Bengal.
(c) Against the Britishers' victory in World War II
(d) None of the above

(ii) The Rowlatt Act was oposed because

(a) this act curbed fundamental rights.
(b) strengthened police power.
(c) curbed the freedom of expression.
(d) All of the above

(iii) The Jallianwala Bagh massacre took place on which date?

(a) 13th April, 1919 (b) 12th March, 1920
(c) 28th April, 1919 (d) 13th April, 1920

(iv) Who renounced his knighthood after Jallianwala incident?

(a) Jawaharlal Nehru (b) Lala Lajpat Rai
(c) Mahatma Gandhi (d) Rabindranath Tagore

Ans. (i) (a) To protest against Rowlatt Act.
(ii) (d) All of the above
(iii) (a) 13th April, 1919
(iv) (d) Rabindranath Tagore

Part II

Very Short Answer Type Questions

1. What were the initial demands of Congress?

Ans. The initial demands of Congress were reduction of revenue and military expenditures and alloting more funds for irrigation.

2. Name the three leading members of radicals.

Ans. The three leader of radical groups were Bipin Chandra Pal, Bal Gangadhar Tilak and Lala Lajpat Rai.

3. Name the Viceroy of India at the time of partition of Bengal.

Or **Who was Viceroy of India when partition of Bengal was announced?** **Diksha**

Ans. Lord Curzon was the Viceroy of India at the time of partition of Bengal.

4. In which year was the Rowlatt Act passed?

Ans. The Rowlatt Act was passed in 1919.

5. Why did the peasants set fire to police station in Chauri Chaura?

Ans. The peasants set fire to police station in Chauri Chaura because the police had fired on their peaceful demonstration.

6. Who was Chitta Ranjan Das?

Ans. Chitta Ranjan Das was a lawyer from East Bengal and a prominent figure in the freedom movement who was specially active in the Non-Cooperation Movement.

7. What does RSS stand for?

Ans. RSS stands for Rashtriya Swayamsevak Sangh.

8. What was the main slogan of the demonstration against the Simon Commission?

Ans. Simon Commission was met with demonstration with banners saying 'Simon Go Back'.

9. What does HSRA stand for?

Ans. HSRA stands for Hindustan Socialist Republican Association.

10. Who was BK Dutt?

Ans. BK Dutt was a fellow nationalist of Bhagat Singh who accompanied with Bhagat Singh in throwing a bomb in the Central Legislative Assembly.

11. What was the slogan of 'Quit India Movement'?

Ans. The slogan of Quit India Movement was Do or Die.

12. Name a significant woman leader of Dandi March.

Ans. Sarojini Naidu was a significant leader of the Dandi March.

13. Who announced 'Direct Action Day' and when?

Ans. The Muslim League announced 'Direct Action Day' on 16th August, 1946.

14. Why did Gandhiji establish the Natal Congress?

Ans. In 1895, along with other Indians, Mahatma Gandhi established the Natal Congress in Durban, South Africa to fight against racial discrimination.

15. Name the Congress leader who did not share Gandhiji's ideal of Ahimsa but respected him as the 'Father of the Nation'.

Ans. Netaji Subhas Chandra Bose did not share Gandhiji's ideal of Ahimsa, but he respected him as the 'Father of the Nation'.

16. Name the President of the Nabrangpur Congress, Orissa in the 1930s.

Ans. Baji Mohammed was the President of the Nabrangpur Congress, Orissa in the 1930s.

Short Answer Type Questions

1. Write a short note about the foundation of the Indian National Congress.

Ans. The Indian National Congress was established when 72 delegates form all over India met at Bombay in December 1885.

The Congress was created to form a platform for civic and political dialogue of educated Indians with the British Raj. A retired British official AO Hume played a significant role in bringing Indians from the various regions together.

During its first several decades, the Congress passed fairly moderate reform resolutions. Some of important leaders of congress early period were Dadabhai Naoroji, Pherozeshah Mehta, Badruddin Tyabji, WC Bonnerji, Surendranath Banerji, Romesh Chandra Dutt, S. Subramania Iyer, etc.

2. Why was Bengal divided by the British in 1905?

Ans. In 1905, Lord Curzon partitioned Bengal, the biggest province of British India. At that time, it included Bihar and parts of Orissa. The British argued for dividing Bengal for reasons of administrative convenience. However, the British really wanted to curtail the influence of Bengali politicians and split the Bengali people. Thus, instead of removing the non-Bengali areas from the province, they separated East Bengal and merged it with Assam.

3. Explain the consequence of the partition of Bengal.

Ans. The consequences of the partition of Bengal were

- The partition of Bengal made people angry all over India.
- All sections of the Congress including moderates and radicals opposed it.
- Large public meeting, demonstrations were organised and new methods of mass protest took place.
- The Swadeshi Movement started which opposed British rule, encouraged the ideas of self-help, Swadeshi enterprise, national education and use of Indian languages.

4. The struggle that unfolded after the division of partition of Bengal came to be known as the Swadeshi Movement. **Competency Based**

(i) What is the meaning of the word Swadeshi?

(ii) Describe how the Swadeshi Movement help against fighting British rule.

Ans. (i) The word 'Swadeshi' comes from two words 'Swa' and 'desh' which means one's own country. The Swadeshi movement was a important aspect of the Indian independence struggle against British rule.

(ii) The Swadeshi Movement, which emerged in India in response to the partition of Bengal in 1905, played a crucial role in the fight against British rule in the following ways

- **Economic Resistance** Indians boycotted British goods and instead supported locally produced items, leading to a significant economic impact on British trade in India.
- **Promotion of Swadeshi Goods** Indians were urged to use and promote locally produced goods. This led to the establishment of swadeshi industries, which aimed to reduce dependence on British imports and stimulate the Indian economy.
- **Boycott of Educational Institutions** As part of the movement, students boycotted British educational institutions, contributing to a sense of defiance and political consciousness among the youth.

5. How did Gandhiji apply the idea of Satyagraha in our country?

Ans. Gandhiji applied the idea of Satyagraha by promoting non-violent resistance. He encouraged people to peacefully disobey unjust laws, boycott British goods, and engage in acts of civil disobedience. His symbolic actions, like the Salt March, aimed to challenge British authority without violence.

Gandhi's emphasis on truth, love, and the constructive program sought not just political freedom but also social transformation. Through these methods, he inspired a powerful and nonviolent movement for India's independence.

6. How did the Non- Cooperation Movement gain momentum through 1921-1922?

Ans. The Non-Cooperation Movement gained momentum through 1921-22 in the following ways

- Many students left government controlled schools and colleges, and joined the movement.

- Many lawyers such as Motilal Nehru, CR Das, C Rajagopalachari and Asaf Ali gave up their practices.
- Professionals gave up their jobs, British titles were surrendered, legislatures were boycotted and foreign clothes were destroyed.

7. What was the Khilafat agitation? Explain.

Ans. The Khilafat agitation is also known as the Khilafat Movement. It was a significant political and religious movement during 1920s. It was launched to protest against the mistreatment of the caliph.

In the First World War, Ottoman Turkey was defeated and a harsh peace treaty was imposed on Turkish Sultan or Khalifa, the spiritual head of the Islamic world by the British. To defend Khalifa's power, a Khilafat Committee was formed in Bombay in March 1919. Mohammad Ali and Shaukat Ali were the leaders of Khilafat agitation.

8. Why did Indians Boycott the Simon Commission? How it was greeted on its arrival?

Ans. Indians boycotted the Simon Commission for several significant reasons. The commission consisted entirely of British members with no Indian representative was one of the reasons. It was headed by Lord Simon to decide India's political future.

Simon Commission arrived in India in 1928. It was greeted with black flags and slogans like 'Simon Go Back'. Both Congress and Muslim League unitedly protested against it.

9. Write a short note on Maulana Azad.

Ans. Maulana Azad was a great leader of the Indian National Movement. He was born in Mecca to a Bengali father and an Arab mother. He was well versed in many languages.

He was a scholar of Islam and an exponent of the belief of Wahadat-i-deen, the essential oneness of all religions. He was an active participant in the movements launched by Mahatma Gandhi. He was a great advocate of Hindu-Muslim unity and never approved Jinnah's two-nation theory.

10. Write a brief note on Khan Abdul Ghaffar Khan.

Ans. Khan Abdul Ghaffar Khan was a Pashtun leader from the North-West frontier province. He was close friend of Mahatma Gandhi and was known as 'Frontier Gandhi'.

He founded the Khudai Khidmatgars ('Servants of God') which was a powerful non- violent movement against the British Raj.

He was a supporter of Hindu-Muslim unity and strongly opposed the Muslim League's demand for the partition of India.

Long Answer Type Questions

1. In 1919, Gandhiji gave a call for a satyagraha against the Rowlatt Act that the British had just passed. What was the Rowlatt Satyagraha? Explain.

Ans. The Rowlatt Satyagraha was an important non-violent protest against the oppressive Rowlatt Act passed by the British colonial government

The Rowlatt Act was passed in 1919 by the Britishers. The Act curbed fundamental rights such as freedom of expression and strengthened police powers. Mahatma Gandhi, Mohammad Ali Jinnah, and other opposed the government's restriction of basic freedoms, calling the Act "devilish" and tyrannical.

The Rowlatt Satyagraha become the first all-India struggle against the British government although it was largely restricted to cities. On 6th April, 1919 nationwide hartal was launched and the day was observed as the day of humiliation and prayer.

In April 1919, there were a number of demonstrations and hartals in the country and the government used brutal measures to suppress them.

2. Those who say religion has nothing to do with politics do not know what religion is Mahatma Gandhi. Discuss the various factors that led to make Gandhiji a mass leader. **Competency Based**

Ans. Certain circumstances made Gandhiji to emerge as a mass leader which were as follows

- Gandhiji arrived in India in 1915 from South Africa where he led Indians in non-violent marches against racialism. Thus, he was already respected leader.
- His struggle in South Africa had brought him in contact with various types of Indians Hindus, Muslims, Parsis and Christians, Gujarati's, Tamils, North Indians, upper-class merchants, lawyers and workers.
- He spent 1915-16 in India travelling throughout the country, understanding the people, their needs and the overall situation.
- Initially, he took part in local movements in Champaran, Kheda and Ahmedabad. During this time he came into contact with Rajendra Prasad and Vallabhbhai Patel.
- In 1918, Gandhiji led a successful millworker's strike in Ahmedabad.

3. Describe Gandhi's march to Dandi. Why Salt March was an effective symbol of resistance against colonialism?

Ans. Mahatma Gandhi and other prominent leaders of the freedom movement thought that it was sinful to tax salt because it is an essential item of our food. In 1930, Gandhiji decided to break this law. Gandhiji felt that his Salt March would become popular and would represent the general desire of freedom from a specific injustice. Gandhiji and his followers marched for over 240 miles from Sabarmati to the coastal town of Dandi where they broke the law by making salt from sea water.

Salt March was an effective symbol of resistance against colonialism because

- All classes could identify with salt as it was an essential food item.
- Monopoly over manufacturing and selling salt was a sign of oppression of the British.
- Breaking the law would affect British economy.

4. What were the factors that contributed to the rise of national consciousness among the people of India ?

Ans. Several factors contributed to the rise of national consciousness among the people of India.

These were

British Control and Exploitation The awareness grew that the British were exercising control over the resources of India and the lives of its people.

This realisation fueled a desire for self-determination and autonomy, as Indians recognised that their country's resources and systems were meant for all its inhabitants.

Political Associations and Leaders After 1850, important groups called political associations started forming and they were really active in the 1870s and 1880s. These groups, led by educated individuals who spoke English, like lawyers, believed that the people of India should have the power to make decisions about their own matters.

Dissatisfaction with British Rule Dissatisfaction with British rule intensified in the 1870s and 1880s due to oppressive policies such as the Arms Act (1878), which disallowed Indians from possessing arms, and the Vernacular Press Act (1878), which aimed to silence critics by allowing the government to confiscate assets of newspapers publishing objectionable content.

The attempt to introduce the Ilbert Bill in 1883, which sought equality in the trial of British and Indian individuals, further highlighted racial attitudes and contributed to Indian discontent.

Picture Based Questions

1. Look at the given picture and answer the following questions.

(i) The event shown in the picture related to which movement?

Ans. The event shown in the picture is related to Quit India Movement .

(ii) In which year this movement was started?

Ans. This movement was started in August, 1942.

(iii) What did happen in this movement?

Ans. In this movement, demonstrators clashed with the police everywhere. Many people were arrested many were killed, many more were injured.

2. Look at the given picture and answer the following questions.

(i) What are demonstrators doing in the above picture?

Ans. Demonstrators are opposing the Simon Commission in the above picture.

(ii) Why did the British send the Simon Commission in 1927?

Ans. Britishers send the Simon Commission in 1927 to decide India's political future.

Case Based Questions

1. **Read the passage given below and answer the following questions.**

In Pursuit of Gold

This is what a Moderate leader, Dinshaw Wacha, wrote to Naoroji in 1887:
Pherozeshah is nowadays too busy with his personal work... They are already rich enough ... Mr. Telang too remains busy. I wonder how if all remain busy in the pursuit of gold can the progress of the country be advanced?

What problems regarding the early Congress does this comment highlight?

Ans. The comment highlights key issues in the early Indian National Congress. The Indian National Congress was created to form a platform for civic political dialogue of educated Indians with the British Raj in 1885. The Congress intially was moderate and demanded a greater voice for Indians in the government and in the administration only.

Initially, it was an educated and wealthy people's institution, most of the members were too busy with their personal work and could not afford time for the progress of the country. This problem was pointed out by Dinshaw Wacha to Dadabhai Naoroji.

2. **Read the passage given below and answer the following questions.**

"It was he who got Bedakhli stopped in Pratapgarh"

The following is an extract from a CID report on the Kisan Movement in Allahabad district, January 1921:
The currency which Mr. Gandhi's name has acquired even in the remotest villages is astonishing. No one seems to know quite who or what he is, but it is an accepted fact that what he says is so, and what he orders must be done. He is a Mahatma or *sadhu*, a Pundit, a Brahmin who lives at Allahabad, even a *deota* the real power of his name is to be traced back to the idea that it was he who got *bedakhli* [illegal eviction] stopped in Pratapgarh as a general rule, Gandhi is not thought of as being antagonistic to Government, but only to the *Zamindars*. We are for Gandhiji and the Sarkar.

According to this report, how did people view Mahatma Gandhi? Why do you think they felt that he was opposed to zamindars, but not to the government? Why do you think they were in favour of Gandhiji?

Ans. According to this report, people had mixed view about Mahatma Gandhi. They saw him as their leader and believe in his words and orders. While they thought of Gandhi as a champion for their rights and problems, they did not saw him as a leader against the British rule because his campaigns and his non-violent approach matched with concerns of the rural population.

They support and favour Gandhi because they felt he could help with their problems and justice and fairness with land issues. Gandhi was a symbol of hope and change for them.

ASSESSMENT EXERCISE

Multiple Choice Questions (MCQs)

1. What slogan was raised by Bal Gangadhar Tilak?
   (a) "Give me liberty or give me death"
   (b) "Inquilab Zindabad"
   (c) "Freedom is my birthright and I shall have it"
   (d) "Swaraj for all"
2. Which regions were separated from Bengal during the partition?
   (a) Bihar and Orissa (b) Punjab and Sindh
   (c) Bihar and Assam (d) Assam and Meghalaya
3. Lala Lajpat Rai belonged to which influential social organisation?
   (a) Indian National Congress
   (b) Muslim League
   (c) Arya Samaj
   (d) All of the above

Subjective Questions (VSA, SA & LA)

1. Who was the leading figure of the Indian National Congress in the early years?
2. Which British officer helped in the formation of the Indian National Congress?
3. When was the All-India Muslim League formed and by whom?
4. How did the partition of Bengal in 1905 impact the rise of nationalism in India?
5. What events led to the Non-Cooperation Movement and what were its key components?
6. Analyse the impact of World War I on the freedom struggle in India.
7. Explain the differences between the "moderates" and "radicals" within the Indian National Congress.

CHAPTER 1

Resources

Resources include anything which have economic value or which become economically valuable with time. In this chapter, we will learn about resources, their types and the ways of conserving the resources. Sustainable development and its principles are also discussed in this chapter.

A resource is anything which has **utility**[1] to satisfy our needs. For example, books, water, air, sunlight, etc.

All the resources have some **value**[2] like **economic** value. For example, metals may have an economic value but a beautiful landscape may not have economic value. However, both are important and satisfy our needs.

Some resource become economically valuable with time. **Time** and **technology** are two important factors that can change substances into resources.

The people's ideas, knowledge, inventions and discoveries lead to the creation of more resources. For example, the discovery of fire and the invention of wheel.

1.1 Types of Resources

Resources are generally classified into three types

(i) Natural resources (ii) Human-made resources

(iii) Human resources

Natural Resources

The resources which are directly obtained from nature and used without modification are called natural resources.

For example, the air we breathe, water in rivers and lakes, soils, minerals, sunlight, animals, etc are natural resources.

The distribution of natural resources is unequal due to differences in the physical factors over the Earth like terrain, climate and altitude.

Natural resources are classified into **renewable and non-renewable resources**

(i) **Renewable Resources** The resources which get renewed or replenished quickly are called renewable resources. For example, solar and wind energy.

(iii) **Non-Renewable Resources** The resources which take thousands of years to get renewed or replenished after exhausting are called non-renewable resources. For example, coal, petroleum and natural gas.

Human-Made Resources

When human beings change the original form of natural resource to make it more useful, it is called human-made resource.

For example, use of natural resources for making buildings, roads, machinery, etc. Technology is also a human-made resource.

Human Resources

Human resource refers to the number and abilities of the people.

1 **Utility** Any thing has utility if it can be used in any way to satisfy human needs.

2 **Value** Worth of any thing is known as its value.

Human Resources

Human resource refers to the number and abilities of the people.

People themselves are human resources. Education and health help in making people a valuable resource.

Improving the quality of people's skills so that they are able to create more resosurces is known as **human resource development.**

1.2 Conserving Resources

The method of using resources carefully and giving them time to get renewed is called **resource conservation.**

The conservation of resources can be done by adopting the steps like reducing consumption of resources and recycling and reusing things.

Sustainable development is another method for conserving resources. It refers to balancing the need to use resources and also conserve them for future.

Some principles of sustainable development are as follows

- Respect and care for all forms of life.
- Improve the quality of human life.
- Conserve the Earth's vitality and diversity.
- Minimise the depletion of natural resources.
- Change personal attitude and practices towards the environment.
- Enable communities to care for their own environment.

RESOURCES

Conservation of Resources

The method of using resources carefully and giving them time to get renewed.

Sustainable Development

It refers to balancing utilisation of resources and also conservation for future

Types of Resources

Human-made Resources

- Natural resources that are transformed by human.
- For example–Buildings, roads, machinery, vehicles, etc.
- Technology is also a human-made resource.

Human Resources

- Human is a resource itself, able to create more resources with knowledge, skill and technology.
- Human Resource Development refers to the development to train human for new skills

Natural Resources

- Resource obtained directly from nature.
- For example-Air, water, soils, minerals, sunlight, animals, etc.

Non-renewable Resources

- Resources that require thousand of years to replenish themselves.
- For example-Coal, petroleum and natural gas, etc.

Renewable Resources

- Resources that renewed or replenishes quickly.
- For example-Soil, water, solar energy, etc.

NCERT FOLDER

Covering Intext Questions and Exercises of NCERT

NCERT ON PAGE 1 (LET'S DO)

Q.1 List out five resources you use in your home and five you use in your classroom.

Ans. Resources used in home

(i) Natural resources in home are
- Air
- Water
- Minerals like: salt, sugar, etc.

(ii) Human-made resources in home are
- Air cooler
- Refrigerator

Resources used in classroom

(i) Natural resources in classroom are
- Air
- Water
- Solar energy/sunlight

(ii) Human-made resources in classroom are
- Desks
- Furniture
- Chalk board

NCERT ON PAGE 2 (ACTIVITY)

Q.2 Circle those resources from Amma's list that have no commercial values as yet.

Amma's List
- Cotton cloth
- Iron ore
- Intelligence
- Medicinal plants
- Medical knowledge
- Coal deposits
- Beautiful scenery
- Agricultural land
- Clean environment
- Old folk songs
- Good weather
- Resourcefulness
- A good singing voice
- Grand mother's home remedies
- Affection from friends and family.

Ans. The resources from Amma's list that have no commercial values are old folk songs, good weather, a good singing voice, grandmother's home remedies and affection from friends and family.

NCERT ON PAGE 3 (LET'S DO)

Q.3 Think of a few renewable resources and mention how their stock may get affected by overuse.

Ans. Renewable resources are things that regenerate/ replenish over time, such as biomass (trees, crops, plants), water, wind, solar energy and geothermal energy.

The stock of these resources may get affected by overuse or over-exploitation which is discussed in the following examples

Natural Vegetation It is a renewable resource which is overused by people for their increasing demands. Trees are cut for wood, housing and other needs at a faster speed due to which problems like environmental pollution emerged.

Water It is a renewable resource which is overused by people for various needs. This overuse led to problems like water shortage in many parts of the world.

Q.4 Make a list of five human-made resources that you can observe around you.

Ans. Five human-made resources that I can observe around me are

(i) Benches
(ii) Pen/pencil
(iii) Buildings
(iv) School bus
(v) Roads

EXERCISES

Q.1 Answer the following questions.

(i) Why are resources distributed unequally over the Earth?

Ans. Resources are distributed unequally over the Earth due to the differences in uneven physical factors on which resource distribution depends. These factors are terrain, climate and altitude which are different from place to place over the Earth's surface.

(ii) What is resource conservation?

Ans. Resource conservation means using the resources carefully and giving them time to get renewed.

(iii) Why are human resources important?

Ans. Human resources are important because nation's development is mostly dependent upon human resources which include human's skill, technology, thinking and knowledge, that leads to a nation's power.

Only human skill and technology change the natural substances into a valuable resource.

(iv) What is sustainable development?

Ans. Balancing the need to use resources and conserve them for the future is called sustainable development.

Q.2 **Tick the correct answer.**

(i) Which one of the following does not make substance a resource?

(a) Utility (b) Value (c) Quantity

Ans. (c) Quantity

(ii) Which one of the following is a human-made resource?

(a) Medicines to treat cancer (b) Spring water (c) Tropical forests

Ans. (a) Medicines to treat cancer

(iii) Complete the statement.

Non-renewable resources are ....

(a) derived from living things.

(b) made by human beings.

(c) derived from non-living things.

Ans. (a) derived from living things.

Q.3 **Activity**

"Rahiman paani raakhiye,
Bin paani sab soon.
Paani gaye na ubere
Moti, manus, choon……"

[Says Rahim, keep water, as without water there is nothing. Without water pearl, swan and dough cannot exist.]

These lines were written by the poet Abdur Rahim Khankhana, one of the nine gems of Akbar's court. What kind of resource is the poet referring to? Write in 100 words, what would happen if this resource disappeared?

Ans. The resource referred to by the poet is water.

Water is one of the most valuable resources of life. It is called 'a life sustaining' resource. It is very essential for the growth and development of living things like plants, human beings and animals, for cooking, for all sorts of activities like agricultural, industrial and household practices, and for our day to day life.

If this resource disappeared, the Earth will turn into desert and without forest cover, all the living things would die due to thirst and hunger. No plant can grow in the absence of water which further affects the lives of animals who depend upon them. In short, no form of life can survive without water.

Q. 4 **For Fun**

(i) Pretend that you live in the pre-historic times on a high windy plateau. What are the uses you and your friends could put the fast winds to? Can you call the wind a resources?

Now imagine that you are living in the same place in the year 2138. Can you put the winds to any use? Can you explain why the wind is an important resource now?

Ans. If my friends and I had lived in the prehistoric period on a high, windy plateau, we would not have understood the utility of the high winds because technology was absent at that time. When the fast winds started blowing, we would have tried to hide in caves or behindrocks to protect ourselves. In this case, winds could not be called a resource because we would have been scared of fast winds, and they would have been of no use to us.

In the year 2138, wind can be important as resource in supplying renewable energy for electricity, supporting wind based transportation and climate control in response to environmental challenges.

(ii) Pick up a stone, a leaf, a paper straw and a twig. Think of how you can use these as resources? See the example given below and get creative!

You can use a stone...	Use/Utility
• To play stapu	toy
• As a paper-weight	tool
• To crush spices	tool
• To decorate your garden/ room	decoration piece
• To open a bottle	tool
• In a catapult	weapon

Ans.

You can use a leaf…	Use/Utility
• For colour printing	tool
• Pasting in drawing pictures	material
• To stick in a scrap book	material
• To write on a dry leaf as a paper	material

You can use a twig…	Use/Utility
• To make fire from dry twig	tool
• To stick in scrap book	material
• To make picture frame for drawing	material

You can use a straw…	Use/Utility
• To make pictures	tool
• To make water bubbles	tool
• To make a book mark	tool
• To make sand pictures with the help of a twig	tool

REVIEW EXERCISE

Including Competency Based Questions

Part I

Multiple Choice Questions (MCQs)

1. The value associated with resources is .....

(a) economic value (b) aesthetic value
(c) legal value (d) ethical value

2. The technology to create .... had turned energy in fast flowing water into an important resource. Diksha

(a) Thermal Power (b) Solar Power
(c) Hydroelectricity (d) Windmill

3. The exclusive right over any idea or invention is called

(a) invention (b) technology
(c) patent (d) stock of resource

4. Sunlight is which type of resource?

(a) Limited (b) Unlimited
(c) Both (a) and (b) (d) None of these

5. .... refers to the number and ability of the people, e.g., knowledge, skills, etc. Diksha

(a) Biotic resources (b) Abiotic resources
(c) Human resources (d) Human-made resources

6. What makes an object or substance a resource?

(a) Utility (b) Value
(c) Usability (d) Both (a) and (c)

7. Resources drawn from nature and used without much modification are called

(a) human-made resources
(b) cultural resources
(c) natural resources
(d) All of the above

8. ....help in making people as a valuable resources. Diksha

(a) Education and food (b) Education and health
(c) Transport and trade (d) Health and power

9. It signifies development of human beings i.e. developing the quality and capacity of people state. Identify Competency Based

(a) Human resources
(b) Human-made resources
(c) Human resources development
(d) None of the above

10. Using resources carefully and giving them time to get renewed is called

(a) resource balancing (b) resource conservation
(c) resource depletion (d) devaluation

11. Balancing the need to use resources and also conserve them for the future is called

(a) development
(b) sustainable development
(c) human resource development
(d) devaluation

12. Consider the following statements and choose the correct option. Competency Based

I. Time and technology are two important factors that can change substances into resources.
II. The invention of the fire led to the development of newer forms of transportation.

Codes

(a) Both I and II (b) Only II
(c) Only I (d) None of these

13. Identify the resources from the information given below.

I. These resources may take thousands of years to be renewed or replenished.
II. Example of these resources are coal and petroleum.

Codes

(a) Renewable (b) Non-renewable
(c) Human made (d) Natural resources

Answers

1. (a)	2. (c)	3. (c)	4. (b)	5. (c)
6. (d)	7. (c)	8. (b)	9. (c)	10. (b)
11. (b)	12. (a)	13. (b)		

Match the Following

1.

List I	List II
A. Water	1. Natural resource
B. Minerals	2. Human-made resource
C. Education	3. Human resource
D. Roads	4. Renewable resource

Codes Competency Based

	A	B	C	D		A	B	C	D
(a)	4	1	3	2	(b)	1	2	3	4
(c)	3	2	1	4	(d)	4	3	1	2

Ans. (a)

Assertion-Reason

1 **Assertion** (A) The discovery of fire resulted in the development of cooking and various other techniques.

Reason (R) The invention of the wheel ultimately resulted in the development of newer modes of transport. **Competency Based**

Codes

(a) Both A and R are true and R is the correct explanation of A
(b) Both A and R are true, but R is not the correct explanation of A
(c) A is true, but R is false
(d) A is false, but R is true

2. **Assertion** (A) Water seems to be an unlimited renewable resource.

Reason (R) The shortage and drying up of natural water sources is a major problem in many parts of the world today. **Competency Based**

Codes

(a) Both A and R are true and R is the correct explanation of A
(b) Both A and R are true, but R is not the correct explanation of A
(c) A is true, but R is false
(d) A is false, but R is true

Ans. 1. (b) Both A and R are true, but R is not the correct explanation of A

2. (a) Both A and R are true and R is the correct explanation of A

Fill in the Blanks

1. Metallic minerals, coal, natural gas and petroleum are some examples of ...... resources.
2. Technology is a .... resource.
3. The discovery of ...... led to the practice of cooking.
4. .... resources are those which get renewed or replenished quickly.

Ans. 1. non-renewable 2. human-made
3. fire 4. Renewable

True/False

1. Water is not precious. We should not bother about its wasteful use.
2. All sources and substances have the equal economic value.
3. We should minimise the depletion of natural resources.
4. People are human-made resources.
5. Technology is a human resource.

Ans. 1. False 2. False 3. True 4. False 5. False

Case Based Question

1. Read the passage given below and answer the following questions.

Resources that are drawn from nature and used without much modification are called natural resources. The air we breathe, the water in our rivers and lakes, the soils and minerals are all natural resources. Many of these resources are gifts of nature and can be used directly. In some cases, tools and technology may be needed to use a natural resource in the best possible way. Natural resources can be broadly categorised into renewable and non-renewable resources.

Renewable resources are those which get renewed or replenished quickly. Some of these are unlimited and are not affected by human activities, such as solar and wind energy. Yet careless use of certain renewable resources like water, soil and forest can affect their stock. Water seems to be an unlimited renewable resource. But shortage and drying up of natural water sources is a major problem in many parts of the world today. Non-renewable resources are those which have a limited stock. Once the stocks are exhausted it may take thousands of years to be renewed or replenished. such resources are considered non-renewable. Coal, petroleum, and natural gas are some examples.

(i) Which of the following is considered a natural resource?
(a) Water (b) Roads
(c) Railway (d) All of these

(ii) Resources can be replenished quickly and are known as ....
(a) human-made
(b) renewable resource
(c) non-renweable resource
(d) human resources

(iii) What is the major problem in today's world?
(a) Shortage of solar energy.
(b) Excess of solar energy.
(c) Shortage of natural water resources.
(d) Excess of natural water resources.

(iv) Identify the resource among the following which is considered as non-renewable.
(a) Coal (b) Petroleum
(c) Water (d) Both (a) and (b)

Ans. (i) (a) Water
(ii) (b) renewable resource
(iii) (c) Shortage of natural water resources.
(iv) (d) Both (a) and (b)

Part II

Very Short Answer Type Questions

1. What is resource?

Ans. A resource is any thing which has utility to satisfy our needs.

2. Mention the different types of resources.

Ans. The different types of resources are
(i) Natural resources
(ii) Human-made resources
(iii) Human resources

3. How can a substance or material become a resource?

***Or* What makes a substance a resource?** **Diksha**

Ans. If a substance or material has some utility, it can become a resource.

4. How would you define the word utility?

Ans. Any thing has utility if it can be used in any way to satisfy human needs.

5. What do you understand by the word technology?

Ans. The application of latest knowledge and skill in doing or making things is called technology.

6. Name the two important factors which are responsible in making any substance into resource.

Ans. Time and technology are two important factors which are responsible in making any substance into a resource.

7. Write the name of natural resources.

Ans. The air, the water, the soils and the minerals are all natural resources.

8. How human-made resources differ from natural resources? **Competency Based**

Ans. Human-made resources are different from natural resources as human-made resources are created by human beings while on the contrary, natural resources are directly obtained by environment/ nature.

9. What do you understand by human resource development?

Ans. Improving the quality of people's skill so that they can be more advanced and useful, is called 'human resource development'.

10. What do you understand by stock of resource ?

Ans. Stock of resources is the amount of resource available for use.

11. How can we conserve the resources? **Diksha**

Ans. We can conserve the resources by reducing consumption, recycling and nursing.

Short Answer Type Questions

1. What is the significance of time and technology in making a substance a resource? Explain.

Ans. Time and technology are two most important factors in making substances as a resource.

With the passage of time, technology became more and more advanced.

As advanced technology is helpful in searching new directions to make life better, this advanced technology changes a useless substance in a useful resource.
For example, hydroelectricity which has made water a source of electricity.

2. Some resources have economic value, while some don't. Explain with example. **Competency Based**

Ans. It is true that some resources have economic value, while some resources do not have economic value. Any resource used for production and is market-oriented has an economic value.

For example, cotton is used in industries to produce textiles and other goods, so cotton has economic value. However, moral values and love for friends and family do not have economic value but have social value.

3. Why people are considered as a resource? What is human resource development?

Ans. People are considered as a resource because with their demands and capabilities, they can create new resources.
People are considered as a special resource as they can make the best use of nature to create more resources when they have the knowledge, skill and the technology to do so.
Education and health help in making people a valuable resource.

Improving the quality of people's skills so that they are able to create more resources is known as human resource development.

4. Distinguish between natural and human resources. **Competency Based**

Ans. The differences between natural and human resources are as follows

Natural Resources	Human Resources
Resources that are drawn from nature and used without much modification are called natural resources.	People are human resources.
Natural resources become resources when people put them into use according to their skill and abilities.	People who are skillful, healthy and intelligent serve their nation well and become human resources.
For example, river, lakes, air, soils, minerals, trees, mountains, plateaus, etc.	For example, doctor, engineer, lawyer, teacher, minister, policeman, cobbler, etc.

5. What do you mean by human-made resources? Give some examples.

Ans. When human beings change the original form of natural resource to make it more useful, it is called human-made resource.

For example, people use natural resources to make buildings, bridges, roads, machinery and vehicles, which are known as human made resources. Technology is also a human made resource.

6. People often got confused and think that human resources are similar to human-made resources. What do you think about it? Justify your answer. **Competency Based**

Ans. People often got confused and think that human resources are similar to human-made resources. However, these types of resources are different from each other.

When human beings change the original form of natural resources for their use, it is known as human-made resource while people themselves are human resources as it refers to the number and abilities of the people.

7. As human beings, how can we ensure sustainable development?

Ans. As human beings, we can ensure sustainable development in the following ways

(i) By ensuring that all uses of renewable resources are sustainable.

(ii) By ensuring that the diversity of life on the Earth is conserved.

(iii) By ensuring that the damage to natural environmental system is minimised.

8. Give four ways in which you can save energy at home. **Competency Based**

Ans. The four ways to save energy at home are

(i) We should put light and fans off when not in use.

(ii) We should not waste water unnecessarily.

(iii) Food should be cooked in pressure cooker.

(iv) Save petrol by following driving rules properly.

9. Resources are essential elements that humans utilise to meet their needs, encompassing natural, human-made, renewable and non- renewable categories. **Competency Based**

(i) Can you provide examples of natural resources and how they contribute to human well-being?

Ans. Some, examples of natural resources are air, water soil, fossil, etc.

Natural resources are important and contribute to human well-being as they provide clean air to breathe, water for drinking and agriculture and materials for industry.

(ii) Why is difference between renewable and non-renewable resource significant for sustainability?

Ans. Difference between renewable and non-renewable resources is significant because it highlights the need for sustainable use of resources to ensure their availability for future generations.

Long Answer Type Questions

1. Briefly describe the different types of resources.

Ans. Resources are generally classified into three types

(i) **Natural Resources** The resources which are directly obtained from nature and used without modification are called natural resources.

For example, the air we breathe, water in rivers and lakes, soils, minerals, sunlight, animals, etc are natural resources.

(ii) **Human-Made Resources** When human beings change the original form of natural resource to make it more useful, it is called human-made resource. For example, use of natural resources for making buildings, roads, machinery, etc.

(iii) **Human Resources** Human resource refers to the number and abilities of the people. People themselves are human resources.

2. An editor is writing an article about the conserving resources. Discuss the key points that should be mentioned in article and also explain some principles of sustainable development. **Competency Based**

Ans. Conserving resources is essential for a sustainable future. It involves sincerly managing our finite natural and human-made resources such as water, forests and minerals. By reducing waste, reusing items and recycling materials, we can minimise our environmental impact and decrease the strain on ecosystems. Sustainable practices, like efficient energy use and responsible consumption, help us safeguard our planet's health and ensure a better quality of life for future generation.

Some principles of substainable development are

- Respect and care for all forms of life.
- Improve the quality of human life.
- Conserve the Earth's vitality and diversity.
- Minimise the depletion of natural resources.
- Change personal attitude and practices towards the environment.
- Enable communities to care for their own environment.

3. Distinguish between renewable and non- renewable resources. **Diksha**

Ans. The differences between renewable and non- renewable resources are as follows

Renewable Resources	Non-Renewable Resources
Renewable resources are naturally replenished over time and can be sustained indefinitely if managed properly. Its examples includes solar energy, wind energy, hydro-power and biomass.	Non-renewable resources are finite and are not naturally replenished . Its examples include fossil (coal, oil, natural gas) and minerals (iron, copper, uranium).
These resources have low environmental impact and are considered eco friendly.	Extraction and use of non renewable resources can have significant environmental consequences, such as pollution and habitat destruction.
Renewable resources are typically abundant and do not deplete with use.	These resources are limited in quantity and will eventually be exhausted with continued consumption.

4. How the resources can be conserved? Explain.

Ans. There are many ways to conserve resources. Some examples include

- **Reducing consumption** This means using less of a resource in the first place. For example, we can reduce your consumption of water by taking shorter showers or turning off the faucet when we brush our teeth.
- **Recycling** This means processing used materials so that they can be used again. For example, we can recycle paper, plastic and metal.
- **Reusing** This means using an item multiple times without throwing it away. For example, we can reuse a water bottle or a reusable shopping bag.

Case Based Question

1. Read the passage given below and answer the following questions.

Value means worth. Some resources have economic value, some do not. For example, metals may have an economic value, but a beautiful landscape may not. But both are important and satisfy human needs. Some resources can become economically valuable with time. Your grandmother's home remedies have no commercial value today. But if they are patented and sold by a medical firm tomorrow, they could become economically valuable. Time and technology are two important factors that can change substances into resources. Both are related to the needs of the people. People themselves are the most important resource. It is their ideas, knowledge, inventions, and discoveries that lead to the creation of more resources. Each discovery or invention leads to many others. The discovery of fire led to the practice of cooking and other processes while the invention of the wheel ultimately resulted in the development of newer modes of transport. The technology to create hydroelectricity has turned energy in fast-flowing water into an important resource.

(i) What are some examples of resources that have economic value?

Ans. Metals, oil, food, and water are all examples of resources that have economic value.

(ii) What are the key factors that can turn substances into valuable resources?

Ans. The key factors that can turn substances into valuable resources are utility, value, time, technology, etc.

(iii) What did the invention of the wheel ultimately result in?

Ans. The invention of the wheel ultimately resulted in the development of newer modes of transport.

ASSESSMENT EXERCISE

Multiple Choice Questions (MCQs)

1. .... resource is a non- living resource.

(a) Abiotic (b) Biotic (c) Human (d) Natural

2. Coal is the example of which resource?

(a) Ubiquitous (b) Localised (c) Both (a) and (b) (d) None of these

3. Which one of the following is a biotic resource?

(a) Plants (b) Soils (c) Roads (d) Coal

Subjective Questions (VSA, SA & LA)

1. Write any two examples of potential resources.

2. Give three examples of actual resources.

3. What is Ubiquitous resource?

4. What do you understand by the word 'value'?

5. What do you mean by resources? Explain with examples.

6. Differentiate between conserving resources and sustainable development.

7. Differentiate between human-made resources and natural resources.

8. What are the different types of resources? Discuss.

9. Why resource conservation are important?

Land, Soil, Water, Natural Vegetation and Wildlife Resources

CHAPTER 2

People in various parts of the world have different lifestyles due to the difference in availability of resources. These resources are land, soil, water, natural plants, animals and technology. In this chapter, we will learn about land, its uses and conservation, soil and its formation, water, natural vegetation and wildlife resources.

2.1 Land

Land is an important natural resource. It covers around 30% of the Earth's surface, but all the parts of this land are not habitable.

There is **uneven population distribution** in different parts of the world, mainly due to differences in characteristics of land and climate.

Land with rugged mountains, steep slopes, low-lying flood-prone areas, deserts and dense forests is usually sparsely populated or uninhabited. On the other hand, plains and river valleys are suitable for agriculture and are densely populated.

KNOWLEDGE PLUS **Ninety per cent** of the world population occupies only thirty per cent of land area. The remaining seventy per cent of the land is either sparsely populated or uninhabited.

Land Use and its Conservation

Land is used for various purposes like agriculture, forestry, mining, housing, roads and setting up industries.

Land use depends on **physical factors** like terrain, soil, climate, minerals, and water, as well as **human factors** like population and technology.

Land can be categorised on the basis of ownership as follows

- **Private Land** It is owned by individuals.
- **Community Land** It is owned by community for common uses like collection of fodder, fruits, nuts or medicinal herbs. The community lands are also called **common property resources.**

Land degradation, **landslides**[1], soil erosion and desertification are major environmental threats that occur due to expansion of agriculture and construction activities.

Afforestation, land reclamation, regulated use of chemical pesticide and fertilisers and checks on overgrazing are some of the common methods used to conserve land resources.

2.2 Soil and its Formation

Soil is the thin upper layer of the Earth's surface. It is composed of organic matter, minerals, and weathered rocks formed through the process of **weathering**[2].

Fertility of soil depends on the right mixture of minerals and organic material.

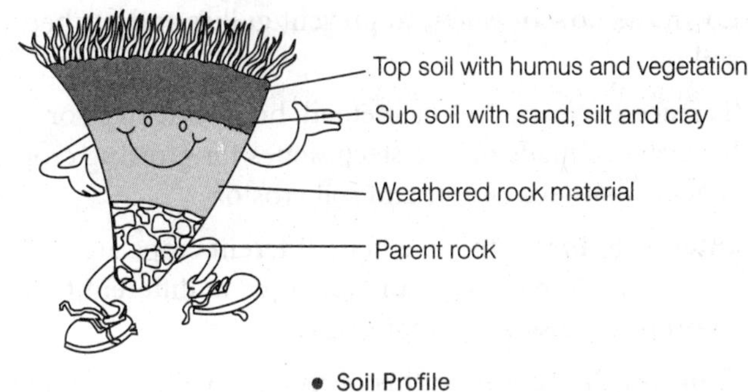

• Soil Profile

1 **Landslide** It refers to the mass movement of rock, debris or Earth down a slope.
2 **Weathering** It is the breaking up and decay of exposed rocks, by changes in temperature, frost action, plants, animals and human activity.

Factors of Soil Formation

Factors affecting soil formation include nature of the parent rock, climate, topography, organic matter and time. All these factors differ from place to place.

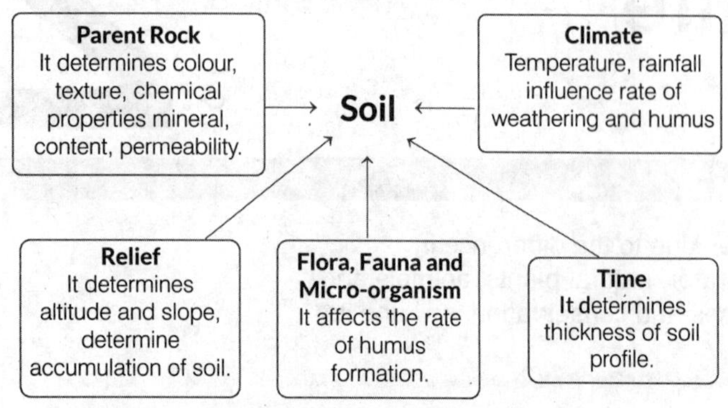

• Factors Affecting Soil Formation

KNOWLEDGE PLUS It takes hundreds of years to make just one centimetre of soil.

Soil Degradation and Conservation Measures

Soil erosion and depletion are major threats to soil. Both **human** and **natural factors** led to degradation of soil. These are

- Deforestation
- Overgrazing
- Overuse of chemical fertilisers or pesticides
- Rain wash
- Floods
- Landslides

Some methods of soil conservation are

- **Mulching** In this method, the clear ground between plants is covered with a layer of organic matter like straw to retain soil moisture.
- **Contour Barriers** In this method, stones, grass, soil are used to build barriers along contours. Trenches are made in front of the barriers to collect water.
- **Rock Dam** In this method, rocks are piled up to slow down the flow of water, to prevent gullies and further soil loss.
- **Terrace Farming** In this method, broad flat steps or terraces are made on the steep slopes for growing crops, reducing surface runoff and soil erosion.
- **Intercropping** In this method, different crops are grown in alternate rows and are sown at different times to protect the soil from rain wash.
- **Contour Ploughing** In this method, ploughing is done parallel to the contours of a hill slope to form a natural barrier for water to flow down the slope.
- **Shelterbelts** In this method, rows of trees are planted to check the wind movement and to protect soil cover, in coastal and dry regions.

2.2 Water

Earth is called the **water planet** because three-fourth part of the Earth's surface is covered with water.

Oceans cover two-third part of the Earth's surface, however ocean water is saline and not suitable for drinking.

Only 2.7% of water is fresh water out of which only 1% is fit for human use. It is found as **groundwater**, in rivers and lakes, and as **water vapour** in the atmosphere.

The total water volume of the Earth remains constant. It remains in continuous motion, cycling through oceans, air, land, and back again, through the processes like evaporation, precipitation and run-off. This is referred to as **water cycle**.

Problems and Conservation of Water Resources

Growing population, rising demand for food and cash crops, urbanisation, and rising standard of living are the major causes of shortages in the supply of fresh water.

There is water scarcity in many regions of the world like Africa, West Asia, South Asia, parts of the USA, Mexico, South America, Australia and countries located in drought-prone areas.

Discharge of sewage, agricultural, chemicals and industrial waste are major contaminants of water.

Afforestation, adopting effective techniques for irrigation like lining canals, using sprinklers or drip irrigation and promoting **rainwater harvesting**[3] can be done for conservation of water resources.

KNOWLEDGE PLUS In 1975, the consumption of water for human use was 3850 cu km/year. It raised to more than 6000 cu km/year in the year 2000.

2.3 Natural Vegetation and WildLife

Natural vegetation and wildlife exist in the **biosphere** which is a narrow zone of contact between the lithosphere, hydrosphere and atmosphere.

In biosphere, living beings are inter-related and interdependent on each other for their survival. This life supporting system is known as the **ecosystem**.

3 **Rainwater harvesting** It is the process of collecting rainwater from rooftops and directing it to an appropriate location, where it is stored for future use.

Natural vegetation and wildlife are valuable resources. Plants provide various things and animals are important for maintaining balance in the ecosystem.

Distribution of Natural Vegetation

The growth of vegetation depends primarily on temperature and moisture. The major vegetation of the world are categorised as forests, grasslands, scrubs and **tundra**[4].

Large trees grow in areas of heavy rainfall. As the amount of moisture decreases, their size and density reduces.

Short trees and grasses grow in areas of moderate rainfall forming the grasslands of the world and thorny bushes and scrubs grow in areas of low rainfall.

Conservation of Natural Vegetation and Wildlife

Changes of climate and human interferences can cause the loss of natural habitats for plants and animals. Deforestation, soil erosion, tsunami, landslide, etc are major causes for extinction of natural vegetation and wildlife.

Poaching[5] is a major concern leading to a decline in animal species, including tigers, lions and elephants. These animals are poached for collection and illegal trade of hides, skins, nails, horns, etc.

Some of the methods for conserving natural vegetation and wildlife are

- **National Parks**[6], **Wildlife Sanctuaries**[7] and **Biosphere Reserves**[8] are made to protect natural vegetation and wildlife.
- Awareness programmes like social forestry and Vanamohatasava should be encouraged at the regional and community level.
- Many countries have passed laws against the trade as well as killing of birds and animals.
- An international convention **CITES** (Convention on International Trade in Endangered Species of Wild Fauna and Flora) has been established.

CITES

It is an international agreement between governments. It lists several species of **animals** and **birds** in which trade is prohibited.

It aims to ensure that international trade in specimens of wild animals and plants does not threaten their survival.

4 **Tundra** It is the type of vegetation found in cold regions like the Arctic.

5 **Poaching** It refers to illegal killing of animals for trade.

6 **National Parks** These are protected areas designated by governments for the conservation of natural landscapes and wildlife.

7 **Wildlife Sanctuaries** These are protected areas which aimed at the protection of a particular animal or general wildlife.

8 **Biosphere Reserves** These are a series of protected areas meant for the conservation of plants and animals. They are linked through a global network and aimed to demonstrate relationship between conservation and development.

LAND, SOIL, WATER, NATURAL VEGETATION AND WILDLIFE RESOURCES

Land
Covers around 30% of the Earth's surface
- Private Land
- Community Land

Land Use

Physical Factors
- Terrain
- Soil
- Topography
- Climate
- Minerals
- Availability of water

Human Factors
- Population
- Technology

Land Conservation
- Afforestation
- Land reclamation
- Regulated use of chemical pesticides and fertilisers
- Checks on overgrazing

Natural Vegetation
Provide us timber, oxygen, shelter to animals

Distribution
- Forests
- Grasslands
- Scrubs
- Tundra

Conservation of Natural Vegetation and Wildlife
- National Parks
- Wildlife Sanctuaries
- Biosphere Reserves

Soil
Thin upper layer of Earth's surface

Formation
- Time
- Relief
- Climate
- Parent rock
- Flora, Fauna and Micro-organism

Degradation
- Deforestation
- Overgrazing
- Overuse of chemical fertilisers/pesticides
- Rain wash
- Floods
- Landslides

Conservation
- Mulching
- Rock dam
- Contour barriers
- Terrace farming
- Intercropping
- Contour ploughing
- Shelter belts

Water
Covers around 3/4 part of Earth's Surface

Distribution
- **Ocean Water** Around 97%
- **Fresh Water** Around 3%

Conservation
- Rainwater harvesting
- Adopting effective techniques of irrigation

NCERT FOLDER

Covering Intext Questions and Exercises of NCERT

NCERT ON PAGE 7 (LET'S DO)

Q.1 Observe the land, type of soil and water availability in the region you live. Discuss in your class, how it has influenced the life style of people there.

Ans. I live in XYZ, city where water availability is limited and the region faces water scarcity, especially during the summer months.

This situation has influenced people's lifestyles by necessitating water conservation practices, such as rainwater harvesting and efficient water usage. It has also led to the dependence on groundwater sources and the need for infrastructure like water tanks and pumps to ensure a regular water supply.

NCERT ON PAGE 8 (LETF'S DO)

Q.2 Talk to some elderly person in your family or neighbourhood and collect information about changes in the land use over the years, in the place where you live. Display your findings on a bulletin board in your classroom.

Ans. I had talked to my neighbor, who has lived in Delhi for over 60 years. They shared that Delhi has witnessed a significant transformation in land use. Previously, there were more open spaces and farmlands, but over the years, these were changed into a busy area due to the construction of residential areas, commercial spaces, and infrastructure.

NCERT ON PAGE 12 (ACTIVITY)

Q.3 In India soils could be alluvial, black, red, laterite, desertic and mountain soil. Collect a handful of different types of soil and observe. How are they different?

Ans. In India, various soil types include alluvial, black, red, laterite, desertic and mountain soil. These soils differ in color, texture and composition as follows

- Alluvial soil is typically light brown and has a fine texture.
- Black soil is dark and has a clay-like texture.
- Red soil is reddish due to iron content and is sandy.
- Laterite soil is red and hard when dry, but soft when wet.
- Desertic soil is pale and sandy,
- Mountain soil varies in color and can be stony or loamy.

NCERT ON PAGE 13 (ACTIVITY)

Q.4 Take two trays A and B of same size. Make six holes at one end of these trays and then fill them with the same amount of soil. Leave the soil in tray A bare while sow wheat or rice grains in tray B. When the grain in tray B has grown a few centimetres high, place both the trays in such a way that they are on a slope. Pour one mug of water from the same height into each tray. Collect the muddy water that trickles down the holes of both trays in two separate containers and compare how much soil is washed out of each tray?

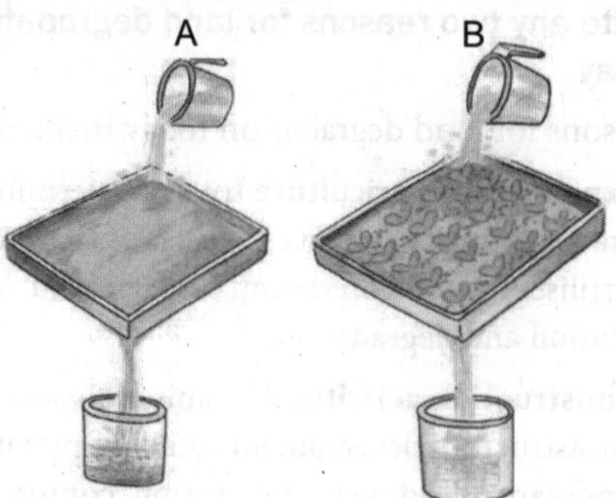

Ans. If we pour one mug of water from the same height into each tray after doing all the activity and collect the muddy water that trickles down the holes of both trays in two separate containers, then tray B, with the growing grains, will have significantly less soil washed out during the water pouring. It is because the roots of the plants hold the soil together, preventing erosion. Tray A, without plants, will experience more soil erosion, leading to a greater amount of soil washed away.

NCERT ON PAGE 14 (ACTIVITY)

Q.5 An average urban Indian uses about 150 litres of water every day.

Use	Litres per person per day
Drinking	3
Cooking	4
Bathing	20
Flushing	40
Washing clothes	40
Washing utensils	20
Gardening	23
Total	150

Can you suggest some ways to bring down this amount?

Ans. Following are the ways to bring down the average every day water consumption of urban India

- Fix any leaky pipes or taps promptly.
- Use a bucket instead of a hose for gardening.
- Close the taps when water is not in use.
- Collect rainwater for various non-drinking purposes.
- Educate family members about the importance of conserving water.

EXERCISES

Q.1 Answer the following questions.

(i) Which are the two main climatic factors responsible for soil formation?

Ans. The two main climatic factors responsible for soil formation are temperature and rainfall which influence the rate of weathering and humus formation.

(ii) Write any two reasons for land degradation today.

Ans. Reasons for land degradation today include

- **Expansion of agriculture** Intensive farming practices, including excessive use of chemical fertilisers and deforestation for farmland, lead to soil erosion and degradation.
- **Construction activities** Urbanisation and infrastructure development can disrupt natural landscapes, leading to soil erosion, compaction and loss of fertile top soil.

(iii) Why is land considered an important resource?

Ans. Land is an important resource because it provides surface for agriculture, building houses, cultivation, construction of mining, setting up industries, etc.

(iv) Name any two steps that government has taken to conserve plants and animals.

Ans. The two steps that government has taken to conserve plants and animals are as follows

(a) Government has established National Parks, Wildlife Sanctuaries and Biosphere Reserves in different parts of India to protect natural vegetation and wildlife.

(b) Awareness programmes like social forestry and Vanamahotasava have been encouraged at the regional and community levels.

(v) Suggest three ways to conserve water.

Ans. Three ways to conserve water are as follows

- Collect rainwater in tanks and use it for various purposes.
- Fix leaky taps and pipes to prevent water wastage.
- Practice responsible irrigation techniques, such as drip irrigation, to minimise water use in agriculture.

Q.2 Tick the correct answer.

(i) Which one of the following is not a factor of soil formation?

(a) Time (b) Soil texture

(c) Organic matter

Ans. (b) Soil texture

(ii) Which one of the following methods is most appropriate to check soil erosion on steep slopes?

(a) Shelter belts (b) Mulching

(c) Terrace cultivation

Ans. (c) Terrace cultivation

(iii) Which one of the following methods is not in favour of the conservation of nature?

(a) Switch off the bulb when not in use.

(b) Close the tap immediately after using.

(c) Dispose polypacks after shopping.

Ans. (c) Dispose polypacks after shopping.

Q.3 Match the following.

	List I		List II
A.	Land use	1.	Prevent soil erosion
B.	Humus	2.	Narrow zone of contact between the lithosphere, hydrosphere and atmosphere.
C.	Rock dams	3.	Productive use of land
D.	Biosphere land	4.	Organic matter deposited on top soil
		5.	Contour ploughing

Ans. (a) A-3, B-4, C-1, D-2

Q.4 State whether the given statement is true or false. If true, write the reasons.

(i) Ganga-Brahmaputra plain of India is an overpopulated region.

Ans. True, as the land is very fertile and suitable for cultivation.

(ii) Water availability per person in India is declining.

Ans. True, because of ever growing population, wastage, drying-up of water resources and increasing water pollution.

(iii) Rows of trees planted in the coastal areas to check the wind movement is called intercropping.

Ans. False, it is called shelter-belts, whereas intercroping means growing different crops in alternates rows and sown at different times to protect the soil from rain-wash.

(iv) Human interference and changes of climate can maintain the ecosystem.

Ans. False, it will deteriorate the ecosystem.

Q.5 Discuss some more reasons which are responsible for changes of land use pattern. Has your place undergone any change in the land use pattern in recent years?

Find out from your parents and elderly people. You can conduct an interview by asking the following questions.

Place	When your grand parents were in their 30s	When your parents were in their 30s	Why do you think this is happening?	Are common areas and open spaces disappearing?
Rural				
Number of cattle and poultry owned				
Number of trees and ponds in the village				
Main occupation of the head of the family				
Urban				
Number of cars owned				
Number of rooms in the house				
Number of metalled roads				
Number of flyovers in the city				
Number of parks and playgrounds				

Based on the table you have just completed, draw a picture of land use patterns that you foresee in your neighbourhood after 20 years. Why do you think that land use patterns change over the years?

Ans.

Place	When your grand parents were in their 30s	When your parents were in their 30s	Why do you think this is happening?	Are common areas and open spaces disappearing?
Rural				
Number of cattle and poultry owned	Cattle:02 per family	01	Because of shifting to other jobs from agriculture.	Yes
Number of trees and ponds in the village	Trees: 150 Ponds:12	10 01	Because of ever increasing population.	Yes
Main occupation of the head of the family	Agriculture	Small shop	Due to unproductive land and its small size.	NIL
Urban				
Number of cars owned	NIL	01 car per household	Due to increase in income.	NIL
Number of rooms in the house	4	2	Due to division among members.	Yes
Number of metalled roads	1	4	Due to increase in transport facilities.	Yes
Number of flyovers in the city	NIL	4	Due to congestion on the road.	Yes
Number of parks and playgrounds	2 and 4	2 and 2	Due to growth of population.	Yes

Some other reasons responsible for change in land use pattern are rise in population and increase in demand for land for agriculture, transport, housing complexes, industries, etc.

Yes, my area has also undergone changes in land use patterns. It has evolved from a primarily green agricultural land and spacious city to a bustling metropolis.

Land use patterns change over the years due to urbanisation, agriculture evolution, technological advances and economic shifts, impacting natural and human environments.

REVIEW EXERCISE

Including Competency Based Questions

Part I

Multiple Choice Questions (MCQs)

1. Common property resource is also known as

(a) industrial land (b) agricultural land
(c) community land (d) private land

2. 90% of the world population occupies only ....% of land area. Diksha

(a) 30 (b) 33 (c) 32 (d) 27

3. It takes hundreds of years to make just one centimetre of .... Diksha

(a) rock (b) soil (c) sand (d) land

4. The breaking up of rocks is known as .... Diksha

(a) erosion (b) reclamation
(c) degradation (d) weathering

5. The total Earth's surface cover with water is about ....

(a) one-fourth (b) two-third
(c) three-fourth (d) one-third

6. What is the percentage of usable water for human consumption?

(a) 97 (b) 12 (c) 1 (d) 10

7. Which is not an example of ground water?

(a) Water flowing in rivers
(b) Water through hand pumps
(c) Water through submersible pumps
(d) Water through wells

8. Which of the following factors influences the type and distribution of natural vegetation?

(a) Landforms (b) Soil
(c) Climate (d) All of these

9. The major vegetation types of the world are grouped as forests, grasslands, tundra and

(a) shrubs (b) herbs
(c) scrubs (d) trees

10. Vanamohatasava is celebrated to create awareness about

(a) conservation of forests
(b) conservation of minerals
(c) recycling of water
(d) preserving historical monuments

11. Ravi, a student of class VIII, told his friend Naveen that natural vegetation and wildlife exist only in the narrow zone of contact between lithosphere, hydrosphere and atmosphere. What is the from used for that? Competency Based

(a) Biosphere (b) Stratosphere
(c) Ecosystem (d) Environment

12. Rahul, a resident of Rajasthan, see a major extinction of natural vegetation and wildlife in his town and nearby area. Which of the following is/are reasons for the changing? Competency Based

(a) Deforestation (b) Constructional activities
(c) Poaching (d) All of these

13. What is a biosphere reserve ?

(a) Protected area linked through global network
(b) Land use for production
(c) Farmers land
(d) None of the above

14. Species of some animals are on the verge of extinction as their population has decreased considerably. Such species are known as Diksha

(a) Endangered species (b) Extinct species
(c) Dying species (d) Dead species

15. The use of land is determined by factors such as

(i) topography (ii) soil
(iii) climate (iv) mineral

Choose the correct option.

(a) (i), (ii) and (iii) (b) (i), (iii) and (iv)
(c) (ii), (iii) and (iv) (d) All are correct.

16. Consider the following statements.

I. Community land is owned by the community for common uses like a collection of fodder, fruits, nuts, or medicinal herbs.
II. The quality of land also differs from place to place.

Which of the above statements is/are correct?

(a) I and II both (b) Only II
(c) Only II (d) None of these

17. Consider the following statements.

I. The thin layer of grainy substance covering the surface of the Earth is called the biosphere.
II. Only human factors can lead to the degradation of soils.

Which of the above statements is/are correct?

(a) I and II both (b) Only I
(c) Only II (d) None of these

Answers

1. (c)	2. (a)	3. (b)	4. (d)	5. (c)
6. (c)	7. (a)	8. (d)	9. (c)	10. (a)
11. (a)	12. (d)	13. (a)	14. (a)	15. (d)
16. (a)	17. (d)			

Match the Following

1.

	List I		List II
A.	Parent rock	1.	Method of soil conservation
B.	Mulching	2.	Method of land resources conservation
C.	Afforestation	3.	One of the main factors of soil formation
D.	Flora-Fauna	4.	Affect the rate of humus formation

Codes

	A	B	C	D		A	B	C	D
(a)	3	1	2	4	(b)	2	4	3	1
(c)	1	2	4	3	(d)	4	3	1	2

Ans. 1. (a)

Assertion-Reason

1. **Assertion** (A) Land with rugged mountains and dense forests is usually sparsely populated.

   Reason (R) Plains and river valleys are suitable for agriculture and are densely populated.

   Codes

   (a) Both A and R are true and R is the correct explanation of A

   (b) Both A and R are true, but R is not the correct explanation of A

   (c) A is true, but R is false

   (d) A is false, but R is true

2. **Assertion** (A) The ocean water is saline and not fit for human consumption.

   Reason (R) Fresh water accounts for only about 2.7 per cent.

   Codes

   (a) Both A and R are true and R is the correct explanation of A

   (b) Both A and R are true, but R is not the correct explanation of A

   (c) A is true, but R is false

   (d) A is false, but R is true

Ans. 1. (b) Both A and R are true, but R is not the correct explanation of A

2. (b) Both A and R are true, but R is not the correct explanation of A

Fill in the Blanks

1. The process responsible for soil formation is called ..... .
2. The percentage of freshwater on the Earth is ......
3. The colour, texture, etc of soil is determined by ....
4. Climatic factors influencing rate of weathering include .... and ....
5. 70% of fresh water exists as ....

Ans. 1. weathering 2. 2.7 3. parent rock 4. rainfall, temperature 5. ice sheets

True/False

1. The growing population is not a cause of soil erosion.
2. Forests and other vegetation reduce surface run-off.
3. Most of Africa and entire Australia are facing shortages in fresh water supply.
4. Vegetation and wildlife are valuable resources.
5. It takes hundreds of years to make just one centimetre of soil.

Ans. 1. True 2. True 3. True 4. True 5. True

Picture Based Questions

1. **Look at the picture provided below and answer the following question.** **Competency Based**

Which of the following is one of the factor of landslides?

(a) Evaporation (b) Rock dam
(c) Mulching (d) Earthquakes

2. **The given picture represents a type of farming in which broad flat steps are made on the steep slopes. Which type of farming is this?** **Competency Based**

(a) Contour ploughing (b) Shift farming
(c) Terrace farming (d) Intercrop farming

Ans. 1. (d) Earthquakes 2. (c) Terrace farming

Case Based Question

1. Read the given passage and answer the following questions.

Forests are our wealth. Plants give shelter to the animals and together they maintain the ecosystem. Changes in climate and human interference can cause the loss of natural habitats for plants and animals. Many species have become vulnerable or endangered and some are on the verge of extinction. The animals are poached for collection and illegal trade of hides, skins, nails, teeth, horns as well and feathers. Some of these animals are tiger, lion, elephant, deer, black buck, crocodile, rhinoceros, snow leopard, ostrich, and peacock. These can be conserved by increasing awareness. National parks, wildlife sanctuaries, and biosphere reserves are made to protect our natural vegetation and wildlife. Conservation of creeks, lakes, and wetlands is necessary to save the precious resource from depletion.

(i) What is the primary reason for the loss of natural habitats for plants and animals?

(a) Earthquake (b) Human interference
(c) Forest fires (d) Landslides

(ii) What is/are the primary reason for poaching of animals ?

(a) Scientific research
(b) Food consumption
(c) Collection and illegal trade of various body parts
(d) For their trade

(iii) Which among the following is the international convention that prohibits the trade of several species of animals and birds?

(a) CITES (b) UNESCO
(c) WWF (d) IUCN

(iv) What is the purpose of national parks, wildlife sanctuaries, and biosphere reserves?

(a) To control population
(b) To encourage tourism
(c) To protect natural vegetation and wildlife
(d) None of the above

Ans (i) (b) Human interference
(ii) (c) Collection and legal trade of various body pails
(iii) (a) CITES
(iv) (c) To protect natural vegetation and wildlife

Part II

Very Short Answer Type Questions

1. Define the term land use. Diksha

Ans. The term land use means use of land for different purposes such as agriculture, forestry, mining, building houses.

2. Which two factors mainly determine the use of land?

Ans. The factors which determine land use are physical factors such as topography, soil, climate, minerals and availability of water and human factors such as population and technology.

3. What is soil?

Ans. Soil is the thin upper layer of the Earth's surface.

4. Define water scarcity.

Ans. Water scarcity refers to shortage of water as compared to its demand.

5. What are the threatened species?

Ans. All the species which are listed in endangered, critically endangered and vulnerable group are altogether called threatened species.

6. Name the regions of the world which are facing water scarcity.

Ans. The regions of the world which are facing water scarcity are Africa, West Asia, South Asia, parts of Western USA, North-West Mexico, parts of South America and entire Australia.

7. Why are animals poached?

Ans. The animals are poached for collection and illegal trade of hides, skins, nails, teeth, horns as well as feathers.

8. Protected forests too are not completely safe for wild animals. Why? Competency Based

Ans. Protected forests too are not completely safe for wild animals because poachers have found access in these areas and are killing animals.

9. What do you understand by national park?

Ans. National parks are protected areas dessignated by governments for the conservation of natural landscapes and wildlife.

10. What do you understand by Biosphere Reserve?

Ans. Biosphere reserves are a series of protected areas meant for the conservation of plants and animals. They are linked through a global network and aimed to demonstrate relationship between conservation and development.

Short Answer Type Questions

1. Comment on the statement, "Land is the most important resource". Competency Based

Or What is the importance of land as resource?' Diksha

Ans. Land is the most important resource because

(i) All agricultural and industrial processes depend on it.

(ii) All living beings, animals and plants are found on the surface of land.

(iii) Land serves as a links between atmosphere and hydrosphere.

2. Why is there uneven distribution of population?

Or What are the reasons for uneven distribution of population in different parts of the world ? **Diksha**

Ans. The uneven distribution of population is because of the following reasons

(i) **Geographic Features** Uneven distribution is influenced by land characteristics like rugged mountains, deserts, and dense forests which tend to be sparsely populated, while plains and river valleys are suitable for habitation.

(ii) **Climate** Harsh climates such as extreme cold or dry regions are not preferred by population, while temperate and fertile areas attract settlements.

(iii) **Resource Availability** Areas with abundant resources like fertile soil and freshwater sources tend to have higher populations, while resource-scarce regions have lower populations.

3. Why is land use pattern changing?

Ans. Land use pattern is changing because of the following reasons

- People started encroaching the common lands to build up commercial areas, housing complexes in the urban areas.
- Changes in agricultural practices, such as mechanisation and crop diversification affect land use pattern.
- Cultural changes which are taking place in our society also changes land use pattern.

4. How is vegetation useful to us?

Ans. Vegetation is useful to us as

- It provide us with timber.
- It give shelter to animals.
- It produce oxygen that we breathe.
- It protect soils so essential for growing crops.
- It act as shelter belts.
- It help in storage of underground water.

5. The Indian subcontinent boasts of serving as the natural habitat of a large and varied wildlife. We can find some of the most magnificent as well as the rarest wildlife species of the world in the country. **Competency Based**

(i) What are the major factors that led to the extinction of these wildlife species?

Ans. Cutting of forests, change in climate condition, constructional activities, forest sizes and poaching are some major factors that led to the extinction of wildlife species.

(ii) What are some major species that are on extinction and need to protect?

Ans. Tiger, lion, elephant, black buck, rhinoceros are some major that are on extinction species which need to be protected.

6. Why should we conserve biodiversity?

Ans. We should conserve biodiversity because

(i) Biodiversity ensures resilience, stability and adaptability in ecosystems.

(ii) It provides essential resources, such as food, medicine and clean water and supports economic activities like agriculture and tourism.

(iii) Biodiversity has intrinsic value, contributing to cultural heritage, scientific knowledge and the appreciation of Earth's beauty.

7. Why is it important to raise awareness about the conservation of natural vegetation and wildlife and what measures are taken to conserve these resources?

Ans. It is important to raise awareness about natural vegetation and wildlife as they are on the verge of extinction.

To conserve these, following measures are taken by government

- National parks, wildlife sanctuaries, biosphere reserves are made to protect our natural vegetation and wildlife.
- Awareness programmes such as social forestry and Vanamohatasava are encouraged, at regional and community level.
- Government policies like Tiger Conserve Act, 1972 and International convention like CITES are made to protect wildlife.

Long Answer Type Questions

1. Define the following

(i) Common Property Resource (ii) Biosphere

(iii) Ecosystem

Ans. (i) **Common Property Resource** Community land is owned by the community for common uses like collection of fodder, fruits, nuts or medicinal herbs. These community lands are also called common property resources.

(ii) **Biosphere** It is a narrow zone of contact between the lithosphere, hydrosphere and atmosphere.

(iii) **Ecosystem** In the biosphere, living beings are inter-related and inter-dependent on each other for survival. This life supporting system is known as the ecosystem.

2. What are the factors responsible for soil formation? Diksha

Ans. The factors responsible for soil formation are

(i) **Parent rock** It determines the physical and chemical properties of the soil. It also controls the porosity of the soil.

(ii) **Relief** It determines the layer of accumulation or depth of the soil.

(iii) **Climate** Temperature and rainfall influence the rate of weathering. Weathering accelerates the rate of soil formation.

(iv) **Flora, Fauna and Microorganism** These influence the rate of humus formation.

(v) **Time** It is a very important factor in determining the depth or thickness of the soil.

3. What are the different methods of soil conservation? Diksha

Ans. The different methods of soil conservation are

- **Mulching** In this method, the clear ground between plants is covered with a layer of organic matter like straw, to retain soil moisture.
- **Contour barriers** In this method, stones, grass, soil are used to build barriers along contours. Trenches are made in front of the barriers to collect water.
- **Rock dam** In this method, rocks are piled up to slow down the flow of water, to prevent gullies and further soil loss.
- **Terrace farming** In this method, broad flat steps or terraces are made on the steep slopes for growing crops, reducing surface runoff and soil erosion.
- **Intercropping** In this method, different crops are grown in alternate rows and are sown at different times to protect the soil from rain wash.
- **Contour ploughing** In this method, ploughing is done parallel to the contours of a hill slope to form a natural barrier for water to flow down the slope.
- **Shelterbelts** In this method, rows of trees are planted to check the wind movement and to protect soil cover, in coastal and dry regions.

4. What is rainwater harvesting? Give some advantages of rainwater harvesting. Diksha

Ans. Rainwater harvesting is the process of collecting rainwater from rooftops and directing it to an appropriate location, where it is stored for future use.

The advantages of rainwater harvesting are as follows

- It reduces the consumption of groundwater.
- It is free from pollutants as well as salts, minerals and other natural and man-made contaminants.
- It is considered as the purest form of natural water.
- The stored water is a reliable source of water when other sources dried up.

5. How can we reduce excess use of water ?

Ans. Following methods can be used to reduce the excess use of water

(i) Promoting afforestation and reforestation, as vegetation cover slow the surface run off and increase the ground water storage.

(ii) Water harvesting through root top tanks and bamboo channels.

(iii) Promoting canal irrigation for agricultural field.

(iv) Use of sprinklers for watering plants.

(v) Drip irrigations can be used in dry regions.

6. What are the factors responsible for distribution of natural vegetation?

Ans The factors responsible for the distribution of natural vegetation include

- **Temperature and Moisture** These are primary determinants, with heavy rainfall supporting dense forests, moderate rainfall leading to grasslands, and low rainfall resulting in thorny shrubs and scrubs.
- **Climate Change** Alterations in climate patterns can disrupt the natural habitats for plants and animals.
- **Human Interferences** Deforestation, soil erosion and other activities like poaching can lead to changes in natural vegetation distribution.
- **Soil erosion, Tsunamis and Landslides** Natural disasters and soil erosion also impact the distribution of vegetation.
- **Loss of Habitat** Human activities and environmental changes can lead to the endangerment and extinction of various species of plants and animals.

7. What are the reasons for the extinction of different species? Diksha

Ans The reasons for the extinction of different species include

- **Climate change and Habitat Destruction** Alterations in temperature and moisture levels can disrupt ecosystems, making them unsuitable for certain species.
- **Human Interference** Activities like deforestation, poaching, and illegal wildlife trade can directly harm and deplete animal populations.
- **Pollution** Contamination of natural habitats and water sources can adversely affect species and their habitats.
- **Over-exploitation** Excessive hunting or fishing for resources like hides, skins, horns and tusks can drive species to extinction.
- **Loss of Natural Habitats** Factors such as soil erosion, landslides, and human development can lead to the loss of critical habitats for plants and animals, making them vulnerable to extinction.

8. **Landslides are simply defined as the mass movement of rock, debris or earth down a slope. Mention some methods to mitigate landslides.** **Competency Based**

Ans. Some methods to mitigate landslides are
- Hazard mapping to locate areas prone to landslides. Hence, such areas can be avoided for building settlements.
- Construction of retention wall to stop land from slipping.
- Increase in the vegetation cover to stop landslide.
- The surface drainage control works can be implemented to control the movement of landslide along with rain water and spring flows.

Picture Based Question

1. **Read the given articles carefully and give answer to the following questions.**

(i) Read the news item and find out how fire started in California? Could it be avoided?

(ii) Write some measures to avoid this kind of hazard.

Ans. (i) The main cause of fire in California was human fault. A child burnt a match stick and threw it carelessly.

(ii) This hazard could have been avoided if the match was kept in safe custody of the family.

Case Based Question

1. **Read the passage given below and answer the following questions.**

A massive landslide hit Pangi village near Reckong Peo in Kinnaur district of Himachal Pradesh and damaged a 200-metre stretch of old Hindustan- Tibet road, National Highway- 22. This landslide was triggered by intense blasting at Pangi village. Due to the blasting, this weak zone of slope collapsed and caused intense damage to the road and nearby villages. The Pangi village was completely vacated to avoid any possible loss of life.

(i) What do you understand by 'landslide'?

Ans. Landslide is the mass movement of rock, debris or Earth down a slope. They often take place in conjunction with earthquakes, volcanoes and so on.

(ii) What are the factors responsible for landslide?

Ans. The factors which are responsible for landslide are
- earthquake
- floods
- volcanoes
- human factors and so on.

(iii) What type of topography gives rise to a major and widely spread landslide?

Ans. Hilly terrain with steep slope, unstable geographical conditions and also the weak zones give rise to the major and widely spread landslides.

ASSESSMENT EXERCISE

Multiple Choice Questions (MCQs)

1. The Earth's total land is about .... per cent of the total area of Earth's surface.
(a) 20 (b) 25
(c) 30 (d) 32

2. Living beings are inter-related and inter-dependent on each other for survival called ....
(a) Lithosphere (b) Biosphere
(c) Hydrosphere (d) Atmosphere

3. What is/are the major threats to environment?
(a) Climate change
(b) Soil erosion
(c) Promoting tourism
(d) Both (a) and (b)

Subjective Questions (VSA, SA & LA)

1. Define weathering.
2. What do you mean by community land?
3. Write one method of water conservation.
4. What is Parent Rock?
5. Explain Afforestation.
6. Explain water cycle and its uses.
7. Define CITES.
8. Difference between National Park and Biosphere Reserve.
9. Explain how land are classified broadly?
10. Discuss the factors of soil formation.

Agriculture

CHAPTER 3

The science and art of cultivation on the soil, raising crops and rearing livestock is known as agriculture. The word agriculture is derived from Latin words **ager** or **agri** meaning soil and **culture** meaning cultivation. There are three types of economic activities that are involved in the transformation from a plant to a finished product. These are **primary**[1], **secondary**[2] and **tertiary**[3] activities.

Agriculture is a **primary activity**. It includes growing of fruits, crops, vegetables, flowers and rearing of livestock. About 50% of the world's population is engaged in agriculture, and in India, two-thirds of the population depend on it.

Agriculture depends on favorable topography of soil and climate. The land on which the crops are grown is known as **arable land.**

3.1 Farming System

Agriculture or farming system includes **inputs** like seeds, fertilisers, machinery and labour and **outputs** such as crops, wool, dairy and poultry products. It also involves, operations like ploughing, sowing, and harvesting.

Farming is practised in various ways across the world. On the basis of the geographical conditions, demand of produce, labour and level of technology, farming can be classified into two main types. These are **subsistence farming** and **commercial farming**.

Subsistence Farming

Subsistence farming is practised to meet the needs of the farmer's family. It can be classified as **intensive subsistence** and **primitive subsistence farming**. These are discussed below

Intensive Subsistence Farming

In this type of farming, a small plot of land is cultivated using, simple tools and more labor. It requires climate with a large number of days having sunshine and fertile soils. Rice is mainly grown through intensive subsistence farming. Other crops include wheat, maize, pulses and oilseeds. It is common in densely populated monsoon regions of South, South-East and East Asia.

Primitive Subsistence Farming

It includes shifting cultivation and nomadic herding. These are discussed below

- **Shifting Cultivation** It is practised in thickly forested areas of the Amazon basin, tropical africa, etc. It involves clearing of land by felling of trees and burning them.

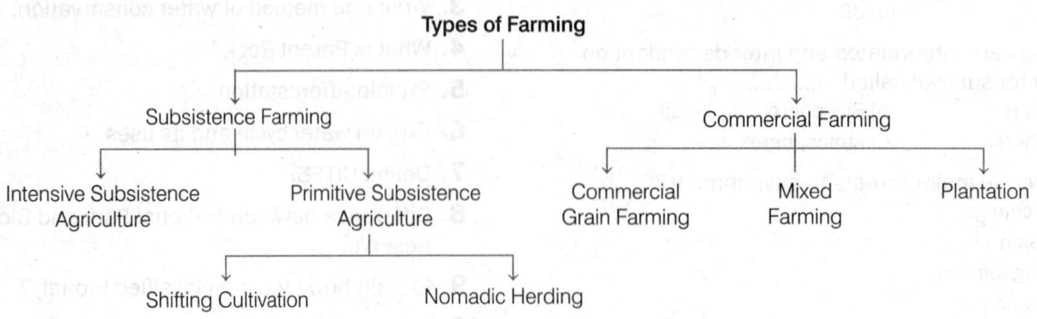

1 **Primary Activities** These involve activities related to extraction and production of natural resources, e.g. agriculture, fishing and gathering.

2 **Secondary Activities** These involve processing of the resources produced through primary activities, e.g. manufacturing steel, baking bread, and weaving cloth.

3 **Tertiary Activities** These provide support services to the primary and secondary sectors, e.g. transport, trade, banking, insurance and advertising.

Then, the ashes remained are mixed with soil to grow crops like maize and potatoes.

After the soil loses its fertility, the land is abandoned and a new land is cleared. Shifting cultivation is also known as **slash and burn agriculture**, **Jhumming** (North-East India), **Milpa** (Mexico), **Roca** (Brazil) and **Ladang** (Malaysia).

- **Nomadic Herding** It is practised in semi-arid and arid regions like Sahara, Central Asia, Rajasthan, and Jammu and Kashmir. In this type of farming, herdsmen move from place to place with their animals in search of fodder and water.

  Animals like sheep, camel, yak and goats are commonly reared by herders which provides milk, meat, wool, hides and other products to their families.

Commercial Farming

Commercial farming involves growing of crops and rearing of animals for sale in the market. It requires large cultivated land, large amount of capital, and use of machines.

It includes commercial grain farming, mixed farming, and plantation agriculture.

These are discussed below

- **Commercial Grain Farming** In this farming, crops are grown for commercial purposes, e.g. wheat and maize. It is mainly practised in sparsely populated temperate grasslands of North America, Europe and Asia.
- **Mixed Farming** It involves growing food and fodder crops along with rearing of livestock.

  It is practised in regions like Europe, Eastern USA, Argentina, South-East Australia, New Zealand and South Africa.
- **Plantations Farming** In this farming, single crops like tea, coffee, sugarcane, are grown. It requires large amount of labor and capital.

  Major plantations are found in tropical regions of the world, such as rubber plantations in Malaysia, coffee plantations in Brazil, and tea plantations in India and Sri Lanka.

KNOWLEDGE PLUS **Organic farming** is a type of farming in which organic manure and natural pesticides are used instead of chemicals.

3.2 Major Crops

A large variety of crops are grown for fulfilling the needs of the growing population and other purposes like supplying raw material for agro-based industries.

Major food crops are wheat, rice, maize and millets. Jute and cotton are major fibre crops and tea and coffee are major beverage crops. These are discussed below

- **Wheat** It requires moderate temperature and rainfall while growing and bright sunshine at the time of harvest. It grows best in loamy soil.

  Major producers of wheat include the USA, Canada, Argentina, Russia, Ukraine, Australia and India. It is grown in India in winter season.
- **Rice** It is a major food crop and the staple diet of tropical and sub-tropical regions. It requires **high temperature**, humidity and rainfall.

  It grows best in alluvial clayey soil that can retain water. China is the top producer of rice, followed by India, Japan, Srilanka and Egypt.
- **Maize** Maize also known as **corn** requires moderate temperature and rainfall. It requires lots of sunshine and well-drained fertile soils.

  It is grown in North America, Brazil, China, Russia, Canada, India and Mexico.
- **Millets** Millets including jowar, bajra and ragi are hardy crops also known as **coarse grains**. They require low rainfall and high to moderate temperature.

  They can be grown on less fertile and sandy soils. They are grown in India, Nigeria, China and Niger.
- **Jute** It is known as the **Golden Fibre**. It is grown in tropical areas and requires high temperature, heavy rainfall and humid climate.

  It grows well in alluvial soil. India and Bangladesh are its major producers.
- **Cotton** It requires high temperature, light rainfall, 210 frost-free days and bright sunshine for its growth.

  It grows best in black and alluvial soils. Its major producers are China, USA, India, Pakistan, Brazil and Egypt.
- **Tea** It is a beverage crop grown on plantations. It requires a cool climate and well distributed high rainfall for the growth of its tender leaves. It is grown well-drained loamy soil.

  Kenya, India, China, Sri Lanka produces the best quality of tea in the world.

- **Coffee** It requires a warm and wet climate and well-drained loamy soil. It is mostly grown on hill slopes. Brazil is the leading producer of coffee, followed by Colombia and India.

KNOWLEDGE PLUS In about AD 850, **Kaldi**, an Arab goat-herder, discovered the coffee while tasting the berries of evergreen bush on which the goats were feeding.

3.3 Agricultural Development

Agricultural development refers to efforts made for increasing farm production, in order to meet the growing demand of increasing population. Its ultimate aim is to increase **food security**.

Agricultural development can be achieved through methods like

- increasing the cropped area
- increasing the number of crops grown
- improving irrigation facilities
- using fertilisers
- adopting high-yielding variety seeds
- mechanising agriculture

Developing countries with large populations practice intensive agriculture in which crops are grown on small holdings. On the other hand, commercial agriculture is practised in countries like USA, Canada and Australia, in which crops are grown on larger landholdings.

KNOWLEDGE PLUS Food security exists when all people have access to sufficient, safe and nutritious food at all times.

A Farm in India

A typical Indian farmland is about 1.5 hectares in area. The **High Yielding Varieties** (HYVs) of seeds are purchased from market. The land is fertile and at least two crops in a year can be grown, which are mainly wheat, rice and pulses.

The government agricultural officers, villagers and family give advice and help the farmers in various farm activities. Usually farmers in India use conventional methods of farming like bullocks for ploughing or some farmers take tractors and tubewells on rent.

In spite of having storage facilities, some farmers are forced to sell the produce in mandi even when the market is not favourable to them. In recent past, the government has taken some steps to develop storage facilities.

A Farm in the USA

The average size of a farm in the USA is much larger than that of an Indian farm. A typical farm size in the USA is about 250 hectares. Adequate measures are taken to control pests that can damage the crop.

Farmers send soil samples periodically to a soil testing laboratory to check whether the nutrients are sufficient or not. In case of having a negative result, farmers plan a **scientific fertilisers programme**.

For the proper sprinkling of chemical fertilisers and pesticides on the field, farmers use computer programme which provides a satellite picture of the field. The farmers in the USA works like a businessman and not like a peasant farmer in India..

Mind Map

AGRICULTURE

Types of Farming

Subsistence Farming
Practiced to meet the needs of the farmer's family

Primitive Subsistence Farming

Nomadic Herding
Herdsmen move with their animals in search of food and reared sheep, camel, yak for milk, meat, wool

Shifting Cultivation
- Clearing of land by felling of trees and burning them
- Other names- Jhumming, milpa, roca, slash and burn, ladang

Intensive Subsistence Farming
A small plot of land is cultivated using simple tools and more labour

Commercial Farming
Involves growing of crops and rearing of animals for sale

Commercial Grain Farming
Crops are grown for commercial purposes, e.g. wheat and maize

Mixed Farming
Growing food and fodder crops along with rearing of livestock

Plantation Farming
Single crop is grown which requires large amount of labour and capital, e.g. tea, coffee, sugarcane, etc

Agricultural Development
- Efforts to increase farm production
- Adopting HYV seeds
- Mechanising agriculture
- Using fertilisers

Crops

Food Crops

Rice
- High temperature, humidity and rainfall
- Grown in alluvial clayey soil

Wheat
- Moderate temperature and rainfall
- Grown in loamy soil

Millet
- Low rainfall and high to moderate temperature
- Grown in less fertile and sandy soils

Maize
- Moderate temperature and rainfall
- Grown in lots of sunshine and well drained fertile soils

Beverages

Tea
- Cool climate and high rainfall
- Grown in well drained loamy soil

Coffee
- A warm and wet climate
- Grown in well drained loamy soil

Fibre Crops

Jute
- High temperature, heavy rainfall, humid climate
- Grown in alluvial soil

Cotton
- High temperature, light rainfall, 210 frost-free days and bright sunshine
- Grown in black and Alluvial soils

NCERT FOLDER

Covering Intext Questions and Exercises of NCERT

EXERCISES

Q.1 Answer the follwing questions.

(i) What is agriculture?

Ans. The word agriculture is derived from Latin words ager or agri meaning soil and culture meaning cultivation. Agriculture includes growing of fruits, crops, vegetables, flowers and rearing of livestock.

(ii) Name the factors influencing agriculture.

Ans. The factors influencing agriculture include topography, soil quality, climate and the availability of arable land.

(iii) What is shifting cultivation? What are its disadvantages? Diksha

Ans. Shifting cultivation involves clearing of land by felling of trees and burning them. Then, the ashes remained are mixed with soil to grow crops like maize and potatoes. After the soil loses its fertility, the land is abandoned and a new land is cleared.

The disadvantages of shifting cultivation are as follows

- It leads to large extent of deforestation.
- It leads to soil erosion and soil loss.
- It makes the land infertile.

(iv) What is plantation agriculture? Diksha

Ans. Plantation agriculture is a type of commercial farming where a single crop like tea, coffee, sugarcane, cashew, rubber, banana or cotton is grown. It requires large and labour capital.

(v) Name the fibre crops and name the climatic conditions required for their growth.

Ans. The fibre crops are cotton and jute.

The favourable climatic conditions for their growth are as follows

- **Cotton** It requires high temperature, light rainfall, 210 frost free days and bright sunshine for its growth.
- **Jute** It requires high temperature, heavy rainfall and humid climate for its growth.

Q.2 Tick the correct answer.

(i) Horticulture means

(a) growing of fruits and vegetables
(b) primitive farming
(c) growing of wheat

Ans. (a) growing of fruits and vegetables.

(ii) Golden fibre refers to

(a) tea (b) cotton (c) jute

Ans. (c) jute

(iii) Leading producer of coffee is

(a) Brazil (b) India (c) Russia

Ans. (a) Brazil

Q.3 Give reasons.

(i) In India, agriculture is a primary activity.

Ans. Agriculture is considered a primary activity in India because the majority of its population (two-third population) is engaged in agriculture. The favourable soil and climate conditions in many regions of India further support and encourage agricultural activities.

(ii) Different crops are grown in different regions.

Ans. Different crops are grown in different regions because growing of crops depends upon the geographical conditions, demand of produce, labour and level of technology.

Q.4 Distinguish between the following.

(i) Primary activities and tertiary activities

Ans. The differences between primary and tertiary activities are as follows

Primary Activities	Tertiary Activities
Primary activities are those activities which are associated with the extraction and production of natural resources.	Tertiary activities are those activities which provide support to primary and secondary activities through services.
For examples, Agriculture, fishing,gathering, poultry, etc.	For examples, Transport, trade, advertising, banking, etc.

(ii) Subsistence and intensive farming

Ans. The differences between subsistence and intensive farming are

Subsistence Farming	Intensive Farming
In this farming, farmers produce crops to meet the needs of their family.	In this farming, farmers produce a crop for the purpose of sale in the market.
It is done generally on a traditional basis using low level of technology and household labour.	It is done on a small plot of land using simple tools and more labour.

Q.5 Activity

(i) Collect seeds of wheat, rice, jowar, bajra, ragi, maize, oilseeds and pulses available in the market. Bring them to the class and find out in which type of soil they grow.

Ans. The different type of seeds and the soil on which they grow are as follows

- **Wheat** It grows best in loamy soil.
- **Rice** It grows best in alluvial clayey soil that can retain water.
- **Jowar (Sorghum) and Bajra (Pearl Millet)** They can be grown on less fertile and sandy soils.
- **Ragi** (Finger Millet) Ragi grows in well-drained sandy loam soil and can also grow in rocky and hilly terrain.
- **Maize** Maize grows in well-drained, loamy soil with good organic content. It requires fertile soil for optimal growth.
- **Oilseeds (e.g. sunflower, soybean, groundnut)** Many of the oilseeds grow in well-drained loamy or sandy loam soils.
- **Pulses (e.g., lentils, chickpeas, mung beans)** Pulses grow in well-drained loamy soils with good organic matter.

(ii) Find out the difference between the life style of farmers in the USA and India on the basis of pictures collected from magazines, books, newspapers and the Internet.

Ans. The differences of lifestyle of farmers in the USA and India are

Lifestyle of Farmers in India	Lifestyle of Farmers in USA
It is characterised by small-scale farming, with a majority of farmers owning relatively small plots of land.	In the USA the farmers have significantly much larger farms.
Farmers in India are engaged in subsistence agriculture. Commercial farming is also prevalent in certain areas.	Farmers in USA are engaged in commercial agriculture, with a focus on maximising production and profit.
Their technology adoption varies; some use tractors, drip irrigation and mobile apps, while others rely on traditional methods	They employ advanced technologies, including soil testing, computer-assisted planning, and the use of chemical fertilisers and pesticides.
They often face challenges related to a lack of storage facilities. This leads to selling produce in the mandi even when market conditions may not be favourable.	They have access to automated grain storage and efficient market agencies.

NCERT ON PAGE 31 (FOR FUN)

Q.6 For Fun

Across		Down	
1.	Crop that needs well-drained fertile soil, moderate temperature and lots of sunshine (5)	1.	Coarse grains are also called (7)
2.	Increasing production through use of HYV seeds, chemical fertilisers and pesticides (10, 5)	3.	Cultivation involving slash and burn (8)
4.	USA, Canada, Russia, Australia are major producers of this crop (5)	5.	Growing of crops, fruits and vegetables (11)
10.	Type of farming to meet family needs (11)	6.	Tea, coffee, sugarcane and rubber are grown in (11)
13.	Rearing of animals for sale (9)	7.	Requires 210 frost- free days for growth (6)
14.	Growing grapes for wines (11)	8.	Growing of flowers (12)
		9.	Also called 'Golden Fibre' (4)
		11.	Also known as paddy (4)
		12.	Activity concerned with extraction of natural resources (7)

Ans.

1. Maize, Millets
2. Commercial grain
3. Shifting
4. Wheat
5. Agriculture
6. Plantations
7. Cotton
8. Horticulture
9. Jute
10. Subsistence
11. Rice
12. Primary
13. Livestock
14. Viticulture

REVIEW EXERCISE

Including Competency Based Questions

Part I

Multiple Choice Questions (MCQs)

1. Which type of activity agriculture is? Diksha

(a) Primary activity
(b) Secondary activity
(c) Tertiary activity
(d) None of the above

2. .... activity is concerned with processing and manufacturing.

(a) Primary (b) Secondary
(c) Tertiary (d) None of these

3. .... percentage of population in the world depends on agriculture.

(a) 20 (b) 50
(c) 75 (d) 35

4. The land on which crops are grown is known as

(a) Arable land (b) Wet land
(c) Dry land (d) None of these

5. The type of agriculture largely practiced in India is

(a) subsistence farming
(b) extensive farming
(c) commercial farming
(d) mixed farming

6. Slash and burn practice of agriculture is also known as

(a) intensive farming (b) extensive farming
(c) shifting farming (d) nomadic farming

7. Factors influencing the crop cultivation is/are

(a) temperature (b) fertile soil
(c) rainfall (d) All of these

8. The two most important staple food crops of the world are

(a) ragi and bajra (b) tea and coffee
(c) rice and wheat (d) millets and maize

9. .... is grown in winter. It requires rainfall during growing season and bright sunshine at the time of harvest.

(a) Rice (b) Watermelon
(c) Wheat (d) Bajra

10. Sujata, a student of class VIII is talking about a crop which requires moderate temperature and rainfall. She says that in India it is grown in winter in loamy soil. Which crop she was talking about? Competency Based

(a) Rice (b) Wheat
(c) Millets (d) Maize

11. Which among the following is not a millet crop?

(a) Jowar (b) Ragi
(c) Wheat (d) Bajra

12. Cultivation of grapes is also known as ....

(a) viticulture (b) horticulture
(c) sericulture (d) pisciculture

13. Growing vegetables, flowers, fruits and decorative plants for commercial use is known as Diksha

(a) viticulture (b) horticulture
(c) sericulture (d) pisciculture

14. Identify the type of farming from the information given below. Competency Based

(i) In this farming, cultivated area is large.
(ii) Machines are used to do most of the work.
(iii) It is mainly popular in North America, Europe and Asia.

Codes

(a) Shifting (b) Nomadic
(c) Commercial (d) Plantation

15. Consider the following statements and choose the correct option.

I. Manufacturing steel, baking bread, and weaving cloth are examples of secondary activities.
II. Tertiary activities provide support to the primary and secondary sectors through services such as transportation, trade, banking, insurance and advertising.

Codes

(a) Both I and II (b) Only II
(c) Only II (d) None of these

16. **Consider the following statements and choose the correct option.**

I. Wheat requires moderate temperatures and adequate rainfall during the growing season, as well as bright sunshine at the time of harvest.

II. Rice is also known as the 'Golden Fiber.'

Codes

(a) Both I and II (b) Only II
(c) Only I (d) None of these

17. **Arrange the following countries in terms of coffee production.**

I. Brazil II. India III. Columbia

Codes

(a) III, II, I (b) II, I, III
(c) I, II, III (d) I, III, II

Answers

1. (a) **2.** (b) **3.** (b) **4.** (a) **5.** (a)
6. (c) **7.** (d) **8.** (c) **9.** (c) **10.** (b)
11. (c) **12.** (a) **13.** (b) **14.** (c) **15.** (a)
16. (c) **17.** (d)

Match the Following

1.

List I	List II
A. Cotton	1. A type of commercial farming
B. Millets	2. Golden fibre
C. Plantation	3. 210 frost free days
D. Jute	4. Low rainfall, high to moderate temperature

Codes

	A	B	C	D		A	B	C	D
(a)	4	1	2	3	(b)	4	2	3	1
(c)	2	3	4	1	(d)	3	4	1	2

2.

List I	List II
A. Rice	1. The staple diet of the tropical and sub-tropical regions
B. Wheat	2. Loamy soil
C. Millets	3. Sandy soil

Codes

	A	B	C		A	B	C
(a)	1	3	2	(b)	3	2	1
(c)	2	3	1	(d)	1	2	3

Ans. 1. (d) 2. (d)

Assertion-Reason

1. **Assertion** (A) China, USA, India, Pakistan, Brazil and Egypt are the leading producers of cotton.

Reason (R) Brazil is the leading producer of coffee followed by Columbia and India.

Codes

(a) Both A and R are true and R is the correct explanation of A
(b) Both A and R are true, but R is not the correct explanation of A
(c) A is true, but R is false
(d) A is false, but R is true

2 **Assertion** (A) Developing countries with large populations usually practice intensive agriculture where crops are grown on small holdings mostly for subsistence.

Reason (R) Larger holdings are more suitable for commercial agriculture in the USA, Canada, and Australia.

Codes

(a) Both A and R are true and R is the correct explanation of A
(b) Both A and R are true, but R is not the correct explanation of A
(c) A is true, but R is false
(d) A is false, but R is true

Ans. 1. (b) Both A and R are true, but R is not the correct explanation of A
2. (b) Both A and R are true, but R is not the correct explanation of A

Fill in the Blanks

1. Favourable topography of soil and .... are essential for agricultural activity.

2. In ...., no genetic modification is done to increase the field of the crop.

3. Primitive subsistence agriculture includes shifting cultivation and ....

4. In commercial grain farming, crops are grown for .... purpose.

5. .... and .... are fiber crops.

6. .... is the commercial rearing of silkworms.

7. Cotton grows best in .... and .... soil.

Ans. 1. climate 2. organic farming
3. nomadic herding, 4. commercial
5. Cotton, jute 6. Sericulture
7. black, alluvial

True/False

1. Land on which crops are grown Is known as arable land.
2. Fishing and agricultural activities are secondary in nature.
3. The type of cultivation in which a plot of land is cleared by felling the trees and burning them is called shifting cultivation.
4. Coffee does not require warm and wet climate and well-drained loamy soil.
5. Maize is also known as corn.

Ans. 1. True 2. False 3. True
4. False 5. True

Picture Based Questions

1. **Image shown below is of women in rice field. What are the key environmental factors required for rice cultivation?**

(a) Low temperature, low humidity, and no rainfall
(b) High temperature, high humidity, and rainfall
(c) Moderate temperature, low humidity, and rainfall
(d) High temperature, low humidity, and no rainfall

2. **Image shown below is of wheat farm. In which season is wheat grown in India?**

(a) Summer (b) Winter (c) Spring (d) Fall

Ans. 1. (b) High temperature, high humidity, and rainfall
2. (b) Winter

Case Based Question

1. **Read the given passage and answer the following questions.** **Competency Based**

Agricultural development refers to efforts made to increase farm production in order to meet the growing demand of increasing population. This can be achieved in many ways such as increasing the cropped area, the number of crops grown, improving irrigation facilities, use of fertilizers and high-yielding variety of seeds. The mechanisation of agriculture is also another aspect of agricultural development. The ultimate aim of agricultural development is to increase food security.

Agriculture has developed in different places in different parts of the world. Developing countries with large populations usually practice intensive agriculture where crops are grown on small holdings mostly for subsistence. Larger holdings are more suitable for commercial agriculture as in the USA, Canada and Australia.

(i) Which of the following is an aspect of achieving agricultural development?
(a) Mechanisation
(b) Use of fertilisation
(c) Improve irrigation
(d) All of the above

(ii) Which type of agriculture is typically practiced in USA?
(a) Commercial agriculture
(b) Intensive agriculture
(c) Extensive agriculture
(d) Subsistence agriculture

(iii) Which factors could influence the success of agricultural development in both developing and developed countries?
(a) Climate change
(b) Government policies
(c) Availability of high-yielding seeds
(d) Cultural preferences

(iv) Why is intensive agriculture practiced in developing countries?
(a) To feed large population
(b) It is less water consuming
(c) To maintain soil fertility
(d) It is profitable

Ans (i) (d) All of the above
(ii) (a) Commercial agriculture
(iii) (c) Availability of high-yielding seeds
(iv) (a) To feed large population

Part II

Very Short Answer Type Questions

1. How did the word agriculture originate?

Ans. The word 'agriculture' is derived from two Latin words i.e. 'ager' meaning soil and 'culture' meaning cultivation.

2. What are tertiary activities?

Ans. Tertiary activities are those which provide support to primary and secondary activities through services.

3. What is a farm system? Diksha

Ans. Farm system is a system of agricultural practices combining various elements and resources.

4. What is arable land?

Ans. Arable land is the land on which crops are grown. It is also known as cultivable land or tilled land.

5. Enumerate the areas of nomadic herding.

Ans. Nomadic herding is practised in arid regions of Sahara, Central Asia and some parts in India like Rajasthan, Jammu and Kashmir.

6. What is the main feature of plantation agriculture?

Ans. The main feature of plantation agriculture is the large scale cultivation of single crop with significant labour and capital need.

7. What is mixed farming?

Ans. In mixed farming, land is used for growing food and fodder crops and rearing livestocks. It is mainly practiced in USA, Argentina, etc.

8. Name the major agricultural crops.

Ans. The major agricultural crops are rice, wheat, millets and maize.

9. Which countries are known for rice productions?

Ans. China, India, Japan, Sri Lanka, Bangladesh and Egypt are known for rice production.

10. Name the golden fibre. Where is it grown?

Ans. Jute is known as golden fibre. It is grown mainly in India and Bangladesh.

11. What is pisciculture?

Ans. Breeding of fish in specially constructed tanks and ponds is known as pisciculture.

12. Which countries are known for wheat productions?

Ans. The USA, Canada, Argentina, Russia, Ukraine, India and Australia are known for wheat production.

13. Which two countries lead in the production of jute?

Ans. India and Bangladesh are the leading producers of jute.

Short Answer Type Questions

1. Name the inputs, outputs and processes of agriculture in general. Also mention the various operations involved. Diksha

Ans. The inputs in agriculture are seeds, fertiliser, machinery and labour, etc.

The processes involved in the agricultural operations are ploughing, sowing, irrigation, weeding and harvesting.

The outputs from the system include crops, wool, dairy and poultry products.

2. What is meant by subsistence farming? Explain the types of subsistence farming.

Ans. Subsistence farming is practiced to meet the needs of the farmer's family.

The types of subsistence farming are as follows

Intensive Subsistence Farming In this type of farming, a small plot of land is cultivated using, simple tools and more labor.

Primitive Subsistence Farming It includes shifting cultivation and nomadic herding.

Shifting cultivation involves clearing of land by felling of trees and burning them. The ash that remains is mixed with the soil to regain fertility.

In nomadic herding, herdsmen move from place to place with their animals in search of fodder and water.

3. Nomadic herding is a traditional form of livestock management practiced by nomadic or semi-nomadic communities. Explain this type of farming. Competency Based

Ans. Nomadic herding is a traditional form of livestock management practiced by nomadic or semi-nomadic communities.

In this method, herders continuously move their livestock, including sheep, camels, yaks and goats, from one grazing area to another in search of fodder and water. These herders have defined migratory routes and adapt to the seasonal availability of resources.

Nomadic herding provides essential products such as milk, meat, wool, hides and other resources for the herders' families and is commonly practiced in arid and semi-arid regions, including the Sahara, Central Asia, Rajasthan and Jammu and Kashmir.

4. Shifting cultivation is considered to be primitive and destructive to environment. Yet it is still prevalent in the North-Eastern regions of the country. Competency Based

(i) What do you mean by shifting cultivation?

Ans. Shifting cultivation involves clearing of land by felling of trees and burning them. Then, the ashes remained are mixed with soil to grow crops like maize and potatoes. After the soil loses its fertility, the land is abandoned and a new land is cleared.

(ii) By what name is shifting cultivation known in North-East region ?

Ans. Shifting cultivation is known as Jhumming cultivation in North-East region of India.

5. Define the following. **Diksha**

(i) Food security

(ii) Organic farming

Ans. (i) Food security means all people, at all times, have access to sufficient, safe and nutritious food to meet their dietary needs and food preferences for an active and healthy life.

(ii) Organic farming, organic manure and natural pesticides are used instead of chemicals. No genetic modification is done to increase the yield of the crop.

6. Define the following

(i) Sericulture (ii) Pisciculture

(iii) Viticulture (iv) Horticulture

Ans. (i) **Sericulture** It is the commercial rearing of silk worms. It may supplement the income of the farmer.

(ii) **Pisciculture** It is the breeding of fish in specially constructed tanks and ponds.

(iii) **Viticulture** It involve the cultivation of grapes.

(iv) **Horticulture** It involves growing vegetables, flowers and fruits for commercial use.

7. What do you understand about agricultural development? Why is agricultural development required?

Ans. Agricultural development refers to efforts made to increase farm production in order to meet the growing demand of increasing population.

Agricultural development required for the following reasons

- **Meeting Food Demand** Agricultural development addresses the increasing global population's need for more food.
- **Improving Food Security** Agricultural development enhances food security by increasing production and stabilising the food supply.
- **Economic Growth and Livelihoods** Agricultural development fosters economic growth and provides livelihoods, especially in developing countries by raising agricultural productivity and generating related job opportunities.

Long Answer Type Questions

1. What are the types of commercial farming? **Diksha**

Ans. The types of commercial farming include commercial grain farming, mixed farming, and plantation agriculture. These are discussed below

- In commercial grain farming crops are grown for commercial purposes. Wheat and maize are common commercially grown grains. Major areas where commercial grain farming is practiced are temperate grasslands of North America, Europe and Asia.
- In mixed farming, the land is used for growing food and fodder crops and rearing livestock. It is practiced in Europe, the Eastern USA, Argentina, south-east Australia, New Zealand and South Africa.
- Plantations are a type of commercial farming where single crops of tea, coffee, sugarcane, cashew, rubber, banana or cotton are grown. Large amounts of labour and capital are required. Major plantations are found in the tropical regions of the world.

2. What is shifting cultivation ? What are its advantages?

Ans. Shifting cultivation, also known as slash-and-burn agriculture, is a traditional farming practice in which farmers clear land by cutting and burning vegetation to create fields for crop cultivation.

Some of the advantages of shifting cultivation are

- Shifting cultivation promotes biodiversity as it allows the forest to regenerate during fallow periods.
- Burning plant material in shifting cultivation returns nutrients to the soil, enhancing soil fertility.
- It is a sustainable farming method when practiced in low population density areas, as the land can recover during the fallow period.
- It can be adapted to suit local conditions and is well-suited for hilly or forested regions.
- It often requires minimal external inputs such as fertilisers and pesticides.
- It allows for a variety of crops to be grown in different cycles, diversifying farmers' livelihoods

3. What are fiber crops and the climate conditions required for their growth?

Ans. Fiber crops are plants cultivated for their fibers, which are used in various industries, such as textiles and paper production.

The climatic conditions required for their growth vary depending on the specific fiber crop. For example,

Climatic Conditions for Cotton Growth

- Cotton requires a warm climate.
- It requires high temperatures and bright sunshine.

- It grows in regions with 210 or more frost-free days.
- Light rainfall is preferred during the growing season of cotton.

Climatic Conditions for Jute Growth

- Jute requires a tropical climate.
- It needs high temperatures, heavy rainfall and a humid climate.
- It is typically grown in areas with monsoon seasons.

4. An agriculturalist is writing an article for a journal on the pattern of farming in different regions of the world. Take the example of Indian farming system and American farming system and discuss the major differences between them, that could be discussed in article. **Competency Based**

Ans. Different regions of the world practice different types of farming system according to their geographical location, accessibility of resources and various other factors. for example, the differences between the Indian farming system and American farming system are follows

- Indian farms are generally small. They mainly vary from 1 to 5 hectare.

  While average size of farm in America is larger than that of an Indian farm. A typical farm size in the USA is about 250 hectares.
- Indian farmers resides in the main village while American farmers generally resides in the farm.
- Indian farmers grow at least two crops in a year which are normally wheat or rice and pulses. While USA farmers grow many types of crops such as corn, soyabean, wheat and cotton.
- Indian farmer generally produces crops for self consumption. They sold some part of cultivation in mandi located in nearby town. American farmers store grains in the automated grain storage or despatch them to the market agencies.

Picture Based Question

1. Look at the picture given below of a farm in USA and answer the following questions.

(i) What is the average size of a farm in USA?

Ans. The average size of a farm in USA is about 250 hectares.

(ii) What machines are used in these farms for performing agricultural operations? Where are the grains stored?

Ans. Tractors, seed drills, leveller, combined harvester and thresher are used to perform various agricultural operations in these farms.

The grains are stored in the automated grain storage or despatched to market agencies.

Case Based Question

1. Read the given passage below and answer the questions.

In commercial farming, crops are grown and animals are reared for sale in the market. The area cultivated and the amount of capital used is large. Most of the work is done by machines. Commercial farming includes commercial grain farming, mixed farming and plantation agriculture. In commercial grain farming crops are grown for commercial purposes.

Wheat and maize are common commercially grown grains. Major areas where commercial grain farming is practiced are temperate grasslands of North America, Europe and Asia. These areas are sparsely populated with large farms spreading over hundreds of hectares. Severe winters restrict the growing season and only a single crop can be grown.

(i) What does commercial farming primarily focused on?

Ans. Commercial farming is primarily focused on growing crops and raising animals for sale in the market.

(ii) Name the crops that are commonly grown in commercial grain farming.

Ans. **Wheat** and **maize** are commonly grown in commercial grain farming.

(iii) Name the major areas where commercial grain farming is located.

Ans. The major areas for commercial grain farming are temperate grasslands in North America, Europe, and Asia.

Map Based Question

1. The map below represents the world distribution of Arable land. Explain why the agricultural activities are concentrated in these regions of the world?

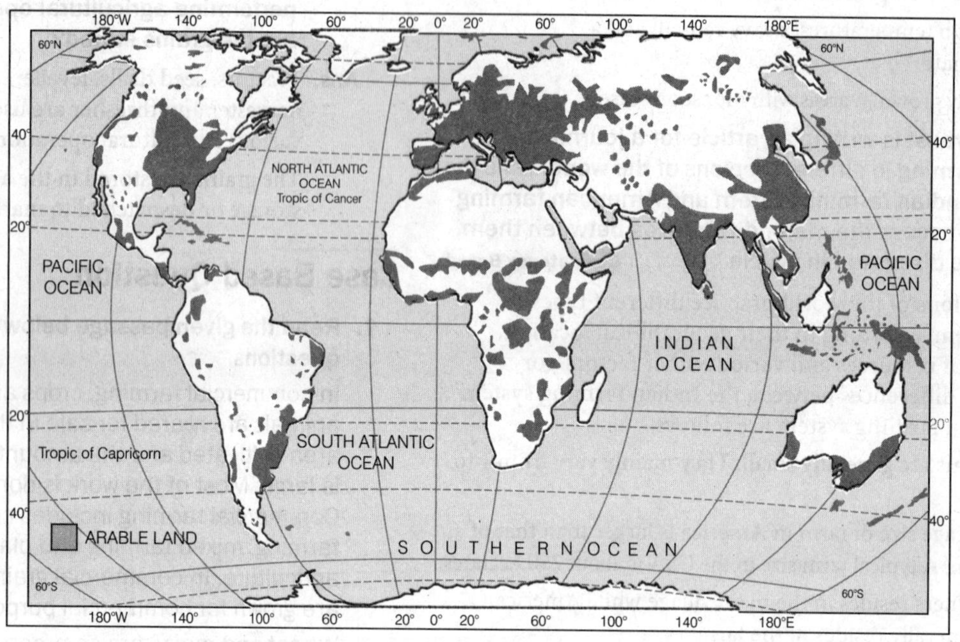

Ans. The agricultural activities are concentrated in these regions of the world because they provide topography of soil and climate for the growth of the crops.

ASSESSMENT EXERCISE

Multiple Choice Questions (MCQs)

1. An activity which is related directly to the extraction and production of natural resources is called

(a) Secondary activity (b) Primary activity
(c) Tertiary activity (d) None of these

2. Shifting cultivation is known as Milpa in which country?

(a) Asia (b) Mexico
(c) Brazil (d) Malaysia

3. Which crops called beverage crops?

(a) Tea (b) Wheat
(c) Rice (d) Cotton

4. Paddy is another name of which crops?

(a) Wheat (b) Rice
(c) Tea (d) Cotton

5. Which one of the following is the single crop?

(a) Banana (b) Jute
(c) Rice (d) Wheat

6. Leading producer of tea

(a) Brazil (b) Srilanka
(c) India (d) Russia

Subjective Questions (VSA, SA & LA)

7. Give two example of secondary activity.

8. Name the land on which crops are grown.

9. Which types of favourable conditions required in agricultural practices?

10. What do you mean by horticulture?

11. Name two fibre crops.

12. Write a short note on Nomadic Herding.

13. Explain Commercial farming.

14. Differentiate substansive farming and intensive farming.

15. Discuss, farming and its types in detail.

16. Discuss agricultural development.

CHAPTER 4

Industries

Industry refers to an economic activity that is concerned with production of goods, extraction of minerals or the provision of services. For example, iron and steel industry (production of goods), coal mining industry (extraction of coal) and tourism industry (service provider).

Industry is included in **secondary activities**. Secondary activities or manufacturing change raw materials into products which can be more valuable to people. For example, pulp changed into paper and paper into a note book. These represent the two stages of the manufacturing process.

4.1 Classification of Industries

Industries can be classified on the basis of raw materials, size and ownership.

Industries on the Basis of Raw Materials

On the basis of raw material industries can be classified in to the following.

- **Agro-Based Industries** These use plant and animal based products as their raw materials. For example food processing, vegetable oil, cotton textile, dairy products and leather industries.
- **Mineral Based Industries** These are the primary industries that use mineral ores as their raw materials. The products of these industries provide raw material to other industries.
  For example, iron made from iron **ore**[1] is the product of mineral based industry. This is used as raw material for the manufacture of a number of other products such as heavy machinery, building materials and railway coaches.
- **Marine Based Industries** These industries use products from the sea and oceans as raw materials. For example, industries processing sea foods or manufacturing fish oil.
- **Forest Based Industries** These use forest produce as raw materials. The industries associated with forests are pulp and paper, **pharmaceuticals**[2], furniture and buildings.

Industries on the Basis of Size

Size refers to the amount of capital invested, number of people employed and the volume of production.

On the basis of size, industries can be classified into the following

- **Small-Scale Industries** These industries use less amount of capital and technology. **Cottage** or **household industries** are a type of small-scale industry where the products are made by hands, by the artisans For example, basket weaving, silk weaving, food-processing, and pottery and other handicrafts industries.
- **Large-Scale Industries** These industries use large amount of capital investment and superior technology to produce large volumes of products. For example iron and steel industries, heavy electricals, production of automobiles and heavy machinery.

Industries on the Basis of Ownership

On the basis of ownership, industries can be classified into the following

- **Private Sector Industries** These industries are owned and operated by individuals or a group of individuals. For example, Tata Iron and Steel Industry, Jamshedpur.
- **Public Sector Industries** These industries are owned and operated by the government. For example, Hindustan Aeronautics Limited and Steel Authority of India Limited.

1 **Ore** It is a type of rock that contains sufficient minerals with important elements including metals that can be economically extracted from the rock.

2 **Pharmaceuticals** Pharmaceuticals are medicines and drugs that are specially made to treat, cure, or prevent diseases and health problems in people.

- **Joint Sector Industries** These industries are owned and operated by the state and individuals or a group of individuals. For example, Maruti Udyog Limited.
- **Co-operative Sector Industries** These industries are owned and operated by the producers or suppliers of raw materials, workers or both. For example, Anand Milk Union Limited and Sudha Dairy.

4.2 Factors Affecting Location of Industries

The factors affecting the location of industries are the availability of raw material, land, water, labour, power, capital, transport and market. Industries are situated where some or all of these factors are easily available.

Sometimes, the government offers incentives like subsidised power, lower transport cost and other infrastructure to encourage industries to set up in backward areas. **Industrialisation** often leads to development and growth of towns and cities.

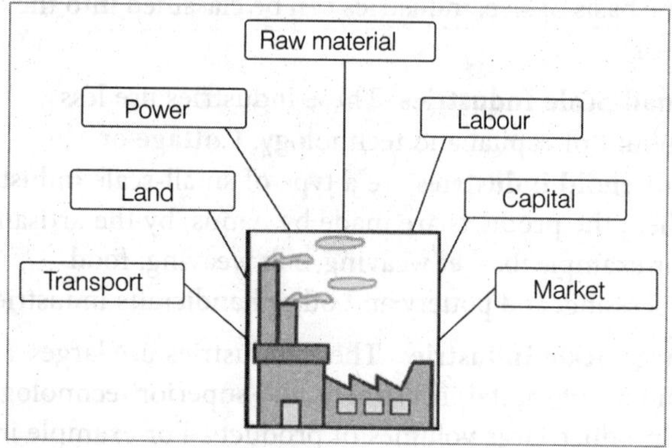

• Factors Affecting Location of Industries

4.3 Industrial System

An industrial system consists of the following

- **Input** It includes the raw materials, labour and costs of land, transport, power and other infrastructure.
- **Process** It includes a wide range of activities that convert the raw material into finished products.
- **Output** It is the end product and the income earned from it.

For example, in textile industry, the inputs may be cotton, human labour, factory and transport cost. The processes include ginning, spinning, weaving, dyeing and printing and the output is the shirt.

4.4 Industrial Regions

Industrial regions emerge when a number of industries locate close to each other and share the benefits of their closeness.

Major industrial regions of the world are

- Eastern North America
- Western and Central Europe
- Eastern Europe
- Eastern Asia

Such areas are usually located in temperate areas near sea ports and coal fields.

India has several Industrial regions like

- Mumbai-Pune cluster
- Bangalore-Tamil Nadu region
- Hugli region
- Ahmedabad-Baroda region
- Chottanagpur industrial belt
- Visakhapatnam-Guntur belt
- Gurgaon-Delhi-Meerut region
- Kollam-Thiruvanathapuram industrial cluster

Industrial Disaster

In industries, accidents or disasters mainly occur due to technical failure or irresponsible handling of hazardous material.

Some of the worst industrial disasters include **Bhopal Gas Tragedy** on 3rd December, 1984, and an incident of gas well blowout in Gao Qiao, Chongging, China on 23rd December, 2005.

Some measures for reducing the risk of industrial disaster are

- Densely populated residential areas should be separated far away from the industrial areas.
- People staying in the vicinity of industries should be aware of the storage of toxins or hazardous substances and their possible effects in case if an accident occurs.
- Fire warning and fighting system should be improved.
- Storage capacity of toxic substances should be limited.
- Pollution dispersion qualities in the industries should be improved.

Try These

1. **Give an example of an industry related to the production of goods.**
2. **What are mineral-based industries?**
3. **Give an example of large-scale industry.**
4. **Name any two industrial regions of the world.**

4.5 Distribution of Major Industries

The world's major industries are the iron and steel industry, the textile industry and the information technology industry.

Iron and steel industries are located in Germany, USA, China, Japan and Russia. Textile industries are mainly located in India, Hong Kong, South Korea, Japan and Taiwan.

The major hubs for the information technology industry are Silicon Valley in California and the Bangalore region in India.

Iron and Steel Industry

Iron and steel industry is a **feeder industry**[3] whose products are used as raw material for other industries.

The inputs for this industry include raw materials such as iron ore, coal and limestone, along with labour, capital, site and other infrastructure.

The process of converting iron ore into steel involves many stages which include putting raw material in the blast furnace where it undergoes **smelting**[4] and then **refining**[5] it.

The output that is obtained after refining is steel which may be used by other industries as raw material.

Before 1800 AD, iron and steel industries were located in areas where raw materials, power supply and running water were easily available.

Later, the ideal location for the industry was near coal fields and close to canals and railways.

After 1950, iron and steel industry began to be located on large areas of flat land near sea ports. This is because steel works had become very large and iron ore had to be imported from overseas.

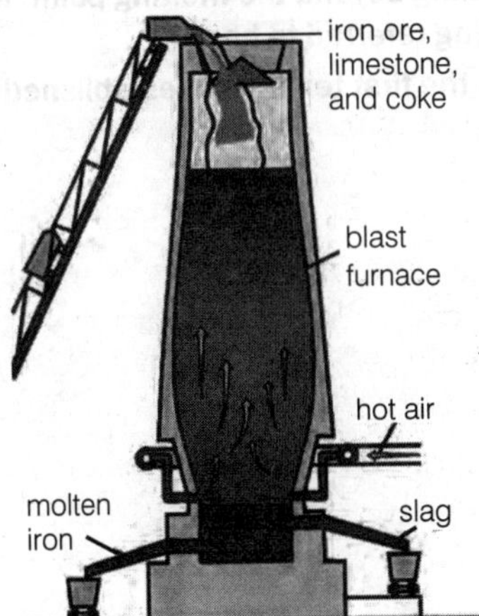

• Processing of Iron Ore into Steel

Steel and Its Uses

Steel is tough and can easily be shaped, cut, or made into wire. Special alloys of steel can be made by adding small amounts of other metals such as aluminium, nickel, and copper. These alloys provide steel unusual hardness, toughness, or ability to resist rust.

Steel is often called the **backbone of modern industry**. Almost everything we use is made of iron or steel. For example, ships, trains, trucks, autos are made largely of steel. Even the safety pins and needles are made from steel.

Oil wells are drilled with steel machinery and steel pipelines are used to transport oil. Minerals are mined with steel equipments and farm machines are mostly made up of steel. The framework of large buildings is also made up of steel.

Iron and Steel Industries in India

In India, the iron and steel industry has grown due to access to raw materials, cheap labour, transport, and markets.

The important steel producing centres in India include Bhilai, Durgapur, Burnpur, Jamshedpur, Rourkela and Bokaro. All these important centres are situated in a region that spreads over four states which are West Bengal, Jharkhand, Odisha and Chhattisgarh.

Bhadravati and **Vijay Nagar** in Karnataka, **Visakhapatnam** in Andhra Pradesh, **Salem** in Tamil Nadu are other important steel centres.

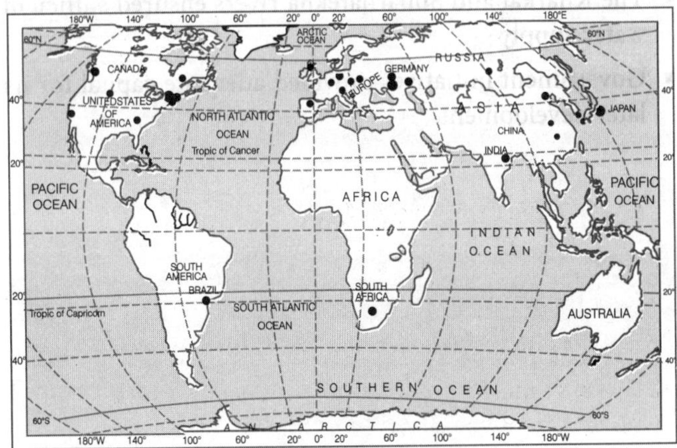

• World's Major Iron Ore Producing Areas

3 **Feeder Industry** It is an industry that supplies raw materials or semi-finished goods to another industry.

4 Smelting It is the process in which metals are extracted from their ores by heating beyond the melting point.

5 Refining It is the process of purifying or improving a substance, like crude oil by removing impurities to make it cleaner and more useful.

The development of the iron and steel industry led to rapid industrial development in India. The Indian iron and steel industry consists of large integrated steel plants as well as mini steel mills. It also includes secondary producers, rolling mills and **ancillary industries**[6].

KNOWLEDGE PLUS Information technology, wellness, hospitality and knowledge are emerging industries which are also known as **Sunrise Industries.**

Jamshedpur

Geographically, Jamshedpur is the most conveniently situated iron and steel centre in India. It was previously known as **Sakchi.**

Tata Iron and Steel Company Limited (TISCO) is the only iron and steel industry started before independence. TISCO was privately owned and started in 1907 at Sakchi, near the confluence of the rivers Subarnarekha and Kharkai in Jharkhand.

Sakchi was chosen to set-up the steel plant for several reasons

- This place was only 32 km away from Kalimati station on the Bengal-Nagpur railway line.
- It was close to the sources of raw material like coal from Jharia coalfields, and iron ore, limestone, dolomite and manganese from Odisha and Chhattisgarh.
- Kolkata provides a large market to this region.
- The Kharkai and Subarnarekha rivers ensured sufficient water supply.
- Government initiatives provided adequate capital for its later development.

Pittsburgh : Steel City of USA

Pittsburgh is an important steel city of the United States of America. As other steel plants, it also enjoys favourable geographical conditions such as

- Raw material like coal is available locally. Iron ore comes from the iron mines at Minnesota, about 1500 km from Pittsburgh.
- The famous **Great Lakes waterway** provides one of the best routes for shipping ore cheeply between Minnesota and Pittsburgh. Trains carry the ore from Great Lakes to Pittsburgh.
- The Ohio, the Monogahela and Allegheny rivers provide adequate water supply to this region.

Today, a small number of large steel mills are located in Pittsburgh. These are located in the valleys of Monogahela and Allegheny rivers above Pittsburgh and along the Ohio river below it.

Many factories other than steel mills are also located in Pittsburgh. These factories use steel as their raw material to make many different products such as railroad equipment, heavy machinery and rails.

KNOWLEDGE PLUS The names of Great Lakes are Superior, Huron, Ontario, Michigan and Erie. Lake Superior is the largest of these five lakes. It lies higher upstream than others.

Try These

1. **Which Indian city is known as the 'Manchester of India'?**
2. **Mention the inputs used in iron and steel industry.**
3. **This is a process in which metals are extracted from their ores by heating beyond the melting point. Name the process being referred to here.**
4. **Where was the first textile mill established in India and when?**

6 Ancillary Industries They are also known as support industries and play crucial role in supporting and complementing the operations of primary industries. These industries provide goods and services that are essential for the functioning of larger industries.

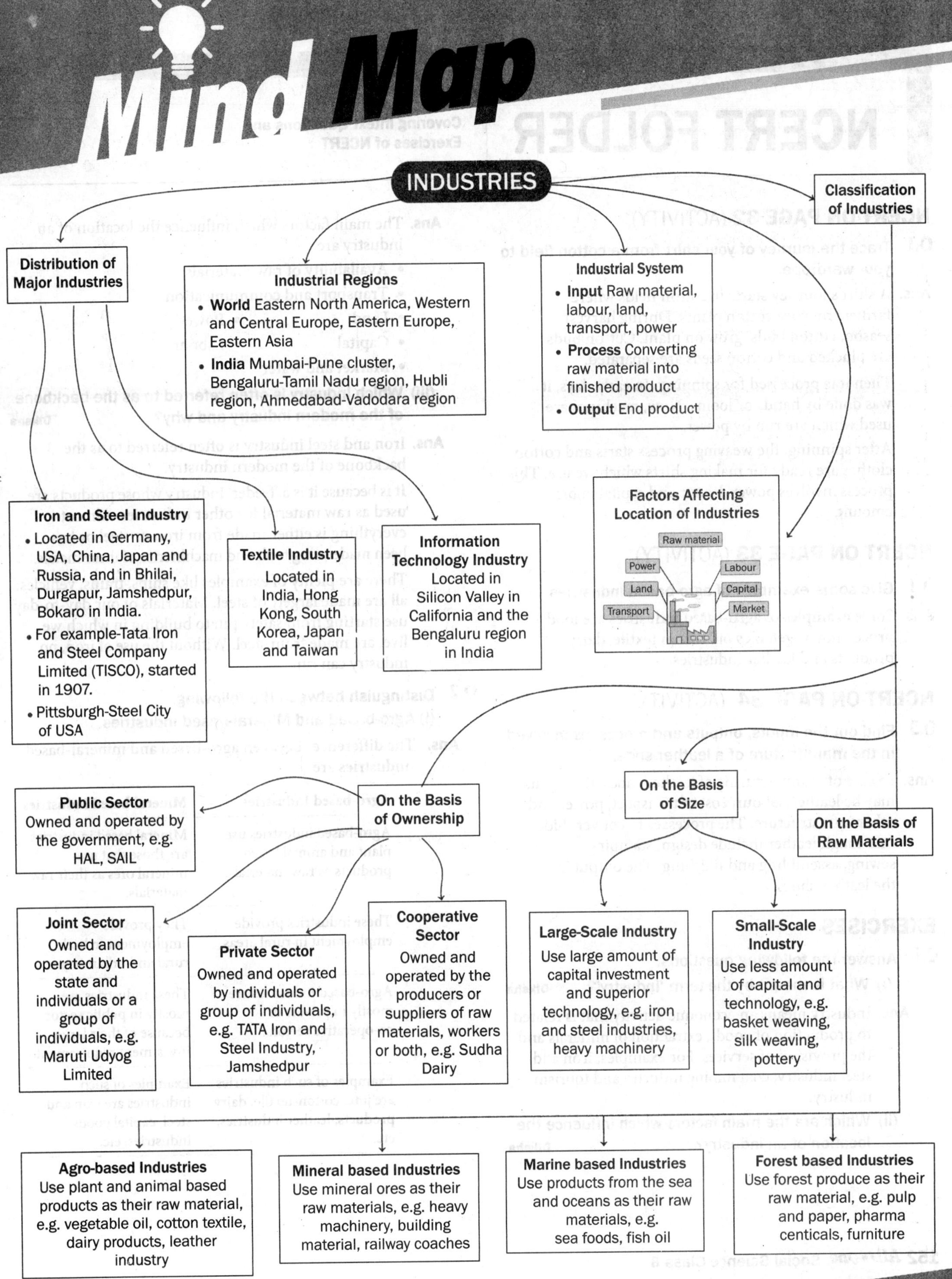
Mind Map
Covering intext questions and Exercises of NCERT
INDUSTRIES
Distribution of Major Industries
Industrial Regions
• World Eastern North America, Western and Central Europe, Eastern Europe, Eastern Asia
• India Mumbai-Pune cluster, Bengaluru-Tamil Nadu region, Hubli region, Ahmedabad-Vadodara region
Industrial System
• Input Raw material, labour, land, transport, power
• Process Converting raw material into finished product
• Output End product
Classification of Industries
Factors Affecting Location of Industries
Raw material
Power
Labour
Land
Capital
Transport
Market
Iron and Steel Industry
• Located in Germany, USA, China, Japan and Russia, and in Bhilai, Durgapur, Jamshedpur, Bokaro in India.
• For example-Tata Iron and Steel Company Limited (TISCO), started in 1907.
• Pittsburgh-Steel City of USA
Textile Industry
Located in India, Hong Kong, South Korea, Japan and Taiwan
Information Technology Industry
Located in Silicon Valley in California and the Bengaluru region in India
Public Sector
Owned and operated by the government, e.g. HAL, SAIL
On the Basis of Ownership
On the Basis of Size
On the Basis of Raw Materials
Joint Sector
Owned and operated by the state and individuals or a group of individuals, e.g. Maruti Udyog Limited
Private Sector
Owned and operated by individuals or group of individuals, e.g. TATA Iron and Steel Industry, Jamshedpur
Cooperative Sector
Owned and operated by the producers or suppliers of raw materials, workers or both, e.g. Sudha Dairy
Large-Scale Industry
Use large amount of capital investment and superior technology, e.g. iron and steel industries, heavy machinery
Small-Scale Industry
Use less amount of capital and technology, e.g. basket weaving, silk weaving, pottery
Agro-based Industries
Use plant and animal based products as their raw material, e.g. vegetable oil, cotton textile, dairy products, leather industry
Mineral based Industries
Use mineral ores as their raw materials, e.g. heavy machinery, building material, railway coaches
Marine based Industries
Use products from the sea and oceans as their raw materials, e.g. sea foods, fish oil
Forest based Industries
Use forest produce as their raw material, e.g. pulp and paper, pharma centicals, furniture

NCERT FOLDER

Covering Intext Questions and Exercises of NCERT

NCERT ON PAGE 32 (ACTIVITY)

Q.1 Trace the journey of your shirt from a cotton field to your wardrobe.

Ans. A shirt's journey starts in cotton fields where farmers nurture cotton plants. During harvest season, cotton buds, grow on plant. Cotton buds are plucked and cotton seeds are separated.

Then it is processed for spinning. In early days, it was done by hands or looms. Now, machines are used which are run by power.

After spinning, the weaving process starts and cotton clothes are ready for making shirts which we use. This process involves power, labour and capital in big amount.

NCERT ON PAGE 33 (ACTIVITY)

Q.2 Give some examples of agro-based industries.

Ans. Some examples of agro-based industries are food processing, vegetables oil, cotton textile, dairy products and leather industries.

NCERT ON PAGE 34 (ACTIVITY)

Q.3 Find out the inputs, outputs and processes involved in the manufacture of a leather shoe.

Ans. In case of manufacturing of leather shoes, the inputs may be leather, labour, cost of transport, power and other infrastructure. The processes to convert hides into tough leather include design, stamping, sewing, assembling and finishing. The output is the leather shoes.

EXERCISES

Q.1 Answer the following questions.

(i) What is meant by the term 'industry'? Diksha

Ans. Industry means an economic activity that is related to production of goods, extraction of minerals and the provision of services. For examples, iron and steel industry, coal mining industry and tourism industry.

(ii) Which are the main factors which influence the location of an industry? Diksha

Ans. The main factors which influence the location of an industry are

- Availability of raw materials
- Transport and communication
- Land
- Power
- Capital
- Labour
- Market and water

(iii) Which industry is often referred to as the backbone of the modern industry and why? Diksha

Ans. Iron and steel industry is often referred to as the backbone of the modern industry.

It is because it is a 'feeder' industry whose products are used as raw material for other industries. Almost everything is either made from iron or steel or has been made using tools and machineries of these metals. There are plenty of examples like ships, trains, vehicles; all are made largely of steel. Materials of our day-to-day use starting from safety pin to building in which we live, are made from steel. Without the use of iron, no industry can run.

Q.2 Distinguish between the following.

(i) Agro-based and Mineral-based industries.

Ans. The differences between agro-based and mineral-based industries are

Agro-based Industries	Mineral-based Industries
Agro-based industries use plant and animal based products as raw materials.	Mineral based industries are those that use mineral ores as their raw materials.
These industries provide employment in rural areas.	They provide employment to both rural and urban areas.
Agro-based industries are mostly in private or co-operative sectors.	These industries are mostly in public sector because of their large investment requirement.
Examples of such industries are jute, cotton-textile, dairy products, leather industries, etc.	Examples of such industries are iron and steel, capital goods industries, etc.

(ii) Public sector and Joint sector industries

Ans. The differences between public sector industries and joint sector industries are

Public sector industries	Joint sector industries
The industries which are owned and operated by State Government or Central Government are called public sector industries.	The industries which are owned and operated by government and an individual or a group of individuals are called joint sector industries.
These industries are managed and run by workforce appointed by government.	Both government servants and private employees run these industries.
For example Steel Authority of India Limited (SAIL), Hindustan Aeronautics Limited (HAL), etc.	For example Maruti Udyog Limited (MUL).

Q.3 Give two examples of the following in the space provided.

(i) Raw materials: .... and ....

(ii) End products: .... and ....

(iii) Tertiary activities: .... and ....

(iv) Agro-based industries: .... and ....

(v) Cottage industries: .... and ....

(vi) Co-operatives: .... and ....

Ans. (i) iron-ore, cotton

(ii) car, notebooks

(iii) banking, transport

(iv) Pottery and bn

(v) Pottery and basket weaving

(vi) amul butter, khadi industry

REVIEW EXERCISE

Including Competency Based Questions

Part I

Multiple Choice Questions (MCQs)

1. Maruti Udyog industry comes under

(a) Private Sector (b) Public Sector
(c) Joint Sector (d) Cooperative Sector

2. These industries are owned and operated by the producers or suppliers or both. Indentify them.

(a) Private industries (b) Public industries
(c) Joint industries (d) Co-operative industries

3. Which of these factor(s) affect the location of industries ? Diksha

(a) Power (b) Availability of raw material
(c) Transport (d) All of these

4. Ankur, a resident of Noida, decided to establish a industry in an effective manner. Which of the following factors significantly influences the location of industry? Competency Based

(a) Government Policies (b) Market
(c) Labour (d) All of the above

5. Why is steel called the backbone of modern industries? Diksha

(a) Steel is cheaper
(b) Steel is available everywhere in the world
(c) Everything we use is related with steel
(d) None of the above

6. In which of the following countries are the world's major iron and steel industries located ? Diksha

(a) Germany (b) China
(c) Russia (d) All of these

7. TISCO was started in the year .... at Sakchi.

(a) 1907 (b) 1980 (c) 1807 (d) 1954

8. .... is an important steel city of the United States of America.

(a) New York (b) Pittsburgh
(c) Washington (d) None of these

9. Industrial disaster occurred in Bhopal on Diksha

(a) 3rd December, 1974 (b) 3rd December, 1980
(c) 3rd December, 1983 (d) 3rd December, 1984

10. On the night of 2nd December, 1984, one of the biggest industrial disasters to ever take place began unfolding in Bhopal, Madhya Pradesh.

Source - Indian Express

Which gas was leaked in Bhopal gas tragedy from a nearby Union Carbide Pesticide plant? Competency Based

(a) Methyl Isocyanate
(b) Carbon monoxide
(c) Methane
(d) Oxygen

11. **Which one of the following statements is/are incorrect?**
   I. Manufacturing is known as a tertiary activity.
   II. The iron and steel industry is known as Sunrise Industry.

   Codes
   (a) Only I (b) Both I and II (c) Only II (d) None of these

12. **Which one of the following statements is/are correct?**
   I. Public sector industries are owned and operated by the government.
   II. Private sector industries are owned and operated by a group or individuals.

   Codes
   (a) Both I and II (b) Only II
   (c) Only I (d) None of these

13. **Identify the city that describes the area given below.**
   I. It is an important city of the United States of America. **Competency Based**
   II. It is one of major steel industry city.
   III. The Ohio, the Monagahela and Allegheny rivers provide water supply to this area.

   Codes
   (a) New York (b) Washington
   (c) Baltimore (d) Pittsburgh

Answers

1. (c)	2. (d)	3. (d)	4. (d)	5. (c)
6. (d)	7. (a)	8. (b)	9. (d)	10. (a)
11. (b)	12. (a)	13. (d)		

Match the Following

1.

List I	List II
A. Hindustan Aeronautics Ltd	1. Joint sector
B. Sudha Dairy	2. Agro-based
C. Maruti Udyog Ltd	3. Public sector
D. Vegetable Oil	4. Co-operative sector

Codes

	A	B	C	D		A	B	C	D
(a)	2	3	1	4	(b)	4	1	2	3
(c)	3	4	1	2	(d)	1	2	3	4

2.

List I	List II
A. Steel city of the USA	1. TISCO
B. Jameshedpur	2. Industrial disaster
C. Silicon Valley	3. Pittsburgh
D. Bhopal	4. California

Codes

	A	B	C	D		A	B	C	D
(a)	1	2	3	4	(b)	3	1	4	2
(c)	4	3	2	1	(d)	2	4	1	3

Ans. 1. (c) 2. (b)

Assertion-Reason

1. **Assertion** (A) Capital and labour are the inputs required for the steel industry.
   Reason (R) Capital is essential for infrastructure and equipment, while labour is needed for manufacturing process.

   Codes
   (a) Both A and R are true and R is the correct explanation of A
   (b) Both A and R are true, but R is not the correct explanation of A
   (c) A is true, but R is false
   (d) A is false, but R is true

2. **Assertion** (A) TISCO was originally established in 1907 in Sakchi, near the confluence of the rivers Subarnarekha and Kharkai.
   Reason (R) Sakchi, where TISCO was founded, was later renamed as Jamshedpur.

   Codes
   (a) Both A and R are true and R is the correct explanation of A
   (b) Both A and R are true, but R is not the correct explanation of A
   (c) A is true, but R is false
   (d) A is false, but R is true

Ans. 1. (a) Both A and R are true and R is the correct explanation of A
2. (b) Both A and R are true, but R is not the correct explanation of A

Fill in the blanks

1. Industries can be classified on the basis of raw materials, size and ....
2. Basket weaving, handicrafts and pottery are examples of .... industry.
3. The process of smelting is done in a ....
4. Market is one of the .... factors for setting up of industries. **Diksha**

Ans. 1. owernship 2. small-scale/cottage 3. blast furnace 4. locational

True/False

1. Production of automobiles and heavy machinery are small scale industries.
2. An industrial system consists of input processes and outputs.
3. Smelting is the process in which metals are extracted from their ores by heating beyond the melting point.

4. Mineral based industries use plant and animal based products as their raw materials.

Ans. 1. False 2. True
3. True 4. False

Picture Based Questions

1. Which type of industry can be seen in the picture?

(a) Mineral-based industry
(b) Agro-based industry
(c) Marine-based industry
(d) Forest-based industry

2. The below given image represent a co-operative sector industry. Who owns and operates co-operative sector industries?

(a) Government authorities
(b) Private investors
(c) Suppliers of raw materials, workers
(d) None of the above

Ans. (i) (b) Agro-based industry
(ii) (c) Suppliers of raw materials, workers

Case Based Question

1. Read the passage given below and answer the following questions.

Industrial regions emerge when a number of industries are located close to each other and share the benefits of their closeness. Major industrial regions of the world are Eastern North America, Western and Central Europe, Eastern Europe and Eastern Asia. Major industrial regions tend to be located in temperate areas, near seaports and especially near coal fields. India has several industrial regions like Mumbai-Pune cluster, Bangalore-Tamil Nadu region, Hugli region, Ahmedabad-Baroda region, Chota Nagpur industrial belt, Visakhapatnam-Guntur belt, Gurgaon-Delhi-Meerut region and the Kollam-Thiruvananthapuram industrial cluster.

(i) Which of the following is not a major industrial region in the world?
(a) Western Europe (b) Eastern Asia
(c) Southern Africa (d) Eastern Europe

(ii) In which type of areas are major industrial regions often located?
(a) Polar areas (b) Tropical areas
(c) Temperate areas (d) Arid areas

(iii) Which of the following is/are an industrial region in India?
(a) Mumbai-Pune cluster
(b) Bangalore-Tamil Nadu region
(c) Hugli region
(d) All of the above

(iv) When does the industrial regions energy?
(a) When industries are scattered across a country.
(b) When industries are located close to each other and share the benefits of closeness.
(c) When Iidustries are located far from each other.
(d) When industries are solely based on agricultural production.

Ans (i) (c) Southern Africa
(ii) (c) Temperate areas
(iii) (d) All of the above
(iv) (b) When industries are located close to each other and share the benefits of closeness.

Part II

Very Short Answer Type Questions

1. What do you understand by the word manufacturing?

Ans. Manufacturing is an activity which changes raw material into products of more value to people.

2. What are the stages of making notebook from pulp?

Ans. The stages of making a notebook from pulp include cutting of trees, and transporting them to the pulp mill. There the wood of the tree was processed and converted into wood pulp which was mixed with chemicals. Finally it was changed into paper by machines and bound into a notebook.

3. Name three common methods of classifying industries.

Ans. Industries are classified according to raw material used, size and ownership.

4. Mention the major industrial regions of the world.

Ans. The major industrial regions of the world are

- Eastern North America
- Western and Central Europe
- Eastern Europe
- Eastern Asia

5. What does industrial system consists of?

Ans. Industrial system consists of three things

(i) Inputs (ii) Processes (iii) Outputs

6. Which public sector steel plant of India is located near a port ?

Ans. Visakhapatnam steel plant of India is located near a port.

7. What is industrial region ? **Diksha**

Ans. An industrial region is a place where a number of industries are located close to each other and share the benefits of their closeness. For example, Mumbai-Pune cluster and Bangalore-Tamil Nadu region.

8. Give one reason for industrial disaster. **Diksha**

Ans. Technical failure or irresponsible handling of hazardous material could be one reason for industrial disaster.

9. Name four common processes involved in a textile industry.

Ans. Ginning, spinning, weaving and dyeing are processes involved in a textile industry.

10. Which industry is one of the oldest industries in the world? **Diksha**

Ans. Cotton textile and iron and steel industries are the oldest industries in the world.

11. What is smelting?

Ans. Smelting is the process in which metals are extracted from their ores by heating above the melting point.

12. When was TISCO started and where was it located?

Ans. TISCO was started in 1907 at Sakchi, near the confluence of the rivers Subarnarekha and Kharkai in Jharkhand.

Short Answer Type Questions

1. What do you understand by secondary activities? Give an example.

Ans. Secondary activities or manufacturing change raw materials into products of more value to people. For example, pulp was changed into paper and paper into a note book. These represent the two stages of the manufacturing process.

The paper made from pulp and cloth made from cotton have had value added to them at each stage of the manufacturing process. In this way the finished product has more value and utility than the raw material that it is made from.

2. Classify industries on the basis of their size.

Ans. On the basis of size, industries can be classified into the following

- **Small-Scale Industries** These industries less amount of capital and technology. Cottage or household industries are a type of small-scale industry where the products are made by hands, by the artisans For example basket weaving, silk weaving, food-processing, and pottery and other handicrafts industries.
- **Large-Scale Industries** These industries use large amount of capital investment and superior technology to produce large volumes of products. For example iron and steel industries, heavy electricals, production of automobiles and heavy machinery.

3. Write a short note on the various classifications of industries. **Diksha**

Ans. Industries can be classified on the basis of raw materials, size of industry and ownership. Industries can be further classified on the basis of these criteria.

(i) On the basis of raw materials, industries can be classified into

- Agro based industries
- Mineral based industries
- Forest based industries

(ii) On the basis of size, industries can be classified into

- Large-scale industries
- Small-scale industries

(iii) On the basis of ownership, industries can be classified into

- Private sector industries
- Public sector industries
- Joint sector industries

4. List the major industries of the world and where they are located?

Ans. The world's major industries are the iron and steel industry, the textile industry and the information technology industry.

Locations of iron and steel industry are

- Germany
- USA
- China

Locations of textile industry are

- India
- Hong Kong
- South Korea
- Japan

Locations of information technology industry are

- Silicon Valley of Central California
- Bangalore region of India.

5. Write a short note on industrial regions.

Ans. Industrial regions emerge when a number of industries locate close to each other and share the benefits of their closeness.

Major industrial regions of the world are

- Eastern North America
- Western and Central Europe
- Eastern Europe
- Eastern Asia

Such areas are usually located in temperate areas near sea ports and coal fields.

6. Suggest some measures to reduce industrial risk.
Or Describe the risk reduction measures. **Diksha**

Ans. To reduce industrial risk, the following measures should be followed

- Densely populated residential areas should be separated far away from the industrial areas.
- People staying in the vicinity of industries should be aware of the storage of toxins or hazardous substances and their possible effects in case if an accident occurs.
- Fire warning and fighting system should be improved.

7. What are the inputs, process and output of iron and steel industry ?

Ans. Inputs, process and output of a iron and steel industry are

- **Inputs** Iron ore is the main raw material that is used in this industry. Other inputs needed are labour, capital, coal, infrastructural facilities, etc.
- **Process** The process of converting iron-ore into involves steel many stages. The raw material is put in the blast furnace where it undergoes smelting, then it is refined.
- **Output** The output obtained after refining is steel which may be used by other industries as raw material.

8. "The iron and steel industry is the basic as well as heavy industry." Support the statement with suitable examples. **Competency Based**

Ans. The iron and steel is called basic industry because all other industries depend on it for their machinery.

Steel is needed to manufacture a variety of engineering goods, construction material, defence, medical, telephones, scientific equipment and variety of consumer goods.

Iron and steel is a heavy industry because all the raw materials and finished goods are heavy. They are bulky also. They are entailing heavy transportation costs.

9. Steel is often called the backbone of modern industry. Almost everything we used is either made of iron or steel or has been made with tools and machinery of these metals. **Competency Based**

(i) What was the ideal location for iron and steel industry?

Ans. Ideal location for the iron and steel industry is near coal fields and close to canals and railways.

(ii) What are the uses of steel that are essential part of the world today?

Ans. Steel has become very essential part of industry and our life. Ships, trains, trucks and autos are made largely of steel. Even safety pins and the needles are made of steel. Oil wells are drilled with steel machinery. Minerals are mixed with steel equipment. Large buildings also have steel framework.

10. Explain the favourable factors for the location of steel plant at Jamshedpur.

Ans. Iron and steel industry is located at Jamshedpur due to the following factors

- Manganese is obtained from Keonjhar district of Odisha.
- Well-developed network of transport is available.
- Kolkata provides port facilities to steel plant at Jamshedpur.
- Cheap and skilled labour is available from the nearby states.

11. Pittsburgh is an important steel city of the United States of America. Explain the steel industry of Pittsburgh. **Competency Based**

Ans. Pittsburgh is an important steel city of the United States of America. It enjoys favourable geographical conditions such as

- Raw material like coal is available locally. Iron ore comes from the iron mines at Minnesota, about 1500 km from Pittsburgh.
- The famous Great Lakes waterway provides one of the best routes for shipping ore cheeply between Minnesota and Pittsburgh. Trains carry the ore from Great Lakes to Pittsburgh.
- The Ohio, the Monogahela and Allegheny rivers provide adequate water supply to this region.

12. What do you mean by information and technology? **Diksha**

Ans. Information Technology (IT) refers to the use of computers, software, and telecommunications to store, transmit, and manipulate data.

It includes activities like computer programming, networking, and using digital tools to process and manage information, making our lives more efficient and connected.

Long Answer Type Questions

1. Manufacturing industries are important for the economic development of the country. Discuss? **Competency Based**

Ans. Manufacturing industries play a crucial role in the economic development of a country for a variety of reasons

- **Job Creation** Manufacturing industries provide employment opportunities to a large number of people, contributing to a reduction in unemployment rates.
- **Increased Production** These industries produce a wide range of goods, from consumer products to machinery, which are essential for the growth of various sectors of the economy.
- **Foreign Exchange Earnings** Exports of manufactured goods can bring in significant foreign exchange, helping to stabilise a country's balance of payments.
- **Technological Advancement** Manufacturing industries often drive technological innovation and advancement, leading to increased productivity and efficiency.

- **Infrastructure Development** The growth of manufacturing industries requires infrastructure development, such as roads, railways, and power supply, which benefits not only the industries but also the overall development of the country.

2. Classify industries on the basis of raw material. Diksha

Ans Industries can be classified based on the type of raw materials they use into the following categories

- **Agro-Based Industries** These use plant and animal-based products as their raw materials. Their examples include food processing, vegetable oil extraction, cotton textile manufacturing product processing and leather industries
- **Mineral-Based Industries** These utilise mineral ores as their primary raw materials. These industries produce materials like iron, steel, cement and chemicals that are used in various sectors. Products from mineral-based industries often serve as inputs for other industries.
- **Marine-Based Industries** These use products derived from the sea and oceans as their raw materials. Their examples include seafood processing, fish oil extraction and industries related to marine resources.
- **Forest-Based Industries** These utilise forest produce as their raw materials. These industries produce items like pulp and paper, pharmaceuticals, furniture, and building materials, primarily using wood and other forest resources.

3. Classify industries on the basis of their ownership.

Ans. Industries can be classified based on ownership into the following categories

- **Private Sector Industries** These are owned and operated by individuals or a group of individuals. Their examples include privately-owned manufacturing companies, small businesses and corporations.
- **Public Sector Industries** These are owned and operated by the government. Their examples include government-run enterprises like Hindustan Aeronautics Limited and Steel Authority of India Limited
- **Joint Sector Industries** These are owned and operated by both the state government and individuals or a group of individuals. Their examples include Maruti Udyog Limited, where the government and private individuals collaborate in ownership and management,
- **Co-operative Sector Industries** These are owned and operated by the producers or suppliers of raw materials, workers, or both, who form cooperatives. Their examples include Anand Milk Union Limited (AMUL) and Sudha Dairy, which are successful cooperative ventures where farmers and dairy workers collectively own and manage the industry.

4. What is industrial disaster? Give some steps to minimise the risks of industrial disaster. Competency Based

Ans. Industrial Disaster is a term used for accidents or disaster which some times happen in industries mainly due to technical failure or irresponsible handling of hazardaus materials.

The steps of risk reduction measures are as follow

- **Zoning and Separation** Densely populated residential areas should be located far away from industrial areas to minimise the risk to human life in the event of an industrial accident. Proper zoning regulations can help to achieve this separation.
- **Public Awareness** People living near industrial areas should be educated and made aware of the presence of toxic or hazardous substances in vicinity. Public awareness campaigns can help residents to understand the potential risks and how to respond in case of an accident.
- **Improved Safety Systems** Fire warning and fighting system should be improved.
- **Limiting Storage** The storage capacity of toxic substances within industrial facilities should be limited to the minimum necessity. Reducing the quantity of hazardous materials on-site can reduce the potential for accidents and their serverity.

5. Explain about Industrial System in detail with an example. Diksha

Ans An industrial system consists of inputs, processes and outputs. The inputs are the raw materials, labour and costs of land, transport power and other infrastructure, such as communication networks, waste disposal systems and security measures. The processes includes a wide range of activities that convert the raw material into finished products. The processes include a wide range of activities that convert the raw material into finished products. The outputs are the end product and the income earned from it.

For example, in the case of the textile industry, the inputs are cotton, human labour, factory space and transport costs. The processes include ginning, spinning, weaving, dyeing and printing. The output is the shirt you wear.

Picture-based Questions

1. Look at the picture given below and answer the questions.

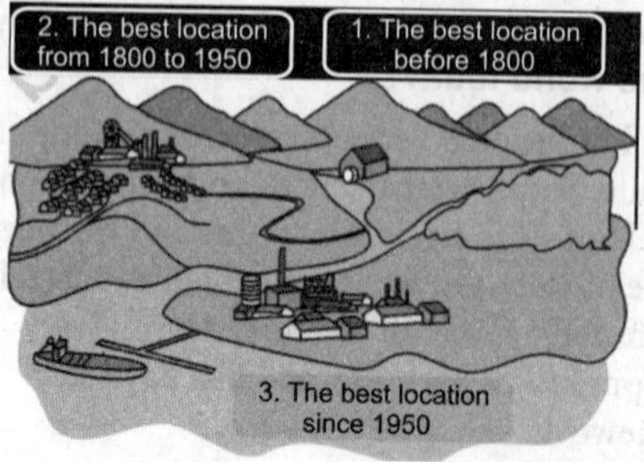

(i) **What significant change occurred in the location of the iron and steel industry after 1950?**

Ans. After 1950, the iron and steel industry began to be located on large areas of flat land near seaports.

(ii) **Where was the iron and steel industry located before 1800 AD?**

Ans. Before 1800 AD, the iron and steel industry was located near the availability of raw materials, power supply and running water.

(iii) **Why did the iron and steel industry started to concentrate near seaports after 1950?**

Ans. The iron and steel industry started to concentrate near the seaport because steelworks had become very large, and iron ore had to be imported from overseas, making seaports more convenient for transportation.

2. Look at the picture given below and answer the questions.

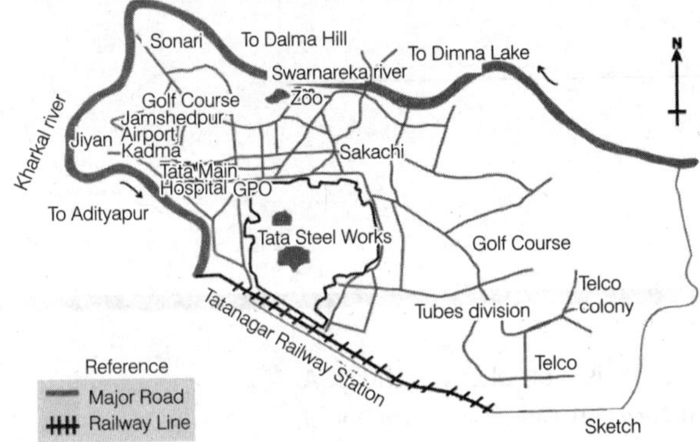

(i) **Which was the only iron and steel plant in the country before 1947?**

Ans. Tata Iron and Steel Company Limited (TISCO) was the only iron and steel plant in the country before 1947, which was privately operated.

(ii) **Where does TISCO get its coal from?**

Ans. TISCO gets its coal from the Jharia coal fields.

Case Based Question

1. Read the source given below and answer the following questions.

Pittsburgh is an important steel city of the United States of America. The steel industry at Pittsburgh enjoys locational advantages. Some of the raw material such as coal is available locally, while the iron ore comes from the iron mines at Minnesota, about 1500 km from Pittsburgh. Between these mines and Pittsburgh is one of the world's best routes for shipping ore cheaply – the famous Great Lakes waterway. Trains carry the ore from the Great Lakes to the Pittsburgh area.

The Ohio, the Monogahela and Allegheny rivers provide adequate water supply. Today, very few of the large steel mills are in Pittsburgh itself. They are located in the valleys of the Monogahela and Allegheny rivers above Pittsburgh and along the Ohio river below it.

Finished steel is transported to the market by both land and water routes. The Pittsburgh area has many factories other than steel mills. These use steel as their raw material to make many different products such as railroad equipment, heavy machinery and rails.

(i) **How is iron ore transported from the iron mines in Minnesota to Pittsburgh?**

Ans. Iron ore is transported from the iron mines in Minnesota to Pittsburgh by trains, using the Great Lakes waterway as one of the best routes for cost-effective shipping.

(ii) **What are the locational advantages of Pittsburgh for the steel industry?**

Ans. Locational advantages in Pittsburgh include the availability of local coal, proximity to iron ore mines in Minnesota connected via the Great Lakes waterway, and access to the Ohio, Monogahela, and Allegheny rivers for water supply.

(iii) **Where are most of the large steel mills located in relation to Pittsburgh today?**

Ans. Today, most of the large steel mills are located in the valleys of the Monogahela and Allegheny Rivers above Pittsburgh and along the Ohio river below it.

Map Based Questions

1. With the help of an atlas, identify some iron and steel industries in India and mark their location on an outline map of India. **NCERT**

Ans.

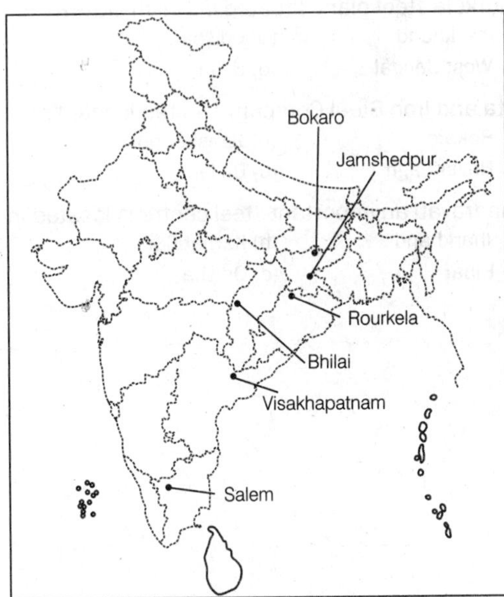

2. On an outline map of the world, mark the countries in which iron and steel industry is located.

Ans. Countries with iron and steel industry are USA, India, China, Russia, Germany and Japan.

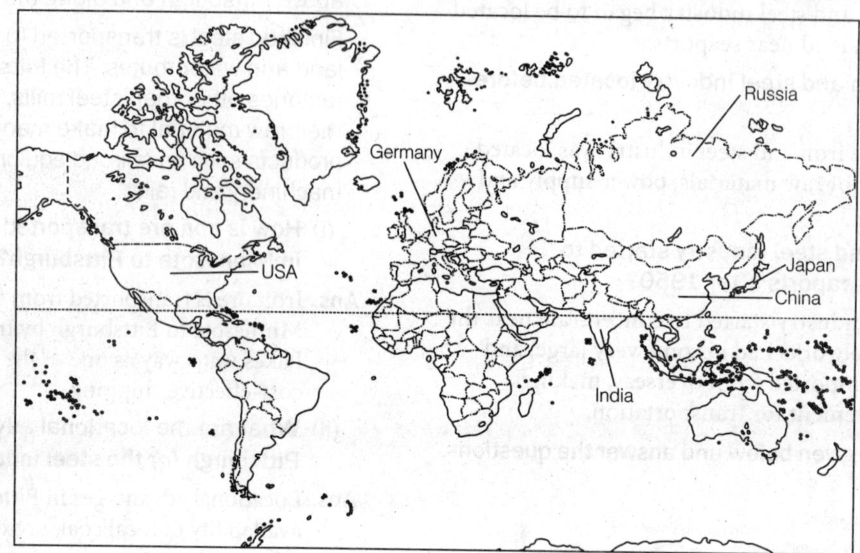

ASSESSMENT EXERCISE

Multiple Choice Questions (MCQs)

1. Industries use products from the sea and oceans as a raw material is
(a) forest based industries
(b) marine based industries
(c) agro based industries
(d) mineral based industries

2. Rourkela steel plant situated in which state?
(a) Jharkhand (b) Odisha
(c) West Bengal (d) Bihar

3. Tata and Iron Steel Company Limited located at
(a) Bokaro (b) Jamshedpur
(c) Hazaribagh (d) Bhilai

4. Bhadravati an important steel centre is located in
(a) Jharkhand (b) Karnataka
(c) Bihar (d) Odisha

5. .... is a steel city in the USA.
(a) New York City (b) Detroit
(c) Pittsburgh (d) Ohio

Subjective Questions (VSA, SA & LA)

6. Name the major industrial regions of the world.

7. Name the industrial regions of India.

8. Give three examples of uses of steel.

9. Define 'Sunrise Industries'.

10. Explain small-scale industries.

11. Write a note on petrochemical industry.

12. Explain the characteristics of steel.

13. Discuss the economic activity of industries.

14. What is the significance of industries?

15. What are the factors that contribute to the success of TISCO?

Human Resources

CHAPTER 5

People are nation's most important resource. They make use of nature's gifts and turn them into resources with their demand and abilities. Thus, **human resources**[1] are the ultimate resources. Healthy, educated and motivated people can develop resources according to their requirements.

Human resources are not equally distributed over the world. They vary in their educational levels, age and sex. Their numbers and characteristics keep changing.

5.1 Distribution of Population

The way in which people are spread across the Earth's surface is known as the pattern of population distribution. Over 90% of the world's population lives on only about 30% of the land.

Population distribution is uneven. Some areas are very crowded, like South and South-East Asia, Europe and North-Eastern North America and some areas have very few people, like high latitude areas, tropical deserts, high mountains, and equatorial forests.

More people live in the North of the Equator in the South. About three-quarters of the world's population live in Asia and Africa. 60% of world's population live in just 10 countries having more than 100 million people.

Factors Affecting Distribution of Population

Factors affecting distribution of population can be divided into geographical factors and social, cultural and economic factors. These are

Geographical Factors

- **Topography** People like to live on plains over mountains and plateaus because plains are better for farming, manufacturing and services. The Ganga plains are more populated than mountains like Andes and Alps.
- **Climate** People avoid extreme hot or cold climates, such as the Sahara desert and Polar regions of Russia, Canada and America.
- **Soil** Fertile soils provide suitable land for agriculture. Thus, fertile plains such as Ganga and Brahmaputra in India, Hwang-He and Chang Jiang in China, and the Nile in Egypt are heavily populated.
- **Water** People prefer to live in areas where fresh water is available. Thus, river valleys are densely populated, while deserts have fewer people.
- **Minerals** Areas with mineral deposits are more populated. Thus, diamond mines of South Africa and discovery of oil in the Middle East lead to people settling in these areas.

Social, Cultural and Economic Factors

- **Social** Areas of better housing, education and health facilities are more densely populated, e.g. Pune.
- **Cultural** Places with religious or cultural importance, like Varanasi, Jerusalem, and Vatican City are more populated.
- **Economic** The industrial areas that provide employment opportunities are more populated, e.g. Osaka in Japan and Mumbai in India.

5.2 Density of Population

Population density is the number of people living in a unit area of the Earth's surface. It is normally expressed in **per square km**.

The average population density in the world is 51 persons per square km. **South Central Asia** has the **highest density**, followed by East and South East-Asia.

KNOWLEDGE PLUS Average density of population in India is 382 persons per square km.

1 Human Resource Human resources are groups of individual who use nature to creak more resources.

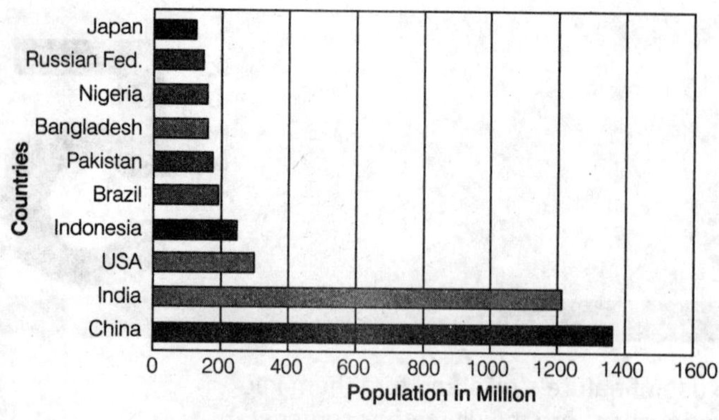

• World's Most Populous Countries

5.3 Population Change

The population change refers to change in the number of people during a specific time. World population is unstable due to changes in the number of births and deaths.

Unitil 1800s, world population used to grow slowly because many babies were born, although they died early due to poor health facilities and food shortages.

In 1804, the world had 1 billion people, which reached to 3 billion in 1959. This is often called **population explosion.** In 1999, population doubled to 6 billion due to better food supplies and medicine, high number of births and low number of deaths.

Factors Affecting Population Change

The factors that affect population change are birth rate, death rate, natural growth rate and migration.

Birth Rate is the number of live births per 1,000 people. **Death Rate** is the number of live deaths per 1,000 people.

The difference between the birth rate and the death rate of a country is called the natural growth rate. The increase in natural growth rate led to increase in world population.

Migration is the movement of people in and out of an area. It is another way by which population size changes. It is classified as

- **Immigrants or in-migration** When a person enters a new country, it is known as in-migration.
- **Emigrants or out-migration** When a person leaves a country, it is know as emigration.

Countries like the United States and Australia have gained more population due to immigration while Sudan has experienced a loss in population due to emigration.

The trend of **international migration**[2] is from less developed nations to more developed nations for better employment opportunities and within countries. People often move within countries from rural to urban areas for employment, education and healthcare.

Patterns of Population Change

The rates of population growth vary across the world. World total population is increasing rapidly, but not all countries are experiencing this growth.

Some countries like **Kenya** have high population growth rates due to high birth and death rates in the past. However, with better healthcare, death rates have decreased, but birth rates remain high, resulting in high growth rates.

In other countries like the **United Kingdom**, population growth is slowing down because of both low death and low birth rates.

5.4 Population Composition

People vary greatly in their age, sex, literacy level, health condition, occupation and income level.

Population composition refers to the structure of the population. It helps us to know more about the people in a country, like how many are males or females, their ages, education, occupations, income levels and health conditions.

Population Pyramid

Population pyramid, also called an **age-sex pyramid**, is a way to study the population composition of a country. It shows the following.

- The total population divided into various age groups, e.g. 5 to 9 years, 10 to 14 years.
- The percentage of the total population, subdivided into males and females, in each of those groups.
- The shape of the population pyramid give information about the people living in a particular country. The number of children (below 5 years) are shown at the bottom and reflect the level of births. The size of the top of pyramid shows the number of aged people (above 65 years) and the level of deaths.
- The population pyramid gives information about the number of dependents in a country. There are two types of dependents, **young dependents** (below 15 years of age) and **elderly dependents** (above 65 years of age). The people of working age are economically active.

2 International Migration It is the movement of people across international borders for the purpose of settlement.

Population Pyramid of Different Countries

Kenya

In countries with high birth and death rates like Kenya, the pyramid is broad at the base and narrow towards the top. This is because many children are born, but a large percentage of them die in their infancy. Relatively, some of these children become adult and there are very few old people.

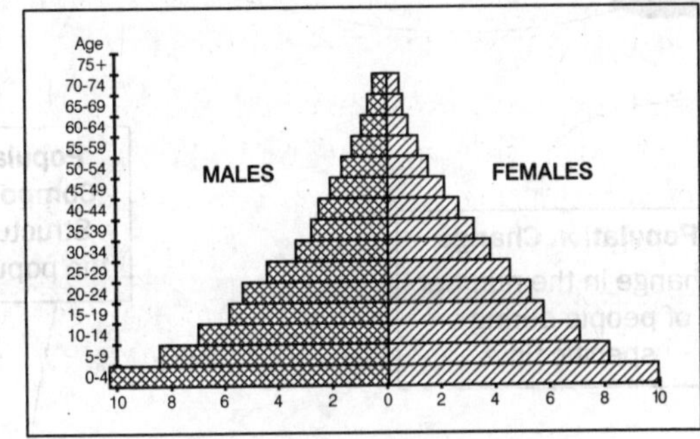

• Population Pyramid of Kenya

India

In countries with decreasing death rates like India, the pyramid is broad in the younger age groups because more children survive to adulthood. Such populations consists of a large number of young people which means a strong and expanding labour force.

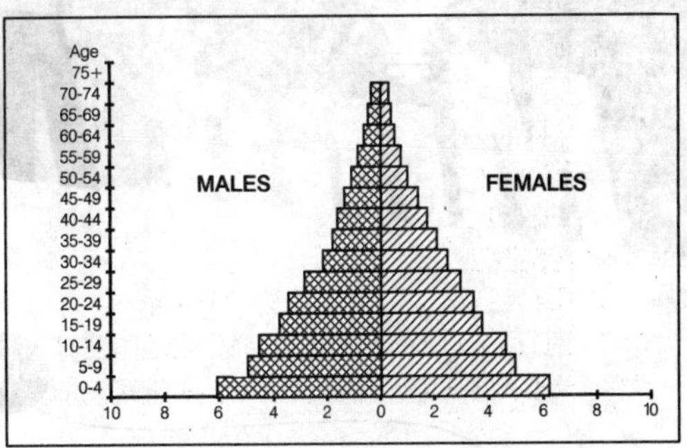

• Population Pyramid of India

Japan

In countries with low birth rates and low death rates like Japan, the pyramid is narrow at the base and they have more old age people.

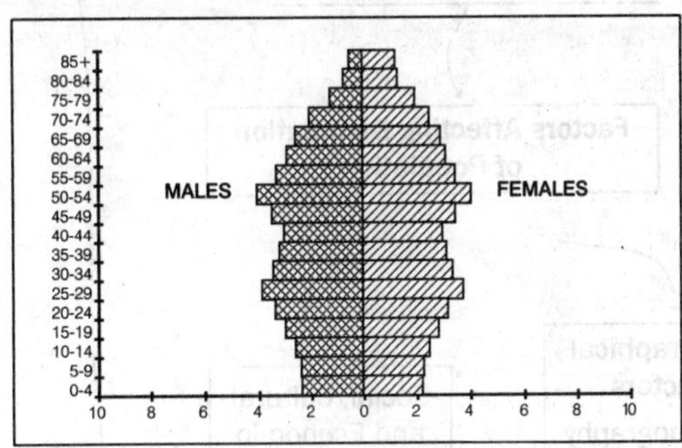

• Population Pyramid of Japan

Mind Map

HUMAN RESOURCES

Population Distribution
The way in which people are spread across the Earth's surface

Factors Affecting Distribution of Population

Geographical Factors
- Topography
- Climate
- Soil
- Water
- Minerals

Social, Cultural and Economic Factors

Population Density
- Number of people living in a unit area of the Earth's surface
- Average density of the world- 51 persons per sq km
- Highest population density in the world-South Central Asia.

Population Change
Change in the number of people during a specific time

Factors Affecting Population Change
- Births
- Deaths
- Migration

Natural Growth Rate
Difference between the birth rate and the death rate

Population Composition
Structure of the population

Variation of the Population based on Various Aspects
- Age
- Sex
- Literacy level
- Occupation
- Income level
- Health condition

Population Pyramid or Age-Sex Pyramid

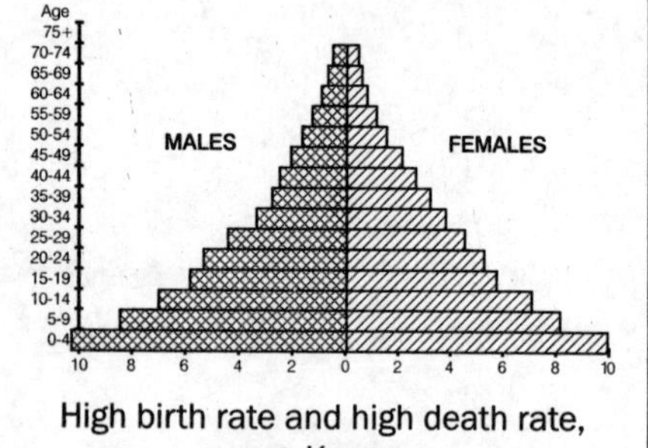

High birth rate and high death rate, e.g. Kenya.

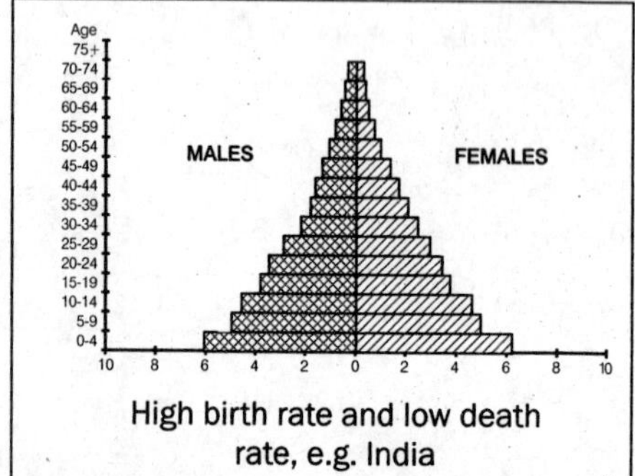

High birth rate and low death rate, e.g. India

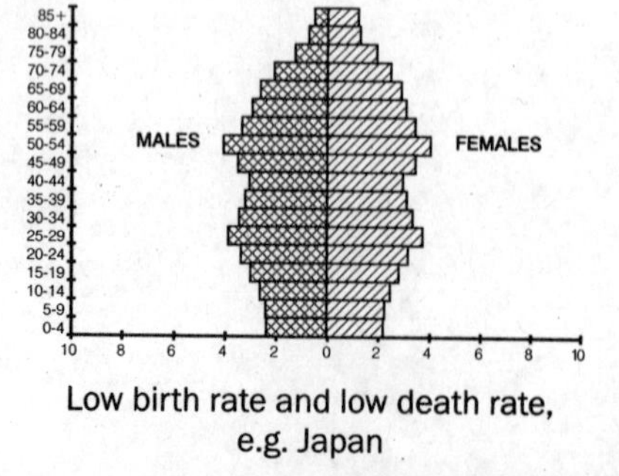

Low birth rate and low death rate, e.g. Japan

NCERT FOLDER

Covering Intext Questions and Exercises of NCERT

NCERT ON PAGE 45 (ACTIVITY)

Q.1 Study figure 5.1 (NCERT textbook page 45) and find out of the world's total population which continent has.

(a) Only 5 per cent (b) Only 13 per cent
(c) Only 1 per cent (d) Only 12 per cent

Ans. (a) North America (b) Africa
(c) Oceania (d) Europe

EXERCISES

Q.1 Answer the following questions

(i) Why are people considered a resource?

Ans. People are considered a resources because they have the knowledge, skills and abilities to create, use and manage other resources.

Nature's resources becomes important only when people find it and make it useful for them.

(ii) What are the causes for the uneven distribution of population in the world?

Ans. The causes and factors for the uneven distribution of population in the world are

- **Topography** People like to live on plains over mountains and plateaus because plains are better for farming, manufacturing and services. The Ganga plains are more populated than mountains like Andes and Apls.
- **Climate** People avoid extreme hot or cold climates, such as the Sahara desert and Polar regions of Russia, Canada and America.
- **Soil** Fertile soils provide suitable land for agriculture. Thus, fertile plains such as Ganga and Brahmaputra in India, Hwang-He and Chang Jiang in China, and the Nile in Egypt are heavily populated.
- **Water** People prefer to live in areas where fresh water is available. Thus, river valleys are densely populated, while deserts have fewer people.
- **Minerals** Areas with mineral deposits are more populated. Thus, diamond mines of South Africa and discovery of oil in the Middle East lead to people settling in these areas.

(iii) The world population has grown very rapidly. Why?

Ans. The world population has grown very rapidly because of many factors which are as follows

- Rapid increase in natural growth rate.
- Eradication of many deadly dangerous diseases. i.e. improvement in medical facilities.
- Migration of the people from developing countries to developed nations.
- Growth in food supplies.

(iv) Discuss the role of any two factors influencing population change.

Ans. The main factors influencing population change are

- **Birth Rate** It is the number of live births per 1,000 people. High birth rates increases the population rapidly. A slow birth rate leads to a slow increase in the population
- **Death Rate** It is the number of live deaths per 1,000 people. A high death rate leads to a slow increase in population. A low death rate (as a result of increased healthcare facilities), along with no decrease in the birth rate, leads to an increase in population.

(v) What is meant by population composition? Diksha

Ans. Population composition refers to the structure of the population. It helps us to know the people in a country, like how many are males or females, their ages, education, occupations, income levels and health conditions.

(vi) What are population pyramids? How do they help in understanding about the population of a country?

Ans. Population pyramids are visual representations that help us understand the population of a country. It is also called an age-sex pyramid.

It help to understand the population of a country in the following ways

- Population pyramids divide the total population into age groups, like 5-9 years or 10-14 years, showing how many people are in each group.
- They also show the percentage of males and females in each age group, helping us see the gender balance in the population.
- The pyramid's shape reveals important information. A wide base indicates births of many children, while a wide top means deaths of more elderly people.
- By looking at the pyramid, we can see how many young dependents (below 15 years) and elderly dependents (above 65 years) are there.

- Population pyramids help us to understand the country's economic potential. A broad base with more young people can mean a strong labor force, while a narrow base with more elderly people may indicate an aging population.

Q.2 Tick the correct answer.

(i) What does the term population distribution refer to?

(a) How population in a specified area changes over time.

(b) The number of people who die in relation to the number of people born in a specified area.

(c) The way in which people are spread across a given area.

Ans. (c) The way in which people are spread across a given area.

(ii) Which are three main factors that cause population change?

(a) Births, deaths and marriage.

(b) Births, deaths and migration.

(c) Births, deaths and life expectancy.

Ans. (b) Births, deaths and migration.

(iii) In 1999, the world population reached

(a) 1 billion (b) 3 billion (c) 6 billion

Ans. (c) 6 billion

(iv) What is a population pyramid? **Diksha**

(a) A graphical presentation of the age, sex composition of a population.

(b) When the population density of an area is so high that people live in tall buildings.

(c) Pattern of population distribution in large urban areas.

Ans. (a) A graphical presentation of the age, sex composition of a population.

Q.3 Complete the sentences below using some of the following words.

(sparsely, favourable, fallow, artificial, fertile, natural, extreme, densely)

When people are attracted to an area, it becomes (i) .... populated. Factors that influence this include (ii) .... climate; good supplies of (iii) .... resources and (iv) .... land.

Ans. (i) densely (ii) favourable

(iii) natural (iv) fertile

Q.4 Discuss the characteristics of a society with "too many under 15's" and one with "too few under 15's"

Hint : Need for schools, pension schemes, teachers, toys, wheel chairs, labour supply, hospitals.

Ans. People of different age groups have different requirements. If a society has too many under 15s, it will require more teachers, toys, schools as per the needs of children and labour supply will be less.

If a society has too few under 15s, it implies that it has more adult population which will require more pension schemes, hospitals, wheel chairs and labour supply will be more.

REVIEW EXERCISE

Including Competency Based Questions

Part I

Multiple Choice Questions (MCQs)

1. Human resources differ from one another in respect of

(a) age (b) educational level

(c) sex (d) All of these

2. The highest density of the population in the world is in

(a) South Central Asia (b) Europe

(c) South America (d) None of these

3. What is the average population density of the world? (Persons per sq. km).

(a) 10 (b) 100

(c) 51 (d) 300

4. Most of the people usually prefer to live in

(a) plains (b) equatorial forest area

(c) high mountains (d) high altitude areas

5. The factors which influence population change are

(a) birth rate (b) death rate

(c) migration (d) All of these

6. The country which have high growth rate of population is

(a) Kenya (b) New Zealand (c) Brazil (d) Egypt

8. **Raj and Neha were talking about the high birth and death rate in their country. What would the population pyramid of their country look like?** Competency Based

(a) Broad at the base and rapidly narrows towards the top.
(b) Broad at the base and top.
(c) Narrow at the base and broad towards the top.
(d) Narrow at the base and narrower at the top.

9. **Identify the country from the information given below.** Competency Based

(i) Both birth and death rates are high.
(ii) Population pyramid is broad at the base and rapidly narrows towards the top.

(a) Kenya (b) Japan (c) India (d) U.S.A

10. **Which one of the following statements is incorrect?**

I. Human resources like other resources are equally distributed over the world.
II. South and South-East Asia, Europe and North-Eastern part of North America are the crowded areas.

Codes

(a) Only I (b) Both I and II
(c) Only II (d) None of these

11. **Which one of the following statements is correct?**

I. The people avoid living in extreme climatic conditions.
II. The United Kingdom is a country with a low population growth rate.

Codes

(a) Only I (b) Both I and II
(c) Only II (d) None of these

12. **Arrange the following countries, according to their population from larger to smaller.**

I. Nigeria II. Pakistan
III. India IV. USA
V. Japan

Codes

(a) III, II, I, IV, V (b) I, II, III, V, IV
(c) III, IV, II, V, I (d) III, IV, II, I, V

13. **Arrange the following countries, according to their area from larger to smaller.** Competency Based

I. Russia II. India
III. China IV. United States
V. Brazil VI. Argentina

Codes

(a) I, II, IV, VI, III, V (b) I, III, IV, V, II, VI
(a) IV, III, VI, II, I, V (d) III, IV, I, VI, V, II

Answers

1. (d)	**2.** (a)	**3.** (c)	**4.** (a)	**5.** (d)
6. (a)	**7.** (d)	**8.** (a)	**9.** (a)	**10.** (a)
11. (b)	**12.** (d)	**13.** (b)		

Match the Following

1.

	List I		List II
A.	Social Place	1.	Mountain
B.	Cultural Place	2.	Plains
C.	Ganga	3.	Varanasi
D.	Himalaya	4.	Pune

Codes

	A	B	C	D		A	B	C	D
(a)	4	3	2	1	(b)	3	2	1	4
(c)	2	1	4	3	(d)	1	2	4	3

2.

	List I		List II
A.	Migration	1.	Geographical factor
B.	Life Expectancy	2.	People leaving the country
C.	Climate	3.	Number of years for which an average man expect to live
D	Emigrants	4.	The movement of people in and out of an area

Codes

	A	B	C	D		A	B	C	D
(a)	4	3	1	2	(b)	3	2	1	4
(c)	2	1	4	3	(d)	1	2	4	3

Ans. 1. (a) 2. (a)

Fill in the Blanks

1. The .... are the most densely populated areas of the world.

2. ...... in Japan and ...... in India are two densely populated areas.

3. Varanasi, Jerusalem and Vatican city are some examples of .... factors.

4. In 1999, less than 30 years later, the population doubled to .... billion.

5. The government of India has Ministry of Human Resource Development which was created in.... . Diksha

Ans. 1. Ganga Plains 2. Osaka, Mumbai
3. religious or cultural 4. 6 5. 1985

True/False

1. Population is unevenly distributed in the world.

2. Deaths are usually measured using the death rate.

3. Emigrants are people who arrive in a country.

4. The age group 0-15 comes under the economically dependent group.

5. Green land has the lowest population density.

Ans. 1. True 2. True 3. False 4. True 5. True

3. Emigrants are people who arrive in a country.
4. The age group 0-15 comes under the economically dependent group.
5. Green land has the lowest population density.

Ans. 1. True 2. True 3. False 4. True 5. True

Assertion-Reason

1. **Assertion** (A) The population pyramid can help determine the dependency ratio in a country.

   Reason (R) Dependents in a population pyramid are categorised into young dependents and elderly dependents, while those of working age are economically active.

   Codes
   (a) Both A and R are true and R is the correct explanation of A
   (b) Both A and R are true, but R is not the correct explanation of A
   (c) A is true, but R is false
   (d) A is false, but R is true

2. **Assertion** (A) In countries like Japan, low birth rates make the population pyramid narrow at the base.

   Reason (R) Decreased death rates allow a significant number of people to reach old age.

   Codes
   (a) Both A and R are true and R is the correct explanation of A
   (b) Both A and R are true, but R is not the correct explanation of A
   (c) A is true, but R is false
   (d) A is false, but R is true

Ans. 1. (a) Both A and R are true and R is the correct explanation of A
2. (a) Both A and R are true and R is the correct explanation of A

Picture Based Questions

1. **Look at the picture given below and answer the question that follows.**

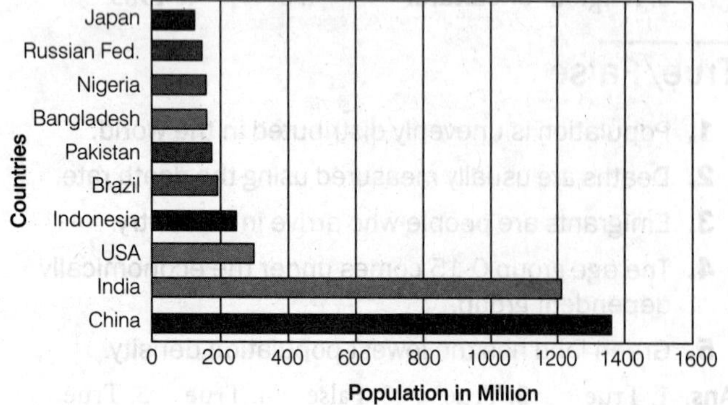

According to the population chart, what is Brazil's rank in the world?
(a) 2nd (b) 4th (c) 5th (d) 3rd

2. **Look at the picture given below and answer the question that follows.**

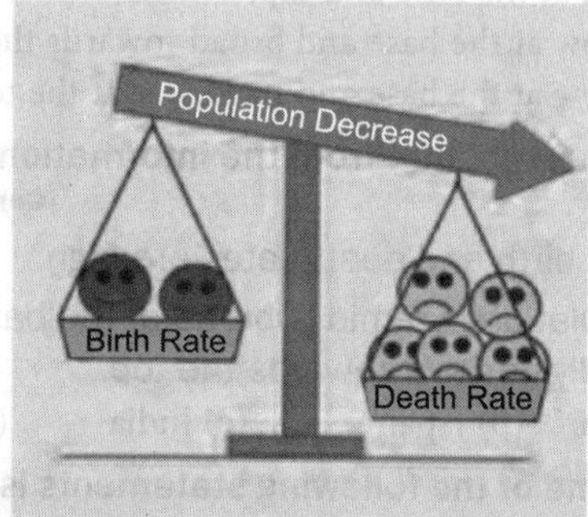

Which factor has contributed to high population growth rates in Kenya?
(a) High birth rates and low death rates
(b) Low birth rates and high death rates
(c) High birth rates and high death rates
(d) Low birth rates and low death rates

Ans. 1. (c) 5th
2. (a) High birth rates and low death rates

Case Based Question

1. **Read the given passage and answer the following questions.**

The way in which people are spread across the Earth's surface is known as the pattern of population distribution. More than 90 per cent of the world's population lives in about 30 per cent of the land surface. The distribution of population in the world is extremely uneven. Some areas are very crowded and some are sparsely populated. The crowded areas are South and South-East Asia, Europe and North-Eastern North America. Very few people live in high-latitude areas, tropical deserts, high mountains and areas of equatorial forests. Many more people live North of the Equator than South of the Equator. Almost three- quarters of the world's people live in two continents Asia and Africa. Sixty per cent of the world's people live in just 10 countries. All of them have more than 100 million people.

(i) **What does the text imply about the distribution of the world's population?**
(a) It is evenly spread across all regions.
(b) It is primarily concentrated in low-lying areas.
(c) It is highly uneven, with some areas densely populated and others sparsely populated.
(d) It is mostly located in regions with a Mediterranean climate.

(ii) **What is the significance of the distribution of population in relation to a country's economic development?**

(a) It has no impact on a country's economic development.

(b) It is the primary factor determining a country's economic development.

(c) It can affect a country's economic development, but other factors also play a role.

(d) It is directly correlated with a country's political stability.

(iii) **Which of the following factors is not mentioned in the text as contributing to uneven population distribution?**

(a) Health conditions (b) Occupation

(c) Income level (d) All of the above

(iv) **What does a narrow population pyramid at the base and a wider top indicate in a country's population distribution?**

(a) High birth rates and low death rates

(b) Low birth rates and high death rates

(c) High birth rates and high death rates

(d) Low birth rates and low death rates

Ans (i) (c) It is highly uneven, with some areas densely populated and others sparsely populated.

(ii) (c) It can affect a country's economic development, but other factors also play a role.

(iii) (d) All of the above

(iv) (b) Low birth rates and high death rates.

Part II

Very Short Answer Type Questions

1. What do you understand by population distribution?

Ans. Population distribution is the way in which people are spread across the Earth's surface.

2. Which geographical factors are responsible for distribution of population? Diksha

Ans. Geographical factors responsible for population of distribution are topography, climate, availability at water, mineral deposits, soil.

3. What do you mean by population ?

Ans. Population refers to the number of people living in a particular region.

4. What are the people called who have come from other countries?

Ans. People who have come from other countries are called immigrants.

5. What is emigration? Diksha

Ans. Emigration is the movement of people to other countries.

6. What is the general trend of international migrations ?

Ans. The general trend of international migration is from less developed nations to more developed nations in search of better employment opportunities.

7. What do you understand about life expectancy?

Ans. Life expectancy is the number of years that an average person can expect to live.

8. Name the country with slowing growth rate of population.

Ans. United Kingdom is the country with slowing growth rate of population.

9. What do you mean by population explosion?

Ans. Population explosion is a sudden and rapid increase in population.

10. Define the sex ratio.

Ans. Sex ratio is the proportion of males and females in a given population. It is expressed as the number of males per 100 females.

11. What is a population pyramid? Diksha

Ans. Population pyramid, also called an age-sex pyramid, is a way to study the population composition of a country.

12. What kind of youth is the future of our country? Competency Based

Ans Skilled, spirited and hopeful youth endowed with a positive outlook is the future of any country.

Short Answer Type Questions

1. Factors affecting population distribution can be divided into geographical and social, cultural and economic factors. Explain the social, cultural and economic factors of population distribution. Competency Based

Ans. Social, cultural and economic factors of population distribution are

- **Social** Areas of better housing, education and health facilities are more densely populated, e.g. Pune.
- **Cultural** Places with religious or cultural importance, like Varanasi, Jerusalem, and Vatican City are more populated.
- **Economic** The industrial areas that provide employment opportunities. Thus these areas are more populated, e.g. Osaka in Japan and Mumbai in India.

2. Explain why the Ganga plains have high population density and polar regions have low population density? Diksha

Ans. Ganga plains have high population density because plains have fertile soils for agriculture, abundant water resources from rivers and rainfall for agricultural and other human activities. These also have favourable climate for human habitation.

Low population density of Polar regions is due to their extreme climate with very cold weather. It makes difficult for people to live in these regions.
Polar regions also lack many resources that are essential for human habitation such as food, water and shelter.

3. What is birth rate? How can we measure births?

Ans. Birth rate is one of the influencing factors of population change.

Births are usually measured using the birth rate i.e. the number of live births per 1000 people. When birth rate is more than death rate, it is population increase.

4. What do you understand by the term death rate? How deaths are measured?

Ans. Death rate is an influencing factor of population change.

Deaths are usually measured using the death rate i.e. the number of deaths per 1000 people. When death rate is more than birth rate, it is population decrease.

5. Why is the population pyramid of Kenya broad at the base and narrow towards the top? Competency Based

Ans. The population pyramid of Kenya is broad at the base and narrow towards the top because of the following

- Many children are born, but a large percentage of them die in their infancy.
- Some of these children become adult and there are very few old people.

6. Explain the population pyramid of Japan.

Ans. The population pyramid of Japan is narrow at the base which indicates that there are a relatively small number of young people in the population and Japan has low birth rate. Decreased death rates allow less number of people to reach old age. The working population is more compared to the children and old population in Japan.

7. Analyse the population pyramid of India.

Ans. In countries with decreasing death rates like India, the population pyramid is broad in the younger age groups because more children survive to adulthood. Such populations consists of a large number of young people which means a strong and expanding labour force.

Long Answer Type Questions

1. Describe the distribution of population in the world.

Ans. The distribution of population in the world is extremely uneven. Some areas are very crowded and some are sparsely populated. It can be understood from the following points.

- More than 90 per cent of the world's population lives in about 10 per cent of the land surface.
- The densely populated areas are South and South-East Asia, Europe and North-Eastern North America.
- The sparsely populated areas are high latitude areas, tropical deserts, high mountains and areas of equatorial forests.
- Almost three-quarters of the world's people live in two continents Asia and Africa.
- Sixty per cent of the uneven distribution of people stay in just 10 countries. All of them have more than a 100 million people.

2. The quality of people is more important than quantity. Eludicate. Competency Based

Ans. The quality of people is more important than quantity for several reasons

- Quality human resources, including education, skills, and motivation, lead to higher productivity, boosting a nation's economy.
- Educated individuals drive innovation and technological progress.
- Quality human resources address societal challenges, promote social harmony, and contribute to community development.
- Healthy, educated individuals need less government assistance.
- A high-quality workforce attracts investment and participates effectively in global markets.
- Quality human resources adapt to changing landscapes for long-term sustainability.

3. Migration has positive and negative impact on a country or an area. Describe. Competency Based

Ans. Migration can have both positive and negative impacts on a country or an area.

On the positive side,

- Migrants often bring new skills and ideas to their new countries, which can boost the economy.
- Migration can help to introduce new cultures and perspectives to a country.
- Migrants can help to fill labour shortages in certain industries.
- Migrants pay taxes, which can help to fund government programs and services.

On the negative side,

- Migrants can compete with native-born workers for jobs and housing which can lead to social tensions.
- Some studies have shown that crime rates are higher in areas with high levels of immigration.
- Migration can lead to cultural clashes and social tensions between different groups of people.
- Migration can lead to increased urbanisation and population.

4. What are the bad effects of population explosion on society? **Competency Based**

Ans. Bad effects of population explosion on our society are

- Population explosion creates pressure upon resources as there are more people and their quick depletion.
- An increased number of poverty-stricken individuals as little food is distributed among more people, then starvation, malnutrition or poor diet with ill health and diet-deficiency diseases would increase.
- Loss of natural environment (forests and such) and loss of ecosystems because they are destroyed to make way for farming and urban developments to accommodate the rising population.
- Irreversible loss of fertile land and increase in decertification.

5. How does population pyramid help in understanding the population of the country? **Competency Based**

Ans. Population pyramid help in understanding the population of the country in the following ways

- It shows the total population which is divided into various age groups. For example, 5 to 9 years, 10 to 14 years.
- it shows the percentage of the total population, sub divided into males and females, in each of those groups.
- It shows the numbers of children (below 15 years) at the bottom and reflect the level of births.
- The size of the top of population pyramid shows the numbers of aged people (above 65 years) and reflects the number of deaths.

6. What do you mean by population composition? Explain in detail. **Diksha**

Ans. Population composition refers to the structure of a population, which helps us understand the characteristics of the people living in a particular area

Population composition includes information about the different age groups within a population, such as children, adults, and the elderly. It involves understanding the gender balance within the population, specifying the number of males and females.

Population composition looks at the literacy and educational levels of the people, indicating the extent of education in the area. It provides details about the types of jobs people are engaged in and their income levels, which are vital for assessing the economic activity in a region.

Population composition also considers the health conditions of the population, helping in evaluating the overall well-being and healthcare needs of the community.

Picture Based Question

1. Given below image is the population pyramid of Kenya.
Briefly elaborate what does the population pyramid of Kenya signifies?

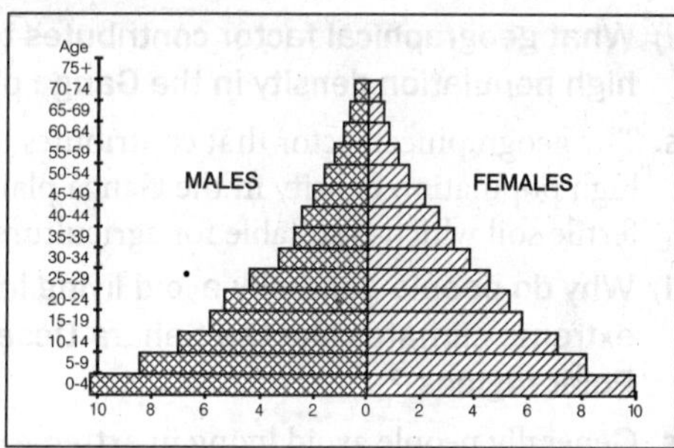

Ans. The population pyramid of Kenya represents that birth rate and death rates both are high in Kenya. It is represented by broad base and rapidly narrow towards top in the pyramid.

Case Based Question

1. Read the source given below and answer the following questions.

Topography People always prefer to live on plains rather than mountains and plateaus because these areas are suitable for farming, manufacturing and service activities. The Ganga plains are the most densely populated areas of the world while mountains like Andes, Alps and Himalayas are sparsely populated.

Climate People usually avoid extreme climates that are very hot or very cold like the Sahara Desert, polar regions of Russia, Canada and Antarctica.

Soil Fertile soils provide suitable land for agriculture. Fertile plains such as Ganga and Brahmaputra in India, Hwang-He, Chang Jiang in China and the Nile in Egypt are densely populated.

Water People prefer to live in areas where fresh water is easily available. The river valleys of the world are densely populated while deserts have spare populations.

Minerals Areas with mineral deposits are more populated. Diamond mines in South Africa and the discovery of oil in the Middle East led to the settling of people in these areas.

Social Areas of better housing, education and health facilities are more densely populated e.g., Pune.

Cultural Places with religion or cultural significance attract people. Varanasi, Jerusalem and Vatican City are some examples.

Economic Industrial areas provide employment opportunities. A large number of people are attracted to these areas. Osaka in Japan and Mumbai in India are two densely populated areas.

(i) What geographical factor contributes to the high population density in the Ganga plains ?

Ans. The geographical factor that contributes to the high population density in the Ganga plains is the fertile soil which is suitable for agriculture.

(ii) Why do people generally avoid living in extreme climates like the Sahara Desert or Polar regions ?

Ans. Generally people avoid living in extreme climates because they are very hot or very cold and are unfavourable for humans.

(iii) What economic factor can lead to higher population density in industrial areas ?

Ans. The economic factor that can lead to higher population density in industrial areas are that industrial areas provide employment opportunities, attracting a large number of people.

Map Based Question

1. Look at the given figure and find out :
Of these countries how many are in Asia? Locate them on a world map.

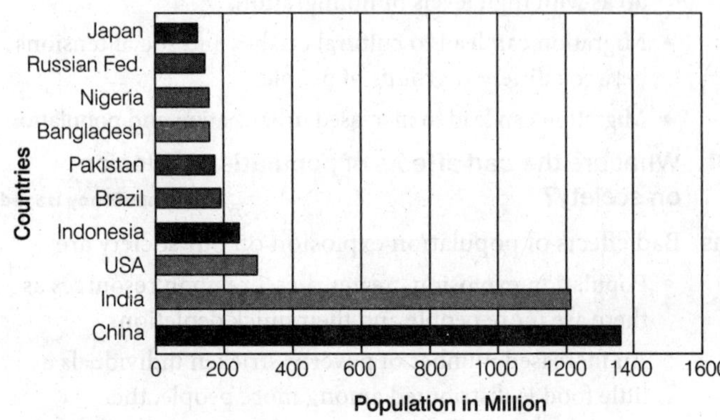

Ans. The countries in Asia are China, India, Indonesia, Pakistan, Bangladesh and Japan.

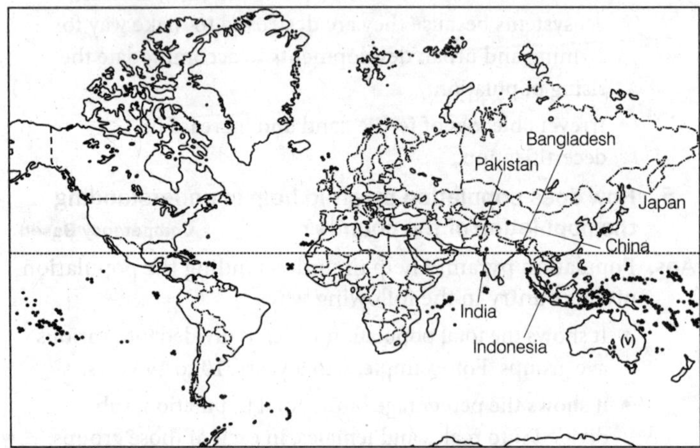

ASSESSMENT EXERCISE

Multiple Choice Questions (MCQs)

1. The world's population reached one billion in
(a) 1804 (b) 1904 (c) 1885 (d) 1850

2. Population pyramid tells us about
(a) senior citizens (b) males-females
(c) youngsters (0-18) (d) estimate the birth rate

3. The population pyramid of which country shows decreasing death rates?
(a) Japan (b) India (c) Kenya (d) Malaysia

4. Osaka is in
(a) India (b) Japan (c) Korea (d) China

5. What is the population density of India?
(a) 350 (b) 382 (c) 282 (d) 300

6. The ratio of male and female in population is called
(a) longevity (b) sex ratio
(c) infant morlality rate (d) None of these

Subjective Questions (VSA, SA & LA)

1. Define death rate.

2. Explain immigration.

3. Explain human resources.

4. What is population composition?

5. Define migration.

6. Define population density.

7. Why people prefer to live on plains rather than mountain? Explain.

8. Explain cultural factors with examples.

9. What are the factors which affect the population change?

10. Describe the factors affecting the distribution of population.

11. What are the characteristics of population pyramid? Discuss.

CHAPTER 1

The Indian Constitution

Every society has certain set of rules that makes it different from the other societies. These rules are formulated through common consent among different communities in large societies.
A Constitution is a **written document** containing such rules.

1.1 Need of Constitution

The need of the Constitution can be understood from the following points

- The Constitution contains rules and principles which forms the basis of the governance of a country. Such rules and regulations are agreed upon by all the citizens of a country.
- The Constitution determines the nature of a country's political system whether it will have democratic system or **monarchy**[1]. The Constitution lays down the rules that protect against the misuse of power by political leaders. In India, such provision have been made in the section on **Fundamental Rights.**
- The Constitution ensures that a dominant group does not use its power against other less powerful groups or people. It ensures that minorities are not excluded from anything that is generally available to the majority.
  Thus, it prevents the domination by the majority of a minority. This domination can be **inter- community domination**[2] or **intra- community domination**[3].
- The Constitution lays down guidelines that governs decision-making process in a democratic country.
  It prevents us from taking any harmful decision that can adversely effect the rights and freedom of the citizens.

Democracy in Nepal

Nepal had seen various struggles by people demanding democracy. Democracy was first established in Nepal in 1990 after a people's struggle, which lasted till 2002.

In February 2005, **King Gyanendra** took over the government. However, due to the people's movement of 2006, Nepal again became a democracy in 2008 after abolishing the **monarchy**.

1.2 The Indian Constitution

The Indian Constitution describes the procedure of setting up the government in the country. It also contains the rules that determines its functioning.

The Indian Constitution was prepared by a group of around 300 people who became the members of **Constituent Assembly**, formed in December 1946.

Dr Rajendra Prasad was the President of the Constituent Assembly. The members of the Constituent Assembly met periodically for the next 3 years to write India's Constitution.

The challenges that Constituent Assembly faced while preparing Constitution were

- The country was made up of different communities who spoke different languages, belonged to different religion and had different cultures.
- The country was about to divide into India and Pakistan and some of the Princely States remained undecided about their future.

Besides these challenges, the Constituent Assembly prepared the Constitution that reflects a respect for maintaining diversity while preserving unity in the country. It also reflects upon eradicating poverty through socio-cultural reforms and incorporating the role of people in choosing their **representatives**[4].

KNOWLEDGE PLUS Dr Bhimrao Ambedkar is known as the father of the Indian Constitution.

1 **Monarchy** It is the system of government or rule by a King or rule of the single person.
2 **Inter-community Domination** It refers to one community dominating another community.
3 **Intra-community Domination** It refers to one community dominating others within the same community.
4 **Representative** It refers to the person who is elected by the people through general elections to represent a constituency in a governance system.

Key Features of Indian Constitution

The key features of the Indian Constitution are discussed below

1. Federalism

Federalism is the existence of more than one level of government in a country.

India has **three levels of government** – at centre, state and village level. Panchayati Raj is the third tier of the government at the village level.

The Constitution contains different lists for different tiers of government. These lists have specific subjects on which each tier of government can make laws.

States have authority in making laws on certain issues. However, on subjects related to national concern, only Central government can make laws.

The Constitution also specifies the source of money for each tier of government.

State

The term 'State' refers to a political institution that represents a **sovereign**[5] people who occupy a definite territory.

It is different from the term **Government**. The government is a part of the state which is responsible for administering and enforcing laws.

2. Parliamentary form of Government

Parliamentary form of government is a type of government which is run by representatives chosen by the people.

The Constitution of India grants **universal adult suffrage** to all citizens. This means that every citizen of the country can take part in elections irrespective of their caste, gender, race or social background.

3. Separation of Power

There are three organs of government in India namely **Legislature, Executive and Judiciary.**

The Legislature consists of elected representatives. The Executive is a smaller group of people who are responsible for implementing laws and running the government. The judiciary refers to the system of courts in the country.

The Constitution of India specifies separate set of powers for each of these organs. This separation of power prevents misuse of power by any one organ and ensures balance between all three organs.

4. Fundamental Rights

Fundamental rights are a set of written rights in the Indian Constitution that protects the citizens from **arbitrary**[6] and absolute exercise of power by the state. There are six Fundamental Rights in the Indian Constitution which are as follows

(i) **Right to Equality** It states that all persons are equal before the law. This means that all person shall be equally protected by the laws of the country. This right states that no citizen can be discriminated on the basis of their religion, caste or sex.

(ii) **Right to Freedom** It includes freedom of speech and expression, right to form associations, right to move freely and reside in any part of the country, and the right to practise any profession, occupation or business.

(iii) **Right Against Exploitation** It prohibits against **human trafficking**[7], forced labour and employment of children under 14 years of age.

(iv) **Right to Freedom of Religion** Under this right , every person has the right to practise, profess and propagate the religion of their choice.

(v) **Cultural and Educational Rights** It provides the right to all minorities (both religious and linguistic) to set up their own educational institutions for preserving and developing their culture.

(vi) **Right to Constitutional Remedies** It allows citizens to appeal in the court if any of their Fundamental Rights have been violated by the state.

Apart from these Fundamental Rights, the Constitution also include **Directive Principles of State Policy.** These ensure greater social and economic reforms. They also serve as a guide to the independent Indian State to make laws and policies to help reduce the poverty of the masses.

5. Secularism

The Indian Constitution has provided for a **secular state.** A secular state is one which does not officially promote any one religion as the state religion. Hence, in India equal treatment is given to all religions.

5 **Sovereign** It is the term used to describe the people of India who are independent and free to decide their country's destiny.

6 **Arbitrary** It is a situation when nothing is fixed and instead left to one's judgement or choice.

7 **Human Trafficking** It is the practice of illegal trade in human beings, particularly women and children.

THE INDIAN CONSTITUTION

Constituent Assembly

- Formed in December 1946.
- Independent body and included 300 members at the time of formation.
- Prepared the Constitution that reflects a respect for maintaining diversity while preserving unity in the country.

Need of Constitution

- Contains rules and principles which forms the basis of the governance of a country.
- Determines the type of political system in a country.
- Prevents misuse of power.
- Prevents the domination by the majority of a minority.

Features of the Indian Constitution

Describes the procedure of setting up the government in the country.

Parliamentary Form of Government

The Constitution of India grants universal adult suffrage

Fundamental Rights

- Right to Equality
- Right to Freedom
- Right to Freedom of Religion
- Right Against Exploitation
- Right to Constitutional Remedies
- Cultural and Educational Rights

Federalism

- Existence of more than one level of government in a country.
- In India, at centre, state and village level.

Secularism

It means state does not officially promote any one religion as the state religion

Separation Of Power

Executive

Responsible for implementing laws and running the government.

Legislature

Consists of elected representatives.

Judiciary

Refers to the system of courts in the country.

NCERT FOLDER

Covering Intext Questions and Exercises of NCERT

NCERT ON PAGE 6

Q.1 Discuss with your teacher what you understand by the term 'constitutive'. Provide one example of 'constitutive rules' from your everyday life.

Ans. The term 'constitutive' refers to fundamental structure or basic formation of a system.

In my school, the 'constitutive rules' guide students to wear proper uniform and reach school on time.

Q.2 Why did the people of Nepal want a new Constitution?

Ans. The people of Nepal wanted a new Constitution because the previous Constitution of 1990 was not fully democratic as the King still had authority over the country's administration.

They aspire to establish Nepal as a fully democratic nation.

NCERT ON PAGE 7

Q.3 In which of the following situations is a minister misusing his power?

(a) Refuses to sanction a project of his ministry for sound technical reasons.

Ans. The minister is not misusing his power in this situation as he has a valid reason for not sanctioning a project.

(b) Threatens to send his security staff to rough up his neighbour.

Ans. The minister is misusing his power in this situation as he is using his position for his personal rivalry with the neighbour.

(c) Calls up the police station asking them not to register a complaint that is likely to be filed against his relative.

Ans. The minister is misusing his power here by not letting an authority perform its duty.
He is preventing fair procedure and justice.

NCERT ON PAGE 9

Q.4 Why was Shabnam happy that she had not watched TV? What would you have done in a similar situation?

Ans. Shabnam was happy that she had not watched TV because she had used that time to revise her chapters for the test.

I would also have done the same as Shabnam, in a similar situation.

NCERT ON PAGE 10

Q.5 Let us recap the reasons why the Constitution plays an important role in democratic societies by recalling the constitutive rules that you have read about through these examples

Example	Constitutive Rules
The people of Nepal are writing a new Constitution after the success of the people's movement for democracy.	It lays down ideals that define the kind of country that we want to live in.
Suresh, the class monitor wrongly picks on Anil, his classmate. It states rules that prevent misuse of power by persons in authority.	
Shabnam decides to revise her chapters instead of watching TV.	

Ans.

Example	Constitutive Rules
The people of Nepal are writing a new Constitution after the success of the people's movement for democracy.	It lays down ideals that define the kind of country that we want to live in.
Suresh, the class monitor wrongly picks on Anil, his classmate. It states rules that prevent misuse of power by persons in authority.	The girls do not get to play basketball because the boys are a majority in class. It protects the rights of minorities so that they do not get repressed by the majority.
Shabnam decides to revise her chapters instead of watching TV.	It guards against taking any decision which may go against the larger interest.

NCERT ON PAGE 13

Q.6 Discuss the difference between state and government with your teacher.

Ans. The differences between the state and government are as follows

State	Government
A state is a political entity with defined borders and sovereignty.	A government is a group of people with the authority to make laws and run the administration of the state.
State is not a part of the government.	Government is a part of the state.

NCERT ON PAGE 14

Q.7 Which Fundamental Rights will the following situations violate?

(a) If a 13 year old child is working in a factory manufacturing carpets.

Ans. In this situation, the Right against Exploitation would be violated which states that the Constitution prohibits human trafficking, forced labour and children working under 14 years of age.

(b) If a politician in one state decides to not allow labourers from other states to work in his state.

Ans. In this situation, the Right to Freedom would be violated as it provides for the right to move freely and reside in any part of the country and the right to practise any profession, occupation or business.

(c) If a group of people are not given permission to open a Telugu medium school in Kerala.

Ans. In this situation, the Cultural and Educational Rights would be violated as it states that all minorities, (religious or linguistic), can set-up their own educational institutions in order to preserve and develop their own culture.

(d) If the government decides not to promote an officer of the armed forces for being a woman.

Ans. In this situation, the Right to Equality would be violated as it states that all persons are equal before the law. It also states that no citizen can be discriminated against on the basis of their religion, caste or sex.

NCERT ON PAGE 15

Q.8 The Constitution also mentions Fundamental Duties. Find out with the help of your teacher what these include and why it is important for citizens in a democracy to observe these.

Ans. The Part IV A of the Constitution of India contains the Fundamental Duties. The duties are listed under Article 51-A.

The Fundamental Duties are as follows

(i) To abide by the Constitution and respect its ideals and institutions, the National Flag and the National Anthem.

(ii) To cherish and follow the noble ideals which inspired our national struggle for freedom.

(iii) To uphold and protect the sovereignty, unity and integrity of India.

(iv) To defend the country and render national service when called upon to do so.

(v) To promote harmony and the spirit of common brotherhood amongst all the people of India.

(vi) To value and preserve the rich heritage of our composite culture.

(vii) To protect and improve the natural environment including forests, lakes, rivers and wildlife and to have compassion for living creatures.

(viii) To develop the scientific temper, humanism and the spirit of inquiry and reform.

(ix) To safeguard public property and to abjure violence.

(x) To strive towards excellence in all spheres of individual and collective activity so that the nation constantly rises to higher levels of endeavour and achievement.

(xi) It is the duty of all parents or guardians to provide opportunities for education to his child or ward between the age of six and fourteen years.

It is important for the citizens in a democracy to observe fundamental duties as they serve as a reminder to the citizens that while enjoying their rights, they should also be aware of their duties towards their country and fellow citizens. Fundamental duties serve as a source of inspiration for the citizens, and encourage a sense of discipline and commitment among them.

EXERCISES

Q.1 Why does a democratic country need a Constitution? Diksha

Or **Does a country need a Constitution? State any five reasons.** Diksha

Ans. A democratic country needs a Constitution due to its following purposes

- The Constitution contains rules and principles which forms the basis of the governance of a country. Such rules and regulations are agreed upon by all the citizens of a country.
- The type of political system in a country (i.e democracy or monarchy) is determined by the Constitution.
- Political leaders who are chosen by people as their representatives in a democracy can misuse their power. The Constitution prevents such misuse of authority.
- The Constitution prevents the domination by the majority of a minority. This domination can be inter-community domination or intra-community domination.
- The Constitution lays down guidelines that governs decision-making process in a democratic country. It prevents us from taking any harmful decision that can adversely effect the rights and freedom of the citizens.

Q.2 Look at the wordings of the two documents given below. The first column is from the 1990 Nepal Constitution. The second column is from the more recent Interim Constitution of Nepal. Diksha

1990 Constitution of Nepal Part 7 : Executive	2015 Constitution of Nepal Part-7: Federal Executive
Article 35 : Executive Power : The Executive power of the kingdom of Nepal shall be vested in his majesty and the Council of Ministers.	Article 75: Federal Executive : The Executive Power : The executive power of Nepal shall, pursuant to this Constitution and law be vested in the Council of Ministers.

What is the difference in who exercises 'Executive power' in the above two Constitutions of Nepal?

Ans. The difference in who exercises 'Executive power' in the given two situations in the Constitution of Nepal is that in the 1990 Constitution, the executive power was vested in the King and his Council of Ministers. However, in the 2015 Constitution, the executive power of Nepal, was vested in the Council of Ministers.

Q.3 What would happen if there were no restrictions on the power of elected representatives? Diksha

Ans. If there were no restrictions on the power of elected representatives, the leaders might misuse the powers given to them.

The Constitution has certain safeguards against the misuse of powers by our leaders.

Q.4 In each of the following situations, identify the minority. Write one reason why you think it is important to respect the views of the minority in each of these situations.

(a) In a school with 30 teachers, 20 of them are male.

Ans. In this situation, the female teachers are in minority.

The female teachers must be allowed to express their opinion in matters concerning teaching and the students, so that their efforts are not wasted because they are a minority.

(b) In a city 5 per cent of the population are Buddhists.

Ans. In this situation, the Buddhist population is in minority.

Every citizen of India has a right to follow a religion of his/her choice. People of other faith must respect the religion other than the religion they follow.

(c) In a factory mess for all employees, 80 per cent are vegetarians.

Ans. In this situation, non-vegetarians are a minority.

The choice of food a person eats is a personal choice. Every person has the freedom to choose the food that he or she eats.

(d) In a class of 50 students, 40 belong to more well-off families.

Ans. In this situation, the economically weaker sections or the under privileged are a minority.

Citizens cannot be discriminated based on their financial status. Their views and rights have to be respected.

Q.5 The column on the left lists some of the key features of the Indian Constitution. In the other column, write two sentences, in your own words, on why you think this feature is important.

Key Feature	Significance
Federalism	
Separation of powers	
Fundamental Rights	
Parliamentary Form of Government	

Ans.

Key Feature	Significance
Federalism	It prevents the concentration of powers in one government at the centre. Under this feature, the vast number of communities are adequately represented in multiple levels of government.
Separation of powers	It prevents the misuse of power by any one organ of the state. It also ensures balance of power between different organs.
Fundamental Rights	It protects citizens against the arbitrary and absolute exercise of power by the state. It guarantees the rights of minorities against the majority.
Parliamentary Form of Government	It gives direct role to people to elect their representatives. It gives opportunity to every citizen of the country to take part in elections.

REVIEW EXERCISE

Including Competency Based Questions

PART I

Multiple Choice Questions (MCQs)

1. Which of the following is a set of fundamental rules according to which a country functions?

(a) Fundamental rights
(b) Constitution
(c) Directive Principles of State Policy
(d) A law

2. Which among the following is not a function of the Constitution? Competency Based

(a) To determine the type of political system in a country.
(b) To prevent the misuse of power by any one group.
(c) To determine dietary preferences of the citizens.
(d) To provide rules and regulations for administration of a country.

3. The political system in Nepal till 2006 was

(a) democracy (b) dictatorship
(c) Panchayati Raj (d) monarchy

4. In which year did Nepal adopt the new constitution?

(a) 2013 (b) 2014
(c) 2015 (d) 2016

5. Who was the President of the Constituent Assembly of India at the time of its formation?

(a) Dr BR Ambedkar (b) Pt Jawaharlal Nehru
(c) Mahatma Gandhi (d) Dr Rajendra Prasad

6. Who among the following was/were members of the Constituent Assembly?

(a) Jawaharlal Nehru (b) AK Ayyar
(c) Sardar Vallabhbhai Patel (d) All of these

7. Which of the following is not a key feature of the Indian Constitution?

(a) Federalism (b) Secularism
(c) Separation of powers
(d) Presidential form of government

8. Which of the following is a part of the state and is responsible for administering and enforcing laws?

(a) Judiciary (b) Government
(c) Army (d) Police

9. Which of the following is not a feature of the parliamentary form of government? Competency Based

(a) People have a direct role in the election of government.
(b) The representatives in government are directly accountable to the people.
(c) Every citizen of India can take part in the formation of government.
(d) Parliamentary form of government is unable to prevent discrimination on the grounds of caste.

10. Which of the following is not one of the three organs of the government in India?

(a) Executive
(b) Bureaucracy
(c) Judiciary
(d) Legislature

11. According to the Fundamental Rights mentioned in the Indian Constitution, which of the following is prohibited?

(a) Human trafficking
(b) Forced labour
(c) Children under 14 years of age working in hazardous occupations
(d) All of the above

12. Right to Freedom includes

(a) right to make children under 14 years of age work.
(b) right to discriminate between the upper caste and lower caste.
(c) right to freedom of speech and expression.
(d) None of the above

13. All minorities, religious or linguistic, can set up their own educational institutions in order to preserve and develop their own culture. This is mentioned in which part of the Constitution ? Competency Based

(a) Fundamental Rights
(b) Directive Principles of State Policy
(c) Fundamental Duties
(d) Preamble

14. Which one of the following statements is incorrect?

I. The Indian Constitution does not determine the Monarchy system in the country.

II. The Indian Constituent Assembly was set up in 1946.

Codes

(a) Only I (b) I and II both (c) Only II (d) None of these

15. Which one of the following statements is correct?

I. Federalism is a system of government in which power is shared between one or more levels of government.

II. The right to equality ensures that everyone is treated equally.

Codes

(a) Only I (b) I and II both (c) Only II (d) None of these

16. Arrange the following events in correct chronological sequence.

I. First people's movement in Nepal for democracy
II. First demand for Constituent Assembly by the INC
III. Restoration of third parliament by King Gyanendra
IV. Adoption of the New Constitution of Nepal

Choose the correct option.

(a) I, III, IV, II (b) II, I, III, IV
(c) IV, I, III, I (d) II, III, I, IV

17. Identify the feature of the Constitution with the help of following information. **Competency Based**

I. This feature grant Universal Adult Franchise to the citizens of India.
II. This feature allows direct participation of people in electing their representatives.

Codes

(a) Federalism (b) Secularism
(c) Fundamental rights
(d) Parliamentary form of government

18. Arun, an 18 year old boy went to a restaurant with his family. However, the hotel staff did not allow his family to enter there because they belonged to the dalit community. **Competency Based**

Which of the following fundamental rights have been deprived from the Arun's family in the above situation?

(a) Right to Freedom
(b) Right against Exploitation
(c) Right to Equality
(d) Cultural and Educational Rights

Answers

1. (b)	2. (c)	3. (d)	4. (c)	5. (d)
6. (d)	7. (d)	8. (b)	9. (d)	10. (b)
11. (d)	12. (c)	13. (a)	14. (d)	15. (b)
16. (b)	17. (d)	18. (c)		

Match the Following.

1.

List I	List II
A. Legislature	1. System of courts
B. Executive	2. Our elected representatives
C. Judiciary	3. Implementation of laws

Codes

	A	B	C		A	B	C
(a)	2	3	1	(b)	1	3	2
(c)	1	2	3	(d)	3	1	2

2.

List I	List II
A. Fundamental Rights	1. Dr Rajendra Prasad
B. Head of the Constituent Assembly	2. Dr BR Ambedkar
C. Father of the Constitution	3. Cultural and educational rights

Codes

	A	B	C		A	B	C
(a)	1	2	3	(b)	3	1	2
(c)	1	3	2	(d)	2	3	1

Ans. 1. (a) 2. (b)

Assertion-Reason

1. Assertion (A) India is a secular country.

Reason (R) India is the only Hindu kingdom of the world.

Codes

(a) Both A and R are true and R is the correct explanation of A
(b) Both A and R are true, but R is not the correct explanation of A
(c) A is true, but R is false
(d) A is false, but R is true

2. Assertion (A) The Constitution of India defines three organs of government i.e. the Legislature, the Executive and the Judiciary.

Reason (R) The three organs have separate powers and functions to prevent the misuse of power by any single branch of government, ensuring a balance of power.

Codes

(a) Both A and R are true and R is the correct explanation of A
(b) Both A and R are true, but R is not the correct explanation of A
(c) A is true, but R is false
(d) A is false, but R is true

Ans. 1. (c) A is true, but R is false
2. (b) Both A and R are true, but R is not the correct explanation of A

Fill in the Blanks

1. In ...., the Indian National Congress made the demand for a Constituent Assembly. **Diksha**

2. .... was the Chairman of the Drafting Committee of the Indian Constitution. **Diksha**

3. The Constitution prohibits human trafficking, forced labour and employment of children under .... years of age. **Diksha**

4. A secular state has no .... of its own.

5. Buddhists in India are counted as ....

Ans. 1. 1934 2. Dr. Babasaheb Ambedkar 3. 14
4. religion 5. minority

True/False

1. The Indian Constitution guarantees the rights of minorities against the majority.
2. Discrimination is a part of the Indian Constitution.
3. The Constitution of India came into force on 15th August, 1947.
4. The Universal Adult Franchise was adopted much before the independence of India.

Ans. 1. True 2. False 3. False 4. False

Picture Based Questions

1. Look at the picture given below and answer the question that follow.

Which of the following movements is shown in the above picture?

(a) Movement for the Right to Education
(b) Indian Independence Movement
(c) People's movement in Bangladesh
(d) People's movement in Nepal

2. Identify the famous personality in the below picture.

(a) Jawaharlal Nehru (b) Dr Rajendra Prasad
(c) Sardar Vallabhbhai (d) Mahatma Gandhi

Ans. 1. (d) People's movement in Nepal
2. (b) Dr. Rajendra Prasad

Case Based Questions

1. Read the given passage below and answer the questions that follow.

The section on Fundamental Rights has often been referred to as the 'conscience' of the Indian Constitution. Colonial rule had created a certain suspicion of the State in the minds of the nationalists and they wanted to ensure that a set of written rights would guard against the misuse of State power in independent India. Fundamental Rights, therefore, protect citizens against the arbitrary and absolute exercise of power by the State.

The Constitution, thus, guarantees the rights of individuals against the State as well as against other individuals. Moreover, the various minority communities also expressed the need for the Constitution to include rights that would protect their groups. The Constitution, therefore, also guarantees the rights of minorities against the majority. As Dr. Ambedkar has said about these Fundamental Rights, their object is two-fold. The first objective is that every citizen must be in a position to claim those rights. Secondly, these rights must be binding upon every authority that has got the power to make laws.

(i) Which of the following provisions of the Indian constitution acts as a guide for the moral and ethical behavior of the citizens and protects them from the tyranny of the government?

(a) Fundamental Rights (b) Directive Principles
(c) Preamble (d) Fundamental Duties

(ii) In relation to the state, what is the objective behind incorporation of Fundamental Rights into the Constitution?

(a) To protect the rights of the State
(b) To guard against the misuse of State power
(c) To promote the absolute exercise of power by the State
(d) To establish a monarchy

(iii) Fundamental rights provides several protections to the citizens of India. These protections are provided against which of the following?

(a) Only the State
(b) Only other individuals
(c) Both the State and other individuals
(d) Only minority communities

(iv) What was the main concern of the Indian nationalists regarding the State?

(a) They believed the State would promote atheism.
(b) They feared the State would impose a single language
(c) They were worried about the State's potential for abuser of power
(d) They wanted the state to control all aspects of citizens' lives.

Ans. (i) (b) Directive Principles
(ii) (b) To guard against the misuse of State power
(iii) (c) Both the State and other individuals
(iv) (c) They were worried about the State's potential for abuser of power

PART II

Very Short Answer Type Questions

1. What is a Constitution?

Ans. A Constitution is a written document containing a set of rules for governing a nation or a state.

2. When did the Indian National Congress make the demand for a Constituent Assembly?

Ans. The Indian National Congress made the demand for a Constituent Assembly in 1934, and it was formed in 1946.

3. Who is known as the father of the Indian Constitution? Diksha

Ans. Dr BR Ambedkar is known as the father of the Indian Constitution.

4. Who was the first Prime Minister of free India?

Ans. The first Prime Minister of free India was Pt Jawaharlal Nehru.

5. Which neighboring country of India was under monarchy till 2006?

Ans. Nepal was under monarchy till 2006.

6. What are the three-tiers of government in India?

Ans. The three tiers of government in India are the Central Government, State Government and Panchayati Raj at the village.

7. What is Universal Adult Franchise? Diksha

Ans. Universal Adult Franchise means every adult citizen has the right to vote irrespective of caste, creed, sex, education and financial status.

8. Which fundamental right in the Indian constitution allows citizens to move the court if they believe that any of their fundamental rights have been violated by the state? Competency Based

Ans. Right to constitutional remedies allows citizens to move the court if they believe that any of their Fundamental Rights have been violated by the state.

9. How does the Indian Constitution safeguard the interests of the minorities of the country? Diksha

Ans. The Indian Constitution safeguard the interests of the minorities by ensuring that the dominant group does not use its power against other less powerful people or groups.

10. What is the characteristic of a secular state?

Ans. A secular state is one in which the state does not officially promote any religion as the state religion.

11. What is secularism? Diksha

Ans. Secularism is the right of the citizens to practice any religion.

12. Define the following.
(a) Tyranny (b) Polity Diksha

Ans. (a) Tyranny is the cruel and unjust use of power or authority.

(b) Polity means a society that has an organised political structure. For example, India is a democratic polity.

Short Answer Type Questions

1. The Constitution in a democracy is the supreme law that outlines the basic structure of government and the fundamental right of citizens. It plays a crucial role in laying out guideline for decision making and providing safeguard against the misuse of power by leaders. Competency Based

(i) How does the Constitution help to ensure that leaders exercise power responsibly?

Ans. The Constitution helps to ensure that leaders exercise power responsibly by providing safeguards against the misuse of power and by outlining the basic principles of democracy.

(ii) What can citizens do to hold leaders accountable and ensure that they respect the Constitution?

Ans. Citizens can hold leaders accountable and ensure that they respect the Constitution by voting, participating in the political process, and speaking out against injustice.

2. Differentiate between Democratic and Monarchy government. Diksha

Ans.

Monarchy	Democracy
In monarchy, the government is headed by a monarch or a king.	In democracy, the government is headed by elected representatives.
The power and position in this government is passed through heritage.	The democracy principally supports elections (people's choice).
Same king can rule for several years in a monarchy.	The government is changed every few years through regular elections in a democracy.

3. What are the factors the Drafting Committee had to take into consideration while drafting the Constitution? Diksha

Ans. The Drafting Committee had to consider the following while drafting the Constitution

- India was a land of diversity with many communities, languages and many religions.
- Thus, diverse cultures and the princely states in India had to be considered.

- The partition of the country into India and Pakistan was about to happen and the drafting committee had to bear this in mind.
- The socio-economic condition of a majority of Indians which was in a bad state had to be considered.

4. Dr BR Ambedkar urged Scheduled Caste to join the government as well as the Civil Services. Comment **Competency Based**

Ans. Dr Bhimrao Ambedkar or Baba Saheb is known as the Father of the Indian Constitution.

He believed that his participation in the Constituent Assembly helped the Scheduled Castes get some safeguards in the draft Constitution. But he also stated that although the laws might exist, Scheduled Castes still had reason to fear because the administration of these laws were in the hands of 'Caste Hindu Officers'. Thus, he urged Scheduled Castes to join the government as well as the Civil Services.

5. What did AK Ayyar remark when the Constituent Assembly adopted the principle of Universal Adult Franchise (UAF)?

Ans. When the Constituent Assembly adopted the principle of Universal Adult Franchise, AK Ayyar, a member of the Constituent Assembly, remarked that this was done with an abundant faith in the common man and the ultimate success of democratic rule.

He also remarked that this was done in the belief that the introduction of democratic government on the basis of adult suffrage will bring enlightenment and promote the well-being of the common man.

6. What are the three organs of the government? Explain. **Diksha**

Ans. The three organs of the government are the Legislature, the Executive and the judiciary.

The Legislature consists of elected representatives. The Executive is a smaller group of people who are responsible for implementing laws and running the government. The Judiciary refers to the system of courts in our country.

7. "The Constitution contains the lists that detail the issues that each tier of government can make laws on. In addition, the Constitution also specifies where each tier of government can get the money from for the work that it does."

(i) What are the provisions in the Constitution related to different tiers of the government?

Ans. The Constitution of India has several provisions related to distribution of powers between the different tiers of the government. It has specified different subjects for each tier to make laws. The Constitution also give details of the finance that each tier can get for their respective works.

(ii) The arrangement in the statement given above points towards which feature of the Constitution ?

Ans. The arrangement in the statement given above points towards Federalism which is an important feature of the Constitution.

8. What is the importance of Fundamental Rights? **Diksha**

Ans. The importance of Fundamental Rights are as follows

- It protects the liberties and freedom of the citizens.
- It prevents the establisment of the authoritarian and dictatorial rule in the country.
- It protects the citizens of the country from the arbitary and unjust decisions taken by the government.

9. What are Directive Principles of State Policy? Why have they been added to the Constitution?

Ans. The Directive Principles of State Policy are referred to as the guidelines for the government in law-making and governance to ensure welfare of the people. They are contained in Part IV of the Constitution. They were added to ensure greater social and economic reform and work as a guide to the state to make laws and policies that help reduce poverty of the masses.

Long Answer Type Questions

1. What are the Fundamental Rights given by the Constitution of India? Explain briefly.

Ans. The six fundamental rights given by the Indian Constitution are

(i) **Right to Equality** All persons are equal before the law and there shall be no discrimination on the basis of religion, caste or sex etc.

(ii) **Right to Freedom** This includes the right to freedom of speech and expression, the right to form associations, the right to move freely and reside in any part of the country and the right to practise any profession, occupation or business.

(iii) **Right against Exploitation** Under this right human trafficking, forced labour and children under 14 years of age working in hazardous occupations are prohibited.

(iv) **Right to Freedom of Religion** Under this right, all citizens have the right to practise, profess and propagate the religion of their choice.

(v) **Cultural and Educational Rights** Under this right, all minorities, religious or linguistic, are free to set up their own educational institutions in order to preserve and develop their culture.

(vi) **Right to Constitutional Remedies** Under this right a citizen can appeal in the court if he/she believes that any Fundamental Right has been violated by the state.

2. Explain the journey of Nepal from being a Monarchy to achieving democracy.

Ans. Nepal had witnessed several people's struggles for democracy. A people's struggle in Nepal in 1990 established democracy. The democratic government that fomed lasted for 12 years until 2002.

In 2002, there was Maoist uprising in the countryside. King Gyanendra with the help of army began to take up various aspects of the administration of Nepal during this uprising.

In February 2005, King Gyanendra finally took over as the head of the government. In November 2005, the Maoists joined other political parties to sign a 12-point agreement.

In 2006, the people's movement for democracy began. Finally, in April 2006, the people's movement succeeded in putting an end to the powers of the King. The King restored the Third Parliament and asked the political parties to form a government. The Nepal finally abolished monarchy and established democracy in 2008.

3. "In 1946 the constituent assembly was formed which then met periodically for the next three years to draft India's constitution." Explain the key features of the Indian Constitution. **Competency Based**

Ans. Following are some of the key features of the Indian Constitution

- **Federalism** The Constitution establishes a federal system of government, with power divided between the central government and the state governments.
- **Parliamentary form of Government** The Constitution establishes a parliamentary form of government, with the Prime Minister as the head of government.
- **Separation of Powers** The Constitution separates the powers of the government into three branches: the legislature, the executive, and the judiciary.
- **Fundamental Rights** The Constitution guarantees six fundamental rights to all citizens. These are the right to equality, the right to freedom, the right against exploitation, the right to freedom of religion, the cultural and educational rights, and the right to constitutional remedies.
- **Directive Principles of State Policy** The Constitution lays down a set of directive principles of state policy, which are guidelines for the government to follow in order to achieve social and economic justice.
- **Fundamental Duties** The Constitution lays down a set of fundamental duties for all citizens, such as respecting the Constitution and the national flag, defending the country, and promoting fraternity among all citizens.

Picture Based Questions

1. In what way is the class monitor misusing his power? **NCERT**

Ans. Suresh, the class monitor, is misusing his power by acting unfairly with his classmate. He complains against Anil to the teacher even though Anil had not done anything wrong. Hearing the class monitor's complain the teacher got annoyed and punished Anil.

2. Who is in a minority in the above storyboard? In what way is this minority being dominated by the decision taken by the majority? **NCERT**

Ans. The girls of the class are in minority in the above storyboard. The minority has to comply with the decision taken by the majority even if they do not agree with it. In this way, the minority is always dominated by the decisions taken by the majority.

Case Based Question

1. Read the given passage and answer the following questions.

The Constitution plays a crucial role in laying out the ideals that we would like all citizens of the country to adhere to, including the representatives that we elect to rule us. Just like in the game of football, a change of constitutive rules will affect the game. Indian Constitution has been amended over the years to reflect new concerns of the polity. Often a major change in the Constitution means a change in the fundamental nature of the country. We saw this in the case of Nepal and how it needed to adopt a new Constitution after it became a democracy. The different features of the Indian Constitution outlined above, involve complicated ideas that are often not easy to grasp. Don't worry too much about this for the moment. In the rest of the book as well as in your higher classes, you will read more about these different features of the Indian Constitution and understand more substantively what they mean.

(i) What role does the Constitution play in a country?

Ans. The Constitution lays out the ideals for citizens and representatives to adhere to, shaping the fundamental principles of the nation.

(ii) Why is it important for a country to amend its Constitution over time?

Ans. It is important for a country to amend its Constitution over time because amendments reflect evolving concerns, ensuring that Constitution remains relevant and adaptable to changing societal needs.

Map Based Question

1. Write down the names of the Indian states, which share boundary with the following neighbouring nations **NCERT**

(a) Bangladesh (b) Bhutan (c) Nepal

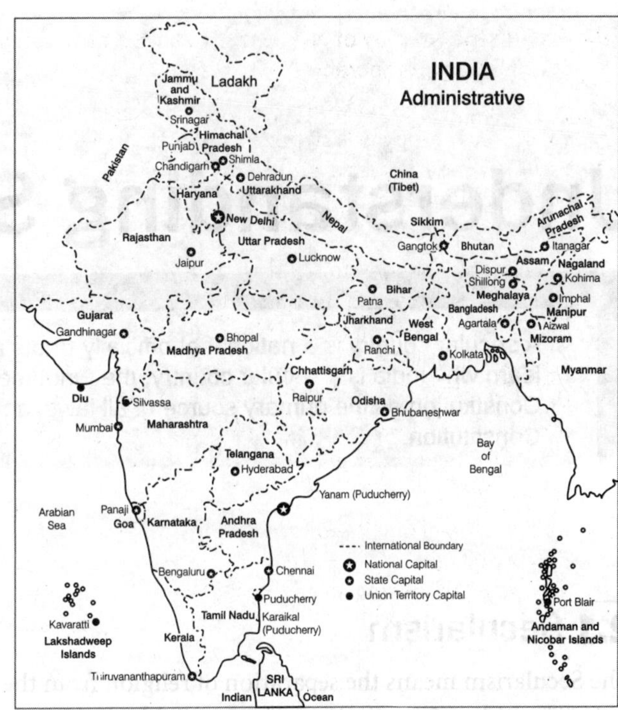

Ans. (a) The states sharing boundary with Bangladesh are West Bengal, Assam, Tripura and Mizoram.

(b) The states sharing boundary with Bhutan are West Bengal, Sikkim, Assam and Arunachal Pradesh.

(c) The states sharing boundary with Nepal are Uttarakhand, Uttar Pradesh, Bihar, West Bengal and Sikkim.

ASSESSMENT EXERCISE

Multiple Choice Questions (MCQs)

1. Which organs of government ensures the balance of power between all organs?
(a) Judiciary (b) Executive
(c) Legislature (d) Both (b) and (c)

2. The President of the Constituent Assembly was
(a) Dr. B R Ambedkar (b) Dr. Rajendra Prasad
(c) Jawaharlal Nehru (d) Mahatma Gandhi

3. In which year, the National Congress made the demand for a Constituent Assembly?
(a) 1930 (b) 1934
(c) 1935 (d) 1940

4. The Father of India Constitution is
(a) B R Ambedkar (b) J L Nehru
(c) Mahatma Gandhi (d) S V Bhai Patel

Subjective Questions (VSA, SA & LA)

1. Define federalism.

2. Name the third tier of government.

3. Name the three organs of state.

4. Explain Judiciary.

5. Define secular state.

6. Write a short note on Fundamental Rights.

7. What are the challenges came while preparing Constitution?

8. Differentiate parliamentary form of government and presidential form of government.

9. How Directive Principle of State Policy is different from Fundamental Rights?

10. What are the key features of the Indian constitution? Discuss.

Understanding Secularism

CHAPTER 2

A secular country is a nation that officially treats all religions equally. In this chapter, we will learn why India is a secular country, the fundamental right of religious freedom, the Constitution as the primary source of all laws, and the vision and values of the Indian Constitution.

2.1 Secularism

The Secularism means the separation of religion from the state. The Indian Constitution allows individuals the freedom to follow their religious beliefs and practices. India has adopted a strategy of separating the power of religion and the power of the state.

Importance of Separating Religion from State

It is important to separate religion from the State because of the following reasons

- Discrimination of one religious group by another takes place more easily when one of the religion is given official recognition by the state. Thus, it is important to separate religion and state.
- The separation of religion from state prevents the tyranny of majority and violation of fundamental rights of minorities.
- It helps to protect freedom of individuals to adopt another religion or **freedom to interpret**[1] the religious teachings differently.

2.2 Indian Secularism

The Indian Constitution mandates Indian State to be a secular. **Secularism**[2] has been adopted in the Indian Constitution with the following objectives

- To prevent the domination of one religious community over another.
- To prevent the domination of some members over the other members of same religious group.
- To prevent the state from supporting any particular religion or discriminating against other religions.

India has adopted various ways for achieving the above objectives. These are

- Indian state does not support or promote any religion. For example, government schools are not allowed to celebrate any religious festivals neither they can include religious songs in morning prayer.
- Indian state has adopted a **policy of non- interference** in religious matters. In order to respect the sentiments of all religions equally, India has made certain exceptions for some religious groups.

For example, Sikhs are exempted from wearing helmets, as wearing a pugri or turban is considered important part of their religion.

- India has adopted a **strategy of intervention** in the religious matters in two ways

(i) Firstly, it **intervenes**[3] to prevent discrimination.

For example, **untouchability**[4] is a Hindu social practice, however Indian state intervenes to end this practice as it violates the fundamental rights of lower castes.

---

1 **Freedom to Interpret** It means giving freedom to everyone to understand things in their own way.

2 **Secularism** Secularism is the separation between the power of religion and the power of the state.

3 **Intervene** It means to influence or involve in any particular matter.

4 **Untouchability** It is the practice of discriminating individuals and groups on the basis of their caste and jobs done by them.

(ii) Secondly, it intervenes in the form of support in the religion based personal laws of communities.
For example, the Indian Constitution grants the right to religious communities to set up their own educational institutions. It also provides financial help for the same purpose.

Difference between Indian and American Secularism

There is a strict separation of religion and state in the United States of America. The state does not prohibit the practice of any religion and it does not interfere in the religious matters in any way.

On the other hand, in Indian secularism, the state can interfere in religious affairs. However, this interference has to be based on the ideals laid out in the Constitution. The Indian Constitution guarantees Fundamental Rights that are based on secular principles.

Secularism in America

The first amendment of the US Constitution laid the foundations of secularism in America. This amendment prohibited the state from declaring any religion as the official religion and also giving preference to any religion.

In USA, the separation between state and religion means that neither the state nor the religion can interfere in the affairs of one another.

UNDERSTANDING SECULARISM

Importance of Separating Religion from the State

- Prevents the tyranny of majority and violation of Fundamental Rights of minorities.
- Protect freedom of individuals to adopt another religion

Difference between Indian and American Secularism

In USA, there is strict separation of religion and state. The state does not interfere in the religious matters in any way and does not prohibit practice of any religion.

On the other hand, the state can interfere in religious affair in Indian secularism, but the interference has to be based on the ideals of the Constitution.

Objectives of Secularism

- Prevents the domination of one religious community over another.
- Prevents the domination of some members over the other members of same religious group.
- Prevents the state from supporting any particular religion or discriminating against other religions

Ways to Achieve Objectives of Secularism

- India has adopted a strategy of intervention.
- Intervenes to prevent discrimination.
- Intervenes in the form of support in the religion
- Indian state does not support or promote any religion. based personal laws of communities.
- Indian state has adopted a policy of non-interference in religious matters.

Indian Secularism

- Secularism means the separation of religion from state.
- The Indian Constitution mandates Indian State to be a secular.

NCERT FOLDER

Covering Intext Questions and Exercises of NCERT

NCERT ON PAGE 19

Q.1 Re-read the introduction to this chapter. Why do you think retaliation is not the proper response to this problem? What would happen if different groups followed this path?

Ans. I think, retaliation would not be a proper response to the problem as it would create disorder in the society which would further lead to loss of peace.

If all the different groups followed this path then it would result in destruction of harmony in the nation. It will also promote violence.

NCERT ON PAGE 20

Q.2 Can there be different views within the same religion?

Ans. Yes, there can be different views within the same religion.

For example, in Hindu religion, some people have faith in observing fast and following rituals which might not be considered important by a group of people of another religion.

NCERT ON PAGE 23

Q.3 Government schools often have students from different religious backgrounds. Re-read the three objectives of a secular state and write two sentences on why it is important that government schools do not promote any one religion?

Ans. It is important that government schools do not promote any one religion because

(i) If government schools promote or prohibit any religion, then it will result in discrimination between the students belonging to different religious backgrounds.

(ii) India is a secular country and promotion of any particular religion by the government schools would violate the principle of secularism.

NCERT ON PAGE 25

Q.4 Can you think of a recent incident, from any part of India, in which the secular ideals of the Constitution were violated and persons were persecuted and killed because of their religious backgrounds?

Ans. There are many recent incidents where people were persecuted because of their religious backgrounds. For example, the communal riots of 2002 in Gujarat and persecution of Kashmiri pandits in Kashmir during 1990s.

EXERCISES

Q.1 List the different types of religious practice that you find in your neighbourhood. This could be different forms of prayer, worship of different gods, sacred sites, different kinds of religious music and singing etc. Does this indicate freedom of religious practice?

Ans. Different types of religious practices are observed in my neighborhood by people belonging to different religions such as Hindu, Muslims, Christians, etc.

Hindus worship idols of gods while Muslims worship the shrine built over the grave of Muslim saints. Christians worship the god through their religious symbol and prayers.

Yes, this indicates freedom of religious practice as all the religious groups free to practice their religion.

Q.2 Will the government intervene if some religious group says that their religion allows them to practise infanticide? Give reasons for your answer.

Ans. The government will surely intervene in the above case as infanticide violates the fundamental right to life of the infant.

The government has right to intervene in religious matters if a practice is of criminal nature or is harmful for the society.

Q.3 Complete the following table:

Objective	Why is this important ?	Example of a violation of this objective
One religious community does not dominate another.		
The state does not enforce any particular religion nor take away the religious freedom of individuals.		
That some members do not dominate other members of the same religious community.		

Ans.

Objective	Why is this important ?	Example of a violation of this objective
One religious community does not dominate another.	It is important because if this objective is not met then there would be discrimination and even violence in the society.	A Hindu religious procession is not allowed to pass through the road where a mosque is located.
The state does not enforce any particular religion nor take away the religious freedom of individuals.	It is important because this objective is the essence of a secular state. It is also an important feature of a democratic society. It gives the scope to individuals to embrace other religion.	When a state government does not allow the celebration of festival of any one religion while promoting the festivals of the other religion.
That some members do not dominate other members of the same religious community.	It is important as it allows every individual of the same religion to interpret the religion in their own way.	Making vegetarianism as an essential feature of Hinduism or discrimination against the Dalits by dominant Hindu castes.

Q.4 Look up the annual calendar of holidays of your school. How many of them pertain to different religions? What does this indicate?

Festivals	Religion	Number of Holidays
Lohri	Sikhism	1
Holi	Hinduism	3
Good Friday	Christianity	1
Mahavir Jayanti	Jainism	1
Buddha Jayanti	Buddhism	1
Dussehra	Hinduism	3
Diwali/ deepawali	Hinduism	3
Guruparv	Sikhism	1
Christmas	Christianity	1
Muharram	Islam	1
Id-ul-zoha	Islam	1
Guru Gobind Singh Jayanti	Sikhism	1
Id-ul-fitr	Islam	1

Ans. In my school calender there are nine holidays for Hindu festivals, three holidays each for Islamic festivals and Sikh festivals, two holidays for Christian festivals, and one holiday each for Buddhist and Jain festivals.

This indicates that there are variety of religions in India and it also shows that Hindus are in majority while other religions such as Islam, Christianity, Buddhism, etc are in minority.

Q.5 Find out some examples of different views within the same religion.

Ans. Some examples of different views within the same religion are as follows

- Vaishnavite are worshippers of Vishnu and Shaivites are worshippers of Shiva within the Hindu religion.
- Buddhists are divided into the Hinayana and Mahayana sects.
- Muslims are divided into the Shia and Sunni sects.
- Within Christianity, people belong to the Protestant and Catholic sects.

Q.6 The Indian State both keeps away from religion as well as intervenes in religion. This idea can be quite confusing. Discuss this once again in class using examples from the chapter as well as those that you might have come up with.

Ans. It is true, that the Indian State both keeps away and intervenes in matters of religion.

Instances of the State keeping away from matters of religion are as follows

- The State does not officially promote any religion.
- Institutions of the government like offices, schools, police stations, etc are not allowed to celebrate any religious festival in their premises.
- The State does not interfere with the essential religious practices of the religions. For example, Sikhs are exempted from wearing helmet, as wearing pugri is an important part of their religion.

Instances of the State intervening in matters of religion are as follows

- The State has banned untouchability, a practice of the Hindu community, as it discriminates against one section of the community.
- Some seats have been reserved for the Scheduled Castes (backward section of the Hindu community).
- The state has banned triple talaq practice of Islam for the welfare of Muslim women.

REVIEW EXERCISE

Including Competency Based Questions

Part I

Multiple Choice Questions (MCQs)

1. What happened in Germany during Hitler's rule?
(a) Bombing of Nagasaki
(b) End of World War II
(c) Assassination of Mahatma Gandhi
(d) Killing of Jews

2. Majority of the population of Israel belong to which religion?
(a) Christian (b) Jewish
(c) Muslim (d) No majority religion in Israel

3. Which of the following correctly explains the meaning of secularism?
(a) Separation of religion from state power.
(b) Separation of one community from another.
(c) Separation of politics from religion.
(d) Mixing of religion with politics.

4. The Indian state is secular and works in various ways to prevent religious **Diksha**
(a) domination (b) conflict
(c) disputes (d) problems

5. India opted secularism to ensure **Diksha**
(a) that one religious community does not dominate another.
(b) that some members do not dominate other members of the same religious community.
(c) that the state does not enforce any particular religion not take away the religious freedom of individuals.
(d) All of the above

6. Which of the following activities cannot be done in government schools? **Competency Based**
(a) Singing the national song
(b) Celebrating national festivals
(c) Celebrating religious festivals
(d) None of the above

7. Indian Constitution does not contain which of the following provisions?
(a) Equality (b) Fundamental rights
(c) Reservations (d) Discriminations

8. Which of the following is correct with reference to Saudi Arabia? **Competency Based**
(a) It is a secular country.
(b) All religions are treated equally.
(c) Non-muslims are free to practise their religion in the way they want.
(d) Non-muslims cannot gather in public spaces for prayer.

9. Mukesh, a Hindu citizen of the United States of America, lives in a part of the country where Christian fundamentalism is very powerful. No one is willing to rent their house to him.
Which of the following statements best reflects the situation? **Competency Based**
(a) Mukesh is facing housing discrimination due to his religious beliefs.
(b) Mukesh has successfully rented a house in the area despite religious differences.
(c) Mukesh is a Christian fundamentalist himself.
(d) Christian fundamentalism has no impact on housing in the area.

10. Identify the type of freedom from the information given below. **Competency Based**
I. Indian police stations and government schools do not promote any one religion.
II. The Indian state allows Sikhs an exception to the law of wearing helmets while riding two-wheelers.
III. The Constitution of India grants religious communities the right to set up their own schools and colleges.

Codes
(a) Right to Equality.
(b) Right to Freedom of Religion
(c) Cultural and Educational Rights
(d) Both (b) and (c)

11. Recently, some of the Members of the Lok Sabha have claimed that the words "Socialist" and "Secular" were omitted in the New Copies of the Preamble of the Constitution of India.
Source : Mint **Competency Based**
Why is the term 'secular' particularly significant in a country with a diverse religious population?
(a) It is important for the country to function democratically.
(b) Secularism emphasises on to separation of religion from the state.
(c) Secularism emphasise that one religious community does not dominate another.
(d) All of the above

12. **Consider the following statement and choose the correct option.**

Which one of the following statements is correct?

I. The Indian Constitution guarantees religious freedom to all citizens.

II. India adopted a strategy of separating religion and the state.

Codes

(a) Only I (b) I and II both
(c) Only II (d) None of these

Answers

1. (d)	**2.** (b)	**3.** (a)	**4.** (a)	**5.** (d)
6. (c)	**7.** (d)	**8.** (d)	**9.** (a)	**10.** (d)
11. (d)	**12.** (b)			

Match the Following

1.

	List I	List II
A.	Hinduism	1. Shwetambars
B.	Christianity	2. Protestant
C.	Islam	3. Vaishnavites
D.	Jains	4. Shias

Codes

	A	B	C	D		A	B	C	D
(a)	4	3	1	2	(b)	3	2	4	1
(c)	2	4	3	1	(d)	1	2	4	3

Ans (b)

Assertion-Reason

1. **Assertion** (A) India is a secular State.

Reason (R) People are free to practice their religion freely in India without interference from the government.

Codes

(a) Both A and R are true and R is the correct explanation of A

(b) Both A and R are true, but R is not the correct explanation of A

(c) A is true, but R is false

(d) A is false, but R is true

2. **Assertion** (A) The Indian State distances itself from religion and support one religion.

Reason (R) Government spaces in India, such as law courts, police stations, government schools, and offices, are not supposed to display or promote any one religion.

Codes

(a) Both A and R are true and R is the correct explanation of A

(b) Both A and R are true, but R is not the correct explanation of A

(c) A is true, but R is false

(d) A is false, but R is true

Ans. 1. (a) Both A and R are true and R is the correct explanation of A

2. (d) A is false, but R is true

Fill in the Blanks

1. ...... is important for a country to function democratically.

2. The intervention of the State can also be in the form of ....

3. The Indian State is not ruled by a .... group, nor does it promote any .... on its own.

4. ....refers to a persons's liberty to develop their own understanding and meaning of the religion they practice. **Diksha**

5. Indian Constitution bans ....to prevent discrimination of lower castes.

Ans. 1. Secularism 2. support
3. religious, religion 4. Freedom to interpret
5. untouchability

True/False

1. In Indian Secularism, the State is not strictly separated from religion.

2. The Indian Constitution does not allow religious communities to set-up their own schools and colleges.

3. The police stations in India are supposed to display and profess the religion of the police superintendent.

4. The Fundamental Rights guaranteed by the Indian Constitution are based on secular principles.

Ans. 1. True 2. False 3. False 4. True

Picture Based Question

1. **Look at the picture given below and answer the questions that follow.**

Which of the following is recited during the 'Pledge of Allegiance' in US government schools?

(a) "One nation, indivisible" (b) "Under God"
(c) "Liberty and justice for all" (d) "In God we trust"

Ans. (b) "Under God"

Case Based Question

1. Read the passage given below and answer the questions that follow.

In February 2004, France passed a law banning students from wearing any conspicuous religious or political signs or symbols such as the Islamic headscarf, the Jewish skullcap, or large Christian crosses. This law has encountered a lot of resistance from immigrants who are mainly from the former French colonies of Algeria, Tunisia and Morocco. In the 1960s, France had faced a shortage of workers and, therefore, had provided visas for these immigrants to come and work in the country. The daughters of these immigrants often wear headscarves while attending school. However, with the passing of this new law, they have been expelled from their school for wearing headscarves.

(i) The new law was passed in France with which of the following objectives?

(a) To reduce religious tensions in the country.
(b) To reduce immigration from Muslim countries.
(c) To promote secularism in the country.
(d) To promote French culture.

(ii) What were the views of the immigrant community regarding the new law?

(a) They were generally supportive of the law.
(b) They were generally opposed to the law.
(c) They were divided in their opinion on the law.
(d) None of the above

(iii) Which of the following situations encouraged France to encourage immigrants into the country?

(a) To address a shortage of workers.
(b) To promote cultural exchange.
(c) To encourage tourism.
(d) To boost diplomatic relations.

(iv) What was the consequence of not adhering to the new law that was passed in France in 2004?

(a) Daughters of the immigrants were asked to leave the school.
(b) The parents of Jewish students were fined.
(c) Daughters of immigrants started a protest against this law.
(d) All of the above

Ans. (i) (c) To promote secularism in the country.
(ii) (b) They were generally opposed to the law.
(iii) (a) To address a shortage of workers.
(iv) (a) Daughters of the immigrants were asked to leave the school.

PART II

Very Short Answer Type Questions

1. What is the position of minorities in Israel?

Ans. The position of minorities is very poor in Israel as they are treated unfairly.

2. What is discrimination?

Ans. Discrimination refers to the practice, when people are treated differently on grounds of religion, sex, caste, etc.

3. Can India be regarded as a non-religious country? **Competency Based**

Ans. No, it is wrong to consider India as a non-religious country as it gives religious freedoms to its citizens. India also protects and respects the religious sentiments of the people.

4. Can the Indian State intervene in religious affairs?

Ans. Yes, the Indian State can intervene in religious affairs when it is considered necessary in the interest of the society.

5. Give examples of one secular state and one non-secular state.

Ans. India is an example of a secular state and Israel is an example of a non-secular state.

6. When did France pass a law banning students from wearing any conspicuous religious or political signs or symbol?

Ans. In February 2004, France passed a law banning students from wearing any conspicuous religious or political signs or symbols.

7. What do you mean by untouchability?

Ans. Untouchability is the practice of discriminating individuals and groups on the basis of their caste and jobs done by them.

8. What laid the foundation of secularism in America?

Ans. The first amendment of the US Constitution laid the foundation of secularism in America.

Short Answer Type Questions

1. What are the objective of secularism? **Competency Based**

Ans. The objectives of secularism are

- To prevent the domination of one religious community over another.
- To prevent the domination of some members over the other members of same religious group.
- To prevent the state from supporting any particular religion or discriminating against other religions.

2. What does religious freedom mean to you? How do you exercise it? **Competency Based**

Ans. For me, religious freedom means the ability to follow my religion, observe its practices and celebrate its festivals without the fear of any repression or discrimination.

I exercise my religious freedom by worshipping the god of my religion in the way prescribed by my religion and celebrating the festivals of my religion freely.

3. How are people of different religions viewed in your society?

Ans. In our society, people belonging to different religions live together in harmony. We not only celebrate the festivals of our religion but participate wholeheartedly in the religious festivals of other religions also.

On happy occasions as well as difficult times, the whole society comes together. We have unity in diversity. All this is possible because our society believes in secularism.

4. What does the Indian Government do to promote secularism?

Ans. The Indian Government ensures equal status for all religions and religious freedom for all in order to promote secularism. It gives financial aid to minority religions for setting up their institutions.

The Indian Government also sets-up a mechanism to help the religions undertake pilgrimage, visit religious places etc. In this way, different citizens of the country get to follow their different religions freely.

5. In what way does Indian secularism differ from others? **Competency Based**

Ans. There is one significant way in which Indian secularism differs from others.

There is a strict separation of religion and state in the United States of America. The state does not prohibit the practice of any religion and it does not interfere in the religious matters in any way.

On the other hand, in Indian secularism, the state can interfere in religious affairs. However, this interference has to be based on the ideals laid out in the Constitution.

6. Suggest some ways in which you can work to promote secularism in your country.

Ans. As a citizen of my country, I also can work towards promoting the ideal of secularism in the following ways

- Respecting the faith of people following a religion different from mine.
- Not offending the things that are considered sacred by the followers of a certain religion.
- Helping people of a religion different from mine and celebrating their festivals by giving them holiday from work/school, etc.

7. "History has instances of religious discrimination, like the Nazi persecution of Jews and mistreatment of religious minorities in Israel. Saudi Arabia restricts non-Muslim places of worship and gatherings for non-Muslim prayer." **Competency Based**

(ii) What is religious discrimination?

Ans. Religious discrimination is the unjust or prejudicial treatment of people or groups on the basis of their religious beliefs or affiliations.

(i) Why is religious discrimination wrong?

Ans. Religious discrimination is wrong because it violates people's fundamental right to religious freedom. Religious freedom is the right to practice one's religion freely, without interference from the state.

8. Read the passage given below and answer the following questions. **Diksha**

The Indian Constitution contains Fundamental Rights that protect us against State power as well as against the tyranny of the majority. The Indian Constitution allows individuals the freedom to live by their religious beliefs and practices as they interpret these. In keeping with this idea of religious freedom for all, India also adopted a strategy of separating the power of religion and the power of the State. Secularism refers to this separation of religion from the State.

(i) Define secularism

Ans. Secularism is the separation between the power of religion and the power of the state.

(ii) What does the Indian Constitution mention about religious beliefs?

Ans. The Indian constitution allows individuals the freedom to live by their religious beliefs and practices.

Long Answer Type Questions

1. Why is it necessary to separate religion from the State?

Ans. For a country to function democratically, it is important to separate religion from the State because

- Discrimination of one religious group by another takes place more easily when one of the religion is given official recognition by the state. Thus, it is important to separate religion and state.
- The separation of religion from state prevents the tyranny of majority and violation of fundamental rights of minorities.
- It helps to protect freedom of individuals to adopt another religion or freedom to interpret the religious teachings differently.

2. Discuss the nature of the concept of secularism that is being followed in India.

Ans. The nature of secularism in India is unique in the way that the State follows the policy of distancing as well as intervention in matters of religion as follows

(i) **Distancing** The Indian State distances itself from all religions. It gives equal respect to all religions yet does not officially promote any one particular religion on its own. This is to maintain neutrality.

(ii) **Intervention** Though the Indian State follows the policy of keeping away from religious matters, it may intervene in exceptional cases. This happens when the State feels that some citizen's/citizens' Fundamental Rights have been violated by religion.

3. What is the nature of the State in Israel and Saudi Arabia? How is it different from India? **Competency Based**

Ans. The countries of Israel and Saudi Arabia have a non-secular type of State. The States of Israel and Saudi Arabia profess and promote the Jewish and Islamic religion respectively in their programmes and policies.

Israel and Saudi Arabia are completely different from India in the way that India is a secular State where all religions are treated equally. Unlike India, the position of religious minorities is very bad in Israel and Saudi Arabia. Minorities are not free to follow their religion freely nor can they assemble in public spaces for prayer, religious gatherings, etc. In Saudi Arabia, the followers of other religions cannot set-up their places of worship. he people of minority religions live in constant fear and are even killed and persecuted as is the case in Israel.

4. "The Indian Constitution guarantees religious freedom for all and separates the power of religion and the State. Secularism refers to this separation of religion from the State."
What does it mean for India to be a secular state **Competency Based**

Ans. India is a secular state, which means that the government does not discriminate on the basis of religion and treats all religions equally. This is enshrined in the Indian Constitution, which guarantees the freedom of religion to all citizens.

Some specific examples of what it means for India to be a secular State are

- The government does not promote any particular religion or set of religious beliefs.
- The government does not fund religious institutions or activities.
- All citizens are free to practice their religion in public or in private.
- The government does not interfere in the internal affairs of religious groups.
- The government does not discriminate against people on the basis of their religion in matters such as employment, education, or housing.

5. Discuss the practice of untouchability as a social evil.

Ans. Untouchability is a very age old social practice among the Hindu society. It is considered as a social evil as it involves the exploitation of a particular caste by the higher caste of the same religion. This practice violates the Fundamental Rights of the Dalits or scheduled caste.

Untouchability is a social evil characterised by

- **Caste-Based Discrimination** It is rooted in the caste system, leading to the discrimination and segregation of individuals based on their birth into specific castes.
- **Historical Persistence** Untouchability has deep historical roots and has been practiced for centuries in parts of India, contributing to the perpetuation of social inequalities.
- **Economic Exploitation** It involves the marginalisation of Dalits into menial and degrading occupations, resulting in their economic exploitation and limited access to opportunities.

Picture Based Questions

1. In the given storyboard, discuss the answer given by the teacher. **NCERT**

Ans. The answer given by the teacher in the above storyboard is in accordance with the law of country.

All government institutions, including government schools, offices etc, are prohibited from displaying or promoting any one religion. Thus, the teacher in the storyboard says that government schools cannot celebrate any religious festival in the school premises.

2. This poster below highlights the need for 'Peace'. It says "Peace is a never-ending process ... it cannot ignore our differences or overlook our common interests." Write in your own words what you think the above sentences are trying to convey?

How does it relate to the need for religious tolerance? **NCERT**

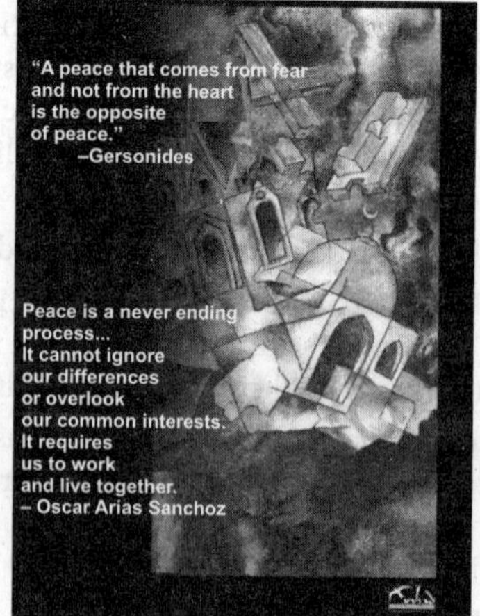

Ans. The given sentences in the poster are trying to convey that peace is a long-cherished goal of all citizens. It is a basic human need as it helps to maintain harmony, security and lets people live with dignity.

Peace is related to the need for religious tolerance as peace does not come on its own. We have to work towards upholding peace by being tolerant of each other, respecting our differences and focus on achieving the larger common interest. Being tolerant to other religions should become a part of our nature. Only then can we truly achieve peace and unity in diversity.

Case Based Question

1. Read the passage given below and answer the questions that follow.

The most important aspect of secularism is its separation of religion from State power. This is important for a country to function democratically. Almost all countries of the world will have more than one religious group living in them. Within these religious groups, there will most likely be one group that is in a majority. If this majority religious group has access to State power, then it could quite easy to use this power and financial resources to discriminate against and persecute persons of other religions. This tyranny of the majority could result in the discrimination, coercion and at times even the killing of religious minorities. The majority could quite easily prevent minorities from practising their religions. Any form of domination based on religion is in violation of the rights that a democratic society guarantees to each and every citizen irrespective of their religion. Therefore, the tyranny of the majority and the violation of Fundamental Rights that can result is one reason why it is important to separate the State and religion in democratic societies.

(i) What are some of the benefits of secularism?

Ans. Some benefits of secularism, are that it promotes religious freedom, equality and tolerance. It also helps to prevent conflict and violence.

(ii) What is the relationship between secularism and democracy?

Ans. Secularism and democracy are two closely related concepts. Secularism is essential for democracy to function properly. Without secularism, the majority religious group could use State power to oppress religious minorities.

(iii) What is the potential outcome if the majority religious group has access to State power without separation?

Ans. If the majority religious group has access to state power without separation, the majority may use its power and resources to discriminate against and even harm religious minorities, preventing them from practicing their religions.

ASSESSMENT EXERCISE

Multiple Choice Questions (MCQs)

1. State's efforts to influence a particular matter in accordance with the principles of the Constitution is called

(a) Intervene (b) Coercion
(c) Secularism (d) None of these

2. Which of these is not a secular value?

(a) Treating all religions equally.
(b) Allowing minorities to pressure their culture.
(c) Freedom to follow or exit from a religion.
(d) Collection of taxes by the government for promoting any religion.

3. The force used by a legal authority is

(a) secular (b) allegiance
(c) coercion (d) None of these

Subjective Questions (VSA, SA & LA)

1. Mention one objectives of Secular state.

2. Mention the holiday in a school calendar for different religions: Hindu, Muslim, Sikh and Christian

3. Define Freedom to interpret.

4. Why separation between religion and state is important? Give reason.

Or Why it is said that, it is important to separate the state and religion in democratic societies?

5. Differentiate Indian Secularism from other countries.

6. What are the most important aspect of Secularism?

7. What are the objectives of secular state? Discuss.

8. Describe the ways to prevent domination of one community on the other.

Parliament and the Making of Laws

CHAPTER 3

Parliament is the most important symbol of Indian democracy and a key feature of the Constitution. It enables citizens of India to participate in decision making and control the government.The Parliament was created after 1947. It has immense powers because it is the representative of the people.

The Parliament of India (Sansad) is the **supreme law-making** institution. It consists of two houses (the **Rajya Sabha** and the **Lok Sabha**) and the **President**.

The Rajya Sabha is also known as the **Council of States**. It has a total strength of 245 members. It is presided over by the Vice-President of India. The Lok Sabha or the **House of the People** has a total membership of 545. It is presided over by the Speaker.

3.1 People's Participation in Decision Making

India gained it's independence on 15th August, 1947 after a long period of struggle. Many people from different sections of the society participated in this struggle. People in this struggle were inspired by ideas of freedom, equality and participation in decision-making.

Under the colonial rule, the people could not participate in decision making and criticise the decision taken by the British government. However, the struggle for freedom allowed people to openly **criticise**[1] the British Government and make demands.

During colonial rule, the people were also not allowed to vote. However, the Constitution of India laid down the principle of **Universal Adult Franchise** which meant that all adult citizens of the country have the right to vote.

People and their Representatives

The decision of people is important for creating a democratic government and deciding about its functioning. An individual citizen gives approval to the government through elections.

People elect their representatives to the Parliament. One of the group from these elected representatives then forms the government.

This government is controlled and guided by the Parliament which is made up of all the representatives together. As these representatives are chosen by the people, it is the people themselves who forms the government and also controls it.

3.2 Election to the Parliament

The elections to the Parliament are similar to the elections organised for the state legislature.

The country is divided into a number of constituencies for the purpose of elections. One person is elected to the Parliament from each **constituency**[2]. The candidates of different political parties contest in the elections.

The candidates after being elected to the Parliament becomes the Members of Parliament or MPs. These MPs together form the Parliament.

After the Lok Sabha elections, the political party having the majority of elected MPs, i.e. 272 or more members forms the government.

MPs of other political parties who do not belong to the majority party or the **coalition**[3] forms the opposition. The largest among these parties is called the **opposition party**.

The Lok Sabha is usually elected once in every five years.

1 **Criticise** It means to find fault in something or disapprove of a person or thing.
2 **Constituency** It refers to the division of a territory in a country for the purpose of elections.
3 **Coalition** It refers to the alliance formed by political parties after elections when no party has been able to get adequate seats to form a clear majority.

The Rajya Sabha consists of 233 elected members who are elected by legislative assemblies of various states. Apart from these, the President nominates 12 member to the Rajya Sabha.

KNOWLEDGE PLUS Electronic Voting Machines (EVMs) were used throughout India for the first time in 2004 general elections.

3.3 The Role of the Parliament

The parliament performs the following functions

- **To Select the National Government** The Lok Sabha in the Parliament selects the executive, who is responsible for the implementation of the laws made by the Parliament.

  The Prime Minister who is the **head of the ruling party** in Lok Sabha select ministers from the MPs of his party. These ministers together head different areas of government like health, education, finance, etc. The Rajya Sabha in the Parliament functions as the representative of the states of India in Parliament. It can initiate legislation and play crucial role in passing of a bill to become a law. It plays an important role in **reviewing**[4] and altering the laws initiated by the Lok Sabha.

- **To Control, Guide and Inform the Government** The parliament controls, guides and informs the government in the following ways

  Question Hour A session of Parliament begins with question hour in which MPs can obtain information about the working of the government. Asking of questions is an important task for every MP. It makes the government alert about its shortcomings.

  Opposition Parties They highlight the drawbacks of various policies and programmes of the government, and mobilise popular support for their own policies. They also provide valuable feedback to the government.

  Approval of Parliament The Parliament's approval is important for the government in all matters dealing with finances.

3.4 Making of Laws

Parliament makes laws for the entire country. Parliament needs to be sensitive to the problems faced by the people while making laws.

The citizens play a crucial role in helping the Parliament to frame laws related to the concerns of the people.

The citizens can impact every stage of law making process by raising their issues through TV reports, newspaper editorials, radio broadcasts, local meeting, etc.

For example, the people played an important role in the implementation of the **Protection of Women from Domestic Violence Act**, 2005.

The Protection of Women from Domestic Violence Act, 2005

Domestic violence refers to the physical and emotional abuse of the women by an adult male, usually her husband. It also includes verbal , sexual and economic abuse. This issue was brought to the notice of Parliament by the people.

Thus, Parliament passed the Protection of Women from Domestic Violence Act, 2005. It extends to all women who 'live or have lived together in a shared household' with the male member who is commiting the violence. This act came into effect in 2006.

3.5 Unpopular and Controversial Laws

Sometimes laws passed by the Parliament became unpopular and unacceptable by the people.

Sometimes, a law can be constitutionally valid and hence legal but it can continue to be unpopular among the people because they feel that the intention behind it is unfair and harmful.

If the law favours one group and disregards the other it will be controversial and lead to conflict. Thus, people might criticise the laws. In a democracy like India, the people can express their views against **repressive laws**[5] in the following ways

- Write their views in newspapers
- Hold public meetings
- Report to TV news channels
- Approach the court that has the power to modify or cancel laws if they don't adhere to the Constitution.

When such views are shared by a large number of people, then there is pressure on the Parliament to change such laws.

For example, various municipal laws on the use of space within municipal limits often make hawking and street-vending illegal. However, hawkers and vendors provide essential services cheaply and efficiently many people. Besides, it is their means of livelihood. Thus, the municipal law prohibiting street vending became unpopular.

4 **Reviewing** It means to think or revisit anything again or to make changes to any decision after thinking over it again.

5 **Repressive Laws** It refers to the laws that prevent the persons from exercising their fundamental rights.

PARLIAMENT AND THE MAKING OF LAWS

Election to the Parliament

- After the Lok Sabha elections, the political party having the majority of elected MPs form the government.
- MPs not belonging to the majority form the opposition party.

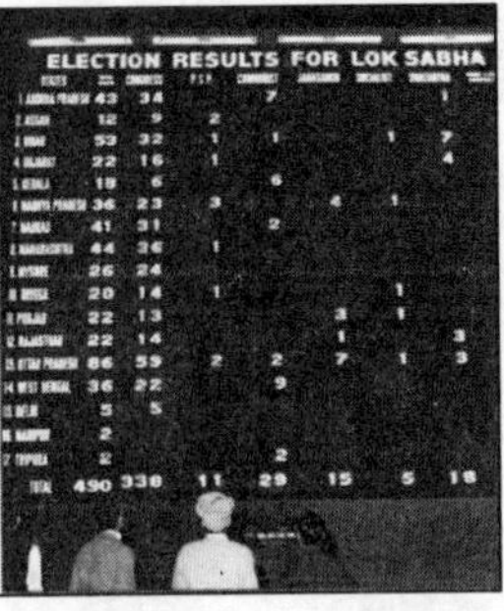

Unpopular and Controversial Laws

People can express their views against repressive laws by

- writing their views in newspaper
- hold public meetings
- report to TV news channel
- approach the court.

People's Participation in Decision-Making

The Constitution of India established Universal Adult Franchise, granting all the citizens the Right to Vote.

Making of Laws

Parliament makes laws for the entire country, e.g. Protection of Women from Domestic Violence Act, 2005

The Role of the Parliament

To select the National Government

- Rajya Sabha functions as the representative of the states of India.
- Lok Sabha selects the executive.
- PM selects the Council of Ministers from MPs.

To Control, Guide and Inform the Government

Question Hour

MPs obtain information about the working of the government.

Opposition Parties

Highlight the drawbacks of various policies and programmes of government and provide feedback to the government.

Approval of Parliament

Important for the government in all matters dealing with finances.

NCERT FOLDER

Covering Intext Questions and Exercises of NCERT

NCERT ON PAGE 32

Q.1 Give one reason why you think there should be Universal Adult Franchise?

Ans. There should be Universal Adult Franchise because it gives opportunity to every adult citizens to vote and participate in the decision making process of the government.

Q.2 Do you think there would be any difference if the class monitor was selected by the teacher or elected by the students? Discuss.

Ans. Yes, there will be difference in the above two cases as teacher may be partial in selecting monitor and choose the student who is closed to him/her. While in the other case the monitor elected by the class has the representation of whole class. It also gives equal chance for everyone to participate.

NCERT ON PAGE 33

Q.3 Use the terms 'constituency' and 'represent' to explain who an MLA is and how the person gets elected?

Ans. A candidate who gets the highest number of votes in elections from a particular constituency of a state gets elected as an MLA and he represents this constituency in the legislative assembly.

Q.4 Discuss with your teacher the difference between a State Legislative Assembly (Vidhan Sabha) and the Parliament (Lok Sabha).

Ans. The major differences between a State Legislative Assembly and the Parliament are as follows

State Legislative Assembly	Parliament
The members elected in the Legislative Assembly are known as MLAs.	The members elected to the Parliament are known as MPs.
It may consists of one house or two houses.	It consists of two houses.
It is less powerful than the Parliament	The Parliament is more powerful than the State Legislative Assembly.

Q.5 From the list below, identify the work of a State Government and that of a Central Government.

(i) The decision of the Indian Government to maintain peaceful relations with China.

Ans. It is the work of Central Government.

(ii) The decision of the Madhya Pradesh Government to discontinue Board Exams in class VIII for all schools under this Board.

Ans. It is the work of State Government.

(iii) Introduction of a new train connection between Ajmer and Mysore.

Ans. It is the work of Central Government.

(iv) Introduction of a new 1000 rupee note.

Ans. It is the work of Central Government.

Q.6 Fill in the blanks with the following words:

Universal Adult Franchise; MLAs; representative; directly.

Democratic governments in our times are usually referred to as representative democracies. In representative democracies, people do not participate (i) .... but, instead, choose their (ii) .... through an election process. These (iii) .... meet and make decisions for the entire population. These days, a government cannot call itself democratic unless it allows what is known as (iv) .... This means that all adult citizens in the country are allowed to vote.

Ans. (i) directly
(ii) representatives
(iii) MLAs (iv) Universal Adult Franchise

Q.7 You have read that most elected members whether in the Panchayat or the Vidhan Sabha or the Parliament are elected for a fixed period of five years. Why do we have a system where the representatives are elected for a fixed period and not for life?

Ans. Representatives are elected for a fixed period so that people have the choice to vote them out when people are dissatisfied with their performance. This also prevents the misuse of power by the representatives.

NCERT ON PAGE 35

Q.8 Use the following table to answer the questions below.

Results of the 17th Lok Sabha Election, (May 2019)

Political Party	No. of MPs
Bhartiya Janata Party (BJP)	303
Indian National Congress (INC)	52
Dravida Munnetra Kazhagam (DMK)	24
All India Trinamool Congress (AITC)	22
Yuvajana Sramika Rythu Congress Party (YSRCP)	22
Shiv Sena (SS)	18
Janata Dal (United) (JD (U))	16
Biju Janata Dal (BJD)	12
Bahujan Samaj Party (BSP)	10
Telangana Rashtra Samithi (TRS)	9
Lok Jan Shakti Party (LJSP)	5
Samajwadi Party (SP)	5
Independents (Ind.)	4
Nationalists Congress Party (NCP)	4
Communist Party of India (Maxist) (CPI) (M)	3
Indian Union Muslim league (IUML)	3
Jammu and Kashmir National Conference (J&KNC)	3
Telugu Desam Party (TDP)	3
All India Majlis-e-Ittehadul Muslimeen (AIMIM)	2
Apna dal (Apna dal)	2
Communist Party of India (CPI)	2
Shiromani Akali dal (SAD)	2
Aam Aadmi Party (AAP)	1
AJSU Party (AJSU)	1
All India Anna Dravida Munnetra Kazhagam (AIADMK)	1
All India United Democratic Front (AIUDF)	1
Janata dal (Secular) (JD (s))	1
Jharkhand Mukti Morcha (JMM)	1
Kerala Congress (M) (KC (M))	1
Mizo National Front (MNF)	1
Naga people Front (NPF)	1
National People's Party (NPP)	1
Nationalist Democratic Progressive Party (PDPP)	1
Rashtriya Loktantrik Party (RLP)	1
Revolutionary Socialist Party (RSP)	1
Sikkim Krantikari Morcha (SKM)	1
Viduthalai Chiruthaigal Katchi (VCK)	1
Grand total	**543**

(i) Who will form the government? Why?

Ans. Bhartiya Janata Party will form the government because it has secured a majority in the Lok Sabha.

(ii) Who will be present for discussions in the Lok Sabha?

Ans. The elected Members of Parliament (MPs) will be present for discussions in the Lok Sabha.

(iii) Is this process similar to what you have read about in class VII?

Ans. Yes, it is similar.

NCERT ON PAGE 38

Q.9 The following is an example of a question asked in Parliament.

Lok Sabha

Unstarred Question No : 48 Answered On : 15.12.2017

Converge of Schemes for Children

Manoj Rajoria

Will the Minister of Women and Child Development be pleased to state

(a) Whether the Government proposes to converge various schemes and policies for children in the country;

(b) If so, the details thereof; and ;

(c) If not, the reasons therefor?

(a) and (c) The Ministry has developed the National Plan of Action for Children 2016 which largely draws upon the existing programmes and schemes of various Ministries/Departments. It provides a framework for convergence and co-ordination between Ministries/Departments. If provides a framework for convergence and co-ordination between Ministries/Departments and State/UTs Governments and encourages collective action from all stakeholders to address multi-dimensional vulnerabilities experienced by children.

The National Plan of Action for children 2016 categorises children's rights under four key priority areas; (i) Survival, Health and Nutrition, (ii) Education and Development, (iii) Protection and (iv) Participation. It identifies key programmes, schemes and policies as well as stakeholders for the implementation of different strategies.

In the above question, what information is being sought from the Minister of Women and Child Development?

Ans. In the above question, the Minister of Women and Child Development is being asked questions related to the convergence of various schemes related to children's health, education, protection, etc.

Q.10 If you were a Member of Parliament (MPs), list two questions that you would like to ask.

Ans. If I were a Member of Parliament (MPs), I would ask the following two questions

(i) What has the government done to ensure education for all?

(ii) What steps has the government taken for women's upliftment?

NCERT ON PAGE 39

Q.11 State one reason why you think the Sedition Act of 1870 was arbitrary? In what ways does the Sedition Act of 1870 contradict the rule of law?

Ans. The Sedition Act of 1870 was arbitrary because the definition of sedition was very broad and according to it, the British could arrest and detain any person they wanted.

The Sedition Act of 1870 contradicted the rule of law because there was no scope for holding a proper trial to adjudge whether a person was indeed guilty of the offence he had been convicted for or not. The Act permitted arresting Indians without due trial if they protested or criticised the British Government.

NCERT ON PAGE 42

Q.12 (i) What do you understand by 'domestic violence'? List the two rights that the new law helped achieve for women who are survivors of violence.

Ans. Domestic violence refers to the injury, harm or threat of injury or harm caused by an adult male, usually the husband, against his wife. Injury may be caused by physically beating up the woman or by emotionally abusing her. Abuse of the woman includes verbal, sexual and economic abuse.

Two rights that the new law of Protection of Women from Domestic Violence Act 2005 helped achieve for women survivours of violence are

(a) Right of women to live in a shared household with protection against violence.

(b) Right of women who have survived domestic violence to receive monetary relief in order to meet their expenses including medical costs.

(ii) Can you list one process that was be used to make more people aware of the need for this law (The Protection of Women from Domestic Violence Act)?

Ans. The process of public discussions was used to make more and more people aware of the need for this law.

EXERCISES

Q.1 Why do you think our Nationalist Movement supported the idea that all adults have a Right to Vote?

Ans. The Nationalist Movement fought for independence from British rule. The people of India wanted freedom from the British rule because they had no role in the decision making process. Also they could not criticize the decisions of the government.

During the Nationalist movement the people openly criticised the government and also made several demands. This developed confidence in the mind of nationalists that all persons in independent India would be able to participate in making decisions. This was the reason due to which our Nationalist Movement supported the idea that all adults have right to vote.

Q.2 You have read in chapter 1 that the parliamentary form of government that exists in India has three tiers. This includes the Parliament (Central Government) and the various State Legislatures (State Governments).

Fill in the following table with information on the various representatives from your area.

	State Government	Central Government
Which political party/parties is/are currently in power?		
Who (name) is the current representative from your area?		
Which political parties currently form the opposition?		
When were elections last held?		
When will the next elections be held?		
How many women representatives are there (from your state)		

Ans. Do it yourself.

Q.3 Re-read the storyboard on how a new law on domestic violence got passed. Describe in your own words the different ways in which women's groups worked to make this happen.

Ans. The law on domestic violence got passed after going through the following successive stages. These are

- When more and more complaints of domestic violence were received, the need for a new law was felt.
- The need for a new civil law to address the issue of domestic violence was raised at different public forums.
- In December 2002, the Parliamentary Standing Committee, which had accepted most of the demands of the women's groups, submitted its recommendations to the two Houses of Parliament.
- Finally a new bill, was reintroduced in Parliament in 2005. Afterbeing passed in both houses of Parliament, it was sent to the President for his assent.

Women's group had an important role in the passage of the domestic violence act. Throughout 1990s they participated in several movements that demanded a new civil law for domestic violence. National commission for women made submissions to the parliamentary standing committee to protest against the new bill that was introduced in 2002 because it did not had provisions which they wanted. Finally, the committee accepted most of the demands of the womens's group and this bill was passed into the Act in 2006.

REVIEW EXERCISE

Including Competency Based Questions

Part I

Multiple Choice Questions (MCQs)

1. The Upper House of Parliament is termed as

(a) Lok Sabha (b) Vidhan Sabha
(c) Rajya Sabha (d) Executive

2. The total membership of the Lok Sabha is

(a) 243 (b) 543
(c) 100 (d) 250

3. What is the term/tenure of Lok Sabha?

(a) 1 year (b) 3 years
(c) 5 years (d) It is a permanent house

4. Who is the head of the Indian state?

(a) The President
(b) Prime Minister
(c) Both 'a' and 'b'
(d) Neither 'a' nor 'b'

5. Who presides over the Lok Sabha?

(a) President (b) Prime Minister
(c) Speaker (d) People

6. How are the members of Lok Sabha chosen? **Competency Based**

(a) Nominated by President
(b) Nominated by Prime Minister
(c) Elected by the people
(d) Chosen on first-come-first-serve basis

7. When were the EVMs were first used in India?

(a) 1985 (b) 2001
(c) 2004 (d) 2010

8. Abuse of a woman in the domestic sphere could be in the form of

(a) verbal abuse (b) sexual abuse
(c) economic abuse (d) All of these

9. Dinesh, a college going student is unhappy with the recent laws that were drafted for the women's safety. He finds that many of his friends were also upset with the laws. **Competency Based**

In which of the following ways, Dinesh and his friends can show views to the government ?

(a) By taking the help of a news channel
(b) By publishing articles in a newspaper
(c) By holding public meetings
(d) All of the above

10. When was the Sedition Act passed?

(a) 1858 (b) 1860
(c) 1870 (d) 1919

11. Identify the feature of Parliament from the following information **Competency Based**

I. It is the part of every session of the parliament.
II. It is of one hour duration.
III. Important questions are asked to the government by the MPs during this.

Codes

(a) Zero Hour (b) Question Hour
(c) Adjournment Session (d) Discussion Hour

12. **Twenty-seven years after the Women's Reservation Bill was first introduced in Parliament, the Lok Sabha on September 20 passed a Bill with near unanimity to amend the Constitution and provide one-third reservation to women in the Lok Sabha and State Assemblies."** **Competency Based**

Source The Hindu

Which of the following statements is correct for Women Reservation Bill, 2023?

I. It would increase the number of women in political office, which would lead to better representation of women's interests in policymaking.

II. It is a significant step towards ensuring that women have equal representation in government and that they can fully exercise their right to equality.

III. It would help to break down gender stereotypes.

Codes

(a) I and II (b) Only II (c) II and III (d) All of these

13. **Consider the following statement and choose the correct option.**

Which one of the following statements is correct?

I. India is a non-democratic country.

II. The Constitution of independent India laid down the principle of Universal Adult Franchise.

Codes

(a) Only I (b) I and II both
(c) Only II (d) None of these

14. **Which one of the following statements is correct?**

I. The country is divided into numerous constituencies, each of which elects one person to the Lok Sabha.

II. Elections to the Lok Sabha are held in a similar manner as they are for the state legislature.

Codes

(a) Only I (b) I and II both
(c) Only II (d) None of these

Answers

1. (c)	2. (b)	3. (c)	4. (a)	5. (c)
6. (c)	7. (c)	8. (d)	9. (d)	10. (c)
11. (b)	12. (d)	13. (c)	14. (b)	

Match the Following

1.

	List I		List II
A.	Rajya Sabha	1.	Lower House
B.	Lok Sabha	2.	Upper House
C.	Prime Minister	3.	Law making body
D.	Parliament	4.	Leader of the ruling party

Codes

	A	B	C	D		A	B	C	D
(a)	2	1	4	3	(b)	1	2	3	4
(c)	4	3	2	1	(d)	1	2	4	3

Ans. (a)

Assertion-Reason

1. **Assertion** (R) The Prime Minister is responsible for selecting ministers from among the MPs of her party to help implement government decisions.

Reason (A) The Prime Minister of India is the leader of the ruling party in the Lok Sabha.

Codes

(a) Both A and R are true and R is the correct explanation of A
(b) Both A and R are true, but R is not the correct explanation of A
(c) A is true, but R is false
(d) A is false, but R is true

2. **Assertion** (A) A specific process was adopted for the issue of domestic violence to become a law.

Reason (R) The issue of domestic violence was brought to the attention of Parliament.

Codes

(a) Both A and R are true and R is the correct explanation of A
(b) Both A and R are true, but R is not the correct explanation of A
(c) A is true, but R is false
(d) A is false, but R is true

Ans. 1. (b) Both A and R are true, but R is not the correct explanation of A

2. (a) Both A and R are true and R is the correct explanation of A

Fill in the Blanks

1. ...... parties are crucial to keep a check on the ruling party.

2. Democratic government is formed with the decision of ....

3. The number of elected members in the Lok Sabha is ....

4. There are ...... nominated members in the Rajya Sabha.

Ans. 1. Opposition, 2. People.
3. 543 4. 12

True/False

1. The Parliament consists of the Lok Sabha, Rajya Sabha and the Prime Minister.

2. The Rajya Sabha is also known as the Council of States. **Diksha**
3. The Lok Sabha is a permanent house.
4. A Parliament session begins with Zero Hour.
5. People cannot criticise a law already passed by the Parliament.

Ans. 1. False 2. True 3. False 4. False 5. True

Picture Based Question

1. Look at the picture given below of Rajya Sabha and answer the questions that follow.

Who chairs the proceedings of Rajya Sabha?

(a) Prime Minister
(b) Vice-President
(c) President
(d) Education Minister

Ans. (b) Vice-President

Case Based Question

1. Read the passage given below and answer the questions that follow

Various municipal laws on the use of space within municipal limits often make hawking and street vending illegal. No one will dispute the necessity for some rules to keep the public space open so that people can walk on the pavements easily. However, one also cannot deny that hawkers and vendors provide essential services cheaply and efficiently to the millions living in a large city. This is their means of livelihood. Hence, if the law favours one group and disregards the other it will be controversial and lead to conflict. People who think that the law is not fair can approach the court to decide on the issue. The court has the power to modify or cancel laws if it finds that they don't adhere to the Constitution.

(i) Which of the following is the reason behind the unpopularity of the municipal laws?

(a) Because they favour one group and disregard the other.
(b) Because they are not necessary to keep public spaces open.
(c) Because they are not fair to hawkers and vendors.
(d) All of the above

(ii) Which of the following statements is true with respect to the hawkers and vendors?

(a) They provide essential services cheaply and efficiently.
(b) They contribute to the local economy.
(c) They provide jobs
(d) None of the above

(iii) Which of the following is not a power of the court?

(a) Modify laws (b) Enact laws
(c) Uphold laws (d) Cancel laws

(iv) What is the best way to resolve a conflict over a law?

(a) To approach the court
(b) To protest
(c) To negotiate with the government
(d) To ignore the law

Ans. (i) (d) All of the above
(ii) (a) They provide essential services cheaply and efficiently.
(iii) (b) Enact laws
(iv) (a) To approach the court

Part II

Very Short Answer Type Questions

1. Name the two houses of Parliament.

Ans. The two houses of Parliament are Lok Sabha and Rajya Sabha.

2. What makes the Indian Parliament powerful?

Ans. The participation of the people in the form of their representatives in the decision making process makes the Indian Parliament powerful.

3. What do you mean by constituency?

Ans. The division of the territory of the country for the purpose of elections is known as the constituency.

4. What is a coalition government? **Diksha**

Ans. When a single political party, joins together with different political parties to get the majority to form a government, it is called a coalition government.

5. What is the meaning of opposition party?

Ans. Opposition is formed by the MPs of the parties who do not belong to the majority party or coalition that forms government. The largest among these parties is called the opposition party.

6. Identify the function of the Executive.

Ans. The Executive works on implementing the laws made by the Parliament.

7. Mention the composition of Rajya Sabha.

Ans. The Rajya Sabha is composed of 233 elected plus 12 nominated members.

8. Is the Protection of women from Domestic Violence Act' a Civil law or Criminal law ? Competency Based

Ans. The 'Protection of Women from Domestic Violence Act 2005' is a Civil law.

9. What does 'rule of law' mean?

Ans. Rule of law means that no one is above law and all laws apply equally to all citizens of the country.

10. What do you mean by controversial law ?

Ans. The law that favors one group and disregards the other is known as controversial law.

Short Answer Type Questions

1. Discuss about the composition of the Parliament.

Ans. The Parliament is the supreme law making body. It consists of the two houses (the Rajya Sabha and the Lok Sabha) and the President.

The Rajya Sabha is also known as the Council of states and it has a total strength of 245 members. The Rajya Sabha is presided over by the Vice-President. The Lok Sabha is also known as the house of people, has a total membership of 545. It is presided over by the Speaker.

2. What was the significance of the Freedom Movement regarding the people's participation in decision making ?

Ans. During the Freedom Movement, people from various backgrounds joined the struggle to break the power of the British rule.

Under colonial rule, people lived in fear of the British Government, they were made to follow repressive rules even if they did not agree with it. The Freedom Movement changed this situation. Inspired by the ideas of freedom, equality and participation in decision-making, people openly criticised the government and made demands.

3. What is Universal Adult Franchise? Why it is important?

Ans. Universal Adult Franchise means the right of all adult citizens to vote irrespective of caste, creed etc.

It is important, especially in a democracy, because through this, all citizens of India have the equal right to select their political representatives.

4. What is the composition of the Indian Executive? Competency Based

Ans. The Indian Executive is comprised of the President, Vice-President and Prime Minister and other ministers appointed by President on the advice of the Prime Minister. These ministers are accountable to the Prime Minister, who himself is answerable to the Lok Sabha. The President is the nominal head of the state.

5. What is the role of the Prime Minister in the Parliament?

Ans. The Prime Minister is the head of the ruling party in the Lok Sabha.

He selects ministers from the MPs of his party. These ministers together head different areas of government. In this way the Prime minister has an important role in the Parliament.

6. Analyse the role of Rajya Sabha with respect to the Lok Sabha.

Ans. The Rajya Sabha plays a crucial role complementary to that of the Lok Sabha in the following ways

- While the Lok Sabha represents the people directly through elections, the Rajya Sabha represents the States and Union Territories, providing a federal character to the legislative process.
- The Rajya Sabha acts as a revising chamber, reviewing and suggesting amendments to legislation initiated in the Lok Sabha.

7. 'The Rajya Sabha primarily functions as the representative of the states of India in the Parliament. The Rajya Sabha can also initiate legislation and a bill is required to pass through the Rajya Sabha to become a law.'

(i) What does the above statement signify regarding the powers of the Rajya Sabha?

Ans. The Rajya Sabha has equal powers with respect to Lok Sabha in matters of passing a bill.

(ii) What is the function of the Rajya Sabha with regard to the passage of a bill?

Ans. The Rajya Sabha can initiate a bill. It can also review and alter the laws initiated by the Lok Sabha. The passage of bill through the Rajya Sabha is necessary for it to become a law.

8. What is the role of people in bringing about the withdrawal of the unpopular laws by the parliament? Competency Based

Ans. The role of people is important in bringing about the withdrawal of the unpopular laws by the Parliament.

If they disapprove of any of their actions, they can voice their criticism. They might criticise this law, hold public meetings, write about it in newspapers, report to TV news channels, etc.

The criticism of the people with regard to unpopular laws leads to rethinking and even withdrawal of such laws by the government.

Long Answer Type Questions

1. How is government formed in a democracy?

Ans. In a democracy, government is formed after elections. After the Lok Sabha elections, the political party having the majority of elected MPs (i.e. 272 or more members) form the government.

MPs of other political parties who do not belong to the majority party or the coalition forms the opposition. The largest among these parties is called the opposition party.

The Parliament also selects the executive, which is responsible for the implementation of the laws made by the Parliament. The Prime Minister who is the head of the ruling party in Lok sabha select ministers from the MPs of his party. These ministers together head different areas of government.

2. Opposition plays an important role in democracy. Justify. Competency Based

Ans. Opposition parties play a pivotal role in any democratic system due to several key reasons

(i) Opposition parties act as a check and balance on the government. This role is critical in preventing the concentration of power in the hands of a single entity, which could lead to authoritarianism or unchecked decision-making.

(ii) Secondly, opposition parties offer an alternative perspective and a different set of policies and ideas. This diversity of viewpoints is essential in a democracy, as it encourages healthy debate and fosters the exploration of various solutions to societal challenges.

(iii) Opposition parties hold the government accountable for its actions. By scrutinizing policies, decisions, and actions, they help expose corruption, inefficiency, or any potential abuses of power. This scrutiny encourages transparency and discourages the ruling party from acting in an arbitrary or self-serving manner.

3. Explain how the Parliament control, guide and inform the government.

Ans. The parliament controls, guides and informs the government in the following ways

- **Question Hour** A session of Parliament begins with question hour in which MPs can obtain information about the working of the government. Asking of questions is an important task for every MP. It makes the government alert about its shortcomings.
- **Opposition Parties** They highlight the drawbacks of various policies and programmes of the government and mobilise popular support for their own policies. They also provide valuable feedback to the government.
- **Approval of Parliament** The Parliament's approval is important for the government in all matters dealing with finances.
- **Making of Laws** Parliament makes laws for the entire country. Parliament needs to be sensitive to the problems faced by the people which making laws.

The citizens play a crucial role in helping the Parliament to frame laws related to the concerns of the people. The citizens can impact every stage of law making process by raising their issues through TV reports, newspaper editorials, radio broadcasts, local meeting, etc.

4. "The Parliament has an important role in making laws. There are many ways through which this takes place and it is often different groups in society that raise the need for a particular law."
How does a new law come into force in India? Discuss with a suitable example. Competency Based

Ans. A new law comes into force in India when it is passed by both houses of Parliament (Lok Sabha and Rajya Sabha) and assented to by the President of India. Once a bill is passed by both houses of Parliament, it is sent to the President for his assent.

The President can either assent to the bill, veto it, or return it to Parliament for reconsideration.

If the President assents to the bill, it becomes an Act of Parliament and comes into force on the date specified in the Act.

For example, in 2013, the Parliament of India passed the Right to Education Act, 2009, which guarantees free and compulsory education to all children aged 6 to 14 years. The Act was assented to by the President of India on 4th August, 2009, and came into force on 1st April, 2010. The Act has also helped to improve the quality of education in India.

Picture Based Questions

1. Observe the image of the Parliament given below. **NCERT**

What do you think the artist is trying to convey through this image?

Ans. Through this image of the Parliament, the artist is trying to convey that the Parliament is based on the people strength. The Parliament is the supreme law-making body of Indian democracy and it is composed of representatives elected directly by the people who come from different religions and backgrounds. So, it is ultimately the people who make rules for their country.

2. The photograph shows results from the third Lok Sabha elections held in 1962. Use the photograph to answer the following questions.

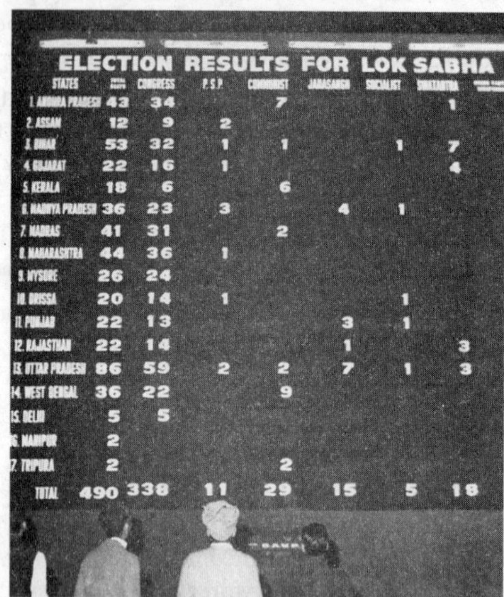

ELECTION RESULTS FOR LOK SABHA

STATES		CONGRESS	P.S.P.	COMMUNIST	JANASANGH	SOCIALIST	SWATANTRA
1. ANDHRA PRADESH	43	34		7			1
2. ASSAM	12	9	2				
3. BIHAR	53	32	1	1		1	7
4. GUJARAT	22	16	1				4
5. KERALA	18	6		6			
6. MADHYA PRADESH	36	23	3		4	1	
7. MADRAS	41	31		2			
8. MAHARASHTRA	44	36	1				
9. MYSORE	26	24					
10. ORISSA	20	14	1			1	
11. PUNJAB	22	13			3	1	
12. RAJASTHAN	22	14			1		3
13. UTTAR PRADESH	86	59	2	2	7	1	3
14. WEST BENGAL	36	22		9			
15. DELHI	5	5					
16. MANIPUR	2						
17. TRIPURA	2			2			
TOTAL	490	338	11	29	15	5	18

(i) Which state has the highest number of MPs in the Lok Sabha? Why do you think this is so?

Ans. The state of Uttar Pradesh has the highest number of MPs in the Lok Sabha.

I think this is because Uttar Pradesh has the highest population compared to other states.

(ii) Which state has the least number of MPs in the Lok Sabha?

Ans. Manipur has the least number of MPs in the Lok Sabha.

(iii) Which party do you think will form the government? Give reasons, why?

Ans. The Congress Party will form the government because it has got clear majority in the Lok Sabha.

3. From the below storyboard, can you list two different ways in which people lobbied Parliament? **NCERT**

Ans. Following are the ways in which people lobbied Parliament

(i) Public debates and discussion

(ii) Petition to the government

4. In the following poster, what do you understand by the phrase 'Equal Relationships are Violence Free'? **NCERT**

Ans. Equal relationship means that both the husband and the wife enjoy equal rights in the household. Neither the husband nor the wife tries to suppress or use violence against the other. Such relationships are based on equality and are free of violence.

5. List the three forms of protest that you seen in the given photos. NCERT

Ans. The three forms of protest seen in the above photos are (i) Hunger strike (ii) Dharna (iii) Public rally

Case Based Question

1. Read the passage given below and answer the questions that follow.

In December 2002, the Standing Committee submitted its recommendations to the Rajya Sabha and these were also tabled in the Lok Sabha.

The Committee's report accepted most of the demands of the women's groups. Finally a new bill, was reintroduced in Parliament in 2005. After being passed in both houses of Parliament, it was sent to the President for his assent. The Protection of Women from Domestic Violence Act came into effect in 2006.

(i) How does Parliament become aware of the need of new laws?

Ans. Different groups in society raise the need for a particular law which is then brought to the attention of the Parliament. In this way, the Parliament become aware of the need of new laws.

(ii) In what ways is the new law on domestic violence important for women?

Ans. The Protection of Women from Domestic Violence Act, 2006 is important for women as it recognises the women's right to live in a shared household. She also gets protection from further violence. The act also has provisions for monetary relief for women to meet their expenses..

ASSESSMENT EXERCISE

Multiple Choice Questions (MCQs)

1. The Lok Sabha is elected for
   (a) 5 years (b) 3 years
   (c) 7 years (d) 4 years
2. The elected members of Rajya Sabha is
   (a) 233 (b) 243
   (c) 231 (d) 241
3. The other name of Rajya Sabha is
   (a) Upper house (b) Council of States
   (c) Lower house (d) Both (a) and (b)
4. Who nominates the 12 members of Rajya Sabha?
   (a) Prime Minister (b) Speaker
   (c) President (d) Council of Ministers

Subjective Questions (VSA, SA & LA)

1. How many nominated members are there in Rajya Sabha?
2. What do you mean by Lower House?
3. Explain coalition.
4. Give one function of Lok Sabha.
5. What are EVMs?
6. What are the functions of Parliament? Explain.
7. Explain Government and the function of the Rajya Sabha.
8. What is Parliament and how it plays an vital role in democratic country?

Judiciary

CHAPTER 4

In India, there is a rule of law. To enforce this rule of law, there is judicial system consisting of the courts that a citizen can approach when a law is violated.

Judiciary is independent in its functioning i.e. there is no interference of government in the functioning of judiciary.

4.1 Role of the Judiciary

The judiciary performs the following roles

- **Dispute Resolution** Judiciary provides a mechanism for resolving dispute between citizens, between citizens and the government, between two states governments, and between the centre and state government.
- **Judicial Review** Judiciary is the final interpreter of the Constitution. It has the power of **judicial review**[1] which means that it can strike down particular laws passed by the government if it believes that these violates the basic structure of the Constitution.
- **Upholding the Law and Enforcing Fundamental Rights** Every citizen of India can approach the Supreme Court or the High Court if they believe that their Fundamental Rights have been violated.

4.2 Independent Judiciary

Indian Constitution has provided for an independent judiciary through the provision of **separation of power**. It means that the other branches of government (the legislature and the executive) cannot interfere in the work of judiciary. The courts are not under the government and do not act on their behalf.

It is also essential for this separation of power to work well that,

- All judges in the High Court as well as the Supreme Court are appointed with very little interference from other branches of government.
- It is very difficult to remove a judge, once he/she is appointed to the office.
- Independence of judiciary allows the courts to ensure that there is no misuse of power by the legislature and the executive.
- It also plays a crucial role in protecting Fundamental Rights of citizens because anyone can approach the courts if they believe that their rights have been violated.

4.3 Structure of Courts in India

There are three different levels of courts in India. These include several courts at the lower level and only one court at the apex level.

- **District Court** The District or Subordinate Courts are at the district or tehsil or town level. Most of the people interact with these courts. Each state is divided into districts that are presided over by a **District Judge**.
- The subordinate court is more commonly known by many different names. These include the Trial Court or the Court of the District Judge, the Additional Sessions Judge, Chief Judicial Magistrate, Metropolitan Magistrate, Civil Judge.
- **High Court** High Courts exist at the state level and they are the **highest court of the state.**
- **Supreme Court** It is the court at the top level in India. It is presided over by the **Chief Justice of India**. It is located at New Delhi and was established on 26th January, 1950. The decisions made by the Supreme Court are binding on all other courts in India.

All these different courts are connected to each other. In India, there is an integrated judicial system. It means that the decision made by higher courts are binding on the lower courts.

---

1 **Judicial Review** Judicial review refers to the power of judiciary to modify or cancel the laws framed by the Parliament.

This integration can also be understood by the **appellate system** that exists in India. In this system, a person can appeal to a higher court if they are not satisfied with the judgement of the lower court.

Evolution of Courts in India

The first High Courts were established in the three Presidency cities of Calcutta, Bombay and Madras in 1962. In 1966, the Delhi High Court was established.

There are 25 High Courts at present in India. Some of the states share common High Court such as Punjab and Haryana share a common High Court at Chandigarh and the four North Eastern States (Assam, Nagaland, Mizoram and Arunachal Pradesh) have a common High Court at Guwahati.

Andhra Pradesh and Telangana have separate High Courts from 1st January, 2019 at Amaravati and Hyderabad, respectively.

4.4 Different Branches of the Legal System

There are two branches of the legal system in India which are **Criminal Law** and **Civil Law**.

The differences between the two system are listed below

Criminal Law	Civil Law
It deals with conduct or acts that the law defines as offences.	It deals with any harm or injury to the rights of individuals.
The examples of cases under criminal law are theft, harrasment of women for dowry, murder, etc.	The examples of cases under civil law are sale of land, rent matters, divorce cases, etc.
It begins with lodging an FIR with the police who investigates the crime. After the investigation the case is filed in the court.	A petition has to be filed in the relevant party by the affected party only.
Under this law, if the accused is found guilty, he/she can be sent to jail and also fined.	Under this law, if the accused is found guilty, the court gives specific relief that is asked for.

4.5 Access to the Courts

Every citizen of India has the right to seek justice through courts. However, access to the courts in reality has always been difficult for a vast majority of the poor in India due to several reasons

Legal procedures involve a lot of money and paperwork as well as take up a lot of time. This legal procedure is difficult for a poor person who cannot read and whose family depends on a daily wage.

Another issue that affects the common people's access to justice is long time taken by courts to hear a case. The phrase **'justice delayed is justice denied'** is often used to characterise this extended time period that courts take to hear a case.

Despite of these issues, judiciary has played a crucial role in our country by keeping a check on the powers of the executive and the legislature and protecting the Fundamental Rights of citizens.

Public Interest Litigation

To increase the access to justice, Supreme Court devised the mechanism of Public Interest Litigation or PIL in the early 1980s. The features of the PIL are as follows

- PIL allows any individual or organisation to file a PIL in the High Court or the Supreme Court on behalf of those whose rights were being violated.
- It had simplified the legal process as even a letter or telegram addressed to the Supreme Court or High Court could be treated as a PIL.

PIL was used to secure justice on many issues such as

- Rescuing bonded labourers from inhuman work conditions.
- Securing the release of prisoners in Bihar who had been kept in jail even after their punishment term was complete.
- Providing the mid-day meal in government and government-aided schools.

KNOWLEDGE PLUS The Supreme Court was earlier located in the **Chamber of Princes** in the Parliament House. It moved to its present building on Mathura Road in New Delhi in 1958.

JUDICIARY

Structure of Courts in India

District Court
Courts at the district/tehsil/ town level

High Court
Highest court of the state

Supreme Court
- Court at the top level in India.
- Presided by the Chief Justice of India.

Independent Judiciary
- The Judiciary plays independent role with no interference of the Executive and the Legislative.
- It protects the Fundamental Rights of the citizens.

Access to the Courts
- All citizens have the right to seek justice through courts.
- The court interprets Fundamental Rights.
- Public Interest Litigation (PIL) can be filed in the court on behalf of those whose rights are violated.

Role of the Judiciary

Upholding the Law and Enforcing Fundamental Rights
Every citizen of India can approach the Supreme Court/High Court if his /her Fundamental Rights have been violated.

Judicial Review
- Judiciary is the final interpreter of the Constitution.
- Judiciary can strike down particular laws passed by the government.

Dispute Resolution
Resolves disputes between
- citizens
- citizen and the government
- two state governments
- the centre and the state government

Different Branches of the Legal System

Criminal Law
- Deals with conduct or acts that the law defines as offences.
- For example-Theft, harassment of women for dowry, murder, etc.

Civil Law
- Deals with any harm or injury to the rights of individuals.
- For example-Sale of sand, rent matters, divorce cases, etc.

NCERT FOLDER

Covering Intext Questions and Exercises of NCERT

NCERT ON PAGE 50

Q.1 With the help of your teacher, fill in the blank spaces in the table below.

Type of Dispute	Example
Dispute between centre and the state	
Dispute between two states	
Dispute between two citizens	
Laws that are in violation of the Constitution	

Ans.

Type of Dispute	Example
Dispute between centre and the state	Dissolution of Bihar Assembly
Dispute between two states	Kaveri (cauvery) water dispute between Karnataka and Tamil Nadu
Dispute between two citizens	Dispute between landowner and tenant
Laws that are in violation of the Constitution	Sealing of business establishments in Delhi.

Q.2 Do you think that any ordinary citizen stands a chance against a politician in this kind of judicial system? Why not?

Ans. No, an ordinary citizen does not stand a chance against a politician in this kind of judicial system. This is because the Judiciary does not enjoy the power to function independently as the politician has the power to appoint and dismiss a judge from his office.

NCERT ON PAGE 51

Q.3 List two reasons why you believe an Independent Judiciary is essential to democracy?

Ans. Independent judiciary is essential to democracy due to the following reasons

- It provides impartial judgement which is integral to democracy.
- It prevent the misuse of power by Legislature and Executive.

NCERT ON PAGE 53

Q.4 Write two sentences of what you understand about the appellate system from the case 'State (Delhi Administration) vs Laxman Kumar and other (1985)' mentioned in the text.

Ans. I understood the following about the appellate system from the given case

- The appellate system of the Indian Judiciary is one through which an appeal is made in the higher court against the judgement of the lower court if the person is not satisfied with the verdict.
- The verdict of different courts may differ from each other.

NCERT ON PAGE 54

Q.5 Fill in the table given below based on what you have understood about criminal and civil law.

Description of violation	Branch of law followed	Procedure to be followed
A group of girls are persistently harassed by a group of boys while walking to school.	—	
A tenant who is being forced to move out files a case in court against the landlord.	—	—

Ans.

Description of violation	Branch of law followed	Procedure to be followed
A group of girls are persistently harassed by a group of boys while walking to school.	Criminal	Filing of an FIR in the police station and the police after investigation will file a case in the court.
A tenant who is being forced to move out files a case in court against the landlord.	Civil	Tenant has to file a petition before the relevant court.

NCERT ON PAGE 57

Q.6 Discuss the impact of the shortage of judges on the delivery of justice to the litigants.

Ans. The impact of the shortage of judges on the delivery of justice is as follows

- Shortage of judges led to pendency of cases in the courts which in turn results in delay of justice.
- The accused and criminal persons gets enough time to turn the case in their favour by using their influence.
- Many times the victims and eyewitness are attacked and murdered because of the delay in judgement.

EXERCISES

Q.1 You read that one of the main functions of the Judiciary is upholding the law and enforcing Fundamental Rights. Why do you think an independent judiciary is necessary to carry out this important function?

Ans. An independent judiciary is essential to carry out its function of upholding the law and enforcing Fundamental Rights beacause only a judiciary independent of outside interference can give fair trial to citizens without being influenced by the politicians or other powerful persons. Hence, the Constitution has separated the powers of judiciary, executive and legislature.

Q.2 Re-read the list of Fundamental Rights provided in Chapter 1. How do you think the Right to Constitutional Remedies connects to the idea or judicial review ?

Ans. The Right to Constitutional Remedies guarantees citizens the right to approach the court directly if they believe that any of their Fundamental Rights have been violated by the state.

The judiciary has the power to remove any law passed by the Parliament which, according to it, violates the basic structure of the Constitution, i.e. the Fundamental Rights. In this ways, the two ideas of Right to Constitutional Remedies and Judicial Review are connected to each other.

Q.3 In the following illustration, fill in each tier with the judgements given by the various courts in the Sudha Goel case. Check your responses with other in class.

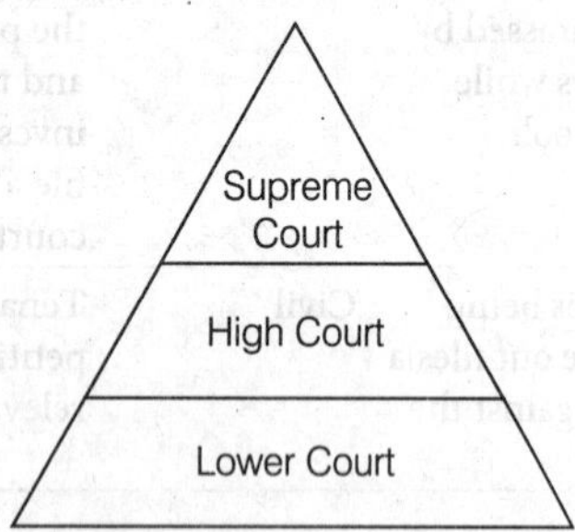

Ans. The judgement given by the various courts in the Sudha Goel case were

- **Supreme Court** It sentenced Laxman and Shakuntala for life and acquitted his brother- in-law, Subhash due to lack of evidence.
- **High Court** It acquitted Laxman, Shakuntala and Subhash Chandra.
- **Lower Court** It convicted Laxman, his mother Shakuntala and his brother-in-law Subhash Chandra and sentenced all three of them to death.

Q.4 Keeping the Sudha Goel's case in mind, tick the sentences that are true and correct the ones that are false.

(a) The accused took the case to the High Court because they were unhappy with the decision of the Trial Court.

Ans. True

(b) They went to the High Court after the Supreme Court had given its decision.

Ans. False

They cannot go to the High Court after the Supreme Court has given its decision.

(c) If they do not like the Supreme Court verdict, the accused can go back again to the Trial Court.

Ans. False

The verdict of the Supreme Court cannot be appealed in lower courts.

Q.5 Why do you think the introduction of Public Interest Litigation (PIL) in the 1980s is a significant step in ensuring access to justice for all?

Ans. The introduction of the mechanism of Public Interest Litigation (PIL) by the Supreme Court in early 1980s gave increased access to justice.

Before the 1980s, litigation in courts was a costly and time consuming affair. As a result of this, the poor could not afford going to courts and get justice. However, the introduction of PIL allowed any individual or organisation to file a PIL in the High Court or the Supreme Court on behalf of those whose rights had been violated.

Q.6 Re-read excerpts from the judgement on the Olga Tellis vs Bombay Municipal Corporation case. Now write in your own words what the judges meant when they said that the Right to Livelihood was part of the Right to Life.

Ans. Right to livelihood is an important part of the Right to Life because no person can live without the means of living, or the means of livelihood.

Q.7 Write a story around the theme, 'Justice delayed is justice denied'.

Ans. Do it yourself.

Q.8 Make sentences with each of the glossary words given on the back page.

Ans. **Acquit** The court acquitted Mohan of all charges.

To Appeal Tina is going to appeal against the judgement given by the lower court in domestic violence case.

Compensation The court awarded Deepak's widowed wife a compensation of ₹ 1 lakh.

Eviction The court has ordered the eviction of tenant who has not paid his rents for the last 10 years.

Violation Practicing untouchability is a violation of the Constitution of India.

REVIEW EXERCISE

Including Competency Based Questions

Part I

Multiple Choice Questions (MCQs)

1. The number of courts at the apex level is

(a) one (b) two
(c) three (d) four

2. Which is the highest judicial authority in a state?

(a) The Supreme Court
(b) The High Court
(c) The District Court
(d) Subordinate Court

3. The Supreme Court was established on-

(a) 26th January, 1930
(b) 26th January, 1950
(c) 15th August, 1952
(d) 30th January, 1947

4. The High Court of Delhi came up in which year?

(a) 1950 (b) 1952
(c) 1966 (d) 1970

5. Total number of High Courts in India is

(a) 19 (b) 24
(c) 25 (d) 28

6. Which two states share a common High Court?

(a) Punjab and Haryana
(b) Delhi and Punjab
(c) Delhi and Haryana
(d) Madhya Pradesh and Chhattisgarh

7. The High Court of Andhra Pradesh and Telangana was established in which year?

(a) 2016 (b) 2017
(c) 2018 (d) 2019

8. Which law is violated in the case of a dowry death? Diksha

(a) Society law (b) Civil law
(c) Criminal law (d) None of these

9. The Supreme Court in the early 1980s, devised a mechanism of PIL to increase access to .... Diksha

(a) justice (b) development
(c) employment (d) trade

10. What is the full form of PIL?

Or What is the expansion at PIL? Diksha

(a) Public Interest Litigation
(b) Private Interest Litigation
(c) Public Information Litigation
(d) Public Information Law

11. Mayank sharma married to Damini Sharma in 1999. On 17th August 2000, Damini was found dead in her apartment. She has several injuries on her body. Her family filed a case in court. The trial Court acquitted Mayank and his family members and did not gave any sentence against them. Competency Based

The family members of Damini can appeal in which of the following courts?

(a) Appeal to a higher court
(b) Appeal in Parliament
(c) Appeal in District Court
(d) Appeal to the President of India

12. 'The district judiciary is the primary interface between the justice system and the people.'

Which of the following statements best explains this statement? Competency Based

(a) The district judiciary is the first level of the judiciary that most people come into contact with.
(b) The district judiciary is the most affordable level of the judiciary.
(c) The district judiciary is the most convenient level of the judiciary.
(d) All of the above

13. Consider the following statement and choose the incorrect option.

I. The Indian Courts are under the government.
II. The Indian Constitution does not protect the independence of the judiciary.

Codes

(a) Only I (b) I and II both
(c) Only II (d) None of these

14. Which of the following statements is correct?

I. The Supreme Court of India is the highest judicial authority.
II. District-level courts are the only courts where the appellate system is applicable.

Codes

(a) Only I (b) I and II both (c) Only II (d) None of these

Answers

1. (a)	2. (b)	3. (b)	4. (c)	5. (c)
6. (a)	7. (d)	8. (c)	9. (a)	10. (a)
11. (a)	12. (d)	13. (b)	14. (a)	

Match the following

1.

	List I		List II
A.	Supreme Court	1.	District Court
B.	State	2.	Dispute between the Centre and State
C.	District	3.	High Court

Codes

	A	B	C		A	B	C
(a)	2	3	1	(b)	3	2	1
(c)	1	2	3	(d)	3	1	2

2.

List I		List II
A. Judiciary	1.	Key feature of the Constitution
B. Separation of Powers	2.	Criminal law cases
C. FIR	3.	Increased access to justice
D. PIL	4.	Uphold the law of the land

Codes

	A	B	C	D		A	B	C	D
(a)	3	2	1	4	(b)	4	1	2	3
(c)	2	1	4	3	(d)	2	1	3	4

Ans. 1. (a) 2. (b)

Assertion-Reason

1. **Assertion** (A) Every citizen of India can approach the Supreme Court or the High Court if they believe that their Fundamental Rights have been violated.

   Reason (R) The judiciary is responsible for upholding the law and enforcing fundamental rights.

   Codes

   (a) Both A and R are true and R is the correct explanation of A

   (b) Both A and R are true, but R is not the correct explanation of A

   (c) A is true, but R is false

   (d) A is false, but R is true

2. **Assertion** (A) All citizens of India have a right to justice through the courts.

   Reason (R) Access to courts is difficult for a vast majority of the poor in India.

   Codes

   (a) Both A and R are true and R is the correct explanation of A

   (b) Both A and R are true, but R is not the correct explanation of A

   (c) A is true, but R is false

   (d) A is false, but R is true

Ans. 1. (a) Both A and R are true and R is the correct explanation of A

2. (b) Both A and R are true, but R is not the correct explanation of A

Fill in the Blanks

1. Only an .... Judiciary can give verdict against the government.
2. The .... play a significant role in protecting our Fundamental Rights.
3. The decisions made by the .... are binding on all other courts of India.
4. The Supreme Court acts as the court of .... also.
5. The mechanism of PILs was devised in the early ....

Ans. 1. independent

2. Supreme Court and High Court

3. Supreme Court

4. record

5. 1980s

True/False

1. District courts are the highest court in a state.
2. There is only one Supreme Court in India.
3. A citizen can appeal against a decision made by Supreme Court.
4. The decisions made by the lower courts are binding on the higher courts.
5. The seven North-Eastern states have a common High Court.

Ans. 1. False 2. True 3. False 4. False 5. False

Picture Based Questions

1. **Observe the below picture carefully andidentify the building from the given options.**

(a) High Court of Delhi (b) Prime Minister Office
(c) Supreme Court of India (d) None of these

2. Look at the below picture of the High Court of Madras and choose the correct option. When was the High Court of Madras established?

(a) 1870 (b) 1860
(c) 1865 (d) 1862

Ans. 1. (c) Supreme Court of India
2. (d) 1862

Case Based Question

1. Read the given passage below and answer the questions that follow.

High Courts were first established in the three Presidency cities of Calcutta, Bombay and Madras in 1862. The High Court of Delhi came up in 1966. Currently, there are 25 High Courts. While many states have their own High Courts, Punjab and Haryana share a common High Court at Chandigarh and four North-Eastern states of Assam, Nagaland, Mizoram and Arunachal Pradesh have a common High Court at Guwahati. Andhra Pradesh (Amaravati) and Telangana (Hyderabad) have separate High Courts from 1st January, 2019. Some High Courts have benches in other parts of the state for greater accessibility.

(i) When was the first High Court established in India?

(a) 1862 (b) 1866
(c) 1966 (d) 2019

(ii) A High Court bench located outside the state capital serves which primary purpose?

(a) To handle legal matters related to a specific region within the state.
(b) To reduce the work load on the main court in the capital city.
(c) To provide easier access to justice for citizens in remote areas.
(d) All of the above

(iii) Which of the following statements is not true about the establishment of High Courts in India? Diksha

(a) The first High Courts were established in 1862 in Calcutta, Bombay and Madras.
(b) The High Court of Delhi was established in 1966.
(c) Currently, there are 25 functioning High Courts in India.
(d) All states have their own High Courts.

(iv) What is the purpose of having benches of High Courts in other parts of the state?

(a) To make access to justice easier for people living in remote areas.
(b) To reduce the workload on the main HighCourt.
(c) To provide specialised courts for certain types of cases.
(d) All of the above

Ans. (i) (b) 1866
(ii) (b) To reduce the work load on the main court in the capital city.
(iii) (d) All states have their own High Courts.
(iv) (d) All of the above

Part II

Very Short Answer Type Questions

1. What does the judiciary do?

Ans. The judiciary is that organ of the state which upholds the law of the land.

2. How many levels of courts are there in our country?

Ans. There are three different levels of courts in our country.

3. What do you mean by apex court?

Ans. Apex court refers to the court at the highest level in the Indian judicial system i.e. the Supreme Court.

4. Which court are in numerous numbers and interact with most of the people?

Ans. The courts that most people interact with are called subordinate or district courts.

5. Who presides over the Supreme Court?

Ans. The Chief Justice of India presides over the Supreme Court.

6. In which cities were the first High Courts of India established?

Ans. The first High Courts were established in the three Presidency cities of Bombay, Calcutta and Madras.

7. Name some offences which comes under criminal law.

Ans. Theft, murder, harassing a woman for dowry are some offences which comes under criminal law.

8. Name some issues which comes under civil law.

Ans. Disputes related to sale or purchase of land or other goods, rent matters, divorce cases etc comes under civil law.

9. Who introduced PILs in Indian judicial system and when?

Ans. The Supreme Court introduced PILs in the Indian judicial system in the early 1980s.

10. Who acts as a check on the powers of the Executive and Legislative?

Ans. The judiciary acts as a check on the powers of the Executive and Legislative.

11. What is the full form of FIR? Competency Based

Ans. The full form of FIR is First Information Report.

Short Answer Type Questions

1. What is the meaning of Judiciary?

Ans. Judicial system or Judiciary consists of the mechanism of courts that enforces the rule of law. That means, any citizen can approach a court when a law is violated. As an organ of government it plays an important role in the functioning of India's democracy.

2. Describe the functions of the Indian judiciary.

Ans. The judiciary performs the following functions

- **Dispute Resolution** Judiciary provides a mechanism for resolving dispute between citizens, between citizens and the government, between two state governments and between the Centre and State government.
- **Judicial Review** Judiciary can strike down particular laws passed by the government if these violates the basic structure of the Constitution.

3. 'The judiciary has played a crucial role in democratic India.' Justify the statement. Competency Based

Ans. The judiciary in democratic India has been important, ensuring the protection of constitutional principles and safeguarding citizens rights. It acts as a check on the executive and legislative branches, upholding the rule of law.

Through landmark judgements, the judiciary has addressed social issues, promoted equality, and interpreted the Constitution, contributing significantly to the country's democratic framework. The judiciary's independence and commitment to justice reinforce its crucial role in upholding democratic values in India.

4. What do you understand by integrated judicial system?

Ans. The different courts in India are connected to each other in an integrated judicial system. This integration of courts is through the following mechanisms

- The decision made by higher courts are binding on the lower courts.
- The appellate system exists in India where a person can appeal to a higher court if they are not satisfied with the judgement of the lower court.

5. What values can be learned from the functioning of Indian judiciary? Competency Based

Ans. From the Indian judiciary, several values can be learnt as follows

- **Equality and Justice** The judiciary's commitment to upholding the Constitution and its principles of equality before the law, regardless of background, fosters a sense of fairness and justice.
- **Rule of Law** Its emphasis on due process and adherence to legal procedures reinforces the idea that everyone is subject to the same laws, promoting a society governed by law, not by individuals.
- **Critical Thinking and Debate** Its open court system and engagement with diverse perspectives encourage critical thinking and healthy debate on important issues, strengthening democratic discourse.
- **Accountability and Transparency** Its role in holding individuals and institutions accountable for their actions promotes transparency and prevents the abuse of power.

6. Describe the evolution of courts in India.

Ans. The first High Courts were established during the British rule in 1862. They were set-up in the three presidency cities of Calcutta, Bombay and Madras.

The Supreme Court of India was established as a federal court under British rule. It was established as Supreme Court on 26th January, 1950.

The Delhi High Court was established in 1966. Now, the country has one Supreme Court at the top and 25 High Courts.

7. 'The decisions made by the Supreme Court are binding on all other courts in India.' Justify the statement. Competency Based

Ans. The statement is justified because the Supreme Court holds the highest authority in the Indian judicial system. Its decisions set legal precedents and interpretations that guide lower courts. The doctrine of judicial precedent ensures consistency and uniformity in legal rulings throughout the country.

As the apex court, its judgements are binding on all other courts, establishing a hierarchical structure that maintains the integrity and coherence of the Indian legal system.

8. What do you mean by criminal cases? Explain.

Ans. Criminal case deals with conduct or acts that the law defines as offences. The examples of criminal cases are theft, harrasment of women for dowry, murder, etc. It begins with lodging an FIR with the police who investigates the crime. After the investigation the case is filed in the court. Under this law, if the accused is found guilty, he/she can be sent to jail and also fined.

9. Explain civil law as a branch of the legal system.

Ans. Civil case deals with any harm or injury to the rights of individuals.

The examples of civil cases are sale of land, rent matters, divorce cases, etc. A petition has to be filed in the relevant party by the affected party only. Under this, if the accused is found guilty, the court gives specific relief that is asked for.

10. Explain the role of the judge in the Indian criminal system. Diksha

Ans. The role of the judge in the Indian criminal system is as follows

- To conduct the trial in an impartial and open court.
- To see all evidences and hear all witnesses
- To give a judgement on the innocence or guilt of the accused person.
- To pronounce the sentence if the accused is convicted.

11. "While the courts are available for all, in reality access to courts has always been difficult for a vast majority of the poor in India. Legal procedures involve a lot of money and paperwork as well as take up a lot of time."

(i) How did the Supreme Court tried to solve these problems? Competency Based

Ans. The Supreme Court tried to solve these problems by devising the concept of Public Interest Litigation or PIL.

It made the access to courts easy for poor people by allowing anyone to file a case on behalf of victims. It also simplified the judicial procedures.

(ii) Give example of any one success story of this initiative of Supreme Court.

Ans. One of the successful examples of the PIL includes the Mid-day meal programme in schools. Under this programme, the children in government and government aided schools are provided with free meals.

Long Answer Type Questions

1. Discuss the ways through which the independence of judiciary is ensured.

Ans. The independence of judiciary is ensured in the following ways

- The independence of the judiciary shall be guaranteed by the State and enshrined in the Constitution or the law of the country. It is the duty of all governmental and other institutions to respect and observe the independence of the judiciary.
- The judiciary shall decide matters in accordance with the law, without any restrictions, improper influences, pressures, threats or interferences.
- The judiciary shall have jurisdiction over all issues of a judicial nature and shall have exclusive authority to decide whether an issue submitted for its decision is within its competence as defined by law.
- It is essential that all the judges shall be appointed without any interference from other branches of the government.
- It is the duty of each Member State to provide adequate resources to enable the judiciary to properly perform its functions.

2. District courts are the most accessible courts for litigants, and High Courts and the Supreme Court are the higher courts that hear appeals from district courts. Describe the structure of courts in India. Competency Based

Ans. The structure of courts in India is pyramidal, with the Supreme Court at the apex, followed by the High Courts, and then the District Courts and Subordinate Courts.

The three different levels of courts in India are as follows

(i) **District Court** The District or Subordinate Courts are at the district /tehsil/ town level. They are presided over by a District Judge. The district court is known by several names such as the Trial court or the court of district judge, the additional sessions judge, Chief Judicial Magistrate, Metropolitan Magistrate, Civil Judge.

(ii) **High Court** High Courts exist at the state level and they are the highest court of the state. There are 25 High Courts in India. The first High Courts were established in the three presidency states of Bombay, Calcutta and Madras in 1862.

(iii) **Supreme Court** It is the top most court in India which is located at New Delhi. It was established on 26th January, 1950 and is presided over by the Chief Justice of India. The decisions made by the Supreme Court are binding on all other courts in India.

3. What are the differences between different branches of the legal system?

Ans. The legal system is divided into two main branches i.e. criminal law and civil law.

The differences between them are as follows

Criminal Law	Civil Law
It deals with conduct or acts that the law defines as offences.	It deals with any harm or injury to the rights of individuals.
The examples of criminal cases are theft, harrasment of women for dowry, murder, etc.	The examples of civil cases are sale of land, rent matters, divorce cases, etc.
It begins with lodging an FIR with the police who investigates the crime. After the investigation the case is filed in the court.	A petition has to be filed in the relevant party by the affected party only.
Under this law, if the accused is found guilty, he/she can be sent to jail and also fined.	Under this law, if the accused is found guilty, the court gives specific relief that is asked for.

4. Discuss the role of PIL in Indian judiciary. What values have you learnt from the of PIL in Indian judicial system?

Ans. The role of PIL in Indian judiciary is to increase the access to justice of the people. Through PIL, any individual or organisation can approach the court on behalf of those whose rights have been violated.

It had simplified the legal process as even a letter or telegram addressed to the Supreme Court or High Court could be treated as a PIL.

The values which I have learnt from the PIL in Indian judicial system are as follows

- **Justice for all** The system of PIL provides justice to all people even if they cannot read or write or they are poor.
- **Equality** PIL has established equality in the justice system by easing the access to courts even for the lower strata of the society.
- **Fairness** PIL upholds fairness by providing necessary and correct justice.

Picture Based Question

1. The following is a poster made by the Right to Food campaign. NCERT

Read this poster and list the duties of the government to uphold the Right to Food.

How does the phrase "Hungry stomachs, overflowing godowns! We will not accept it!!" used in the poster relate to the photo essay on the Right to Food on.

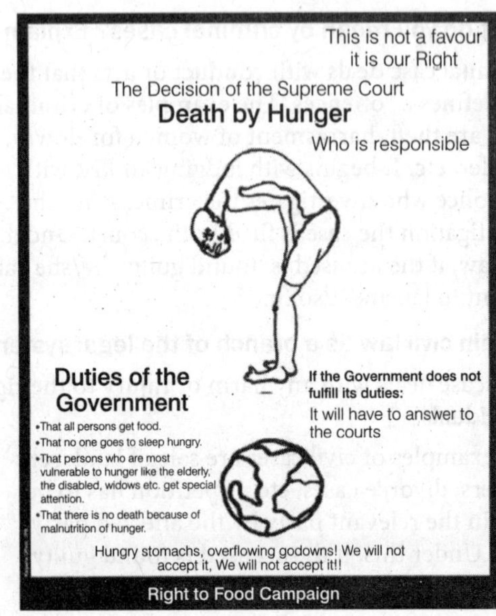

Ans. Duties of the government to uphold the Right to Food are

- All persons should get food.
- No one should go to sleep with a hungry stomach.
- Persons who are most vulnerable to hunger like the elderly, disabled, widows etc., should get special attention.
- There should not be any death because of malnutrition or hunger.

The Phrase "Hungry stomachs, overflowing godowns! We will not accept it!!" is related to the photo essay on the Right to Food as both captured the same sentiments of people.

According to the photo essay, in 2001, millions of people faced shortage of food due to drought in Rajasthan and Orissa. However, the government godowns were full of grains and even getting wasted. This situation of hunger amidst plenty of food was not acceptable to people. This sentiment is also captured in the poster for 'Right to Food' campaign.

Case Based Question

1. Read the passage given below and answer the questions that follows.

The judgment of the Olga Tellis vs. Bombay Municipal Corporation established the Right to Livelihood as part of the Right to Life. The following excerpts from the judgment point to the ways in which the judges linked the issue of the Right to Life to that of livelihood:

The sweep of the Right to Life, conferred by Article 21 is wide and far-reaching. 'Life' means something more than mere animal existence. It does not mean merely that life cannot be extinguished or taken away as, for example, by the imposition and execution of the death sentence, except according to procedure established by law. That is but one aspect of the Right to Life. An equally important facet of that right is the right to livelihood because no person can live without the means of living, that is, the means of livelihood. That the eviction of a person from a pavement or slum will inevitably lead to the deprivation of his means of livelihood, is a proposition which does not have to be established in each individual case .... In the present case that facts constituting empirical.evidence justify the conclusion that the petitioners live in slums and on pavements Becouse they have small jobs to nurse in the city and for them there is nowhere else to live. They choose a pavement or a slum in the vicinity of their place of work and to loose the pavement or the slum is to loose the job.

The conclusion therefore is that the eviction of the petitioners will lead to deprivation of their livelihood and consequently to the deprivation of life.

(i) What is the Right to Life?

Ans. The Right to Life is a fundamental right enshrined in Article 21 of the Indian Constitution. It guarantees the right to life and personal liberty to all persons in India.

(ii) What do you mean by the Right to Livelihood?

Ans. The Right to Livelihood is the right to earn a living and to have the means to support oneself and one's family.

(iii) How did the judges in the Olga Tellis case link the Right to Life to the Right to Livelihood?

Ans. The judges in the Olga Tellis case linked the Right to Life to the Right to Livelihood by stating that life cannot be lived without the means of livelihood.

They held that eviction from a pavement or slum would lead to the deprivation of livelihood and consequently to the deprivation of life.

ASSESSMENT EXERCISE

Multiple Choice Questions (MCQs)

1. Judiciary provides a mechanism for resolving disputes between
(a) citizen and government (b) two states
(c) Centre and State Governments (d) All of these

2. The final interpreter of the Constitution is
(a) Executive (b) Legislative
(c) Judiciary (d) None of these

3. The highest Judicial authority in our country is
(a) Supreme Court (b) High Court
(c) Tehsil Court (d) None of the above

4. Harassing a woman to bring more dowry comes under
(a) Criminal Law (b) Civil Law
(c) Both (a) and (b) (d) None of these

Subjective Questions (VSA, SA & LA)

1. What is Judicial system?

2. Define PIL.

3. Define separation of power.

4. How many High Courts are there in India?

5. Name the three levels of court.

6. Write a short note on Judicial Review.

7. Write a short note on Independent Judiciary.

8. Differentiate Civil and Criminal law.

9. List two reasons why Public Interest Litigation is important in judiciary.

10. What is Appellate system? Discuss.

Understanding Marginalisation

CHAPTER 5

Marginalisation means when a certain person or a sect of people are made to feel of lesser importance, by those in power. Their demands are usually overheard and their desires and dreams are ignored by society. In this chapter, we will learn about few sections of our society that have faced marginalisation which includes, Adivasis and various minorities.

Marginalisation is a situation where a group of people or community are excluded from the society or treated differently from majority.

People or community can be marginalised because they speak a different language, follow different customs or belong to a different religious group from the majority community.

They may also feel marginalised because they are poor, considered to be of 'low' social status and viewed as being less human than others. Sometimes, marginalised groups are viewed with hostility and fear.

The **sense of difference** and **exclusion** leads to communities not having access to resources and opportunities and in their inability to assert their rights.

Economic, social, cultural and political factors work together to make certain groups in society feel marginalised.

5.1 Adivasis

The term Adivasis literally means **original inhabitants**. They are the communities who lived and often continue to live in close association with forests.

In India, there are 500 different Adivasi groups and they constitute 8% of the India's population. Many of India's most important mining and industrial centres are located in Adivasi areas like Jamshedpur, Rourkela, Bokaro aand Bhilai.

Adivasis exist in large numbers in Chhattisgarh, Jharkhand, Madhya Pradesh, Odisha, Gujarat, Maharashtra, Rajasthan, Andhra Pradesh, West Bengal, and in the North-Eastern states of Arunachal Pradesh, Assam, Manipur, Meghalaya, Mizoram, Nagaland and Tripura. There are more than 60 different tribal groups in Odisha.

Characteristics of Adivasis

Some of the features of Adivasis are as follows

- They practice a range of tribal religions that are different from Islam, Hinduism and Christianity.
- They worship ancestors, village and nature spirits. The ancestors are worshipped at home while the village spirits are often worshipped at specific sacred groves within the village boundary.

  The nature spirits are associated with and resides in various sites in the landscape like 'mountain-spirits', 'river-spirits', 'animal-spirits', etc.
- Adivasis have their own languages like **Santhali** which has the largest number of speakers. The languages of Adivasis have deeply influenced the formation of **mainstream**[1] Indian languages, like Bengali.
- There is very little hierarchy among adivasis. This makes them completely different from communities organised around principles of jati-varna (caste) or those that were ruled by kings.
- Adivasis have been influenced by surrounding religions such as Buddhist, Shakta, Vaishnav, Bhakti and Christianity, etc.
- Adivasi religion have also influenced the dominant religions of the empires around them. For example, Jagannath cult of Odisha and Shakti, and tantric traditions in Bengal and Assam.

KNOWLEDGE PLUS Tribals are also referred to as adivasis. The term 'Scheduled Tribe' is used for Adivasis by the Indian government in various official documents.

1 **Mainstream** It means the most common or popular things or ideas that most people follow or are aware of in a society or culture.

5.2 Adivasis and Stereotyping

In India, Adivasi communities are portrayed in very stereotypical ways. They are shown in colourful costumes, headgears and through their dancing, etc.

There is very limited information about the realities of the lives of Adivasis due to which people believed that they are exotic, primitive and backward.

Adivasis are criticised for their lack of advancement as they are believed to be resistant to change or new ideas.

Adivasis and Development

Forests covered the major part of India till the nineteenth century. In the middle of 19th century, adivasis had access to forests and had a deep knowledge about them. They were not ruled by large states and empires. Rather, empires heavily depended on adivasis for access to forest resources.

In the pre-colonial world, adivasis were hunter-gatherers and nomads and lived by shifting agriculture. However, for the past 200 years, adivasis have been increasingly forced to migrate to live as workers in plantations, at construction sites, in industries and as domestic workers.

Importance of Forests

Forests were important to the development of all empires and settled civilisations in India in the following ways

- Metal ores like iron and copper, and gold and silver, coal and diamonds were extracted from forests.
- Timber, most of the medicinal herbs and animal products were obtained from forests.
- Animals like elephants which were essential for imperial armies were acquired from the forests.
- The continuation of life depended on forests because these help to recharge many of India's rivers, and are essential for the availability and quality of air and water.

Displacement of Adivasis

Previously, adivasis lived in areas that are rich in minerals and other natural resources. However, the lands of Adivasis are taken over for mining and other large industrial projects which led to their**displacement** [2]. Forest lands have been cleared for timber and to get land for agriculture and industry.

According to official figures, more than 50 per cent of persons displaced due to mines and mining projects are tribals. Another recent survey report shows that 79 per cent of the persons that are displaced from the states of Andhra Pradesh, Chhattisgarh, Odisha and Jharkhand, are tribals.

In the North east, Adivasis' lands remain highly **militarised** [3]. India has 101 national parks covering 40,564 sq km and 543 wildlife sanctuaries covering 1,19,776 sq km. These are areas where tribals originally lived. When Adivasis continue to stay in these forests, they are termed as**encroachers** [4].

Result of Displacement of Adivasis

Adivasis have lost their main sources of livelihood and food as a result of losing their lands and access to the forest. Thus, many Adivasis have migrated to cities in search of work where they are employed for very low wages in local industries or at building or construction sites.

Adivasis get caught in a cycle of poverty and deprivation. 45 per cent of tribal groups in rural areas and 35 per cent in urban areas live below the poverty line. This leads to deprivation in other areas.

Many tribal children face**malnourishment** [5]. Literacy rates among tribals are also very low.

When Adivasis are displaced from their lands, they also lose their traditions and customs.

5.3 Minorities and Marginalisation

The term **minority** is used to refer to communities that are numerically small in comparison to the rest of the population. This concept also includes the issue of power, access to resources and has social and cultural dimensions.

Minority communities may feel insecure about their lives, assets and well-being. This sense of insecurity may increase if the relations between the minority and majority communities become strained.

The Constitution of India provides safeguards to minorities to protect them against the possibility of being culturally dominated by majority. These safeguards also protects them against any discrimination and disadvantage.

The Constitution provides these safeguards because it is committed to protecting India's cultural diversity and promoting equality as well as justice.

---

2 **Displacement** It refers to the act of moving someone from its original or current place to a different place.

3 **Militarised** It refers to an area where the presence of the armed forces is considerable.

4 **Encroachers** It refers to a person who occupies a piece of land unlawfully.

5 **Malnourishment** It is a condition where a person or organism does not receive the proper nutrients such as vitamins, minerals and calories needed for their overall health and well-being.

Muslims and Marginalisation

Muslims are a marginalised community in India which constitute 14.2 per cent of India's population as per the 2011 census. They are considered as a marginalised community because they have been deprived of the benefits of the **socio-economic development**.

They are deprived of basic amenities, literacy and public employment. They are lagging behind on the a range of social, economic and educational indicators.

The economic and social marginalisation that Muslims experience also have other dimensions. The customs and practices of Muslims like other minorities, are different from the mainstream.

For example, some may wear a ***burqa***, sport a long beard and wear a ***fez***. Due to these practices they are identified differently and thought to be different from rest of the population. This leads to their unfair treatment and discrimination against them. The effects of this social marginalisation of the Muslims are

- Migration of the community leading to **ghettoisation**[6].
- Hatred and violence against them in some cases.

Justice Rajinder Sachar Committee

It was a high level committee that was set up in 2005 to examine the social, economic and educational status of the Muslim community in India. It was chaired by **Justice Rajinder Sachar.**

It suggests that the situation of Muslims is comparable to other marginalised communities like Scheduled Castes and Scheduled Tribes, on a range of social, economic and educational indicators.

Conclusion

Marginalisation is a complex phenomenon requiring a variety of strategies, measures and safeguards to redress it. There are different reasons for each of these communities being marginalised. Each experiences marginalisation in different ways.

Marginalisation is linked to experiencing disadvantage, prejudice and powerlessness. It results in having a low social status and not having equal access to education and other resources.

6 **Ghettoisation** It refers to the process or result of isolating or segregating a particular group of people, often based on social, economic or cultural factors, into a specific area or neighbourhood.

UNDERSTANDING MARGINALISATION

Minorities and Marginalisation

- Minorities refers to communities, numerically small in comparison to the rest of the population.
- Muslims constitute 14.2% of the India's population forming a marginalised community.
- The customs and practices of Muslims are thought to be different from rest of the population which leads to discrimination.

Marginalisation

When a group of people or community are excluded from the society or treated differently from majority.

Adivasis and Development

Adivasis previously survived as hunter gatherers and nomads, later they live as workers at construction sites, industries, etc.

Adivasis

- Refer to original inhabitants.
- There are 500 different adivasi groups and constitute 8% of India's population.
- There are more than 60 tribal groups in Odisha.

Displacement of Adivasis

- More than 50% of persons are displaced due to mines and mining projects.
- In North-East, Adivasis lands remain highly militarised.

Adivasis and Stereotyping

- Adivasis are potrayed by colourful costumes, headgears and through their dancing, etc.
- Adivasis are criticised for their lack of advancement.

NCERT FOLDER

Covering Intext Questions and Exercises of NCERT

NCERT ON PAGE 65

Q. 1. Explain at least three different reasons why groups may be marginalised.

Ans. Groups may be marginalised because of the following reasons

(i) Different spoken languages

(ii) Different customs and religions

(iii) Low social status

Q. 2. Why was Dadu forced to leave his village in Orissa?

Ans. Dadu was forced to leave his village in Orissa because the company wallahs took away his ancestral land there for mining the iron ore under it.

Q.3 In your own city or village, who would you think are the marginalised groups? Discuss.

Ans. In my city, Dalits are the marginalised groups because the Dalits are forced to employ themselves in unclean occupations and treated unfairly by the society. Also they face discrimination by the society.

Q.4 (i) Can you name some Adivasi communities that live in your state?

Ans. Bhil and gond are some Adivasi community that live in my state.

(ii) What languages do they speak?

Ans. They speak their own languages. The Gonds speak Gondi and the Bhils speak their own language.

(iii) Do they live close to the forest?

Ans. Yes, they live close to the forests.

(iv) Do they migrate to other regions looking for work?

Ans. Yes, when the forest officials and contractors evict them from their lands, they migrate to other regions for work.

NCERT ON PAGE 67

Q.5 What metals are important in present-day India? Why? Where do they come from? Are there Adivasi populations there?

Ans. Metals like iron and aluminium are important in present-day India.

They are important as they are required for building infrastructure including roads, bridges, rail-lines, aeroplanes, etc.

They come from the mines of iron ore and aluminium ore under forest lands.

Yes, there are Adivasi populations inhabiting these places.

Q.6 List five products that you use at home that come from the forest.

Ans. Five forest based products that we use at home are gum, lac, honey, fruit and timber.

Q.7 By whom were the following demands being made on forest land?

(i) Timber for construction of houses and railways

Ans. Builders, contractors and timber merchants

(ii) Forest land for mining.

Ans. Private and public sector companies.

(iii) Forest land for agriculture by non-tribal people.

Ans. Rich farmers.

(iv) Reserved by government as wildlife parks.

Ans. Government department

(v) In what ways would this affect tribal people?

Ans. This would affect the lives of tribal people as they will be forced to migrate elsewhere in search of work.

NCERT ON PAGE 69

Q. 8 In your opinion, why is it important that Adivasis should have a say in how their forests and forest lands are used?

Ans. Adivasis should have a say in how their forests and forest lands are used because the decisions of the government agencies on these matters affect their lives and livelihood directly.

NCERT ON PAGE 70

Q. 9 Why do we need safeguards for minorities?

Ans. We need safeguards for minorities in order to protect them from any discrimination or domination by the majority because of their smaller numbers. Also these safeguards will help to protect India's cultural diversity.

Q.10 Study the following data.

Access to Basic Amenities, 2008-2009

Religious community	Pucca house	Electricity	Tap water
Hindu	65.4	75.2	43.7
Muslim	63.8	67.5	35.8
Christian	69.3	86.2	48.0
Sikh	91.3	96.0	49.3

Source – India Human Development Report, 2011 Towards social inclusion, Oxford University Press for Institute of Applied Manpower Research, Planning Commission, Government of India, New Delhi.

Which of these communities have the most and the least access to basic amenities?

Ans. Sikhs have the most access to basic amenities while the Muslims have the least access to basic amenities.

NCERT ON PAGE 71

Q.10 Study the following data

Literacy Rate by Religion, 2011 (Percentages)

All	74
Hindus	63
Muslims	57
Christians	74
Sikhs	67
Buddhists	71
Jains	86

Source - Census of India, 2011

Which of these communities have the highest and the lowest literacy rate ?

Ans. Jains have the highest literacy rate while the Muslims have the lowest literacy rate.

Q.11 Study the following data

Public Employment of Muslims (percentages)

Population	IAS	IPS	IFS	Central Public Sector Unit (PSU)	State PSU	Banks and RBI
13.5	3	4	1.8	3.3	10.8	2.2

Source – Social, Economic and Educational Status of the Muslim Community of India, Prime Minister's high level committee report 2006.

What do these figure convey?

Ans. These figures convey that in comparison to their total population, Muslims do not have proper representation in public employment. Share of employment of Muslims in state PSU is better than in other sectors.

Q.12 Read the data related to schooling provided by the Sachar Committee Report:

25 per cent of Muslim children in the 6-14 years age group have either never been enrolled in school or have dropped out. This percentage is much higher than that of any other socio-religious community.

Do you think special measures are required to address this situation?

Ans. Yes, special measures are required to address this situation. Government can introduce free school books, school dresses, nutritious food for all to attract the children.

EXERCISES

Q.1 Write in your own words two or more sentences of what you understand by the word 'marginalisation'.

Ans. Marginalisation refers to the low social status of minorities and their unequal access to public resources. Members of minority communities face marginalisation because of their smaller numbers. Marginalisation can be social, economic, political and cultural.

Q.2 List two reasons why Adivasis are becoming increasingly marginalised.

Ans. Two reasons why Adivasis are becoming marginalised are as follows

(i) They have distinct culture and traditions.

(ii) Their religious practices are different from that of the majority community.

Q.3 Write one reason why you think the Constitutions' safeguards to protect minority communities are very important.

Ans. The Constitution's safeguards to protect minority communities are very important because they are numerically small in number and could possibly be dominated and discriminated against by the majority.

Q.4 Re-read the section on 'Minorities and Marginalisation'. What do you understand by the term minority?

Ans. The term minority refers to any community which is numerically smaller in number in comparison to the rest of the population.

Q.5 You are participating in a debate where you have to provide reasons to support the following statement : 'Muslims are a marginalised community.' Using the data provided in this chapter, list two reasons that you would give.

Ans. Muslims are a marginalised community because-

(i) The representation of Muslims in public employment is not in proportion to their population.

(ii) The literacy rate of Muslims is the least in India as compared to the other communities and much below the national average.

Q.6 Imagine that you are watching the Republic Day parade on TV with a friend and she remarks, "Look at these tribals. They look so exotic. And they seem to be dancing all the time." List three things that you would tell her about the lives of Adivasis in India.

Ans. I would tell her the following about the lives of Adivasis in India

(i) Adivasis have a distinct culture of their own that is different from the mainstream.

(ii) They speak in their own language and have their own customs.

(iii) They live in close association with forests.

Q.7 In the storyboard you read about how Helen hopes to make a movie on the Adivasis story. Can you help her by developing a short story on Adivasis?

Ans. Do it yourself.

Q.8 Would you agree with the statement that economic marginalisation and social marginalisation are interlinked? Why?

Ans. Yes, I agree with the statement that economic and social marginalisation are interlinked as the social marginalisation of a particular community does not allows them to enjoy the economic benefits. Hence, they also become economic marginalised.

REVIEW EXERCISE

Including Competency Based Questions

PART I

Multiple Choice Questions (MCQs)

1. A group can be marginalised on what among the following aspects?

(a) Language (b) Customs
(c) Religion (d) All of these

2. Where did Adivasis live?

(a) Kutcha houses (b) Pacca houses
(c) Colonies (d) In/near forests

3. Tribals are also referred to as

(a) Adivasis (b) Muslims (c) Minorities (d) Dalits

4. Stereotyping particular communities can lead to people discriminating against such groups. **Diksha**

(a) False (b) Partially False
(c) True (d) Partially True

5. What percentage of India's total population is comprised of Muslims (2011)?

(a) 7 Per cent (b) 15 Per cent
(c) 14.2 Per cent (d) 45 Per cent

6. A ghetto is an area / locality populated by

(a) poor people
(b) members of a particular community
(c) malnourished people
(d) displaced people

7. The Justice Sachar Committee was set-up in the year ....

(a) 1995 (b) 2001 (c) 2005 (d) 2008

8. Poonam, a girl from Jharkhand belongs to the Santhal tribal community. Recently she along with her family was forced to migrate to a new city after a company bought their land for setting up an oil refinery.

Which of the following will likely be experienced by Poonam's family? **Competency Board**

(a) A comfortable environment in the new city.
(b) A very low wage employment in the new city.
(c) Enjoyment of their traditional festivals in the new city.
(d) Whole hearted welcome of her family by the people of majority community in the new city.

9. Recently, the Minister of Culture, Tourism and Development of the North-Eastern Region in Rajya Sabha has pointed out various schemes and programmes that are introduced by the government with an aim of protecting, preserving, and promoting the country's tribal cultural heritage. **Competency Board**

Source: Times of India

Which of the following issues are faced by the Tribes in India? Choose the correct options.

I. One of the most significant issues faced by tribal communities is the lack of secure land rights.

II. Tribal populations often experience socio-economic marginalisation, including poverty and lack of access to quality education and healthcare.

III. Rapid urbanisation and modernisation can lead to the erosion of tribal cultures, languages and traditional practices.

Options

(a) I and II (b) II and III
(c) I and III (d) I, II, III

10. Identify the correct option through the following description. **Competency Board**

I. It refers to a fixed belief about a group of people based on generalisation.

II. It disregards the individual charateristics.

Options

(a) Marginalisation (b) Ghettoisation
(c) Stereotypes (d) Displacement

11. **Which one of the following statements is correct?** **Competency Board**

I. Marginalisation is often experienced in both economic and social spheres.

II. The most important mining and industrial centres in India are located in Adivasi areas.

Codes

(a) Only I (b) Both I and II
(b) Only II (d) None of these

12. **Which one of the following statements is correct?** **Competency Board**

I. Adivasis practice a range of tribal religions that are different from Islam, Hinduism and Christianity.

II. Adivasi societies are often less hierarchical than communities organised around principles of jati-varna (caste) or those that were ruled by the king.

Codes

(a) Only I (b) Both I and II
(c) Only II (d) None of these

Answers

1. (d) **2.** (d) **3.** (a) **4.** (c) **5.** (c)
6. (b) **7.** (c) **8.** (b) **9.** (c) **10.** (c)
11. (b) **12.** (b)

Match the Following

1.

	List I		List II
A.	Muslim	1.	Industrial area
B.	Adivasis	2.	Rural areas
C.	45% of tribal groups	3.	Burqa
D.	Bokaro	4.	Scheduled tribe

Codes

	A	B	C	D		A	B	C	D
(a)	3	4	2	1	(b)	2	4	3	1
(c)	4	1	2	3	(d)	4	2	3	1

2.

List I	List II
A. Minorities	1. Muslim educational institutions
B. Muslim community	2. Constitutional safeguard
C. Dongarriya Konds	3. Sachar Committee
D. Madarsas	4. Odisha

Codes

	A	B	C	D		A	B	C	D
(a)	4	3	2	1	(b)	1	4	3	2
(c)	2	3	4	1	(d)	3	1	2	4

Ans. 1. (a) 2. (c)

Assertion-Reason

1. **Assertion** (A) Adivasi have a strong connection to the land.

Reason (R) Adivasis traditionally rely on the land for their livelihood and believe that the land is sacred.

Codes

(a) Both A and R are true and R is the correct explanation of A
(b) Both A and R are true, but R is not the correct explanation of A
(c) A is true, but R is false
(d) A is false, but R is true

2. **Assertion** (A) Forests are important for the environment.

Reason (R) Forests help to clean the air and water and they provide habitats for many different plants and animals.

Codes

(a) Both A and R are true and R is the correct explanation of A
(b) Both A and R are true, but R is not the correct explanation of A
(c) A is true, but R is false
(d) A is false, but R is true

Ans. 1. (a) Both A and R are true and R is the correct explanation of A

2. (a) Both A and R are true and R is the correct explanation of A

Fill in the Blanks

1. According to official figures, more than 50 per cent of persons displaced due to mining projects are ....

2. The tribal language .... has the highest number of speakers.

3. 45 per cent of tribal groups in rural areas and 35 per cent in urban areas live below the .... line.

4. .... have been cleared to get land for agriculture and industry.

Ans. 1. tribals 2. Santhali
3. poverty 4. Forests

True/False

1. Adivasis are exotic, primitive and backward.

2. Many tribal children are well-nourished.

3. Adivasi languages are influenced by mainstream Indian languages.

4. Literacy rates among tribals are very low.

5. Dalits in India are a marginalised community.

Ans. 1. False 2. False
3. False 4. True
5. True

Picture Based Questions

1. Look at the picture given below and answer the questions that follow.

Which of the following is not a reason why it is important to respect tribal cultures and traditions?

(a) Tribal people have their own unique cultures and traditions.
(b) Tribal people have a right to live their lives according to their own beliefs.
(c) Tribal cultures and traditions are often sustainable and harmonious with nature.
(d) Tribal cultures and traditions can help to promote diversity and cultural enrichment.

2. This is a photo of the Niyamgiri Hills. Where are the Niyamgiri Hills located?

(a) Odisha (b) Jharkhand (c) Tamil Nadu (d) Chhattisgarh

Ans. 1. (d) Tribal cultures and traditions can help to promote diversity and cultural enrichment.
2. (a) Odisha

Case Based Question

1. Read the given passage below and answer the questions that follow

In India, we usually 'showcase' Adivasi communities in particular ways. Thus, during school functions or other official events or in books and movies, Adivasi are invariably portrayed in very stereotypical ways – in colourful costumes, headgear and through their dancing. Besides this, we seem to know very little about the realities of their lives. This often wrongly leads to people believing that they are exotic, primitive and backward. Often Adivasi's are blamed for their lack of advancement as they are believed to be resistant to change or new ideas.

(i) Which of the following options correctly describes the portrayal of the tribal communities during public events?

(a) In modern clothing and lifestyles
(b) In traditional costumes and headgear, often dancing
(c) Through high-tech gadgets and technology
(d) As urban professionals

(ii) What misconception can arise from the stereotypical portrayal of Adivasis?

(a) They are highly advanced and urbanised.
(b) They are the most educated group in India.
(c) They are responsible for India's economic growth.
(d) They are exotic, primitive, and backward.

(iii) Which of the following is a stereotype related to the Adivasi community?

(a) They are highly receptive to change.
(b) They are given too many opportunities.
(c) They are resistant to change or new ideas.
(d) They have access to modern technology.

(iv) Which of the following is not a stereotypical way in which Adivasi are portrayed in India?

(a) In colourful costumes, headgear and through their dancing
(b) Intelligent and progressive
(c) Exotic, primitive, and backward
(d) Being resistant to change or new ideas

Ans. (i) (b) In traditional costumes and headgear, often dancing
(ii) (d) They are exotic, primitive, and backward.
(iii) (c) They are resistant to change or new ideas.
(iv) (b) Intelligent and progressive

Part II

Very Short Answer Type Questions

1. Which states do the Shakti and Tantric traditions belong to?

Ans. The Shakti and Tantric traditions belong to the states of West Bengal and Assam.

2. How many Adivasi groups are there in India?

Ans. There are over 500 different Adivasi groups in India.

3. How many tribal groups are there in Orissa?

Ans. There are over 60 different tribal groups in Orissa.

4. What do you mean by the term 'Scheduled Tribes'?

Ans. 'Scheduled Tribes' is a term used to refer to Adivasis. This term is used by the Indian Government in official documents.

5. What is the general perception about Adivasis?

Ans. The general perception about Adivasis is that they are primitive, backward and resistant to change.

6. Why have many Adivasis migrated to cities?

Ans. Adivasis have migrated to cities in search of work after losing their land and livelihood.

7. "When Adivasis are displaced from their lands, they lose much more than a source of income." Justify this statement by giving one argument. **Competency Board**

Ans. When Adivasis are displaced from their lands, apart from a source of income, they also lose their traditions and customs i.e. a way of living and being.

8. What was the lifestyle of Adivasis in pre-colonial India?

Ans. In pre-colonial India, Adivasis were traditionally hunter-gatherers and nomads.

9. How are Muslims usually identified?

Ans. Muslims are usually identified by their burqa, long beard and fez.

10. Which factor leads to ghettoisation of the Muslim community?

Ans. The social marginalisation of the Muslim community leads to its ghettoisation.

11. Who chaired the Sachar Committee?

Ans. The Sachar Committee was chaired by Justice Rajindar Sachar.

12. What do you mean by ghettoisation

Ans. Ghettoisation refers to the process or result of isolating or segregating a particular group of people, often based on social, economic or cultural factors, into a specific area or neighbourhood.

Short Answer Type Questions

1. How are Adivasi societies different from the mainstream?

Ans. Adivasi societies are distinctive because there is often very little or no hierarchy among them. This makes them radically different from mainstream communities organised around principles of jati–varna (caste) or those that were ruled by kings. They have their own culture, customs, religions, etc.

2. What do you mean by 'stereotyping'? Is it good or bad? Why?

Ans. Stereotyping means seeing and presenting a community of people in particular ways without having full knowledge of the reality of their lives. For example, Adivasis are usually depicted in colourful costumes and headgear.

Stereotyping is not good because it leads to wrong notions about a particular community and on that basis, discriminating against it.

3. Explain how the Adivasis are portrayed in India.

Ans. In India, Adivasi communities are portrayed in very stereotypical ways. They are shown in colourful costumes, headgears and through their dancing, etc.

There is very limited information about the realities of the lives of Adivasis due to which people believed that they are exotic, primitive and backward.

Adivasis are criticised for their lack of advancement as they are believed to be resistant to change or new ideas.

4. Write a short note on displacement of the Adivasis.

Ans. Previously, Adivasis lived in areas that are rich in minerals and other natural resources. However, the lands of Adivasis are taken over for mining and other large industrial projects which led to their displacement. Forest lands have been cleared for timber and to get land for agriculture and industry.

According to official figures, more than 50 per cent of persons displaced due to mines and mining projects are tribals. Another recent survey report shows that 79 per cent of the persons that are displaced from the states of Andhra Pradesh, Chhattisgarh, Odisha and Jharkhand, are tribals.

5. According to the 2011 Census, what percentage of India's population is Muslim, and why are they considered a marginalised community?

Ans. Muslims are a minority community in India who constitute 14.2 per cent of India's population as per the 2011 census.

They are also considered as a marginalised community because they have been deprived of the benefits of the socio-economic development. They are lagging behind on a range of social, economic and educational indicators.

6. What are the main challenges faced by the Muslim community in India? **Competency Board**

Ans. Muslims face the following challenges in India

- Unfair treatment and discrimination.
- Migration of the community leading to ghettoisation.
- Hatred and violence in some cases.

7. Why was the Sachar committee set up ? What did it suggests?

Ans. Sachar committee was a high level committee that was set up in 2005 to examine the social, economic and educational status of the Muslim community in India.

It suggests that the situation of Muslims is comparable to other marginalised communities on a range of social, economic and educational indicators.

8. **"Adivasis use around 10,000 plant species – approximately 8,000 species are used for medicinal purpose; 325 are used as pesticides; 425 as gums, resins and dyes; 550 as fibres; 3,500 are edible. This entire knowledge system gets wiped out when Adivasis lose their forest lands."** **Competency Based**

(i) **What does the above paragraph tells about the Adivasis?**

(ii) **What causes led to the loss of forest land of the Adivasis?**

Ans. (i) The above paragraph shows that Adivasis have a close connection with forests and their entire life and well being depends on forest as they use various forest resources for different purposes. This also shows the importance of forests in their life and livelihood.

(ii) Various developmental activities such as mining, large industrial projects, construction of big dams, etc led to the loss of the lands of Adivasis. It also led to their displacement.

Long Answer Type Questions

1. **Explain the concepts of minorities and marginalisation in detail.** **Diksha**

Ans. The term minority is used to refer to communities that are numerically small in comparison to the rest of the population. This concept also includes the issue of power, access to resources and has social and cultural dimensions.

Marginalisation is a complex phenomenon requiring a variety of strategies, measures and safeguards to redress it. There are different reasons for each of these communities being marginalised. Each experiences marginalisation in different ways.

Marginalisation is linked to experiencing disadvantage, prejudice and powerlessness. It results in having a low social status and not having equal access to education and other resources.

2. **Explain how economic, social, cultural and political factors work together to make certain groups in society feel marginalised?** **Diksha**

Ans. Economic, social, cultural and political factors work together to make certain groups in society feel marginalised in the following ways.

- **Social & Cultural** Certain groups are marginalised because they speak a different language, follow different customs or belong to a different religious group from the majority community.
- **Economic** Certain groups may also feel marginalised because they are poor, considered to be of 'low' social status and viewed as being less human than others.
- **Political** Certain groups experience a sense of disadvantage and powerlessness while more powerful and dominant sections of society who own land, are wealthy, better educated and politically powerful.

3. **Write a short note on Adivasis.**

Ans. The term Adivasi means 'original inhabitants'. They are the communities who lived and often continue to live in close association with forests. Some of the features of Adivasis are as follows

- They practice a range of tribal religions.
- They worship nature , village and ancestral spirits.
- They have their own distinct languages. For example, the Santhali language has the largest number of speakers.
- They have been influenced by surrounding religions such as Buddhists, Shakta, Vaishnav, etc.
- Their religions have also influenced dominant religions. For example, Jagannath cult of Odisha and Shakti and tantric traditions in Bengal and Assam.

4. **Destruction in one sphere naturally impacts the other. Often this process of dispossession and displacement can be painful and violent. How does the Adivasis' life affected due to their displacement? Explain.** **Competency Based**

Ans. Adivasis have lost their main sources of livelihood and food as a result of losing their lands and access to the forest. Thus, many Adivasis have migrated to cities in search of work where they are employed for very low wages in local industries or at building or construction sites.

Adivasis get caught in a cycle of poverty and deprivation. 45 per cent of tribal groups in rural areas and 35 per cent in urban areas live below the poverty line. This leads to deprivation in other areas.

Many tribal children face malnourishment. Literacy rates among tribals are also very low.

When Adivasis are displaced from their lands, they also lose their traditions and customs.

5. **"Marginalised groups feel disadvantaged and powerless compared to wealthier, educated, and politically powerful sections of society. Marginalisation encompasses economic, social, cultural, and political dimensions, reinforcing their sense of exclusion."** **Competency Based**

Who are marginalised groups in India? Discuss.

Ans. Some of the most marginalised groups in India include

- **Scheduled Castes (SCs) and Scheduled Tribes (STs)** SCs and STs are also known as Dalit's and Adivasi's, respectively. They are the most disadvantaged groups in Indian society, and they have historically faced severe discrimination and oppression.
- **Other Backward Classes (OBCs)** OBCs are a diverse group of people who are considered to be socially and educationally backwards.

  They face discrimination in many areas of life, including education, employment and housing.

- **Minorities** Religious minorities in India, such as. Muslims, Christians and Sikhs, often face discrimination and prejudice. They may be denied access to education and employment opportunities and they may be victims of violence.
- **Women** Women in India face a number of challenges, including gender-based discrimination, violence, and lack of access to.education and employment opportunities.
- **People with Disabilities** People with disabilities in India often face discrimination and prejudice. They may be denied access to education and employment opportunities and they may be victims of violence.

Picture Based Question

1. Look at the picture given below and answer the following questions.

(i) What is the literal meaning of the term Adivasi?

Ans. Adivasi literally means original inhabitants.

(ii) In which states of India are Adivasis particularly numerous?

Ans. Adivasis are particularly numerous in states like Chhattisgarh, Jharkhand, Madhya Pradesh, Odisha, Gujarat, Maharashtra, Rajasthan, Andhra Pradesh, West Bengal and in the North-Eastern states of Arunachal Pradesh, Assam, Manipur, Meghalaya, Mizoram, Nagaland and Tripura.

Case Based Question

1. Read the given passage below and answer the questions that follow

From the 1830s onwards, Adivasis from Jharkhand and adjoining areas moved in very large numbers to various plantations in India and the world

Mauritius, the Caribbean and even Australia. India's tea industry became possible with their labour in Assam. Today, there are 70 lakh Adivasis in Assam alone. The story of this migration is full of extreme hardship, torture, heartbreak and death. For example, In the 19th century alone five lakh Adivasis had perished in these migrations. The song below captures the hopes of the migrants and the reality they faced in Assam.

Come Mini,let's go to Assam
Our country has so much suffering
The country of Assam, oh Mini
Has tea gardens full of greenery ....
The Sardar says work, work
The Babu says catch and bring them in
The Saheb says I'll take off the skin of your back
Hey Jaduram, you deceived us by sending us to Assam

What do you think is the poem trying to convey? **NCERT**

Ans. This poem conveys that Adivasis migrated to Assam in hope of getting better work and conditions but in reality they faced different kinds of torture in the plantation.

ASSESSMENT EXERCISE

Multiple Choice Questions (MCQs)

1. Adivasis are particularly numerous in states like
(a) Rajasthan (b) Odisha/Orissa
(c) Jharkhand (d) All of these

2. During 19th century, adivasis converted to which religion?
(a) Hinduism (b) Jainism
(c) Christianity (d) None of these

3. ...... women are an important part of woman's movement in India.
(a) Hindu (b) Muslim
(c) Adivasi women (d) All of these

4. Adivasis are
(a) Schedule Tribe (b) Schedule Caste
(c) Both 'a' and 'b' (d) None of these

Subjective Questions (VSA, SA and LA)

1. Define shifting cultivation.
2. Explain Ghettoisation.
3. What do you mean by Sachar Committee?
4. Name the place where mining and industrial centres are located.
5. Explain Marginalisation with example.
6. Who are called original inhabitants, give some facts related to them?
7. Describe the characteristics of Adivasis.
8. What actions government should take for the betterment of Adivasis?

Confronting Marginalisation

CHAPTER 6

The Adivasis, Dalits, Muslims, women etc come under the marginal groups. Various ways are used by them for **confronting**[1] marginalisation.

These groups argue that as they are citizens of a democratic country, they possess equal rights that must be respected. Many of them look up to the Constitution to address their concerns.

6.1 Invoking Fundamental Rights

The Constitution of India contains Fundamental Rights which are equally available to all the Indians. The marginalised groups have utilised these rights in the following two ways

- They have forced the government to recognise the injustice done to them, by insisting on their Fundamental Rights.
- They have insisted the government to enforce these laws.

Sometimes, the struggles of marginalised groups against the injustice have influenced the government to frame new laws in accordance with the principles of the Fundamental Rights.

Marginalised community like **Dalits**[2] can invoke or use some of the Fundamental Rights in situations where they feel that they have been treated badly by some individual or community, or even by the government. These rights are

- **Article 17** abolished **untouchability**[3] and made it an unlawful and punishable act which is not supported by the democratic government.
  According to it, **no one can prevent Dalits from educating** themselves, entering temples, using public facilities, etc.
- Article 17 is further supported by **Article 15** which states that **no citizen of India shall be discriminated against on the basis of religion, race, caste, sex or place of birth**.

The Fundamental Rights used by the other minority groups include the **right to freedom of religion** and **cultural and educational rights**.

The Constitution grants different forms of cultural rights to ensure cultural justice to minority groups, so that the culture of these groups is not dominated by the culture of the majority groups.

6.2 Laws for the Marginalised

Certain laws and policies have been made especially for the marginalised groups in our country. The government promotes such policies in order to give opportunities to specific groups.

Promoting Social Justice

There are several ways through which the government promotes **social justice**[4]

- Both State and Central governments create specific schemes for implementation in tribal areas or in areas that have a high Dalit population.

For example, the government provides for free or subsidised hostels for students of Dalit and Adivasi communities, so that they can avail of education facilities that may not be available in their localities.

- The government formulates laws to end inequity in the system. One such law/**policy**[5] is the reservation policy. It reserves seats in education and government employment for Dalits and Adivasis.

---

2 **Dalits** Dalit means 'broken'. Dalits belong to the lowest caste group and have often been subjected to social discrimination, segregation and economic hardship.

3 **Untouchability** It refers to the social practice of discriminating against certain groups based on their caste and low social status within the Indian caste system.

4 **Social Justice** It is the concept of ensuring that all individuals and groups in a society have fair and equal access to resources, opportunities and rights.

5 **Policy** It is a predetermined course of action or set of principles that guide decision-making and behaviour within an organisation, government, or society.

Both the Central and State governments have their own list of Scheduled Caste (Dalits), Scheduled Tribes and backward and most backward castes.

If a particular Dalit caste or a certain tribe is mentioned on the government list, then a candidate from that caste or tribe can avail the benefit of reservation.

6.3 Protecting the Rights of Dalits and Adivasis

In addition to policies, our country also has specific laws that guard against the discrimination and exploitation of marginalised communities. One such law is the **Scheduled Castes and the Scheduled Tribes (Prevention of Atrocities) Act** that was framed in 1989.

This act was framed in response to the demands of Dalits and others that the government must take seriously the ill-treatment and humiliation faced by them everyday.

This act lists several levels of crimes against the Dalits and Adivasis which includes the following

- **Modes of Humiliation** It includes both physically and **morally reprehensible**[6] humiliations. For example, forcing a member of a Scheduled Caste or a Scheduled Tribe to drink or eat any inedible or obnoxious (distasteful) substance, forcibly removing their clothes, parading them naked or with painted face, etc.
- **Actions of Dispossession** It includes action like occupying or cultivating any land that is owned by or allotted to a member of a Scheduled Caste or Scheduled Tribe and force them to perform slave labour.
- **Crimes against Women** It includes assaulting or dishonouring any woman belonging to a Scheduled Caste or Scheduled Tribe.

KNOWLEDGE PLUS The central government passed the **Scheduled Tribes and Other Traditional Forest Dwellers (Recognition of Forest Rights) Act, 2006.** This Act recognises the forest dwellers their right to homestead, cultivable and grazing land, and to non-timber forest produce.

6.4 Adivasis Demand and the 1989 Act

The 1989 Act is also important for the Adivasis or the tribals. It confirms that the land belonging to tribal people cannot be sold to or brought by non-tribal people.

The Adivasi activists refer to this law to defend their right to occupy land that was traditionally belonged to them. They demand that those who have forcibly occupied tribal lands should be punished under this law.

A tribal activist named **CK Janu** points out that some State Governments are violators of the constitutional rights of the tribals. It is because they allow non-tribal enchroachers to exploit tribal forest land and forcibly evict the tribals from their lands.

The Scourge of Manual Scavenging

Manual scavenging is the practice of removing human and animal waste/excreta from dry latrines using manual methods and carrying it on head to disposal grounds.

A **manual scavenger** is the person who does the job of carrying this waste. This job is mainly done by people from Dalit communities.

There are several problems faced by manual scavengers which include

- Manual scavengers are exposed to subhuman conditions of work and face serious health hazards.
- They are constantly exposed to infections that affect their eyes, skin, respiratory and gastro-intestinal systems.
- They get very low wages for the work they perform.
- They often live in separate settlements on the outskirts of the village and are denied access to the temple, public water facilities, etc.
- The practice of untouchability has been abolished however, manual scavengers in different parts of the country, like the Bhangis in Gujarat, Pakhis in Andhra Pradesh and the Sikkaliars in Tamil Nadu, continue to be considered untouchable.

In 1993, the **Employment of Manual Scavengers and Construction of Dry Latrines (Prohibition) Act** was passed which prohibits the employment of manual scavengers as well as the construction of dry latrines.

On 6th December, 2013, the **Prohibition of Employment as Manual Scavengers and their Rehabilitation Act** came into force.

Conclusion

It is evident that the existence of a right or a law or even a policy does not mean that it exists in reality. People have to constantly work on or make efforts to translate these into principles that guide the actions of their fellow citizens and political leaders. The desire for equality, dignity and respect is not new and has existed in different forms. Similarly, even in a democratic society, similar processes of struggle, writing, negotiation and organising need to continue.

6 **Morally Reprehensible** It is a term used to describe actions, behaviours, or decisions that are widely considered to be deeply unethical, offensive, or morally wrong.

CONFRONTING MARGINALISATION

Invoking Fundamental Rights

- **Article 17** No one can prevent Dalits from educating themselves, entering temples, using public facilities, etc.
- **Article 15** No citizen of India shall be discriminated against on the basis of religion, race, caste, sex or place of birth.

Laws for the Marginalised

- The government provides for free or subsidised hostels for students of Dalit and Adivasi communities.
- It provides reservation of seats in education and government employment for Dalits and Adivasis.

Adivasis Demand and the 1989 Act

- Land belonging to the tribal people cannot be sold to or brought by non-tribal people.
- Those who have forcibly occupied tribal lands should be punished.

Protecting the Rights of Dalits and Adivasis

- Scheduled Castes and the Scheduled Tribes Act, 1989
- Levels of crimes against the Dalits and Adivasis includes
  - Modes of Humiliation
  - Actions of Dispossession
  - Crimes against Women

NCERT FOLDER

Covering Intext Questions and Exercises of NCERT

NCERT ON PAGE 77

Q.1 State one reason why you think reservations plays an important role in providing social justice to Dalits and Adivasis.

Ans. Reservations plays an important role in providing social justice to Dalits and Adivasis as these create special opportunities for Dalits, Adivasis and other marginalised communities to get seats in educational and professional institutions.

Q.2 Complete the following table.

List of schemes	What is this scheme about?	How do you think it will help to promote social justice?
Scholarships for students		
Special police stations		
Special schemes for girls in government schools		

Ans.

List of Schemes	What is this Scheme about?	How do you think it will help to promote social justice?
Scholarships for students	It provides financial aid to students belonging to weaker sections of society.	It will help students from marginalised and backward sections to get equal education and hence will promote social justice.
Special police stations	It provides special police stations for women , Dalits, etc to record crimes.	It aids in quicker access to justice, faster disposal of cases for marginalised communities.
Special schemes for girls in government schools	These schemes provide nutritional aid, scholarships to meritorious students.	It encourages girls education and promote their welfare in order to bring them at par with boys.

NCERT ON PAGE 79

Q.3 In your opinion does the force put on Rathnam to perform this ritual violate his Fundamental Rights?

Ans. Yes, the force put on Rathnam to perform this ritual violates his Fundamental Rights.

Q.4 Why do you think the Dalit families were afraid of angering the powerful castes?

Ans. The Dalit families were afraid of angering the powerful castes because they depended on them for their livelihood and they were smaller in number.

NCERT ON PAGE 80

Q.5 Can you list two different provisions in the 1989 Act?

Ans. The two different provisions in the 1989 Act are

(i) The act recognises crimes against Dalit and tribal women.

(ii) It lists actions that dispossess Dalits and Adivasis of their meagre resources or which force them into performing slave labour.

Q.6 Look up the glossary and write in your own words what you understand by the term 'morally reprehensible'.

Ans. Morally reprehensible is a term used to describe actions, behaviours, or decisions that are widely considered to be deeply unethical, offensive, or morally wrong.

NCERT ON PAGE 81

Q.7 What do you understand by manual scavenging?

Ans. Manual scavenging refers to the practice of removing human and animal waste/excreta from dry latrines and carrying it on the head to the disposal grounds.

Q.8 Re-read the list of Fundamental Rights provided on page 14 of NCERT and list two rights that this practice violates.

Ans. Two rights that the practice of manual scavenging violates are

(i) Right to Equality (ii) Right to Freedom.

Q.9 Why did the Safai Karamchari Andolan file a PIL in 2003? What did they complain about in their petition?

Ans. The Safai Karamchari Andolan filed a PIL in 2003 to get manual scavenging banned.

They complained that manual scavenging still existed and it continued in government undertakings like the railways. The petitioners sought enforcement of their Fundamental Rights.

Q.10 What did the Supreme Court do on hearing their case in 2005?

Ans. The Supreme Court directed every department/ ministry of the Union and State Government to verify the facts stated in the PIL filed by the Safai Karamchari Andolan within six months, and if found true they have to take up the rehabilitation and liberation programmes.

EXERCISES

Q.1 List two Fundamental Rights in the Constitution that Dalits can draw upon to insist that they can be treated with dignity and as equals. Re-read the Fundamental Rights listed on page 14 of NCERT to help you answer this question.

Ans. Two Fundamental Rights in the Constitution that Dalits can draw upon to insist that they can be treated with dignity and as equals are as follows

(i) Article 15 which includes Right to Equality.

(ii) Article 17 which abolishes untouchability.

Q.2 Re-read the story on Rathnam as well as the provisions of the 1989 Scheduled Castes and Scheduled Tribes (Prevention of Atrocities) Act. Now list one reason why you think he used this law to file a complaint.

Ans. Rathnam used this law to file a complaint to protest against the domination and violence of the powerful castes in his village, as this law contains provisions that makes humiliation of the scheduled castes illegal.

Q.3 Why do Adivasi activists, including CK Janu, believe that Adivasis can also use this 1989 act to fight against dispossession? Is there anything specific in the provisions of the act that allows her to believe this?

Ans. Adivasi activists, including CK Janu, believe that Adivasis can also use the 1989 Act to fight against dispossesion because this act provide them the right to occupy lang that was traditionally belonged to them.

Yes, there is an specific provision of the act which that land belonging to tribal people cannot be sold to or brought by non-tribal people. In cases where this has happened, the Constitution guarantees the right of tribal people to repossess their land.

Q.4 The poems and the song in this unit allow you to see the range of ways in which individuals and communities express their opinions, their anger and their sorrow. In class, do the following two exercises.

(a) Bring to class a poem that discusses a social issue. Share this with your classmates. Work in small groups with two or more poems to discuss their meaning as well as what the poet is trying to communicate.

Ans. Classroom activity. Students are encouraged to do this task themselves.

(b) Identify a marginalised community in your locality. Write a poem, or song, or draw a poster, etc to express your feelings as a member of this community.

Ans. Students are suggested to do this task themselves.

REVIEW EXERCISE

Including Competency Based Questions

PART I

Multiple Choice Questions (MCQs)

1. Which of the following is a marginalised group in our Indian society?

(a) Women (b) Men (c) Children (d) None of these

2. Which article of the Indian Constitution prohibits untouchability? Diksha

(a) Article 14 (b) Article 15 (c) Article 16 (d) Article 17

3. "Dr. Ambedkar was not allowed to sit with his classmates in school. He often faced discrimination in matters as simple as drinking water from the same source as the upper-caste children. "

Choose the option which shows the discrimination faced by Dr Ambedkar. Competency Based

(a) Untouchability (b) Religious discrimination

(c) Racialism (d) Age discrimination

4. The right of equality assures that no citizen shall be discriminated against on the ground of .... Diksha

(a) colour (b) sex

(c) caste (d) All of these

5. How does the government ensure an end to inequality in the country? Competency Based

(a) Through laws (b) Through reservations

(c) Both (a) and (b) (d) None of these

6. Which of the following is a step to promote social justice?

(a) Manual scavenging (b) Untouchability

(c) Reservations (d) None of these

7. Who among the following can avail reservations?

(a) Dalits (b) Muslims

(c) Brahmins (d) None of these

8. Who among the following is an Adivasi activist?

(a) Kabir (b) CK Janu
(c) Chokhamela (d) Rathnam

9. Which community has been mainly employed in manual scavenging?

(a) Adivasis (b) Children (c) Poor women (d) Dalits

10. "Incidents of suicide by students from marginalised communities are becoming common, these numbers are not just a statistic they are stories sometimes of centuries of struggle." **Competency Based**

Source : The Hindu

Which of the following can be a measure to help students of marginalised communities access education?

(a) By giving them financial aid in the form of scholarships.
(b) By giving them reservations in educational institutions.
(c) By giving them subsidised gas cylinder.
(d) Both (a) and (b) are correct

11. Identify the concept using the following information. **Competency Based**

I. It is a course of action that provides direction for the future.
II. It sets the future goals to be achieved and set the principles to be followed.
III. It provides guidelines for a particular thing or place.

(a) Movement (b) Confrontation
(c) Policy (d) Scheme

12. Which one of the following statements is/are correct?

I. Fundamental Rights are an important part of the Constitution and are available to all Indians equally.
II. The Constitution lays down the principles that make our society and polity democratic.

Codes

(a) Only I (b) Both I and II
(c) Only II (d) None of these

13. Which one of the following statements is/are correct?

I. It is wrong to practice untouchability and this practice is not tolerated by the Indian government.
II. Dalits are not allowed to enter temples in India.

Codes

(a) Only I (b) Both I and II
(c) Only II (d) None of these

14. Which of the following are the correct sequence?

I. The Prohibition of Employment as Manual Scavengers and their Rehabilitation Act came into force.
II. The government passed the Employment of Manual Scavengers and Construction of Dry Latrines (Prohibition) Act.
III. The Scheduled Castes and the Scheduled tribes (Prevention of Atrocities) Act was framed.

Codes

(a) I, III, II (b) III, II, I (c) II, III, I (d) I, II, III

Answers

1. (a)	**2.** (d)	**3.** (a)	**4.** (d)	**5.** (c)
6. (c)	**7.** (a)	**8.** (b)	**9.** (d)	**10.** (d)
11. (c)	**12.** (b)	**13.** (a)	**14.** (b)	

Match the Following

1.

List I	List II
A. PIL filed by Safai Karamchari Andolan	1. 1989
B. Scheduled Tribes and other Traditional Forest Dwellers (Recognition of Forest Rights) Act.	2. 2003
C. Employment of Manual Scavengers and Construction of Dry Latrines (Prohibition) Act	3. 1993
D. Scheduled Castes and Scheduled Tribes (Prevention of Atrocities) Act	4. 2006

Codes

	A	B	C	D		A	B	C	D
(a)	4	1	2	3	(b)	2	4	3	1
(c)	1	2	4	3	(d)	3	1	4	2

Ans. 1. (b)

Assertion-Reason

1. Assertion (A) Article 17 of the Constitution of India declares the abolition of untouchability.

Reason (R) Article 17 ensures that Dalits have the right to education, access to temples, and the use of public facilities, while also making the practice of untouchability a punishable crime.

Codes

(a) Both A and R are true and R is the correct explanation of A
(b) Both A and R are true, but R is not the correct explanation of A
(c) A is true, but R is false
(d) A is false, but R is true

2. Assertion (A) Adivasis are confronting marginalisation in India.

Reason (R) Marginalised groups follow a different culture, language and traditions from mainstream.

Codes

(a) Both A and R are true and R is the correct explanation of A
(b) Both A and R are true, but R is not the correct explanation of A
(c) A is true, but R is false
(d) A is false, but R is true

Ans. 1. (c) A is true, but R is false
2. (b) Both A and R are true, but R is not the correct explanation of A

Fill in the Blanks

1. The ...... Government passed the Scheduled Tribe and Other Traditional Forest Dwellers Act in ....
2. Untouchability is a .... crime.
3. The law for prohibition of manual scavenging was passed by the government in ....
4. The task of .... is mainly done by Dalit women and young girls.

Ans. 1. Central, 2006 2. punishable
3. 1993 4. Manual scavenging

True/False

1. Rathnam united with other Dalit families of his village to fight against discrimination.
2. The reservation policy of the government is for Dalits and Adivasis.
3. Adivasis usually live in or near forest and mountainous tracts.
4. Dalits have been using Article 22 to seek equality where it has been denied to them.

Ans. 1. False 2. True 3. True 4. False

Picture Based Question

1. Which of the following movements is shown in the picture?

(a) Safai Karamchari Andolan
(b) Railway Karamchari Andolan
(c) Jungle Bachao Andolan
(d) None of the above

Ans. (a) Safai Karamchari Andolan

Case Based Question

1. **Read the given passage below and answer the questions that follow.**

Manual scavenging refers to the practice of removing human and animal waste/excreta using brooms, tin plates and baskets from dry latrines and carrying it on the head to disposal grounds some distance away. A manual scavenger is the person who does the job of carrying this filth. This job is mainly done by Dalit women and young girls. According to the Andhra Pradesh-based Safai Karamchari Andolan, an organisation working with manual scavengers, there are one lakh persons from Dalit communities who continue to be employed in this job in this country and who work in 26 lakh private and community dry latrines managed by municipalities. Manual scavengers in different parts of the country, the Bhangis in Gujarat, Pakhis in Andhra Pradesh and the Sikkaliars in Tamil Nadu, continue to be considered untouchable. They often live in separate settlements on the outskirts of the village and are denied access to the temple, public water facilities, etc.

(i) Which of the following statements best describes the manual scavenging?
(a) Cleaning the streets
(b) Removing human and animal waste from dry latrines.
(c) Sweeping floors
(d) All of the above

(ii) Manual scavenging is being practiced by several communities in India. Which of the following are among those communities?
(a) Bhangis (b) Pakhis (c) Sikkaliars (d) All of these

(iii) Which of the following is not a challenge faced by manual scavengers in India?
(a) They are often considered untouchable.
(b) They are often denied access to temples and public water facilities.
(c) They are often paid low wages.
(d) They are often exposed to health hazards.

(iv) Which of the following is not a way through which manual scavengers are marginalised in India?
(a) They are often denied access to education and employment.
(b) They are often stereotyped and discriminated against.
(c) They are often denied access to temples and public water facilities.
(d) They are often treated as equals to other castes.

Ans. (i) (b) Removing human and animal waste from dry latrines.
(ii) (d) All of these
(iii) (c) They are often paid low wages.
(iv) (d) They are often treated as equals to other castes.

Part II

Very Short Answer Type Questions

1. Which principles are ensured by our Constitution?

Ans. Our Constitution ensures democratic principles which are defined in and through the list of the Fundamental Rights.

2. Name two distinct cultural and religious groups in the country.

Ans. Two distinct cultural and religious groups in the country are Parsis and Muslims.

3. How does our Constitution ensure cultural justice to minority groups?

Ans. Our Constitution ensures cultural justice to minority groups by granting cultural and educational rights to them.

4. What do the powerless people do against the powerful? **Competency Based**

Ans. Powerless people attempt to overcome their situation by fighting, protesting and struggling against their powerlessness and exclusion.

5. What does 'Dalit' refer to?

Ans. The word 'Dalit' literally means 'broken' and is used by certain groups to highlight the centuries of discrimination they have experienced within the caste system.

6. What does the government do to promote social justice?

Ans. The government promotes social justice by formulating various policies and laws for the marginalised groups.

7. What is the government's reservation policy?

Ans. Government's reservation policy involves reserving seats in educational institutions and government employment for Dalits and Adivasis.

8. Which act was passed by the Government of India in 1993?

Ans. The government passed the Employment of Manual Scavengers and Construction of Dry Latrines (Prohibition) Act in 1993.

9. What is Safai Karamchari Andolan?

Ans. Safai Karamchari Andolan is Andhra Pradesh based organisation working for the rights of manual scavengers.

10. What does a manual scavenger do?

Ans. A manual scavenger does the work of carrying human and animal waste/excreta on their head to disposal grounds.

Short Answer Type Questions

1. How have minority groups drawn on the Fundamental Rights to highlight their causes?

Ans. Minority groups have particularly drawn upon the Fundamental Rights like the Right to Freedom of religion and cultural and educational rights to highlight their causes.

According to these rights, distinct cultural and religious groups like Muslims and Parsis have the right to be the guardians of the content of their culture as well as the right to decide how best this content is to be preserved.

2. "Article 17 of the Constitution states that untouchability has been abolished – what this means is that no one can henceforth prevent Dalits from educating themselves, entering temples, using public facilities, etc. Article 15 of the Constitution notes that no citizen of India shall be discriminated against on the basis of religion, race, caste, sex or place of birth." **Competency Based**

(i) What is untouchability and who were called untouchables?

Ans. Untouchability refers to the social practice of discriminating against certain groups based on their caste and low social status within the Indian caste system. These oppressed groups were called untouchables, but today, they are referred to as Dalits.

(ii) How have Dalits used Article 15 of the Constitution to seek equality?

Ans. Dalits have used Article 15 to seek equality due to its provision that no citizen of India shall be discriminated against on the basis of religion, race, caste, sex or place of birth.

3. Why was the Scheduled Castes and the Scheduled Tribes (Prevention of Atrocities) Act, 1989 framed? **Diksha**

Ans. The Scheduled Castes and the Scheduled Tribes (Prevention of Atrocities) Act, 1989 was framed in response to demands made by Dalits and other groups. They wanted the government to stop the ill treatment and humiliation Dalits and tribal groups face everyday.

4. The existence of a right or a law or even a policy on paper does not mean that it exists in reality. What do you understand by this statement? **Competency Based**

Ans. The given statement means that even if the law or policy has been passed by the goverment, it is not followed or exists in reality.

For example, when the Constitution for India was framed, it guaranteed the Fundamental Right to equality to every citizen. However, six decades later, our country is yet to accord equality to all its citizens. Discriminations on the basis of religion, caste, sex still continue to exist.

5. 'The desire for equality, dignity and respect is not new'. Explain in your own words. Competency Based

Ans. Every individual desires to live a life of dignity and respect and this can happen only when he/she is treated as an equal citizen in society. If he/she is deprived of this, he/she will fight for it because it is fundamental to a dignified life.

When different people and communities co-exist, there is bound to be some dispute and both will demand equality and dignity. So struggle will be continued as long as all groups do not enjoy equal status in society.

6. Discuss the criticism of the tribal activist CK Janu about the state governments.

Ans. The tribal activist CK Janu criticised that some State Governments are violators of the constitutional rights of the tribals because they themselves allow non-tribal enchroachers into the forests and forcibly evict the tribals from their lands in the process of declaring the forests as reserved or as sanctuaries.
She also noted that in cases where tribals have already been evicted and cannot go back to their lands , they must be compensated.

7. How 1989 Act is important for the Adivasis or the tribals?

Ans. The 1989 Act is also important for the Adivasis or the tribals. It confirms that the land belonging to tribal people cannot be sold to or brought by non-tribal people.
The Adivasi activists refer to this law to defend their right to occupy land that was traditionally belonged to them. They demand that those who have forcibly occupied tribal lands should be punished under this law.

Long Answer Type Questions

1. "The Constitution lays down principles that make our society and polity democratic. They are defined in and through the list of Fundamental Rights that are an important part of the Constitution." Competency Based **Discuss how the marginalised communities have drawn on Fundamental Rights. Also, discuss the influence of these struggles on the government. Mention any one instance from this chapter where the demands of these communities have been fulfilled in the form of law.**

Ans. The Constitution of India contains Fundamental Rights which are equally available to all the citizens. The marginalised groups have utilised these rights in the following two ways

- They have forced the government to recognise the injustice done to them by insisting on their Fundamental Rights.
- They have insisted the government to enforce these laws.
- Sometimes, these struggles of marginalised groups against the injustice have influenced the government to frame new laws in line with the principles of the Fundamental Rights.

One example where the demands of these marginalised communities have been fulfilled by the government in the form of law is the passage of the Scheduled Castes and the Scheduled Tribes (Prevention of Atrocities) Act, 1989. The demand for this act became strong during 1970s and 1980s in the Southern India.

2. What are the clauses of the Scheduled Castes and the Scheduled Tribes (Prevention of Atrocities) Act, 1989?

Ans. The clauses of the Scheduled Castes and the Scheduled Tribes (Prevention of Atrocities) Act, 1989 are

- **Modes of Humiliation** It includes both physically and morally reprehensible humiliations. For example, forcing a member of a Scheduled Caste or a Scheduled Tribe to drink or eat any inedible or obnoxious distasteful substance, forcibly removing their clothes, parading them naked or with painted face, etc.
- **Actions of Dispossession** it includes action wife occupying or cultivating any land that is owned by or allotted to a member of a Scheduled Caste or Scheduled Tribe and force them to perform slave labour.
- **Crimes against Women** It includes assaulting or dishonouring any woman belonging to a Scheduled Caste or Scheduled Tribe.

3. What does the government do to promote social justice in order to implement the Constitution?

Ans. The government do the following to promote social justice in order to implement the Constitution

- Both State and Central governments create specific schemes for implementation in tribal areas or in areas that have a high Dalit population.

  For example, the government provides for free or subsidised hostels for students of Dalit and Adivasi communities, so that they can avail of education facilities that may not be available in their localities.

- The government formulates laws to end inequity in the system. One such law/policy is the reservation policy. It reserves seats in education and government employment for Dalits and Adivasis.

  Both the Central and State governments have their own list of Scheduled Caste (Dalits), Scheduled Tribes and backward and most backward castes.

  If a particular Dalit caste or a certain tribe is mentioned on the government list, then a candidate from that caste or tribe can avail the benefit of reservation.

4. What benefit does the government policy of reservation provide to the margindised communities?

Ans. The government policy of reservation provides the following benefits to the marginalised communities

- **Education** The government provides for free or subsidised hostels for students of Dalit and Adivasi communities so that they can avail of education facilities that may not be available in their localities. The government also reserves a certain percentage of seats in educational institutions for Dalit and Adivasi students.
- **Employment** The government reserves a certain percentage of seats in government employment for Dalit and Adivasi candidates.
- **Other Benefits** The government also provides other benefits to Dalits and Adivasis, such as scholarships, land grants, and subsidies for housing and business development.

5. Write a short note on Manual scavenging and also mention the laws that have been passed against it.

Ans. Manual scavenging is the practice of removing human and animal waste/excreta from dry latrines using manual methods and carrying it on head to disposal grounds.

A manual scavenger is the person who does the job of carrying this waste. This job is mainly done by people from Dalit communities.

The laws that have been passed against manual scavenging are

- In 1993, the Employment of Manual Scavengers and Construction of Dry Latrines (Prohibition) Act was passed which prohibits the employment of manual scavengers as well as the construction of dry latrines.
- On 6th December, 2013, the Prohibition of Employment as Manual Scavengers and their Rehabilitation Act came into force.

Picture Based Question

1. Look at the picture given below and answer the questions that follow.

(i) Who was Kabir?

Ans. Kabir was a fifteenth-century poet and weaver who also belonged to the Bhakti tradition.

(ii) What was Kabir's view on caste and religion?

Ans. Kabir believed that caste and religion were not important factors in determining a person's worth. He believed that everyone had the ability to reach the highest level of spiritual salvation.

(iii) Why is Kabir's poetry still popular today?

Ans. Kabir's poetry is still popular today because it expresses the universal human desire for equality and justice.

His poetry is also a reminder of the importance of challenging social hierarchies and religious hypocrisy.

Case Based Question

1. Read the passage given below and answer the questions that follow.

The 1989 Act is important for another reason - Adivasi activists refer to it to defend their right to occupy land that was traditionally theirs.

As you read in the previous chapter, Adivasis are often unwilling to move from their land and are forcibly displaced. Activists have asked that those who have forcibly encroached upon tribal lands should be punished under this law.

They have also pointed to the fact that this act merely confirms what has already been promised to tribal people in the Constitution - that land belonging to tribal people cannot be sold to or bought by non-tribal people.

In cases where this has happened, the Constitution guarantees the right of tribal people to re-possess their land. C.K. Janu, an Adivasi activist, has also pointed out that one of the violators of Constitutional rights guaranteed to tribal people are governments in the various states of India - for it is they who allow non-tribal encroachers in the form of timber merchants, paper mills etc, to exploit tribal land, and to forcibly evict tribal people from their traditional forests in the process of declaring forests as reserved or as sanctuaries. She has also noted that in cases where tribals have already been evicted and cannot go back to their lands, they must be compensated. That is, the government must draw up plans and policies for them to live and work elsewhere.

(i) What does C.K. Janu say about the role of State Governments in violating the constitutional rights of Adivasi people?

Ans. C.K. Janu says that State Governments are violators of the constitutional rights guaranteed to tribal people because they allow non-tribal encroachers to exploit tribal land and forcibly evict tribal people from their traditional forests.

(ii) What does the Constitution guarantee tribal people in terms of their land?

Ans. The Constitution guarantees tribal people the right to re-possess their land if it has been sold to or bought by non-tribal people.

(iii) Why are Adivasis often unwilling to move from their land?

Ans. Adivasis are often unwilling to move from their land because they have a deep cultural and spiritual connection to their land. They also rely on their land for their livelihoods.

ASSESSMENT EXERCISE

Multiple Choice Questions (MCQs)

1. Scheduled Tribe and other traditional Forest Dwellers Act was passed in
(a) 2005
(b) 2000
(c) 2006
(d) 2003

2. The Safai Karamchari Andolan filed a PIL in
(a) 2002
(b) 2003
(c) 2005
(d) 2001

3. Article 15 of Constitution states
(a) right to speech
(b) right to freedom
(c) right against discrimination
(d) None of the above

4. Which caste did Soyrabai belong to?
(a) Gonds tribe group (b) Adivasis
(c) Mahar castes (d) All of these

Subjective Questions (VSA, SA & LA)

1. Who comes under marginal groups?

2. What do you mean by Article 15?

3. Define Government Reservation Policy.

4. Explain the rights of marginalised communities.

5. Write a short note on Manual Scavenger.

6. Explain the role of government for Dalit community.

7. Which types of subsidised facilities are provided to Dalits by governments ? Discuss.

8. Discuss 'the Scheduled Caste and the Scheduled Tribes (Prevention of Atrocities) Act, 1989'.

Public Facilities

CHAPTER 7

Public facilities are services provided by the government. The government takes overall responsibility to provide these services or facilities for common Indian citizens which is seen as a part of the basic fundamental right. These facilities are important to sustain and lead a comfortable life. In this chapter, we will learn about how the government provides different public facilities such as water.

7.1 Meaning and Benefits of Public Facilities

Public facilities are the **basic needs**[1] or facilities that need to be provided to everyone. Water, healthcare, **sanitation**[2], electricity, public transport, schools and colleges are some of the public facilities.

The benefits of public facilities can be shared by many people. For example

- A school in the village will enable many children to get educated.
- The supply of electricity to an area can be useful for many people.

Role of the Government

The government has the responsibility to ensure that public facilities are made available to everyone.

Private companies also provide public facilities but they operate for profit in the market. So, they charge a price for these facilities. Only some people can afford these paid facilities and hence these are not available to everyone. The public facilities provided by the private companies are as follows

- Schools
- Hospitals
- Supply water through tankers
- Supply drinking water in sealed bottles

As the Right to Life guaranteed by the Constitution is for all persons living in this country, thus the responsibility to provide public facilities must be that of the government.

Money for Public Facilities

Every year, the government present budget in the Parliament. The budget is an account of the expenses the government has made on its programmes in the past year and how much it plans to spend in the coming year.

In the budget, the government also announces the various ways in which it plans to meet these expenses. The main source of revenue for the government is the taxes collected from the people.

The government collect taxes from the people and use them for providing public facilities. For example, to supply water, government partly collects taxes and partly charge a price for water which is affordable to everyone.

7.2 Water as Part of the Fundamental Right to Life

Water is essential for life and for good health. It is needed for various daily activities. Safe drinking water can prevent many water-related diseases.

The Indian Constitution recognises the Right to Water as being a part of the **Right to Life** under Article 21. This means that it is the right of every person to have sufficient amount of water to fulfill his/her daily needs irrespective of his/her social status. Thus, there should be **universal access**[3] to water.

Both the Supreme Court and the High Court have ruled in several cases that the right to safe drinking water is a Fundamental Right.

1 **Basic needs** These are fundamental requirements that are essential for human survival, well-being and dignity. For example, food,water, shelter, sanitation, etc.

2 **Sanitation** It refers to the provision of facilities and services for the safe disposal of human waste and the promotion of cleanliness and hygiene.

3 **Universal access** It refers to the idea that all individuals, regardless of their background, should have equal and unrestricted access to essential services, opportunities and resources.

7.3 Water Supply to Chennai

There is shortage of water supply in Chennai. Municipal supply meets only about half of the needs of the people in the city. There is disparity in water supply in Chennai as

- Some areas get water more regularly than others.
- The areas closer to the storage points get more water than the colonies located far away.

Mostly the poor is affected by this shortage of water as the middle class are able to cope the shortage of water through a variety of private means such as digging borewells, buying water from tankers and using bottles water for drinking.

Safe drinking water is also accessible only to wealthy people who can afford it. Thus, it is only the people with money who have the right to water, and this posed a challenge to the goal of universal access to 'sufficient and safe' water.

Search for Alternatives of Water Supply

According to standard set by the **Urban Water Commission**, the supply of water per person in an urban area in India should be about **135 litres per day** (about 7 buckets).

However in **slums**, it is less than **20 litres per day per** person (1 bucket) and in luxury hotels, it is as much as **1600 litres (80 buckets) of water per day**.

The shortage of municipal water is considered as a failure of the government. Thus, some people argue that since government is unable to supply the amount of water that is needed, the private companies should be allowed to perform the task of water supply.

Some fact regarding water supply in the world are given below

- Throughout the world, water supply is the primary responsibility of the government and there are very few instances of private water supply.
- Public water supply has achieved universal success in some areas of the world.
- In some cases of private water supply, the prices of water increased greatly, making it unaffordable for many people.
- There are some cases of success in government water departments in India, though they are few and limited to certain areas of their work.
- In some cases, the government uses the services of private companies for transporting and distributing water **on contract**[4] but the rate for water tankers is decided by the government water supply department.

Sanitation Coverage in India

The sanitation coverage in India is even lower than that of water. According to official figures for 2011, 87% of household in India have access to drinking water while 53% have access to sanitation.

Sulabh is a non-government organisation which has been working to address the problems of sanitation faced by low-caste and low-income people in India.

Sulabh enters into contracts with municipalities or other local authorities to construct toilet blocks with government funds. Local authorities provide land and funds for setting up the services, whereas maintenance costs are sometimes financed through user charges.

7.4 Conclusion

Public facilities relate to our basic needs and the Indian Constitution recognises the right to water, health, education, etc as being a part of the **Right to Life**.

There is a shortage in supply and there are inequalities in distribution of public facilities. However, giving the responsibility of providing these facilities to private companies is not the best solution.

Any solution needs to consider the fact that every citizen of the country has an equal right to these facilities.

4 **On Contract** Being 'on contract' typically means that an individual or a party has entered into a contractual agreement with another party to perform specific tasks or provide certain goods or services for a defined period.

Role of the Government

- To ensure that public facilities are made available to everyone.
- Meet expenses partly from taxes and partly by charging for water.
- Collect taxes and use them for public facilities.

Meaning of Public Facilities

- Basic necessities and facilities for everyone.
- For example-Water, healthcare, sanitation, electricity, public transport, schools and colleges.

PUBLIC FACILITIES

Water as a Part of the Fundamental Right to Life

- The Indian Constitution recognises the Right to Water as part of Article 21, the Right to Life.
- Right to safe drinking water is a Fundamental Right.

Water Supply to Chennai

- Disparity in water supply in Chennai
- The Municipal Corporation meets only half of the city's needs.
- The water shortage primarily affects the poor, while the middle class can cope with it.

Search for Alternatives

- The shortage of municipal water considered as failure of the government.
- Private companies should take over the task of water supply.
- Sulabh is a non-government organisation working for the problem of sanitation.

NCERT FOLDER

Covering Intext Questions and Exercises of NCERT

NCERT ON PAGE 88

Q.1 You have seen the four situations on pages 86 and 87. Based on these, what impression do you get of the water situation in Chennai?

Ans. From the given four situations, we get the impression that water situation is not good in Chennai. There is shortage of supply and demand is high. As a result of this, only those who can afford to pay more have sufficient access to water and those who are poor can not get sufficient access to water.

Q.2 Pick out the various sources of water for household use from the description alongside.

Ans. Municipal water, private borewell, water tanker, tubewells, piped water, etc are some of the various sources of water for household use.

Q.3 What, in your view, is similar and what is different in Subramanian's and Padma's experiences?

Ans. The similarity in Subramanian's and Padma's experiences is that both face the shortage of water.

The difference in Subramanian's and Padma's experiences is that Subramanian is economically strong and can afford to buy water from a tanker but Padma cannot afford this, so she depends on borewell water.

Q.4 Write a paragraph describing the water supply situation in your area.

Ans. In our locality, the water supply situation is not very good. We get municipal water for 2-3 hours a day. The quality of the water is not very good. Many people have submersible pump in their home to get water. We buy bottled water for drinking and cooking purposes.

Q.5 Why does water flow in a trickle in summer in most places of India? Find out.

Ans. Water flows in a trickle in summer in most places of India because the demand for water is much higher and supply is very limited.

The underground water levels also dry up because of the hot weather and therefore, yield less water.

Q.6 Discuss : Is there a general shortage of water for everyone in Chennai? Can you think of two reasons why different people get varying amounts of water?

Ans. Yes, there is a general shortage of water in Chennai.

Two reasons why different people get varying amounts of water are as follows

(i) Location from the source of water.

(ii) Different economical status.

NCERT ON PAGE 91

Q.7 Amu : Did you notice that the roads in Saidapet were so bumpy and without treetlights? I wonder what the place is like at night.

Kumar : What better can you expect in a slum!

Amu : Why should slums be like that? Shouldn't they have public facilities?

Kumar : I think public facilities are for all those who live in proper houses in colonies. They are the people who pay taxes. Amu: Why do you say that! Slum dwellers are also citizens and they have rights too.

Kumar : Arrey! The government will go bankrupt this way!

Amu : Well, it has to find a way. Can you imagine what it would be like to live in a slum without proper roads, water, electricity?

Kumar : Err....

Amu : Our Constitution recognises many of the public facilities as being a part of the Right to Life. The government must see that these rights are protected so that everyone can lead a decent life.

Whose point of view do you agree with?

Ans. I agree with the viewpoint of Amu.

The Constitution of India is the law of the land. It recognises many of the public facilities as a part of the Right to Life. The government has the responsibility to ensure that these rights are protected, so that everyone can lead a life of dignity.

NCERT ON PAGE 92

Q.8 What are public facilities? Why should the government be responsible for providing public facilities?

Ans. Public facilities are the basic needs or facilities that need to be provided to everyone. Water, healthcare, sanitation, electricity, public transport, schools and colleges are some of the public facilities.

It is the government which has to take the responsibility of providing public facilities as these facilities are a part of the right to life.

Q.9 The government can get private companies to deliver some of the public facilities. For instance, contracts for building roads are given to private contractors.

Distribution of electricity in Delhi is done by two private companies. However, the government must keep a close watch on these and ensure that they fulfil their commitment to reach these facilities to all people and at affordable prices.

Why do you think the government must assume the overall responsibility for public facilities even when it gets private companies to do part of the job?

Ans. The government must assume the overall responsibility for public facilities even when it gets private companies to do part of the job because private companies work for profits and they do not have people's welfare as their priority.

It is the responsibility of the government to monitor the work of the private companies and ensure that it is done well. This is important to ensure the affordability of public facilities for all.

Q.10 Look at your water bill and find out what the minimum rate is for municipal water in your area. Does the rate increase as the use of water increases? Why do you think the government charges a higher rate for greater use of water?

Ans. Yes, the rate increases as the use of water increases. The government charges a higher rate for greater use of water because higher consumption of water has higher operative costs. It is also done to make people use water responsibly and not waste it.

Q.11 Find out the various kinds of taxes people pay to the government by talking to a salaried person, a person running his/her own factory/ business and a shopkeeper. Share your findings in the classroom with your teacher.

Ans. Various kinds of taxes paid by salaried persons include Income tax, House tax, Water tax, etc.

Taxes paid by business persons/ shopkeepers include Service tax, VAT, Excise, GST and Custom duties.

NCERT ON PAGE 94 AND 95

Q.12 Do you think this would be a right step? What do you think would happen if the government withdraws from the task of supplying water?

Ans. I don't think it would be a right step. If the government withdraws from the task of supplying water, then it would fail to perform its duty. Only the government can ensure public facilities for all. If the private companies take over the task of supplying water, then they would do it with profit motive and charge higher prices.

Q.13 Discuss the main ideas in the above section. What do you think can be done to improve water supply?

Ans. The above section highlights that government is responsible for proper water supply.

The government should improve its working by improving water supply. It should also find ways to increase its revenue collection. The use of rainwater harvesting and groundwater levels should also be improved.

Q.14 Do you think it is also important to conserve resources like water and electricity and to use more public transport?

Ans. Yes, it is important to conserve resources like water and electricity and use more public transport. These steps can save money as well as the resources.

NCERT ON PAGE 96

Q.15 Do you think that lack of access to proper sanitation facilities affects people's lives ? How?

Ans. Yes, lack of access to proper sanitation facilities affects people's lives by spreading water borne diseases.

Q.16 Why do you think that this would impact women and girls more acutely?

Ans. Lack of access to proper sanitation facilities compels women and girls to travel long distances. This is neither safe nor healthy for women and girls.

EXERCISES

Q.1 Why do you think there are so few cases of private water supply in the world?

Ans. There are so few cases of private water supply in the world because of the following reasons

- Private companies work for profit and not for public welfare.
- In some cases, where water supply was handed over to the private companies, there was a steep rise in the price of water.
- Some places saw huge protests by the people against the water supply by private companies. For example, in Bolivia.

Q.2 Do you think water in Chennai is available to and affordable by all? Discuss.

Ans. No, in Chennai, water is not available to all equally and it is not affordable by all. The Municipal water supply meets only half of the needs of the people in the city. There are areas which receive more water than others as they are closer to the storage point.

The poor people are the worst sufferers as they do not have a water connection and even the brackish water from borewell is available for only 20 minutes everyday. They cannot afford to buy bottled water, so they have to use poor quality and limited supply of water. On the other hand, the middle classes get submersible pumps installed and buy bottled water.

Q.3 How is the sale of water by farmers to water dealers in Chennai affecting the local people? Do you think local people can object to such exploitation of groundwater? Can the government do anything in this regard?

Ans. The sale of water by farmers to water dealers in Chennai has affected the lives of local people adversely as they are facing severe water shortages.

Yes, the local people can object to such exploitation of groundwater as it is a public good.

Yes, the government can stop the private companies.

Q.4 Why are most of the private hospitals and private schools located in major cities and not in towns or rural areas?

Ans. Most of the private schools and hospitals are located in major cities because people there can afford to pay higher for the services whereas people living in towns and rural areas cannot afford these.

Q5 Do you think the distribution of public facilities in our country is adequate and fair? Give an example of your own to explain.

Ans. No, the distribution of public facilities in our country is not adequate and fair.

All persons living in our society do not have equal access to public facilities. For example, water supply system is better in localities comprising wealthy people. In poor localities, there is always a problem of water shortage. The situation is same with regard to healthcare and hospitals too.

Q.6 Take some of the public facilities in your area, such as water, electricity, etc. Is there a scope to improve these? What in your opinion should be done? Complete the table.

	Is it available ?	How can it be improved?
Water		
Electricity		
Roads		
Public Transport		

Ans.

	Is it available?	How can it be improved?
Water	Yes	The quality of the water should be checked and maintained.
Electricity	Yes	It can be improved by checking illegal connections and power theft.
Roads	Yes	Roads can be improved by ensuring regular repair and maintenance.
Public Transport	Yes	Public transport can be improved by introduction of more buses, metro rails, etc.

Q.7 Are the above public facilities shared equally by all the people in your area? Elaborate.

Ans. No, the above public facilities are not shared equally by all the people.

Rich people have better access to these facilities as the areas where they live are better maintained by the authorities. However, the slums and areas where poor people live are not maintained, neither they have access to equal facilities.

Q.8 Data on some of the public facilities are collected as part of the census. Discuss with your teacher when and how the census is conducted.

Ans. Do it yourself.

Q.9 Private educational institutions– schools, colleges, universities, technical and vocational training institutes are coming up in our country in a big way. On the other hand, educational institutes run by the government are becoming relatively less important. What do you think would be the impact of this ? Discuss.

Ans. The private educational institutions are coming up in a big way in our country today. But if this continues, then there would be a monopoly of private educational institutions. Since private institutions work with profit motive, they keep the prices high. The high fees will deprive poor people from getting education.

Thus, it is important for government to run educational institutions to work towards providing affordable education to all.

REVIEW EXERCISE

Including Competency Based Questions

Part I

Multiple Choice Questions (MCQs)

1. Public facilities relate to our basic needs and the Indian Constitution recognises the right to water, heath, education, etc. under .... Diksha
   (a) Right to Life
   (b) Right to Equality
   (c) Cultural and Educational Right
   (d) None of the above

2. The benefits of a public facility can be shared by
   (a) only richer people (b) only poor people
   (c) everyone in the society (d) None of these

3. Which of the following is not a public facility?
   (a) Water (b) Schools
   (c) Electricity (d) None of these

4. What is the most important form of public transport over short distances? Diksha
   (a) Bus (b) Car
   (c) Metro (d) Rickshaw

5. Which of the following is not a source of water in rural areas?
   (a) Wells (b) Handpumps
   (c) Overhead tanks (d) Borewells

6. Aqua water is a private company that provides water to residents and businesses in Chennai, India. It is one of the largest water suppliers in the city, with a fleet of over 1,000 water tankers. The company takes water from nearby towns and villages and pays farmers an advance each month for the right to exploit the water sources on their land. Competency Based

   Which of the following will this growing practice in Chennai most likely lead to in the near future?
   (a) Reduced water pollution
   (b) Increased water resources in Chennai
   (c) Decreased groundwater
   (d) All of the above

7. This summer may not be harsh for Chennai residents in terms of drinking water supply. The Chennai Metropolitan Water Supply and Sewerage Board (CMWSSB) hopes to maintain the present level of water supply as Krishna water from Andhra Pradesh is set to be released to the city in May.

   Source The Hindu Competency Based

   What is/are the challenge(s) regarding water management in India?
   (a) Water scarcity
   (b) Inefficient water use
   (c) Uneven distribution of water resources
   (d) All of the above

8. Rama, is a 13 year old girl who lives in a village. In her village, there are very few toilets and that too belong to some rich people in the area. She along with her mother and other females has to travel to a place to defecate in the open.

   What do you think , the females of this village are most prone to?
   (a) Diabetes (b) Dysentery
   (c) Hypertension (d) HIV AIDS

9. Which one of the following statements is/are correct?
   I. Safe drinking water can prevent many water-related diseases.
   II. Water-related diseases are only problem in developing countries.

   Codes
   (a) Only I (b) Both I and II
   (c) Only II (d) None of these

10. Which one of the following statements is/are incorrect?
    I. Once a public facility is provided, its benefits can be shared by many people.
    II. Public facilities are only beneficial for a small number of people.

    Codes
    (a) Only I (b) Both I and II
    (c) Only II (d) None of these

Answers

1. (a)	2. (c)	3. (d)	4. (a)	5. (c)
6. (c)	7. (d)	8. (b)	9. (a)	10. (c)

Match the Following

1.

List I	List II
A. Article - 21	1. Set-up water standard
B. Budget	2. Water shortage
C. Chennai	3. Safe drinking water
D. Urban Water Commission	4. Financial plan

Codes

	A	B	C	D		A	B	C	D
(a)	1	2	3	4	(b)	3	4	2	1
(c)	2	1	4	3	(d)	4	3	2	1

2.

List I	List II
A. Polio	1. Sulabh
B. Cholera	2. Water-borne disease
C. Basic Needs	3. Preventable disease
D. Sanitation	4. Public facilities

Codes

	A	B	C	D		A	B	C	D
(a)	1	2	3	4	(b)	3	1	4	2
(c)	3	2	4	1	(d)	2	3	4	1

Ans. 1. (b) 2. (c)

Assertion-Reason

1. Assertion (A) The right to water is a Fundamental Right in India.

Reason (R) The Constitution of India recognises the right to water as being a part of the Right to Life under Article 21.

Codes

(a) Both A and R are true and R is the correct explanation of A

(b) Both A and R are true, but R is not the correct explanation of A

(c) A is true, but R is false

(d) A is false, but R is true

2. Assertion (A) The government is not responsible for providing education to the people.

Reason (R) Education is essential for individual and social development.

Codes

(a) Both A and R are true and R is the correct explanation of A

(b) Both A and R are true, but R is not the correct explanation of A

(c) A is true, but R is false

(d) A is false, but R is true

Ans. 1. (a) Both A and R are true and R is the correct explanation of A

2. (d) A is false, but R is true

Fill in the Blanks

1. Providing adequate public facilities for everyone is a major role of the ....

2. Every citizen has a right to ...... facilities.

3. About .... of Indian households have access to sanitation.

4. Safe drinking water can prevent many water-related ....

5. There should be ...... access to water.

Ans. 1. government 2. public 3. 53% 4. diseases 5. universal

True/False

1. 99% of Indian households have access to safe drinking water.

2. Right to water, health and education are a part of the Right to Life.

3. The situation of water crisis is worse in urban areas than rural areas.

4. Public facilities relate to people's basic needs.

Ans. 1. False 2. True 3. False 4. True

Picture Based Questions

1. Look at the picture given below and answer the questions that follow

Which of the following is the least common source of water in rural areas of India?

(a) Wells (b) Hand pumps

(c) Piped water supply (d) Ponds

2. What can be done to improve the life of the woman in the picture and other people who do not have access to a safe and reliable water supply?

(a) Build more piped water systems.
(b) Provide water storage tanks and rainwater harvesting systems.
(c) Educate people about water conservation and sanitation practices.
(d) All of the above

Ans. 1. (c) Piped water supply
2. (d) All of the above

Case Based Question

1. Read the passage given below and answer the questions that follow

Porto Alegre is a city in Brazil. Though there are many poor people in this city, what is remarkable is that it has a far lower number of infant deaths as compared to most other cities of the world. The city's water department has achieved universal access to safe water and this is the main reason behind the lower number of infant deaths. The average price of water is kept low, and the poor are charged half the basic rate. Whatever profit the department makes is used to improve the water supply.

The working of the water department is transparent and people can have a direct say in deciding which projects the department should take up. Through a process of public meetings, people hear what the managers have to say and also vote on their priorities.

(i) Which of the following feature(s) is/are found in Porto Alegre?
(a) It has a far lower number of infant deaths than most other cities of the world.
(b) It has a large population of poor people.
(c) It has a universal water supply.
(d) All of the above

(ii) The water department of Porto Alegre has done a significant job by achieving
(a) universal access to safe water
(b) universal access to education
(c) universal access to healthcare
(d) All of the above

(iii) How does the water department of Porto Alegre utilise its profit?
(a) It is used to improve the water supply.
(b) It is used to fund other government programs.
(c) It is divided among the employees of the water department.
(d) None of the above

(iv) Which of the following is/are the primary reason behind the successful working of the water department in Porto Alegre?
(a) It is managed by a team of experts who are appointed by the government.
(b) It is managed by a committee of elected representatives.
(c) It is managed through a process of public meetings and voting.
(d) All of the above

Ans. (i) (d) All of the above
(ii) (a) universal access to safe water
(iii) (a) It is used to improve the water supply.
(iv) (c) It is managed through a process of public meetings and voting.

Part II

Very Short Answer Type Question

1. What do you mean by right to water?

Ans. It means that it is the right of every person to have equal access to safe drinking water irrespective of his/her caste, class, gender, religion, etc.

2. What is the most important characteristic of public facilities?

Ans. The most important characteristic of a public facility is that once it is provided, its benefits can be shared by many people.

3. Whose responsibility is it to ensure public facilities to everyone?

Ans. It is the government's responsibility to ensure public facilities for everyone.

4. Where does the government get funds for providing public facilities?

Ans. The government gets funds for providing public facilities by collecting taxes viz. income tax, service tax, sales tax, etc.

5. Who bears the maximum burden of shortage in water supply?

Ans. Poor people bear the maximum burden of shortage in water supply.

6. What does the shortage in supply of municipal water lead to?

Ans. When there is shortage in municipal water, private companies try to fill it by selling water for profit. This leads to great inequalities in water use.

7. Name the NGO which has been working for five decades to address the problem of sanitation.

Ans. Sulab, the Non-Government Organisation (NGO) has been working for five decades to address the problems of sanitation.

8. What are the main sources of water in urban areas?

Ans. The main sources of water in urban areas are municipal water, borewells, packaged water, tankers, etc.

9. How can we prevent the spread of water-borne diseases? **Competency Based**

Ans. Water-borne diseases can be prevented if people have access to safe drinking water and proper sanitation facilities.

10. How does the government set the price for the water supplied by it? **Competency Based**

Ans. The government sets the price of water in such a way that most people can afford a certain minimum amount of water for daily use.

11. What is often regarded as a sign of the failure of the government?

Ans. A shortage of basic public facilities like water, electricity is often regarded as a sign of the failure of the government.

Short Answer Type Questions

1. Why is access to safe drinking water important in India?

Ans. Safe drinking water is important in India as it can prevent many water-related diseases.

India has one of the largest number of cases of diseases such as diarrhoea, dysentery, cholera. Many people in India, mostly including children below the age of 5, die everyday because of water-related diseases. These deaths can be prevented if people have access to safe drinking water.

2. What happens when there is a great shortage of public facilities like water?

Ans. When there is a great shortage of public facilities like water, mostly the poor is affected as the middle class are able to cope the shortage of water through a variety of private means such as digging borewells, buying water from tankers and using bottles water for drinking.

Safe drinking water is also accessible only to wealthy people who can afford it. Thus, it is only the people with money who have the right to water, and this posed a challenge to the goal of universal access to 'sufficient and safe' water.

3. How have private companies exploited the situation of water shortage in Chennai?

Ans. The shortage of water in Chennai has opened up opportunities for private companies. Many private companies are providing water to cities by buying it from places around the city. In Chennai, water is taken from nearby towns like Mamandur, Palur, Karungizhi and from villages to the North of the city using water tankers.

Every month the water dealers pay farmers an advance for the rights to exploit water sources on their land. This water is taken away not just from agriculture but also from the drinking water supplies of the villagers. As a results, ground water levels have dropped drastically in all these towns and villages.

4. 'The supply of water per person in an urban area in India should be about 135 litres per day (about seven buckets)- a standard set by the urban water commission. Whereas people in slums have to make do with less than 20 litres a day per person (one bucket), people living in luxury hotels may consume as much as 1,600 litres (80 buckets) of water per day.' **Competency Based**

(i) What does the above paragraph represent about the access of water by different classes?

Ans. The given paragraph indicates that availability of water to poor people living in slums is way lower than the standard set by the urban water commission whereas rich people in luxury hotels use many times more water than the standard.

(ii) What in your view should be the action taken by the government to solve this problem?

Ans. The government should set a limit for water use in luxury hotels and they should be penalized in case of excessive usage. The water supply in slums should be more regular to ensure these mandated amount of water availability.

5. Why it is important for government and private sector to work together to provide public facilities? Explain how it is possible.

Ans. There are many cases where government alone is not successful in efficiently providing public facilities. The private sector on the other hand is efficient but it is not concerned with the public welfare.

Thus, if both the private companies and the government work together, both the efficiency and public welfare objective will get achieved.

It is possible when the government work with private sector 'on contract' basis. In this arrangement, government uses the services of private companies for transporting and distribution of public facilities.

Long Answer Type Questions

1. "A public facility is one whose benefits can be shared by many people once it is provided. Examples include schools, electricity and roads. These facilities improve people's lives and contribute to economic development."
Discuss about the public facilities and their characteristics. Also provide some examples of such facilities. **Competency Based**

Ans. Public facilities are essential services provided by a government to its citizens. They are typically funded by taxes and are accessible to everyone, regardless of income or social status. Public facilities play an important role in improving people's lives and promoting economic development.

Examples of public facilities include

- Education schools, libraries, universities.
- Healthcare hospitals, clinics, public health programs.
- Transportation roads, bridges, public transportation systems.
- Infrastructure water supply, wastewater treatment, electricity, telecommunications.
- Parks and recreation parks, playgrounds, museums, sports facilities.
- Public safety police, fire departments, emergency services.

2. What is budget? Where does the government get money for public facilities? Explain.

Ans. The budget is an account of the expenses the government has incurred on its programmes in the past year and how to spend in the forth coming year.

The government get money for public facilities from the various taxes it collected from the people. The government also charges a price for water. For instance, to supply water, the government has to incur costs in pumping water, carrying it over long distances, laying down pipes for distribution, treating the water for impurities and finally, collecting and treating waste water. This price is set in a way that most people can afford a certain minimum amount of water for daily use.

3. Should private companies be allowed to take over the task of water supply? Explain with examples. **Competency Based**

Ans. No, the private companies should not be allowed to take over the task of water supply.

If private companies are given the responsibility of providing public facilities such as water, they will charge more. In such a situation, only some people will be able to afford to buy water.

There are several examples in the world and in India which shows that water supply by private companies is not sustainable

- Throughout the world , water supply is the primary responsibility of the government.
- Public water supply has achieved universal success in some area of the world.
- In some cases of private water supply, the prices were very high making it unaffordable for many.
- There are some cases of success in government water departments in India though they are few and limited to certain areas of work.

4. What is the situation of water supply in different localities of Chennai? Is water available to all?

Ans. The situation of water supply in Chennai is not very good. All citizens do not have equal access to water. For example, in Anna Nagar, senior government officials live in lush green with-maintained lawns due to generous spraying of water. The bungalows here have tap water for major part of the day. In case the water supply is inadequate, residents here get water tankers arranged easily for themselves.

On the other hand, Mylapore suffers from water shortage. This area gets municipal water once in two days. Residents meet their water needs with the help of private borewells. Borewell water is however brackish, so residents use it in their toilets and for washing. For other uses, water is purchased from tankers. For drinking water, residents have installed water purification systems in their homes.

In Madipakkam, houses get water once in four days. Water shortage is an accepted way of life in this area. Residents buy bottled water for drinking.

In Saidapet, slum dwellers near Saidapet live in hutments that do not have water taps. They collect water for their daily needs from a common tap at the corner of the street. Water is supply to this common tap from a borewell for 20 minutes, twice daily. They get about 3 buckets of water daily. During summer months even this meagre supply is reduced.

Picture Based Question

1. Look at the picture given below and answer the questions that follow.

(i) What is Sulabh's mission?

Ans. Sulabh is a non-governmental organisation working to address the problems of sanitation facing low-caste, low-income people in India.

(ii) How does Sulabh finance its construction work?

Ans. Sulabh enters into contracts with municipalities or other local authorities to construct toilet blocks with government funds.

Case Based Question

1. Read the passage given below and answer the questions that follow.

Senior government officials like Mr. Ramagopal live in Anna Nagar, Chennai. This area looks lush and green with lawns maintained by a generous spraying of water. Bungalows here have tap water for major part of the day. On days when the water supply is inadequate, Mr. Ramagopal speaks to a senior official whom he knows in the municipal water board and a water tanker is easily arranged for his house.

Like most areas of the city, Subramanian's apartments in Mylapore suffers from water shortage. This area gets municipal water once in two days. A private borewell meets some of the resident's water needs. Borewell water is, however, brackish so the residents use it in their toilets and for washing. For other uses, water is purchased from tankers. Subramanian spends upto ₹ 500-600 per month on buying water from the tankers. For drinking water, residents have installed water purification systems in their homes.

(i) What is the water situation in Mr. Ramagopal's neighborhood?

Ans. Mr. Ramagopal's neighborhood, Anna Nagar, has a good water supply. Bungalows in this area have tap water for most of the day.

(ii) What are some of the challenges that people in Chennai face due to water shortage?

Ans. People in Chennai face a number of challenges due to water shortage, which include

- People have to wait long hours for water tankers.
- They have to purchase water from tankers, which can be expensive.
- They have to use brackish water for washing and other non-drinking purposes.
- They have to ration water usage.

(iii) What is the water situation in Mylapore?

Ans. Mylapore is a residential area in Chennai that gets municipal water once in two days.

Borewell water is also available, but it is brackish and used mainly for toilets and washing. Residents spend up to ₹ 500-600 per month on buying water from tankers.

ASSESSMENT EXERCISE

Multiple Choice Questions (MCQs)

1. Budget is presented by the government in
(a) Parliament (b) Rajya Sabha
(c) Lok Sabha (d) All of these

2. Which article included Right to Water Supply?
(a) Article 20 (b) Article 21
(c) Article 16 (d) Article 22

3. Which one is not a water-borne disease?
(a) Diarrhoea (b) Cholera
(c) Dysentery (d) Thyroid

4. The sources of water in rural areas are
(a) wells
(b) handpumps
(c) ponds
(d) All of the above

Subjective Questions (VSA, SA & LA)

1. Define Sulabh.

2. Name the nearby town of Chennai from where water is taken.

3. Why water is necessary for us?

4. What does Article 21 states?

5. Explain public facilities.

6. What are the main source of revenue of government?

7. Write a short note on Right to Education.

8. Describe the role of government to ensure that public facilities are made for everyone.

9. Is the right to safe drinking water a Fundamental Right? Discuss.

Law and Social Justice

CHAPTER 8

A place where buying and selling of goods and services takes place is known as **market**. People are exploited in markets everywhere either they are workers, consumers or producers. Thus, government makes certain laws to protect people from the exploitation or unfair practices in the market. In this chapter, we will learn how laws, the guiding principles of our society, play a crucial role in promoting social justice.

Laws for the Workers, Consumers and Producers

In the market the exploitation happens because the private companies, contractors, businesspersons want to make maximum profit. To realise this profit they might deny workers their rights and not pay them wages.

To protect workers from such practices, a law on **minimum wages**[1] was framed. The minimum wages are revised upwards every few years.

Similar laws are also present to protect the interests of the **producers**[2] and **consumers**[3].

These laws help to ensure that the relations between these three parties (the worker, consumer and producer), are governed in such a manner where no one is exploited by other.

Implementation of the Laws

After making laws, their implementation or enforcement is more important. Through making, enforcing and upholding these laws, the government can control the activities of individuals or private companies and thus, ensure **social justice**[4].

For example, in order to make sure that every worker gets fair wages, the government has to regularly inspect work sites and punish those who violate the law. When workers are poor or powerless, the fear of losing future earnings or facing reprisals often forces them to accept low wages.

Laws by the Indian Constitution

The fundamental rights guaranteed by the Indian Constitution serves as the basis for many of these laws. For example, **Right Against Exploitation** provide that no one can be forced to work on low wages or under bondage.

Similarly the constitution lays down that no child below the age of 14 years shall be employed to work in any factory or mines or engaged in any other hazardous employment.

KNOWLEDGE PLUS In 2016, Parliament amended the **Child Labour (Prohibition and Regulation) Act, 1986**. It banned the employment of children below the age of 14 years in all occupations and of adolescents (14-18 years) in hazardous occupations and processes.

8.1 Worker's Worth

In India, the worth of an Indian worker is very low as one worker can easily replace another.

There is so much unemployment in India that many workers are willing to work in unsafe conditions in return for a wage. Many foreign companies come to India for cheap labour. The wages that these companies pay to workers in other countries like USA, are higher than the wages they pay to the workers in poorer countries like India.

These companies can get longer hours of work for lower pay, and the additional expenses for workers such as for housing facilities, are also fewer. These companies also often ignore safety in workplaces, so they can save costs and earn higher profits.

1 **Minimum wage** It is the amount of wage below which no worker can be paid. The government fixes this wage every year keeping in view the cost of living index.

2 **Producer** It refers to a business or entity that creates or manufactures goods or services for sale to consumers or other businesses.

3 **Consumer** It is an individual or entity that purchases and uses goods or services to satisfy their needs or wants.

4 **Social Justice** It is a concept and movement that aims to promote fairness, equality, and the equitable distribution of resources and opportunities in society.

An example of these companies is the **Union Carbide** (UC), an American company that had set up a plant in Bhopal in which it produced pesticides.

The UC plant included lower working conditions and lower safety measures for cost cutting. Other ways through which this plant cut costs were

- In the UC plant, every safety device was malfunctioning or was in short supply.
- Between 1980 and 1984, the number of workers for the MIC (Methyl-isocyanite) plant was decreased from 12 to 6 workers.
- The period of safety training for workers was also reduced from 6 months to 15 days.
- The post of night-shift worker for the MIC plant was abolished.

These low safety measures led to the leakage of highly poisonous gas, Methyl-isocyanite gas, from the UC plant on 2nd December, 1984. This incident led to a disaster which is known as **Bhopal Gas Tragedy**.

8.2 Enforcement of Safety Laws

The government is the maker and enforcer of laws, thus it is supposed to ensure that safety laws are implemented.

It is the duty of the government to ensure that the **Right to Life** guaranteed under **Article 21** of the Constitution is not violated.

Despite these, there was violation of safety standards in the Union Carbide Plant. This violation occurred because of the following reasons

- The safety laws were weak in India and even these weak safety laws were not enforced.
- The government officials did not recognised the plant as hazardous and allowed it to operate in populated locality.
- Some municipal officials raised objection to the installation of an MIC production unit in 1978 because of safety violations. However, the government allowed the factory to start production as it was providing jobs and investment.
- The government did not ask UC to shift to cleaner technology or safer procedures.
- Government inspectors continued to approve the procedures in the plant despite repeated incidents of gas leaks.

In this case, instead of protecting the interests of the people, their safety was being disregarded both by the government and by the private company.

As more industries are being set up both by local and foreign businesses in India, there is a great need for stronger laws protecting workers' rights and better enforcement of these laws.

8.3 New Laws to Protect the Environment

In India, there were very few environment laws in 1984 and there was hardly any enforcement of these laws. The environment was regarded as a free entity and any industry could pollute the air and water without any restrictions.

In Bhopal Gas Tragedy, several people who were not directly related to the factory in any way, were greatly affected by the poisonous gases leaked from the plant.

Thus, it was realised by the people that the existing environment laws only cover individual worker and did not cover those persons who might be injured due to industrial accidents.

The Indian government introduced new laws after the Bhopal Gas Tragedy because of the pressure from environmental activists. Under these laws, the **polluter**[5] was to be held accountable for the damage done to the environment.

The Supreme Court in **Subhash Kumar Vs. State of Bihar** (1991) ruled that the Right to Life is a Fundamental Right under Article 21 of the Constitution and it includes the right to the enjoyment of pollution-free water and air.

The government is responsible for setting up laws and procedures that can check pollution, clean rivers and introduce heavy fines for those who pollute.

8.4 Conclusion

Laws are necessary in many situations. Private companies, contractors, businesspersons use unfair practices like paying low wages, employing children for work, ignoring work conditions and the environment in order to make higher profits.

It is the duty of the government to pass laws and enforce them strictly to protect the citizens from being exploited.

It is also the duty of the common people to support the government. People must demand stronger laws for protecting workers' interests, so that the Right to Life is achieved for all.

5 Polluter It refers to a person or thing responsible for contaminating or polluting the environment with harmful or poisonous substances.

LAWS AND SOCIAL JUSTICE

Need for Laws

- By enforcing the laws, the government can control activities of individuals or private companies.
- Inspect work sites and to ensure social justice.
- Under fundamental rights, Indian Constitution guarantees Right against Exploitation.
- Child labour (Prohibition and Regulation) Act, 1986 amended to ban Child Labour.

Worker's Worth

- Due to unemployment in India workers are ready to work in unsafe conditions.
- Companies from developed nations like USA comes to India for cheap labour.
- For example-Union carbide pesticide company from America. They avoid safety rules and regulation. Low safety measures led to disaster such as Bhopal Gas Tragedy.

Enforcement of Safety Laws

- Government is maker and enforcer of laws.
- It is duty of government to ensure 'Right to Life' under Article 21 of Indian Constitution.
- Safety of people is disregarded both by the government and private companies.
- There is a great need for stronger laws protecting workers' rights.

New Laws to Protect the Environment

- The existing laws did not cover those persons who injured due to industrial accidents.
- The Indian Government introduced new laws after the Bhopal Gas Tragedy. Under these laws, the polluter is to be held accountable for the damage done to the environment.

NCERT FOLDER

Covering Intext Questions and Exercises of NCERT

NCERT ON PAGE 101

Q.1 Why do we need a law on minimum wages?

Ans. We need a law on minimum wages to ensure that workers are duly paid and not exploited by their employers.

Q.2 Find out:

(a) What is the minimum wage for a construction worker in your state?

Ans. The minimum wage for a construction worker in my state is at least ₹150 daily.

(b) Do you think the minimum wage for a construction worker is adequate, low or high?

Ans. The minimum wage for a construction worker is not adequate. It is very low.

(c) Who sets the minimum wages?

Ans. The Labour Ministry sets the minimum wages.

NCERT ON PAGE 102

Q.3 The table given below provides some important laws relating to the protection of various interests. Columns (2) and (3) in this table state why and for whom these laws are necessary. Based on discussions in the classroom, you have to complete the remaining entries in the table.

Law	Why is it necessary?	Whose interests does the law protect?
Minimum wages act specifies that wages should not be below a specified minimum.	Many workers are denied fair wages by their employers. Because they badly need work, workers have no bargaining power and are paid low wages.	This law is meant to protect the interests of all workers; particularly, farm labourers, construction workers, factory workers, domestic workers, etc.
Law specifying that there be adequate safety measures in workplaces. For example, alarm system, emergency exists, properly- functioning machinery.		
Law requiring that the quality of goods meet certain prescribed standards. For example, electrical appliances have to meet safety standards.	Consumers might be put to risk by the poor quality of products such as electrical appliances, food, medicines.	
Law requiring that the prices of essential goods are not high – For example, sugar, kerosene, foodgrains.		The interests of the poor who will otherwise be unable to afford
Law requiring that factories do not pollute air or water.		
Laws against child labour in workplaces.		
Law to form workers unions/ associations.	By organising themselves into unions, workers can use their combined power to demand fair wages and better working conditions.	

Ans.

Law	Why is it necessary?	Whose interests does the law protect?
Minimum wages act specifies that wages should not be below a specified minimum.	Many workers are denied fair wages by their employers. Because they badly need work, workers have no bargaining power and are paid low wages.	This law is meant to protect the interests of all workers; particularly, farm labourers, construction workers, factory workers, domestic workers, etc.
Law specifying that there be adequate safety measures in workplaces. For example, alarm system, emergency exists, properly- functioning machinery.	Workplaces have lower safety measures for workers because companies want to cut costs and increase profits.	This law protects the interests of workers as it is meant for the health, safety and welfare of the workers.
Law requiring that the quality of goods meet certain prescribed standards. For example, electrical appliances have to meet safety standards.	Consumers might be put to risk by the poor quality of products such as electrical appliances, food, medicines.	This law protects the interests of the consumers from the unfair and high prices. It also enables the poor to afford necessary goods.
Law requiring that the prices of essential goods are not high – For example, sugar, kerosene, foodgrains.	To keep the prices of essential items stable and prevent middle-men from making profits.	The interests of the poor who will otherwise be unable to afford
Law requiring that factories do not pollute air or water.	To keep the environment, including air and water clean.	This law protects the interests of the public. Clean air and water is necessary for healthy living.
Laws against child labour in workplaces.	Children might be exploited and forced to work in dangerous conditions which would harm their life.	This law protects the interests of children and prevents them from being exploited.
Law to form workers unions/ associations.	By organising themselves into unions, workers can use their combined power to demand fair wages and better working conditions.	This law protects the worker's interest by giving them a way to address their grievances.

NCERT ON PAGE 107

Q.4 Why do you think enforcement of safety laws is important in any factory?

Ans. Enforcement of safety laws is important in any factory for the security of its workers and people living near the factory.

It is important to protect the people from any disastrous incident such as the Bhopal Gas Tragedy.

Q.5 Can you point to a few other situations where laws (or rules) exist but people do not follow them because of poor enforcement? (For example, over-speeding by motorists). What are the problems in enforcement? Can you suggest some ways in which enforcement can be improved?

Ans. Yes, some situations where laws (or rules) exist but people do not follow are the following

- Zebra lines for road crossing
- Giving and taking of dowry
- Employing children under 14 year's age

The problems in enforcement are

- Lack of adequate staff
- Untrained staff
- Irresponsible citizens

Some ways in which enforcement can be improved are

- Strict punishments for breaking laws.
- Deployment of adequate number of staff for enforcing the laws.

NCERT ON PAGE 108

Q.6 'A clean environment is a public facility'. Can you explain this statement?

Ans. A clean environment is a public facility which provides numerous benefits to the community in the following ways

- It helps maintain good public health by reducing the spread of diseases, improving air quality, and ensuring access to safe drinking water.
- It environment also contributes to the overall well-being and quality of life of individuals.
- It offers recreational opportunities such as parks, beaches which promotes good physical and mental health.
- It attracts tourism, which can boost the local economy and create employment opportunities.

Q.7 Why do we need laws?

Ans. We need laws for the welfare of people and bring order in society.

Q.8 Why are companies and contractors able to violate environmental laws?

Ans. Companies and contractors are able to violate environmental laws because there is no strict enforcement of those laws by the government.

EXERCISES

Q.1 Talk to two workers (for example, construction workers, farm workers, factory workers, workers at any shop) to find out if they are receiving the minimum wages laid down by law.

Ans. The following information was received on talking to two workers

- Construction workers do not receive the minimum wages.
- Factory workers do get minimum wages.

Q.2 What are the advantages to foreign companies in setting up production in India?

Ans. The advantages to foreign companies in setting up production in India are as follows

(i) Cheap labour

(ii) Fewer additional expenses (housing facilities, etc.)

(iii) No strict safety standards to follow.

Q.3 Do you think the victims of the Bhopal Gas Tragedy got justice? Discuss.

Ans. No, the victims of the Bhopal Gas Tragedy did not get justice.

The victims of the gas leak have still not been rehabilitated. They are still fighting for safe drinking water, health standards and jobs for living. They are yet to get adequate compensation for the suffering caused. Their cases are still pending in numerous courts.

Q.4 What do we mean when we speak of law enforcement? Who is responsible for enforcement? Why is enforcement so important?

Ans. Law enforcement means implementation of the laws made by the government without discrimination. The government is responsible for enforcement of the laws.

Enforcement of laws is important because

(i) Rules and procedures would be violated excessively without it.

(ii) The Bhopal gas tragedy took place because of lax safety laws in the country.

Q.5 How can laws ensure that markets work in a manner that is fair? Give two examples to support your answer.

Ans. Laws can ensure that markets work in a fair manner in the following ways

(i) Enforcing the law against black-marketing by regular surprise checks to curb hoarding of items.

(ii) Anti Child Labour Act must be enforced to check exploitation of children by sealing shops and industries that employ children.

Q.6 Imagine yourself to be a worker working in a chemical factory, which has received orders from the government to move to a different site 100 kms away from the present location. Write about how your life would change. Read out your responses in the classroom.

Ans. Do it yourself

Q.7 Write a paragraph on the various roles of the government that you have read about in this unit.

Ans. The government performs various roles such as

- providing public facilities for a decent standard of living of all citizens
- making laws for the protection of people from exploitation by the market
- enforcing laws to ensure their proper implementation
- punish those who disobey the laws.

Q.8 What are the sources of environmental pollution in your area? Discuss with respect to

(a) Air (b) Water (c) Soil

What are the steps being taken to reduce the pollution? Can you suggest some other measures.

Ans. Sources of environmental pollution in my area are as follows

(a) **Air** Vehicular emissions and factories emitting hazardous gases.

(b) **Water** Disposal of industrial waste in the rivers and throwing of garbage.

(c) **Soil** Industrial effluents and pesticides.

Steps being taken to reduce pollution are

- Old vehicles emitting polluting gases have been banned.
- Disposal of industrial and household waste/garbage into the rivers prohibited.
- Crackdown on factories emitting pollutants.

Some other suggestions to reduce environmental pollution are as follows

- Promote the use of public transport as much as possible.
- Promote environment friendly ways of disposing waste. e.g. composting.
- Generate awareness among citizens about the harmful effects of polluting the environment.

Q.9 How was environment treated earlier? What has been the change in perception? Discuss.

Ans. Before 1984, there were very few laws for the protection or treatment of environment and there was very weak enforcement of these laws. There was no restriction on the pollution of environment by industries.

However after the Bhopal gas tragedy in 1984, the importance of environment was realised and laws were made for its protection. The courts also gave judgements that emphasized the protection of environment under right to life.

Q.10 **You have read about the Bhopal Gas Tragedy and the on-going struggle. Students from countries across the world have come together to support this struggle for justice. From protest marches to awareness campaigns, you can read about their activities on the website www.studentsforbhopal.com. The website also has resources such as photos, posters, documentaries, victims' statements etc.Use this and other resources to make a wallpaper/exhibition on the Bhopal gas tragedy for your classroom. Invite the whole school to see and talk about it.**

Ans. Do it yourself.

REVIEW EXERCISE

Including Competency Based Questions

PART I

Multiple Choice Questions (MCQs)

1. Enforcement of law become important Diksha

(a) when law seeks to protect the government.
(b) when law seeks to protect the children only.
(c) when law seeks to protect the ministers.
(d) when law seeks to protect the weak from strong.

2. Name the poisonous gas that leaked from Union Carbide's plant leading to a serious disaster.

(a) Methyl Isocyanite (MIC)
(b) Sulphuric Acid (H_2SO_4)
(c) Carbon Monoxide (CO)
(d) None of the above

3. What did the Union Carbide's Bhopal plant produce?

(a) Pesticides (b) Fertilisers
(c) Both (a) and (b) (d) Neither (a) nor (b)

4. Safety measures are workplace which include Diksha

(a) alarm system
(b) emergency exits
(c) properly functioning machinery
(d) All of the above

5. Who ensures that the laws are implemented?

(a) The people (b) Private companies
(c) The government (d) None of these

6. New law on environment are introduced due to Diksha

(a) Bhopal Gas Tragedy
(b) UC factory tragedy
(c) Both (a) and (b)
(d) None of the above

7. Which type of pollution was caused by the Bhopal Gas Tragedy?

(a) Air pollution (b) Water pollution
(c) Neither (a) nor (b) (d) Both (a) and (b)

8. Right to a healthy environment is intrinsic to the Fundamental Right of Competency Based

(a) Right to Equality
(b) Right against Exploitation
(c) Right to Life
(d) Right to Freedom

9. "Delhi's air quality was in 'severe' category on Saturday, with several areas having an AQI above 400. Meanwhile, the demand for air purifiers and masks has surged due to the rise in pollution levels."

***Source* India Today** Competency Based

Which of the following is not one of the causes of air pollution?

(a) Burning of firecrackers
(b) Exhaust from vehicle
(c) Discharge of industrial effluents
(d) Smoke from the chimney of steel industry

10. Jindal Fertilisers, a renowned company, faced growing concerns about pollution caused by its operations within the city. Determined to be environmentally responsible, the company decided to shift its operations outside the city limits." Competency Based

When a company shifts its operations outside the city limits, workers may face which of the following problems?

(i) Job losses
(ii) Dislocation
(iii) Increased commuting costs
(iv) Reduced job opportunities
(v) Safety concerns

Codes

(a) i, ii, iii, v (b) ii, iv, v, iii
(c) i, ii, iv, v (d) All of these

11. **Which one of the following statements is correct?**

I. The government passed many laws to guarantee that workers are not exploited.

II. A person or organisation that produces goods for sale in the market is known as a producer.

Codes

(a) Only I (b) Both I and II
(c) Only II (d) None of these

12. **Which one of the following statements is incorrect?**

I. Foreign companies came to India for cheap labour.

II. Union Carbide is an American company.

Codes

(a) Only I (b) Both I and II
(c) Only II (d) None of these

13. **Arrange the following in the correct sequence.**

I. Bhopal Gas Tragedy. **Competency Based**

II. The Indian Parliament amended the Child Labour (Prohibition and Regulation) Act, 1986.

Iii. Subhash Kumar vs State of Bihar case.

Codes

(a) II, I, III (b) I, III, II,
(c) I, II, , III (d) I, II, III

Answers

1. (d)	2. (a)	3. (a)	4. (d)	5. (c)
6. (c)	7. (d)	8. (c)	9. (c)	10. (d)
11. (b)	12. (d)	13. (b)		

Match the Following

1.

List I	List II
A. Minimum wages	1. Poisonous gas
B. Methyl-Isocyanite	2. Fundamental right
C. Right against Exploitation	3. Source of pollution
D. Industries	4. To protect workers

Codes

	A	B	C	D		A	B	C	D
(a)	1	2	4	3	(b)	2	1	3	4
(c)	4	1	2	3	(d)	3	2	1	4

Ans. (c)

Assertion-Reason

1. **Assertion** (A) Foreign companies come to India for cheap labour.

Reason (R) Wages in India are significantly lower than wages in developed countries like the United States.

Codes

(a) Both A and R are true and R is the correct explanation of A
(b) Both A and R are true, but R is not the correct explanation of A
(c) A is true, but R is false
(d) A is false, but R is true

2. **Assertion** (A) The environment is a 'free' entity.

Reason (R) We all have a right to a clean and healthy environment.

Codes

(a) Both A and R are true and R is the correct explanation of A
(b) Both A and R are true, but R is not the correct explanation of A
(c) A is true, but R is false
(d) A is false, but R is true

Ans. 1. (a) Both A and R are true and R is the correct explanation of A

2. (d) A is false, but R is true

Fill in the Blanks

1. The government makes .... to protect people from exploitation.
2. Markets deny workers their rights in the drive for ....
3. There is a law on .... to ensure that workers are not under paid.
4. Emissions from vehicles are a major cause of .... pollution.
5. Laws ensure that the relations between workers, consumers and producers are not ....
6. Bhopal Gas Tragedy occurred on .... **Diksha**

Ans. 1. laws
2. profits
3. minimum wages
4. air
5. exploitative
6. 2nd December, 1984

True/False

1. The minimum wages are revised up wards every few years.
2. Within three days of the Bhopal Gas Tragedy, more than 8,000 people were dead.
3. Accidents are rare in construction sites.
4. The victims of the Bhopal Gas Tragedy finally got justice.

Ans. 1. True 2. True 3. False 4. False

Picture Based Questions

1. Observe the picture carefully and choose the correct statement.

I. According to the 2011 Census, over 4 million children in India aged between 5 and 14 work in various occupations, including hazardous ones.

II. Children under the age of 14 are prohibited from working in any occupation, and adolescents aged 14-18 are prohibited from working in hazardous occupations and processes.

III. Anyone found violating against Child Labour Prevention Act, the ban must be penalised with a jail term of six months to two years or a fine of ₹ 20,000 to ₹ 50,000, or both.

Codes

(a) I and II (b) II and III
(c) I, II and III (d) None of these

2. This given photo is of Disneyland. Where is Disneyland located?

(a) New York (b) Shanghai (c) New Delhi (d) Paris

Ans. 1. (c) 2. (d)

Case Based Question

1. Read the passage given below and answer the questions that follow.

The Bhopal disaster brought the issue of the environment to the forefront. Several thousands of persons who were not associated with the factory in anyway were greatly affected because of the poisonous gases leaked from the plant. This made people realise that the existing laws, though weak, only covered the individual workers and not persons who might be injured due to industrial accidents. In response to this pressure from environmental activists and others, in the years following the Bhopal gas tragedy, the Indian government introduced new laws on the environment. Henceforth, the polluter was to be held accountable for the damage done to environment. The environment is something that people over generations will share, and it could not be destroyed merely for industrial development. The courts also gave a number of judgments upholding the right to a healthy environment as intrinsic to the Fundamental Right to Life. In Subhash Kumar vs. State of Bihar (1991), the Supreme Court held that the Right to Life is a Fundamental Right under Article 21 of the Constitution and it includes the right to the enjoyment of pollution-free water and air for full enjoyment of life. The government is responsible for setting up laws and procedures that can check pollution, clean rivers and introduce heavy fines for those who pollute.

(i) There are several Fundamental Rights in the Indian Constitution. Name the fundamental right that includes pollution free environment.

(a) Right to Education
(b) Right to Property
(c) Right to Freedom of Speech
(d) Right to Life under Article 21

(ii) The responsibility of imposing fines for environmental pollution lies with which of the following authorities/individuals?

(a) Environmental activists (b) The Supreme Court
(c) The government (d) Industrialists

(iii) The right to a healthy environment was recognised as which of the following in one of the Supreme Court judgements?

(a) A Fundamental Right under Article 21 of the Constitution
(b) A human right under international law
(c) A right that can be enforced through the courts
(d) All of the above

(iv) In the context of the Fundamental Right to Life, what did the Supreme Court affirm as part of this right in Subhash Kumar vs. State of Bihar (1991)?

(a) Right to own property
(b) Right to clean rivers
(c) Right to free education
(d) Right to pollution-free water and air

Ans. (i) (d) Right to Life under Article 21
(ii) (c) The government
(iii) (d) All of the above
(iv) (d) Right to pollution-free water and air

Very Short Answer Type Questions

1. What does the Constitution say about child labour?

Ans. The Constitution states that no child below the age of 14 years shall be employed to work in any factory or mines or engaged in any other hazardous employment.

2. What is the Minimum Wages Act?

Ans. The Minimum Wages Act specifies that wages should not be below specified minimum limit.

3. Why foreign companies come to India? Give one reason.

Ans. The foreign companies come to India for cheap labour.

4. Which incident brought the issue of environment to the forefront in India?

Ans. The Bhopal Gas Tragedy (1984) brought the issue of environment to the forefront in India.

5. Name the company which was involved in the Bhopal gas tragedy.

Ans. Union Carbide was the company responsible for the Bhopal gas tragedy.

6. Who were the victims of the Bhopal gas tragedy?

Ans. The victims of the Bhopal gas tragedy were poor, working-class families living near the plant.

7. What happened to the Union Carbide (UC) plant following the disaster? **Competency Based**

Ans. UC stopped its operations in that plant following the disaster, leaving behind tons of toxic chemicals.

8. Apart from making laws, what are the other responsibilities of the government? **Diksha**

Ans. Apart from making laws the other responsibilities of the government is ensuring the implementation and enforcement of these laws.

9. Name the South Asian countries which have become centres for industries producing pesticides, asbestos or processing zinc and lead. **Competency Based**

Ans. India, Bangladesh and Pakistan are three South Asian countries which have become centres for industries producing perticides, asbestos or processing zinc and lead.

Short Answer Type Questions

1. Was the Bhopal gas tragedy an accident? Give reasons for your answer.

Ans. The Bhopal gas tragedy was not an accident as Union Carbide had deliberately ignored the essential safety measures in order to cut costs. Much before the Bhopal disaster in 1984, there had been incidents of gas leak killing a worker and injuring several others.

2. The right against Exploitation says that no one can be forced to work for low wages or under bondage. **Competency Based**

(i) Explain the Right against Exploitation.

Ans. The Right against Exploitations is a Fundamental Right in the Indian Constitution that prohibits human trafficking, forced labour and child labour. It ensures that individuals are protected from exploitation and guarantees their dignity and freedom.

(ii) What is the Child Labour Act in India?

Ans. The Child Labour (Prohibition and Regulation) Act, 1986, in India is a legal framework that prohibits the employment of children below the age of 14 years in all occupations and of adolescents (14-18 years) in hazardous occupations and processes.

3. As per your understanding of the chapter, state how the workers are exploited?

Ans. The workers are exploited in the following ways

- By giving them low wages
- Employing child as a labour
- Poor, unhygienic and unsafe conditions of work
- No job security

4. What are the reasons for the sharp differences in safety standards between the two Union Carbide factories in the USA and India? **Diksha**

Ans. The reasons for the sharp differences in safety standards between the two Union Carbide factories in the USA and India are as follows

- Workers in India are easily replaceable because of high unemployment rate.
- Workers are willing to work in unsafe conditions for wages.
- There is ignorance and vulnerability of Indian workers.

5. Why is the perceived worth of an Indian worker so low?

Ans. The perceived worth of an Indian worker is so low because the worker in India is easily replaceable due to high unemployment rate where many workers agree to work in unsafe conditions for wages. As a result, the employers ignore the safety at workplaces.

6. In your view, what can the government do to ensure that laws are fully implemented? **Competency Based**

Ans. The government can ensure that laws are fully implemented by conducting surprise raids and checks the workplace.

It can, for instance, ensure that every worker gets fair wages by regularly inspecting work sites and punish those who violate the law.

Through implementation of laws, the government can control the activities of individuals or private companies so as to ensure social justice.

Long Answer Type Questions

1. What is the status of child labour in India as per Census of 2011? Diksha

Ans. According to the 2011 Census, over 40 million children in India, aged between 5 and 14 years work in various occupations including hazardous ones.

In October 2016, the government amended the Child Labour Protection Act, banning children under 14 years of age from working as domestic servants or as workers in dhabas, restaurants, tea shops etc. It made employing these children a punishable offence.

Anyone found violating the ban must be penalised with a punishment ranging from a jail term of three months to two years and/or fine of ₹ 20,000 to ₹50,000. The Central Government has asked State Governments to develop plans to rescue and rehabilitate children who are working as domestic servants.

2. Compare and contrast UC's safety systems in Bhopal with that of its other plant in the USA.

Ans. There was huge difference in the safety system installed in the UC plant at America and Bhopal.

In West Virginia plant in America, computerised warning system and monitoring system as well as emergency evacuation plans were present.

On the other hand, the UC plant in Bhopal relied on manual gauges and the human senses to detect gas leaks. The emergency evacuation plans were also non-existent in Bhopal.

Apart from these, the Company cut its costs by seriously compromising on safety in the Bhopal plant. Every safety device was either malfunctioning or in short supply. Between 1980 and 1984, the number of workers for the plant was decreased in half from 12 to 6 workers. The period of safety training for workers was reduced from 6 months to 15 days and the post of night-shift worker for the plant was abolished.

3. Why do foreign companies come to India?

Ans. Many foreign companies come to India for cheap labour. The wages that these companies pay to workers of other countries like USA, are higher than the wages they have to pay to workers in poorer countries like India.

These companies can get longer hours of work for lower pay, and the additional expenses for workers such as for housing facilities, are also fewer. These companies also often ignore safety in workplaces, so they can save costs and earn higher profits.

An example these companies is the Union Carbide (UC), an American company that had set up a plant in Bhopal in which it produced pesticides.

The UC plant included lower working conditions and lower safety measures for cost cutting.

4. "As a law making and enforcement agency, it was the responsibility of the government to implement safety law." How has the government failed in its responsibility to enforce safety laws? Competency Based

Ans. As a law making and enforcement agency it was the responsibility of government to implement safety laws. However, there was violation of safety laws in the Union Carbide plant. This violation occurred because of the following reasons

- The safety laws were weak in India and even these weak safety laws were not enforced.
- The government officials did not recognised the plant as hazardous and allowed it to operate in populated locality.
- Some municipal officials raised objection to the installation of an MIC production unit in 1978 because of safety violations. However, the government allowed the factory to start production as it was providing jobs and investment.

  The government did not ask UC to shift to cleaner technology or safer procedures.
- Government inspectors continued to approve the procedures in the plant despite repeated incidents of gas leaks.

Thus, the government thus failed in its responsibility to protect the interests of the people and seriously compromised on their safety.

5. "The Bhopal disaster brought the issue of environment to the forefront. Several thousands of persons who were not associated with the factory in any way were greatly affected because of the poisonous gases leaked from the plant." Competency Based
Discuss how the environmental laws evolved in India?

Ans. In India, there were very few environment laws in 1984 and there was hardly any enforcement of these laws. The environment was regarded as a free entity and any industry could pollute the air and water without any restrictions.

In Bhopal gas tragedy, several people who were not directly related to the factory in any way were greatly affected by the poisonous gases leaked from the plant.

Thus, it was realised by the people that the existing environment laws only covered individual worker and did not cover those persons who might be injured due to industrial accidents.

The Indian government introduced new laws after the Bhopal gas Tragedy because of the pressure from environmental activists. Under these laws, the polluter was to be held accountable for the damage done to the environment.

The Supreme Court in Subhash Kumar Vs. State of Bihar(1991) ruled that the Right to Life is a Fundamental Right under Article 21 of the Constitution and it includes the right to the enjoyment of pollution-free water and air.

Picture Based Questions

1. Look at the picture given below and answer the question that follow. 

It's really cruel burdening kids like this. I had to hire that boy to help my son!

What do you think the famous cartoonist RK Laxman is trying to convey in this cartoon? How does it relate to the 2016 law that you read about (NCERT Textbook) on page 103?

Ans. The cartoonist is trying to convey the issue of child labour in our society. Another issue that he is trying to convey is heavy load of schoolbags on today's children. This cartoon relates to Child Labour (Prohibition and Regulation) Act, 1986 which banned the employment of children below the age of 14 years in all occupations and of adolescents (14-18 years) in hazardous occupations and processes.

2. Look at the picture and information given below and answer the questions that follow.

Emissions from vehicles are a major cause of environmental pollution. In a series of rulings (1998 onwards), the Supreme Court had ordered all public transport vehicles using diesel were to switch to Compressed Natural Gas (CNG). As a result of this move, air pollution in cities like Delhi came down considerably. But a recent report by the Center for Science and Environment, New Delhi, shows the presence of high levels of toxic substance in the air. This is due to emissions from cars run on diesel (rather than petrol) and a sharp increase in the number of cars on the road.

(i) What are the challenges of balancing environmental protection and workers' livelihoods?

Ans. The challenges include the loss of jobs, the relocation of workers to polluted areas, and the safety of workers.

(ii) What is one example of an environmental issue that has negatively affected workers livelihoods?

Ans. One example is the closure of polluting industries in residential areas in Delhi.

While this action solved the problem of pollution in those areas, it also resulted in many workers losing their jobs.

Case Based Question

1. Read the passage given below and answer the question that follow. NCERT

Environment as Public Facility

In recent years, while the courts have come out with strong orders on environmental issues, these have sometimes affected people's livelihoods adversely. For instance, the courts directed industries in residential areas in Delhi to close down or shift out of the city. Several of these industries were polluting the neighbourhood and discharge from these industries was polluting the river Yamuna, because they had been set up without following the rules. But, while the court's action solved one problem, it created another. Because of the closure, many workers lost their jobs. Others were forced to go to far-away places where these factories had relocated. And the same problem now began to come up in these areas-for now these places became polluted. And the issue of the safety conditions of workers remained unaddressed.

Recent research on environmental issues in India has highlighted the fact that the growing concern for the environment among the middle classes is often at the expense of the poor. So, for example, slums need to be cleaned as part of a city's beautification drive, or as in the case above, a polluting factory is moved to the outskirts of the city. And while this awareness of the need for a clean environment is increasing, there is little concern for the safety of the workers themselves. The challenge is to look for solutions where everyone can benefit from a clean environment. One way this can be done is to gradually move to cleaner technologies and processes in factories.

The government has to encourage and support factories to do this. It will need to fine those who pollute. This will ensure that the workers livelihoods are protected and both workers and communities living around the factories enjoy a safe environment.

(i) Do you think everyone got justice in the case cited above?

Ans. No, everyone did not get justice because the welfare of workers was ignored. They were deprived of their livelihood.

(ii) Can you think of other ways in which the environment can be protected? Discuss in class.

Ans. Some other ways in which the environment can be protected are as follows

- Afforestation
- Use of public transport
- Ban use of polybags
- Proper disposal of sewage

ASSESSMENT EXERCISE

Multiple Choice Questions (MCQs)

1. No child below the age of .... years shall be employed to work in any factory or mines.

(a) 14 (b) 15
(c) 18 (d) All of these

2. The Bhopal gas tragedy took place on

(a) 10th October, 2002
(b) 2nd December, 1986
(c) 2nd November, 2004
(d) 4th December, 1985

3. An individual who buys goods for personal use and not for resale called as

(a) producer (b) consumer
(c) wages (d) None of these

Subjective Questions (VSA, SA & LA)

1. Define Market.

2. Name the South Asian Countries.

3. Which chemical is responsible for Bhopal gas tragedy?

4. What is the full form of UC?

5. Write a short note on Child Labour?

6. What do 'Right against Exploitation' Says?

7. What were the reasons by which Bhopal gas tragedy took place?

8. Describe the law for producer and consumers.

9. What are the new laws made by government to protect the Environments?

Being Prepared-A Vital Part of Disaster Management

CHAPTER 1

India is a unique geo-physical entity with a vast population. It is also known as one of the world's most disaster-prone countries because various types of natural disasters such as cyclones, drought, earthquake, floods or landslides strike in different parts of India in varying intensity making us vulnerable in different degrees.

1.1 Hazard Prone Regions

There are certain regions where one hazard is more likely to happen than another. These are

- **Coastal areas** which are frequently hit by cyclones.
- **Plateaus and mountainous regions** which are under the threat of landslides and earthquakes.
- **Ganga-Brahmaputra** and most other river valley regions which are mostly affected by floods.
- Severe drought is often experienced by Rajasthan and Western Odisha.
- To combat these situations, communities must be prepared themselves beforehand, so that they can be tackled in a better way.
- **Disaster preparedness**[1] is a process involving activities that help us to face disasters efficiently.
- Whenever a disaster strikes, it is the **community**[2] which faces it first, which is called the **first responder**.
- The Government and International Agencies like United Nations, or Red Cross, and Panchayats in rural areas assist the first responders.
- So, it is our responsibility to get prepared for the upcoming disasters beforehand in order to minimise the damage to life and property.
- The areas which are vulnerable to more than one disaster are considered as **multi-hazard** zone.
- India is divided into various disaster prone zones. When these zones overlap, then that overlapped area is called multi-hazard zone. For example, coastal areas may face flood and cyclones frequently.
- A hazard is considered a disaster only when it becomes a cause of loss of life and property, but if people are equipped to face it or adopt some safety measures beforehand, then it is called a hazard. For example when a flood occurs and people are not prepared to face it, it may cause huge destruction to life and valuables. Then the flood becomes a disaster. But if people are evacuated along with valuables to a safe shelter, then the flood remains a hazard and not a disaster.

1.2 Types of Disasters

Disasters are of two types

Natural Disasters

Natural disasters include all those hazards which are naturally generated and cannot be prevented but mitigated. Disasters are sometimes referred to as calamities. For example, earthquakes, volcanic eruptions, tsunami, droughts, floods, cyclones etc. These are described below

Earthquake

The Earth we live on is made-up of large plates that float over an ocean of semi-molten rock. Due to their movements, the Himalayas emerged 65 million years ago. When two plates collide with each other, energy is released and earthquake takes place; it shakes the Earth for some seconds sometimes with great or low intensity. For example, Delhi is situated near a fault.

1 **Disaster Preparedness** It refers to the set of activities and precautions that a community collectively takes before a disaster occurs, in order to reduce the impact of a disaster, and to cope with it efficiently.

2 **Community** It refers to the people who live together in a village or urban area, who can be identified as a local group with a common way of life.

As earthquakes are more likely to occur along **faults**[3], Delhi, which has a dense population is more vulnerable to disaster.

Tsunami

Tsunami is an under water earthquake which causes huge waves generally running across the ocean with a speed of 8000 km/h.

Drought

Drought is a natural phenomenon, which occurs when an area receives less than **normal rainfall**[4] rate.

It is characterised by a deficiency of surface or sub-surface water leading to acute shortage of water.

Causes of Drought

Environmental degradation[5] is a major factor that intensifies drought situation.

Other causes are deforestation, soil erosion (by wind and water), loss of biodiversity and excessive use of ground or surface water.

Floods

Floods are the most frequent and often the most devastating disaster in India. Floods usually occur due to excessive rainfall when water rises above its normal course or level. This results in submerging of places under water for prolonged or short periods of time. The Ganga and Brahmaputra rivers cause the largest floods in India. Besides this, areas of the West, East and South are also called flood-prone regions.

Cyclones

A cyclone is a storm that occurs due to a difference in temperature and pressure of air, over the warm waters of the oceans. It comes with strong winds and lashing rain. Tidal waves also cause floods in coastal regions.

A cyclone is powerful enough to destroy all the elements which are on its way such as

- Trees
- Concrete buildings and houses

Man-made Disasters

Man-made disasters can be caused inadvertently or by major accidents or by deliberate actions of individuals, groups or government.

Following are some types of man-made disasters

Nuclear Attacks

The nuclear attack on Hiroshima and Nagasaki in Japan in 1945 caused a lot of destruction through the generation of heat, fire and radiation. Besides this, military or navy missile or war testing may also cause these disasters.

Biological Disasters

Biological disasters can be caused by preserving and releasing germs of deadly diseases such as small pox, jaundice or by polluting water. For example, terrorists used Anthrax to eliminate people in the USA in 2002. It was a biological weapon.

Due to Dangerous Chemicals

Man-made disasters are caused by the misuse or spread of dangerous chemicals. For example, Bhopal gas tragedy in 1984 was an industrial accident caused by the release of Methyl Iso- Cyanate or MIC, a lethal gas. It caused the death of many persons almost instantly and after two decades, people are still suffering from the after effects of this disaster.

Other Disasters

Other disasters are major fires land, air or water accidents caused by collisions, breakdown etc., and collapse of bridges and buildings.

1.3 Mitigation of Disasters

Man-made disasters can be prevented by adhering to rules which govern the way a building must be constructed. These are called **Building Bye Laws**[6]. By following these rules, the community can be ensure that all constructions in the country are made-up of disaster resistant designs as well as layout.

At international level, countries sign agreements on Nuclear Non-Proliferation Treaties mutually agreeing not to develop nuclear weapons for mass destruction. Further, the industrial disasters and accidents can also be reduced and mitigated by adhering conscientiously to safety measures.

---

3 **Faults** These are places in the Earth where the rocks are broken and the rocks on one side have moved in some direction relative to the other. Faults are planes, not lines.

4 **Normal rainfall** When the rainfall for the monsoon season of June to September for a place is within +/– 19% of its long period average. It is categorised as normal. When the monsoon rainfall deficiency exceeds 19%, it is categorised as deficient or scanty.

5 **Environmental degradation** In simple terms, it is the reduction or deterioration of environmental resources that harms us in many ways.

6 **Building Bye Laws** It is a set of rules and regulations that prescribe the standards for construction of, spacing between and access to buildings. The purpose of these laws is to ensure that all constructions in the country conform to disaster resistant designs, as well as layout.

Mitigation of Natural Disasters

Natural disasters can be mitigated if we prepare communities to face and respond to disasters effectively. Taking care of our environment is a big responsibility of all of us due to which we can mitigate the different types of calamities. So, economic development should be done a way that it not only meets the needs of our demands but also ensures not to become a cause of environmental degradation. Only then we can be succeeded in conserving lives and valuables. Thus, disaster management helps us to adapt ourselves to nature and learn to use it to our advantage.

Role of Different Agencies

To face disasters better, at first we should be aware about its causes and effects, and also by creating a more disaster-resilient society . Many different agencies, the government and communities are ready to help in coping with the after-effects of the disaster.

These agencies are called **civil-society** which together work in making an effective Disaster Management Plan.

Community Contingency Plan

It is a series of assessments and evaluations followed by the development of proposed plans of action in anticipation of a natural or human-made disaster.

This involves

- Identification of the potential threat, for example proximity to an active volcano, settlements on seismic faults or flood plains, history of drought, food shortages, or epidemics etc. Identification of likely impact of disaster, for exmaple number of people potentially affected, disruption of food or water supply, transportation system, or communication channels, damage to property, roads, health facilities, duration of disaster and its effects.
- Identifying methods to mitigate the disasters such as shelter-belt plantations to break the intensity of cyclones along the coast. Anticipating and developing optimum response to such a threat. For example educate/ alert population to potential risk, develop notification and evacuation plans, provide means of transporting people, food and medical supplies.
- Identification of existing resources. For example areas where shelters could be established, sources of food, water and medical supplies, communication and transportation systems, location of reconstruction equipment. Conducting periodic mock drills, which are a simulation of a disaster to assess and improve the effectiveness of the disaster preparedness plan of a community or system.

REVIEW EXERCISE

Covering Textbook Questions

Q.1 What do you understand by disaster preparedness? In India, which are the common disasters we have to be prepared for?

Ans. Disaster preparedness activities are designed to minimise loss of life and damage, for example by removing people and property from a threatened location and by facilitating timely and effective rescue, relief and rehabilitation. Preparedness is the main way of reducing the impact of disasters. In India, there are various disasters which affect the lives people and their valuable such as earthquakes, landslide, cyclone, flood, forest fire, drought, avalanche, tsunami and so on.

Q.2 What role do you see for yourself in making your community disaster-resilient? Discuss in groups and share your findings with the class.

Ans. Students can play a great role in making the community disaster-resilient. Students can spread awareness among citizens about the disaster hazards and steps that are needed to be taken after a disaster has occurred. Small tasks like providing first aids to the victims can be done by them.

Q.3 Discuss some methods to organise yourselves to manage disasters.

Ans. Some methods to organise ourselves to manage disasters are

- Spreading understanding about impending natural calamities and disasters.
- Teach people about survival techniques in case of natural disasters.
- Basic preparedness must be shared.
- Spreading awareness about first aid and ways to prepare first aid boxes.
- A list of important offices and officials phone numbers should be distributed in case of calamity.

Q.4 When does a hazard transforms into a disaster?

Ans. A hazard transforms into a disaster when the impact of a hazard on the community is such that the people are not able to cope up with the disaster causing injury, loss of property and death.

Earthquakes

CHAPTER 2

An earthquake is a sudden trembling or shaking movement of the Earth's surface (**crust**[1]). Earthquake have varying degrees of intensity. Most earthquakes are minor **tremors**[2].

Large earthquakes begin with slight tremors but suddenly change into more violent shocks and leave vibrations of gradually diminishing force called aftershocks.

Focus is the subterranean point of origin of an earthquake. The point on the surface directly above the focus is the epicentre. **Epicentre**[3] is the most sensitive place where intensity of the earthquake is felt the most.

The **Richter scale**[4] and the **Modified Mercalli scale**[5] are used to measure the magnitude and intensity of an earthquake.

2.1 Causes of Earthquake

- The Earth's crust is made of massive interlocking blocks of rocks called tectonic plates. These plates float on a layer of semi-liquid rock called the **mantle**[6].
- When tectonic plates collide with each other, pressure is released which causes a **fault**[7]. Then these movements may result in vibrations which pass through and around the Earth in waveform, as ripples are generated when a pebble is dropped into water and earthquakes happen.
- Earthquakes are natural phenomena. They cause the most sudden of all disasters, without any warning time.
- It damages life and property in urban and semi-urban areas because of high rise concrete structures.
  For example, the incident of the Gujarat earthquake in 2001, ruined more lives and properties because of the high-rise buildings which were built without adhering to the required structural engineering norms during the construction and design of these buildings.

Effect on People Due to Earthquakes

The effects of earthquakes are diverse. About 95 per cent of people killed in an earthquake are killed by falling buildings. If earthquake happens at night, it affects people more adversely because when people are asleep, they are not prepared for the first tremors (foreshocks), which may cause huge destruction of life and valuables. The broad zone surrounding the epicentre is the most affected zone in times of earthquake. Earthquakes may lead to other dangerous hazards such as landslides, floods, fires and huge ocean waves called tsunami.

People More at Risk during Earthquake

Some people are usually more at risk because of their location or socio-economic condition. Earthquakes occur mostly along a geological fault (a place where two sections of the Earth's crust join). Bedrock areas with flexible structures (buildings, houses) receive fewer effects of earthquake and are also more persistent than rigid structures built on loose soil or river deposits.

The worst affected people are the poor communities who suffer a lot and have no choice to live in a well-structured place. In poorer regions, people may not have access to information about how to make their houses safer.

Some people even do have information, but due to lack of money, they are unable to afford stronger, better-quality building materials. After a disaster, due to the loss of livelihoods, physical injuries, destruction, no availability of means of transportation and no insurance, the poor communities find it very difficult to regain the position they were in before the disaster struck.

1 **Crust** It is the solid surface of the Earth.
2 **Tremor** It refers to shaking of the ground.
3 **Epicentre** It is the place on the surface of the Earth directly above the hypocentre.
4 **Richter scale** It is a scale which classifies the magnitude (force) of an earthquake.
5 **Modified Mercalli Scale** It is a scale which classifies the intensity (effects) of an earthquake.
6 **Mantle** It is the semi-liquid layer of rock below the Earth's crust.
7 **Fault** It is a place where two or more blocks of the Earth's crust join.

KNOWLEDGE PLUS In parts of Iran, which are vulnerable to earthquakes, the days are hot and the nights are cold. Houses are often designed with thick walls and heavy roofs, which are excellent for insulating people from extreme temperatures, but not so good at resisting earthquakes.

2.2 Earthquakes in India

The Himalayan region being the world's youngest fold mountain ranges, as well as geologically active, is the earthquake prone area. India is divided into five seismic zones (in descending order), among which the Himalayan region is in the highest earthquake risk zones. The entire North-East region and the Kutch region of Gujarat are in zone 5 which means that people of these areas are most vulnerable to earthquakes.

Five Seismic zones are as follows

- Zone - 5 (very high risk)
- Zone-4 (high risk)
- Zone-3 (moderate risk)
- Zone-2 (low risk)
- Zone - 1 (very low risk)

Measuring Earthquakes

Magnitude refers to severity of an earthquake, that is, the seismic energy recorded on a seismograph. Intensity means the observed effects that the ground shaking has on people, buildings, man-made structures and natural features.

There are two different ways of measuring earthquake. These are

(i) The Richter scale
  (a) It is an open-ended scale.
  (b) It measures the energy or intensity of an earthquake means (how strong it is).

(ii) The Modified Mercalli scale
  (a) It has twelve classes.
  (b) It measures the effects of an earthquake (how damaging it is).

An earthquake that is small in magnitude (low on the Richter scale, can still cause a lot of damage (high on the Modified Mercalli scale).

- Some of the classes on the Mercalli scale are explained as follows

Class I - III	Not felt, except by very few people.
Class IV-VI	Felt by nearly everyone. Some windows broken. Unstable objects fall over. Pendulum clocks may stop.
Class VII-X	Everybody runs outdoors. Buildings designed to resist earthquakes and made of strong materials are hardly damaged; ordinary buildings are moderately damaged; buildings not designed to resist earthquakes, or made from weaker materials, are severely damaged. Earthquake is noticed by people driving cars.
Class XI - XII	Total devastation. Earthquake waves are seen on the surface of the ground. Objects are thrown upwards into the air.

2.3 Preparing for an Earthquake

We can be prepared for an earthquake by following these steps:

Step-1 Train Ourselves

When an earthquake occurs, it is important to help survivors quickly. First responders usually carry out most of the first-aid and rescue work. So, we have to train ourselves in basic rescue and first-aid functions.

Drop, Cover and Hold in the event of tremors

If you are indoors when an earthquake strikes, stay there. **Drop, cover and hold**, protecting your eyes by pressing your face against your arm, until the shaking stops. If unable to drop, cover and hold because there's no table or desk nearby, take other protective action. *For example*, sit on the floor against an interior wall away from windows, skylights, doors and things that could fall.

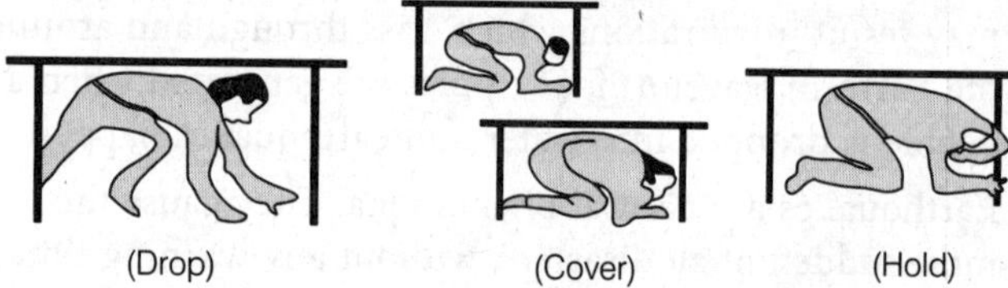
(Drop) (Cover) (Hold)

Step-2 Appropriate Technology in Buildings

We must ensure retrofitting our existing buildings and strengthen their structures to make them earthquake resistant. We can do this by applying appropriate technology in building material and also adhering to safety norms in new constructions including the Building Bye Laws.

Step-3 In Case of Tremors

When tremors occur, one should duck, i.e. bend down under the desk and stay away from heavy objects like windows, bookcases, filing cabinets, heavy mirrors, hanging plants, fans and other such objects the shaking stops. When you are in a school building or home, rush to open fields for safety and away from trees, signs, buildings, electrical wires and poles.

If living in a high rise building, move against an interior wall and cover the head with arms and a helmet. Do not use the lifts in case of earthquake. If one is driving during an earthquake, just pull over to the road side and get out of the car, and move away from flyovers, power lines and advertisement boards.

If you are sitting in a stadium, theatre or auditorium, do not rush at the time of earthquake, just cover your head with your arms and stay calm till the shaking is over. Then let younger children, elderly and disabled people leave first in an orderly manner.

Step-4 After the Tremors Subside

When earthquake stops, people should be prepared for aftershocks. When injured, check yourself first and then help others who are distressed. In case of fire, keep a bucket of sand ready to put out the fire and call the Fire Department (101) or Police Control Room (100).

Step-5 Relief Centre

In the areas of moderate to very high risk zone, buildings like schools, hospitals, etc could become a relief centre.

At relief centres, the following things are required to cope with the trauma the people have been through

- **Activity kits** including books, papers, colour pencils and chalk for drawing and writing purpose.
- **Sewing kits** to repair and stitch clothes.
- **Cleaning and Utilities kit** that is very essential for health and hygiene.

2.4 Conclusion

Earthquakes are destructive but sometimes they give an opportunity to communities to start afresh and improve on their pre-disaster conditions by adopting adequate mitigation and preparedness measures through concerted efforts.

A student has an important role to play in educating his/her community on earthquake risk, as well as creating awareness on how to cope with sudden disasters.

The given tips are very much useful to understand and cope up with the sudden earthquake phenomena and face it with confidence.

REVIEW EXERCISE

Covering Textbook Questions

ACTIVITIES

Q.1 Which zone does your village or city fall in? Has your village or city ever experienced an earthquake?

Ans. Attempt yourself.

Q.2 What is a seismograph? Where is it usually kept in your city? If you live in a village, can you find out where the nearest seismograph is kept?

Ans. Seismograph is an earthquake sensitive detection or an instrument used for recording the intensity and duration of seismic waves. It is usually kept at geological centre.

Q.2 What would you do if you find that someone is trapped inside a building under the rubble and you can hear the person, though you can't see him or her? Can you find out if your village or Gram Panchayat or Block/Taluka has specialised search and rescue teams for disasters, if you live in a rural area? If you live in a city, do you know if such teams exist?

Ans. Attempt yourself with the help of your teacher.

Q.3 How would you deal with a person who has lost everything in an earthquake and is shocked? Find out more about trauma counselling? Who can be a good counsellor?

Ans. When a person has lost everything in a disaster (like an earthquake, etc) and undergoes a severe emotional shock and pain caused by extremely upsetting experience which is called trauma', then the person needs 'trauma counselling' which means a short-term intervention. It is appropriate for such people who are suffering traumatic incidents like joblessness, death, car accident, illness and facing a disaster. Trauma counselling supports people in identifying and coming to terms with the feeling and emotions one may feel during and after a traumatic experience.

Objective

To get your life back on track and to move you from being a victim to being a victor.

A person can be a good counsellor if he has these traits:

- Listening to what you are saying (and not saying).
- Supporting your coping mechanisms. Exploring with you and validating your feelings and emotions.
- Supporting you to make sense of the incident.
- Preventing the use of suppression as a defense.
- Integrating the event into your life.

Q.4 How would you prevent bleeding from a wound on the arm?

Ans. Applying pressure with cotton and bandage is very effective in preventing bleeding from a wounded arm.

Q.5 Make posters to tell people what to do when there are tremors. Display them in prominent places in your village or area, if in zones 3-5.

Ans. Do it yourself with the help of your teacher and peer group.

Q.6 Make an illustrated comic type information sheet on the DROP, COVER and HOLD routine for people or children who cannot read and explain it to them.

Ans. Attempt yourself.

Q.7 What precautions should one take when one enters a building that has cracked or collapsed because of an earthquake?

Ans. When entering a building which has been cracked or collapsed because of an earthquake, one should keep away from unconsolidated items and walls, keep in mind the possibility of aftershocks and rush outside with the survivor as quickly as he can.

Q.8 Are there Ham Radio Operators in your village or area? Find out more about Ham Radio.

Ans. Ham Radio or Amateur radio is basically a social hobby and a radio communication service provider in which the users which are called **hams** must pass an examination in order to operate this.

People get connected with Ham radio whether they are in remote, obscure locations or trapped during a disaster.

Ham radio operators are allowed to use every mode of communication: AM, FM, CW, SSB and so on, worldwide.

Amateur radio includes a vast array of activities like

- Talking around the world without wires.
- Talking locally through repeaters.
- Emergency communications.
- Public service communications.
- Amateur radio satellites in space and so on.
- According to an estimation, six million people are regularly involved with ham radio, worldwide.

Q.9 Draw a map of your village or, area locating your school, houses, ponds, tanks, etc., as well as open spaces and high rise buildings. Mark an emergency evacuation route plan, for use in case of an earthquake. Take your plan to your local DMT. Take their help to locate possible relief centres and cattle protection areas (if in a village). If your village or area does not have a DMT yet, your teachers could help your with this exercise.

Ans. Do with the help your teacher.

EXERCISES

Q.1 Which earthquake vulnerability zones do you live in? (Use the map)

Ans. Students should refer their area's zonal map and try to identify their place where they live in.

Q.2 What would you do if you were going home from school and there was an earthquake?

Ans. If an earthquake strikes while going homes from school, the student should try to rush to an open ground or area away from high-rise buildings, towers, etc.

Q.3 Where would you go if you were in the games field and there was an earthquake?

Ans. It is better to stay in the games field rather than move to another place.

Q.4 What activities would you do with children who have witnessed and experienced an earthquake when they come to a relief camp or shelter?

Ans. I would conduct fun activities including games and story-telling sessions to cheer-up the children who had witnessed the earthquake.

Q.5 List simple do's and don'ts in the event of tremors or an earthquake.

Ans. Do's

- In the event of an earthquake, use the drop, cover and hold method to protect yourself.
- If living in a high-rise building, you must protect your head with arms and wear a helmet for safety.
- Move to open fields.
- If you are driving a vehicle, pull over to the side of the road and stop and get out of the car.
- Move away from flyovers, power lines and advertisement boards.

Dont's

- Do not stay near unstable objects like fans, windows, mirrors as they may shatter and cause injury.
- Do not stand near buildings, trees, poles, towers etc.

Q.6 How does preparedness help you and your community when an earthquake occurs?

Ans. When people and communities are made aware about earthquake's causes and effect, they prepare themselves beforehand. That saves their lives as well as valuables and properties and reduces the damage. People can be ready to volunteer and cope up with the after-effects.

Cyclones

CHAPTER 3

A cyclone is a large air mass that rotates around a strong center of low atmospheric pressure. The Indian subcontinent is the worst cyclone-affected part of the world, as a result of low-depth of the Ocean bed and the way our coast is shaped. The Indian Ocean is one of the six major cyclone-prone regions of the world.

3.1 Meaning of Cyclone

A cyclone is a region of low atmospheric pressure which travels at a wind speed of over 300 km/h. Cyclones are classified as extra tropical cyclone (also called temperate cyclone) and tropical cyclone.

It follows different directions in different hemispheres; it blows in a clockwise direction in the Northern hemisphere and anti-clockwise direction in the Southern hemisphere. Cyclones are accompanied by heavy rains and huge waves in the oceans. They may occur in the regions where a combination of warm sea temperature, high relative humidity and atmospheric instability are found. Cyclones have a centre called **eye of the cyclone**, which is a zone having a calm, good weather and cloudy sky.

In the edge of the eye, also called the **wall of the eye,** with a radius of 20-30 kilometres, where the worst and devastating wind conditions prevail. Cyclones have diameters of several hundreds of kilometres. The eye varies from 20 to 50 km in diameter and covers all of the **troposphere**[1] with a cloudy mass.

Dangers from a Cyclone

There are various devastating situations during a cyclone such as

- Strong winds and gales uproot trees, destroy telephone lines and electricity poles that may disable power and communication and the whole civic life.
- Torrential rain accompanying high tidal waves, which are also known as **storm surges**[2], may cause rising water level in coastal areas, which may result in coastal inundation or severe flooding.

Preparing for Cyclones

- Preparedness is very essential to be safe from a hazard.
- One should always be aware about the cyclone prone regions.
- Generally, cyclones occur between 5-20 degrees latitude, North and South of the equator.
- Around 80 per cent of the total cyclones are generated in the Eastern coastline.
- Cyclone-related hazards like strong winds, floods and storm surges are experienced by West Bengal, Odisha, Andhra Pradesh and Tamil Nadu which are situated along the Bay of Bengal.
- On the other hand, on the West Coast along the Arabian sea, the most vulnerable states are Gujarat, Maharashtra coastal regions.
- These two seas i.e. Arabian Sea and Bay of Bengal Sea, have the greatest frequency of tropical cyclones as compared to other cyclone-prone areas in the world.

---

1 **Troposphere** The layer of the Earth's atmosphere that is closest to its surface, between 0-10 km. Most (90%) of the Earth's atmosphere lies within the troposphere.

2 **Storm Surge** It is simply water that is pushed toward the shore by the force of winds swirling around the cyclone. This advancing surge combines with the normal tides to create a cyclonic tidal wave, which can increase the mean water level by more than 15 feet. The slope of the continental shelf also determines the level of surge. A shallow slope of the coast causes deeper inundation and flooding.

Indian Subcontinent : Cyclone Prone Regions 12th May, 1990

Andhra Pradesh coast was hit by a severe cyclonic storm on 8th May, 1990 with wind speed about 240-250 km/h and 5-6 metre-high storm surges. The area all along the coast of Krishna and Guntur districts was affected severely by the storm, which was accompanied by gales and heavy rainfall. Other areas were affected by flooding due to heavy rainfall.

The cyclone affected 9 of the total 23 districts, while the number of villages affected was 5,923. The cyclone killed 928 persons and around 24,000 cattle. A total of about of 7.8 million people were affected by the cyclone. About 8,27,100 houses were partially damaged while 5,69,000 were completely destroyed. More than 5,00,000 hectares of agricultural and horticultural land was affected. Total damage to property was worth ₹125 million.

According to the various evidences, the Indian subcontinent is the worst cyclone-affected region of the world. Along with the Indian ocean which is one of the six major cyclone-prone regions of the world. The reasons behind this vulnerability are low depth of the ocean bed and the shape of our coast. In India, the entire East coast is vulnerable to cyclones.

3.2 Cyclones and Environmental Degradation

Forests work as a natural windbreaker and water barriers shielding the coastal communities from the destructive power of cyclone and storm surges.

But this coastal shelter belt is depleting day by day because of the destructive activities like deforestation and encroachment by paddy cultivators, prawn farmers, etc.

Vulnerability of Odisha

True, natural calamities are hard to avert. But in Orissa, the ordeal was also man-made. There has been a systematic destruction of mangrove and other tropical trees having branches that send down roots. This growth protected the coastal areas. Greedy people have deforested the coastal areas, leaving no impediment between the sea and habitations.

3.3 Cyclone Forecasting and Warning

Dissemination of cyclone warnings and tracking are done by the Indian Meteorological Department (IMD). The INSAT satellite and 10 cyclone detection radars are being used in tracking process. The warning system provides two important informations to people such as cyclone alert within 48 hours and cyclone warning within 24 hours.

The special Disaster Warning System (DWS) is used for dissemination of cyclone warning through INSAT satellite at various isolated places in local languages.

Cyclone Warning and Mock-Drills Work Wonders

This is evidenced from the difference in loss suffered during cyclones of comparable intensity that hit the Andhra Pradesh coast in 1977 and 1990. The cyclones were accompanied by high storm surges of huge intensity. The number of deaths in 1977 was over 10,000 whereas the loss of human lives in 1990 was less than 1,000. Timely warnings issued by the IMD enabled the administration in evacuating and transporting over half a million people from the affected areas, who had practised their disaster preparedness and response plans over and over.

3.4 Managing Cyclones

In hazard mitigation, the community plays an important role by making a **Community Contingency Plan** with the help of civil society, government functionaries and elected representatives of the people. This plan is consisting of a number of activities which people decide to follow, to prevent loss of life, livelihood and property in case of an emergency. Students can also play an important role in creating awareness and disseminating information.

In the Cyclone Seasons

- Listen to radio or TV weather reports and in case of a cyclone warning, ensure that everyone is alerted. This is usually done through loudspeakers or by going from house to house.
- Identify safe shelters (cyclone shelters, pucca buildings, etc) in your area, and the closest and safe route to reach them.
- Keep an emergency kit ready at home.
- Check your house and surrounding areas to see if it is secure. Doors, windows, the roof and walls should be strengthened before the cyclone season through retrofitting, repair, etc.

- Store adequate food grains and water in safe places.
- Keep your important papers in the emergency kit.
- Keep a list of emergency addresses and phone numbers such as the local police station, Block or taluka office (in rural areas) on display.
- Conduct mock drills for yourselves, imagining that a warning has been given.

Upon a Cyclone Warning

- Listen to your local radio, TV or community warning system for further information.
- Close all windows and doors. Secure doors and stay indoors.
- Keep food items in waterproof bags.
- Prepare or update a list of assets and belongings of your house and give information to volunteers and other authorities about your near and dear ones.
- Get the emergency kit ready and in case of warning of a severe cyclone, move with your family to a strong pucca building or cyclone shelter.
- Do not venture into the sea.
- Wear warm clothing for protection.

If You Have to Evacuate

- Keep track of radio updates and advice.
- If the wind suddenly drops, do not venture out, as this could be the eye of the cyclone. Wait till the official 'all clear' declaration.
- If in a vehicle, stop, but away from the sea and trees, power lines and water courses.

After the Cyclone

- Do not go out till officially advised that it is safe. If evacuated, wait till advised to go back. Use the recommended route for returning and do not rush.
- Check for gas leaks before using the stove.
- Dry electric appliances thoroughly before use.
- Be careful of snakebites.
- Beware of fallen power lines, damaged bridges, buildings and trees.
- Do not enter floodwaters.

REVIEW EXERCISE

Covering Textbook Questions

Q.1 What causes a cyclonic storm?

Ans. Cyclonic storm is a result of a combination of warm sea temperature, high relative humidity and atmospheric instability, which converts it into a low atmospheric pressure region.

Q.2 What are the hazards associated with cyclones?

Ans. The hazards which are associated with cyclones are: strong winds and gales, torrential rains, high tidal waves or storm surges, severe floods, etc.

Q.3 What is the 'eye of a cyclone' and what are its characteristics?

Ans. Eye of the cyclone is the centre of the cyclone which is a zone of calm, good weather and a cloud cover.

Q.4 List the steps in preparing for a cyclone.

Ans. The steps in preparing for a cyclone are as follows

- In the cyclone seasons, people in coastal areas should always be alert by updating themselves through listening to radio or TV weather reports about a cyclone warning.
- Identify safe shelters in your area and the closest and safe route to reach them.
- After updating themselves about a cyclone warning, fishermen should avoid going to the sea.
- Make sure there is an emergency kit ready at home and also keep all your important documents in that.
- Store adequate food grains and water in safe places.
- Also try to keep a list of emergency addresses and phone numbers of the local police station, Block or taluka office (in rural areas).

Q.5 Besides natural causes, what are the man-made reasons, which have contributed to increase in the impact of cyclones?

Ans. Human activities affect the whole environment. As in coastal areas which are cyclone-prone regions, paddy cultivators, prawn farmers and other human beings, through their various activities like encroaching and cutting trees, are increasing the levels of deforestation. In spite of making people aware about the fact that forests work as a natural water barrier, windbreakers and shielding the coastal communities from the destructive power of cyclone and storm surges, there has been widespread deforestation.

Q.6 Which are the cyclone-prone areas of our country?

Ans. In India, the East and West coastal regions along the Bay of Bengal and Arabian Sea, respectively, are two of the worst affected cyclone-prone regions of the world.

As compared to West coast, East coast is more cyclone-prone region in India.

On the East coast (Bay of Bengal Sea), West Bengal, Odisha, Andhra Pradesh and Tamil Nadu are the worst affected states.

On the West coast (Arabian Sea), Gujarat and Maharashtra are the most vulnerable states.

Q.7 Hundreds Feared Killed as Cyclone Devastates Odisha Coast

Several hundred people were feared killed as the super cyclone with a velocity of more than 260 kph battered 10 coastal districts of Odisha for more than eight hours today. The state government called in the army and the air force to help carry out relief and rescue operation. "You cannot imagine the devastation. More than 2,00,000 houses have been destroyed and vast tracts in the coastal areas submerged," Chief Minister Giridhar Gamang told the United News of India on telephone. He also spoke to Defence Minister George Fernandes to send in troops, air force helicopters and transport aircraft. All the 10 affected districts remained cut off from the rest of the country with power supply and telecommunication links cut off. According to initial reports, heavy damage has been reported in the affected areas. Road links in certain areas have been cut off. The cyclone hit Paradip port this morning at a speed of 260 kph. The diameter of the cyclone was very big and all nine coastal districts of Odisha were affected badly. The storm of rare intensity left petrified residents fearing for their lives in the capital and the thickly populated areas along the coast. Massive loss of life and property was feared, but a clear picture will emerge only after the storm abates.

The hardiest of trees fell to the ferocity of the gales, which swept away much of what came in their way. Torrential rains continued to lash the capital city, which is about 65 km from the Puri coast. The flat terrain along the coast allowed the strong tidal waves to reach far inland without obstruction. The cyclone stormed Bhubaneswar at around 0830 IST. The gale speed had touched a howling 260 kph by 1500 IST. Telephone and electricity poles snapped like matchsticks, leaving the telecommunication network in shambles. Power breakdowns plagued the affected areas with little prospects of early restoration of supply. The air traffic control tower in Bhubaneswar reportedly suffered damage, leaving little scope for early resumption of air traffic. Fallen trees blocked the roads and the highway between Cuttack and Bhubaneswar.

The army moved in to provide immediate relief. Two signal attachments were flown in with INMARSAT terminals to re-establish telecommunication links. Electrical and mechanical engineers of the army are already trying to restore power supply.

Huts and other fragile structures collapsed, forcing the inmates to seek shelter in temples and schools. Tidal waves rose two-storeys high, breaking embankments at Talachua in Paradip and Erasama. Large parts were inundated in the coastal areas. But details were not immediately available. Ships had been taken off the harbour. Several buildings, including the state secretariat complex, were damaged. Eyewitnesses said no tall tree was standing in the entire city anymore. Old-timers said they had never seen such devastation.

The building housing the UNI offices in the heart of the city was among the structures damaged. It forced the agency to shut down its computerised news operations. The only means of communication available was the telephone line, which also threatened to go off anytime.

Full details of the havoc wrought by the cyclone are yet to come in, but it was feared to have left a ghastly trail, especially in the coastal areas. Meanwhile, the railways cancelled 14 passenger and mail trains scheduled to run in the cyclone-affected areas.

Source : United News of India

(a) Imagine that you were in Bhubaneswar when the storm struck ... Write down what you experienced and saw around you in a page. Share your experiences with your classmates.

Ans. Attempt yourself with help of your teachers.

(b) In your view, what preventive actions could Odisha have taken to reduce the damage caused when the Super Cyclone struck?

Ans. Odisha Government could have taken the following cyclone damage reducing measures

(i) At first, the meteorological department should broadcast the early cyclone warning news through radio or TV, so that people could be alerted and made ready for the up-coming hazard.

(ii) After broadcasting the warning, the government should have disaster management rescue team, like air force helicopters and transport aircrafts ready to evacuate people from the cyclone-prone regions.

(iii) Hence, if the whole system had taken these essential actions, the cyclone hazard would not become a disaster.

(iv) Indeed, we cannot prevent cyclones, but these measures can help in reducing the damage.

Floods

A flood is an overflow of water that submerges land that is usually dry. Floods are an area of study of the discipline hydrology and are of significant concern in agriculture, civil engineering and public health.

4.1 Meaning of Flood

A flood is a natural phenomena which occurs due to rise of the river water beyond its normal place or course. The danger this causes to people and buildings is called the **flood hazard**[1].

When a river overflows its banks and water spreads on to the surrounding land, it is called a **riverine flood**[2]. The amount of water that a river can hold before a flood starts is known as **channel capacity**[3].

Causes of Floods

- Rainwater or melting snow, Strong tides
- Storms, Cyclones, Tsunami
- Sediment deposition or silting of river beds
- Blocking of river channels by landslides
- Narrowness of the river
- Change in the course of the river
- Inefficient engineering design in the construction of embankments, dams and canals.

Regions Where Floods Occur

Floods, unlike cyclones, are common to all countries. In India, North and Eastern parts are more flood-prone regions. The Flood-prone regions of India are as follows

Most Flood-Prone Regions

The most flood-prone areas are the **Brahmaputra**, **Ganga** and **Meghana basins** in the Indo-Gangetic-Brahmaputra plains in the North and North-East regions, which carry 60 per cent of India's total river flow. This basin is spread over 15 states and is densely populated consisting of about 47 per cent of India's total population.

Other Flood-Prone Regions

North-West regions consisting of West-flowing rivers i.e. the Narmada and Tapi, Central India and Deccan Plateau regions consisting of major East-flowing rivers like the Mahanadi, Krishna, Godavari and Cauvery.

Seasons of Floods

Floods are active in India in the West monsoon period of June to September. Nearly 75 per cent of the total rainfall is concentrated over a short monsoon of these four months.

Effects of Flooding

Flooding is one of the most destructive forms of natural disasters.It causes heavy economic and human losses.

Floods are an annual feature in some parts of India. Flooded areas may get isolated from the rest of the country. Regions near coastal areas and rivers are more vulnerable to flooding.

Economically and socially backward communities are more vulnerable to the destructive effects of floods. These communities take longer to come back to the kind of life they were leading before the disaster struck.

Indians Flee Monsoon Floods

Parts of Assam and the neighbouring state of Arunachal Pradesh remain cut off from the rest of the country, as flooding waters have destroyed transport links. Floods in the North-East of India are an annual phenomenon.

In August 2000, floods in the region killed 100 people, and left 70,000 people homeless in Assam alone. Environmentalists blame soil erosion, the silting of riverbeds and the increasing population in the flood plains.

Sunday, 7th June, 2002, The Hindu

1 **Flood Hazard** It is the risk of damage to life, livelihoods or property from flooding.

2 **Riverine Flood** It is a flood caused when a river overflows its banks.

3 **Channel Capacity** It is the maximum flow of water in a river.

4.2 Flood Preparedness

Indeed, we cannot stop a flood as it is a natural hazard, but we can stop it from becoming a disaster by flood preparedness. Disaster Management Teams (DMTs) are responsible for preparedness and response for hazards in village and urban cities. But as responsible citizens, we all have the responsibility to get involved in the process of preparedness, creation of awareness and working with skilled emergency response teams. This would reduce loss of life and minimise human suffering.

Before Flooding Occurs

In seasons of flooding, people should identify the nearest safe shelters. An emergency kit containing useful objects like a first-aid kit, torch, water-proof bags, etc should be kept handy.

When You Hear a Flood Warning or If Flooding Appears Likely

After a flood warning is issued, the radio and the TV should be constantly used for further information. Dry food, drinking water and warm clothes should be kept handy.

If You Need to Evacuate

Use water-proof bags to carry emergency kit with valuables and other useful items. Before evacuating, the local volunteers or DMTs should be informed the address of the place you are going to. Turn off power and raise electrical items on to the highest place available and furniture, clothing, appliances on to other high places. Whether leaving or staying, put sandbags in the toilet bowl and cover all drain holes to prevent sewage back-flow. Do not get into water of unknown depth and current; it may be dangerous for you.

During Floods

Consume boiled water. Food should be kept covered, don't eat heavy meals. In case of diarrhoea, use raw tea, rice water, tender coconut water etc. Children should not be remain on empty stomach.

The surrounding area should be disinfected by using bleaching powder and lime. Avoid getting into floodwater; if you have to then cover yourself properly and check depth and current with a stick. Do not enter water over knee-deep depth.

Consume dry food and avoid food which has got wet in the floodwaters. Snakebites are common during floods, so be careful.

Students have also a very major role to play in preparing for disasters. In recent past, volunteers in the country have played an important role in helping victims to rebuild their lives whenever disasters have tormented the country. They also have played a key role in creating awareness among people on disaster preparedness.

REVIEW EXERCISE

Covering Textbook Questions

Q.1 List the causes for floods.

Ans. There are various causes of floods such as

- Rainwater or melting snow
- Strong tides, Storms
- Cyclones, Tsunami

Other causes of floods are

- Blocking of river channels by landslides
- Narrowness of the river
- Change in the course of the river

Q.2 Suggest measures to prevent damage from frequent flooding.

Two measures have been suggested, add more.

(i) Raising the height of public and private building in low lying areas.

(ii) De-silting river beds regularly.

Ans. Some other measures to prevent damage from frequent flooding are as follows

(i) Find higher safe areas than the surrounding, or get built an earthen mound for evacuating in the event of a flood.

(ii) Building structures should be based on sound engineering design.

(iii) People must have an emergency kit ready.

Q.3 How can communities prepare to face floods?

Ans. Communities can play an important role at the time of floods

- In seasons of flooding, the food-prone areas should identify the nearest safe shelters.
- An emergency kit containing useful objects like a first-aid kit, torch, water proof bags, etc should be kept handy.
- Dry food, drinking water and warm clothes should be kept handy.
- Taking these steps can be helpful in minimising the damage due to floods.

Q.4 What should a community do in order to be prepared before every flood season?

Ans. People should know the nearest safe shelter's route. People must have ready an emergency kit containing first aid kit, strong ropes, a radio, torch, spare batteries, stocks of fresh water, dry food, salt, sugar, kerosene, matchboxes, water-proof bags to store clothing and valuables.

People must be connected with the local radio or TV for warnings and advice and keep themselves alert. Take bullock-carts, agricultural equipments and domestic animals to a safer place.

Q.5 Read the newspaper extract of 2002 below

In Assam, soldiers have helped rescue thousands of people marooned in remote villages, and more troops have been put on 'standby' for relief operations. An army spokesman said that disaster management squads in speedboats and helicopters were also on standby. This is just the beginning of India's monsoon season, but the rains have been unusually heavy so far.

(i) Find out which are the agencies and organisations that play an important role in flood preparedness and response.

(ii) Make a list of their local offices and people heading them. Ask your teacher to contact Red Cross or any of the other agencies to come and tell you how they prepare for floods and other disasters.

Ans. (i) Trained Disaster Management Teams (DMTs) are responsible for preparedness and response in each village or urban neighbourhood.

(ii) Students are advised to attempt themselves with the help of their subject teacher by using survey technique.

Q.6 Given below are the names of common rivers in India. Against each river, tick in the appropriate box to indicate whether it floods frequently or not.

River	Floods frequently	Does not flood frequently
GODAVARI		
BRAHMAPUTRA		
MAHANADI		
CAUVERY		
GANGA		
SUTLEJ		

Ans. Ganga and Brahmaputra rivers flood frequently, whereas Godavari, Mahanadi, Cauvery and Sutlej do not.

NCERT ON PAGE 37

Q.7 Read the following newspaper reports.

Assam Several embankments on the main Brahmaputra River have been breached, with water engulfing more than 600 villages. About 30,000 hectares of crops were also submerged. All rivers in Assam are flowing at dangerous levels threatening several new areas, officials said. The Eastern district of Dhemaji was among the worst affected by a breach in the embankment, with at least 2,50,000 people stranded by the rising waters.

Uttarkashi Heavy monsoon rains have triggered flash floods in parts of Northern and Western India. A cloudburst that hit nearby Uttarkashi district created a torrent of muddy water that swept away at least six villages while flowing down the mountains, said DK Gupta, from the state control room.

Maharashtra Flooding in the Western state of Maharashtra where a few cases of cholera have been reported close to Mumbai.

Himachal Pradesh More than 100 people were reported to have died in flash floods in the Northern state of Himachal Pradesh earlier this week.
The river Sutlej, which runs through the state, was reported to have risen to more than 40 feet above its not level in some places.

Bihar Water from two of India's biggest rivers—the Brahmaputra and the Ganges—has engulfed thousands of villages. According to some estimates, nearly half a million people have been made homeless in the Northern states of Bihar and Assam.

Identify the states and areas that are vulnerable to floods by the following rivers

(i) Brahmaputra

(ii) Ganga

(iii) Sutlej

Ans. The states that are vulnerable to floods by these rivers are as follows

(i) Brahmaputra - Assam, Bihar

(ii) Ganga - Bihar

(iii) Sutlej - Himachal Pradesh

Drought

CHAPTER 5

A drought is a phenomenon in which there is deficiency of surface or sub-surface water and rainfall. Its consequences include acute shortage of water, food, fodder crop failure and employment. Drought creates an acute scarcity of water on a large scale for every kind of activity such as agricultural operations, including lack of moisture in soil to grow crops, affecting production and causing crop failure, scarcity of food, fodder, employment and starvation.

5.1 Are We All Vulnerable to Drought

Drought is one of the most widespread disasters that India faces, affecting more than 70 per cent of cultivable land. The reaction to droughts is not like disasters such as earthquakes, cyclones and floods. Drought conditions develop over a period of time, hence we call it a **slow onset disaster**.

Drought-Prone Regions

In India, 191 districts out of 543 are severely drought-prone. Drought-prone areas are as follows

Worst Affected Regions

The Western belt of India like Rajasthan and Gujarat are frequently affected by droughts.

The main causes of vulnerability are weak monsoon and degraded environment. For example in 2003, most parts of Rajasthan were experiencing the fourth consecutive year of drought.

Other Affected Regions

Western Odisha, Rayalaseema and Telangana areas of Andhra Pradesh, Chhattisgarh, Jharkhand, Central Maharashtra, Interior Karnataka, West Bengal, parts of Tamil Nadu and even water rich states such as Punjab, Haryana, Bihar and Uttar Pradesh are other prominent pockets of drought-prone regions.

People living in rural areas, who wholly depend on agriculture and animal husbandry, and tribals who depend on forest produce are the worst affected and most vulnerable to the hazards of droughts.

KNOWLEDGE PLUS Non-availability of moisture over most parts of the year, makes 68 per cent of the land vulnerable to drought in India. In 2001, more than eight states suffered the impact of severe drought.

5.2 Indirect Aggravators of Drought

Environmental degradation, especially the loss of green cover, affects rainfall received in the region increasing the possibility of water stress. Drought affects us in different ways, some of which are described below

Drought Affects Farmers

It causes crop failure, lack of fodder and no or less water to feed their cattle.

Drought Affects Poor Families

Constant drought causes crop failure and reduces agricultural productivity. As a result, insufficient availability or supply of crops in the market raises the price in the market because, as we read in economics, higher the demand higher the price.

The people who suffer the most are from deprived sections, as they are unable to get even their daily basic need food because of inadequate purchasing power.

Drought Affects Women

Since unknown past, women never or hardly got the same status as men in society. In areas of drought, especially in rural societies, women are the last to eat at home as there is a dearth of food, no access to health, education facilities etc. They are usually the last and have the least to eat at home hence they suffer from malnutrition.

Drought increases women's work burden and they have to work longer to earn the same wages and travel longer to fetch water, fodder and fuel-wood.

Drought Affects People Living in Desert Land

They depend more on animal husbandry than on agriculture.

Severe scarcity of fodder and water and degradation of vegetation are reasons for zero agricultural activity there.

Drought Affects Employment

A fall in agricultural production leads to a fall in employment opportunities for rural people who depend on agricultural labour for a living. It also causes people to migrate to other places in search of employment. These are called distress migrations.

Drought Affects Children

Lack of food means malnutrition in drought affected areas making these regions more prone to various kinds of infections and diseases. Migrations due to constant drought conditions lead to higher school drop-out rates and affect child health and education.

As a result, it gives a society a number of wage earners and increases child labour.

5.3 Coping with Drought

Drought is a slow onset disaster, thus giving us time to cope with mitigation, preparedness and response.

The Indian Meteorological Department forecasts the amount of rainfall expected every year and this indicates the possibility of droughts. Since we have ample time, we can try to mitigate the ill-effects. We can reduce the intensity and impact of droughts through collective and individual actions.

It is important to remember that any step taken to mitigate drought must be sustained for a long period of time.

Such involvement should be from a cross-section of people such as community, Panchayat representatives, volunteers, government functionaries, teachers and students.

KNOWLEDGE PLUS There is over 100 million hectares of degraded land in the country. Protecting, regenerating and restoring degraded land can reduce the pressure of population on cultivated land and keep forests and pastures safe to supply fodder for the animals.

Long-term Drought Mitigation Strategies

In the long term, effects of droughts can be mitigated by promoting community based rainwater harvesting, watershed programmes, increasing forest cover, adopting drought resistant varieties of paddy and other crops and encouraging seed insurance schemes.

REVIEW EXERCISE

Covering Textbook Questions

Q.1 Choose the right answer to the following questions

(i) The greatest amount of fresh water on the Earth is found in ....

(a) the oceans
(b) ice caps and glaciers
(c) aquifers
(d) surface water

Ans. (b)

(ii) Groundwater is ....

(a) not usable because it is dirty.
(b) another name for watershed.
(c) too far beneath the Earth's surface to be used.
(d) another name for an aquifer.

Ans. (d)

(iii) Surface water ....

(a) is used to produce electricity.
(b) can be easily contaminated.
(c) can be used for recreation.
(d) All of the above

Ans. (d)

Q.2 How does drought affect our lives?

Ans. Drought creates a large-scale scarcity of water for every kind of activity such as agricultural operations including lack of moisture in soil to grow crops, thereby affecting production and causing crop failure, scarcity of food, fodder, employment and causes starvation. Thus it affects human lives in various ways.

Q.3 List ways to conserve water in day-to-day use.

Ans. We can conserve water by preventing wastage and misuse of water through the following ways

- Recycling of water by using waste water of washing machines for cleaning home or washing cars and directing water from the wash area to the fields or garden.
- Harvest rainwater at home and in schools.
- Plant trees (afforestation)

Use traditional methods such as

- **Guhls** In the Western and Central Himalayas, 1 to 15 km long traditional diversion channels also known as guhls were built to draw water from hill streams or springs. They carried 15 to 100 litres discharge of water per second.
- **Bamboo Pipes** In Meghalaya, bamboo pipes function like a drip irrigation system. These pipes are used to tap spring water for irrigation purposes, which reduces to 20-80 drops per minute at the site of the plant.
- **Ahar-Pyne** Ahars are rectangular catchment basins and pynes are channels which fetch the water flowing from the seasonal streams. This system of irrigation is found mainly in South Bihar.
- **Kunds** The structure of kunds is shaped like a bowl with a lid. This method belongs to Thar desert where kunds are covered underground tanks with an artificially prepared catchment area to improve run-off.
- **Surangam** A tunnel dug through a laterite hillock is known as surangam. People collect water which seeps out from the tunnel. It is found in Malabar area.

Q.4 What actions will help us to mitigate drought, individually as well as collectively?

Ans. Drought is a slow onset disaster, thus giving us time to cope with it in the following ways

- Through preparedness and response, the drought-affected societies certainly can reduce its intensity.
- People have to take effective steps which must be sustained for a long period of time.
- Such involvement should be from a cross-section of people such as community, Panchayat representatives, volunteers, government functionaries, teachers and students.

People must have long-term drought mitigation strategies such as

- Construction of community based rain water harvesting structures.
- Promoting watershed programmes.
- Increasing forest cover through plantations.
- Adopting drought resistant variety of paddy and other crops.
- Using alternative crops in drought conditions.
- Capacity building of communities in Drought Management and introducing livelihood options besides agriculture and animal husbandry which are water intensive.
- Encouraging crop and seed insurance schemes.
- Students can also play a key role in many ways like conserve water through preventing wastage and misuse of water, recycling of water, etc.

Q.5 What do you understand by 'rainwater harvesting'?

Ans. Rainwater harvesting is a technique used for collecting, storing and using rainwater for drinking water supply, landscape irrigation and other uses. The rainwater is collected from various hard surfaces such as roof tops and/or other types of man-made structures above ground with hard surfaces.

This ancient practice is currently growing in popularity throughout our communities due to interest in reducing the consumption of potable water and the inherent qualities of rainwater.

Rainwater Harvesting Advantages

Some advantages of rainwater harvesting are as follows

- It makes use of a natural resource and reduces flooding, storm water run-off, soil erosion and contamination of surface water with pesticides, sediments, metals and fertilisers.
- It reduces the need for imported water.
- It is an excellent source of water for landscape irrigation, with no chemicals such as fluoride and chlorine, and no dissolved salts and minerals from the soil.
- Home systems can be relatively simple to install and operate and may reduce your water bill.
- It promotes both water and energy conservation.
- No filtration system is required for landscape irrigation.
- It inculcates a culture of water conservation.

CHAPTER 6

Man-made Disasters

Disasters can also be created by human actions including major accidents, deliberate or inadvertent actions of individuals or groups. For example, rail road or air accidents are man-made disasters.

Moreover, humans also use dangerous weapons in wars causing huge destruction of life and environment. For example, use of weapons such as nuclear bombs or the atom bomb that was dropped in Japan during World War II.

A vast level of human suffering, loss of life and long-term damage to a nation's economy and productive capacity are the cost of man-made disasters.

6.1 Types of Man-made Disasters

WMD (Weapons of Mass Destruction)

Weapons like nuclear bombs or atom bombs are commonly called 'Weapons of Mass Destruction' (WMD). These weapons lead to a huge disastrous breakdown and collapse of social, political and economic system which are the key elements sustaining communities. As a result agriculture and food production become major casualties.

WMD can be broadly classified into three categories

(i) Nuclear disaster

Scientific research and development has enabled nations to produce nuclear arms instead of atomic bomb. Nuclear arms are more destructive and harmful than the atom bomb, which was used more than a half century ago.

These nations considered themselves most powerful in the world after producing these arms and there is also a risk of accidental exposure to harmful radiation from several nuclear reactors.

Nuclear material can also be used for creating crude bombs commonly known as 'dirty bombs'. Usually, theft of nuclear material enables terrorists and other anti-social elements whose only aim is to create war conditions among countries.

An example of nuclear arms is the use of nuclear bomb on Hiroshima and Nagasaki in World War-II, on 6th August, and 9th August, 1945, respectively.

Protect ourselves from Nuclear Radiation

Common symptoms of radioactivity are nausea, dizziness, vomiting and disorientation, with no odour but a wave of heat. A nuclear explosion is followed by a blast with thick gaseous cloud cover and can cause instant blindness if viewed. Doors and windows should be closed.

Radioactive rays do not penetrate solid structures though buildings may be damaged by fires.

(ii) Chemical Disasters

Chemical disasters are caused by industrial accidents, irresponsible handling of chemical substances. They may occur by deliberate action also to cause destruction.

As chemical agents are easily available and their chemical processes are simple to use, these chemical WMD are manufactured on a large scale by several nations in the world.

These weapons are difficult to detect since they are colourless and odourless but release poisonous gases which can cause widespread devastation because they spread easily and affect large area.

The Bhopal Gas Tragedy of December, 1984

The Bhopal Gas Tragedy is a catastrophe that has no parallel in industrial history. In the early hours of 3rd December, 1984 a rolling wind carried a poisonous gray cloud past the Union Carbide Plant in Bhopal, Madhya Pradesh. Forty tons of Methyl Isocyanate (MIC) spread throughout the sleeping city. An estimated 2500 people died, people whose hopes and dreams were ironically bound with the technology and affluence which the plant symbolised. About 300,000 suffered from agonising injuries from the disastrous effects of the massive poisoning.Residents awoke to clouds of suffocating gas and began a desperate flight through the dark streets. No alarm ever sounded a warning and no evacuation plan was prepared. When victims arrived at hospitals breathless and blind, doctors did not know how to treat them since emergency information on antidotes was not available.

(iii) Biological Disasters

Biological weapons are easy to manufacture and they also target a large number of people. Effects of such weapons usually take time to show up. They are called a "Poor man's nuclear bomb". They deliberately infect people with harmful biological species.

Accidental Disasters

Accidental disasters are disasters such as train accidents, road accidents, bus accidents etc. Major accidents take place due to collision of rails or derailments and cause huge mass destruction inflicting injuries with disabilities to many more. For example, Gaisal rail Tragedy of August 1999, in West Bengal.

According to various studies and analysis of occurence of various kinds of disasters, fire accidents are very high in number in India.

REVIEW EXERCISE

Covering Textbook Questions

Q. 1 Find out how potassium Iodate tablets can be used to counter exposure to radioactivity.

Ans. Potassium iodate can be used to protect the thyroid against accumulation of radioactive iodine. It does this by saturating the body with a stable source of iodine prior to this exposure.

Q. 2 What causes man-made disasters?

Ans. Man-made disasters are caused by human actions including major accidents, deliberate or inadvertent actions of individuals or groups.

Q. 3 How do man-made disasters affect us?

Ans. Man-made disasters are considered more devastating than natural disasters. A vast level of human suffering, loss of life and long-term damage to a nation's economy and productive capacity are the cost of man-made disasters.

There are various examples of this devastation such as

- The Bhopal gas Tragedy, on 3rd December, 1984, in Madhya Pradesh was an industrial accident in which 2500 people died and about 300,000 suffered from agonising injuries from the disastrous effects of the massive poisoning.
- Another example of man-made disaster is a nuclear attack on two cities of Japan, Hiroshima and Nagasaki, on 6th August, 1945 and 9th August, 1945 respectively. In Hiroshima 66,000 people were killed and 69,000 injured and in Nagasaki, 39,000 persons were killed and 25,000 injured.

Q. 4 How would you protect yourself and your family in the case of a nuclear disaster?

Ans. One can recognise nuclear attack or accident through common symptoms of radioactivity which are nausea, dizziness, vomiting and disorientation, with no odour but a wave of heat.

A nuclear explosion is followed by a 'blast' with thick gaseous cloud cover and can cause instant blindness, if viewed.

So, if a nuclear accident or attack occurs do not panic just close all doors and windows at times of explosions, do not go outside but stay indoors till further communication from the government comes.

It is noteworthy that radioactivity does not penetrate solid structure, but fire can cause damage to buildings and human life.

Q.5 What simple Do-s and Don't-s can you list in case of a biological disaster?

Ans. Do's in the event of biological disasters

- Follow regular hygienic methods as before every principal meal wash your hands with antibiotic soap.
- Before cooking always wash vegetables properly. Follow active immunisation.
- If sickness occurs, immediately contact health authorities without any delay. In case of mosquitoes use nets or repellants at night.

Don'ts in the event of biological disasters

- Do not panic and be calm.
- Do not allow waste material to gather in or around your locality.
- Do not allow stagnant water accumulated around you.
- Do not eat stale food items.

Q.6 How would you recognise the presence of a poisonous gas in the air? What precautions would you take to protect yourself and your family against its harmful effects?

Ans. Poisonous gases are colourless and odourless, but their presence can be recognised through which we can save ourselves and our family too. These are now

(i) The first symptoms of a possible chemical leakage are irritation, burning and redness in the nostrils and eyes, followed by nausea, dizziness and disorientation. Pungent or bitter-sweet smells indicate the presence of a gas in the air.

(ii) That panic induced fleeing during a gas leakage is harmful. Stay calm in the same place, put a wet cloth on your face and breath through it. Most gases will dissolve in water.

(iii) Lying down close to the ground may help since most hazardous gases are lighter than air and will tend to rise upwards.

Q.7 Describe how you would help people involved in a road accident in your neighbourhood.

Ans. Attempt yourself with the help of your teacher and group discussion.

SAMPLE QUESTION PAPERS

Sample Question Paper 1 (Solved)

Social Science

Time : 3 hrs	M.M. : 80

General Instructions

1 All questions are compulsory.

2 Marks for each question are indicated against the question.

Multiple Choice Questions (MCQs)

1. What was the primary purpose behind the establishment of botanical gardens and natural history museums by the British in colonial territories? (1)

(a) To preserve native plant specimens.
(b) To gather information about local artists.
(c) To collect and document plant specimens and their uses.
(d) To showcase British artistic talents.

2. What was the primary advantage granted to the East India Company by the charter it acquired from Queen Elizabeth I in 1600? (1)

(a) Exclusive rights to trade with the West.
(b) Permission to establish colonies in the East.
(c) Sole authority to trade with the East, barring competition from other English trading groups.
(d) Authorisation to trade freely with any country in Europe.

3. Identify the primary reason for European cloth manufacturers to initially rely on woad instead of Indian indigo for dyeing cloth. (1)

(a) Indian indigo was unavailable in the European market.
(b) Woad produced a more vibrant blue colour than Indian indigo.
(c) Indian indigo was cheaper and more easily accessible in Europe.
(d) European governments imposed a ban on the import of Indian indigo.

4. Among the mentioned tribal groups in India, which community was primarily involved in rearing goats? (1)

(a) Van Gujjars of the Punjab hills
(b) Labadis of Andhra Pradesh
(c) Gaddis of Kulu
(d) Bakarwals of Kashmir

5. Which of the following is an example of an unlimited renewable resource not significantly affected by human activities? (1)

(a) Solar energy (b) Forests
(c) Water (d) Soil

6. What percentage of the world's population inhabits approximately 30 per cent of the total land area? (1)

(a) 70% (b) 90% (c) 60% (d) 10%

7. Which agricultural practice involves the commercial rearing of silk worms? (1)

(a) Agriculture (b) Sericulture
(c) Pisciculture (d) Viticulture

8. Which category do mineral-based industries primarily belong to? (1)

(a) Secondary industries (b) Tertiary industries
(c) Quaternary industries (d) Primary industries

9. What is the term used to describe the variance between a country's birth rate and death rate that leads to population change? (1)

(a) Population difference (b) Demographic shift
(c) Natural growth rate (d) Population equilibrium

10. Match the following. (1)

	List I		List II
A.	Right to Equality	1.	Equal protection under the law and prohibition of discrimination
B.	Right to Freedom	2.	Prohibition of human trafficking and forced labour
C.	Right to Freedom of Religion	3.	Every person's right to practice any profession or occupation
D.	Right against Exploitation	4.	Establishment of educational institutions by minorities

Codes

	A	B	C	D		A	B	C	D
(a)	1	3	4	2	(b)	1	2	3	4
(c)	4	3	2	1	(d)	2	1	3	4

11. Assertion (A) The Indian Constitution grants the right to religious communities to establish their own educational institutions and provides them with non-preferential financial aid.

Reason (R) The intervention of the state can be in the form of support, and this includes the provision for religious communities to set up schools and colleges while receiving financial assistance on a non-preferential basis, as outlined in the Indian Constitution. **(1)**

Codes

(a) Both A and R are true and R is the correct explanation of A

(b) Both A and R are true, but R is not the correct explanation of A

(c) A is true, but R is false

(d) A is false, but R is true

12. Consider the following statements and choose the correct option. (1)

I. Indian judiciary resolves disputes among citizens, citizens and government, state governments, and between the center and state governments.

II. Judiciary can invalidate Parliament-passed laws if they violate the basic structure of the Constitution, known as judicial review.

III. Every Indian citizen can approach the Supreme Court or High Court if they believe their Fundamental Rights are violated.

Options

(a) Statements I, II, and III are all true.

(b) Statements I and III are true, but statement II is false.

(c) Statements II and III are true, but statement I is false.

(d) Statement I is true, but statements II and III are false.

13. What is the significance of Niyamgiri hill for the Dongarria Konds, an Adivasi community residing in the Kalahandi district of Odisha? (1)

(a) It is a historical site with ancient artefacts.

(b) It holds immense religious and cultural significance as the sacred mountain for the Dongarria Konds.

(c) It is an ideal location for a modern residential development.

(d) It serves as a natural reserve for endangered species.

14. According to the Constitution of India, the right to water is (1)

(a) recognised as a separate fundamental right under Article 19.

(b) part of the right to life under Article 21.

(c) a privilege accessible only to economically disadvantaged individuals.

(d) limited to specific geographical regions within the country.

15. Arrange the following in the correct sequence. (1)

I. Kol rebelled in Chotanagpur

II. Warli revolt in Maharashtra

III. Forest Satyagraha in Assam

IV. Birsa Munda arrested

Codes

(a) I, II, III, IV (b) III, IV, II, I

(c) IV, II, I, III (d) I, IV, III, II

16. Identify the correct option that describe the given statements. (1)

I. He founded a reform association known as the Brahmo Sabha.

II. He began a campaign against the practice of Sati.

III. He was given the title of Raja of Akbar II.

Options

(a) Raja Rammohan Roy

(b) Ishwar Chandra Vidyasagar

(c) Dayanand Saraswati

(d) Narayan Guru

Fill in the Blanks

1. A company is a form of business set up by people or .... **(1)**

2. It is also the duty of the government to ensure that the right to life guaranteed under .... of the constitution is not violated. **(1)**

3. In 1817, _______a Scottish economist and political philosopher, published a massive three-volume work, A History of British India. **(1)**

True or False

1. Bahadur Shah Zafar and his sons being arrested by Captain Hodson. **(1)**

2. Coffee does not require warm and wet climate and well-drained loamy soil. **(1)**

3. The Supreme Court was established on 26th January, 1950, the day India became a Republic. (1)

Very Short Answer Type Questions

1. When was the Pradhan Mantri Kaushal Vikas Yojna (PMKVY) initiated? What was its primary goal? (2)
2. Where was the first English factory established in 1651? How did it evolve into the city of Kolkata? (2)
3. According to an official release by the Ministry of Law and Justice, "Now we have all three tiers of Indian judiciary on NJDG portal. NJDG is recognised as a significant innovation under the ease of doing business initiative of the Government of India." (2)

   Source : Economic Times

   (i) What is the role of the judiciary?

   (ii) Is the judiciary independent in India or not?

Or What does criminal law address? What follows after the lodging of an FIR in a case?

4. What defines human resource and its significance in resource transformation? (2)

Or What are non-renewable resources? Give examples.

5. How did Ram Mohan Roy influence the ban on Sati practice in 1829? (2)

Short Answer Type Questions

1. Why was the Scheduled Castes and the Scheduled Tribes (Prevention of Atrocities) Act, 1989 framed? What are its key provisions? (3)
2. How does the concept of an independent judiciary function within the Indian Constitution? (3)

Or What is the hierarchical structure of courts in India? How does the integrated judicial system function?

3. How are industries classified based on raw materials? Explain. (3)
4. What is the significance of natural vegetation and wildlife within the ecosystem? (3)
5. What were some reasons for discontent among Indian sepoys and peasants during British rule in India? (3)
6. How did the First World War contribute to the growth of mass nationalism in India? (3)

Or The struggle that unfolded after the partition of Bengal came to be known as the Swadeshi Movement.

   (i) What is the meaning of the word 'Swadeshi'?

   (ii) Describe how the Swadeshi Movement helped against fighting British rule.

Long Answer Type Questions

1. How did the East India Company establish its presence in Bengal? What led to conflicts with the Nawabs? (5)

Or What led to the Battle of Plassey? What were its consequences for the British East India Company in India?

2. How can farming be categorised? What are the key characteristics of subsistence and commercial farming? (5)

Or What are the major characteristics and geographical requirements for the cultivation of rice, wheat, millets, maize, cotton, jute, coffee, and tea as highlighted in their production regions?

3. Why is the separation of religion from the state crucial in democratic societies? (5)

Or "The Indian Constitution guarantees religious freedom for all and separates the power of religion and the state. Secularism refers to this separation of religion from the State."

What does it mean for India to be a secular state?

Case Based Questions

1. **Read the given passage and answer the questions that follow.** (4)

   The way in which people are spread across the Earth surface is known as the pattern of population distribution. More than 90 per cent of the world's population lives in about 30 per cent of the land surface. The distribution of population in the world is extremely uneven. Some areas are very crowded and some are sparely populated. The crowded areas are South and South-East Asia, Europe and North Eastern North America. Very few people live in high latitude areas, tropical deserts, high mountains and areas of

Equatorial forests. Many more people live North of the Equator than South of the Equator. Almost three-quarters of the world's people live in two continents Asia and Africa. Sixty per cent of the world's people stay in just 10 countries. All of them have more than a 100 million people.

(i) Where are the densely populated areas in the world? (1)

(ii) Which continents hold most of the world's population? (1)

(iii) What characterises nations with significant populations? (2)

2. Read the given passage and answer the questions that follow. (4)

The practice of surveying also became common under the colonial administration. The British believed that a country had to be properly known before it could be effectively administered. By the early nineteenth century, detailed surveys were being carried out to map the entire country. In the villages, revenue surveys were conducted. The effort was to know the topography, the soil quality, the flora, the fauna, the local histories, and the cropping pattern – all the facts seen as necessary to know about to administer the region. From the end of the nineteenth century, census operations were held every ten years. These prepared detailed records of the number of people in all the provinces of India, noting information on castes, religions and occupation. There were many other surveys – botanical surveys, zoological surveys, archaeological surveys, anthropological surveys, forest surveys.

(i) How did the British view surveying in colonial administration? (1)

(ii) What were the key objectives of Census operations in India? (2)

(iii) Which diverse surveys were conducted under colonial rule? (1)

3. Read the given passage and answer the questions that follow. (4)

The government has to ensure that these laws are implemented. This means that the law must be enforced. Enforcement becomes even more important when the law seeks to protect the weak from the strong. For instance, to ensure that every worker gets fair wages, the government has to regularly inspect work sites and punish those who violate the law. When workers are poor or powerless, the fear of losing future earnings or facing reprisals often forces them to accept low wages. Employers know this well and use their power to pay workers less than the fair wage. In such cases, it is crucial that laws are enforced. Through making, enforcing and upholding these laws, the government can control the activities of individuals or private companies so as to ensure social justice. Many of these laws have their basis in the Fundamental Rights guaranteed by the Indian Constitution.

(i) Why is law enforcement crucial, especially in protecting vulnerable workers? (1)

(ii) Why do workers agree to low wages ? (1)

(iii) What role does government play in ensuring social justice through laws? (2)

Map Based Question

1. (a) On the political map of India, locate the following. (3)

(i) Locate the region of Awadh

(ii) Locate Hugli

(iii) The place where first school for girls was started by Jyotirao Phule and his wife Savitribai Phule.

(b) On the given political outline map of India, identify and label the following. (2)

(i) State in which Tata Iron and Steel Company Limited (TISCO) located

(ii) City of lakes

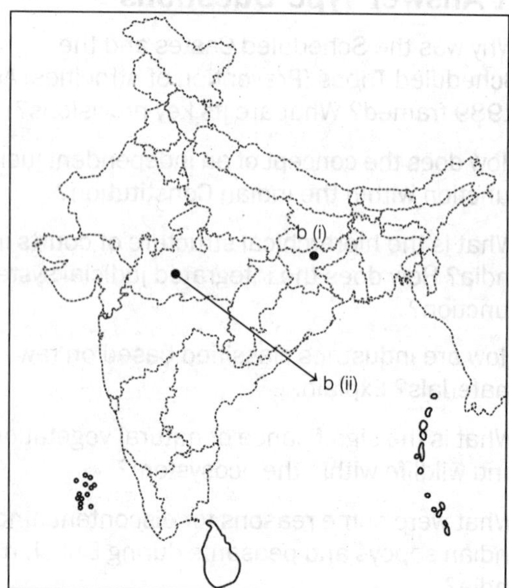

Answers

Multiple Choice Questions

1. (c)	2. (c)	3. (a)	4. (d)	5. (a)
6. (b)	7. (b)	8. (a)	9. (c)	10. (a)
11. (a)	12. (a)	13. (b)	14. (b)	15. (d)
16. (a)				

Fill in the Blanks

1. by Government
2. Article 21
3. James Mill

True or False

1. True 2. False 3. True

Very Short Answer Type Questions

1. The Pradhan Mantri Kaushal Vikas Yojna (PMKVY) was initiated in 2015. The primary goal was to train young people in India, so they could learn skills that would help them get jobs or improve their existing job skills.

2. The first English factory was established on the banks of the River Hugli in 1951. Over time, it expanded into a settlement, leading to the fortification and acquisition of zamindari rights, evolving into Calcutta (now Kolkata).

3. (i) The role of the judiciary is to interpret and uphold the law, ensure justice, resolve disputes and protect individual rights and freedoms.

   (ii) Yes, the judiciary is independent in India.

Or Criminal Law handles offences like theft, dowry harassment, and murder.

After lodging an FIR, police investigate, leading to court cases where guilty individuals can face jail or fines.

4. Human resources refer to the people who contribute their skills, abilities and knowledge to get things done.

   The significance of the human resource is to making use of materials and turning them into valuable resources. These people bring different qualities and strengths, which are essential in transforming raw materials into something useful or valuable for society.

Or The non-renewable resources are limited in quantity and require thousands of years to replenish themselves.

Coal, petroleum and natural gas are examples of non-renewable resources as they replenish over extremely long periods beyond human lifetimes.

5. Ram Mohan Roy used his language skills to argue against the practice of sati, where widows were forced to burn themselves on their husbands' funeral pyres. He convinced British officials that this practice was wrong and didn't fit with Indian customs. His efforts got their support, leading to the ban on sati practice in 1829.

Short Answer Type Questions

1. The Scheduled Castes and the Scheduled Tribes (Prevention of Atrocities) Act, 1989, was framed because Dalit and tribal groups faced harsh treatment and violence from dominant castes.

   It was in response to the growing violent acts against these assertive Dalit groups, highlighting the ongoing practice of untouchability.

   The key provisions of the Act are

   - **Defining Atrocities** The act identifies various forms of atrocities against Dalits and Adivasis.
   - **Prohibited Acts** It prohibits acts like force-feeding inedible substances and humiliating practices targeted at these communities.
   - **Penalisation** It penalises the dispossession of their resources and forced labour, aiming to safeguard the dignity and rights of marginalised communities.

2. Functioning of Independent Judiciary in the Indian Constitution are as follows

   - **Separation of Powers** The independent judiciary ensures a balance among different branches of government.
   - **Appointment Autonomy** Judges in High Courts and the Supreme Court are appointed with little interference from the legislature or executive.
   - **Safeguarding Rights** This independence helps prevent the misuse of power and protects citizens' Fundamental Rights.
   - **Impartial Judgments** Independence ensures fair decisions, free from influence by powerful individuals.
   - **Maintaining Integrity** Independence secures the integrity of the judicial system.

Or The judicial system in India consists three tiers of courts, which are as follows

- **Local Level** At the grassroots, there are subordinate or district courts.
- **State Level** Each state has its own High Court.
- **Apex Court** The highest authority is the Supreme Court in New Delhi, headed by the Chief Justice of India.

The integrated judicial system functions in the following ways

- **Binding Decisions** Rulings made by higher courts are mandatory for lower courts to follow.
- **Appeals Process** If someone disagrees with a decision in a lower court, they can appeal to higher courts.
- **Ensuring Justice** This system ensures fairness and provides a way to seek justice.
- **Hierarchical Appellate System** It creates a structured way to challenge and review legal decisions.

3. Classification of industries based on raw materials are as follows

- **The agro-based industries** utilise plant or animal products, such as food processing industries involved in making juice from fruits or cotton textile industries.
- **The mineral-based industries** rely on mineral ores as their primary materials. Examples include using iron for machinery or steel production.
- **The marine-based industries** derive materials from the sea. Examples encompass seafood processing industries dealing with fish or other marine products.
- **The forest-based industries** utilise forest produce as raw materials. These industries produce items like pulp for paper or pharmaceuticals from medicinal plants.

4. Significance of natural vegetation and wildlife in the ecosystem are as follows

- Natural vegetation and wildlife are interconnected and crucial components within the biosphere, forming an ecosystem vital for sustaining life.
- Vegetation plays an essential role by providing essential resources such as timber, oxygen, shelter, fruits, and medicinal plants necessary for various life processes.
- Wildlife contributes significantly by offering resources like milk, meat, and aiding in essential ecological functions like pollination by insects.
- Birds, insects, and animals are essential in maintaining ecological balance by serving as decomposers, scavengers, and integral parts of the food chain.
- Their collective presence ensures the ecosystem's harmony, playing a critical role in sustaining life and preserving the environment's balance and stability.

5. Some reasons for discontent among Indian sepoys and peasants during British rule in India were as follows

- Indian sepoys, who were soldiers, felt unhappy because they didn't get enough pay and were forced to do things against their religious beliefs, like going overseas.
- Peasants were also upset because they had to pay high taxes, were burdened by loans, and lost their lands that had been in their families for a long time.
- In 1824, when sepoys refused to go overseas, they were punished. Then, in 1856, a law was passed that made them serve abroad, making them even more upset.
- Both sepoys and peasants felt like the British reforms were taking away their religion, customs, and the way they traditionally lived, and that made them really unhappy.

6. The First World War changed India's economic situation, leading to increased government expenditure and taxes, causing hardships for common people while benefitting certain business groups.

The war boosted Indian industries due to increased demand for goods, reducing imports. Villages faced pressure to supply soldiers, creating awareness among them about imperial exploitation. Also, the influence of the Russian Revolution and the spread of socialist ideas inspired Indian nationalists towards collective struggles.

Or

(i) The word 'Swadeshi' comes from two words 'Swa' and 'desh' which means one's own country. The Swadeshi Movement was an important aspect of the Indian independence struggle against British rule.

(ii) The Swadeshi Movement, which emerged in India in response to the partition of Bengal in 1905, played a crucial role in the fight against British rule in the following ways

- **Economic Resistance** Indians boycotted British goods and instead supported locally produced items, leading to a significant economic impact on British trade in India.
- **Promotion of Swadeshi Goods** Indians were urged to use and promote locally produced goods. This led to the establishment of Swadeshi industries, which aimed to reduce dependence on British imports and stimulate the Indian economy.
- **Boycott of Educational Institutions** As part of the movement, students boycotted British educational institutions, contributing to a sense of defiance and political consciousness among the youth.

Long Answer Type Questions

1. The East India Company established trading in Bengal way back in 1651. They set up their first trading center near the Hugli river. Over time, they expanded their settlements and got special rights from the Mughal rulers, like being allowed to trade without paying taxes.

The East India Company caused trouble by not paying the taxes they owed and by refusing to follow some rules set by the Nawabs, like not allowing them to make their money. This led to problems with Bengal's Nawabs such as Murshid Quli Khan, Alivardi Khan, and Siraj-ud-Daulah. The Nawabs felt like the Company was causing them to lose money and challenging their authority. They accused the Company of not following the rules and causing financial losses.

On the other hand, the Company thought that the demands of the Nawabs were unfair and hindered their trade. This conflict made tensions rise, leading to clashes between the East India Company and the Nawabs in Bengal.

Or The Battle of Plassey took place on 23rd June, 1757, in Bengal, India.

Factors leading to the Battle of Plassey

- **Economic Interests** The British East India Company was seeking to expand its influence and control over trade in India, particularly the lucrative trade in Bengal's textiles.
- **Political Instability** The weakening of the Mughal Empire in India created a power vacuum in certain regions, including Bengal.
- **Disloyal Association** Siraj-ud-Daulah, the Nawab of Bengal, suspected the British of interfering in regional politics and undermining his authority. The Company also developed alliances with some of Siraj-ud-Daulah's disaffected officials, worsening the relations between the Nawab and the British.
- **Military Conflict** The growing tensions between the British East India Company and Siraj-ud-Daulah's forces led to confrontations, culminating in the Battle of Plassey.

Consequences for the British East India Company

- **Victory and Control** The British East India Company emerged victorious in the Battle of Plassey, largely due to the betrayal of Siraj-ud-Daulah's commander-in-chief, Mir Jafar, who sided with the British.
- **Political Influence** The British gained substantial political influence in Bengal after the battle.
- **Economic Exploitation** The Company exploited its newfound power to extract economic concessions from Bengal. They imposed heavy taxes, manipulated trade, and controlled the administration, leading to economic exploitation and impoverishment of the region.
- **Expansion of Influence** The Battle of Plassey marked the beginning of the Company's expansion in India.

2. Farming can be categorised on the basis of the geographical conditions, demands of produce, labour and level of technology. Farming is classified into two main types. These are subsistence farming and commercial farming.

The key characteristics of subsistence farming are as follows

- Subsistence farming aims to meet the needs of the farmer's family using low levels of technology and household labour.
- It includes intensive subsistence farming, cultivating small plots with simple tools and more labour for multiple annual crops in suitable regions like Asia.
- The primitive subsistence farming is another form of subsistence farming. It involves shifting cultivation in forested areas and nomadic herding in arid regions.

Characteristics of commercial farming are as follows

- Commercial farming focuses on producing crops and rearing animals for sale in the market.
- It requires large cultivated areas, significant capital investment, and extensive use of machinery.
- The types of commercial farming include commercial grain farming, primarily in temperate grasslands, and mixed farming involving both crops and livestock.

Or The major characteristics and geographical requirements for the crops are as follows

- **Rice** It requires high temperature, humidity, and alluvial clayey soil. China leads in the production because of these factors. India, Japan, Sri Lanka, and Egypt, with West Bengal and Bangladesh yielding multiple crops annually.
- **Wheat** It requires moderate temperatures and well-drained loamy soil. It is extensively cultivated in USA, Canada, Argentina, Russia, Ukraine, Australia, and India during Winter.
- **Millets** (Jowar, Bajra, Ragi) These grow on less fertile sandy soils. They need low rainfall and moderate to high temperatures. The are commonly grown in India, Nigeria, China, and Niger.
- **Maize** It requires moderate temperature, sunlight, and fertile well-drained soil. It is cultivated in North America, Brazil, China, Russia, Canada, India, and Mexico.
- **Cotton** It requires high temperature, light rainfall, and 210 frost-free days, black and alluvial soils. It is primarily produced in China, USA, India, Pakistan, Brazil, and Egypt, vital for the textile industry.
- **Jute** It grows in humid, high-temperature regions with heavy rainfall. It grows on alluvial soil. It is mainly cultivated in India and Bangladesh. It is known as the 'Golden Fibre'.
- **Coffee** It requires warm, wet climates. It is grown on hilly slopes, led by Brazil, Columbia, and India.
- **Tea** It requires cool climate, distributed high rainfall, well-drained loamy soils, and abundant labour for leaf picking. It is produced predominantly in Kenya, India, China, and Sri Lanka.

3. In democratic societies, keeping religion separate from the government is crucial because it helps stop the majority from bossing around or mistreating religious minorities.

If the government is controlled by the majority religion, it might lead to unfair treatment of other religions, breaking the basic rules of democracy. This separation allows people to believe what they want without the government controlling them. It also lets people challenge unfair traditions or practices in religions without any trouble from those in power. By doing this, democratic societies make sure that everyone keeps their individual freedoms, no matter what religion they follow.

Or India is a secular state, which means that the government does not discriminate on the basis of religion and treats all religions equally. This is enshrined in the Indian Constitution, which guarantees the freedom of religion to all citizens.

Some specific examples of what it means for India to be a secular state are

- The government does not promote any particular religion or set of religious beliefs.
- The government does not fund religious institutions or activities.
- All citizens are free to practice their religion in public or in private.
- The government does not interfere in the internal affairs of religious groups.
- The government does not discriminate against people on the basis of their religion in matters such as employment, education or housing.

Case Based Questions

1. (i) The densely populated areas in the world are South/South East Asia, Europe, and North-Eastern North America. These places have a lot of people because they offer good conditions to live in, resources, and chances for jobs.

(ii) Asia and Africa hold most of the world's population, about three-quarters of them. Places like the high latitudes, deserts, and Equatorial regions have fewer people.

(iii) Around 60% of the world's population lives in only 10 countries such as China, India, and the USA. These countries have more than 100 million people each. They have big populations because of their history, diverse cultures, and different government policies.

2. (i) The British considered surveying essential for effective administration, believing that understanding a country's details i.e. topography, soil, flora, fauna, and local histories. They believe it was helpful for proper governance in colonial India.

(ii) The key objectives of Census operations in India were to conduct a count of the population every ten years in every area of the country. During these counts, detailed information about people's castes, religions, and occupations was recorded. This process aimed to create comprehensive records for each province, aiding in more effective and organised administration across the regions.

(iii) Under colonial rule, the British conducted various surveys covering different aspects. These surveys encompassed studies on plants, animals, archaeological remains, people (anthropology), and forests.

3. (i) Law enforcement is crucial as it ensures that workers get fair wages by checking workplaces regularly and punishing those who break the law. This prevents the exploitation of vulnerable workers.

(ii) Workers accept lower wages because they are afraid of what might happen to them if they ask for more money. If they speak up, they were worried that they might lose their job or face other problems.

(iii) The government ensures fairness by creating, enforcing, and upholding laws. By doing this, it stops private companies from doing unfair things, which helps to make society fair for all, just like the rights written in the Constitution.

Map Based Question

1.

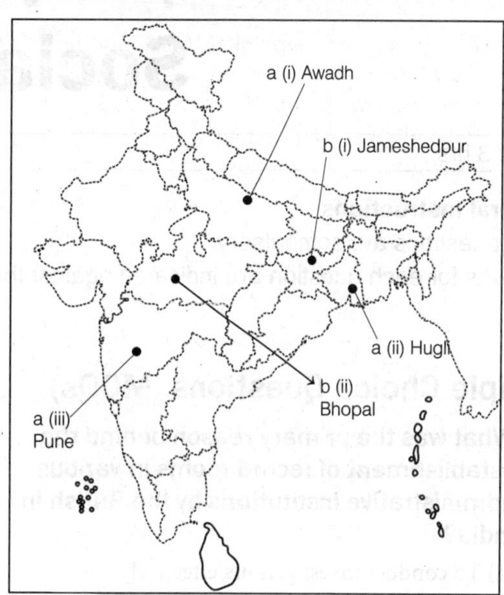

Sample Question Paper 2 (Unsolved)
Social Science

Time : 3 hrs	M.M. : 80

General Instructions

1 All questions are compulsory.

2 Marks for each question are indicated against the question.

Multiple Choice Questions (MCQs)

1. What was the primary reason behind the establishment of record rooms in various administrative institutions by the British in India? (1)

(a) To conduct investigations effectively
(b) To encourage debates and discussions
(c) To preserve important documents and letters
(d) To develop administrative culture

2. Who was considered the leader during the rebellion against British rule in 1857? (1)

(a) Aurangzeb
(b) Bahadur Shah Zafar
(c) Captain Hodson
(d) None of the above

3. What significant event occurred on 12th August, 1765, involving the East India Company? (1)

(a) The appointment of the East India Company as the Diwan of Bengal
(b) The signing of a peace treaty with the Mughal emperor
(c) The British occupation of Indian territories
(d) The establishment of a trading post in Bengal

4. Match the following. (1)

List I	List II
A. Fallow	1. A flower used for consumption or alcohol production
B. Sal	2. Indigenous and separated by Gangetic plain.
C. Mahua	3. A field left uncultivated for soil fertility recovery

Codes

	A	B	C		A	B	C
(a)	3	2	1	(b)	1	2	3
(c)	1	3	2	(d)	2	1	3

5. What event took place on 9th May, 1857, related to the Indian soldiers? (1)

(a) The hanging of Mangal Pandey
(b) The refusal of sepoys in Meerut to use new cartridges
(c) The dismissal of eighty-five sepoys for disobeying officers
(d) The sentencing of sepoys to ten years in jail

6. Which principle of Sustainable Development emphasises empowering communities to take care of their own environment? (1)

I. Respect and care for all forms of life
II. Improve the quality of human life
III. Conserve the Earth's vitality and diversity

Codes

(a) I and II (b) II and III
(c) Only I (d) I, II and III

7. Consider the following statements and choose the correct option. (1)

I. Wheat requires moderate temperatures and adequate rainfall during the growing season, as well as bright sunshine at the time of harvest.
II. Rice is also known as the 'Golden Fiber'.

Codes

(a) I and II (b) Only II
(c) Only I (d) None of these

8. Which of the following statements best describes organic farming? (1)

(a) It uses chemical fertilisers and pesticides for crop cultivation.
(b) It involves genetic modification to enhance crop yield.
(c) It utilises organic manure and natural pesticides rather than chemicals.
(d) It relies on artificial means to increase crop production.

9. **Identify the city that describes the area given below.** **(1)**
   I. It is an important city of the United States of America.
   II. It is one of the major steel industry city.
   III. The Ohio, the Monagahela and Allegheny rivers provide water supply to this area.

   Options
   (a) New York (b) Washington
   (c) Baltimore (d) Pittsburgh

10. **What is the term used for people who leave a country?** **(1)**
   (a) Emigrants (b) Immigrants
   (c) Residents (d) Nomads

11. **Which principle did the Constituent Assembly adopt with the belief in the potential of the common man and the success of democratic rule?** **(1)**
   (a) Universal adult franchise
   (b) Censorship of media
   (c) Selective suffrage
   (d) Limited electoral participation

12. **How many members a political party needs in Lok Sabha to have a majority and to form a Government?** **(1)**
   (a) 543 members (b) 272 members
   (c) 300 members (d) 200 members

13. **What does the judicial system primarily offer regarding dispute resolution in India?** **(1)**
   (a) Solely resolves disputes between citizens and the government.
   (b) Resolves disputes between citizens and state governments.
   (c) Resolves disputes exclusively between two state governments.
   (d) Provides a mechanism to resolve various disputes involving citizens, governments at different levels, and between state and central governments.

14. **Assertion** (A) Adivasi languages, such as Santhali, significantly influenced the development of 'mainstream' Indian languages like Bengali.

   Reason (R) These languages are distinct from Sanskrit and possibly as ancient, leading to a significant impact on the formation and evolution of other Indian languages. **(1)**

   Codes
   (a) Both A and R are true and R is the correct explanation of A
   (b) Both A and R are true, but R is not the correct explainatio of A
   (c) A is true, but R is false
   (d) A is false, but R is true

Fill in the blanks

1. High Courts and the Supreme Court have held that the Right to Safe Drinking Water is a .... **(1)**
2. Balancing the need to use resources and also conserve them for the future is called .... **(1)**
3. In .... the colonial government in India was trying to put down a mutiny that broke out on the ships of the Royal Indian Navy. **(1)**

True or False

1. The use of land is determined by physical factors such as topography, soil, climate, minerals and availability of water. **(1)**
2. Lala Lajpat Rai, a nationalist from West Bengal, was one of the leading members of the Radical group which was critical of the politics of petitions. **(1)**
3. The Indian Constitution guarantees Fundamental Rights that are based on secular principles. **(1)**

Very Short Answer Type Questions

1. How did the Hindu Mahila Vidyalaya in the nineteenth century challenge the traditional curriculum for girls? **(2)**
2. What exclusive rights did the East India Company acquire in 1600? How did it impact its trading operations? **(2)**
3. Define sustainable development and its core principle. **(2)**
4. "When Adivasis are displaced from their lands, they lose much more than a source of income".

   Justify this statement by giving one argument. **(2)**

   Or

   What is ghettoisation? What factors contribute to the formation of ghettos within communities?

5. Define emigrants and immigrants in the context of population changes due to migration. (2)

Or

How is population density calculated? What regions have the highest population densities according to global averages?

Short Answer Type Questions

1. How have Fundamental Rights been utilised by marginalised groups, particularly in India? What significance does Article 17 of the Constitution hold in addressing untouchability? (3)

Or

How do governments support Dalit and Adivasi communities? What crucial policy addresses educational and employment disparities for these groups?

2. What broader aspects define the term 'minority'? Why are safeguards essential for these communities according to the Indian Constitution? (3)

3. What components constitute an industrial system? How do these components function within the context of the textile industry? (3)

4. Which is the primary factors of contributing to soil formation? How do they vary in different locations? (3)

5. "The British had regained control of the country by the end of 1859, but they could not carry on ruling the land with same policies."
   (i) How did the British regain control on India by the end of 1859?
   (ii) Why the British changed their policies after the 1857 rebellion?

Or

How did the 1857 rebellion escalate beyond Delhi? Who were some prominent leaders and their roles in various regions like Kanpur, Lucknow, Jhansi and Mandla during this uprising?

6. How did Mahatma Gandhi establish himself as a prominent leader upon his return to India from South Africa in 1915 ? (3)

Long Answer Type Questions

1. What are the primary roles of the judiciary in India? How do they contribute to the functioning of the legal system? (5)

Or

What is the hierarchical structure of courts in India? What are their functions at various levels?

2. An editor is writing an article about the conserving resources. Discuss the key points that should be mentioned in article and also explain source principles of sustainable development. (5)

Or

What are the primary causes of soil degradation? What methods are employed for soil conservation?

3. Explain key figures in the tradition of Orientalism in India? What were their contributions towards understanding Indian heritage? (5)

Or

Describe the educational system prevalent in Bengal and Bihar during the 1830s, as observed by William Adam.

Case Based Questions

1. **Read the given passage and answer the questions that follow.** (4)

Industries may be agro based, mineral based, marine based and forest based depending on the type of raw materials they use. Agro based industries use plant and animal based products as their raw materials. Food processing, vegetable oil, cotton textile, dairy products and leather industries are examples of agro-based industries. Mineral based industries are primary industries that use mineral ores as their raw materials. The products of these industries feed other industries. Iron made from iron ore is the product of mineral based industry. This is used as raw material for the manufacture of a number of other products, such as heavy machinery, building materials and railway coaches. Marine based industries use products from the sea and oceans as raw materials. Industries processing sea food or manufacturing fish oil are some examples. Forest based industries utilise forest produce as raw materials. The industries associated with forests are pulp and paper, pharmaceuticals, furniture and buildings.

(i) What are the classifications of industries based on raw materials? (1)

(ii) Give examples of agro-based, mineral-based, marine-based, and forest-based industries. (1)

(iii) How do these industries differ in raw material usage and the products they produce? (2)

2. Read the given passage and answer the questions that follow. (4)

Shifting cultivators were found in the hilly and forested tracts of North-East and Central India. The lives of these tribal people depended on free movement within forests and on being able to use the land and forests for growing their crops. That is the only way they could practise shifting cultivation.The Khonds were such a community living in the forests of Orissa. They regularly went out on collective hunts and then divided the meat amongst themselves. They ate fruits and roots collected from the forest and cooked food with the oil they extracted from the seeds of the sal and mahua. They used many forest shrubs and herbs for medicinal purposes, and sold forest produce in the local markets. The local weavers and leather workers turned to the Khonds when they needed supplies of kusum and palash flowers to colour their clothes and leather.

(i) Where were shifting cultivators mainly located? How did their livelihood rely on forests? (2)

(ii) What were the primary forest resources utilised by the Khond community for livelihood ? (1)

(iii) How did local artisans benefit from the Khond community's forest resources, particularly in supplying materials for colouring clothes and leather? (1)

3. Read the given passage and answer the questions that follow. (4)

According to the 2011 census, over 4 million children in India aged between 5 and 14 work in various occupations including hazardous ones. In 2016, Parliament amended the Child Labour (Prohibition and Regulation) Act, 1986, banning the employment of children below the age of 14 years in all occupations and of adolescents (14-18 years) in hazardous occupations and processes. It made employing these children or adolescents a cognizable offence. Anyone found violating the ban must be penalised with a punishment ranging from a jail term of six months to two years and/or fine of ₹ 20,000 to ₹ 50,000. The Central Government had asked State Governments to develop plans to rescue and rehabilitate children who are working.

(i) How many children in India, according to the 2011 census, were involved in various occupations, including hazardous ones? (1)

(ii) What was the significant change made by Parliament in the Child Labour (Prohibition and Regulation) Act, 1986, in 2016? (1)

(iii) What actions were urged upon state Governments by the Central Government regarding children engaged in labour? (2)

Map Based Question

1. (a) On the political map of India, locate the following.

(i) Mahatma Gandhi's earliest local movement

(ii) Locate major iron and steel industries in India.

(ii) The pesticide factory of Union Carbide

(b) On the given political outline map of India, identify the following. (2)

(i) A National Park known for one-horned rhinoceros.

(ii) Major tribal group in Uttarakhand, also referred to as Raghuvanshi Rajput.

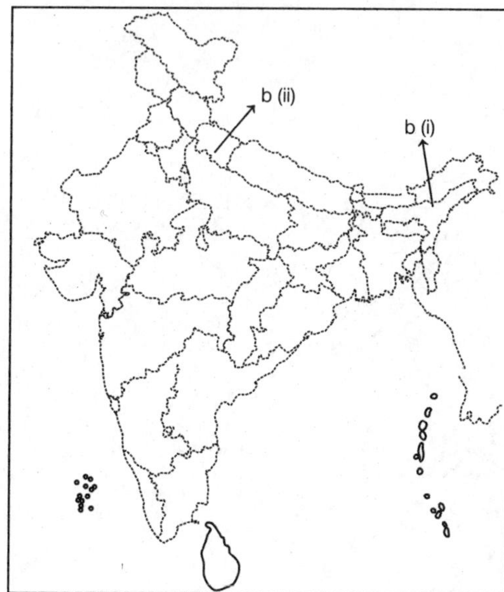

Answers

Multiple Choice Questions

1. (c)	**2.** (b)	**3.** (a)	**4.** (a)	**5.** (b)
6. (d)	**7.** (c)	**8.** (c)	**9.** (d)	**10.** (a)
11. (a)	**12.** (b)	**13.** (d)	**14.** (a)	

Fill in the Blanks

1. Fundamental Right
2. Sustainable Development
3. 1946

True or False

1. True
2. False
3. True

Map Based Question

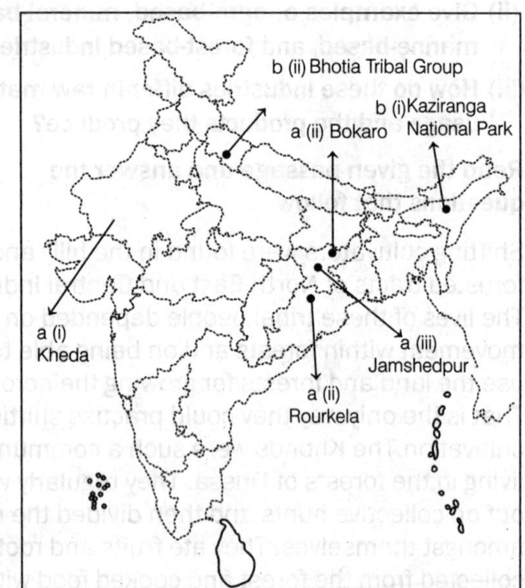

Sample Question Paper 3 (Unsolved)

Social Science

Time : 3 hrs	M.M. : 80

General Instructions

1 All questions are compulsory.

2 Marks for each question are indicated against the question.

Multiple Choice Questions (MCQs)

1. Who was commissioned by Robert Clive to create maps of Hindustan? (1)

(a) William Rennel (b) Robert Clive
(c) British Conquerors (d) Hindustan Explorers

2. Where was the location of the first English factory established in 1651? (1)

(a) Banks of River Thames (b) Banks of River Ganges
(c) Banks of River Hugli (d) Banks of River Nile

3. Who received the Diwani of Bengal, Bihar, and Orissa from the Mughal ruler in 1765? (1)

(a) William Rennel (b) Robert Clive
(c) Siraj-ud-Daulah (d) Warren Hastings

4. Which one of the following statements is/are correct? (1)

I. Public sector industries are owned and operated by the government.

II. Private sector industries are owned and operated by a group or individuals.

Codes

(a) Both I and II (b) Only II
(c) Only I (d) None of these

5. Match the following. (1)

	List I		List II
A.	Removal of Mughal king's name from coins	1.	Governor-General Dalhousie in 1849
B.	Declaration of Bahadur Shah Zafar as the last Mughal king	2.	Governor-General Canning in 1856
C.	Imposition of a law for overseas service by Company's army	3.	Company's policy in 1856

Codes

	A	B	C		A	B	C
(a)	2	1	3	(b)	1	2	3
(c)	3	2	1	(d)	1	3	2

6. What does "Stock of Resource" refer to? (1)

(a) The discovery of new resources
(b) The potential capacity of available resources
(c) The amount of resources available for use
(d) The rate of resource consumption

7. What is the process of weathering primarily attributed to? (1)

(a) Chemical reactions in the atmosphere
(b) Human-made alterations in the environment
(c) Temperature changes, frost action, plants, animals, and human activity
(d) Geological shifts and tectonic movements

8. Where is the origin of the word 'agriculture'? (1)

(a) From Greek words related to land and technology
(b) Derived from Latin words "ager" or "agri" meaning soil, and "culture" meaning cultivation
(c) A combination of Sanskrit terms for farming and growth
(d) Adapted from Chinese terminology for land management

9. Which of the following chemicals was primarily responsible for the Bhopal disaster in 1984? (1)

(a) Sulphur dioxide (b) Methyl Isocyanate (MIC)
(c) Carbon monoxide (d) Nitrogen dioxide

10. What does 'life expectancy' refer to? (1)

(a) The maximum age a person can live
(b) The number of years an individual has already lived
(c) The average number of years an average person can expect to live
(d) The minimum age required for retirement

11. When did the Indian National Congress make the demand for a Constituent Assembly? (1)

(a) 1924 (b) 1932 (c) 1934 (d) 1940

12. Which of the following statements accurately reflects the concept of 'freedom to interpret' in religious practice? (1)

Statement I 'Freedom to Interpret' pertains to the liberty of individuals to explore multiple religions simultaneously.

Statement II It signifies a person's freedom to form their own comprehension and significance of the religion they follow.

Codes

(a) Both the Statements I and II are correct
(b) Both the statements I and II are incorrect
(c) Statement I is true, but Statement II is false
(d) Statement I is false, but Statement II is true

13. Assertion (A) The Indian Parliament symbolises the Indian people's trust in democratic principles like participation in governance.

Reason (R) The Parliament, with substantial powers, is elected every five years with each constituency choosing one representative. **(1)**

Codes

(a) Both A and R are true and R is the correct explanation of A
(b) Both A and R are true, but R is not the correct explanation of A
(c) A is true, but R is false
(d) A is false, but R is true

14. According to the Sachar Committee Report's findings, what did it reveal about the prevalent belief regarding Muslim education choices? (1)

(a) The report confirmed that Muslims predominantly send their children to Madarsas.
(b) The report remained silent about the education preferences of Muslims.
(c) The report discredited the common belief that Muslims prefer Madarsas for their children's education.
(d) The report endorsed the belief that Muslims primarily rely on conventional schools for their children's education.

15. How the hunter-gatherer tribes got their supplies of rice and other grains? (1)

(a) By buying these grains with their meagre earnings from selling forest produce.
(b) By exchanging them for forest produce.
(c) By doing odd jobs
(d) All of the above

Fill in the Blanks

1. .... refers to an economic activity that is concerned with production of goods, extraction of minerals or the provision of services. **(1)**
2. The last powerful ruler of Mughal was .... **(1)**
3. The Lok Sabha is usually elected once every .... years. **(1)**

True or False

1. The Government of India Act 1919, allowed for some elected representation. **(1)**
2. A group of Muslim landlords and nawabs formed the All India Muslim League at Dacca in 1906. **(1)**
3. Sericulture is the breeding of fish in specially constructed tanks and ponds. **(1)**

Very Short Answer Type Questions

1. What distinguishes private land from community land, and what are their respective functions or purposes? **(2)**
2. When and where did the world's worst industrial tragedy occur? What substance leaked from the Union Carbide factory responsible? **(2)**
3. How did the 1850 law regarding conversion to Christianity impact property inheritance for Indians who converted? **(2)**

Or What were the events involving Mangal Pandey and Meerut sepoys that ignited the 1857 rebellion?

4. What purpose do Fundamental Rights serve inthe Indian Constitution? **(2)**
5. How is Subsistence farming categorised based on production methods and output? **(2)**

Or What is sericulture? How does it benefit farmers?

Short Answer Type Questions

1. What was the sequence of events leading to the formation of the Indian Constituent Assembly? How did its members approach the monumental task of drafting the country's constitution? **(3)**

Or How does a democratic Constitution, like India's, safeguard against potential misuse of authority by political leaders, particularly concerning discrimination?

2. How do governments in India promote social justice for marginalised communities? What significant policy addresses historical inequities in education? **(3)**
3. "In 1946 the constituent assembly was formed which thin met periodically for the next three years to draft India's constitution". Explain the key features of the Indian Constitution. **(3)**

Or What issues arose from the Permanent Settlement in India, particularly concerning zamindars and land improvement? **(3)**

4. How did the Khonds tribe rely on forests for sustenance? What roles did they play in the local economy? **(3)**

5. What are the densely populated and sparsely inhabited region globally? Which contiments and countries have the largest share of the world population? **(3)**

6. Shifting cultivation is considered to be primitive and destructive to environment. Yet it is still prevalent in the North-Eastern region of the country.

(i) What do you mean by shifting cultivation?

(ii) By what name is shifting cultivation known in North-East region? **(3)**

Long Answer Type Questions

1. What ideals emerged from Indian political associations post-1850? How did they contribute to nationalism? **(5)**

Or What was the Swadeshi movement in response to the partition of Bengal? What were its main objectives and methods?

2. Explain the industrial system, and what factors contribute to the formation of industrial regions globally and in India? **(5)**

Or What caused the Bhopal industrial disaster in 1984? What are the key measures suggested to reduce such risks in industrial areas?

3. In 1946 the Constituent Assembly was formed which then met periodically for the next three years to draft India's key features Constitution . Explain the Indian Constitution. **(5)**

Or How is the government formed in India post Lok Sabha elections? What roles do the Lok Sabha and the Prime Minister play in this process?

Case Based Questions

1. Read the given passage and answer the questions that follow. (4)

The tradition of Orientalism in 1783, a person named William Jones arrived in Calcutta. He had an appointment as a junior judge at the Supreme Court that the company had set up. In addition to being an expert in law, Jones was a linguist. He had studied Greek and Latin at Oxford, knew French and English, had picked up Arabic from a friend, and had also learnt Persian. At Calcutta, he began spending many hours a day with pandits who taught him the subtitles of Sanskrit language, grammar and poetry. Soon he was studying ancient Indian texts on law, philosophy, religion, politics, morality, arithmetic, medicine and the other sciences.

(i) What languages did William Jones prior to arriving in Calcutta? (1)

(ii) How did William Jones spend his time in Calcutta, and what subjects did he focus on with the pandits? (1)

(iii) What diverse languages and subjects did William Jones study? What ancient Indian texts did he delve into during his time in Calcutta? (2)

2. Read the given passage and answer the questions that follow. (4)

Nomadic herding is practised in the semi-arid and arid regions of Sahara, Central Asia and some parts of India, like Rajasthan and Jammu and Kashmir. In this type of farming, herdsmen move from place to place with their animals for fodder and water, along defined routes. This type of movement arises in response to climatic constraints and terrain. Sheep, camel, yak and goats are most commonly reared. They provide milk, meat, wool, hides and other products to the herders and their families.

(i) What are the primary regions where nomadic herding is practiced according to the passage? (1)

(ii) How does nomadic herding contribute to the livelihood of herdsmen and their families? (1)

(iii) What factors influenced the movement patterns of nomadic herders as mentioned in the passage? (2)

3. Read the given passage and answer the questions that follow. (4)

There are three different levels of courts in our country. There are several courts at the lower level while there is only one at the apex level. The courts that most people interactive and called subordinate or district courts. These are usually at the district or tehsil level or in towns and they hear many kinds of cases. Each state is divided into districts that are presided over by a District Judge. Each state has a High Court which is the highest court of that state. At the top is the Supreme Court that is located in New Delhi and is presided over by the Chief Justice of India. The decisions made by the Supreme Court are binding on all other courts in India.

(i) What are the hierarchical levels of courts in India, and how do they differ in terms of jurisdiction and authority? (1)

(ii) What is the role and responsibility of the District Judge in the Indian judicial system as outlined in the passage? (1)

(iii) How does the Supreme Court's authority extend over other courts in India, and what implications does this have for the legal system? (2)

Map Based Question

1. **(a) On the political map of India, locate the following.**
   (i) State where Dongria Kondha tribe is found.
   (ii) Place where Sepoys refuses army drill in 1857.
   (iii) State of shifting cultivation is done state of North-East

   (b) On the given political outline map of India, identify and label of the following. (2)
   (i) Region from Gujarat completely dependent on purchasing water from the near by Talukas.
   (ii) State where Mala Irular tribe is found

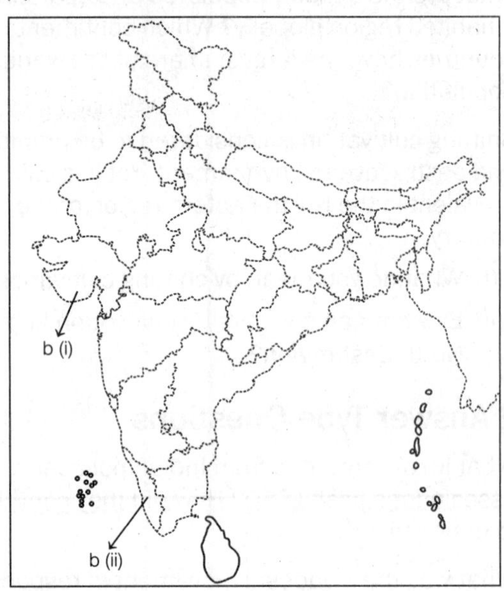

Answers

Multiple Choice Questions

1. (a)	2. (c)	3. (b)	4. (a)	5. (b)
6. (c)	7. (c)	8. (b)	9. (b)	10. (c)
11. (c)	12. (b)	13. (a)	14. (c)	15. (d)

Fill in the Blanks

1. Industry
2. Aurangzeb
3. five

True or False

1. False
2. True
3. False

Map Based Question

1.

a (ii) Meerut
a (iii) Assam
b (i) Saurashtra
a (ii) Orissa
b (ii) Kerala